Ohio and Its People

Map 1. Ohio Counties

Ohio and Its People

George W. Knepper

THE KENT STATE UNIVERSITY PRESS
Kent, Ohio, and London, England

© 1989, 1997 by The Kent State University Press, Kent, Ohio 44242
All rights reserved
Library of Congress Catalog Card Number 97-5446
ISBN 0-87338-595-0
Manufactured in the United States of America

Second edition

05 04 03 02 01 00 99 98 97   5 4 3 2 1

Unless otherwise noted, photographs are reproduced through the courtesy of the Ohio Historical Society. The author wishes to thank the Ohio Historical Society for permission to borrow
substantially from his earlier book, *An Ohio Portrait* (Columbus: Ohio Historical Society, 1976),
for material used in chapter sixteen.

Library of Congress Cataloging-in-Publication Data
Knepper, George W., 1926–
    Ohio and its people / George W. Knepper. — 2nd ed.
     p.   cm.
    Includes bibliographical references and index.
    ISBN 0-87338-595-0 (pbk. : alk paper) ∞
     1. Ohio—History. I. Title.
F491.K63   1997
977.1—dc21   97-5446

British Library Cataloging-in-Publication data are available.

This book is dedicated to
"The People of Ohio for their accomplishments"

Contents

Preface to the Second Edition

It is astonishing how quickly change occurs in the fluid American society. While recognizing that the nation has always had a love affair with tomorrow, it is nonetheless a thing of wonder to document the rapidity and magnitude of change within the State of Ohio in just under one decade's time.

As I finished writing *Ohio and Its People* in the late 1980s, the state was still reeling from severe economic blows. Almost daily we read of yet another business merging, downsizing, or relocating. The state's great industrial base was crumbling, leaving hundreds of thousands of workers to find new jobs within Ohio or to leave the state for more promising prospects elsewhere. And on the political front, the Democratic party still held power in Columbus. Their leaders, especially Speaker of the House of Representatives Vernal G. Riffe, Jr., were power brokers who wielded disproportionate influence.

Now, less than ten years later, Ohio's economy is resurgent. Its political destiny is, for the moment, in the hands of Republicans in both the executive and legislative departments. Such turnarounds may seem at first glance to be unique to this time and this place; but as this book shows, especially those chapters dealing with the industrial age, such rapid transitions are common to Ohio's experience. Its heavy industry–based economy made it particularly susceptible to capitalism's boom and bust cycles. The diversity and balance of its population made it a two-party state capable at any time of switching political leadership.

In the social realm, all the major concerns of an earlier time are still much in evidence. Prominent among them are the funding of public education, busing, crime control, welfare reform, medical costs, and the care of indigents of all ages. Environmental protection is still as much a focus of debate as it was in the 1980s, for the suburbanization of the state moves apace as open land is developed for residential, commercial, and industrial purposes.

In the past decade, most of Ohio's major cities and many of its smaller ones have made great progress in renewing portions of their downtown areas and, in some cases, their neighborhoods. The same cannot be said for all too many small communities, especially those located in areas hardest hit by mining, industrial, and agricultural dislocations. The playing field is uneven: one small community may be thriving while its next-door neighbor falls further into decay. But such has always been the norm in America.

A decade ago, while Ohio was laboring in the late stages of economic malaise, I finished my story on an optimistic note. I wrote: "It may be that Ohio's best years are yet to come." Since then the Buckeye State has indeed regained much of its vitality. I remain optimistic for Ohio's future, although there will undoubtedly be cycles of bad times along with the good. This state has a long tradition of bouncing back from tough times; it bends but it does not break. Ohio will continue to bring to America what it has always offered— a solid, workmanlike performance characteristic of the best the nation can offer.

I would like to thank John Green, director of the Ray Bliss Institute at the University of Akron, for his comments on chapter 18.

George W. Knepper
November 1996

Preface to the First Edition

On July 4, 1827, the canal boat the *State of Ohio,* filled with revelers, made its way into the village of Cleveland, thus inaugurating traffic on the first leg of the Ohio and Erie Canal. In the day-long festivities that followed, Alfred Kelley, a young Cleveland businessman and a state canal commissioner, proposed a toast: "The PEOPLE of the state of Ohio for their accomplishments despite their youth, poverty, diversity, and sectional jealousies." Youth and poverty were soon overcome, but the diversity of Ohio's people and their resulting sectional jealousies would continue to be a feature of the seventeenth state for decades to come.

States love to boast of their unique aspects, but Ohio's claim to fame is the antithesis of uniqueness. Indeed, Ohio's most important quality has been its representative character, and probably no other state contained so broad a sampling of American types in the nineteenth and early twentieth centuries. Ohio was a salad bowl of peoples, not a melting pot. Within its borders were significant numbers of New Englanders, Middle States people, and Upland southerners, as well as smaller representations from the Tidewater. Quakers, Pennsylvania Dutch (Pietist Germans), free blacks, and escaped slaves added to the mix from the beginning of statehood. Every significant immigrant group contributed to the state's social mix, with the German and Irish contingents among the earliest and most significant.

Most of these newcomers tended to settle close by others of their kind, each group bringing along its distinct "cultural baggage." Yet no single group was strong enough to impose its traditions upon the others. Until well into the twentieth century many of these cultural enclaves retained enough of their original character that they continued to exhibit distinct social and political behavior; the various groups remained distinct, standing out from their neighbors. Ultimately America's common cultural dressing as represented by movies, radio, television, mass circulation magazines, and the like muted these distinctions. Yet even today, to know Cleveland in no way prepares one to understand Cincinnati, and Columbus is different still. No single population center dominates the state as in Michigan or Illinois. No single crop dominates its agriculture; no one industry dominates its manufacturing.

Such diversity poses problems for the historian. Except on the broadest levels of human behavior, one cannot generalize about the people of Ohio. In the following pages the discerning reader will note when distinctions have been made among groups and when a generalization can be made without doing great violence to regional distinctions.

If the diversity of its people gives Ohio a representative quality, so does its unusual balance between northern and southern influences, between agriculture and industry, between rural and urban. Ohio has been called the westernmost of the eastern states and the easternmost of the western states. Historically it was influenced by the settled qualities of the East while embracing the social improvisation of the West.

This balance and representative quality has made Ohio a favorite testing ground for measuring everything from political preferences to consumer taste. If a new product catches on in an Ohio test market, it is supposed to sell nationally. Ohio cities have often been selected to represent "typical" American settings. Mount Vernon, Springfield, Mansfield, and others have been written about in this vein. Peter Davis, author of *Hometown: A Portrait of an American Community,* chose Hamilton to represent an American city of medium size; a U.S. Census Bureau official advised him to select Hamilton because it was northern enough to be industrial, southern enough to have a gently rural aspect, western enough to have once been on the frontier, and eastern enough to have a past.

Those who write state history tread on shaky ground. Inevitably their story tends to give the unwary reader an inflated idea of the state's centrality in American affairs. If writing about Ohio industry, for example, one cannot afford the time and distraction of following what transpired in its sister states as they industrialized. Thus Ohio's experience may appear to be more unique than it was. Though I have been alert to this fallacy, it creeps in from time to time. Another problem rests with state-nation relationships. I have depended upon the logic of each situation in determining whether to tell Ohio's story first, then relate it to the nation's, or to tell the story of national events and show how Ohio reacted.

The most recent history that attempted to tell the Ohio story in a single volume was published almost a half century ago, with new material added in

1953 and 1967. Since that time the state has experienced striking change. Furthermore, a generation of historians has revised many of the old "truths" about Ohio. It is time, then, to tell its story anew and to bring it up to date.

This text rests on more than three decades of reading, travel, and research. In the process I have been fortunate to have access to numerous libraries, archives, and scholars. Ohio is well-served by all three. I have had assistance from many persons. Portions of the manuscript have been read by Fred Blue, Kenneth Davison, Richard Hopkins, Roger Grant, David Kyvig, Carl Lieberman, Phillip Shriver, Richard Smith, and Everett Walters. John Hubbell, director of the Kent State University Press and an occasional teacher of Ohio history, read the entire manuscript. Margaret Geib and The University of Akron Cartographic Laboratory executed the maps. Wimonrat Soonthornrojana served ably as a research assistant. Jeanne West and Julia Morton, editors of the Kent State University Press, and Laura Nagy provided outstanding editorial services. To each of them, my profound thanks. They are not responsible for the choices I have made or for any errors. Mrs. Mia Hahn O'Connor put the text on a word processor and faithfully executed its many revisions. Her work was extraordinary. She was ably assisted by Edie Richeson. I am also grateful to The University of Akron for a Faculty Improvement Leave in spring term, 1984, and for a research grant in that year.

George W. Knepper
Stow, Ohio, 1988

Ohio and Its People

A Favored Land

Before the American War for Independence, the Ohio Country was but a shadowy image in the minds of eastern colonials. Only a few traders willing to risk their lives for profits knew its forest trails and the Indians who traveled them. But soon after the war ended, Americans surged westward in irresistible numbers. Ohio was located directly in the mainstream of this migration, and as America grew, so did Ohio. All the productive energy of an emerging nation was focused in Ohio's experience. And that experience begins with the land itself.

To the English traveler Morris Birkbeck, who passed through the state in 1817, Ohio was "a country beautiful and fertile, and affording . . . all that nature had decreed for the comfort of man." Long before Birkbeck saw it, the region was part of the Ohio Country, which stretched along the great river that Iroquois Indians called "O-Y-O" (great water or principal river). The French explorer René Robert Cavelier Sieur de La Salle was the first known European to see the Ohio River. Struck by its beauty, he called it *la belle riviere,* the beautiful river.

Geological Structuring

Ohio's geological history can be read with a high degree of certainty. For at least the last 570 million years Ohio's bedrock has been building up, eroding, and building up again in an endless cycle. This ancient bedrock is sedimentary; it was formed over eons of time by the deposition of materials in compacted layers.

Each of the sedimentary formations has yielded commercially valuable materials. Clinton sand (actually a sandstone formed of outwash from eroding mountains), a valuable source of oil and natural gas, is confined to the southeastern and south central part of the state. Another valuable rock from the Silurian period (about 400 million years ago) is dolomite, a form of limestone readily accessible in western Ohio which is used for making fire brick and agricultural lime. Dolomite is also used as a fluxing material in the smelting of iron ore, and magnesium compounds and other chemicals are derived from it.

Later depositions in the Silurian period resulted in gypsum and halite. Gypsum, which is mined on the Marblehead Peninsula in one of the world's largest deposits, is used in plaster and in that ubiquitous modern building material, wallboard or plasterboard. Halite (rock salt) underlies parts of northern Ohio in thick veins. It has long been mined at Cleveland and Painesville, where the galleries extend well out under Lake Erie. At Akron, Barberton, and Rittman salt was (and in most cases still is) obtained by injecting superheated water into the salt formations and then pumping up the resulting brine. Rock salt is used to melt ice (a necessity for anyone dealing with northern Ohio winters), to "soften" water, and as a source of industrial chemicals. These commercial sources of salt were unavailable to Ohio's early settlers who, like the Indians before them, "made salt" by boiling the waters of salt springs and runs. Salt was actually imported by pack animal or brought by boat from New Orleans long before Ohio's people learned of the treasure lying deep beneath them.

In the Devonian Period an unusually pure limestone was formed. Called Columbus limestone, this easily accessible material was quarried from Columbus to Kelleys Island, where it was so accessible that it was feared for a time the whole island would become a quarry. Further east, at Barberton, miners had to go down 2,000 feet to reach the formation. Columbus limestone is used in concrete, as a smelting flux, as a building material, and as a source of agricultural lime.

Other Devonian deposits include shale, most of which is commercially useless although certain types, such as "mudstone," are useful for brick making. Sandstone dates from this period. In nineteenth-century Ohio it was an important building material, and Berea sandstone provided about 80 percent of the nation's grindstones and millstones. Vanport flint once had a unique commercial value; Ohio Indians used it and traded it widely. The best deposits are at Flint Ridge in Licking County.

Ohio's most important mineral is coal, and its economic significance will be considered in a later context. All Ohio coal is bituminous, formed from organic matter, but historically it varied in quality. The better grades were shaft mined and were the first to be exploited. Lesser grades exist in huge quantities in eastern Ohio where the coal is obtained by strip mining. Miners will remove up to a hundred feet of overlay to get to a four-foot vein of coal.

Clay of various consistencies and qualities is yet another deposit which has been commercially exploited. Fine clays once supported a chinaware industry of great importance in eastern Ohio. Other clays and shales provided raw material for brick, tile and stoneware. Finally, low-grade iron ore was also once commercially valuable. Found throughout eastern and south central Ohio, it supported an iron industry of major importance.

As our story unfolds we shall see how valuable these mineral resources have been to the state's development.

Glaciation and Its Legacy

If it requires imagination to grasp geologic time, it is also an act of imagination to see in the mind's eye the great glacial ice sheets advancing and contracting across the land.

Early glacial periods known as the Nebraskan, Kansan, and Illinoian affected Ohio, but the Wisconsin Glacier had the greatest effect. Entering Ohio about 25,000 years ago, it spread across two-thirds of the state over a period of 6,000 years, encasing about fifty-five of the state's eighty-eight counties under ice estimated to have been 8,000 feet thick at Cleveland and about 1,000 feet thick near its outer limits.

The glacier had a grinding, filling, smoothing effect which forever altered the topography and the drainage system. It left 400 to 600 feet of fill in the valley of the ancient Teays River, which was once larger than the Ohio and drained much of the state toward the northwest. Similarly, it left 400 feet of fill in the Great Miami Valley and 500 feet in the Cuyahoga Valley. It advanced and retreated, started and stopped, leaving moraines, eskers, and kames, all of which are forms of material deposit which in our own day give pleasing variety to the topography of Ohio and also provide sand and gravel resources. Upon its final retreat, perhaps 12,500 years ago, the glacier left a "calling card" in the form of long parallel grooves scoured in the limestone cap of Kelleys Island, where they remain as a testimony to the glacier's presence and power.

Topographical regions

Ohio shares in four topographical regions: the Allegheny Plateau, which is a westward extension of the Appalachian foothills, the Lake Plains, the Till

Plains, and the Bluegrass Region. Within each of these regions are subdivisions based on contour and soil.

The *Allegheny Plateau* is divided into two parts. The unglaciated portion covers the southeastern and extreme south central sections of the state. This is rugged, hilly land broken by sharp ridges, narrow ravines and numerous creeks. These hills and valleys once supported a magnificent hardwood forest, but generations of cutting, clearing, and burning denuded them; farming broke the soil and the exposed earth eroded. The unproductive hill farms were soon abandoned, and slowly great areas returned to woodland. An occasional broad river valley gives variety to the landscape, and the bottomlands provided some of the best soils in the state. Since they were level, rich, and easily cleared, they were the first lands taken up by settlers, though no large cities developed in the unglaciated plateau.

In contrast, the glaciated part of the Allegheny Plateau contains more people and more industry than any other section of Ohio. It stretches nearly 300 miles in an arc from Ashtabula County in the extreme northeastern section of the state to Ross County in south central Ohio. In addition to many great industrial cities, this region of glaciated soils contains productive farmland like that found in Stark, Wayne, and Licking counties.

The *Lake Plains* border Lake Erie. From Pennsylvania westward to Erie County they extend inland an average of five to ten miles. West of Erie County they fan out in a large lobe which embraces parts of eighteen northwestern Ohio counties. The Lake Plains were once covered by Lake Maumee, an ancient lake much larger than the present Lake Erie. Various shorelines of the ancient lake remain today as sandy ridges. In the western part of the state they support tree clusters known as oak openings. Trails and roads ran along these ridges. North Ridge Road and Center Ridge Road west of Cleveland are contemporary examples of this phenomenon. Most of the western end of the Lake Plains was once known as the Black Swamp, a forbidding place where dense forest growth crowded out the sun from a forest floor that was covered by water much of the year. The early settlers, like the Indians before them, avoided the swamp, settling instead on its fringes or on the high banks of the rivers that drain it. They penetrated the swamp to hunt and trap, but it was not opened to agriculture until it was drained in the nineteenth century. With constant draining, its soil is today among the most productive in the state and nation.

South of the Lake Plains and west of the Allegheny Plateau lie the *Till Plains*, so called because of the glacial debris, or till, which covers most of the region. This gently rolling land is also very fertile. Toward its southern end, piles of glacial material created hills, one of which, Campbell Hill in Logan County, has an elevation of 1,549 feet, making it Ohio's highest point. The lowest elevation in the state—440 feet near the mouth of the Great Miami—is

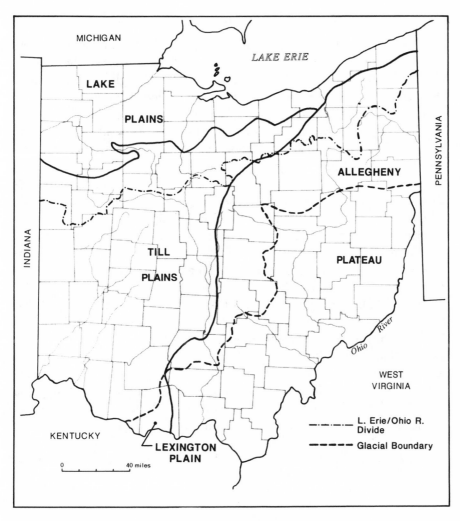

Map 2. Physiographic Features

also in the Till Plains. The soils of this region were among the most fertile that Americans encountered until they reached the soils of Illinois and Iowa. The Corn Belt, of which these two states are so much a part, reaches its easternmost extension in the Ohio Till Plains. In addition to its agriculture, this region boasts several large industrial cities.

A small, northward-pointing triangle of land in Adams, Brown, and Highland counties forms Ohio's *Bluegrass Region.* It is an extension from Kentucky of flat-topped hills and uplands rimmed by cliffs. The Wisconsin glacier did not cover this region but did alter its drainage pattern. This sparsely populated area remains largely rural; tobacco has been its most distinctive crop.

Climate

Weather is of endless concern to humankind. Except for tourists and airline pilots, perhaps no one pays closer attention to it than farmers, whose livelihood depends on it. Ohio weather and climate, although prone to sudden changes, are on the average reasonably predictable. This enabled pioneer farmers to establish the state's large agricultural base; to this day, agriculture is Ohio's largest industry. The growing season varies considerably from an average of 125 frost-free days in Mahoning County to an average of 200 frost-free days in Hamilton County. This season is long enough for farmers to raise nearly every crop common to temperate latitudes. Ohio's rainfall is also adequate, averaging thirty-eight inches per year with considerable local variation. Rain is distributed throughout the year with the heaviest concentrations in spring and early summer. Ohio is well known for the frequency and rapidity of its temperature changes. Nevertheless, average summer highs and winter lows place the state in the temperate range. Ohio's extremes of heat and cold are mild compared with those in many other parts of the United States.

On an average, the southern part of the state receives more rain and has higher temperatures than the extreme northern part. In the north, however, Lake Erie has an important influence on adjacent regions. A resident of the region from 1820 to 1822 wrote, "I never knew so variable and unsettled weather in any part of New England or the Middle States, as I have known in the northern part of Ohio." Lake Erie's waters keep the shoreline colder than surrounding territory in the spring and warmer in the fall. East of Cleveland lie the "snowbelt" counties; Geauga County averages 106 inches of snowfall per year and, with its neighbors, is the snowiest part of Ohio. Winds over Lake Erie also create a cloud cover which restricts northeastern Ohio to fewer clear days than the rest of the state.

Water Resources

While rainfall is of fundamental importance to the state, so also are its other water resources—lakes, rivers, streams, and underground aquifers. Thanks to its long Lake Erie shoreline, Ohio taps into the Great Lakes, the largest surface fresh water system in the world. Historically Lake Erie has served as an important transportation artery conveying Indian canoes, passenger vessels, ore carriers, commercial ships, and an armada of pleasure boats. Its western basin supports one of the world's most productive freshwater fisheries, and the marshes along its shore teem with wildfowl.

Discounting the waters of Lake Erie lying within Ohio's borders, the state ranks forty-second in the surface area of its natural lakes. That statistic may surprise those who live in parts of the state dotted with natural and man-made lakes. Most of these water resources are small, however, and the amount of water they impound is limited.

In contrast to its paucity of large lakes, Ohio contains a comprehensive network of rivers and streams, approximately 44,000 miles of them. These streams belong to two great drainage systems: the Great Lakes-St. Lawrence system to the north and the Ohio-Mississippi system to the south. The retreating ice sheets changed Ohio's drainage pattern and left a continental divide which crosses the state in roughly an east-west direction some thirty to fifty miles south of Lake Erie. Ohio's divide is not at all dramatic to look at. Indeed, it is indistinguishable from the surrounding land, yet it is no less a geographic fact. Rivers rising north of it are short and, except for the Maumee, carry small volumes of water into Lake Erie. Yet these rivers have been much more important historically than their size would suggest. From several of them, notably the Cuyahoga, Sandusky, and Maumee, it was but a short portage across the divide to the waters of the southward-flowing rivers that emptied into the Ohio. The largest of these—the Muskingum, Hocking, Scioto, Little Miami, and Great Miami—were of central importance to the settlement and development of early Ohio.

The Ohio River traces Ohio's eastern and southern borders for more than 400 miles, and is the dominant river of the region. Historically it was the great highway to the West carrying Indian canoes, the flatboats of early settlers, and the keelboats of traders and commercial men. Early in the nineteenth century the first western steamboats plied its currents and gave to the river an indelible aura of romance. By the twentieth century, "towboats" pushed barges carrying enormous tonnage of coal, oil, chemicals, and other bulk cargo.

Ohio rivers and streams provided water to power pioneer mills and to transport pioneer products to market. Later these same streams would turn turbines, supply water to industry, serve as drinking water sources for vast populations, and support recreational activities.

In addition to its billions of gallons of surface water, Ohio is underlain with aquifers containing additional water resources. The west-central and northwestern sections of the state overlie rich yields of underground water as do the valleys of the southward-flowing rivers. Wells provide much of Ohio's rural and urban population with water for drinking, industry, and agriculture. As with the surface systems, underground water sources have been abused through indiscriminate dumping of toxic waste, and public awareness of that fact has led to increased demands for pollution control.

Timber

Water, soil, and timber form the triumvirate basic to the rural economy of Ohio. The historic magnitude of the eastern forests overwhelms the imagination. The naturalist can describe its character and extent; the historian can describe its impact on the lives of those who had to come to terms with it; but

it remains for the novelist to invoke the sense of foreboding, of isolated loneliness that the deep Ohio woods held for many of those who first entered
them. In Conrad Richter's words, pioneers saw "a sea of treetops. . . . As
far as the eye could reach, this lonely forest sea rolled on and on till its faint,
blue billows broke against an incredibly distant horizon." The trees were
hardwoods, mixed in varying concentrations according to soil and climatic
conditions. Conifers—largely hemlock and cedar—grew in the valleys and
ravines formed by steep, rocky ledges.

Natural meadows occasionally broke the forest's monopoly. In central
Ohio prairies of considerable extent were found. An eighteenth-century Indian captive, James Smith, described how Indian hunting techniques kept the
prairies free from forest encroachment.

> We came to the great meadows or prairies that lie between Sandusky and Scioto.
> When we came to this place we met with some Ottawa hunters, and agreed to take
> what they call a ring hunt, in partnership. We waited until we expected rain was
> near falling to extinguish the fire, and then we kindled a large circle in the prai-
> rie. . . . A great number of deer lay concealed in the grass . . . but as the fire
> burned in towards the center of the circle, the deer fled before fire. Indians
> . . . shot them down every opportunity. . . . The rain did not come on that
> night . . . and, as the wind arose, [the fire] extended through the whole prairie,
> which was about fifty miles in length, and in some places near twenty in breadth.

Occasionally, fire burned into the forest floor, cleaning out the underbrush
and creating a parklike environment. This effect was enhanced in some places
by a high canopy of leaves which shut out the sun from the forest floor, thus
inhibiting the growth of underbrush. In such places the ground was covered
by a deep leaf mulch which may account for the Indians' famed ability to
move "noiselessly" through the forest. Other parts of the forest were less
open. Underbrush of all sorts, including vines, made such areas difficult to
traverse except on trails; unwary travelers could easily become lost in the
dense tangles.

Trees reached awesome size in this virgin forest. Only the frequency and
the consistency of reports made by experienced observers lends credibility to
the estimates of tree size. Oaks more than six feet in diameter rose over fifty
feet before branching. Sycamores of gigantic girth often had hollow trunks
large enough to shelter several people and/or horses. Hickory, beech, ash,
chestnut, tulip, cherry, maple, elm, walnut, and many other species were
commonplace.

To early agriculturalists the forest was an enemy to be conquered so that
crops could grow and life proceed along familiar lines. Yet, what was foreboding to some was a land of promise to others. The variety and size of the
trees, they thought, spoke of rich, productive soil. And vast quantities of

timber were available for firewood and for building houses and cabins, barns, sheds, fences, furniture, bridges, barrels, boats, and mills. The pioneer knew the characteristics of various woods. For example, the buckeye tree was especially versatile and easily worked into bowls and benches, chairs and cradles. As one pioneer woman recalled, "So my husband . . . cut down a large sweet buckeye tree and split a part of its body in two, very neatly, and made me two large trays . . . and one of them answered for a wash tub, and when the clothes were dry, it answered to fold them down in, and when ironed served the purpose of a bureau." Ironically, the very popularity of this tree virtually eliminated it from the Ohio scene, but not before lending its identity to the Buckeye State.

Ohio's First Inhabitants

Perhaps as long as 20,000 years ago, during the last Ice Age, peoples from northeastern Asia crossed into Alaska on a land or ice bridge where today the waters of the Bering Strait flow. Recent evidence appears to confirm the likelihood that, while many descendants of these first American immigrants moved southward toward Mexico and South America, others fanned out in an easterly direction toward the Mississippi. Among the latter were the first people known to have reached Ohio.

Discoveries made in an Ohio Valley cave in western Pennsylvania indicate that these *Paleo-Indian People* were present in the area as early as 13,000 B.C. What is known of these and other pre-literate people comes from the work of archeologists who systematically examine and evaluate the minimal traces they left behind. Spear points of the Clovis and Folsom types link these Ohio people with others of their type, whom investigators have more clearly identified and described. Nomadic hunters who lived in rock shelters, they pursued the mastodon, the mammoth, and other large vertebrates. As the ice sheets retreated northward, these species disappeared, and the caribou and musk ox migrated toward the Arctic. The Paleo-Indians disappeared along with these mammals, leaving only stone tools and weapons as evidence of their presence in Ohio over thousands of years.

Archaic People supplanted Ohio's first residents. They, too, were hunters, pursuing with flint-tipped spears game familiar to us today: bear, deer, wild turkeys, and waterfowl. They consumed freshwater clams in abundance, as shell piles or middens testify, and snared fish in crude nets. The Archaic People also gathered plants, nuts, berries, and roots. Some buried their dead in kames (gravel hills) left by the glaciers; archeologists call this group of Archaics the *Glacial Kame People*. By 1000 B.C. the Archaic inhabitants had disappeared from Ohio, but their material culture provided a base for those who followed them.

Sometime around 1000–800 B.C. a more sophisticated culture appeared in the upper Ohio Valley. The *Adena* were so named because evidences of their culture were excavated in 1902 on the grounds of Adena, Thomas Worthington's estate near Chillicothe. Adena culture spread beyond Ohio, but many of its most impressive remnants are found in this state, especially in the southern river valleys, with limited Adena sites identified in the north.

We know something about how the Adena looked and dressed thanks to carved figurines and other artifacts, most notable of which is the celebrated Adena pipe, found in a burial mound. These residents were able to live in semipermanent villages because they were more than hunters and gatherers. They had domesticated certain plants—goosefoot, swartweed, and sunflowers, for example—and they grew squash and possibly corn, which had first been domesticated in Mexico. Adena communities were small, consisting of a few circular houses situated above the river flood plain. These houses were much superior to the smaller, smokier, and more crowded wigwams used by the historic Indians of the eastern forests. By measuring patterns of holes dug for support beams ("postholes"), archeologists have determined that structures as large as forty-five feet in diameter were sometimes built, presumably for community purposes or as dwellings for several families. Most Adena houses were about eighteen to twenty feet in diameter. The roofs were made of heavy thatch while the walls were made of poles covered with woven mats of reeds and grass.

The Adena's sedentary culture supported a population denser than any which had preceded it, since considerable manpower was required to maintain the extensive trade patterns of Adena life. Adena sites reveal copper, seashells, and other materials they received in exchange for Ohio flint and pipestone, which, along with stone tablets inscribed with stylized Adena figures, have been found as far east as Vermont and the Chesapeake Bay and as far west as Wisconsin and the Mississippi Valley.

As wide-ranging as the trade networks were, however, the most impressive remnants of Adena culture are the conical burial mounds, thousands of them both great and small, which they built on the Ohio landscape. The largest is the Miamisburg Mound; sixty-eight feet high and with a base of three acres, it contained burials on several levels. Many small ones were erected over single burials, and hundreds of them remain visible today.

The Adena also built effigy mounds. Ohio's most spectacular mound, indeed America's best known effigy mound, is the Great Serpent Mound in Adams County. Located with its head at the point of an eminence which rises abruptly above the valley of Brush Creek, the writhing serpent measures 1,330 feet from its open jaws to the tip of its coiled tail. The site was carefully chosen and suggests an appropriate setting for ceremonial purposes. This great serpent stimulates the imagination. An oval mound in the serpent's mouth is believed to represent an egg, or it may simply symbolize the open orifice. In the nineteenth century a local minister is reputed to have claimed Adams County as the Garden of Eden, for clearly, he thought, the great serpent represented the infamous snake which had tempted Eve. Most people are content with a less bizarre interpretation. It may well be that the Adena worshipped the snake, believing that the annual shedding of its skin and taking on a new one in its place represented immortality. While looking at this wonderful earthwork, one cannot help but wonder what became of the people who built it. No one knows why, but sometime between A.D. 100 and 300 the Adena disappeared as a society.

Before the Adena passed from the scene, another mound-building culture, the *Hopewell* people, made their appearance. Named for Capt. M. C. Hopewell, on whose Ross County farm their separate cultural identity was first recognized, the Hopewell began to occupy southern Ohio river valleys about 100 B.C. Remnants of Hopewell culture are also found in some northern Ohio river valleys and in the Mississippi watershed. Like the Adena, the Hopewell were hunters, gatherers, and cultivators of domestic plants. Their villages, therefore, were semipermanent, although it appears from remnants found beneath flood deposits that they were sometimes located on flood plains.

The Hopewell maintained a far-flung trade network. Even more than earlier cultures, they exchanged Ohio flint and pipestone for copper nuggets from the Lake Superior region and sea shells from the Atlantic and Gulf coasts. In addition, they secured obsidian (a black, glasslike volcanic rock) and grizzly bear claws from the Rocky Mountains, mica from North Carolina, and silver from Ontario. They fashioned these materials into beautiful ornaments and figurines of considerable aesthetic sophistication. Many of these objects, discovered in burial mounds, are displayed by the Ohio Historical Society, which has the world's finest collection of Hopewell as well as Adena artifacts.

The Hopewells also built exceptional earthworks. Of special note are the geometric forms—circles, rectangles, octagons—which they constructed at Marietta, Newark, Portsmouth, in Hamilton County, and elsewhere. These earthworks, including the concentric rings which gave Circleville its name, were laid out with a precision which suggests that the Hopewells had surveying skills. Many of these impressive constructs have been destroyed, but a large portion of what was once a four-square-mile complex is well preserved in Newark. The Hopewell constructed burial mounds under the direction of shamans or priests who comprised a funerary cult. Hopewell burial mounds were formed by piling dirt over bodies cremated in charnel houses. Some high-status persons were not cremated but were buried in mounds. The Seip Mound in the Paint Creek Valley effectively illustrates Hopewell burial customs. Another impressive group of Hopewell burial mounds is maintained by the National Park Service north of Chillicothe.

The Hopewell people constructed huge hilltop enclosures or "forts" which

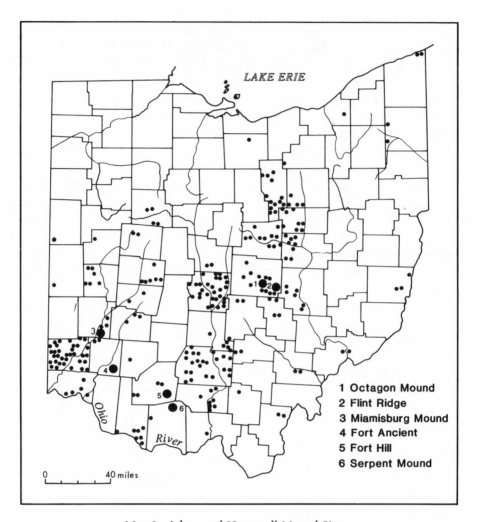

Map 3. Adena and Hopewell Mound Sites

archeologists now know were really not defensive fortifications so much as sites for various ceremonial functions. Large structures in which religious ceremonies could have been enacted were erected within these enclosures. One such site, Fort Ancient in Warren County, is located on a bluff overlooking the Little Miami River. Its massive walls extend three and a half miles and enclose stone pavements, burial mounds, and crescent-shaped mounds. Fort Hill in Highland County encloses a large space within earthen walls that vary from a few feet to more than twenty feet in height.

Hopewell and Adena earthworks first became known to a wide audience in the 1820s when Caleb Atwater of Circleville published a book on Ohio's prehistoric monuments. In 1848 the Smithsonian Institution published *Ancient Monuments of the Mississippi Valley* by Ephraim G. Squier and Edwin H. Davis, both of Chillicothe. This classic work, beautifully illustrated with maps and drawings, set the tone for subsequent scholarly efforts to decipher the secrets of Hopewell and Adena culture.

By A.D. 600 Hopewell culture had all but disappeared from the Ohio Country. As with the Adena, no one knows what accounted for the Hopewell's demise, although there has been no lack of speculation. One thing is certain; the Hopewells brought a cultural sophistication to Ohio that would not be seen again for well over a thousand years, when a European culture was established in the land they had once occupied.

Little is known of the people who immediately followed the Hopewell. They seem to have been oriented toward the north, toward similar peoples living in Ontario and Michigan. However, two distinct cultural groups emerged in Ohio after A.D. 1000 and remained until the historic period. The *Fort Ancient* people occupied southern Ohio, favoring the river valleys as sites for rectangular houses which they enclosed in stockades. They were part of a larger Mississippian culture that demonstrated pronounced similarities to the Indian cultures of central Mexico. New strains of maize (Indian corn), beans, and squash enhanced the food supply which in turn enabled the Fort Ancient people to establish larger, more permanent towns than their predecessors. By the mid-seventeenth century the Fort Ancient culture had disappeared. Some scholars believe the Fort Ancients were ancestors of the historic Shawnee people, or that, at the very least, the historic Shawnees absorbed remnants of these older peoples.

Archeologists have also identified a people they have called *Whittlesey Focus* in the northern part of Ohio. This culture, previously confused with the Eries to the east, has been studied in enough detail to reveal that these people had improved their agricultural skills and become sedentary. In time they built villages on promontories overlooking river valleys. Access to their villages was blocked by stockades. Nonetheless, they may have fallen victim in the seventeenth century to European diseases or to European guns in the hands of invading Iroquois from the east. With the advent of the Iroquois, Ohio's prehistory came to an end.

For some 15,000 years, prehistoric peoples had lived out their lives in the Ohio Country. Yet they left the land essentially unchanged. Unlike the Europeans who followed, they did not cut down the forests, strip the soil, drain the swamps, level the high places, and fill the low, nor did they change the course of river and stream. Least of all did they preempt vast acreage for cities, highways, airports, and all the other works of modern societies. A dynamic "western" culture has transformed their Ohio; yet today one can gaze at their great mounds and earthworks, at their implements and artifacts, and feel a kinship with those distant people who also called Ohio home.

Historic Indians of Ohio

For nearly half a century following the demise of the Fort Ancient and Whittlesey peoples, the Ohio Country was uninhabited. Except for occasional hunting parties, a region which had supported numerous people, organized in impressive cultures, lay virtually empty and unused. Scholars still debate why.

A key force in this abandonment was clearly the Five Nations of the Iroquois Confederacy, based in central and western New York, which after 1720 became the Six Nations. These aggressive people had a more advanced political organization than their neighbors, and early in the seventeenth century they commenced a conquering military sweep which took them to the Mississippi. They dispersed and destroyed tribes from the northern Great Lakes to the Ohio River although they established no settlements in Ohio until the 1740s.

Meanwhile, small, isolated villages occupied by other Indian peoples appeared in Ohio early in the eighteenth century, with more permanent settlements starting to appear in the 1730s. From the north came a people of Iroquoian linguistic stock called *Hurons* by the French and *Wyandots* by the English, who had been driven from their Ontario homeland by the Iroquois during the preceding century. After taking shelter near Fort Pontchartrain, which the French established in 1701 at Detroit, a band of Wyandots led by Orontony (Nicholas) removed in 1739 to Sandusky Bay and established a village named Junundat. Thus the Sandusky River Valley and Sandusky Bay region became the center of Wyandot influence, although they occupied other Ohio locations as well.

The Wyandots, like other Ohio Indians, were already dependent upon European trade goods. The French had been their only source for these goods, but in the 1740s traders from the English colonies to the east were effectively challenging the French traders at Detroit. Anxious to take advantage of this new source of goods, and perhaps to escape indebtedness to French traders, Orontony and some of his people moved further eastward to the Cuyahoga River; there contact could be made with British traders, the most famous of whom was George Croghan, a semiliterate Irishman, who became the most influential British trader among the western tribes. The French commandant at Detroit, anxious to keep the British at bay, authorized a French trader named François Saguin to open a post on the same river. Thus the Cuyahoga became the focus of European trade rivalry in the 1740s and, as a result, attracted an estimated 2,500 Wyandots, Mingoes, and Ottawas to the region. By 1750 trading activity had shifted elsewhere, and few Indians remained along the Cuyahoga. Orontony's Wyandots moved on to villages in eastern Ohio and the Muskingum Valley, where they established Conchake (Coshocton), but soon abandoned these sites for more permanent villages in central

Ohio and the Sandusky region. Through most of the historic period the center
of Wyandot power was Upper Sandusky, located northeast of the modern
city of that name.

The *Miami* Indians came into Ohio from the west: by the 1740s they had
settled in the watersheds of the Great Miami, Little Miami, and the Miami of
the Lake (Maumee). They were of Algonquin linguistic stock, and when first
encountered by French explorers were living near Green Bay, Wisconsin.
Under pressure from other tribes, the Miami moved eastward until they
found new homes in unoccupied lands in western Ohio and eastern Indiana. In

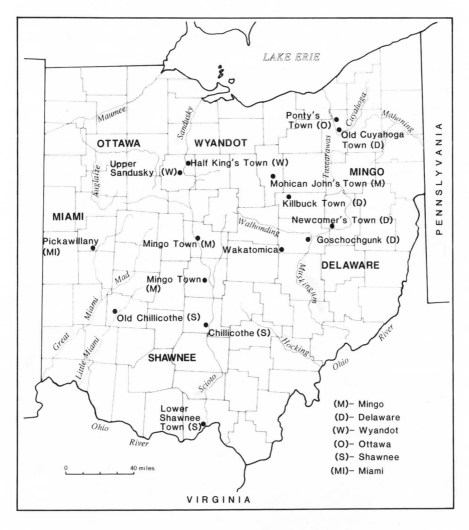

Map 4. Historic Indians (Principal Villages)

an effort to accommodate new relationships with British traders from the East, some Miamis established a village called Pickawillany on the head-waters of the Great Miami. The French, who had controlled Miami trade from Detroit, regarded this as provocation; they would soon take steps to discipline the Miami. British traders called the Miami *Twightwees,* and de-scribed them as a "comely" people, honorable in their trading practices.

Certain bands of Iroquois who had removed from their main villages in New York were found in eastern Ohio in the 1740s and thereafter. In the Ohio Country these people were known as *Mingoes.* Most Ohio Mingoes were Sen-ecas, but among them were Cayugas, Mohawks, Onondagas, Oneidas, and Tuscaroras. A few Mohicans, a non-Iroquoian people, were sometimes in-cluded under this rubric.

These people seem to have drifted into Ohio voluntarily, perhaps seeking new hunting and trapping lands or more favorable access to trading posts. In the 1740s they were located near the trading center along the Cuyahoga, but in the 1750s they withdrew eastward to the Upper Ohio (the Allegheny River and its tributaries in western Pennsylvania). The Mingo also established vil-lages along the west bank of the Ohio River between modern Wellsville and Mingo Junction, and in central Ohio on the Scioto and Olentangy.

The *Ottawa* moved into Ohio from the north about 1740. This Algonquin tribe had been displaced from its Canadian and northern Michigan homeland; some Ottawas settled near the French post at Detroit. Like the Wyandots, they found the Detroit region to be overcrowded and moved into Ohio seek-ing hunting grounds and perhaps new trade opportunities with the British. They too were attracted initially to the Cuyahoga, but their principal villages were located in northwestern Ohio on the fringes of the Black Swamp. Though small in number, they were to play an important part in the forth-coming border warfare of the Great Lakes region.

The *Shawnee* is the most difficult of Ohio tribes to trace in the years prior to their Ohio settlement. Possibly Fort Ancient in ancestry, they were an Al-gonquin people whose five septs, or divisions, occasionally acted indepen-dently of one another. The Shawnee lacked strong central leadership, which may account for the readiness with which separate bands would wander far off from the rest. By the time historic Indians were settling Ohio, the largest number of Shawnees appear to have been in Pennsylvania, and it was mainly these Shawnees who moved into Ohio. Others may have come from Ken-tucky and the south. Early in the eighteenth century, some settled near Portsmouth, but the main body occupied the Scioto Valley in earnest after 1740, making the Pickaway Plains region between Chillicothe (the Shawnee word for village) and Circleville their main focus of settlement.

The Shawnees had been pushed from their Pennsylvania villages by unre-lenting white expansion and by pressure from the Six Nations. In similar fashion their eastern neighbors, the *Delaware,* were forced into a westward movement. By the 1750s, this migration took them into the Tuscarawas and Muskingum valleys of eastern Ohio. The Lenni Lenape (real people) as they called themselves, were among the oldest Algonquin people of eastern America. They inhabited the Atlantic coastal and inland regions of New Jersey when first encountered by English settlers, and these Englishmen named them Delaware for the river valley around which many of their villages centered. While still in Pennsylvania many Delawares were converted to Christianity by Moravian missionaries who later helped direct their converts to Ohio, establishing villages of Christian Indians that have a unique place in Ohio's Indian history.

From time to time between 1750 and 1815, Indians of other tribes played a minor role in Ohio, sometimes establishing short-lived villages, sometimes engaging in hunting and trading, and sometimes becoming involved in military campaigns. Among them were the Pottawatomies and Chippewas (Ojibwas) from the northwest, Kickapoos from the west, and Cherokees from the south. Their impact on Ohio was minimal.

Cultural traits of the Ohio Indians

It is a cultural universal that people stereotype those not of their own kind, and certainly colonial Americans stereotyped American Indians, who were neither the bloodthirsty brutes nor the "noble savages" some thought them to be. Individual Indians represented the whole range of human types. By the time the historic Indians appear in Ohio, their traditional culture was already undermined and irrevocably changed by long contact with European peoples.

Each Indian tribe was distinctive; each had physical traits, traditions, and cultural characteristics which set it apart from the others. There is not room to deal with this diversity here, so some of the more common qualities of Indian society in the Ohio Country will be noted, keeping in mind that these generalizations may not apply in every case.

The historic Indians of Ohio were transients. They moved into Ohio from every point of the compass, some because of pressure from European settlers, some because of pressure from other Indian tribes, some seeking trade opportunities, and some simply because new village and hunting sites were available.

Ohio was a splendid place to relocate. Animals, fish, and fowl were abundant. Although buffalo and elk became scarce after 1790, deer, bear, raccoon, squirrel, and other food animals were plentiful in season. Beaver provided the Indians with furs as did muskrat, raccoon, fox, bear, otter, and mink, whose pelts were avidly sought by British and French traders. As late as 1785, the

Moravian missionary John Heckewelder reported: "a Trader purchased 23 Horseload of peltry from the few Indians then hunting on [Cuyahoga] River."

Ohio waters were rich in fish of many species. Heckewelder noted that just under the falls of the Cuyahoga "the fish crowd together in vast number, and may be taken here the whole year round." Small, clear lakes nearby were "alive with fish." Sturgeon in Lake Erie and catfish in the Ohio River often weighed as much as one hundred pounds. Wildfowl were everywhere. Turkeys of great size, fattened on the nuts and berries of the forest, were favorite targets of Indian hunters as were passenger pigeons, whose numbers were so great as to defy description. Flocks darkened the sky; they roosted in such numbers that tree limbs snapped under their weight. Along Lake Erie's marshy shoreline, and on inland lakes and ponds, ducks and geese provided a ready food supply in season.

Less one exaggerate this picture of abundance, it is well to remember that this natural world contained dangers. Wolves, bears, and wildcats (puma, sometimes called panthers or "painters" by pioneers) were a threat to the unwary. Timber rattlesnakes and copperheads were a deadly threat to man and beast. James Smith reported the Erie Islands to be so infested with "various kinds of serpents (but chiefly rattlesnakes), that it is dangerous landing." Smith reported that the islands were covered with snakes in summer and raccoons in winter leading the Indians to believe that the snakes became transmogrified into raccoons and vice versa as the seasons changed. The swamp rattler (massassauga) was also a threat to the careless. Mosquitoes and other biting, stinging insects were kept at bay by smudge fires, but once away from the fire, the Indians were at their mercy unless protected by the odorous animal fats with which they covered exposed flesh.

The continued abundance of Ohio's wild creatures hinged on several considerations. First was the fact that Indians were present in such limited numbers that the land was not overhunted nor the streams and lakes overfished. It is highly unlikely that the historic Indian population of Ohio ever exceeded 20,000 persons, a population density of one person for every two square miles. (In contrast, in 1990 there were 524 persons for every two square miles of Ohio land.) Second, hunting and fishing equipment was not of the most effective quality. Muskets, which had replaced bows and arrows, were inaccurate and were frequently broken; the rifle, obtained somewhat later, proved a more effective killing instrument. Third, Indians had learned from experience that animals must be protected during certain seasons or else the supply would diminish to an unacceptable level. Hunting and trapping were thus controlled by seasonal constraints, by the shifting of village sites, and by taboos on the taking of totemic animals. Fourth, nature limited kills of certain animals. In severe winter seasons, animals were hard to find. Then Ohio Indians lived on the edge of starvation; they divided into families or small parties and spread out in order to increase their hunting range.

Food supplies were supplemented by gathering natural products. The sap of sugar maples was processed—often by boiling, sometimes by freezing out the water content of the sap—into maple syrup and sugar. Maple syrup poured on a snowbank congealed into a chewy candy beloved by young and old alike. Honey was another natural sweetener, and a "bee tree" was a prized find, possession of which was sometimes contested by bears. Salt for seasoning and curing was extracted from salt springs or "licks." The Indian captive James Smith was taken by his captors to "the buffalo lick, where we killed several buffaloe, and in their small brass kettles they made about half a bushel of salt." Wild grapes and fruits were abundant as were edible berries and nuts. This natural harvest was an important food source. Many roots, stems, leaves, and barks were valued for their medicinal qualities; Indian herbal remedies, in fact, were usually safer and more effective than the medicines and treatments first introduced by white settlers.

Such abundance in available food supplies enabled Ohio Indians to be semi-sedentary. Though they moved frequently, they also established semiperma-nent villages, some of which might remain in place for decades. The more permanent villages contained bark-covered cabins or longhouses constructed by covering a pole frame with bark sheets tied on the frame. Low, dome-shaped wigwams (wegiwas) dominated the less permanent villages. Ottawas and Chippewas used bark or skin-covered tepees as temporary summer hunt-ing shelters. Some villages boasted a large council house; some had log cabins much like those of the white pioneers. By the early eighteenth century Indian villages no longer reflected "pure" Indian lifestyles. In them were found kettles, guns, tools, utensils, blankets, clothing, and ornamentation secured from the whites. Horses secured from whites speeded travel and allowed hunters and trappers to transport large loads.

The Ohio Indians located their principal villages along waterways for ease in communication and also because the rich bottom lands could readily be prepared for crops. Men helped clear fields, but women planted and culti-vated corn, beans of many varieties, squash, gourds, pumpkins, and tobacco. Some of the more permanent villages had orchards. At harvest time, crops were prepared for storage, some being placed in lined storage pits which were secreted around the village.

Within these settlements, tribal organization tended to break down after many years of close contact with whites. However, each tribe had a principal chief and many sub-chiefs. They were usually selected by tribal councils. In the Iroquoian tribes women took a central part in determining this selection. While not so common, one also finds women assuming important leadership roles in certain Algonquin tribes as well. For example, the sister of Cornstalk

(Holaqueska), the principal chief of the Shawnees, was a formidable woman known to the British as the Grenadier Squaw; she was the dominant figure in her village, called Grenadier Squaw's Town. Within each tribe, war chiefs were selected by virtue of their "luck" in battle or their skill in leading raids against frontier settlements, and retained their role only so long as they were successful. If one lost warriors or ran into "bad luck," he might be unable to persuade warriors to follow his lead; thus he ceased to be a war chief.

The Indian concept of property differed markedly from that of the European. Property rights were acknowledged among the members of an Indian family. Everything within the Indian's house or family had a particular owner. The Moravian missionary, John Heckewelder, said of the Christian Delawares:

> Every individual knows what belongs to him, from the horse or cow down to the dog, cat, kitten and little chicken. Parents make presents to their children, and they in return to their parents. A father will sometimes ask his wife or one of his children for the loan of his horse to go out ahunting. For a litter of kittens or brood of chickens, there are often as many different owners as there are individual animals. In purchasing a hen with her brood, one frequently has to deal for it with several children. . . . This is attended with a very good effect; for by this means every living creature is properly taken care of. It also promotes liberality among the children, which becomes a habit with them by the time they are grown up.

While private property was thus recognized for personal possessions, quite a different concept controlled the Indian's attitude toward the land itself. In the words of Turk, a Wyandot, "No one in particular can justly claim this [land]; it belongs in common to us all; no earthly being has an exclusive right to it. The Great Spirit above is the true and only owner of this soil; and He has given us all an equal right to it." Thus Indians felt they had only a use right to the soil, unlike Europeans, who claimed outright ownership of particular parcels. Heckewelder explained that, to the Delaware, the "sale" of land might involve almost any mutually satisfactory change in the relationship of two groups of persons subsisting on the land. In the earliest sales, he said, "the Indians seem to have intended only to give the whites freedom to use the land in conjunction with the native population." However, the white man did not see it this way. When he bought land from the Indians he in effect placed "no trespassing" signs around it and regarded the Indians' continued use for hunting and trapping to constitute a breach of faith. The Indians, of course, were merely continuing their well-established use of the land and did not see how their presence threatened the white man's interests.

Among Indian cultural traits most despised by whites were scalping and the torture of prisoners. Evidence shows that Indians scalped long before their contacts with Europeans, but when Indian tribes were used in European power struggles, the whites paid them to bring in enemy scalps. Thus a practice of ritualistic significance became transformed into a commercial venture. The scalp was originally regarded as a trophy of the chase and the kill. Such trophy-taking was not unique to Indians, but one can appreciate why whites who were targets of this custom failed to take any comfort from that knowledge.

As for torture, Europeans universally condemned it, conveniently forgetting that in their own prisons they tortured prisoners as fiendishly as any Indian, often in the interest of Christianity. Tribes of the Iroquois Confederacy had a particularly fearsome reputation as torturers. The Seneca, for example, allowed a bereaved relative to condemn as many prisoners to slow death as he or she wished. Some tribes rarely tortured prisoners. Even among those that did, there was occasionally an influential Indian leader, like Tecumseh of the Shawnee, who scorned participation in the tormenting of helpless prisoners. For all their condemnation of scalping and torture, ruffian border whites adopted these practices and could wield the knife and the burning brand as effectively as any Indian.

Not all white and black prisoners were condemned to death. Many, especially the young, were adopted in ceremonies which signified the washing away of white or black blood and its replacement with the blood of the Indian. Many of these adoptive relationships were close and enduring. In various treaties with the whites, the Ohio Indians were forced to return captives who had been adopted, and on such occasions there were pitiful scenes as children were torn from their adoptive parents, wives were separated from husbands, and captives who had already experienced one culture shock now faced still another as they were repatriated among those from whom they had been taken.

Religion permeated every aspect of Indian life. The Ohio Indians were animists, believing that every living creature, and also certain inanimate objects like wind and water, contained an "anima," or spirit. It was important to placate these spirits by proper behavior, and to guard against evil spirits and witchcraft. A web of customs and ceremonies evolved to achieve these ends. The shaman, who interpreted the spirits' moods, knew the ceremonies, incantations, and secrets for dealing with them. Omens and dreams were repeated, interpreted, and examined for their significance. Occasionally an unusually influential "prophet" would arise; such was Neolin, the Delaware Prophet, or Tenskwatawa, the Shawnee Prophet. The prophets' messages often included a plea to return to native ways and give up the corrupting influence of the white man's values, his goods, and above all, his liquor.

The Indians' affinity for alcohol, whether French brandy, English rum, or American whiskey, is well documented. As a trader among the Great Lakes Indians observed, alcohol was the first thing and the last thing the Indians asked for. Certain Indian leaders, very much aware of the devastating effects which alcohol had on their people, tried to get white authorities to ban it in the Indian trade. Despite some sincere efforts to cooperate, colonial authorities were never able to enforce such a ban. Greedy traders and unscrupulous squatters continued to ply the Indians with "fire water" for their own nefarious purposes.

Scholars have long pondered the Indians' vulnerability to strong drink. Efforts to explain it include the possibility that Indians had a vitamin deficiency or a chemical imbalance in their blood; or they lacked a social etiquette about when and how to drink; or that Indians had an attraction for the instant visions which the drunk experiences. One recent study maintains that the "drunken Indian," in living up to his stereotype, was engaged in a form of social protest against white society.

In their Ohio setting, Indians who had ready access to alcohol became ever more dependent upon it. They were increasingly vulnerable as white population swelled in the West, bringing with it an increased capacity for distilling and distributing the disabling drink.

Alcohol was second only to disease as the great destroyer of Indian culture. Long before they arrived in Ohio, the Indians had suffered severe population loss from a variety of diseases brought to North America by Europeans. Common diseases such as measles and whooping cough, against which Europeans had developed antibodies, struck the Indians with epidemic force, wiping out entire villages. Smallpox and certain other virulent diseases struck whites and Indians alike with the same deadly force. As late as 1795 the United States secretary of war was warning his commander in the Ohio Country to protect the Indians from smallpox which, he wrote, "would produce the most disastrous consequences" among them.

The call of Indian prophets and reformers to abandon the white man's ways sometimes included religion. Each Ohio tribe had had some experience with Christian missionaries, but the intensity of this experience varied. French Jesuit missionaries—the famous "black robes"—had worked among the Ottawas, Wyandots, and Miamis, but the enduring results of their labor appear to have been modest. Protestant missionary activity was sporadic, often undertaken in conjunction with training Indian boys at "Indian schools."

A notable exception to the transient nature of most missionary work was the activity which the Moravians (a pietistic Protestant group originally from Moravia), carried on with the Delawares. Moravian teachers led the Christian Delawares from their Pennsylvania homes into the Muskingum and Tuscarawas valleys starting in 1772. There they established productive new villages—Schoenbrunn, Gnadenhutten, Lichtenau, Salem. However, these villages and their inhabitants were devastated during the Revolutionary War. Well-meaning white missionaries continued to work among the Indians until their final expulsion from Ohio in the nineteenth century. The more sensitive missionaries performed good works, but even they contributed to the cultural and societal confusion of Indian life.

The Ohio Indians have most often been described as pawns in the white man's power struggles. It is also true that the Ohio Indians played the British and French off against each other. However, the integrity of Indian societies, already seriously corrupted by foreign influences, continued to diminish as they were caught in the Anglo-French political, economic and military competition for control of the Ohio Country.

2.

The Contest for Control
of the Ohio Country

The French Presence

While England was establishing its first permanent colony in North America at Jamestown, Virginia, Frenchmen were gaining what they believed was a permanent foothold on the St. Lawrence. This magnificent river had been explored in the 1530s and 1540s by Jacques Cartier, whose discoveries gave the French monarch a claim to the river and the lands it drained. Samuel de Champlain, in the employ of a French trading company, established a post on the massive rock of Quebec in 1608. In the next two and a half decades, with the assistance of his Huron Indian allies, he established France's claims in the interior of North America. In 1612, accompanied by Huron Indians and a young adventurer named Etienne Brulé, Champlain reached Georgian Bay and established the French presence on the Great Lakes. The party returned to the St. Lawrence via Lake Ontario, but Brulé stayed behind and lived for a time among the Hurons. Some scholars assume that he became the first European to see Lake Erie although no convincing proof has been found to support that claim.

French interest in the new world was largely commercial. Trading companies and, after 1663, the French crown concentrated on profits from the fur trade rather than on establishing a new homeland for French settlers. An important secondary interest was the desire of Catholic orders to establish missions among the Indians. Thus commerce and the cross lured Frenchmen toward the Ohio Country, but the Iroquois Confederacy stood in their way. Ever since 1609, when Champlain and his Huron allies had humiliated a Mohawk war party by overawing them with musket fire, the Iroquois had been implacable enemies of the French. Many brave but foolishly optimistic French missionaries died in hideous fashion while trying to convert the Iroquois and secure them to the French interest.

Shortly after their humiliation by Champlain, the Iroquois obtained firearms from Dutch traders operating along the Hudson River. Thus supplied, they effectively shielded southern Lake Ontario and the approaches to Lake Erie, forcing the French and their Indian allies to take a more northerly route along the Ottawa River in passing between Montreal and the western Great Lakes. Not until 1669 is there evidence of French activity along the fringes of the Ohio Country, and by that time French fur traders had already established posts at Sault Ste. Marie, Michilimackinac, Green Bay, and elsewhere far to the north and west. Unlike Michigan, Indiana, Illinois, and Wisconsin, where the French maintained a presence for a century or more, Ohio had no substantial, lasting French connection.

The use of Ohio's waterways by the French evolved slowly. Although they did not use Lake Erie as a passage to the west until late in the seventeenth century, it is certain that they knew about it much earlier. Jesuits and members of the Recollect order reported the presence of the Erie Indians living along its southeastern shore. A map drawn by the French geographer Nicolas Sanson d'Abbeville in 1650 portrays Lake Erie with surprising accuracy some nineteen years before Adrien Joliet made the first authenticated passage on the lake. On this journey, Joliet encountered an expedition led by René Robert Cavelier Sieur de La Salle, a twenty-six-year-old French aristocrat who had properties near LaChine (China) Rapids above Montreal. La Salle, eager to secure furs and other possible riches, had been told by Senecas of a great river into the interior. It seems likely they were referring to the Allegheny which, joined at Pittsburgh by the Monongahela, forms the Ohio, or they may have been referring to the Mississippi, believing the Ohio to be its headwaters. Scholars have assumed that La Salle discovered the Ohio River, and by 1674 a French map not only depicted the Ohio but attributed knowledge of it to La Salle.

The French called the Ohio *la belle riviere,* the beautiful river. Its strategic importance would be hard to exaggerate since it was an obvious communication route connecting New France along the St. Lawrence with France's Louisiana claims along the lower Mississippi. In the eighteenth century, both La Galissoniere and Duquesne, governor generals of New France, planned to fortify the route of the Allegheny and Ohio, thus confining the British east of that line. However, the French never succeeded in developing this strategic waterway. British pioneers rather than French traders were destined to make the Ohio Valley the great highway into the West.

The British Influx

The French presence in the Great Lakes region and the Ohio River basin did not remain unchallenged. Within a few years of the explorations of Joliet and La Salle, English traders from the Carolinas and Virginia were active along the lower Ohio and its tributaries. Little is known of them. Most were unlettered men; they were not accompanied by literate clergy such as those who left graphic accounts of French efforts among the Indians. As early as 1685 traders out of New York crossed Lake Erie on their way to the upper lakes. When this avenue was closed by the French, New York traders encouraged certain western Indians to bring their furs to Albany or to the new British post at Oswego on Lake Ontario. This was possible only so long as the Iroquois permitted it since they controlled access to these New York posts. But in time the Iroquois, fearful of losing their role as diplomatic and commercial middlemen between the British and the western Indians, began to discourage the practice, so New York traders were forced either to work through them or go into the field themselves as did the traders from other British provinces. Both French and British interests thus "invaded" Indian lands and changed Indian life forever.

The French and the British each claimed a legitimate right to engage in the western trade, and each sought to exclude the other on the basis of these claims. The French claim to the Great Lakes basin and the Ohio-Mississippi watershed rested on the right of discovery and the right of possession. Their people had opened these lands and had established a presence there before any other Europeans. British claims rested on the "sea-to-sea" provisions of colonial charters, which allowed Virginia, Connecticut, Massachusetts, and certain other seaboard colonies to extend their boundaries across the continent to the western sea. It was immaterial to the British case that the king, in making these grants, had no idea of how vast a land he was granting. New York had no "sea-to-sea" charter, but the Iroquois, who claimed the Ohio Country, were located in New York, and that was reason enough for provincial officials to claim a New York interest in the West. Pennsylvania had no legal claim beyond its present western border, but that did not deter Pennsylvania traders and provincial officials from an active involvement in western Indian affairs.

The Indians, on the other hand, clearly thought the land and its resources were theirs, since they had used and occupied the territory long before Europeans came to challenge them. The French and British recognized Indian claims to the extent that they were willing to negotiate with the tribes, seal agreements, and sign treaties. Their traders sought "permission" to establish posts in Indian villages. However, the expansion of European commerce and settlement overrode these gestures when it appeared that Indian stubbornness might frustrate European designs upon tribal land and resources. Both the French and the British manipulated the Indians, considering their own interests to outweigh any consideration due the tribes. Europeans thus established the basis for conflict in the Ohio Country.

The French, having been first on the scene, attempted to consolidate control of the western tribes and to isolate them from what they saw as the insidious activities of British traders. To this end, Antoine de la Mothe Cadillac built a post called Fort Pontchartrain at Detroit in 1701. He planned it to be a center for the fur trade, and he encouraged various tribes to settle in its vicinity. Five years later, Fort Miami (modern Fort Wayne, Indiana) was opened at the head of the Maumee River close by Kekionga and other principal towns of the Miami people. Satellite posts were maintained by French traders in nearby villages.

These French efforts were soon undercut by the initiative of Pennsylvania and Virginia traders. By providing the Indians with goods of equal or better quality at lower prices, these traders became influential in the Ohio Country. They had particular strength at trading posts on the Cuyahoga and Sandusky Bay, at Conchake (Coshocton) on the Muskingum, Lower Shawnee Town (near Portsmouth), and Pickawillany, a Miami village established in 1747 by a chief whom the French called La Demoiselle and the British called Old Briton. La Demoiselle deliberately placed his village on the upper waters of the Great Miami near modern Piqua, east of other Miami villages, in order to be closer to British traders and to remove himself from the influence of the French commandant at Fort Miami, who made repeated efforts to get him to move closer to the Maumee.

From 1744 to 1748 Great Britain and France were formally at war in Europe, on the high seas, and in North America, where the struggle was called King George's War. It was but the most recent in a series of wars fought by these old antagonists for commercial supremacy throughout the world. During this struggle British naval vessels and privateers succeeded in cutting off ships carrying supplies to New France, seriously reducing the French stock of Indian trade goods and giving an advantage to British traders, whose supplies were not affected. Although the war ended in 1748, the tense atmosphere persisted. Therefore the Comte de la Galissoniere, Governor of New France, authorized an armed expedition of some 250 French Canadians and Indians to proceed down the Allegheny and Ohio to impress the Indians with French might and to warn British traders to evacuate French territory.

The leader of this expedition was Célèron de Blainville, a former commandant at Detroit who was thoroughly familiar with the situation in the Ohio Country and experienced in dealing with the Indians. Father Joseph Pierre de Bonnecamps accompanied the expedition and wrote an account of its mission. In the summer of 1749 Célèron made his way to the upper Allegheny. As he proceeded downstream, he stopped at each important river confluence and planted a lead plate several feet deep in the earth. Each plate bore an inscription asserting that the surrounding lands belonged to the king of France. Near the buried plate, a message, impressed on a thin metal plate, was fastened to a tree to alert the curious that the formal claim was buried nearby. This medieval practice of planting a claim makes little sense to modern minds, but it seemed like a good idea and a wise precaution at the time. At least two of the lead plates were later found and now reside in museum collections.

Célèron was alarmed to find British traders in nearly every important Indian village. Logstown, eighteen miles downstream from the forks of the Ohio, and Lower Shawnee Town, at the mouth of the Scioto, were particularly strong centers of British trade. Reaching the Great Miami, Célèron turned northward up the river to Pickawillany, where he tried to bring La Demoiselle back into the French fold. Unsuccessful in this effort, he pressed on to Detroit, and finally returned to Montreal five months after setting out, his expedition a failure. It did not deter British traders in the Ohio Country, nor did it intimidate the Indians.

Célèron's expedition coincided with French efforts to regain the trading initiative in Ohio. For reasons not altogether clear, the Indian concentration along the Cuyahoga had dissipated by 1750; Saguin's post there appears to have been abandoned while a new, fortified post was erected eighty miles to the west at Sandusky. Two years later the French undertook the long-threatened disciplining of the Miamis of Pickawillany. La Demoiselle's village of more than 400 inhabitants contained a stockaded trading post from which British agents worked the Indian villages of the region. In 1752, in what some historians have called the first battle of the French and Indian War, Charles Langlade, a half-breed, led 200 French Canadians and Indians in a surprise raid that destroyed the British post. Five British traders were taken prisoner to Detroit and later released with a warning to stay clear of the Ohio Country. Several Indians were killed, among them La Demoiselle, whose heart was ripped out and eaten and his body boiled and consumed in the ritual cannibalism common to the western tribes. Pickawillany soon fell into disuse as its inhabitants pulled back into Indiana.

To a limited extent, the Ohio Indians had profited from the Anglo-French trade rivalry. But it was not the fur trader who was the ultimate threat to their future; it was the land speculator and the settler. Land speculation was perhaps the oldest profession in North America. Those who followed Columbus cast covetous eyes on some of the world's finest real estate and, in the English colonies especially, speculating in land became a favorite sport of nearly everyone who could afford it, and of many who could not.

Colonials and their associates in the Mother Country were always on the lookout for lands unoccupied by Europeans which could be secured cheaply, developed, and then sold at a profit to settlers. For generations the extensive lands east of the Appalachians provided a theater for their schemes, but the lure of western lands had become irresistible by the early eighteenth century.

In 1748 prominent Virginians organized the Ohio Company, which received from the English crown a grant of 200,000 acres at the forks of the Ohio. In return, the company was to settle a hundred families on this land and erect a fort for their protection. A company storehouse was built at Will's Creek (Cumberland, Maryland) and a crude trail was cut over the mountains toward the Ohio. Christopher Gist was hired as company agent to survey and to open trade with the Ohio Indians. By 1752 the company had abandoned plans to occupy land north of the Ohio River. Instead, company commissioners secured a "deed" from the Indians allowing settlement south and east of the Ohio, in modern-day Pennsylvania and West Virginia. The company promised to build posts between the Monongahela and the Kanawha to supply the Indian trade. The trading post most wanted by the Indians, one at the forks of the Ohio, was not built because of rivalry between the Virginia-dominated company and officials of Pennsylvania who claimed the strategic forks area for their province. Meanwhile French officials in Paris and Quebec had taken alarm and determined upon a course of action that precipitated a showdown between Great Britain and France for possession and control of the heartland of North America.

The governor general of New France in 1753 was the Marquis de Duquesne. He favored vigorous efforts to maintain France's position along the Upper Ohio, and early in that year he dispatched an army of more than 1,500 men to seize possession of the Ohio-Allegheny river valleys and to fortify them as a barrier to British expansion. The expedition sailed to Presqu'isle (Erie, Pennsylvania), where a small stockade was erected. At the headwaters of French Creek they built Fort Le Boeuf and at its mouth they erected Fort Venango. In each of these stockades the French left a small garrison, but they did not secure the forks of the Ohio until the following year.

Meanwhile Robert Dinwiddie, lieutenant-governor of Virginia, moved to counter this French initiative. With the support of the Board of Trade in London, he sent a young and untested Virginian, George Washington, to assure the Ohio Indians of Virginia's friendship and support and to challenge the French presence on the Allegheny. With the veteran woodsman Christopher Gist as guide, Washington carried out his instructions despite enormous difficulties. Upon reaching Fort Le Boeuf, he presented the commander with Governor Dinwiddie's message warning the French to abandon the forts they had erected on land claimed by the king of England. Philippe Joincare,

the commandant at Le Boeuf, agreed to forward Dinwiddie's message to
Quebec, but in the meantime, he said, he had orders to take prisoner any
Englishman attempting to trade on the Ohio or its tributaries.

Winter had set in before Washington, Gist, and their Indian escorts left for
Virginia. The long wilderness journey was a triumph over adversity as Washington and Gist survived hunger, a close-range shot fired by an Indian in
French employ, entrapment for the night on an island in the ice-clogged Allegheny, and the other rigors of a wilderness winter. They finally emerged
from the wilderness at a British trading post on the Monongahela.

Dinwiddie was not pleased by the French response to his message, and in
1754 he dispatched Washington and an expedition to the forks of the Ohio to
support and protect a small post recently built there by William Trent, an
experienced fur trader. Before Washington could act, he received word that
the fort had been seized by a French force that had begun to enlarge and
strengthen it. The post was renamed Fort Duquesne, and its garrison was
strong enough to dominate access to the Ohio Valley. The French consolidated this success by seizing and reinforcing the important British trading
post at Logstown, eighteen miles downstream from the forks.

Washington, meanwhile, did what he could to frustrate French activity.
Moving westward from Wills Creek, he surprised a band of French soldiers
and their Indian allies who, he claimed, had violated Virginia territory. His
force killed the French commander, Sieur de Jumonville, and nine others;
twenty-one prisoners were taken. Washington then retreated to a defensive
position at the Great Meadows southeast of Fort Duquesne where he constructed an inadequate emergency shelter called Fort Necessity. Here he tried
to quiet the fears of panicky Ohio Indians alarmed by French military successes. When Fort Necessity was attacked in July 1754 by an impressive force
of French and Indians, Washington had no recourse but to surrender. In return for a pledge that no forts would be built by Virginians west of the mountains for at least one year, his dispirited force was allowed to march out with
"drums beating and flags flying" on their long road back to Virginia. Thus
began what was to be known as the French and Indian War, the North American portion of a world struggle between France and Great Britain, a struggle
that historian Lawrence Gipson called "The Great War for the Empire."

French success on the Ohio caused the western Indians to reconsider where
their long-range interests lay. British traders had been driven from their land,
and it appeared that the tribes were again dependent upon the French. If
further proof were needed, the ambush and rout of Gen. Edward Braddock's
army in 1755 solidified the French stranglehold. Braddock, ignoring Washington's advice, marched into an ambush by French-led Indians about twelve
miles from Fort Duquesne. The scalp *halloo* rang in Delaware, Shawnee, and

Wyandot villages as warriors returned with grisly trophies; prisoners brought to Fort Duquesne were later tortured and killed in nearby Indian encampments.

For three years French influence was supreme along the Ohio. The French supported Indian war parties that left villages along the Cuyahoga, Muskingum, Scioto, Sandusky, and beyond to descend on the isolated cabins and settlements of Pennsylvania and Virginia. Hundreds, perhaps thousands of frontier men, women, and children were killed or captured. Some captives were slain, but many others were adopted into Indian families. Pennsylvanians James Smith, Charles Stuart, and Mary Campbell were typical of young captives who were treated well. Smith and Stuart each spent about four years with the Ohio tribes before slipping away to white society. Mary Campbell, captured by Delawares, was held at Netawatwees' town near the falls of the Cuyahoga before she was returned to her Pennsylvania family after seven years of captivity.

But by 1758 the military advantage was swinging toward the British. In the autumn of that year a British and colonial army led by Maj. Gen. John Forbes seized Fort Duquesne, which the French had abandoned and burned upon Forbes's approach. On its site the British erected a strong new fortification. They named it Fort Pitt in honor of William Pitt, the able war minister who was organizing British successes on land and sea. By 1759 nearly all important French posts along the northern border had fallen, including Quebec, the administrative heart of New France.

The final blow to France's American empire was delivered in 1760 by Gen. Lord Jeffrey Amherst, who seized Montreal, the center of the western fur trade. The terms of Montreal's capitulation provided that France turn over its western posts to the British. Thus the contraction of French power in the Ohio Country, which had begun with the fall of Fort Duquesne, was now complete. The Ohio Indians, allies of the defeated French, were left in a state of uncertainty and confusion as British redcoats moved to replace French garrisons in the western country.

Among the first French posts occupied were Detroit and Michilimackinac. Maj. Robert Rogers, an experienced and successful Indian fighter from New Hampshire, led the expedition that took control of these posts in 1760. Rogers tried to quiet the Indians' fears, conferring with them on his trip west, but there was a strong undercurrent of belief among some Lakes tribes that the French would return and British occupation would prove temporary. Countering this feeling was the Indians' resentment over the French and British assumption that the land was France's to surrender, an assumption that ignored the Indians' right to control what they saw as their own lands.

Despite some disillusionment with the French, the Ohio Indians much preferred them to the aggressive British, whose uses of the land threatened the Indians' very livelihood. An explosive hostility toward the British began to fester and was soon to seek release.

Pontiac's Rebellion and British Policy in the West

With the signing of the Peace of Paris in 1763, France no longer had an official presence in North America, although the French did retain St. Pierre and Miquelon, tiny islands off Newfoundland on which they could service their fishing fleets. Spain's belated entry in the war as an ally of France cost Spain control of the Floridas. Thus all lands east of the Mississippi were now part of the British Empire. Even before the treaty was signed, Great Britain recognized that she had taken on an awesome new responsibility—the protection, administration, and economic development of the interior lands of North America. An enlarged regular army, stationed in posts which extended in a great arc from Nova Scotia in the north through the Mississippi Valley to the Floridas in the south, was to provide protection from any French or Spanish efforts to seize these exposed lands. Local garrisons would also monitor the Indians and serve as focal points for controlling the Indian trade.

Great Britain had amassed a huge war debt, however, and Parliament was in no mood to pay to maintain adequate forces in North America, a policy that almost cost Great Britain control of the interior. Presents to the Indians were halted. Supplies of gunpowder and shot were curtailed, making it difficult for Indian hunters to secure enough for their needs. British officials seemed on the whole to lack the easy rapport which many French leaders adopted toward the Indians. Were it not for a few skilled diplomats, such as William Johnson among the Iroquois and George Croghan working with the western Indians, the British cause would have been lost.

A challenge to the new British overlords was not long in coming. In 1763 the Ottawa war chief Pontiac attempted to organize an Indian confederacy which would act in concert to drive the British back beyond the eastern mountains. Though a lasting confederacy did not develop, Indians of various tribes did work together temporarily in attacks on every British post in the West. In Ohio, only the fortified post called Fort Sandusky was occupied by British troops. Located on Sandusky Bay, this post was overrun and the tiny garrison of thirteen men slaughtered. All other British-held posts in the West were taken except Detroit and Fort Pitt. Pontiac himself led the five-month siege of Detroit, showing determination in siege warfare unprecedented among Indians.

In response to this challenge, successive British expeditions commanded by Col. John Bradstreet and Col. Henry Bouquet were ordered into the Ohio

Country early in 1764. Bradstreet moved out of Fort Niagara with orders to subdue the Lakes tribes, but he failed to achieve any positive results. On the other hand, Bouquet marched westward from Fort Pitt in October 1764 and succeeded where Bradstreet had failed. He shielded his disciplined line of march from surprise by deploying a screen of experienced Virginia back-woodsmen. Moving to the principal Delaware town of Goshgoshgunk (later Coshocton), near the forks of the Muskingum, Bouquet dictated terms of peace to the Ohio Indians, primarily Shawnees, Delawares, and Wyandots. They were to be protected within their lands north of the Ohio River, they were to bring in all captives, white and black, for repatriation, and they were not to interfere with whites settling south of the Ohio. The tribes adhered to these terms although repatriation of captives was as painful to the Indians as it was to those of the captives who had adjusted well to Indian society.

Bouquet's pacification of the Ohio tribes was but part of a larger British effort to reduce hostilities in the West. In 1763 King George III issued a royal proclamation which established a dividing line down the crest of the Appala-chian Mountains. No settlers were to locate west of that line. This effort to keep the peace by separating settlers and Indians failed, for trying to stop the westward movement of American colonials was like trying to make the tides stand still; it had not worked in the past, and it did not work this time despite British army efforts to administer the rule. The colonial ministry in London had intended to employ up to 10,000 regular troops in the American back country, though actual numbers were far short of that goal. To help pay for their upkeep, Parliament enacted the Sugar Act in 1764, thus setting in motion a series of events which would help to precipitate the American Revolution. Finally, in 1764 king's officials introduced a new Board of Trade policy. It required that traders be licensed, that they refrain from using rum or other "spiritous liquors" in their trading activities, and that they carry on their work through British posts so their actions could be supervised.

The Proclamation Line and the Board of Trade plan were not motivated by love and concern for the Indians. Rather, these efforts were designed to keep the Indians free from the drunkenness and disturbances which had interfered with the profitable fur trade. Peace in the Ohio country would enhance prof-its while reducing Britain's costs in maintaining order. Had these policies succeeded, the bloody encounters soon to come might well have been de-layed; it would be a misreading of frontier attitudes and conditions, however, to suppose that they could have been avoided.

Prelude to the American Revolution

In 1768 the Ohio Indians and the Iroquois Confederacy were prominently represented at councils leading to the Treaty of Fort Stanwix (Rome, New

York). This treaty provided for an Indian reserve in lands set aside north and west of the Ohio River and in northwestern Pennsylvania and western New York. Both royal and provincial officials "guaranteed" the sanctity of the Indian lands, but the gates were opened to settlement in southwestern Pennsylvania, especially along the Monongahela, in western Virginia, and in Kentucky, the Shawnee hunting ground. Ambitious land company schemes were targeted for these areas, and some plans even called for new colonies to be established in the region that the treaty had just vouchsafed to the Indians. Powerful and influential men in Great Britain and in the colonies pushed these schemes. George Washington, rising in wealth and ambition, revisited the western country in 1770, making an exploratory trip down the Ohio to the Kanawha seeking lands which he hoped would be granted him for prior military services. Some of his camp sites were on the Ohio side of the river where he had no right to be. Other whites seeking land or trade or even new mission fields likewise violated the Indian reserve.

Sometimes, however, these whites came as guests under the protection of one or another Indian group. Among the best known of such newcomers to Ohio were the Moravian missionaries. By the late 1750s the Moravians were scouting out Ohio lands. Christian Frederick Post in 1761 knew the lands along the Tuscarawas and Muskingum, and it was there that the Moravians established new missions for Christian Indians. Led by David Zeisberger, John Heckewelder and their associates, Christian Indians (mostly Delawares) migrated westward from Pennsylvania to establish villages far removed from the tensions and distractions which had beset them. Schoenbrunn ("Beautiful Spring") was laid out in 1772 on an orderly plan along the Tuscarawas. Soon Gnadenhutten ("Tents of Grace") and Lichtenau ("Fields of Light") were established further downstream, and other towns followed.

These Moravian villages were under the protection of the Delaware chief White Eyes of the Turkey division, whose principal villages were close by at Goshgoshgunk (Coshocton) and Newcomer's Town. Soon the Moravian towns boasted flourishing fields surrounding orderly villages, each containing a store, a church and a school. The apparent prosperity of the Christian Indians was a goad to certain other Indians who actively opposed the white man's influence with its accompanying loss of Indian tradition and self-sufficiency. Hopocan (Captain Pipe), leader of the wolf division of the Delawares (sometimes called Munsees), was especially hostile to whites, and from his villages along the upper Tuscarawas he attempted to check their growing influence. In a few years, Hopocan would get his chance to strike hard at his enemies.

By 1774 western Pennsylvania and the lands beyond were again centers of conflict. British troops pulled out of Fort Pitt in 1772, leaving a power vacuum which both Pennsylvania and Virginia attempted to fill. Virginia had the better of it. Its aggressive royal governor, James Murray, Earl of Dunmore, sent Dr. John Connolly to be his agent at the forks of the Ohio. In 1774 the fortification there was occupied by Virginia troops, and the area east and south of the Ohio River came under Virginia's active control.

The desire of Virginia and other seaboard colonies to control the lands beyond the Ohio was frustrated, however, when Parliament enacted the Quebec Act of 1774. Though later historians regard it as an enlightened piece of legislation, British colonials thought it anything but. The act attached the lands northwest of the Ohio to the Province of Quebec, which was administered from the old French capital along the St. Lawrence. By doing this, Parliament attached the Ohio Country to a provincial government which, unlike other British colonies in America, was administered by military authority and was free from the assertive elected assemblies which dominated the other colonial governments. Colonials saw this move as an unfair restriction on royal charters that had "sea-to-sea" provisions. On a more practical level, colonials who hoped to profit from exploiting the West—traders, land speculators, missionaries—realized that it would be more difficult to arrange affairs to their liking if control of western lands resided in the autocratic hands of the governor of Quebec. Other terms of the act rankled as well. French residents of Quebec were to be protected in the practice of their Roman Catholic religion and in their recourse to French civil law. These concessions outraged colonials who had fought the French "papists" for generations only to see their former enemies now receive protection from a parliamentary act which, at the same time, seemed to retract their hard-won spoils of victory in the French and Indian War. This perception played no small part in persuading frontier colonials and others with western interests to take up arms against the Mother Country.

Imperial politics had little positive influence on the development of the western frontier. Well-intentioned British and provincial officials tried to control affairs, especially the Indian trade, but they were overwhelmed by the westward surge of new settlers. The valley of the Monongahela filled up quickly with new cabins. Settlers once isolated along the Ohio, the Kanawha, the Greenbrier, and other western Virginia rivers now had neighbors. They no longer shunned Kentucky as "the dark and bloody ground" even though Harrodsborough, Boonesborough, and other frontier posts were on lands which the Cherokee from the south and the Shawnee from the north still claimed as hunting ground. As many as 30,000 persons lived in what is now southwestern Pennsylvania and the panhandle region of West Virginia in 1774–75, with additional thousands starting to pour into Kentucky. In contrast, the entire Indian population of Ohio at that time probably did not exceed 20,000. The Indians would never be more numerous in Ohio, but the white population on lands south of the Ohio River would continue to swell. This central fact was clearly perceived by Indian leaders, especially chiefs of the Mingo, Delaware, and Shawnee tribes who had experienced the effects of white population pressures on their former homes in New York and Pennsylvania.

Opportunities for conflict increased in direct proportion to population. Frustrated young warriors, seeing their hunting grounds threatened, "took up the hatchet" and raided to the east and south of the Ohio. As in the French and Indian War, inhabitants of frontier posts and settlers in isolated cabins became targets of their wrath. Horses were stolen, settlers were killed or captured; life on the western frontier was lived under constant tension. But tough white frontiersmen were hard to intimidate. Some of the best-remembered, men such as Daniel Boone and Simon Kenton, struck hard at the Ohio Indians, although usually in a manner that both Indians and whites thought appropriate to the provocation. Such adversaries were the kind that Indians could respect. Some border "heroes," however, seem not so admirable to later generations. Lewis Wetzel, Sam Brady, David Williamson, and the Poe brothers hunted Indians as one would hunt dangerous beasts. By any standard of civil behavior they were ruffians whose hatred of the Indian was pathological in its unreasoning intensity. All too often, the mythmakers confuse the latter type with the Boones and Kentons.

Amid the growing Indian-white conflicts of 1774, one incident stands out for its viciousness and for its far-reaching consequences. On the Ohio near the mouth of Yellow Creek was a Mingo town led by Tahgajute, known to the whites as Logan. He was the son of the great Cayuga chief Shickellamy, a friend of Pennsylvania provincial authorities. Logan befriended white men; in his own words he was to say, "Such was my love for the whites that my own countrymen pointed as they passed, and said, 'Logan is the friend of white men.' " Indians from Logan's village, including several members of his family, were lured across the Ohio to "Baker's Cabin," where a band of hard-bitten whites plied them with whiskey and then murdered them in cold blood. Logan was so outraged that he sought his own private vengeance and raided the exposed settlements east of the Ohio, not stopping until he had taken dozens of scalps. Some time later Logan poured out his grievances in words which were to become famous as Logan's Lament. Some say he sat under a great elm, later known as the Logan Elm, in Pickaway County while telling Indian agent John Gibson (Logan's brother-in-law), how his friendship for whites had been betrayed. His impressive statement concluded: "There runs not a drop of my blood in the veins of any living creature. . . . Who is there to mourn for Logan? Not one." Logan's Lament was long considered a noble example of Indian expression, and generations of nineteenth-century American school children were required to memorize it. Unfortunately, the embittered Logan, corrupted by liquor, became a drunk who was no longer respected by his people. He was murdered by another Indian about 1780.

Dunmore's War

With the border now aflame, Lord Dunmore set in motion a plan to intimidate the Ohio Indians, especially the Shawnees who were actively resisting further white encroachments upon their hunting grounds. Dunmore led a force of more than 1,000 men down the Ohio to the mouth of the Little Kanawha, where he expected to meet a force of similar size that Col. Andrew Lewis had raised along the Virginia frontier. Lewis was unable to make the planned rendezvous, however, because his camp at Point Pleasant (where the Kanawha joins the Ohio) was attacked by a large Indian army led by Cornstalk, chief of the Shawnees. The ensuing Battle of Point Pleasant, October 10, 1774, lasted many hours and was perhaps the most intense engagement between whites and Indians ever fought along the Ohio. Although both sides fought to exhaustion, the Indian forces withdrew to the Ohio's north bank leaving Lewis in command of the field and claiming the victory.

While Lewis was thus occupied, Dunmore ordered his men forward up the Hocking Valley and then westward to the main Shawnee villages in the Pickaway Plains. Here he established a temporary post called Camp Charlotte and set about negotiating with the Shawnees, who now showed much interest in establishing peace. Just as agreement was imminent, Lewis's army made its belated appearance on the Pickaway Plains and burned some Indian villages near Camp Charlotte. Dunmore handled a dangerous situation well, calming Shawnee fear of the "long knives" (Virginians), and concluding final arrangements for a peace. Foremost among the terms was mutual agreement that in return for leaving the Indians in peace north of the Ohio, whites living south of the river would not be disturbed nor would whites coming down the Ohio be victimized as in the past. Dunmore's army now returned to the Hocking, stopping near its mouth to erect a temporary fortification named Fort Gower. Here, Dunmore's officers promulgated the Fort Gower Resolutions, a series of statements pledging to support the work of the First Continental Congress, which recently had challenged the policies of the Mother Country.

Those who love "firsts" have made somewhat exaggerated claims for the battle of Point Pleasant, which they like to call the first battle of the American Revolution, and for the Fort Gower Resolutions, which have been eulogized as the first endorsement of revolutionary principles. Only by stretching credulity can one accept either of these claims. It is appropriate, however, to remember that British policies for the West alienated frontiersmen and influential provincial politicians. Hence the Ohio Country was bound to figure large in the coming struggle for American independence as an arena in which British control would be challenged, even as it was in the more populous East.

Revolution in the Ohio Country and the West

In the spring of 1775 British soldiers and American "minutemen" fought at Lexington and Concord; in the fall of that year Benedict Arnold and Brig. Gen. Richard Montgomery invaded the St. Lawrence region and brought war to the northern frontier. In Virginia, Lord Dunmore abandoned his post in the face of mounting insurgency and sailed for England. In the West, a self-appointed Committee of Public Safety seized control of Fort Pitt, thus forcing the issue between those who were wavering between support of the "patriot" (American) cause and the "loyalist" (British) cause. Efforts by John Connolly, a loyalist, to rally Indian support for a British-led invasion of western Virginia were frustrated when Connolly was arrested by patriots. Fort Pitt was securely in patriot hands.

The Continental Congress was now directing the expanding war, and George Washington, commander-in-chief of American forces, hoped to secure the support or neutrality of the Ohio Indian tribes. Commissioners from Congress and from Virginia (now free of its royal government) met with a large Indian delegation at Fort Pitt in September 1775 and signed a treaty that called for the Ohio Indians to remain neutral. This hoped-for neutrality was to prove illusory, partly because the Ohio tribes were located squarely between the principal British post at Detroit and the American settlements along the Ohio, with their main supply depot and anchor at Fort Pitt.

Both the Americans and British tried to influence these tribes. Congress authorized Washington to enlist 2,000 Indians and to offer rewards for British prisoners. Meanwhile, Col. Henry Hamilton, commander at Detroit, was trying to sway the Ohio Indians toward the British cause. His efforts were inadvertently aided by the belligerent actions of Pluggy's Band, a Mingo war party that repeatedly raided border settlements in 1776 from its encampments along the Scioto and the Walhonding. These raids helped bring Americans into open conflict with British-backed Ohio Indians. It was impossible for responsible chiefs to restrain their more aggressive young warriors, and by 1777 the three-year border truce came to an end.

The Shawnee chief Cornstalk, alarmed by the increasingly bellicose disposition of his warriors and believing it his duty to warn the Americans that he could no longer maintain his pledge not to molest the Virginia and Kentucky settlements, journeyed to Fort Randolph at Point Pleasant, Virginia. His son accompanied him. While in the fort, Cornstalk, his son, and two other Indians were murdered by militia incensed at reports that a white man had been killed

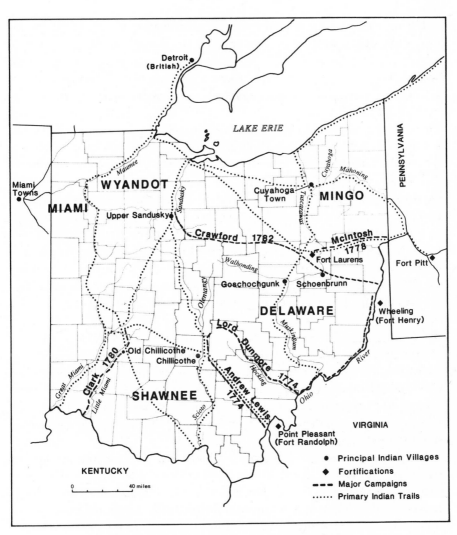

Map 5. Ohio During the American Revolution

nearby by an Indian raiding party. While one can understand the militiamen's anger, one cannot condone or excuse the cold-blooded murder of a noble-minded adversary who was in no way related to that killing. The Ohio Indians did not excuse it either, for now, with few exceptions, they openly chose sides against the Americans.

The Shawnees became the most implacable of foes, in part because their villages were exposed to American military forays and suffered more destruction than villages of other Ohio tribes except, perhaps, the Delawares.

While the Christian Delawares tried to remain neutral, Captain Pipe (Hopocan), chief of the wolf band, persuaded all Delawares except the Moravian converts to join the British. The Wyandots were staunch British supporters, and their villages along the Sandusky became important staging areas for attacks on American settlements. The Miamis joined in opposing the Americans as did the Ottawas and other northern tribes. The Mingoes followed their Iroquois kinsmen in support of the British.

One can readily understand why the Ohio Indians joined the British side during the Revolutionary War. Those aggressive Pennsylvania, Kentucky, and Virginia farmers who came onto the land and changed it forever were nearly all in the American camp. The few loyalists among them had fled to British lines or were silent. The support of British officials and their royal troops was the Indians' best hope for meeting this threat to their lands. Trade relationships, so vital to the Indians, could be maintained through British posts. And, until the Americans won their great victory at Saratoga (October 17, 1777), it had seemed as though the British were telling the truth when they claimed that the Americans could not win the war. The western Indians could not afford to back a loser.

Cornstalk's murder, therefore, set in motion some six years of military activity affecting the Ohio Country. No formal battles were fought, but forest skirmishes were endemic. Action typically involved British-backed Ohio Indians raiding settlements south and east of the Ohio. Each raid was followed by an American counter-movement against the Ohio Indian villages. A recitation of these movements is a dreary chronicle of viciousness and spiteful revenge.

Only an occasional flash of heroism or humaneness relieves the sad tale. For example, Fort Henry, the American post at modern Wheeling, West Virginia, was besieged in 1777 by a force of nearly 300 Indians and British rangers from Detroit. The small garrison held the fort with the kind of bravery that was to be repeated so often in other forest locations in the next half-dozen years. One of the war's heroic tales dates from this engagement. While hotly pursued by Indians, patriot Maj. Samuel McCullough rode his horse down a precipitous 300-foot bluff and escaped his pursuers. Later this exploit became enshrined as "McCullough's Leap" with the artist depicting horse and rider floating free of any supporting ground while his incredulous Indian pursuers watch.

Virginia's George Rogers Clark, the dominant American military figure in the West, made his name immortal along the frontier in 1778. With pitifully meager support from Virginia (Congress could afford none), Clark led a tiny army of frontiersmen down the Ohio to southern Illinois and thence overland to the Mississippi, where they seized Cahokia and Kaskaskia, British posts which were still largely French in character. These posts were not well-defended because they seemed outside the military range of the Americans. Then, early in 1779, Clark led his men through the flooded swamps and bottomlands of Illinois to capture the British fort at Vincennes on the Wabash. Governor Hamilton at Detroit could not permit this threat to British hegemony among the western Indians. He marched to Vincennes and seized it, but then was in turn taken by Clark.

The frontier rejoiced in the capture of Henry Hamilton, whom they had labelled "the hair buyer" for his practice, common among officials of all nations on the frontier, of paying his Indian allies for enemy scalps. Hamilton, who used the Indians even as he despised "savages," was placed in chains, taken to Williamsburg, Virginia, and treated shabbily for an official of his rank. Clark became the great western hero. Unfortunately for him, his fellow westerners now expected Clark to triumph each time he set out against the enemy. Many were confident that he would capture Detroit and end the western war. The strain of trying to live up to these expectations ultimately helped to destroy him.

While Clark had alarmed the British at Detroit, he had done no irreparable damage to the British cause. In the summer of 1778 some 450 Indians and "Canadians" (French *habitants,* traders and half-breeds) besieged Boonesborough in Kentucky. Frustrated by a courageous defense, this force withdrew north of the Ohio after ten days.

Meanwhile, Indian warriors from villages near the Cuyahoga and Sandusky raided the Pennsylvania frontier. Col. Edward Hand, commanding at Fort Pitt, decided to smash these villages. He picked the wrong time of year to try it. In February 1778, he led 500 men out of Fort Pitt intending to sweep through the Cuyahoga villages. Everything went wrong, including the weather. After killing a handful of women and children from small villages along the Beaver and its tributaries, Hand returned to Pittsburgh. His misdirected effort was ridiculed as the "Squaw Campaign."

Perhaps this ineffectual campaign helped persuade several Pittsburgh area men to break with the Americans and take up with the British at Detroit. Among them was Alexander McKee, a Pennsylvanian who became a trusted official of the British Indian department and developed much influence among the Indians. His associate, the Irishman Matthew Elliott, left Pittsburgh for the Shawnee towns and became yet another influential British agent. The most notorious of those who left American employ to serve British masters among the Ohio Indians was Simon Girty, the "renegade." As a youngster in Pennsylvania, Girty had seen his drunken father killed by an Indian. Later, in an Indian raid, he and his brothers were captured and distributed among the participating tribes. Simon was taken by the Senecas. He became well-versed in Indian languages and served the American army as an interpreter. When convinced that he was not properly appreciated, he de-

Girty

fected to the British, who promptly placed him in charge of important actions against the Americans. He performed well, was respected by the Indians, and remained for the rest of his life in British employ. To American frontiersmen who knew him as a leader of bloody forays, he was the devil incarnate.

Meanwhile, the skirmishes that characterized the Ohio Country's involvement in the American Revolution continued. Soon after the "Squaw Campaign," Colonel Hand was replaced at Fort Pitt by Lachlan McIntosh. He authorized construction of Fort Laurens (named for Henry Laurens of South Carolina, president of the Continental Congress) on the west bank of the Tuscarawas a few miles upstream from important Delaware villages. The fort was occupied in the fall of 1778 by a garrison of 150 Virginia and Pennsylvania troops. Their mission was twofold: first, to prepare for an assault on Detroit, and second, to protect neutral Delaware towns in the vicinity. They failed to do either. Early in 1779 Capt. Henry Bird of the British army and Simon Girty led a force of raiders who attacked the fort and held it in siege through bitter winter weather. Both besieged and besieger were near starvation when the British and Indians withdrew upon approach of an American relief column. In August 1779, after surviving a second siege, Fort Laurens was abandoned. It was the only fort built in Ohio during the Revolutionary War.

In May 1778, Virginia's Kanawha Valley was overrun by a force of 400 Shawnee and Mingo warriors who destroyed farms and cabins and terrorized the neighborhood of Fort Randolph (Point Pleasant). In September the Shawnee chief Blackfish besieged Boonesborough, Kentucky, with a force exceeding 400 warriors. After devastating the region around the fort, Blackfish withdrew to his villages north of the Ohio, but these villages proved to be no safe haven.

In May 1779, the Shawnee villages suffered the first of what was to become almost a yearly occurrence. Col. John Bowman led 300 mounted Kentuckians against a new Shawnee village called Chillicothe, on the Mad River, and other villages not far from modern Xenia. Destruction of these villages persuaded some Shawnees, especially those of the Kispokotha and Piqua divisions, to abandon their tenuous position in western Ohio; they soon left for the Spanish lands to the west. But the remaining Shawnees and their Indian allies were far from being defeated. They launched a major raid against the Kentucky settlements in 1780. The expedition was led by Capt. Henry Bird; his British regulars and large Indian war party were equipped with two small field pieces which were expected to breach the wooden palisades protecting Kentucky settlements. The invaders seized two small posts before their attack bogged down. In characteristic fashion the Indians refused to remain in place for a siege; taking horses and such other booty as they could find, they retreated north of the Ohio. This attack so threatened the Kentucky settlements that George Rogers Clark had little trouble raising 1,000 men with whom he crossed the Ohio, burned several Shawnee villages, and scattered a small rearguard in what came to be called the Battle of Piqua (near the present site of Springfield).

As the Shawnees were suffering from quick raids from the south, so the Delawares suffered in their villages along the Muskingum. In 1781 Col. Andrew Brodhead, now commanding at Fort Pitt, led 300 men to Goshgoshgunk (Coshocton) and destroyed this important Delaware village. Cornfields and small villages nearby were put to the torch. Resistance was minimal; a number of Indians were captured without a real fight. Then, in one of those senseless acts that gave a special viciousness to frontier warfare, fifteen Delaware prisoners were murdered in cold blood. The remaining Delawares, except for the Moravian converts, now abandoned their villages on the Muskingum and its tributaries. Some moved to the upper waters of the Scioto while most moved near Captain Pipe's villages, which had been relocated close by the Wyandot villages along the Sandusky.

It was the Indians' turn to inflict suffering. In 1781 Col. Archibald Lochry and 107 militiamen were on their way down the Ohio to join George Rogers Clark at Louisville, where Clark expected to mount still another thrust northward, possibly to Detroit. Lochry's men were under constant surveillance, and a short distance from the mouth of the Great Miami, a superior force of Ohio Indians fell upon them, killing forty-two and capturing the rest, some of whom later died at the stake in Indian camps.

By the end of 1781 the War of Independence was virtually over in the east. Yorktown, in October, was the last major engagement. In the west, however, the war was far from over. Instead it built to a horrid crescendo in 1782; no act of this bloody year was more brutal and shameful than the murder of Christian Indians at Gnadenhutten.

The Moravian villages on the Tuscarawas were close by the Great Trail leading from Fort Pitt, the center of American military efforts, to Detroit, the center of British military activity. Americans and British each suspected the Christian Indians of aiding the enemy although these Indians had long professed and practiced neutrality. Still, it was not possible for them to remain above suspicion. On the one hand, British-allied Indians demanded and received hospitality when in the vicinity of the Christian settlements. On the other, Moravian missionaries passed information along to the Americans from time to time. Suspicion led to action. Late in 1781 the Wyandots and Delawares of the Sandusky forced the Christian Indians to abandon their Tuscarawas villages and move a hundred miles westward to villages close by the Sandusky where they could be watched. David Zeisberger and other missionary leaders charged with aiding the Americans were taken before the British commandant at Detroit. There Maj. Arendt DePeyster found Zeis-

berger and his associates innocent of treasonable activities. They were released and returned to their converts.

Meanwhile, the Christian Indians were starving in their barren new villages. Their captors allowed about a hundred of them to return briefly to their
former villages to harvest corn still standing in the fields. Early in 1782 a
group departed for the Tuscarawas. While the Christian Indians were harvesting their crop, a family of white settlers living to the east along the Ohio
were murdered. Their neighbors, inflamed with hatred for the Indians who
had perpetrated this deed, organized informally under the leadership of Col.
David Williamson and marched to the Tuscarawas where they purportedly
found clothing from the murdered whites. At Gnadenhutten they encountered the Christian Indians and, professing friendship, disarmed them both
literally and figuratively. Based on limited and flimsy evidence, most of the
Americans were convinced that these Indians were either responsible for the
murders, or that they had shielded those who were.

The Christian Indians were confined while the frontiersmen "voted" on
their fate. It appears only seventeen or eighteen of nearly a hundred men
voted to spare the Indians. Informed that they were to die, the Indians spent
the night praying and singing Christian hymns. In the morning they were led
out by twos and killed—twenty-eight men, twenty-nine women, and thirty-
nine children including "13 babies not yet baptized"—their skulls crushed by
mallet blows.

This barbarous act was widely condoned in the West, but it horrified easterners who had been removed for many years from the stark hatreds of border
warfare. Ultimately the Congress of the new United States would attempt to
make amends by setting aside 12,000 acres of land along the Tuscarawas for
use of surviving Christian Indians. Although some survivors returned to the
valley after the war, they did not stay long in this shadowed land. Today a
large shaft in the Gnadenhutten cemetery marks the mass grave. Its legend
says: "Here triumphed in death ninety Christian Indians, March 9, 1782."

The Ohio Indians craved revenge even though they had had their differences with the Christian Indians. They obtained it when they destroyed a
force which was led into their country by Col. William Crawford. Crawford
was well-known on the frontier, having served at one time as a land agent for
George Washington. In May 1782, he led more than 450 mounted volunteers
out of the Mingo Bottoms, intending to destroy the Sandusky towns of the
Wyandots and Delawares. However, Captain Pipe's Delawares, the Half-
King's Wyandots, and their Indian allies were joined by rangers out of Detroit led by Capt. William Caldwell. On June 6, at the Battle of the Olentangy, Crawford checked this British and Indian force. But the American
forces were split, discipline broke down and the Indians, reinforced by new

[handwritten marginal note: Moravian Massacred]

arrivals, captured one segment of the American army the next day at the Battle of the Sandusky. Ironically, the segment which escaped was led by David Williamson. The prisoners included Crawford, who was then made to suffer for Williamson's work at Gnadenhutten. He was taken to a nearby Delaware town and subjected to terrible tortures described in full by Dr. John Knight, a fellow prisoner who was supposed to share Crawford's fate. However, Knight escaped and returned to tell of Crawford's cruel death. The Colonel was remembered by later Ohioans who named a county in his honor.

Another setback for American arms came later in 1782. Captain Caldwell led an Indian force on a successful raid against Bryan's Station in Kentucky. The Kentuckians quickly set out in pursuit of Caldwell's group, but Caldwell's Indian allies ambushed the pursuers at Blue Licks on the Licking River in Kentucky. Sixty-six Kentuckians were killed and several captured.

The last formal thrust of the British and their Indian allies during the War of Independence was directed against Fort Henry at Wheeling. More than 300 Indians and rangers besieged the small fort, whose garrison consisted of eighteen men plus women and young boys. At a critical moment, young Betty Zane ran from the stockade to a nearby cabin, scooped up a supply of gunpowder, and dashed back to the fort under fire. Her precious cargo allowed the defenders to hold out.

The last American campaign in the Ohio Country occurred in November 1782, though too late in the war to accomplish much. George Rogers Clark led more than 1,000 mounted riflemen up the Great Miami Valley. He got as far as the headwaters of that river, where he destroyed a British trading post and the Shawnee villages nearby. This hastened the decision of the Ohio Indians to pull their villages back toward the Maumee, away from further destructive raids by the Kentuckians.

The Peace of Paris (1783), ending the War of Independence, has rightfully been seen as a triumph for American diplomacy. Nowhere is this more evident than in the terms dealing with the western country. John Adams and John Jay took the lead in asserting that the trans-Appalachian west, from Canada to the Floridas and westward to the Mississippi, should belong to the new United States of America. Great Britain had won this grand prize from the French just twenty years earlier; now the British surrendered it to the Americans. The United States claimed it had won this land on the field of battle, but the Earl of Shelburne, head of the British ministry, knew that the expansive energies of westward-moving frontiersmen would culminate in a population surge that the British would be unable to stop or control. Any effort to do so would entail staggering costs, and the recent war had already cost Great Britain dearly. Some historians believe that the military campaigns, particularly those of Clark, north and west of the Ohio River, however minor they

clark

may have been in the total picture of the American Revolution, did substan-
tiate the United States' claim. Though British treaty negotiators rejected it,
they saw the practical limitations of trying to hold on to the western lands.

Furthermore, British interests, especially in the lands northwest of the
Ohio, centered on the lucrative fur trade. The British could continue to control that Indian trade even if the Ohio Country and other western lands were
ceded to the new nation. So the fateful decision was made; the United States
now had her own "colonial" territory, and the new nation set about establishing policies to administer it.

❀

3.

Creating the Northwest Territory

The newly established United States of America faced an awesome array of challenges. Could the thirteen states continue to work together now that they had attained their independence? Could they defend their western lands against Great Britain, France, or Spain? How might the new and poorly developed nation enjoy economic growth and stability? Was the federal system adequate for the government of a scattered and diverse people? The list of vital concerns was extensive, but ranking among the most pressing was: How were the western lands ceded to the United States by Great Britain to be organized, governed, and developed?

This question had been partially answered while the war was still in progress. Assuming that the United States would win the west from the British, Congress adopted a resolution on October 10, 1780, concerning public lands:

Resolved, that the unappropriated lands that may be ceded or relinquished to the United States, by any particular states . . . shall be disposed of for the common benefit of the United States, and be settled and formed into distinct republican States, which shall become members of the Federal Union, and shall have the same rights of sovereignty, freedom and independence, as the other States. . . .

The West, then, was to be developed by Congress as a national resource rather than remain partitioned among the states which still held western land claims by virtue of their colonial charters.

The vision and wisdom inherent in this resolution has been the subject of much commentary from that time to this. For the first time in the modern world, a republican nation decided on its own initiative to convert a colonial region into an integral part of itself. The "colonies" were to be regarded as extensions of the mother country; a dependent wilderness area would become independent, republican states on a basis of equality with the existing states.

Ohio as a Social Laboratory

To give substance to this resolution, Congress had to create republican states out of the public domain. This experimentation was carried out within the first part of the West to become public domain—the area bounded on the east by Pennsylvania, on the south by the Ohio River, on the west by the Mississippi, and on the north by Canada. By 1787 this region was being commonly referred to as the Northwest Territory. Historians of a later day would call it the Old Northwest.

The policies which Congress imposed upon this territory were new, formulated to meet the needs of that region. As with all social evolution, these policies had roots in the past. Congressmen drew upon their experience in making plans for the Northwest, but their experience had not completely prepared them to deal with this unprecedented opportunity. The systems they evolved for land survey and sale and for the government of the territory may have had historic roots, but the application of these systems to the new western land had no exact counterpart in previous practice.

That portion of the new public domain where Congress first tried out its policies—where, in effect, it experimented with them—came in 1803 to be the state of Ohio. The territorial development of Ohio, therefore, is much more complex than that of other new states formed from the public domain. Ohio would be the testing ground. By learning from its Ohio experience, Congress would have a model which it could use, and with modifications did use, to develop additional territories. Congress could proceed after 1803 with a newfound confidence in its policies for developing the public domain.

Creating the Northwest Territory: Five Problems

Congress had to resolve five major problems if the Northwest was to become an effective area for settlement and territorial development: acquiring the lands claimed by the seaboard states; removing Indian title to portions of the land; removing the British presence in the Northwest; choosing a system for the survey and sale of land; and creating territorial governments.

Congress did not have the luxury of dealing with each problem in turn. Rather, the problems overlapped one another. By 1786 the states had ceded

Map 6. Approximate Area of the Ohio Country

their claims in the Northwest, but long after that time the other four problems interacted in a confusing manner. We can exercise the luxury denied Congress and treat each concern separately before dealing with the interrelationships among them.

The States Surrender Their Western Lands to Congress

Four seaboard states claimed portions of the Northwest. New York, acting in 1780, was the first to surrender its land, perhaps because its claim was tenuous at best. Under its 1669 charter, New York had assumed guardianship over the Iroquois Confederacy whose members resided within its borders. The Iroquois had once claimed the Ohio Country and lands beyond as their sphere of influence, but for practical purposes, that claim was ineffective by 1780. Though of little material importance, New York's cession led the way for the other states.

Virginia was next to offer her northwestern lands to Congress. This was a major concession since her 1609 charter gave Virginia a legal basis for claiming the entire region plus the southwestern corner of Pennsylvania and the future West Virginia and Kentucky. From late colonial times, Virginia traders and land speculators had been active in the Northwest. Young George Washington had been sent by the Virginia governor to contest French claims to the Ohio Valley. During the recently concluded War of Independence, Virginia provided such support as she could to the Kentucky and western Virginia settlements. Virginia, rather than the United States, supplied most of the men and materiel which allowed George Rogers Clark to capture Kaskaskia, Cahokia, and Vincennes in 1778–79, and to terrorize the Shawnee villages along the Miami in 1780.

Virginia's offer to relinquish her lands "lying . . . northwest of the river Ohio" was first made in 1781 and was accepted by Congress in 1784 after some adjustment in the terms. In accepting this offer, Congress agreed that Virginia was to reserve "good lands, to be laid off between the rivers Scioto and Little Miami, on the northwest side of the river Ohio." Virginia would use this land to pay bounties to soldiers who had served in the state's military forces should land set aside for this purpose in Kentucky prove insufficient. This Ohio land was called the Virginia Military District (sometimes referred to as the Virginia Military Bounty Lands). It was surveyed in the Virginia fashion (metes and bounds), which set it apart from the rest of Ohio. That fact, and the southern origins of its settlers, gave the region a special flavor which was to have a profound impact upon the later development of the state.

Massachusetts had claims in the Northwest, but, with the exception of a small portion of Lake Erie, they lay north of Ohio. These claims were surrendered to Congress in 1785.

Connecticut was the only other state whose western land claims directly affected the future state. When Congress accepted Connecticut's western lands in 1786, it agreed to a special condition. Connecticut was to retain possession of a "reservation," defined as the lands lying between Lake Erie and the forty-first parallel, extending 120 miles west from the Pennsylvania border. Connecticut authorities expected that this Western Reserve or "New Connecticut" would contain well over 3,000,000 acres. However, Connecticut's geographical information was faulty. Lake Erie's shoreline falls off in a southwesterly direction much more sharply than state officials believed; therefore, the area reserved was smaller than expected.

Eventually, Connecticut sold all but the westernmost portion of the Reserve to a group of thirty-five speculators, organized by Oliver Phelps and others in a loose association called the Connecticut Land Company. The company paid Connecticut $1,200,000 which the state placed in a perpetual fund, the interest of which was to be used to support public education in Connecticut.

The westernmost 500,000 acres of the Reserve (primarily present Erie and Huron counties) was excluded from this sale. Connecticut intended to grant this land to Connecticut people who had suffered losses from British coastal raiders during the war. Hence this area came to be known as the "Firelands" or the "Sufferers' Lands." It was nearly a generation after the Revolution before titles and claims were cleared and land was actually awarded to the sufferers or their heirs.

The survey, sale, and early settlement of the Western Reserve was conducted by the Connecticut Land Company. Indian wars delayed this process until 1796, and the migration which started in that year was largely from New England. This fact gave a distinctly New England flavor to the Connecticut Reserve and has had a substantial impact upon the history of Ohio.

Removing Indian Title

While Congress was still accepting state land cessions in the Northwest it was taking steps to remove Indian title to parts of the region. America's sorry record in dealing with Indian peoples is so well known that one might assume negotiations with the Indians were always carried out in bad faith by American negotiators. Such belief is an oversimplification. Some easterners (but very few westerners) advocated fair treatment of the Indians, but the inevitable reality was that western lands could be acquired only at the expense of the Indians who lived and hunted upon them. Even well-disposed American leaders found themselves pressuring Indians to move from lands coveted by farmers and speculators.

Congressional Indian policy from 1784 to 1789 was frankly coercive; it was based on conquest. Americans claimed to have won a military victory over the British *and* their Indian allies in the Northwest. Congressional commissioners told the Indians that they were "a subdued people . . . overcome in a war which you entered into with us." In response, the Indians said they had never surrendered to the Americans nor had they been conquered. Perhaps the Americans had defeated the British, but they had not beaten the Indians. The Indian argument was futile, however; they knew that, for the moment, they could do little to prevent the Americans from taking what they wanted since the Indians were not organized for resistance.

Congress was determined to secure Indian land beyond the Ohio, but it wanted to cloak this acquisition in legality. Legislators recognized that the Indians had "title" by right of possession and that this title must be removed before western lands could legitimately be developed. The first postwar initiative was taken in 1784 at Fort Stanwix. Congressional commissioners persuaded the Six Nations to relinquish claims they might have on lands lying beyond the Ohio River in a treaty establishing a boundary line which ran along that river. The Six Nations yielded to the United States "all claims to the country west of the said boundary," a reaffirmation of terms agreed on at the earlier treaty of Fort Stanwix in 1768.

In 1785 Congress sent Richard Butler, Arthur Lee, and George Rogers Clark to negotiate with the Wyandots, Ottawas, Delawares, and Chippewas. In bitter winter weather, negotiations dragged on at Fort McIntosh (Beaver, Pennsylvania) on the Ohio River. An American soldier present thought the 400 Indians "a very motley crew—an ugly set of devils all." We have no report of what the Indians thought of the Americans except that they feared and respected Clark, the leader of the Long Knives.

The American commissioners forced the pace of the council. From the Indians' perspective, land was the common possession of the tribe, provided by the Great Spirit for shared use. Only tribal councils involving the principal tribal leaders could alienate land; certainly the minor chiefs who came to Fort McIntosh could not speak for all their people, and they were hesitant to do so. Both the British and the Americans, on the other hand, were apt to think of Indian tribes as "nations" with whose representatives formal negotiations, culminating in treaties, could be carried out. These Indians were proving stubborn, so for two weeks the commissioners stuffed them with food and plied them with hard liquor until the chiefs were semi-comatose, in which state they signed away a huge area of Ohio over much of which they had only the most tenuous of claims.

The Treaty of Fort McIntosh was signed January 21, 1785. The Indians acknowledged that their tribes were "under the protection of the United States and of no other sovereign whatsoever." It isolated the Delawares and the Wyandots in an enclave bounded by a line running from the mouth of the Cuyahoga south to the portage (at modern Akron), across the portage to the Tuscarawas, down that river to the crossing above Fort Laurens (Bolivar), west to the site of Pickawillany on the upper Miami, north over the portage to the St. Mary's River, to the head of the Maumee (Fort Wayne, Indiana), down the Maumee to Lake Erie, and then east to the Cuyahoga. Lands east, south, and west of this enclave were now to be free of Indian claims.

Most western Indians ridiculed what they saw as an outrageous betrayal, and angrily denied the treaty's validity. Those sub-chiefs who had signed it were held in contempt and some were threatened. Congress, however, now proceeded on the assumption that it had clear title to develop the ceded lands.

The Shawnees were most seriously affronted by the Fort McIntosh treaty, which alienated, without their consent, lands they regarded as their own. In order to clarify the position of the Shawnees, Congress sent Richard Butler and Samuel Holden Parsons to negotiate with them in 1785–86. A small stockade named Fort Finney was built at the mouth of the Great Miami to accommodate the negotiators. The Shawnees were slow to arrive at the council site, and the Americans feared that British agents would persuade them to ignore the negotiations. But in time, 230 Shawnee warriors and their women appeared as did a considerable number of Delawares and Wyandots who came to act as go-betweens.

The Shawnees were quite intractable. "God gave us this country," they said. "We do not understand measuring out the lands; it is all ours." When persuasion failed, Butler and Parsons distributed whiskey to the young warriors and threatened the chiefs with the prospect of war. On February 1, 1786, the Shawnees signed the Treaty of Fort Finney, which required them to evacuate southwestern Ohio and adjacent portions of Indiana; most of their principal villages were located in this region. The vacated lands were acknowledged to belong to the United States. This treaty, like those before it, contained an American pledge to keep white trespassers off Indian lands.

The ease and rapidity with which the Delawares, Wyandots, Shawnees, and Ottawas were stripped of their Ohio hunting grounds proved deceptive. While a few chiefs appeared determined to recognize the legitimacy of the recent treaties, most continued to resist American encroachment on the trans-Ohio lands. Hundreds, perhaps thousands of squatters had already taken up farm plots in the rich valleys of the Scioto and other southern and eastern Ohio rivers. They undoubtedly knew the risks they ran, and many paid the price of their temerity by falling to the hatchet and scalping knife. Painted warriors even crossed the Ohio River to attack the Kentucky settlements. Joseph Barker, an early settler in the Ohio Valley, estimated that from 1783 until 1791 Indians on the frontier south of the Ohio killed or took prisoner 1,500 persons, and stole 2,000 horses as well as other property amounting to $50,000. He made no estimate for the region north of the Ohio although it is certain that many settlers, legal and illegal, suffered a similar fate.

Flatboats drifting down the Ohio River with settlers bound for Ohio and Kentucky were ambushed by young warriors. One such warrior was a Shawnee, Tecumseh, who represented a new generation of Indian leadership in the Northwest. Though not yet a chief, Tecumseh's impressive skills and attitudes would soon attract those Indians who felt that force alone could deter the further encroachment of whites on Indian lands.

Tough and determined frontiersmen were perfectly capable of fighting back. In 1786 George Rogers Clark and Benjamin Logan led raids north of the Ohio. Clark took 1,000 men to the Wabash but succeeded only in destroying Indian property. Logan's advance into Shawnee country was closely watched by Indian scouts, and his army found nothing but deserted villages except at Mac-o-chee Creek. Here women and children were trapped in Moluntha's town (Logan County), and most were taken prisoner. The aged Moluntha, an advocate of the recent treaties, was granted protection by Colonel Logan, but a Kentucky militiaman murdered him nevertheless. Following these raids, the Shawnees moved their villages north to the Maumee and its tributaries. Here they were close to the Miami and other tribes and could more readily secure supplies from the British post at Detroit.

The brutality intensified as authorized American settlement began north of the Ohio in 1788. The Northwest Territory had been established, and Congress, through Secretary of War Henry Knox, directed Gov. Arthur St. Clair to secure land cessions from the Ohio Indians, who had formed a loose confederacy in 1786. While the most important members of the confederacy, the Shawnees and Miamis, refused to attend any council to discuss the issue, the Delawares, Wyandots, Ottawas, and three western tribes sent representatives to Fort Harmar, as did the Six Nations. The resulting Fort Harmar treaties (January 1789) reaffirmed the Fort McIntosh boundary line while recognizing the Indians' right to continue to hunt on the ceded lands. A separate pact with the Six Nations reaffirmed the Ohio River boundary of 1784.

In these negotiations the Americans switched from both the policy of coercion and the principle of right-of-conquest. The secretary of war realized that the United States army, consisting of 700 regulars, was in no condition to fight an Indian war, so he encouraged the British method of securing land by purchase. When the Treaty of Fort Harmar had no appreciable effect in stemming further depredations on the Ohio frontier, however, Secretary Knox lost his patience and reverted to force. St. Clair was instructed to hold yet another peace conference and, "the United States would be exonerated from all imputations of injustice in taking proper measures for compelling the Indians to a peace, or to extirpate them." Indeed, Knox felt the United States must "extirpate, utterly, if possible, the said banditti." Lines were now drawn for a bitter new Indian war in the Ohio Country as United States efforts to dispossess the Indians led to great bloodshed.

The British Presence in the West

Meanwhile, negotiations with the Ohio Indians were complicated by Britain's continuing presence in certain border posts located on American soil. Those affecting the Northwest were located at Michilimackinac and Detroit. Later, in 1794, a new post called Fort Miami was erected at Maumee. The British retained possession of these posts, claiming they would hold them until the United States fulfilled all of its commitments under the Peace of Paris.

From the British post at Detroit, Alexander McKee, Matthew Elliott, Simon Girty, and other British agents encouraged the western tribes to defy further American encroachments into the Ohio Country. Congress pressed on despite British interference. Until 1813 that interference would complicate American-Indian relationships in the Ohio Country.

A Model for Developing the Wilderness

State cessions of western lands and congressional negotiations with the Indians were still in their early stages when Congress enacted its first plan for organizing the Northwest. It was called the Report of Government for the Western Territory. Thomas Jefferson was the principal architect of this plan, which Congress adopted in April 1784.

The Ordinance of 1784 is of interest primarily because it shows in broad outline how Congress intended to proceed in fashioning states and the conditions under which they would enter the Union. The plan called for division of the West into prospective states, ten of which were to be located north of the Ohio. Boundaries were drawn on a rectangular grid without respect to natural limits. By stages, each division would proceed toward statehood with the inhabitants enjoying self-government at every stage. The Ordinance of 1784 never took effect, however; it was supplanted by new ordinances which established the territorial system of the United States.

The Land Ordinance of 1785

A list of the most significant legislative acts ever passed by the United States Congress would necessarily include the Land Ordinance of 1785, which laid the foundation for the public land system. Ohio and every state that followed it except Texas, which came into the Union under unique conditions, was influenced by it. It affected the manner in which people possessed the land and were distributed upon it; this, in turn, influenced their outlook on social, political, and economic matters. Today, more than two hundred years after its enactment, its effects are clearly visible from the window of an airplane flying over settled parts of the American Midwest: below a rectangular, checkerboard pattern of roads, lots, and farms still adheres to a pattern set forth in 1785.

Prior to enacting the Land Ordinance, Congress was confronted with a choice of methods for surveying and settling the land. The most widely used pattern was known as the "indiscriminate claim." The land purchaser (perhaps a former soldier holding a land warrant) could enter a designated area and pace off in any configuration the appropriate amount of land. A surveyor then ran "metes and bounds" defining in straight lines the limits of the lot. Frequently natural objects—trees, rocks, fords—were used to define corners. This practice resulted in a jumble of lot lines, running in unpredictable directions, anchored by objects which could readily disappear, change character, or be confused with similar objects nearby. The system produced a landholder's nightmare and a lawyer's dream. Litigation over land and property lines became a flourishing and continuing business wherever the indiscriminate claim was employed, especially in the Virginia Military District, where the state of Virginia, rather than Congress, defined the terms. To its credit, Congress rejected this familiar but unwieldy system in favor of an orderly, rational, rectilinear system of land survey. This rectilinear system, comprised of north-south and east-west lines intersecting at right angles, became the centerpiece of the new ordinance.

The Land Ordinance was passed on May 20, 1785. It provided that land ceded by the states and purchased from the Indians be divided into *townships* six miles square (thirty-six square miles) "by lines running due north and south, and others crossing these at right angles." The first north-south line was to be, in effect, the western boundary of Pennsylvania while the first east-west line (called the Geographer's Line or simply the Base Line) was to begin where the Pennsylvania boundary met the north bank of the Ohio River and was to extend westward "throughout the whole territory." Most townships were to be subdivided into one-mile-square (640 acres) *sections*. North-south rows of townships were called *ranges*. Each range, township, and section was to be numbered according to a regular sequence. The geographer of the United States was to make a return of the survey after completing each seven ranges. However, eastern Ohio's famous Seven Ranges was the only unit completed under the first survey.

From the completed plat of seven ranges, the secretary of war was to take, by lot, one seventh of the land with which to compensate veterans of the Continental regiments who had served in the recent war. The rest of the land was to be sold after authorities in each state had secured copies of the plat. Sales were to be conducted at auction in New York City, the national capital at that time, with the minimum price set at one dollar per acre in specie or loan-office certificates. No land was to be sold on credit. A section of 640 acres was the smallest unit for sale. Some townships were to be sold in their entirety, others by section.

Other provisions of the act were also of enduring importance. Section number sixteen in each township was reserved "for the maintenance of public schools within the said township." It is remarkable that Congress supported this provision since few existing states had as yet provided for public support of education within their own borders. Congress also reserved out of every township the lots numbered 8, 11, 26, and 29 for future sale, anticipating that they would bring a higher price as those around them were sold and improved. Also "one third part of all gold, silver, lead and copper mines" were to be disposed of as Congress might direct.

Survey of the Seven Ranges

Late in 1785, Thomas Hutchins, Geographer of the United States, led a survey team which intended to carry out the plan recently set forth by Congress. It was important to act immediately because large numbers of illegal settlers had come into Ohio following the treaty of Fort McIntosh. Their presence aroused the Indians, making the surveyors' work exceedingly risky.

Illegal settlers, or squatters, were a constant problem on the American frontier. No government had succeeded in keeping unauthorized persons from trespassing on government land or on vast unoccupied tracts owned by private interests. The term "squatter" embraces every human type from the honest and industrious to the thieving and shiftless. Leaders of eastern society tended to take a negative view of squatters. One such easterner characterized them as "too idle, too talkative, too passionate, too prodigal, and too shiftless to acquire either property or character. They are impatient of the restraints of law, religion, and morality." The English traveller Capt. Basil Hall referred to them as "free and easy settlers who are their own lawmakers as the case may be." For every drifter or loser among them there were many of strong character who were simply too poor to purchase land legally. They had rationalized their actions by claiming that it was their natural right to take up unoccupied lands. Congress could not forbid them as it was their "undoubted right" to take up unoccupied lands and there govern themselves by forming a constitution.

The largest part of those crossing the Ohio after 1785 moved west from Pennsylvania and Virginia, or north from the Kentucky settlements. Many of these people were of Scots-Irish stock, characterized by those who knew them as "bold, stout and industrious men, sharp at bargains, fond of religious and political controversy and not strongly attached to government either of the royal or proprietary kind," and, one might add, of any kind which intruded on their self-asserted liberties. "In nearly every cabin," wrote local historian Edgar Hassler, "three articles were to be found: a Bible, a rifle and a whiskey jug. A strong characteristic . . . was their intense hatred of the Indians for whose treatment the extermination policy . . . was generally considered to be the proper model." It was this attitude which made them a threat, for survey and orderly settlement could proceed only if the Indians would remain docile.

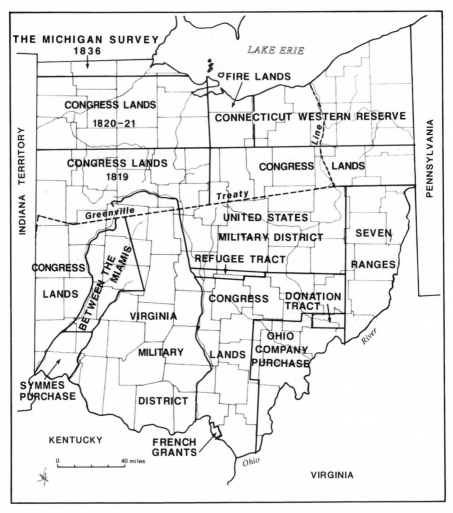

Map 7. Principal Land Subdivisions and Surveys

A congressional proclamation ordering the illegal settlers out of Ohio had little effect, so troops were called in to expel the squatters and preserve Ohio for legal, orderly settlement. Some of the illegals showed a willingness to follow Congress's mandate, especially after Col. Josiah Harmar, commanding at Fort McIntosh, ordered his soldiers to clear them out. Harmar promptly received a petition signed by squatters William Hoagland and John Nixon requesting that they be permitted to gather their crops before leaving. The petitioners claimed that given this leeway they would abide by "the late Proclamation of Congress" and withdraw. Harmar granted "this last indulgence . . . after which if they presume to remain, the Ordinances of Congress will be carried into the most vigorous execution." Remain they did, compelling Harmar's troops to roust them out and burn their cabins. Yet the ashes had scarcely cooled before many tough, determined squatters were already rebuilding a few miles away.

In October 1785, Harmar ordered Maj. John Doughty to establish a fort along the Ohio from which troops could stop squatters from crossing the river. Doughty chose a spot on the west bank of the Muskingum where it empties into the Ohio and there erected Fort Harmar. In 1786 a blockhouse named Fort Steuben was erected on the site of modern Steubenville. Intended to serve the same purpose as Fort Harmar, it also served as a base for surveyors in the Seven Ranges. But neither post succeeded in deterring illegal settlers from taking up the rich bottomlands of eastern and southern Ohio. The squatters' presence sharpened tensions with the Ohio Indians, who now increased efforts to prevent further intrusions on their lands.

Meanwhile, the surveyors, having temporarily abandoned their dangerous work, resumed their task. By December 1786 they had plotted the first four ranges of townships between the Geographer's Line and the Ohio River. Land would soon be available for sale and legal settlement would commence. It was time, therefore, for Congress to provide for government.

Establishing Territorial Government

As we have noted, Congress had enacted an ordinance in 1784 to organize the land northwest of the Ohio. Almost immediately, Congress modified the act by passing the Land Ordinance of 1785. This congressional activity was going on against a backdrop of continuing negotiation with the Indians, final relinquishment of state land claims, and growing pressure from special interest groups seeking land at bargain prices. Moreover, the orderly development of the West was threatened by an ever larger flow of illegal settlers. It was time for Congress to bring order out of the somewhat chaotic conditions, a goal the legislators hoped to achieve by framing a policy for territorial government.

The Northwest Ordinance

On July 13, 1787, Congress enacted the Northwest Ordinance, establishing a government for the Northwest Territory and instituting a magnanimous colonial policy by which the new nation could grow. Nathan Dane and Manasseh Cutler of Massachusetts and Rufus King of New York are usually credited with framing sections of this ordinance, but in several important respects it followed Jefferson's Ordinance of 1784. Although the Northwest Ordinance is one of the most significant documents ever produced by an American Congress, its birth pangs were somewhat overshadowed because at the moment of its creation a convention was framing a new constitution for the United States. Debates over that constitution and its ratification usurped much of the attention that might otherwise have been directed to the Northwest Ordinance.

The ordinance recognized three stages of governmental development as a wilderness area moved toward statehood. In the first stage, Congress would appoint a governor, secretary, and three judges. Each was to reside in the territory and possess a substantial amount of land therein. There was no legislature. The governor and judges, acting together, could select laws from existing state codes. Their selections were to be approved by Congress. The governor would have executive powers over the militia, Indian affairs, and the appointment of civil magistrates.

The second stage of governmental development would be reached when 5,000 "free male inhabitants of full age" resided in the Northwest Territory. Of this number, only those who owned at least fifty acres in the territory could vote for representatives to a territorial legislature. The legislature or "general assembly" was to consist of "the governor, legislative council, and a house of representatives," the latter elected by eligible voters. House members then nominated ten persons for seats in the legislative council; from these ten names, Congress selected five to serve as the council. Electors, representatives, and councilors each had to meet certain residence and property requirements (representatives had to own 200 acres, councilors 500 acres); no squatters were to be enfranchised. Congress clearly intended that in the new west, as in the established east, only those with a stake in society would vote or hold office, and the higher the office, the greater the property required.

The governor and council were both the creatures of Congress; only the house was popularly elected. Furthermore, as a check against popular enthusiasms, the governor had an absolute veto over acts of the territorial legislature. He could also convene or dissolve the general assembly as he saw fit. The general assembly was authorized to elect one delegate to the federal House of Representatives who could introduce and debate legislation, but could not vote "during this temporary government."

The third and final stage of territorial development provided that: "There shall be formed in the said territory, not less than three nor more than five States. . . ." A western state was to extend from the Ohio River to Canada in an area lying between the Mississippi and a line drawn from the mouth of the Wabash River to Post Vincent (Vincennes), then due north to the international boundary; the central state was to lie between that line and a line drawn north from the mouth of the Great Miami to the international border; the eastern state was to lie between that line and the Pennsylvania border. If two more states were added, they were to be formed north of "an east and west line drawn through the southerly bend or extreme of Lake Michigan." This latter provision was to have a profound impact on the future configuration of Ohio.

Whenever any of the three proposed state areas "shall have sixty thousand free inhabitants therein, such State shall be admitted, by its delegates, into the Congress of the United States, on an equal footing with the original States in all respects whatever. . . ." The new state could now form a permanent constitution and state government, "*Provided,* the constitution and government so to be formed, shall be republican. . . ."

Thus the end-point of territorial government was statehood. America had found the key to an orderly process for expansion and growth. This basic framework, much modified over the years, provided the administrative and governmental machinery for converting wilderness into an integral part of a growing nation.

Several other features of the Northwest Ordinance must be noted. It contained six "Articles of Compact," a bill of rights guaranteeing freedom of worship to those who comported themselves "in a peaceable and orderly manner"; the right of *habeas corpus* and trial by jury; the right to make bail except for capital offenses; and other civil rights. This is of special interest because the Constitution of the United States, then being framed in Philadelphia, contained no such civil guarantees, an omission which led to profound discontent in the ratifying conventions until the states were assured that Congress would add a Bill of Rights to the document, as it did in 1791.

Perhaps the most quoted phrase in the Northwest Ordinance provides that "Religion, morality, and knowledge being necessary to good government and the happiness of mankind, schools and the means of education shall forever be encouraged." While revealing Congress's interest in education, it introduced no substantive support for it. The document also addressed two dispossessed groups—Indians and slaves. As to the Indians, "the utmost good faith shall always be observed towards the Indians. Their lands and property shall never be taken from them without their consent; and in their property, rights, and liberty, they shall never be invaded or disturbed *unless in just and lawful wars authorized by Congress*" (italics mine). This expression of good intentions did not interfere with the practical business of securing land. With regard to slaves, Congress decreed: "There shall be neither slavery nor involuntary servitude in the said territory, otherwise than in the punishment of crimes whereof the party shall have been duly convicted." Any slave escaping into the territory "may be lawfully reclaimed" by his master. The Northwest was to be free territory, but it was not to be a haven for runaways.

By adopting the Northwest Ordinance, Congress created a territorial system, the extension and refinement of which continues to this day. In Ohio, the territorial process culminated in 1803 with statehood. For the moment, however, only the grand outline was in place. Much tinkering and adjusting was still to come before Ohio emerged as a state. And while this process was underway, the first permanent, authorized settlements were developing along the north shore of the great river at its southern boundary.

The First Authorized Settlements in Ohio

The survey of the Seven Ranges proceeded slowly. As surveyed land became available, some, though not much, was sold. The minimum sale price of $640 plus fees was simply more than most potential purchasers could afford. Congress passed a number of statutes modifying the plan of 1785 in an effort to speed sales. By December 1786, Thomas Hutchins and his surveying crews, made up of men from each of the existing states (a deliberate move which Congress hoped would stimulate interest and sales among the states), had finished surveying the first four ranges between the Geographer's Line and the Ohio River. Yet eight months later, little more than 70,000 acres of land had been sold for securities valued at $117,108. While the slow pace of land sales satisfied certain eastern interests who were concerned lest too many of the East's finest young people be lured to the beckoning West, Congress desperately wished to increase sales so that the proceeds could be applied against the national debt and the government's expenses. The desire of Congress coincided with steps being taken by private land developers and speculators who were seeking major land purchases in that portion of the Northwest which was to become the state of Ohio. The first successful joining of these interests involved a group of aggressive and resourceful New England war veterans.

The Ohio Company of Associates

Rufus Putnam of Massachusetts was among the Revolutionary War veterans seeking western land in payment for military services. In 1783 he led 288 Revolutionary War officers in signing the Newburgh Petition, which outlined a plan for settling the Ohio Country with veterans. They were to receive lands in compensation for their services, and by their presence they could protect the frontier against Indian assaults. George Washington forwarded the petition to Congress with his endorsement. Congress did not implement the plan but did include some of its features in the Ordinance of 1785.

General Putnam, meanwhile, continued to plan for western settlement. He was joined by his Massachusetts colleague, Brig. Gen. Benjamin Tupper. Both had served with Hutchins on the Seven Ranges survey and were familiar with opportunities in western lands. Putnam and his friends put out a call for interested persons to elect delegates to a meeting to form a plan of action. On March 1, 1786, eleven representatives met in Boston's Bunch of Grapes Tavern and formed the Ohio Company of Associates. Its capital of $1,000,000 in Continental certificates was to be raised by the sale of a thousand shares worth $1,000 each. With Congress's assent, the money would be used to purchase land just west of and adjacent to the Seven Ranges.

Within a year's time, a substantial number of shares had been sold, and the company sent Samuel Holden Parsons to New York City to present a memorial to Congress, calling for that body to sell appropriate lands to them at an attractive price. Parsons was unsuccessful and, when his views of where the purchase should be located began to differ from those of the company, he was relieved of his mission.

The Ohio Company's new advocate (today he would be called a lobbyist) was the Reverend Dr. Manasseh Cutler, one of those multitalented individuals so often brought forth by the Revolutionary generation. His Yale education, his interest in law, the ministry, and the natural sciences, and his service as an army chaplain had given him a broad acquaintance with men and affairs of state. He allied his cause with a larger land purchase scheme headed by William Duer, secretary of the Treasury Board and an influential member of Congress. They then secured the support of Maj. Gen. Arthur St. Clair, the president of Congress, by promising to support him for the soon-to-be created position of governor of the Northwest Territory.

In 1787 Congress approved an arrangement with Cutler, Duer, and associates by which Cutler and Winthrop Sargent, secretary of the Ohio Company, were to make two separate purchases, one for the Ohio Company of Associates and the other for the Duer interests, who called their operation the Scioto Company.

The Ohio Company purchase was bounded on the east by the seventh range, on the south by the Ohio River, and on the west by the seventeenth range (which thus would lie sixty miles to the west of the seventh range once the survey was completed). The tract was to extend as far to the north as was required to give the Company 1,500,000 acres. The land was to be surveyed in a rectilinear pattern (but because its sale was to be controlled by a private company, the survey pattern used varied in detail from that of the Seven Ranges) with one section in each township reserved for the support of schools, one section reserved for the support of religion, three sections reserved for later disposal by Congress, and two entire townships reserved for support of a university. The company was to pay the United States treasury $500,000 immediately and another $500,000 when the survey was complete.

Ultimately the Ohio Company lands embraced 1,781,760 acres, which included lands set aside for special purposes. Congress permitted payment to be made in government securities, which had depreciated in value to such an extent that their actual worth was much diminished. Thus the Ohio Company secured land under most favorable conditions, at a bargain rate (an estimated eight and one-half cents an acre) which undercut the price Congress charged for land in the Seven Ranges. But Congress was being practical instead of doctrinaire. It wanted the West settled. The Revolutionary War veterans of the Ohio Company could be "paid off" for their services while establishing new settlements which could defend themselves against Indian attack. And their success would speed the taming of the frontier and attract other legitimate settlers to the Northwest, thus enhancing land sales.

The associates proceeded to take up their lands in an orderly fashion. Early in 1788, company boat builders moved to Sumrill's Ferry on the Youghiogheny where they prepared an ark, first called the *Union Galley* and later renamed the *Mayflower,* a flatboat named *Adelphia* and three canoes (pirogues). In these craft forty-eight men of the advance parties embarked on April 2, 1788. Five days later, they landed at the mouth of the Muskingum River, on the east bank, across from Fort Harmar. They were greeted by the fort's garrison and by about seventy Wyandots and Delawares who had come to trade. Although these Indians were friendly, troubles in the interior made settlement away from the river and Fort Harmar too risky to contemplate for the time being. Besides, the riverside location they had chosen was convenient to a route eastward through the mountains, a matter of importance for future commerce.

The new arrivals had innumerable practical matters to attend to. Their new village required a name. Adelphia, which meant "brotherhood," was first proposed but soon gave way to Marietta, a graceful compliment to the queen of France, Marie Antoinette. If it seems strange that a group of republican-minded Americans should name their town for the arch-symbol of old world monarchical corruption, it must be remembered that these men were veterans of the Revolutionary armies. They were expressing gratitude for liberal French aid in men and materiel without which the cause of liberty might well have been lost.

Naming a place was one thing; building a town was another. Surveyors went to work laying out a compact community based on the New England ideal of commons, in-lots (town lots), and out-lots (farms). Wide streets separated the lots. To their credit, the planners left intact some of the prehistoric Indian mounds which marked the site. A thirty-foot conical mound remains today as the centerpiece of Marietta's Mound Cemetery, and a residential street, the *Via Sacra,* follows an ancient sacred way leading up from the banks of the Muskingum.

Marietta

A large, uniquely designed fortification dominated the town. Called the *Campus Martius,* this structure provided protection from Indian attack. Fort Harmar, conveniently near, also deterred Indian incursions. The New Englanders who settled Marietta, and those who came in succeeding years, transferred to this new land their classical education, their sense of community order, their organizational skills, their energy and determination. Their culture was little modified by the wilderness. They shaped the wilderness to a much greater extent than it shaped them. While this was true of the Ohio Company settlers, it was not always equally true of others who made new homes in the Ohio Country.

On July 9, 1788, the tiny population of Marietta, joined by soldiers from Fort Harmar, welcomed the arrival of Arthur St. Clair, the governor of the Northwest Territory. In simple but dignified ceremonies, the governor assumed authority over this little settlement and over its enormous hinterland extending to the Mississippi and the northern Great Lakes. As yet, St. Clair had few people to govern, but soon flatboats drifting down the Ohio would discharge their passengers on the Ohio side of the river, and the Northwest Territory would grow accordingly.

Ultimately, settlement of the Ohio Country pushed Native Americans westward. (From *The Biographical Cyclopaedia . . . of the State of Ohio,* (Cincinnati, 1880.)

The Symmes (Miami) Purchase

The second area of permanent Ohio settlement was organized by John Cleves Symmes, a prominent New Jersey judge and member of Congress. He knew something of the West, having traveled down the Ohio to its falls (Louisville, Kentucky). Like the Ohio Company promoters, he and two New Jersey associates, Elias Boudinot and Jonathan Dayton, petitioned Congress for a special purchase of Ohio lands. They sought acreage lying between the two Miami rivers. A soldier and Indian trader named Benjamin Stites had persuaded Symmes of the value of this land. In 1787 Congress sold Symmes a million acres and, in November 1788, Stites erected a few huts on land granted him by Symmes. It lay along the Ohio just below the mouth of the Little Miami River. He called his new settlement Columbia. Ironically, Symmes had no legal right to some of the lands he granted. Congress later restricted Symmes's request for land to a tract considerably smaller than a million acres, yet Symmes acted as though he had received all that he asked for, making any number of unauthorized grants.

The Miami Purchase was settled in a haphazard manner when contrasted with the orderliness of Marietta and the Ohio Company lands. Persons purchasing land from Symmes and his associates back in New Jersey took up their warrants wherever they would. Unwittingly, Symmes in Ohio and his associates in New Jersey sometimes sold the same parcel of land to two different parties. The resulting confusion, aggravated by the outbreak of Indian warfare in 1790, took years to clear up. Furthermore, Congress had imposed the same demands upon Symmes that it had imposed on the Ohio Company. He, too, was required to reserve land for schools, for future sale, for support of a university, and for support of religion. Symmes ignored the requirement that a township across from the mouth of the Licking River be set aside to support a university and, as a result, the university lands were ultimately located to the west of Symmes's purchase. In time, Miami University developed in Oxford, to the dismay of some settlers in the Symmes Purchase who felt that they had been cheated out of their college.

In December 1788, a second community was begun nearby. A New Jersey speculator and two Kentucky associates bought land across from the mouth of the Licking River and there established Losantiville. This fanciful name, attributed to John Filson of Kentucky, one of the founders, was to identify the new settlement as the city across from the mouth of the Licking River (*L* stood for Licking; *os* was Latin for mouth; *anti* was opposite or across from; *ville* was for city). To protect the new settlements, a stockade named Fort Washington was erected and garrisoned by troops from Fort Harmar in the fall of 1789. On January 2, 1790, Governor St. Clair arrived, organized Hamilton County between the two Miami rivers, and declared the new village to be its county seat. He rechristened the town, naming it Cincinnati in honor of the Society of the Cincinnati, the prestigious military society formed by officers who had served in the Revolutionary War. Cincinnati immediately became the dominant town of the region.

Judge Symmes accounted for another early village in southwestern Ohio. North Bend was located where the Ohio River reaches a northern extremity, close by the mouth of the Great Miami. The town's main distinction was that it became the residence of a young career soldier from Virginia, William Henry Harrison. He married Symmes's daughter Anna and went on to a distinguished military and political career, giving North Bend a prominence it would otherwise have lacked. Symmes's last years were spent embroiled in problems largely of his own making. He died a poor man in 1814.

Almost immediately after the founding of Marietta and Cincinnati new settlements were established nearby. It was risky for newcomers to locate at a distance from Fort Harmar and Fort Washington. The Ohio Indians and their northwestern allies had increased their raids into Kentucky and were taking lives and property on the Ohio River. Indian grievances had smoldered since the treaties of Fort McIntosh and Fort Finney stripped them of most of their Ohio land. It was against this backdrop of danger, therefore, that additional outposts were established along the Ohio and a short distance inland.

But new settlements were needed to make room for a continuing flow of new settlers. In 1789, for example, fifty-one men with families and another 101 unaccompanied men reached the Ohio Company settlement; the following year 200 men arrived, thirty-one of them bringing families. Likely spots for new outposts had been scouted out, and in April 1789 the rich bottomlands at Belpre (Beautiful Prairie), just a few miles downstream from Marietta, were occupied. An unusually high percentage of the Belpre pioneers were Revolutionary War veterans, equipped to protect themselves and their neighbors from Indian attack. Upon arrival they built a fortification called Farmer's Castle to provide protection for their families. Other small groups located east of Marietta along the Ohio, a short distance up the Muskingum, and along Duck Creek.

Life was also risky for the squatters and the small number of legitimate settlers who occupied lands in the Seven Ranges. Fort Steuben was the only secure post in that region except for the fortifications at Wheeling on the Virginia side of the river. This area suffered depredations but was spared full involvement in the Indian wars to come because hostile action was confined principally to the central and western sections of the future state.

The Virginia Military District

Despite the outbreak in 1790 of actual warfare between the United States army and the western Indians, settlements were made in the Virginia Military

District. In August 1790, Congress passed an act permitting Virginia to commence use of the district, since all the Kentucky lands initially set forth to redeem soldiers' bounties had been taken up. A few premature entries had already been made north of the Ohio, and these were confirmed in the congressional act.

The opening of the Virginia Military District owed much to the work of Nathaniel Massie. Like so many of the first land developers, he was a surveyor. Having lived in Kentucky since 1780, Massie had much experience with the rigors of frontier life. With a practiced eye he selected a site on the north bank of the Ohio, about twelve miles upstream from Limestone, Kentucky, and in December 1790 contracted with nineteen men who agreed to settle his site in return for grants of in-lots and out-lots. Sometimes called Massie's Station, this first settlement in the Virginia Military District was formally named Manchester. It was the nucleus from which survey and settlement were extended throughout the district.

Since the Virginia Military District operated under Virginia custom, the indiscriminate claim method for selecting land was used. A Virginia veteran could secure a warrant entitling him to the amount of land which was due him, which in turn depended on his rank and length of service. He selected a site and then engaged a surveyor who ran a "metes and bounds" survey of the tract. As noted earlier, the property lines were often highly irregular in shape and the surveyor's markers were casual in the extreme. The surveyor's pay was frequently a portion of the lot surveyed. In this fashion surveyors became backwoods capitalists, acquiring extensive land holdings which they later sold at a profit.

Gallipolis and the French Grant

Unique among Ohio's earliest settlements was Gallipolis. It was an outgrowth of the Scioto Company's efforts to sell land which it expected to acquire from Congress. The Scioto Company was a speculative venture in which William Duer and other influential easterners hoped to reap profits without risking much of their own money. They arranged to purchase over four million acres lying between the Ohio Company lands and the Scioto River, and Congress granted the company favorable terms. Through some complicated machinations the selling of this land fell to a company agent, Joel Barlow, and his English partner, William Playfair. They misrepresented the area as a park-like paradise, and thus sold lots to hundreds of French émigrés who were fleeing the guillotine and associated troubles brought on by the beginnings of the French Revolution. Not content with misrepresentation, Playfair absconded with the funds which the Scioto Company intended to use as payment to Congress, and the company, unable to meet payments, could not acquire title to its lands.

Meanwhile, hundreds of French men and women sailed for America believing that they owned property. When they learned that their "deeds" were valueless, many stayed in the East, but several hundred crossed the mountains, took boats down the Ohio, and arrived at a forest clearing which looked nothing like the arcadian paradise that had been represented to them by Barlow and Playfair.

In fact, the settlement which they found waiting for them in 1790 was not properly located on Scioto Company lands. Rather it was on lands of the Ohio Company. Crude cabins had been erected under the direction of Rufus Putnam, who offered the newcomers both an in-lot and an out-lot much as in his own Marietta settlement. However, the French had to purchase these properties from the Ohio Company. Another option taken up by some was to accept land in the French Grant, established by Congress in 1795. This embraced 24,000 acres located downstream from Gallipolis. It was Congress's way of attempting to mitigate the injuries done to the trusting French *émigrés*.

The crudity of life on the frontier was more than some *émigrés* could stand, and they quickly left the Ohio country. Those who stayed were not well prepared for physical labor, but they persevered, learned the rough new skills which the wilderness required, and created a permanent settlement in 1790. It was named Gallipolis, city of the Gauls, an elegant way of saying Frenchtown.

Men and women living in the tiny authorized settlements stretching along the Ohio from Fort Steuben to North Bend now joined squatters and the inhabitants of the old French posts, north and west of the Ohio Country, to form a small but growing population in the Northwest Territory. In their wilderness condition they were governed under the first stage of territorial government as outlined in the Northwest Ordinance. Thus they became pioneers in a political process which, with many changes through the years, was to guide emerging states and millions of people to full membership in an expanding federal Union.

⚜

4.

From Territory to State

Congress accomplished work of the highest order in establishing a plan for the orderly settlement and government of the Northwest Territory. The proof of its accomplishment is that the plans worked, not perfectly and not always as anticipated, but a wilderness was in fact ultimately transformed into thriving, republican states fully a part of the existing union. Congress's solution to the colonial problem was to eliminate colonies, to bring once-dependent regions into full membership in the brotherhood of states. It was in the "eastern state" of the Northwest Territory that this process first developed in its entirety, and that "eastern state" became Ohio.

First Steps in Territorial Government

On July 9, 1788, Gov. Arthur St. Clair stepped ashore at Fort Harmar to the sound of a fourteen-gun salute. Six days later, accompanied by his official family and the fort's garrison, he crossed the Muskingum to Marietta. There he was met by the learned and patriotic men who formed the core of the Ohio Company. In the ceremonies which followed, Winthrop Sargent, the territorial secretary, read the Northwest Ordinance, the territorial officers' commissions were announced, and St. Clair delivered a short speech. Government was now officially established in the Northwest Territory.

Governing the Northwest Territory was a formidable task. It was a huge area (about 260,000 square miles) whose vast distances were crossed only by water routes or forest trails. The tiny settlements along the Ohio were on the southeastern fringe of a wilderness dotted with old French posts at Detroit, Vincennes, Cahokia, Kaskaskia, and lesser points. Most inhabitants of the interior—barring Indians, who constituted a special case—were of French extraction and tradition. They had been governed under French civil law since the Quebec Act of 1774, and their Roman Catholic religion set them apart from the Protestant settlements along the Ohio. Some inhabitants of these French towns owned slaves, creating a temporary problem in that Congress had excluded that institution from the Northwest Territory.

To be nearer the people of these far-flung outposts, and to be more centrally located within his area of jurisdiction, Governor St. Clair moved his headquarters to Cincinnati in January 1790. Fifty-two years old when he assumed his gubernatorial duties, he had been born in England but grew up in British America and served the colonial cause as a general officer in the Revolutionary War. He was president of the Confederation Congress at the time the Northwest Ordinance was enacted. His best-known portrait shows a

Civil government for the Northwest Territory was inaugurated in 1788.

forceful-looking man of keen eye, sardonic mouth, and determined mien. One senses a hint of the arrogance which riled his political enemies.

While St. Clair held executive authority, Samuel Holden Parsons of Massachusetts, James M. Varnum of Rhode Island, and John Cleves Symmes of New Jersey were invested with judicial power. Together, St.Clair and the judges exercised legislative authority through selection of laws from existing state codes until such time as a suitable population qualified the Territory for an elected legislature. This arrangement proved less than ideal. Varnum was accused of spreading discord in the Ohio Company settlements, and Symmes became outraged when St. Clair later protected the interests of the federal government to Symmes's disadvantage.

St. Clair's administrative duties involved acting as liaison with the federal government, dealing with the Indians, establishing counties, overseeing the militia, and enforcing the territorial ordinances. In the latter instance, however, St. Clair had reservations about the legality of the ordinances since the judges had insisted, apparently with some demurrer on St. Clair's part, that they and the governor could properly legislate for the territory. St. Clair reminded the judges that the Northwest Ordinance simply allowed them to select laws from existing state codes and that these selections must be approved by Congress. However, in the early years of territorial government this provision of the ordinance was largely ignored.

Complicating this picture was the fact that St. Clair was frequently absent from his post. He made trips to the far western settlements, he went east to confer with federal officials, and part of the time he was in the field leading troops. During these absences, executive authority devolved upon the territorial secretary, Winthrop Sargent of Massachusetts. Sargent, a Harvard graduate and soldier, surveyor, and scholar, did not get along well with the judges. He also complained about the lack of respect shown by uncouth westerners whose conduct he called "licentious." His stiff-necked attitude exacerbated the tension which already existed between the governor and the judges. The judges, too, spent much time in the East, to the detriment of law and order in the Territory.

In 1789 the federal government assumed its duties under the new Constitution. Administration of the laws of the land, including the Northwest Ordinance, was now in the hands of the president of the United States. George Washington, long familiar with the western country and its problems, was also a land speculator with the eye of a developer. He visualized the West transformed into a flourishing society peopled by virtuous, republican settlers. But first, there was the Indian problem to be solved, and since the most recent effort at a negotiated settlement, the Treaty of Fort Harmar, had proved inconclusive, military action would be needed to subdue the tribes and open the Northwest.

The Indian Wars

Following the destruction of Shawnee villages by Benjamin Logan in 1786, the Ohio tribes made further changes in their village sites, their relationships with one another, and their dependence on the British. By 1786 a loose confederacy of northwestern Indians was formed around Kekionga (Fort Wayne) and other Miami villages at the head of the Maumee and included villages of other tribes downstream along the Maumee and its tributaries. In addition to the Miamis, this region contained Wyandots, Delawares, Shawnees, Ottawas, Pottawatomies, Kickapoos, Chippewas, and even some renegade Cherokees and Creeks from the south. Efforts by Joseph Brant and the Iroquois nations of New York to exert leadership over the western Indians were rejected on the grounds that ancient Iroquois claims to the Ohio Country were no longer valid.

Each substantial Indian village contained a British trading post. Indeed, Kekionga had a small but flourishing British society in what one visitor regarded as "a very pretty place" where charming women and their men in "fine fur caps" attended gala parties and danced the minuet. Though most British posts were far more primitive, they served as rallying points for Indians resisting American encroachments. Alexander McKee and his associates in the British Indian Department tantalized the Indians with prospects of assistance while carefully avoiding formal commitments. Nevertheless, British arms, ammunition, and trade goods allowed the Indians to maintain their attacks on the exposed frontier.

Early in his tenure, St. Clair decided military force would be required to stop Indian depredations. The secretary of war had ordered him to commence construction of a line of forts northward from Cincinnati, although the first of these, Fort Hamilton, would not be built until 1791. Meanwhile, a frontier army was being assembled at Fort Washington. Commanded by Brig. Gen. Josiah Harmar, this army was composed of 320 regulars and more than 1,100 militia, most of whom were the offscourings of Pennsylvania society, along with undisciplined Kentuckians. In beautiful October weather, Harmar's army arrived at Kekionga and its satellite towns at the head of the Maumee. Warned of Harmar's approach, the Indians had scattered, leaving their unprotected towns and crops to be ravaged and burned.

The American force lingered for four days to complete its destruction, at which time Harmar was informed that Indian bands were in the neighborhood. He detached Col. John Hardin and several hundred men, mostly militia, to disperse them. But Hardin's force stumbled into an ambush, and while his regulars performed well, the militia panicked and ran under assault from the Miami war chief, Little Turtle (Michikinqua), who commanded an Indian force much smaller in size than Hardin's detachment. Commenting on this disgraceful exhibition, Lieutenant Denny, a regular officer, called the militia's behavior "scandalous." Many militiamen, he said, "never fired a shot but ran off at the [appearance of the] first horse of the Indians, and left the few regulars to be sacrificed. Some of them never halted until they crossed the Ohio." Two days later, Harmar sent out another probing strike force, and again Little Turtle's warriors inflicted substantial casualties. Harmar then withdrew his battered army to the safety of Fort Washington, where he submitted an optimistic report of the campaign to Governor St. Clair.

The governor praised Harmar's conduct as did the faithful Lieutenant Denny, who said his commander's conduct during the campaign was "sober, steady, and attentive to the service." However, the general's detractors criticized his use of the militia and accused him of being drunk. Had the campaign been handled properly, they said, the 183 men dead or missing would be alive and accounted for. A court-martial cleared Harmar of wrong-doing, but his effectiveness with the military was at an end. He retired from the army and returned to his Pennsylvania home.

Success rejuvenated the confederation Indians, who now rebuilt their ravaged villages. Less than a month after Harmar's attack, they were beginning "to settle themselves again" along the Maumee. The Shawnee war chief, Blue Jacket, said they were ready to "consult on the measures proper to be taken for their future security." With fresh scalps adorning their lodges, young warriors lusting for honors and loot rampaged across the Ohio Country. They demonstrated the vulnerability of exposed settlements in January 1791 when Wyandots and Delawares surprised families in the exposed settlement at Big Bottom on the Muskingum, about thirty miles above Marietta. They killed more than a dozen settlers; the survivors huddled in a hastily erected stockade called Fort Frye, scarcely daring to tend to their chores outside its walls. The farmers of Washington County now sought protection in fortified posts: Rufus Putnam and his associates urged federal authorities to mount another strike against the Indian confederacy since fear was restricting the flow of settlers and the sale of land in the Northwest.

In the spring of 1791 President Washington and Congress responded to these pleas, authorizing Governor St. Clair, who was also a major general in the army, to raise a force of about 3,000 men against the Indian confederacy. This was to be accomplished by midsummer. Meantime, Maj. Gen. Charles Scott led mounted Kentuckians to the Wabash, where they destroyed Wea villages. The Kentuckians killed a few warriors, but mostly women and children, then returned to the falls of the Ohio having achieved little of lasting consequence. A few weeks later Maj. Gen. James Wilkinson led a similar raid along the Wabash without bringing the Indians to battle. These inconclusive raids did little more than stiffen Indian intransigence and inflame their desire for revenge.

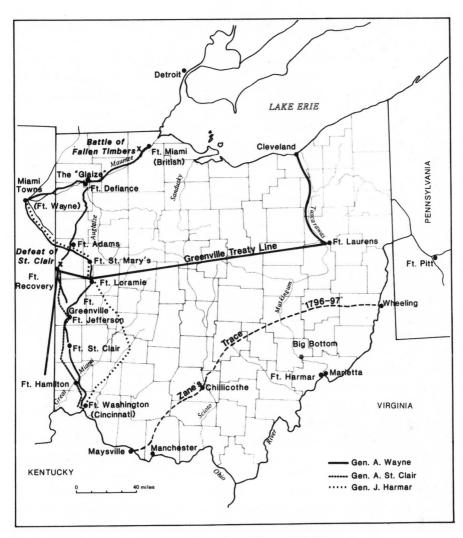

Map 8. The Indian Wars, 1790–95

Hope for destroying the Indian confederacy now rested with St. Clair. Summer was slipping away, and the promised troops had not yet assembled. The regulars were in place at Fort Washington, and as the militia straggled in they were assigned to Fort Ludlow, a temporary training camp nearby. These new recruits were a profound disappointment to St. Clair and his officers. Once more the eastern recruits were intractable, rebellious, undisciplined. Their officers were untrained. A group of 300 rambunctious Kentucky volunteers joined the ranks, adding still another undisciplined force to this unpromising mix of "Indian fighters." Many of them brought along broken guns, or no guns at all.

While the new recruits were receiving elementary drill, St. Clair sent a force to construct a fort on the Great Miami, about twenty-five miles northwest of Fort Washington. The new stockade was named Fort Hamilton and in time would become the nucleus of the city of Hamilton.

On October 4, St. Clair's main army group marched north from Fort Washington, following the western war trail into Indian country. The young Shawnee warrior, Tecumseh, and other Indian scouts watched the advance and noted that the force consisted of a small number of regular troops, mounted volunteers, ragtag eastern recruits, artillery, and supply wagons. A motley group of women camp followers moved with the army. At a point about seventy miles north of Fort Washington, the troops built Fort Jefferson. The need to garrison Forts Washington, Hamilton, and Jefferson eroded St. Clair's strength; so did desertions, which increased as the troops moved deeper into Indian country.

On November 3, the army, now reduced to approximately 1,400 effectives, encamped on a small branch of the Wabash River just east of the present Ohio-Indiana state line. It was intensely cold, and patches of snow covered the ground. Pickets were placed around the camp, but they were not especially alert in the grim and inhospitable weather. Close by were massed Indian defenders supplied with excellent intelligence about St. Clair's situation. Little Turtle and Blue Jacket placed 1,000 warriors in a half-moon formation with Wyandots and Iroquois on the right, Miamis, Shawnees, and Delawares in the center, and the "Lake Indians" (Pottawatomies, Ottawas, Chippewas) on the left.

Early on the morning of November 4, the Indians burst from cover, scattering the pickets and overrunning a militia outpost with ease. The undisciplined militia fled through the main encampment, disrupting efforts to deploy the men in defensive lines. Throughout more than three hours of combat, many undisciplined soldiers gathered aimlessly in the center of the defensive perimeter, and no effort succeeded in returning them to combat. Painted Indians, keyed to a high emotional pitch and shouting fierce war cries, surrounded the beleaguered army and concentrated their fire on officers and artillerymen. The strategy worked, for the potentially dangerous cannon were silenced or captured and surviving officers were too few to organize an effective resistance.

Among the senior officers was Maj. Gen. Richard Butler, who had long been at odds with his commander, St. Clair. Butler had arrogantly imposed harsh terms upon Indian representatives in previous treaty negotiations, but this time the Indians got their revenge. They tomahawked Butler, cut out his heart, and distributed pieces to each tribe engaged in battle. Throughout this vicious melee the warriors found time to scalp the injured and the dead, their exposed flesh smoking in the clear, cold air. Women camp followers and their children were massacred and their bodies desecrated. The wounded were thrown on camp fires to perish horribly.

Throughout this mad encounter, St. Clair conducted himself bravely although he was unable to exercise effective leadership. His horses were shot, so he had to limp about camp on goutty feet, scarcely able to bear the excrutiating pain. A bullet seared his cheek and others struck his clothing. Finally aides shoved him onto a broken-down nag, and he helped lead the breakout from the encircled camp. He left behind 630 officers and men killed and missing, along with uncounted numbers of camp followers and civilian wagoners; 283 men were wounded and a rich supply train was lost. Only the Indians' delay over the spoils kept them from pursuing and destroying St. Clair's broken army.

Safely back in Fort Washington, St. Clair became the target of outraged public opinion. He requested a court of inquiry: in 1792, a committee of the House of Representatives exonerated him of misconduct, praising him for his bravery under fire. Meanwhile St. Clair had resigned his army commission to clear the way for someone else to lead the western troops. St. Clair's Defeat, as the episode came to be known, was the worst defeat ever suffered by an American army at the hands of Indians in a single battle.

The Indians, meanwhile, were savoring their victory. Great quantities of loot had been won. An American captive later reported that Big Cat, a Delaware chief, secured two fine horses, four tents including an officer's marquee (large tent), clothing of all descriptions, axes, guns, "and everything necessary to make an Indian rich."

All was not serene within the tribes, however. American raids and flooded fields had destroyed much of the corn crop so warriors had to hunt instead of engaging in their usual raiding activity. The tribes now further consolidated their villages along the Maumee, especially at "the Glaize," the site of modern Defiance, where the Auglaize River joins the Maumee. Around this focus were at least a dozen Indian villages of various tribes. Despite extensive corn fields which stretched for miles along the river banks, there were too many mouths to feed, and these villages were chronically short of food. Their chiefs begged the British to keep them from starving.

In their newly won confidence that the Americans could be stopped, the northwestern Indians took a hard line toward peace overtures. The Americans, on the other hand, wanted to negotiate a new boundary in the Ohio Country. In 1792, American emissaries Capt. Alexander Trueman and Col. John Hardin were murdered by Indians while on their way to negotiate. The Ohio Indians, with British encouragement, wanted the Ohio River or, at worst, a Cuyahoga-Muskingum line to be the boundary. Although Rufus Putnam succeeded in negotiating a vague agreement with certain Indian leaders at Fort Knox (Vincennes, Indiana), it was essentially a meaningless gesture. The Indians failed to get the guarantees and boundaries they sought. Indian intransigence increased as tribal leaders saw that the Americans were preparing to strike again at the heart of Indian power along the Maumee.

St. Clair's defeat so enraged President Washington that he could hardly keep his famous temper under control. At his insistence, army units were brought up to strength and three additional regiments were enlisted to serve for three years or until the Indians were "pacified." Congress appropriated funds for cavalry and for the recruitment of Indian allies to fight alongside the western army if Washington thought them necessary. To lead this newly augmented army, Washington chose his old Revolutionary War colleague, "Mad" Anthony Wayne. Wayne was not at all "mad" in a clinical sense; he was impetuous and daring, impatient of restraint. His was a controlled madness which had brought him distinction at Stony Point and other battlefields. After the Revolution, Wayne fought against the southern Indians, gaining invaluable experience for his new command.

In late spring, 1792, Wayne's first recruits reported to Pittsburgh and trained until December when Wayne moved operations twenty-two miles down the Ohio to Legionville. The new recruits were drilled and disciplined until Wayne was satisfied they were ready to move to a forward post. In April 1793 he established a new base close by Fort Washington, where preparations continued through the summer. Despite the usual sickness and morale problems, Wayne decided to push northward in order to deter the Indians from hostile action. In October, with about 3,000 men, he reached a spot a few miles north of Fort Jefferson. There he constructed Fort Greene Ville (Greenville) and entered winter quarters. He continued drilling his troops and garrisoned Forts Hamilton, Jefferson, St. Clair (erected 1791–92) and the newly established Fort Recovery, built on the site of St. Clair's defeat.

Exaggerated reports of Wayne's force created consternation among the British and the tribes. As a gesture of support to the Indians the British had constructed Fort Miami at the rapids of the Maumee, but their agents promised more than their government was willing to deliver. British officials wanted no war with America. Meanwhile, Little Turtle, who had enjoyed successes against Harmar and St. Clair, wanted nothing to do with Wayne. "That man never sleeps," he is supposed to have said. Leadership of the Indian confederacy thus fell to Blue Jacket.

In July 1794, having repelled attacks on his supply lines and on Fort Recovery, Wayne moved his army to the Glaize, where he erected Fort Defiance. He then made unsuccessful peace overtures to the Indians. In August, Wayne's army advanced down the Maumee, and on the twentieth they attacked an army of over a thousand Indians lying concealed behind trees felled by a tornado. The Battle of Fallen Timbers was a short one, as Wayne's disciplined cavalry and foot soldiers quickly routed the Indian defenders. Wayne's losses were minimal—33 men killed and about 100 wounded—while estimates of Indian losses range to twice those numbers.

As they retreated, many Indians sought security within Fort Miami, located a mile downstream from the battlefield. Maj. William Campbell, the British fort's commandant, refused to admit them. Although this action embittered the Indians, it was prudent since the major's government wanted no confrontation with American troops. Given Anthony Wayne's impetuous nature, any overt assistance to the Indians might well have resulted in an Anglo-American battle in the Ohio wilderness. Wayne marched to the fort's gates and requested British withdrawal from American territory. Campbell demanded an explanation for the presence of an American force so near a British fortification. Rather than prolong the impasse, Wayne withdrew his troops to Fort Defiance, sent a party to erect a fortress (appropriately named Fort Wayne) at the head of the Maumee, and then returned to Fort Greene Ville from which point he reminded the Indians of their own helplessness as well as that of their British "friends."

The truth of what Wayne said was not lost on leaders of the Ohio tribes and their allies. Gradually various chiefs appeared at Fort Greene Ville to find out his terms for peace. To their dismay, Wayne said the principal basis for peace must be recognition of the treaty line negotiated five years earlier at Fort Harmar, thus dashing Indian hopes that a Cuyahoga-Muskingum line might be acceptable to the Americans. The Indians recognized where power lay, and they returned to their villages to prepare for a peace council.

From June 16 until August 3, 1795, the council fires burned in Fort Greene Ville. Indian representation swelled as each tribal chief and his supporting entourage arrived. Never had there been such a comprehensive gathering of western tribes in a peace negotiation, and Wayne managed the complex affair skillfully, mediating between the instructions he received from federal officials and the sensitivities of Indian leaders. Among the leading participants were Little Turtle of the Miamis, Tarhe of the Wyandots, Blue Jacket and Black Hoof of the Shawnees, and the Delaware chief, Buckongehelas. Wayne led the American contingent, which included the young army officer William Henry Harrison. Also representing the army were William Clark and Merriwether Lewis, whose names would soon become forever linked as leaders of a great western expedition to the Pacific. Others present included the interpreter William Wells, a white man who was also the adopted son of Little Turtle, as well as the influential frontiersman Isaac Zane, son-in-law of Tarhe. Absent from the gathering was Tecumseh, who disdained any accommodation with whites. The talented young Shawnee was destined to lead the last Indian military attacks in Ohio in 1813.

The Battle of Fallen Timbers in 1794.

On August 3, American officials and scores of Indian representatives signed the Treaty of Greenville, which was ratified by the United States Senate in December. The treaty contained the usual clause requiring the Indians to return captives, but most importantly it established a new boundary line separating Indian lands from those now open to Americans. The Greenville Treaty Line ran up the Cuyahoga from its mouth, across the portage, down the Tuscarawas to the crossing above Fort Laurens, then west to Loramie's store on a branch of the Great Miami, northwest to Fort Recovery, and then to a point on the Ohio across from the mouth of the Kentucky River. The Indians were confined to the area north and west of the line. Certain strategic locations within the Indian reserve were set aside for American use. For surrendering their lands, the tribes were to receive $20,000 above and beyond previous payments plus annuities of $9,500, all to be paid in goods. Wayne wisely declined to dictate how the Indians were to divide these payments, leaving that sticky question to the tribes to resolve.

It has been said by various historians that the Greenville Treaty Line "really settled the Indian problem in the Ohio country." Had it been observed in good faith, that might have been true. However, insatiable land hunger led aggressive whites to violate the boundary. Traders and liquor dealers continued to corrupt the tribesmen. Indians continued to hunt, and occasionally to steal a horse or two on the American side of the line. Tecumseh, his brother Tenskwatawa (the Shawnee Prophet), and certain other Indians continued to live for some years in villages below the treaty line. Still, compared to any previous effort to separate Indian and white in Ohio, the Treaty of Greenville was effective, though at the Indians' expense. It opened the way in eastern and southern Ohio for a renewed flood of settlers anxious to clear and cultivate lands which had never known the axe and the plow.

A Renewal of Migration to Ohio

People coming into Ohio immediately after the Treaty of Greenville continued to use the Ohio River as the great avenue to the West. Now, however, outposts were being established far up its tributaries in country protected by the treaty line. Before the Northwest Territory reached its second stage of development in 1799, newcomers had created new population centers in outlying parts of the future state.

Land sales in the Seven Ranges continued to lag, but in 1797 the Virginian Bezaleel Wells established Steubenville on the abandoned site of Fort Steuben. Legal settlers and squatters moved into this region from western Virginia and Pennsylvania, concentrating as before in the narrow valleys where the soil could sustain agriculture. Most were poor people, unable to

purchase land directly from the government, but many could afford to buy
lots and small farms from speculators who had purchased government land in
the Seven Ranges. Some military land warrants were taken up in the surveyed
area, and for years to come squatters and legitimate land owners continued to
share this region.

Downstream, in Ohio Company lands, settlers were pushing farther up the
Muskingum and the Hocking. Here too, fertile agricultural lands were found
only in the river valleys. Indeed, good farm sites were so limited that increases
in population failed to keep pace with more favored areas to the west. Athens,
named after the Greek center of learning and culture and located within the
two college townships, was laid out in 1797 along the Hocking River. In time
it would become a college town and an important regional center for a
sparsely populated section of the state.

In the Virginia Military District Nathaniel Massie was the moving force in
directing settlers into new homes. In 1796 Massie platted a town site on the
west bank of the Scioto just north of the mouth of Paint Creek. It was one of
Ohio's prime town sites, lying in a rich valley that once sheltered Adena and
Hopewell villages and which later was to be the center of Shawnee power.
Generous town lots and four-acre out-lots were laid off; a hundred of these
in-lots and out-lots were offered free to the first settlers. Farm lots of 100 to
200 acres were available in the vicinity for a modest one or two dollars per
acre. It is no wonder that the area boomed as Kentuckians and Virginians
moved in to take advantage of rich new lands and to escape the slave labor
system of their former homes. The new settlement was named Chillicothe;
immediately it became the focus of southern political influence in the
Northwest Territory.

Similar town-building activity was undertaken forty-six miles up the
Scioto. There, at the confluence of the Olentangy (then called the
Whetstone), the surveyor Lucas Sullivant laid out a town on the west bank of
the Scioto. He named it Franklinton, and by 1798 it was a center of population
and influence for the northern portions of the Virginia Military District.

Vigorous expansion was also occurring in the Miami valleys in and near the
Symmes Purchase. Military roads had been cut through this region, giving
settlers access for their wagons and goods. Discharged soldiers returned to
fertile valleys to buy favored pieces of land which they had first seen while
campaigning. Israel Ludlow laid out the town of Hamilton in 1795; it soon
became a prosperous trading center. Later that year Ludlow laid out a town at
the mouth of the Mad River; he named it for Jonathan Dayton, a New Jersey
agent for John Cleves Symmes. Dayton's first settlers arrived in 1796. From
the beginning they encountered difficulties, including the fact that some held
worthless titles and had to renegotiate their deeds at a considerable loss. A
story (which may be apocryphal) claims that Indians warned the settlers that

their cabins were on land that flooded. Nevertheless, the town grew up on the Miami floodplains, and in due time Dayton suffered as the Indians had predicted.

The Connecticut Reserve, or Western Reserve, also attracted its first settlers in the years following the Treaty of Greenville. In 1796 General Moses Cleaveland led a surveying party that laid out lands for the private speculators who formed the Connecticut Land Company. Only that portion of the reserve east of the Cuyahoga could be surveyed since lands to the west were beyond the Greenville Treaty Line. The Connecticut Land Company surveyed its holdings in the rectilinear pattern, but its townships were five-miles-square in contrast to the six-mile-square grid used by Congress in the Seven Ranges. Those who owned shares in the Connecticut Land Company chose their land in the reserve by lot, and an elaborate system was established to equalize the quality of these randomly chosen lands. Near Lake Erie were fertile Lake Plains, but to the south of this region fertile soils were interspersed with extensive bogs, swamps, steep-sided river valleys, and rolling hills.

Surveyors platted a town on the bluffs along the east side of the Cuyahoga's mouth, naming it Cleaveland. By accident or, according to one story, by design, the letter "a" was dropped from the general's name, resulting in the modern spelling of what would for years be a town in name only. Other first settlements in the Western Reserve included Conneaut, Warren, Youngstown, Painesville, Poland, Canfield, Ravenna, and Hudson, none of which attained much influence during the territorial period.

The Western Reserve was the first area of Ohio which settlers from the East reached by routes other than the familiar Ohio River access. The Mahoning Valley, of course, was accessible from the Ohio, but most early settlers in the reserve made the trip from New England via the Mohawk Trail through central New York to the Lake Trail, which ran along ridges paralleling Lake Erie. Some came much of the way by water. In 1799, for example, the land proprietor David Hudson and his party sent livestock along the overland trail while the rest of the party sailed from Oswego across Lake Ontario, dragged their boats and possessions up the Niagara escarpment, battled the stiff currents of the Niagara River, sailed along Erie's shore, dragged their boats up the shallow Cuyahoga, and finally cut their way through virgin forest and around swamps, following surveyors' marks to reach lands purchased sight unseen in old Connecticut. In 1800 Connecticut relinquished all control over her reserve, and the area became an integral part of the Northwest Territory, its 1,000 inhabitants being organized into Trumbull County with Warren as its seat.

Large areas south of the Greenville Line lay outside any previous congressional grant, and disposition of these lands was under continuing discussion.

New Englanders feared a population drain if western lands were sold cheaply. Speculators, many of whom had influence in Congress, wanted public land prices set high enough that they wouldn't undercut the private selling prices. Some congressmen wanted public land sales liberal enough to bring money quickly into the Treasury. Westerners generally favored low prices and easy terms.

After many compromises among these interests, Congress passed two land laws in 1796. The first, enacted May 18, did not fully satisfy anyone. Townships would remain six miles square with land therein sold in quarter townships at public auction with the minimum price set at two dollars per acre, payable within a year. Half the townships would be surveyed into 640-acre sections which would be sold for two dollars an acre at land offices located in Pittsburgh and Cincinnati. Four sections in each township and various salt springs were reserved for future disposal by Congress.

A second act of 1796 established a 2.5 million-acre reserve called the United States Military Tract. Located west of the Seven Ranges, north of the Ohio Company lands and south of the Western Reserve, it was to be surveyed in five-mile-square townships and distributed to satisfy bounties due to veterans of the Continental army. Congress's use of the five-mile-square township (presumably for ease in dividing the land into units consistent with the land bounties granted) is yet another example of that body's willingness to experiment in its patterns of land distribution and survey.

Despite the land acts of 1796, sales continued to lag. The new legislation did not satisfy speculators, and the size of the plots to be sold excluded the small buyer from a reasonable chance of purchase. Clearly some further modification of the land laws would be required to create sales momentum, but before Congress enacted that legislation, territorial government had taken a large step forward.

Moving Toward Self-Government

With the Indian wars now behind them, territorial officials were again able to attend more fully to the civil administration of a growing population. Prior to 1795 the governor and judges had functioned as a legislature by enacting laws despite the terms of the Northwest Ordinance. St. Clair had reminded Secretary Winthrop Sargent and the judges that they exceeded their authority by assuming legislative functions; aside from protesting, however, he did nothing to stop the practice in the early years because practical realities required territorial officials to take quick action in situations, which differed from the more settled conditions of the established states. A certain amount of flexibility and improvisation were needed in governing the region.

In 1795, however, the federal House of Representatives, influenced perhaps by St. Clair's position, disapproved laws which the governor and judges had enacted three years earlier, and even though the Senate failed to concur, the House debates became known in the Northwest and triggered a growing dissatisfaction with what was now perceived as the arbitrary authority of the governor and judges. The territory's first newspaper, the weekly *Centinel of the North-Western Territory* ("Open to all Parties—but Influenced by none"), first published in Cincinnati in 1793, became a medium through which disgruntled people expressed opposition to arbitrary authority.

Nevertheless, during the summer of 1795 Governor St. Clair and judges John Cleves Symmes and George Turner met in Cincinnati as a legislature. They recognized the need to create a comprehensive criminal and civil code, and for this purpose they adopted laws of the existing states. Their work came to be known as Maxwell's Code (named for the code's printer). Twenty-five of its thirty-seven laws were taken from the Pennsylvania code, which was best known to St. Clair, and the remaining laws were drawn from those of four other states. Among its important provisions, Maxwell's Code recognized that English common law was to have force in the Territory. The code restructured certain court practices, protected against excessive taxation, reduced oppressive fees, and imposed a variety of regulatory constraints. Three years later at another legislative session in Cincinnati, Winthrop Sargent, acting in place of the absent St. Clair, joined judges Joseph Gilman and Return Jonathan Meigs, Jr., to adopt eleven new laws including four taken from Kentucky's code. This was irregular in that the borrowed laws were supposed to be taken from the codes of the *original* states, but conditions in frontier Kentucky (which had achieved statehood in 1792) were similar to those north of the Ohio on questions of land, horse breeding, and criminal conduct.

Despite these more orderly approaches to lawmaking, effective administration of the Northwest Territory remained impossible. The governor, secretary, and judges were required to travel long distances to Detroit, Vincennes, and the Illinois towns on the Mississippi. The journeys by boat or horseback were never safe or comfortable, and tested the mettle of men poorly paid for their efforts.

Jacob Burnet, a Cincinnati lawyer who frequently travelled with the judges on circuit, recounted the discomforts and dangers of swimming horses across flooded streams, sleeping in wet snow with only a blanket for protection, and wandering treacherous trails in pitch-black darkness. Once, while on the trail to Detroit, his party stopped at an Indian town on the Auglaize where Buckongehelas, principal chief of the Delawares, resided. They were entertained by a ball game in which about a hundred men opposed an equal number of women, each team attempting to cast a ball between stakes set at the ends of a five-acre field. The game was lively; it ended in victory for the women "by the herculean strength of a mammoth squaw, who got the ball and held it, in spite of the efforts of the men to shake it from the grasp of her uplifted hand, till she approached the goal, near enough to throw it through the stakes." Returning to this village sometime later, the party discovered that whiskey and been brought from Cincinnati, and the Indians were "in a high frolic . . . the whole village, male and female, were drunk."

And so territorial government seemed to bumble along. St. Clair was required to be absent from his duties for considerable stretches of time. Judges wore out, fell ill, or quit in disgust, causing rapid turnover in this key arm of the government. Secretary Sargent appeared to be congenitally unhappy with his salary, his subordination to St. Clair, his relationship with the judges, and the lack of respect shown his person and his office. Within the United States Congress were persons who were none too eager to advance the West, believing that it could only be done at the expense of the East. And by 1797–98 the Ohio settlers were restive, calling more and more frequently for a representative assembly and for self-government.

Governor St. Clair, though distrustful of the ability of most frontier people to govern themselves, recognized that a census should be made to determine if there were now the 5,000 "free male inhabitants of full age" required for progression to the second stage of territorial government. Though he ordered a census, he didn't wait for the count; his travels had convinced him that the number had been reached. He issued a proclamation on October 29, 1798, stating that there were a sufficient number of eligible males, and he then set the third Monday in December as the date for choosing delegates to a territorial legislature.

The newly elected members of the lower house met in Cincinnati in February 1799 to nominate ten persons from whom President John Adams would choose five to comprise the upper house or Legislative Council. The twenty-two members of the lower house represented the entire Northwest Territory. Fifteen of them came from the five counties which later became Ohio; the other seven were from the old French settlements at Detroit, Vincennes, and the Illinois towns. Freeholders owning fifty acres or personal and real property of equivalent worth were eligible to vote for assemblymen; members of the lower house had to own at least 200 acres, and members of the council at least 500 acres. Thus, in what is usually thought of as the most democratic section of the young American republic, large numbers of people had no voice in government.

Restricting participation in government to property holders was consistent with the Federalist philosophy, which advocated government by the able and fit, by those who had a substantial stake in society. But this political philosophy, held by Governor St. Clair and most of the early leadership, was under serious attack by an emerging group of antifederalist Republicans, or Jeffersonians, who, while property owners themselves, still saw virtue in broad popular participation in government. Ironically, once in power many prominent Jeffersonian leaders came to share Federalist doubts about broad popular participation in government. But this tension was not immediately apparent as the newly elected territorial assembly met in its first session.

The Territorial Assembly

On September 24, 1799, the territorial assembly met in Cincinnati for its first formal session. Its affairs were dominated by several remarkable leaders of Virginia background, among them Edward Tiffin, chosen by his colleagues to be president of the new House of Representatives. An English-born physician who had emigrated to Virginia, Tiffin moved to Chillicothe in 1797 with his brother-in-law, Thomas Worthington. Both were men of property who sought a more open society and new economic opportunities in the Northwest. Both wished to escape the baleful influence of slavery; both were committed to the political philosophy of Thomas Jefferson. Their Virginia connections and landed interests made them natural allies of Nathaniel Massie, the most influential man in the Virginia Military District, who, like Tiffin and Worthington, was committed to making Chillicothe preeminent in territorial affairs. Worthington was especially effective in his maneuverings against the Federalist "autocrats," picturing himself and his friends as defenders of the peoples' liberties. No Federalist in the House was a match for him, but in the Legislative Council, Jacob Burnet of Cincinnati, a strong Federalist lawyer who had migrated from New Jersey, played the dominant role.

Despite their political differences, Federalists and Republicans cooperated to set the new government on course. For the moment, Governor St. Clair and the legislature worked together to address their problems, but the governor's absolute veto over acts of the legislature soon undermined mutual trust and respect. To allow the peoples' representatives to be overruled by the judgment of an appointed governor was intolerable in the Republican view. It reminded settlers of the English colonial government they had so recently cast off.

Still, much of the confusion surrounding the loose legislative practices adopted during the first stage of territorial government was now cleared away by statute. The legislature tightened election laws and levied taxes upon land to meet the increased cost of government. First-rate land was taxed at eighty-five cents per 100 acres; second-rate land, sixty cents; and third-rate land, twenty-five cents. County courts were to make the assessments and collect the taxes subject to the final authority of a territorial treasurer and auditor. New laws provided that local county revenues would be raised through a personal property tax and licensing fees. County courts would collect and administer these local revenues. The assembly made appropriations for the expenses of government, with the largest going for the travel and pay of the legislators themselves.

The new legislators also enacted laws dealing with personal conduct and criminal actions. Arson, that bane of a wood-based society, was punishable by death. Territorial officials could no longer make arrests on the Ohio River, all of whose waters were claimed by Virginia or Kentucky. New statutes offered bounties for wolf scalps in an effort to reduce losses of sheep and hogs. Other acts forbade public cursing, "worldly employments" on the Sabbath, gambling, dueling, fighting, and public intoxication. The militia was restructured. Sale of liquor to the Christian Indians was forbidden.

Of special importance for the development of the territory were laws adjusting the highway act that had first been employed in 1792. All able-bodied men were required to work a specified number of days on the roads or be fined seventy-five cents a day. The lawmakers specified the design of roads and bridges and placed implementation in control of the county courts. Signposts, ferries, and tolls were also regulated, as were the rates charged by mill owners, since mills were regarded as public utilities.

Another action of first significance marked this legislature. On two occasions settlers moving into the Virginia Military District petitioned the lower house for permission to bring slave property with them. The legislature rejected the first request out of hand, but debated the second at length, eventually rejecting it nearly unanimously. The morality of slavery was not the central issue. Rather, a majority of representatives believed that the development of the region would be retarded if free labor had to compete with slave labor. Influential Virginians like Tiffin and Worthington had come to the Northwest partly to escape a slave society. Thus these representatives upheld the principle of the Northwest Ordinance—the region north of the Ohio was to remain forever free.

There was, of course, some *de facto* slavery in the Northwest in the early days. Certain French and British settlers in the old French posts held slaves, but in that portion of the territory which became Ohio, only a relative handful of slaves were held by unscrupulous persons who safely ignored the injunction against slavery because they lived in isolation or because their neighbors took no action to restrain them. Other owners concealed some *de facto* slavery as indentured labor, but such abuses tended to disappear with the increase of population and its accompanying controls.

The Press for Statehood

One of the first shots in what was to become a war between Arthur St. Clair and the territorial assembly was fired in October 1799 when St. Clair's son, Arthur, Jr., lost his bid to become territorial representative to the United States House of Representatives. Instead, the territorial legislature, in joint session, chose William Henry Harrison of North Bend. Harrison was a native Virginian, successful Indian fighter, son-in-law of John Cleves Symmes, and friend of the Chillicothe political clique. Harrison was serving as territorial secretary, and he now resigned that position. His successor was Charles Willing Byrd, another Virginian and a brother-in-law of Nathaniel Massie.

Harrison went directly to Philadelphia and took his seat in the House of Representatives as delegate from the Northwest Territory. One of his first acts, in December 1799, was to call attention to reforms needed in the land laws in order to encourage "actual settlers" to purchase and develop lands in the West. Speculators opposed any measure which would undercut the value of their holdings, but on April 15, 1800, the new land act was passed; for the first time, people of modest means had a chance to purchase public lands directly from the government. Under the new Harrison Land Act one could purchase a half-section of 320 acres (west of the Muskingum only) for two dollars an acre, plus surveying and land office fees. A credit system allowed the buyer a down payment of half the cost plus fees (i.e., $330) with the remaining $320 to be paid in four equal installments. Preemption rights—the right of a settler who had "squatted" on unoccupied land to purchase on favorable terms the land he had settled and improved—were extended only to those who had erected a mill. New land offices opened at Marietta, Steubenville, Chillicothe, and Cincinnati to accommodate land seekers.

Purchasers rushed to take advantage of the new terms; soon Thomas Worthington, superintendent of sales and registrar of the land office at Chillicothe, was doing "a land office business." Within two-and-a-half months he sold lands worth $400,000, and by the time Ohio emerged as a state in 1803, the four offices had sold 937,737 acres. For the first time a federal land law produced a rewarding income from sales. A cloud loomed on the horizon, however, for the credit terms encouraged buyers to take up more land than they could pay for, and in time chronic debt and property foreclosures became commonplace. For the time being, however, sales moved briskly and the flow of new residents encouraged the Chillicothe clique to expedite statehood.

Governor St. Clair had long recognized that the Northwest Territory would be divided. The question was, where should the line be drawn? People west of the Great Miami wished to separate from the "eastern state" proposed in the Northwest Ordinance and return to the first stage of territorial government which they believed had better served their interests, and at less cost. St. Clair favored a division of another kind. He wanted to divide his political enemies in the Scioto Valley, strengthen conservative influence, and postpone statehood. And since Marietta, Cincinnati, and Vincennes each wished to become the seat of government for a part of the Territory, the St. Clair faction, with its strength concentrated in Washington County (Marietta) and Hamilton County (Cincinnati), proposed dividing the Territory by a line running north from the mouth of the Scioto to Lake Erie. Marietta would become the seat of government east of that line, Cincinnati west of it.

The Chillicothe Republicans reacted to this plan by urging William Henry Harrison to intercede with Congress to preserve the divisions provided in the Northwest Ordinance. Harrison succeeded in securing the appointment of a House committee which was instructed to examine the question of dividing the Northwest Territory into two "distinct governments." St. Clair urged Harrison to support a division along the Scioto plus another line drawn north from the mouth of the Kentucky River. Cincinnati, Harrison's home area, would become capital of the middle region. Harrison resisted this appeal, and remained true to the interests of the Chillicothe clique. Thomas Worthington, a key actor in that clique, joined him in the federal capital to lobby for maintaining the original division lines.

Harrison and Worthington prevailed, and on May 7, 1800, Congress passed a bill dividing the Northwest Territory along a line running from the mouth of the Kentucky River to Fort Recovery and thence due north to Canada. When a state was formed, the line would revert to one drawn due north from the mouth of the Great Miami. Cincinnati was to be the capital of the region east of this line until the territorial legislature should state otherwise. The region east of the dividing line remained the Northwest Territory while that west of the line was the newly-established Indiana Territory, of which William Henry Harrison was appointed governor. He assumed his new post at Vincennes and relinquished his duties as territorial delegate in Congress.

With the Northwest Territory now limited to the future Ohio and the sparsely populated region to the north of it, the issues separating the governor's supporters (mostly Federalists and conservatives centered in Washington and Hamilton counties) and the Republicans (the Chillicothe clique plus a majority of rural people) were clearly focused. The St. Clair faction wished to retain him as governor and Cincinnati as the seat of government until such time as a division of the territory along the Scioto would separate the Ohio Country, with Marietta the seat of the eastern region and Cincinnati the seat of the western. They hoped to persuade Congress to provide valid titles to inhabitants of Hamilton County who had purchased land from John Cleves Symmes which he had no legal right to sell. They also demanded that Symmes cede one university township as required by Congress in the original Symmes grant. The Chillicothe clique wished to retain the "eastern state" as outlined in the Northwest Ordinance, return the seat of territorial government to Chillicothe, secure St. Clair's removal, and expedite statehood.

The new territorial legislature met in November 1800, with the St. Clair faction controlling the council and holding a slight majority in the House. The legislature elected William McMillan of Cincinnati to serve out Harrison's unexpired term as congressional delegate and selected Paul Fearing of Marietta to serve the full two-year term that followed. Both were St. Clair supporters.

A strong undercurrent of hostility toward the governor marked this session and St. Clair reciprocated in kind. The governor continued to assert his right to establish counties and determine their seats of government. The legislative minority maintained that the legislature had concurrent powers in these matters and resented the governor's cavalier attitude.

Political lines fluctuated in the territorial period, but certain consistencies separated Federalist and Republican. Rufus Putnam, the dominant figure in the Ohio Company lands, and Governor St. Clair were strong nationalists. Nathaniel Massie and Thomas Worthington were regional and state boosters. Putnam and St. Clair believed men of substance, experience, and discipline should rule. Massie and Worthington, though men of immense wealth, believed in a broader popular participation in government. They resisted federal restrictions on their freedom of action, a freedom which they had used to enrich themselves and to consolidate their political influence.

Despite hostility toward St. Clair, the legislature acted on several of the governor's recommendations that were clearly beneficial for the long term. Local self-government was advanced by an act incorporating the town of Marietta. All freeholders and adult male inhabitants who paid taxes could vote in local elections. The lawmakers recognized the town meeting as the locus of decision making for the community, in keeping with Marietta's New England tradition, and granted authority to raise necessary taxes, elect local officials, enact levies in support of schools, and enact regulations for maintaining peace and good order. Thus Marietta became a model to be followed elsewhere in the West as local self-government evolved.

Other important legislative acts established circuit courts at five locations, raised to twenty dollars the limit for hearings before a single justice of the peace, and divided the counties into districts in each of which elections would be held on the same day, with voting to be by written ballot rather than by oral declaration. Jacob Burnet, normally a St. Clair supporter, lamented the removal of "the manly, independent practice of pronouncing audibly and fearlessly, the names of the candidates voted for" in favor of the "secrecy of the ballot box."

Although cooperation between the governor and the legislature had accomplished much, St. Clair announced that the legislative session would end December 9 when his own commission expired. This triggered open hostility in the House, which authorized a committee to sound out the inhabitants of the Northwest Territory with respect to statehood, suggesting that the 60,000 inhabitants required for statehood would be shown in the forthcoming census. Five hundred copies of the address were sent throughout the territory, much to the chagrin of Governor St. Clair.

Meanwhile, on the national scene, Thomas Jefferson won election to the presidency in the famous "revolution of 1800" which removed Federalist power in the executive branch of the federal government. His election was hailed in the Northwest by Republicans who saw a way to enlist powerful support in their statehood drive. Perhaps they could now get rid of the governor and his impediments to statehood; their hopes for the ouster of St. Clair were dashed, however, when the lame-duck president, John Adams, reappointed him to a new term.

St. Clair's supporters in the territorial legislature fanned the flames of the statehood issue when they persuaded Marietta and Cincinnati representatives to pass a bill dividing the Territory along the Scioto, pending Congress's approval. The bill helped clarify political positions. The small Federalist contingent, centered in Cincinnati and Marietta, feared that should the "eastern state" as outlined in the Northwest Ordinance become a new state of the Union, it would be dominated by Republicans and Chillicothe would be its capital. Centering power in Chillicothe could adversely affect the schemes of land speculators. Those banking on the rapid growth of Cincinnati might suffer and those banking on the rapid growth of Chillicothe and the Virginia Military District might gain.

Republicans led by the Chillicothe clique saw that the division bill would leave them isolated along the eastern fringe of a state dominated by Cincinnati. Furthermore, their best hope for expediting statehood and furthering their own political and economic fortunes lay in securing the help of the new president, Thomas Jefferson, and the Congress, now dominated by the Republicans. Led by Nathaniel Massie, the Chillicothe Republicans took their message directly to Congress, stressing that the division bill was in conflict with the Northwest Ordinance and was thus unconstitutional. The federal House took the matter under advisement.

Chillicothe continued to be the main focus of Republican discontent, and when St. Clair and his supporters succeeded in moving the territorial capital to Cincinnati, rioting broke out in Chillicothe. A mob led by a radical clique known as the "Bloodhounds" invaded the rooming house where the governor and his associates were staying, but St. Clair's calm demeanor defused what might have become an ugly confrontation. It was a foretaste of the bitterness that would continue to mark the statehood contest, a contest which now shifted to the new national capital in Washington.

Statehood proponents held a public meeting in Chillicothe and chose

Thomas Worthington and Michael Baldwin (a "Bloodhound" and Worthington's political enemy on local matters) to take the Republican message to Washington. With Jefferson in the presidency and Republican majorities in both houses of Congress, the time seemed right for effective lobbying on behalf of statehood. While Massie, Tiffin, and other Republican leaders furnished them with petitions from home, Worthington and Baldwin lobbied in Washington. Worthington had the ear of William Giles of Virginia, chairman of the House committee considering the territorial division bill. He presented Giles with petitions that gave the impression a selfish minority in positions of power in the Territory was attempting to perpetuate itself rather than supporting the peoples' desire for statehood and republican government. In January 1802, the House overwhelmingly rejected the division bill, retaining thereby the existing configuration of the Territory and improving the chance for speedy development of a state.

With this crisis surmounted, Worthington turned his attention to the ouster of St. Clair as governor. He was in frequent communication with President Jefferson, sometimes dining with him. He described Jefferson as "easy of access and communicative to all—plain in his dress and acting the true part of the first citizen of the Republick." The president was in no hurry to replace St. Clair, perhaps being persuaded by the governor's assertions that he was best able to protect the people from the "misery and ruin" which would follow were statehood to develop too precipitately.

The House of Representatives established a committee to report upon the prospects for statehood. Although the census of 1800 revealed but 45,365 inhabitants in the Territory, the committee noted that rapid increase would drive the population above the 60,000 mark before a new state could be organized. Despite opposition from territorial representative Paul Fearing, A Federalist, the committee proposed that steps be taken to establish a new state, and the House accepted this report. It passed an enabling bill and sent it on to the Senate, where opposition was overcome and a bill reported out. President Jefferson signed the Enabling Act on April 30, 1802.

Statehood Achieved

The Enabling Act assumed that the new state would be created and admitted to the Union. The preamble to the act read:

> That the inhabitants of the eastern division of the territory northwest of the river Ohio, be, and they are hereby, authorized to form for themselves a constitution and State government, and to assume such name as they shall deem proper, and the said State, when formed, shall be admitted into the Union upon the same footing with the original States in all respects whatever.

The state boundaries were set at the Pennsylvania line, the Ohio River to the mouth of the Great Miami, a meridian northward to its intersection with a line projected due east from the southern tip of Lake Michigan, then along that line to the international boundary. In years to come every section of Ohio's boundaries would be a matter for dispute with neighboring states, but for the time being the chief objection to the boundaries came from Detroit, which would now be cut off from its former connection to the "eastern state." It was attached to the Indiana Territory. The Enabling Act also fixed the date for a constitutional convention, and set the terms for voting for delegates to this convention.

Election of convention delegates took place by districts with the franchise limited to adult male taxpayers with at least a year's residence in the territory. The thirty-five delegates so chosen assembled on November 1 in Chillicothe. Twenty-six were Republicans, seven Federalists, and two were undecided. They were young, representing many occupations and professions, but most were involved in land speculations. The strongest pro-statehood politicians, including Chillicothe's Worthington, Massie, Tiffin, and Baldwin, claimed many of the convention's leadership positions. Sixty-four-year-old Rufus Putnam and Ephraim Cutler of Marietta represented the small Federalist minority. Thirty-six-year-old Edward Tiffin—physician, landowner, businessman, and Methodist lay preacher—was a popular choice as president of the convention. One of his first tests came when Governor St. Clair attempted to insinuate his people into the work of the convention, and the convention leadership successfully rebuffed the attempt.

St. Clair was now sixty-eight, in poor health, and somewhat crotchety and out of sorts with the times. His political enemies had lost respect for him. Worthington noted in his diary that on a recent visit to Chillicothe, St. Clair "as usual got very drunk." But they kept a wary eye on the governor's friends, who seemed to hope that St. Clair might become governor of the new state. The governor was given permission to address the convention despite Republican reservations. Nathaniel Massie, one of his bitterest foes, favored allowing the governor to speak, knowing that he would "hang himself" if he spoke against the Enabling Act.

And that is just what St. Clair did. He claimed that Congress could not change the Ordinance of 1787 by later legislation such as the Enabling Act which it had "neither the power nor the right" to pass. He advised the convention to ignore it. This was self-defeating advice, as the federal administration he was criticizing was controlled by his political enemies. Upon completing his speech, St. Clair left the floor and the delegates immediately adopted a resolution which stated that it was "expedient . . . to form a constitution and state government." Thirty-two voted aye; only Ephraim Cutler of Marietta voted nay.

Thomas Worthington and his friends lost no time in acquainting President Jefferson with the details of St. Clair's intemperate speech, and on November 22 Jefferson dismissed the governor from office. Rather than communicate directly with St. Clair, Jefferson enclosed the dismissal in a message to Charles Willing Byrd, who was to succeed St. Clair as governor of the Northwest Territory.

An embittered St. Clair denounced the federal administration, his successor, and his political enemies in the Territory. In December, the "poor old Man" returned to his properties at Ligonier, Pennsylvania, where he spent years unsuccessfully trying to get Congress to reimburse him for personal expenses he accrued while on public business. His old nemesis, Thomas Worthington, now a U.S. senator, voted to reimburse St. Clair, but the vote did not carry. The bitterness of his later years in office overshadowed in the public mind the constructive work St. Clair had done to make territorial government a reality, often at personal sacrifice and under most trying conditions. His tragedy as governor was his inability to adjust to the rising tide of democratic aspiration in the territory. Now he was ill, impoverished, reduced to living in a log cabin; in 1818 he died at age eighty-four.

Meanwhile the convention delegates pressed ahead and completed a constitution by November 29 at which time the convention adjourned. The Republican majority had defeated a proposal to submit the constitution to the people for ratification, fearing that Federalists would use the occasion to throw roadblocks in the way of statehood. The document was entrusted to Thomas Worthington who crossed the mountain trails on horseback, arriving in Washington on December 19. The next day he called on President Jefferson, and on December 22 he delivered the constitution to Congress.

Both houses of Congress appointed committees to consider the document. The Senate committee's report approving the constitution was written into a bill approved by the full Senate. The House adopted the bill, and on February 19, 1803, President Jefferson signed it into law. Ohio was thus officially recognized as a state in the Union. The act stated that, under authority of the Enabling Act, the people had formed "a constitution and State government, and did give to the said State the name of the 'State of Ohio.'" The "said State had become one of the United States of America" and all the laws of the United States "shall have the same force and effect within the said State of Ohio, as elsewhere within the United States."

It is important to emphasize the complete, legal admission of Ohio as a state in February 1803 because a misunderstanding of the facts has led persons, from time to time, to claim that Congress never completed the statehood process. They base their claim on the irrelevant point that Congress did not pass a separate resolution formally declaring Ohio a state as it did with Louisiana and Indiana, the next states to be admitted after Ohio.

But state it was, and in attendant business, Congress approved certain al-
terations which the Ohio convention suggested to propositions contained in
the Enabling Act. These concerned reserving public lands for educational
purposes in the United States Military Tract, the Connecticut Reserve, the
Virginia Military District, and in Indian lands not ceded. A college township
was to be located in the Symmes Purchase. Three percent (instead of the five
percent stated by Congress) of the receipts from the sale of federal lands in
Ohio were to be used for public roads in Ohio and two percent for roads
leading to Ohio. In return for these benefits, Ohio would refrain from taxing
federal lands for a five-year period.

The constitution which the new state had sent for Congress's approval was
a triumph for Republican principles. It was perhaps the most democratic state
constitution yet adopted, with virtually all power in the legislature—the general assembly—vested in a Senate and a House of Representatives. The constitution assured popular control of these bodies through the annual election of
house members and the biennial election of senators. The governor was a
figurehead. Though chosen by popular vote, he had little effective political
power and patronage, and he had no veto power, a provision that was clearly
a reaction to the veto power St. Clair had exercised as territorial governor.
The legislature chose all other state executive officers. The judiciary was also
a creature of the legislature; state and county judges were appointed by the
general assembly and served for a fixed term of seven years.

The constitutional convention had spent considerable time and emotional
energy on issues involving the status of blacks. Although there were only 337
blacks reported in the Northwest Territory at the time, with most of these
apparently living in Detroit, in that section of the Territory that would be cut
off from the state, it took hours of struggle to reconcile opposing viewpoints.
Ephraim Cutler, a staunch New England Federalist from Washington
County, led the move to adopt the article which read that "There shall be
neither slavery nor involuntary servitude in this state, otherwise than for the
punishment of crimes. . . ." The article also placed strict limits on indentured servitude. Thus the first state to emerge from the Northwest Territory
would honor the Northwest Ordinance pledge that slavery should not exist
northwest of the Ohio River.

While the vote on the slavery issue carried by a considerable margin, the
vote to grant the franchise to blacks failed by the narrowest of margins. The
convention delegates had split evenly on the issue, seventeen voting to allow
blacks to vote and seventeen opposing. Edward Tiffin, in his role as president
of the constitutional convention, cast the deciding vote.

The right to vote was limited to white male taxpayers at least 21 years of
age, who elected not only state legislators and the governor but also local
officials, including township trustees, constables, sheriffs, justices of the

peace, and coroners. A bill of rights protected the civil liberties of Ohioans. In short, Ohio's first constitution kept government close to the people. In time, however, problems would arise from giving the legislature too much power at the expense of the executive and judicial branches of government. It would take many decades to rectify this imbalance.

In the meantime, Ohioans were taking the first steps to organize state and local governments. It would prove to be an arduous and contentious process.

5

Early Statehood Issues

Organizing State Government

Before leaving Chillicothe, Republican delegates to the constitutional convention drew up a slate of candidates for governor and the legislature. There was little doubt that the Republicans, with their burgeoning political strength, would elect their candidates; and so they did. Edward Tiffin, fresh from his effective leadership in the constitutional convention, was such a popular gubernatorial candidate that his political opponents cast blank ballots as a gesture of frustration and protest. He won overwhelmingly, but his office under the new constitution was one of prestige rather than power. Power lay with the general assembly, and the Republicans won control of both houses in the January 1803 elections.

Chillicothe, the new state capital, was a lively place on Tuesday, March 1, 1803, when the legislators took their seats. The fourteen senators chose Nathaniel Massie as speaker, and the thirty representatives chose Michael Baldwin as theirs. Both were from Chillicothe as was Secretary of State William Creighton (selected, like other state officials, by the legislature). These men, chosen to lead the state, were young. Governor Tiffin was in his thirty-seventh year; Massie at forty was the oldest of the group; his son-in-law, Creighton, a twenty-five-year-old lawyer and graduate of Davidson College, was the youngest.

Samuel Huntington of Cleveland, Return Jonathan Meigs, Jr., of Marietta (both New Englanders), and William Sprigg of Steubenville represented outlying parts of the state on the supreme court. The presiding justices of the three circuits of the common pleas courts were Calvin Pease of Warren, Wyllys Silliman of Zanesville, and Francis Dunlavy of Hamilton County, learned and distinguished men all. In April, John Smith of Cincinnati and Thomas Worthington of Chillicothe were elected to the United States Senate, and in June, Jeremiah Morrow of Warren County, a quiet, serious Presbyterian of "straightforward common sense," won popular election as Ohio's lone representative in the federal House. A twentieth-century scholar, assessing the character of this group of public servants, wrote that "Ohio could be proud of the quality of its first political leaders."

The legislators set about the task of fleshing out the constitution. First they passed a general statute continuing all territorial laws that were not in conflict with the constitution or with newly enacted laws. With some modifications, territorial tax laws were continued.

Then they turned to some fundamental questions regarding the origination of laws in general. The Northwest Ordinance had provided that the inhabitants of the Northwest Territory and of any states formed from it, "shall always be entitled to judicial proceedings according to . . . the common law." But the Republicans who dominated early state legislatures regarded common law, which is based on the precedent of judicial decisions, as a conservative force that failed to keep pace with social change. Thus they favored statute law, law enacted by the body which they controlled. Even so, the use of English common law was given force in the state in 1805, but growing resentment of this venerable English institution led to its abandonment at the next session of the legislature. Governor Tiffin, "suave in speech and magnetic in personality," led the attack on the common law, and its rejection was the occasion for bitter recriminations from conservatives, including the small Federalist faction in Ohio.

The legislature also dealt with the status of blacks in Ohio. Though slavery was not permitted, blacks were restrained by law from enjoying civil liberties guaranteed to whites. This unhappy condition is described in chapters 8 and 9 as part of a broad consideration of the condition of blacks in pioneer Ohio.

Republican Factionalism and the Fight for Supremacy

For almost a decade Ohio politics were in turmoil as the Republicans pushed aside the Federalist remnant and then split into factions. Massie, Worthington, and many other Republicans of property and power were slowly becoming alienated from the "people," the broad popular party base which in their view had assumed the disruptive, ultra-individualistic stance of the squatters. They saw that their personal fortunes and the health of the new state required order, regularity, and discipline. As their power and property increased, they became further and further removed from their former political associates.

It is an oversimplification to call this a liberal-conservative split. In part it was also a breach between the "southern" and "eastern" elements within the party. The Chillicothe Republicans and their allies continued to dominate the southern group while the opposition had its base in the Western Reserve, the Ohio Company lands, and the eastern counties. One early example of this geographic split occurred in 1807 when Governor Tiffin resigned his office to accept his election, by the state legislature, to the United States Senate. His unexpired term was to be filled by a special election in which Nathaniel Massie represented the "southern" branch of the party and Return Jonathan Meigs represented the "eastern" branch. The Chillicothe clique objected to Meigs partly because he was not one of their own—he was born a Connecticut Yankee. When the votes were counted, it appeared Meigs had won by 170 votes. The Ohio constitution stated that the governor had to reside in the state for four years prior to his election, however, and Meigs had been absent from his Marietta home during part of that period serving as a judge in the Louisiana Territory. On this technicality, the general assembly ruled Meigs ineligible and awarded the acting governor—former Lt. Gov. Thomas Kirker, a Republican—Tiffin's unexpired term.

Further evidence of the southern-eastern party split occurred in the regular gubernatorial election of 1808. Chillicothe's Worthington was opposed by Samuel Huntington of Cleveland, a Connecticut Yankee and a judge of the state supreme court. Worthington's anticipated victory slipped away when Acting Governor Kirker decided to enter the race and took votes away from Worthington. Huntington, with strong support from the Western Reserve, the eastern counties, and the small Federalist remnant, won the election.

While these intraparty struggles were under way, the state supreme court challenged the supremacy of the state legislature. If Republicans had an inviolable political tenet, it was that the legislature, the body representing the people, was supreme. Republican leadership reacted vigorously when it appeared that this political principle was under serious challenge from the court.

In 1804 the legislature passed a law giving justices of the peace jurisdiction in civil suits involving charges up to fifty dollars. Two years later Judge Calvin Pease declared this law unconstitutional since the Ohio Constitution provided for jury trial in cases involving more than twenty dollars. A legislative committee examined Pease's conduct in this matter but took no action against him. The question at issue was whether or not a court could overturn the work of the legislature, representatives of the "sovereign people." That issue had been decided on the national level in *Marbury* v. *Madison* (1803), when the United States Supreme Court assumed the power to determine the constitutionality of legislative acts.

Samuel Huntington was sitting on the Ohio Supreme Court in 1807 when the suit *Rutherford* v. *M'Faddon,* involving the "fifty-dollar law," came before the court. He and his colleague, George Tod, yet another Connecticut man from the Western Reserve, ruled that the "fifty-dollar law" was in violation of the Ohio Constitution and was therefore null and void. Huntington said the court did not wish to alter or repeal any *law,* but the court must compare the legislative act with the Ohio *Constitution.* If the act was in any way contrary to the Constitution, the court must declare it *no law.* Were that not done, said Huntington, either two supreme authorities existed in the state—the legislative and the Constitution—or the Constitution was in itself meaningless since the legislature could unilaterally override it. Both of these prospects were clearly ridiculous in the court's judgment. There was but one supreme authority: the Constitution.

The Chillicothe clique, supporting the concept of legislative supremacy, fought hard in the election of 1808 to portray Huntington as supporting "judicial encroachment" on the rights of the legislature. Huntington's victory at the polls excluded him as a prime target, but a committee of the House reported articles of impeachment against judges Tod and Pease. Tod, brought to trial before the Senate in January 1809, relied on the arguments of Chief Justice John Marshall of the Supreme Court in the Marbury case and Samuel Huntington in the Rutherford case to support his position. On January 20, fifteen senators voted in favor of impeachment, nine voted against, but since Ohio's Constitution required a two-thirds vote for conviction, Tod was spared by a one-vote margin. Pease's trial was decided with the same results, and "the gravest crisis in the history of the Ohio judiciary" was over. The principle of judicial review triumphed for the moment, but bitter divisions in the Republican camp lingered to plague the politics of early statehood; judicial review would have to withstand additional challenges.

By election time in 1810 it appeared as though the Chillicothe Republicans might have overreached themselves. They sponsored a legislative "sweeping resolution" that struck out once more at the judges by removing all incumbents. The resolution also removed the state capital to Zanesville. The latter provision was a bitter dose for the powerful Chillicothe group to swallow, but Zanesville votes were needed to remove the judges, and that community offered a handsome new brick building, complete with cupola, for the capitol. Zanesville's coup was a brief one; in 1812 the capital returned to Chillicothe, where it remained for four more years.

To rally enthusiasm for their cause, the beleaguered Chillicothe Republicans now organized Tammany societies, first in Chillicothe and then elsewhere in the state. Tammany societies (named for Tamanend, a Delaware Indian chief) originated in New York State and embraced some of the secretive trappings which strongly appealed to people on the plain, unadorned frontier. The pages of Chillicothe's *Scioto Gazette* served the Tammany cause well. Tammany "wigwams" (local chapters) backed Thomas Worthington in the gubernatorial race of 1810, while Chillicothe's *Independent Republican* supported his opponent, Return J. Meigs, and warned the people against the machinations of secret societies designed to serve the selfish interests of political cliques. Ross County was thoroughly split into Tammany and anti-Tammany groups, and elsewhere in the southern counties the Tammany society was a focus of division.

Meigs won the election, but the defeated Worthington received a consolation prize when his Tammany friends in the legislature elected him United States Senator. Worthington took up his duties in Washington and performed admirably, becoming one of the nation's authorities on public land policy and western affairs.

The general assembly which met in 1810–11 had strong Tammany representation led by Speaker of the House Edward Tiffin, Grand Sachem of the Chillicothe wigwam. The Tammanyites won a narrow victory over an attempt by moderates to repeal the "sweeping resolution" that had precipitated much of the fuss, but Tammany's influence was waning. The "nefarious cabal" was receiving unfavorable attention, and strains were appearing in its ranks. Massie and Creighton broke with their old allies in the Tiffin-Worthington group and led the outcry against Tammany and secret government. Newspapers around the state joined in the attack on St. Tammany. Charles Hammond, a St. Clairsville Federalist, was especially effective in placing Tiffin and his associates on the defensive. In 1811 there was still a balance in the general assembly between Tammany and anti-Tammany representatives. Finally, however, Republicans of both persuasions came together to repeal the "sweeping resolution" (actually the Commissioning Act, based upon it) in January 1812. The influence of the Tammany societies declined rapidly thereafter, and with the state and nation diverted by an approaching war with Great Britain, the society quickly faded from view.

The Burr Controversy

Ohio's concern with politics was diverted momentarily by a fascinating intrigue that puzzled people at the time and has confounded historians and biographers ever since. The central figure was Aaron Burr, scion of a distin-

Thomas Worthington, known as "The Father of Ohio Statehood."

guished family, officer in the revolutionary armies, and a man of charm and cultivation. By 1805, however, he was something of an outcast from polite eastern society because he had opportunistically challenged Thomas Jefferson for a presidency that was clearly intended to go to the great Virginian; even worse, Burr had shot and killed Alexander Hamilton in a duel.

After retiring from the vice-presidency in 1805, Burr made a western journey that attracted little attention. By the time he made a second trip a year

later, however, rumors were circulating about his intentions. They resulted
in part from the fact that Harman Blennerhassett, a well-to-do Irish *émigré,*
and his charming wife, Margaret, had entertained Burr at their grand estate
on an island in the Ohio River. Nearly all distinguished travellers descending
the Ohio stopped off at Blennerhassett's Island, near Belpre, to enjoy the
conversation, music, books, and wines not available elsewhere in the wilderness. In 1806, however, a Marietta paper published Blennerhassett's articles
advocating the possibility of separating the western states and regions from
the Union. Coupled with earlier speculation about the intentions of Spain,
already suspected of intrigues in the West, the association of Burr with Blennerhassett created questions about Burr's intentions. These suspicions deepened when Blennerhassett subsidized the building of riverboats for Burr at
Marietta, but Burr's calm and convincing replies to inquiries directed at him
forestalled any action.

In November 1806, President Jefferson, no friend of Burr's, sent secret
information concerning western matters to Governor Tiffin, who promptly
informed the legislature, meeting in secret session, of his concerns. With
general assembly approval Tiffin ordered seizure of the boats being built at
Marietta, and he called out the militia for the protection of Cincinnati.
Meanwhile, Virginia militia moved on Blennerhassett's Island, making a
shambles of that once fine property. Blennerhassett and his wife fled into the
interior, ruined and discredited. Burr was captured while fleeing through the
South. Brought to Richmond, Virginia, and tried for treason against the
United States, Burr was acquitted but never again gained the public trust. He
died in 1836. The affair ruined Burr, the Blennerhassetts, and also John Smith
of Cincinnati, one of Ohio's first senators. Smith had befriended Burr and was
later indicted as an alleged accomplice in Burr's schemes. Though found innocent of the charges, his political career was destroyed; he sold his Ohio
property and moved to Louisiana.

The Burr "hysteria" had two possible benefits for Ohio. First, it gave many
people a sense that the state had responded promptly and well to an attempt to
divide the country. The affair, said William Creighton, "has given. . . Ohio
a full and fair opportunity of manifesting her patriotism and attachment to the
general government." Second, the problem of western isolation from effective contact with the developed East was very real. Unless the national government took steps soon to encourage roads and canals connecting the West
to eastern markets, it was possible that the West's commercial ties to the
Ohio-Mississippi waterway could become a political orientation as well.

Indeed, Congress was already taking steps to connect East and West by
way of a national road which was to run from Cumberland, Maryland, on the
Potomac and across the mountains to Wheeling on the Ohio. It would sup-
plant Braddock's Road, scarcely a trace through the wilderness, and supple-

ment Forbes' Road in Pennsylvania as an avenue to the West. Senator Worthington, a strong supporter of the project, had in 1802 helped draft the Ohio Enabling Act which provided that a portion of the proceeds from the sale of federal lands in Ohio should be used for construction of a road to Ohio's borders. In 1806 President Jefferson signed a bill appropriating to the construction project money that had already accrued from Ohio land sales. By 1817 the National Road was completed to Wheeling.

Years before the National Road reached Ohio's borders, however, westerners faced a threat to their security that diverted attention toward the Great Lakes region. War was imminent, and Ohio would become the focus of western military action.

⭢ Ohio in the War of 1812

The Treaty of Greenville had been a satisfactory solution to the Indian problem in the eyes of most Ohio residents except those constantly pushing out into forbidden territory. The old chiefs—Tarhe the Wyandot, Black Hoof the Shawnee, Buckongehelas the Delaware—observed the letter and the spirit of the agreement. These elders continued to submit to American demands on the basis that it was suicidal for the Indians, with their reduced numbers, to oppose the swarming new settlers. Since the Greenville treaty the Indians had been pressured to release much additional Ohio land. In the Treaty of Fort Industry (Toledo), July 4, 1805, the Indians surrendered title to the Western Reserve west of the Cuyahoga and the lands south of it to the Greenville line. Additional treaties at Detroit and Brownstown (in the Michigan Territory) in 1807–8 further reduced Indian land in northwestern Ohio.

As they watched the surrender of their lands, certain younger warriors grew increasingly opposed to the policies of the old chiefs. Foremost among the unreconcilables were the Shawnee warrior, Tecumseh, and his brother Lalawethika, a drunken braggart who had experienced a religious conversion to become Tenskwatawa, reformer and mystic, known to the whites as the Shawnee Prophet.

Tenskwatawa, whose drooping eyelid gave him a sinister look, set in motion an Indian revitalization movement by claiming that the Master of Life had instructed his children to eschew the white man's way—his religion, his whiskey—and return to their own. In the movement's early stages, Tecumseh and Tenskwatawa maintained villages south of the Greenville Treaty Line in Ohio. Initially they got along well with their white neighbors, but as they attracted followers from distant tribes, tension rose and the brothers moved their village to Tippecanoe Creek in western Indiana. From this point Tecumseh ventured among numerous tribes trying to rally them to make a concerted effort to force the whites eastward.

At his Vincennes headquarters, Gov. William Henry Harrison of the Indiana Territory was kept well informed about the activities of Tecumseh and the Prophet. Probably no person had done more than Harrison to weaken the Indians' hold in the Old Northwest. He aggressively pursued treaties of purchase by which the tribes surrendered huge chunks of their traditional lands. He disregarded the fact that he worked through sub-chiefs and other Indian representatives who had no legitimate right to alienate tribal lands, and that the United States government offered but a pittance in annuities for land of inestimable value. On several occasions Tecumseh met with Harrison to object to these policies, but received no satisfaction. Harrison, however, had considerable respect for Tecumseh's talents; he was anxious to find a means of breaking his power among the dissident Indians now gathering in some force at Prophetstown on the Tippecanoe.

Harrison found the excuse he needed. In 1811, he interpreted instructions from Secretary of War William Eustis as authorizing him to disperse the Indians at Prophetstown where, it was reported, large quantities of British goods had recently been received. In September, Harrison led a force of about 1,000 regulars and frontier militia north along the Wabash. On November 6, he camped close by Prophetstown. Tecumseh, before leaving on a trip to rally tribes against white encroachment, instructed Tenskwatawa to avoid a contest with Harrison, but the Prophet now overplayed his hand, convincing his warriors that they would be immune to bullets.

In the dawn of November 7, the Indians attacked Harrison's camp, infiltrating it in an apparent effort to kill Harrison and spread confusion. An alert sentry roused Harrison's men, who had been sleeping with guns at their sides. Brisk fighting followed until the warriors withdrew, having suffered heavy casualties. Furious with the Prophet for misleading them, most returned immediately to their distant villages. After this Battle of Tippecanoe, Harrison's troops burned the cabins, wegiwas, and supplies of Prophetstown and then returned to Vincennes. When Tecumseh reached Tippecanoe and saw the devastation, he realized that an independent Indian confederacy was no longer possible; thus he turned to the British at Fort Malden, constructed at Amherstburg on the Canadian shore of the Detroit River. Soon he would lead Britain's Indian allies in Ohio and the West.

Turning to the British for aid had remained an Indian alternative over several decades. After abandoning Detroit and other posts on American soil in 1796, the British government had divorced itself from any official support of the western Indians, but unofficial support continued from British traders and Indian agents, who supplied the western tribes and encouraged their fears of the Americans. Ohio was still an exposed frontier, and the thought of British-supplied Indians moving against Ohio settlements created anxiety throughout much of the state. The local anti-British sentiment added fuel to smouldering national grievances about to burst into flame. Many complaints against Britain concerned maritime problems—the impressment of American seamen, for example—but these had little direct bearing on westerners except for strengthening the feeling that national honor must be defended. More than one Ohio newspaper hoped to see Great Britain's "overbearing pride" humbled on the high seas. Of more immediate interest to Ohioans, however, was British encouragement of the Ohio Indians and their allies.

Ohio's support for war against Great Britain was not universal; in fact, Ohio's representatives in Congress split on the war issue. Jeremiah Morrow, Ohio's lone representative, voted for war; Sen. Thomas Worthington voted against it because the nation was unprepared. Sen. Alexander Campbell was absent and did not vote. While Worthington cast his vote against war, he admitted that many of his constituents favored it: "those advocating it make much noise, those opposed more quiet."

Congress declared war on Great Britain on June 17. At that moment Gen. William Hull, governor of the Michigan Territory and a superannuated hero of the Revolution, was leading a force composed mostly of Ohio militia northward from Dayton to Detroit. Hull's regimental commanders—Col. Duncan McArthur, Col. James Findlay, and Col. Lewis Cass—were Ohioans. Hull reached Detroit in midsummer, but through carelessness he lost much of his baggage and his confidential papers when his supply boats were seized in the Detroit River. The British and their Indian allies now knew Hull's plans, but more importantly, they knew his apprehensions and fears. In August, the British commander, Gen. Isaac Brock, played upon these fears so skillfully that he convinced Hull he must surrender Detroit or face an Indian massacre. Hull's officers and troops were outraged but powerless to undo the capitulation. An Ohio soldier wrote to his brother that "Old Gen. Hull became panic struck, and in spite of the entreaties of his officers and private soldiers . . . we were made to submit to the most shameful surrender that ever took place in the world." Hull was later court-martialled for his abject surrender and was separated from the army.

Now settlers along Lake Erie could visualize British ships bringing Indian raiders to their shores. The militia was called out in the Western Reserve; new troops were rushed to critical points along the Erie shoreline. Generals Elijah Wadsworth and Simon Perkins organized recruits at Old Portage on the Cuyahoga. From here men and supplies were sent westward to Huron and Lower Sandusky. Blockhouses were built in exposed locations throughout northern and central Ohio. Governor Meigs had energetically rallied troops

and supplies for Hull's expedition, but following Hull's disaster, his call for
more troops was but partially successful, and he considered resorting to a
draft. The availability of Kentucky troops removed that necessity, however.

Confusion in the West was alleviated by the appointment of William
Henry Harrison as commander-in-chief of the Northwestern Army. Harri-
son, slow but steady, was already in the field. He led a force that relieved Fort
Wayne from siege and scattered the Indians engaged in it.

Late in 1812 General Harrison attempted to organize his army in northwestern Ohio. This was Black Swamp country, the least likely place possible

Map 9. Ohio in the War of 1812

for maintaining land transport and supply, but it was on the road to Detroit, now in enemy hands, and to Fort Malden. If Detroit and Malden could be taken, the small British fleet which controlled Lake Erie would be without a port. Harrison's plans fell through in January 1813 when Gen. James Winchester, leading the army's left wing, pushed ahead prematurely to Frenchtown (Monroe, Michigan) on the River Raisin, where he expected to seize supplies. Instead he was surprised and his troops captured by Col. Henry Proctor, who failed to restrain Indians led by the Wyandot chief, Roundhead. Many of Winchester's wounded and captured men were massacred by the Indians. Proctor's name became anathema on the frontier, and "Remember the Raisin" became a western battlecry.

Harrison's seriously weakened force now commenced construction of a supply depot, which was named Fort Meigs in honor of Ohio's wartime governor. By late spring the new post, located on the south bank of the Maumee just below the rapids (Perrysburg), was the center of Harrison's operations on the northern frontier. Across the Maumee were British batteries, and beyond the fort stretched the Black Swamp and hostile Indian country. In May Col. William Dudley with 800 men captured the British batteries and spiked the guns, but Dudley's exuberant Kentuckians rashly followed the retreating enemy into the woods, where Tecumseh's Indians ambushed them. Only about 150 of Dudley's men returned safely to the fort.

Because of the great swamp, Fort Meigs could be reinforced with men and supplies only with great difficulty. Capt. Daniel Cushing of the United States Army left a graphic account of his soldiers, enroute to the fort, finding themselves on wet forest trails, marching behind 450 pack horses carrying flour and salt. On the trail mud and filth was over a foot deep, requiring Cushing and his men to make a four-mile detour through the woods to get ahead of the pack train. Nearing camp, a drove of 4,000 hogs preempted the trail. Other pack trains, carrying urgently needed tents and supplies, dawdled at creek crossings until Captain Cushing shamed their leaders into making a greater effort to reach the fort with this precious cargo. Moving heavy artillery through the Black Swamp was even more onerous. It was best done in winter, but sometimes ice broke under the weight, dumping artillery and supply wagons into the water. Cushing describes such an occasion:

wagons and sleds of every description [broke through the ice], the water, mud and and ice being from two to four feet deep. From the time I first entered the swamp until sundown I did not leave the water, but was from knee deep to waist deep all day wading in mud, water and ice, prying out sleds and wagons, but got to Portage camp about dark. . . . No time to pitch tents; slept out doors this night.

In the summer of 1813, Fort Meigs withstood two strong assaults by British and Indian troops. The attackers, losing heart, then turned their attention eastward to the Sandusky. British ships brought troops and equipment up the Sandusky River to the lower falls (Fremont) where the Americans maintained Fort Stephenson under the command of Maj. George Croghan. General Harrison, moving up from the south, ordered Croghan to abandon the fort if he could, but since the fort was already under attack from Indians and British troops, Croghan and his 150 men remained, fighting a brilliant defensive action aided by the skillful use of the fort's only cannon, "Old Betsey." This heroic defense checked the British and their Indian allies, who now withdrew from northern Ohio. They had heard that an American fleet was abroad on Lake Erie and feared it would cut their supply line to Malden.

The report was true. A young American naval officer, Oliver Hazard Perry, assisted by a handful of shipbuilders, had accomplished the incredible feat of building a fleet in the isolated port of Presque Isle (Erie, Pennsylvania), much of the work being done by unskilled laborers using uncured lumber. Perry had only a few experienced seamen to man his ships, the remainder of the crews being composed of land-lubbers—militia and free blacks mostly—who received but two weeks' training. Late in August Perry's small fleet was at sea, patrolling western Lake Erie, seeking the British fleet under Capt. Robert Barclay. On September 10, 1813, Perry found Barclay's six ships to the northwest of South Bass Island. The two fleets were fairly matched in tonnage, but Perry had a modest advantage in fire power. For three hours the fleets pounded one another; Perry lost his flagship, the *Lawrence,* but he was rowed to the *Niagara* from whose decks he continued the fight. With his flagship, the *Detroit,* a bloody shambles, Barclay surrendered his entire fleet; he had suffered the most thorough defeat experienced to that time by a British fleet.

Perry's victory at the Battle of Lake Erie had profound consequences. He sent a terse dispatch to Harrison—"We have met the enemy and they are ours...," and within days, Perry's ships were ferrying Harrison's troops across the western end of Lake Erie to the Ontario Peninsula. Here they set out in pursuit of the British and Indians who had abandoned Fort Malden for the safety of the Niagara frontier. Tecumseh and his Indians wanted to stay and fight. To Proctor, the Shawnee leader said:

> Father, you have got the arms and ammunition which our great father sent for his red children. If you have an idea of going away, give them to us, and you may go and welcome.
>
> As for us, our lives are in the hands of the Great Spirit. We are determined to defend our lands, and if it be his will we wish to leave our bones upon them.

But Proctor overruled him, and Tecumseh and his followers were forced to retreat with the British to Moravian Town on the Thames where, on October 5, the war's final battle of consequence in the west was fought. Harrison's men won a complete victory, routing the British and scattering the Indians. Tecumseh was killed in the battle. While Shawnee legend claims that Indian warriors buried him in a secret grave so that he could someday rise to lead them back to Chalagawtha, it is reported that Col. Richard M. Johnson of Kentucky shot the Shawnee chief. He reportedly had the body flayed; the skin was then removed, cured, and made into razorstrops which he gave to his friends. Johnson ran successfully for the vice-presidency in 1836; his campaign slogan—"Rumseh dumseh, Johnson killed Tecumseh"—may have contributed modestly to his victory.

Though the theater of war now moved elsewhere in the United States, Ohioans remained cautious. Reports continued to filter into the state capital about Indian atrocities in the nearby Indiana Territory, and rumors circulated that British arms would be supplied to western warriors. The political ambitions of high-ranking officers, notably Duncan McArthur and Lewis Cass, kept Ohio politics in turmoil, and the election of Thomas Worthington as governor in 1814 did nothing to quell discontent.

Meanwhile, fighting continued along the Niagara frontier, on Lake Champlain, and in seacoast towns. The British burned Washington in 1814, but in January 1815 Andrew Jackson dealt a stinging defeat to a British army at New Orleans. The war ended early in 1815 with ratification of the Treaty of Ghent.

The War of 1812 had important consequences for Ohio. It removed for all time the "Indian menace," since the small number of Indians remaining were confined to tiny reservations in the northwestern part of the state. Furthermore, Ohio citizens had cooperated in a national effort, and had gained an enhanced sense of nationhood. On the practical side, Ohioans profited from high wartime prices for goods and services. The western army and fleet provided an immediate market for western products, but Ohio goods which flowed to New Orleans sold at high wartime prices, too. Rich men like Thomas Worthington made money by selling the products of their mills and fields, while poor men, like young John Brown, the future abolitionist, made a living by driving livestock over forest trails to the western army.

Military roads opened northern portions of the state to immigrants who would soon flock to Ohio in record numbers. Hull's Road ran from Dayton to Urbana, Fort Findlay, and on northward; Harrison's Road led through Piqua, St. Mary's, and Defiance; eastern troops had moved westward through Wooster and Upper Sandusky; troops from the Western Reserve marched west through Norwalk and Lower Sandusky (Fremont). Though still far from adequate, these military roads advanced the speed with which settlers occupied north central and northwestern Ohio. As in previous campaigns, soldiers took note of promising locations which they occupied as home sites once the war was over. The Great Lakes, largely free from Indian dangers, could now carry increasing numbers of immigrants moving westward and, as canals developed, goods destined for eastern markets moved across them.

The wartime service records of Ohio military leaders enhanced their political ambitions. William Henry Harrison would become "Old Tippecanoe" and ride his fame into the White House. Duncan McArthur would become governor of Ohio and Lewis Cass governor of the Michigan Territory. The younger men among them represented a new political leadership that would soon replace the generation which had brought Ohio into statehood. At war's end, Ohio was poised for a new spurt of growth.

Filling in the Ohio Frontier

There were 231,000 people in Ohio in 1810. The war slowed growth, but a postwar surge brought the state's population to 581,000 in 1820 and 938,000 in 1830 as newcomers flowed into all of the settled areas and pushed beyond. The new arrivals, like those before them, came from many different geographical and social settings, thus contributing to that diversity which has always been one of Ohio's most distinguishing characteristics.

Nowhere was "Ohio fever" stronger than in New England, where hard times resulted from British naval blockades that had strangled the region's commerce. Farm land was scarce and expensive; taxes were high; social constraints were strong. Young men and women of rural background were especially affected by these conditions. To some the last straw was the "year without a summer," 1816, when, as the result of an atmospheric freak, snow and freezing temperatures struck New England every month of the year. Reports of Ohio's "moderate" climate looked particularly good after that.

In addition to the push of hard times was the pull of rich new lands to be had at reasonable prices. Many of those who had gone before wrote home extolling the soil, climate, size of crops (three-foot long turnips, cornstalks fourteen feet high), and everything else they could think of to convince those who had stayed behind (and perhaps themselves as well) that they had made a wise move. Those who went early to Ohio and were disappointed in what they found tended not to advertise their mistake. Unhappy settlers confided in travellers like John S. Wright, who found some Ohioans "generally disappointed in their expectations, and dissatisfied with the country: many of them declared to me that they would return [east] if they possessed the means."

Most migrating New Englanders in this period went to the Western Reserve. The rigors of the trip had eased since the early days. But it still took forty days of travel through central New York State to the Lake Trail (also called the Ridge Road) or across the Pennsylvania Road (old Forbes Road) to

Pittsburgh where one proceeded by water down the Ohio and up the Beaver and Mahoning to the Youngstown-Warren area. Though many men made a solitary journey westward, the larger number travelled in family groups with all their worldly possessions packed in wagons, on pack animals or on their own backs. The hardships of the journey stretch the imagination of modern travelers moving swiftly through countryside that once tested the mettle of pioneers. It is little wonder that, having made this trip, few returned east; indeed the incredible optimism of the pioneer led many families to move on further west as new lands opened.

Many newcomers to the Reserve now settled west of the Cuyahoga. The Treaty of Fort Industry (1805) had removed Indian title to this land; it was quickly surveyed and villages such as Elyria, Medina, and Lorain began to emerge. The reserved tracts in the Firelands were finally open for settlement; Norwalk became the center of activity in this region where town names, architecture, Calvinist religion, public education, and other cultural characteristics made it the most New England of regions. The Reserve was growing, but it was not until roads and canals opened the interior that it truly flourished.

South of the Reserve and north of the Seven Ranges were Congress Lands which stretched west from Columbiana County beyond Richland County. Small communities of New Jersey, Pennsylvania, and southern Quakers had established themselves at Salem, Alliance, and nearby places early in the nineteenth century, as did the Pennsylvania Germans who settled in modern Stark, Wayne, and nearby counties.

Pennsylvanians dominated the postwar population flow. Among them were pietistic groups—Mennonites, Amish, Dunkards (German Baptist Brethren), Moravians—who were to give a unique flavor to parts of Stark, Wayne, Holmes, Tuscarawas, and Ashland counties. They were joined by others of their faith from Germany and Switzerland. Immigrants from the British Isles, Canada, and Ireland mixed with Scots-Irish Virginians and Pennsylvanians to enrich the local population mix. Lisbon, Salem, Canton, Wooster, Ashland, and Mansfield were developing as the dominant towns of the region.

The end of the war and the completion of the National Road to Wheeling brought new settlers to the Seven Ranges. There they joined the Scots-Irish and Quakers who were early in the area. Population grew along the Ohio River with Steubenville, a center of the wool trade, being the dominant Ohio town in the region. (Wheeling in Virginia preempted much of the valley trade.) St. Clairsville was a small but increasingly influential village in Belmont County.

West of the Seven Ranges lay the United States Military District. Coshocton, Cambridge, and Zanesville, located near the southern extremity of this tract, were the only towns of importance at this early time. Zanesville, described by an 1804 visitor as "a Handsome Place on the Muskingham," developed on land granted to Ebenezer Zane in payment for improving a forest trace in 1796–97 which connected Wheeling with Maysville, Kentucky, on the Ohio River. "Zane's Trace" was southern Ohio's first long-distance "road," although the term is a courtesy word for a crude forest pathway. Zanesville was important enough to have served as state capital from 1810 to 1812. Located near the head of navigation on the Muskingum, it early became an important trading and manufacturing center.

The population of this region was also quite varied, containing Virginians, Pennsylvanians, remnants of the Moravian missions, English immigrants (especially in Guernsey County, where numbers of people from the Isle of Guernsey settled), German pietists, and New Englanders who established Granville and Putnam (now part of Zanesville).

The lands of the Ohio Company did not flourish as they had in their early years. Marietta and Belpre continued to be dominated by New England influences for some years after the war, but increasing numbers of Virginians brought a social and political leaven to this bastion of New England orthodoxy. Marietta continued to be the chief trade center for this part of the Ohio and Muskingum valleys, and the little city continued to have an influence in state affairs disproportionate to its size.

The area between the Ohio Company lands and the Scioto had been formed into Congress Lands in 1798–1802. It was a mineral-rich area whose wealth would be exploited in the second quarter of the nineteenth century and beyond. However, in the immediate postwar years its development lagged except for prosperous areas around Lancaster and Circleville, where both agriculture and manufacturing enterprises developed. Portsmouth was on the verge of assuming a new importance but would have to await the canal and railroad era. Many Virginians and Kentuckians settled in this region. Immigrants from Ireland and Wales formed strong communities in the mining regions, the Welsh in Jackson County and the Irish in Perry County.

The Scioto Valley continued to be dominated by the Virginia-Kentucky influence, as did the Virginia Military District to the west of it where Chillicothe remained the region's most important town. The powerful statemakers—Worthington, Tiffin, Massie, Creighton, *et al.*—remained influential after the war, but waiting in the wings were younger men like Duncan McArthur who were beginning to assert themselves in politics.

A big change occurred in the upper Scioto valley when the general assembly decided to create a new capital city closer to the center of the state. A town was platted on the east bank of the Scioto across from the village of Franklinton. Streets were laid out on the site of a former Wyandot village, the area was organized as a borough, and a new building completed for the legislature's use. In 1816 state government moved to the new capital city, named Columbus. Worthington, ten miles to the north, was older than Columbus by a dozen years. Founded by James Kilbourne, an Episcopal priest and Yankee businessman, it was a New England enclave in an area which was soon to have a population drawn from a variety of sources. Delaware, twelve miles further north (and a few miles east of the Virginia Military District) was a land office site and a supply town for people moving into central Ohio.

At war's end the southwest was among the most vigorous parts of the state thanks to the presence of Cincinnati. It was rapidly emerging as the leading city of Ohio and all the West, having outstripped its Kentucky rivals, Lexington and Louisville, as the center of Ohio River Valley commerce. In the immediate postwar years it was still rather crude, but swift improvements in business and social amenities were to make it the "Queen City of the West." Cincinnati can claim any number of "firsts" for the state of Ohio, in commerce, manufacturing, culture, religion, education, the arts, public services, and other areas. To its original population, dominated by people from New Jersey and Kentucky, it was adding middle states people, New Englanders, Virginians and other southerners, free Negroes and escaped slaves, and Irish and German immigrants. In the 1840s, the German immigration became a flood, stamping Cincinnati with its character to this day.

In the valley of the Great Miami, the towns of Hamilton, Middletown, and Dayton were growing, with Dayton occupying the most strategic position for future development. Lying outside the old Symmes Purchase, lands in this area were organized as Congress Lands between 1798 and 1805. Many former soldiers settled in this region; it also attracted Kentuckians and Virginians in considerable numbers. Some manumitted slaves were settled on land purchased by their former masters. Kentuckians were prominent among settlers of the frontier villages of Springfield and Urbana. North of these settlements, to the state line and Lake Erie, there was little to qualify as a town prior to the 1830s.

Indian Removal

Northwestern Ohio was still a frontier, mostly wet, wooded, and wild. Here were located about sixteen small Indian reservations to which remnants of the Ohio tribes had been confined after the War of 1812 and the treaties of Maumee Rapids (1817) and St. Mary's (1818). Approximately 2,400 Shawnee, Seneca, Delaware, Ottawa, and Wyandot Indians lived in these small clusters while a growing stream of white settlers moved onto their former lands. Much land in this part of the state was still owned by the federal government, the largest part of it being organized as Congress Land in 1819–21.

Life was limited and grim on most reservations. Occasional efforts by federal and state authorities to assist the Indians were minimal and half-hearted. The federal Indian agent for this region was John Johnson, located at Piqua. He was unable to provide the assistance which his charges required, and neither Johnson nor other federal or state authorities could restrain "degraded whites" who sold liquor, stole cattle and hogs, and settled unlawfully on Indian land.

Private efforts to assist the Indians were well-intentioned but often wrongheaded. Moravians, Quakers, Presbyterians, and Methodists competed for advantageous missionary fields. The Quakers sent agents from Pennsylvania to instruct the Indians in the art and science of agriculture since it was believed that Indians could be assimilated into white society as farmers. One frustration piled upon another to defeat this initiative. The Methodists enjoyed considerable success in the Wyandot reservation at Upper Sandusky where they established a mission school and church. John Stewart, a mulatto, led the early phases of these efforts as did the noted circuit rider, James Finley.

Success in assisting the Wyandots was attested to by a British traveller, Thomas Wharton, who liked what he saw of the Upper Sandusky reservation in 1830. The countryside was "most delightful . . . the roads even and good. . . . A vast natural park stretched away on every side . . . flowery prairies, clumps and islets of noble trees, and belts of majestic forest." Cattle grazed in fenced enclosures. The Wyandots, wrote Wharton, were "by long intercourse with the whites," far advanced in civilization. "Many of them speak good English, and are considerable proprietors of cattle, grain, etc." All the Indians he saw on this reserve were "well dressed and mounted, and appeared grave and sedate in their manners."

Despite efforts to adjust to the white man's ways, the Wyandots, like other eastern Indians, were soon forced from their lands. The tragic removal of eastern Indians to the trans-Mississippi West was played out in Ohio as well as in the more publicized South as the administration of President Andrew Jackson pressured the tribes. One by one the Ohio tribal remnants moved west, often under the direction of scurrilous agents who had been the low bidders on federal removal contracts. The last Indians to be forced out by federal policy and state neglect were the Wyandots of Upper Sandusky, who left for the West in 1842. Jacob Burnet, a distinguished citizen of Cincinnati and a veteran of territorial days, captured the pathos of the scene:

> The final catastrophe of that noble race was witnessed by the people of Cincinnati . . . when the remnant of the Wyandots, the last of the braves of the Ohio tribes . . . arrived at the landing, and ascended the steamships that were to convey them from the places of their nativity, into hopeless banishment. To the eye of the human observer, they seemed to linger, and turn to the north, as if to bid a last farewell, to

the tombs in which they had deposited the remains of their deceased children, and in which the bones of their fathers had been accumulating and mouldering for untold ages.

Indians, as organized tribal groups, passed from Ohio forever, but not a day goes by without a reminder that they once possessed Ohio lands. The name of the state and of the river from which that name is borrowed remind us. Counties perpetuate the names of every Ohio tribe except the Shawnee. Many cities—Sandusky, Wapakoneta, Piqua, Coshocton, Chillicothe—share the sites and the names of Indian villages. Ohio's rivers—Muskingum, Cuyahoga, Miami, Scioto, Walhonding, Tuscarawas, and many more—bear Indian names as do parks—Shawnee, Mohican—and innumerable schools and points of interest around the state. Pondering the Indians' fate, one might remember the legend carved on tombstones in rural American cemeteries, "Gone, but not forgotten."

Taking up the Land

Land, inexpensive and fertile, was the magnet which drew most people to Ohio in its early years. Congress revised its land laws frequently, and each revision made it easier for persons of small means to secure acreage directly from the federal government. The Harrison Land Act of 1800 had introduced the principle of credit into federal land transactions. The credit feature stimulated sales, but it also had a pernicious effect. Purchasers were often overly optimistic; they acquired land which they were unable to pay for when income proved insufficient to cover the mortgage payments. During hard times, thousands of persons who had purchased land on credit were unable to meet payments, and they watched in wrathful despair as banks or other lenders foreclosed on their homesteads. The Federal Land Act of 1820 abolished the credit system. However, it helped the small buyer by setting the minimum purchase at eighty acres at a minimum price of $1.25 per acre. Various "relief" acts and "preemption" acts were passed between 1820 and 1854, each designed to meet western demands for cheap lands and "squatters' rights."

By 1821 federal land offices in Ohio had sold 7,360,857 acres, or 66 percent of the federal land available. In addition, sales within the Western Reserve, Ohio Company tract, Virginia Military District, and Symmes Purchase proceeded apace but in each case under terms unique to the particular region.

Although much of the land sold went to speculators, they offered inducements to attract settlers to their tracts, knowing that the value of the remaining lands would accrue as settlements were established. The speculator had to keep his prices in line, for he was in competition with other large landowners and with the state and federal governments. In the latter case he used his political influence in Congress to keep the price of government land high so that he could sell beneath that price and still turn a profit. These tactics earned him the distrust of farmers who wanted inexpensive government land available on liberal credit terms.

In the first years of settlement many of Ohio's large landowners lived outside the state, but increasingly they were Ohio residents. One estimate shows that by 1815 over three-fourths of the state's land was owned by residents. The largest remaining area of nonresident landholding was the Western Reserve, where owners continued to reside in Connecticut, or elsewhere in the East, and disposed of their lands through agents resident in the Reserve.

In the Virginia Military District and in the United States Military District speculators bought bounty warrants from veterans and their heirs at a large discount, thus acquiring enormous holdings. Some migrants into the Virginia Military District—Thomas Worthington and Edward Tiffin, for example— used the money they had acquired from selling their lands east of the mountains to pay for extensive properties in Ohio. Worthington also bought bounty warrants. The most common way for a man to acquire extensive properties was to survey and register lands for other people and take a portion of that land as a fee. Nathaniel Massie, who amassed more than 70,000 acres, and Duncan McArthur with 90,000 acres in the Virginia Military District, are but two of the hundreds of early Ohioans who secured great estates in this fashion.

Some surveyors and land managers became town developers. Bezaleel Wells developed Canton (1805) and Steubenville (1797); Nathaniel Massie started Chillicothe (1796) and Manchester (1791); Simon Perkins and Paul Williams had a plat drawn for Akron (1825). James Kilbourne, land developer, manufacturer, and politician, founded Worthington (1803), helped develop Sandusky and Bucyrus, and "was an indefatigable founder and booster of 'upstart' towns." In every case the developer owned much land, but the town developer was also a man of many talents who did much more than plat new communities. Each found a variety of ways to enrich the life and prospects of his creation.

While many of these early landed rich were worthy and admirable men who deserved the good things that have been said and written about them, others were penurious, greedy, and hard-hearted—absentee landlords who had little appreciation of or sympathy for the problems of the pioneer farmer and artisan. There is little question about the resentment which many settlers felt for the privileged. An 1819 observer described "a certain class of men who are, undoubtedly, in the possession of great advantages. . . . They are the land-jobbers, the speculators, the rich capitalists, the men who were wealthy when they came here—who were able to purchase large tracts and retail them out, reserving, however, every valuable privilege to themselves; men who were able to build mills, machinery and even towns."

Some scholars have attempted to postulate the existence of an economically based class structure in pioneer Ohio. It is one thing to point out the envy and resentment which were quite common when the few had much and the many had little, but it is another thing entirely to demonstrate that there was any sense of social solidarity among the have-nots. They had no effective machinery of protest, no sustained legislative program of reform, no charismatic leaders showing the way to social reorganization. One could make a case for the proposition that envy was at the root of rural dissatisfaction, and that as long as people were free to dream of moving up the socioeconomic scale (and many accomplished it) no true class consciousness was likely to develop among the economically disadvantaged. When times got too tough for the pioneer farmer, he moved, sometimes to another Ohio location, sometimes to Illinois or Iowa or some other "golden" land. However poor and troubled he might be, he saw himself as a free man, even when circumstance had placed him in economic thralldom to the landlord or the bank. If Ohio's promise did not pay off for him today, there was always tomorrow.

6.

The Pioneer State
The Material Side of Life

The large influx of new settlers after the War of
1812 created a population pool of enough density and
variety that, by mid-century, Ohio was in most ways
an up-to-date, mature state. In 1820 Ohio's 581,000
people were in large part migrants from eastern and
southern states or immigrants from overseas. The
census of 1820 did not reveal the birthplace of those
enumerated, but native-born Ohioans were still in the minority. By 1850,
however, about two-thirds of Ohio's nearly two million people had been born
within the state.

This constant swelling and diversification of the population created a dynamic society. While the older settled regions were becoming more stable
and socially sophisticated, there was still a frontier environment in other parts
of the state, especially in the extended region of the Black Swamp.

In this discussion, "pioneer Ohio" refers to a period after the War of 1812
and ending about mid-century, during which the state was reaching a new
maturity in its material and social development. This period spans a little
more than one human generation. Although some generalizations are un-
avoidable and great distinctions are apparent between conditions at the beginning and end of that era, this division highlights the continuity of change
over time in various economic, social, and political activities. We start with
the conditions under which the "typical" landseeker established a homesite in
an Ohio forest clearing.

The Forest Clearing

Having acquired land by purchase from a government land office or a speculator, or by exercising a veteran's bounty warrant, the new settler made his way along established routes until, at the end of his journey, he might have to hack a trail through the forest to reach his land. It was imperative for the new settler to get a crop in the ground. Until he could harvest it, he and his family had to depend on the flour and meal they brought with them, plus whatever game and fish they could catch. For this reason most timed their arrival in Ohio for late winter or early spring. Some new arrivals, especially New Englanders and Pennsylvania Germans, cleared land immediately, clear-cutting the forest and burning the felled trees. Often, however, there was only time to girdle the trees (cut through the bark so sap could not rise and the dying tree would remain leafless). The settlers then planted seeds among the trunks. In time, the dead trees would be felled and burned or would eventually decay and fall of their own weight. Some frontier communities were lucky enough to have a "slasher," a man so skilled with an axe that he could drop trees in wind-rows convenient for burning.

The great fires burned day and night, emitting palls of acrid smoke which hung heavy on the summer air. Stump removal was even more difficult than felling. Stumps were burned without much success; most were grubbed out with the help of oxen. In later years a tripod and pulley device called a "stump puller" was sometimes used. It took years to clear extensive acreage; oftentimes the task remained incomplete. An English traveller, passing through Seneca County in 1830, commented on the "gaunt, naked skeletons of girdled trees, often scathed with fire and standing in vast numbers among the growing grain." The scene gave "an air of bleakness and desolation to the farm lands."

While the farmer was trying to clear land and plant a crop he and his family often lived in a temporary shelter called a "half-faced" camp. It was a lean-to of poles and bark, protected on its open side by a fire which burned day and night. Newcomers who arrived in a group or settled near neighbors were sometimes spared this intermediate step. A "cabin raising" would be held to provide them with a home. This was a community effort which was both functional and social. People working together raised the cabin quickly and in the process enjoyed a social intercourse which gave them an emotional outlet and relief from their solitary tasks. The labor was fueled by copious amounts of whiskey, the great frontier lubricant. No other pay was expected.

The log cabin seems as American as apple pie, but its origins go back to the European forests. Swedes brought this structure with them to Delaware early in the seventeenth century, and it quickly became the standard frontier dwelling. The one-room log cabin had a pitched roof covered with wooden shakes (shingles), a door, one or two windows commonly covered with greased parchment, a dirt floor or one covered with logs split lengthwise with the smooth side up, a stone hearth, and a chimney commonly made of sticks covered with clay. Clay and wood chips were also used to "chink" cracks between the logs. There were endless variations on this basic pattern. Commonly the cabin was added on to as expanding families made more space essential. In time, some were modernized, with siding covering the logs. Many an old Ohio farmhouse, torn down in the twentieth century, revealed its log cabin origins as the siding was removed.

The new settlers tended to be self-sufficient, since they had such limited access to outside goods and supplies. They hoped to feed themselves from the products of the fields and forest, but most had to trade for basics such as coffee, tea, salt, sugar, hardware, implements, and cloth. For these they offered grain (frequently converted into whiskey for convenience in handling), furs and hides, pearl ash and potash made from hardwood ashes, honey collected from "bee trees," ginseng (a root valued by the Chinese as a sovereign drug), and whatever other products they might acquire. Frequently settlers imported livestock from the East. Hogs were valued because they could be turned loose to forage in the woods, then rounded up and driven to market, but their numbers were small in the early pioneer period. Sheep were valued more for their wool than for their flesh; mutton was not a staple food item in pioneer Ohio.

The farmer has always been at the mercy of nature, and these pioneers faced the perils of flood and drought, high winds, hail, and premature frosts. In addition, however, they faced a constant battle against the animal world. Until the forests were extensively cleared, hordes of squirrels nibbled stores of grain. An early Ohio law required men of military age (eighteen to forty-five years) to gather a hundred squirrel "scalps" annually to present to township officials. A bounty was also placed on wolves, which along with other predators such as bears and wildcats, took a toll on livestock. Deer, raccoons, and other browsers and foragers could quickly strip the farmer's garden. As late as 1835 the new president of Oberlin College wrote of his Lorain County home: "The deer were so plentiful that they seemed to look out from the woods . . . to see what we were about."

The pioneer farmer fought back against these incursions by organizing large hunts designed to rid extensive areas of predators and foragers. Most famous of these was the Hinckley Hunt in what is now northern Medina County. On December 24, 1818, more than 500 hunters, stationed along the township's perimeter, moved towards its center as a signal was given, driving game of all sorts before them. As the ring closed, the slaughter increased until a final count revealed the carcasses of 17 wolves, 21 bears, 300 deer, and uncounted hundreds of turkeys, foxes, raccoons, and other small animals. The

Clearing the forests to make a home in the wilderness.

modern city dweller can afford to be sentimental about nature's creatures and feel a pang of regret at such indiscriminate slaughter. The pioneer farmer could not afford sentiment; to him it was a war for survival which he intended to win.

Also threatening man and beast were the poisonous reptiles so abundant in the state. The large timber rattlesnake was especially feared. It was called a "yaller" rattler by pioneers, because its skin looked yellowish during one phase of its annual metamorphosis. Snake hunts were held to rid neighborhoods of these creatures. One weekend's work in Geauga County netted the hunters more than 460 dead rattlers. Hogs were useful in clearing snakes. They were impervious to the snake's venom, and they would kill and sometimes eat poisonous snakes. The Erie Islands were cleared of snakes, in part, by turning hogs loose on them. Rattlesnakes and copperheads continued to thrive in isolated areas but not where man intruded. In 1835 a new resident in the Western Reserve wrote, "it is seldom that a rattle-snake is seen now."

Prior to the introduction of machinery in the 1840s, nearly all Ohio farmers relied on traditional farming methods. Plowing and planting, cultivating and harvesting were still accomplished manually with help from horses, mules, or oxen. The harvested crops were processed by hand. Corn huskings were social occasions which brought neighbors together to speed a tiresome task and, in the process, provide the opportunity to socialize.

In addition to growing crops, settlers had to make or prepare scores of other items. A pioneer in western Ohio recalled how his family provided not only for its basic needs, but also engaged in cottage industries, producing items for sale:

> Our house was a cabin containing a parlor, kitchen and dining room. Connected was a shoe shop, also a broom and repair shop. . . . After supper each knew his place. In our house there were four mechanics. I was a shoemaker and corngrater. My father would make a sledge, and the other two boys could strip corn. My sisters spun yarn and mother knit and made garments. . . . Thus our evenings are spent in our wild home.

Women's work was never done. Families were generally large—ten to fifteen children being quite common early in the century—and, in the well-ordered households, the older children helped care for the younger. The round of cooking and cleaning was endless even in the small cabins that were home to so many rural families in the 1820s and 1830s. Women kept a kitchen garden and raised chickens; the hens provided them with a little "egg money." Household and kitchen equipment was ponderous and took much physical effort to operate. Water had to be pumped, milk and cream separated, butter churned, candles dipped, fireplaces or kitchen ranges supplied with wood and so on in an endless succession. The fruits and vegetables that farm women, and many town and city women as well, canned and preserved were essential to tide the family over the winter and spring months. Women might also help in the fields and stables although some observers thought this improper. If they had any quiet time it might be spent sewing, knitting, weaving, crocheting, or instructing their children in moral and Biblical precepts.

Operating an early nineteenth-century farm was a team project, and the farm wife and mother was an essential part of that team. Early death among women was common due to overwork, poor nutrition, excessive childbearing, primitive medical practices and, perhaps, an emotional malaise which came from the unremitting toil and sameness of their lives. Men, too, were affected by these conditions and were as susceptible to disease as women, but it is probable that they suffered less from social isolation than women did. It is certain that the death of the wife and mother threw the farm family into disarray unless there were girls old enough to fill the breach in household activities. A glance through the biographical sketches found in old county and township histories provides ample evidence that widowers generally remarried after a brief period of mourning, in part, at least, because the woman's role was too essential to go unfilled.

Transportation among rural people was by foot, horseback, or wagon. Only a rich farmer would have a carriage, and use of it would be reserved for church-going, funerals, and other formal occasions. As larger, more prosperous farms supplanted the crudities of the early settlement period, it became an object of pride for the farmer to own a smart team and carriage.

Early Farming Practices

Once the land was cleared by the early settlers, farming began to take hold in the Buckeye State. Ohio attracted all kinds of people from the hunter-farmer and the squatter to the man of sufficient means to purchase cleared land and stock it. Since these people brought with them the diverse practices of their places of origin, it is difficult to generalize about farming practices in pioneer Ohio, but some clear patterns exist.

In the pioneer period the "old cleared farm" was one standard of agricultural use. To work the land required some capital with which to purchase essential tools, seed, livestock, iron goods, emergency supplies, and so forth. One estimate is that, early in the century, $500 would be required for this purpose. Since most farmers were already in debt for their land, this money had to be borrowed, thus increasing financial obligations.

If the farmer was lucky enough to have strong, industrious sons, he might get by without hiring additional help, but the itinerant farm worker—the "hired hand"—was everpresent in rural Ohio. Generally he was a young, single male who lived with the family and was treated as one of them. Though wages were pitifully small, many saved what they could in order to secure their own land. The more eligible among them frequently married the farmer's daughter—thus labor was united with land—a practice which blurred class lines that might have developed had the hired hand been locked forever in his menial status. In prosperous farmsteads a "hired girl" might be employed to assist in the unending household tasks. She too could move on to better things by a fortunate marriage, sometimes with the farmer's son. By mid-century women were seldom seen working in the fields with the men, for with increasing prosperity came more rigidly defined gender roles.

One could often tell from a farmer's buildings, fences, and farming practices from where he had come. The Pennsylvania Germans settled just south of the Western Reserve in the "backbone region," (so-called because it embraced the land separating the northward and southward flowing drainage systems), in the southeastern quadrant, and in the valleys of the Miami rivers north of Hamilton County. They built bank barns which provided room for livestock on the ground level. Doors to the main floor of the barn were reached by a ramp. Pennsylvanians favored sturdy outbuildings, a spring house and heavy-draft horses. New Englanders were partial to well-cleared fields, the three-bay barn, and were early disposed to dairying. The Western

Reserve became an important dairying center after canals gave its New England farmers a market outlet.

No matter what region they hailed from, Ohio farmers were more likely to buy additional land rather than improve the lands already theirs. Thus they were criticized for lagging behind the more efficient (if costly) farming methods of Great Britain and certain other European countries.

The general farmer was a grain grower, concentrating usually on corn and wheat. Other grains were grown in lesser amounts for livestock feed and special uses. Corn was the great crop of the early West, with the chief corn-producing states springing up west of the Appalachians. By 1849 Ohio ranked first in corn production. Even though its production increased substantially in the next decade, Illinois outstripped Ohio and the other big corn producers by an ever-widening margin. Most corn was fed to livestock, so it went to market as beef or pork. Some was eaten by the family and some was distilled. Ross, Pickaway and Butler counties were among the largest producers within the state.

Wheat was important to the early Ohio farmer; in fact, in 1839 Ohio led the nation in wheat production. Thereafter, however, production stabilized while Illinois, Indiana, and Wisconsin moved ahead. By 1859 the western counties were Ohio's largest producers. While relatively inexpensive and easy to raise, wheat was susceptible to smut, fungus, rust, and insects. Nonetheless, wheat contributed to the prosperity of many market distribution points in Ohio. The Lake Erie and Ohio River ports all profited from the grain trade, but so did interior towns opened up by canal—Milan, Massillon, Zanesville, Akron, Chillicothe, Lancaster, and, in the 1850s, towns such as Mansfield and Springfield, which were served by railroads.

Livestock was central to the livelihood of the general farmer. Nearly every farm had milking cows, but in some sections of the state, notably the Western Reserve, dairying became an industry with milk going to nearby markets while butter and great quantities of cheese were sent to southern, eastern, and even foreign markets.

The beef-cattle industry grew in the pioneer period. Cattle grazing flourished, especially in the Virginia Military District and southwestern Ohio, where experienced Kentucky cattlemen raised large herds. As the industry spread, the market centers of Springfield, Columbus, London, Urbana, Marion, and Xenia prospered. Ohio cattlemen seldom raised their own calves; they imported and then grass-fed them, eventually sending them on to feed lots or to market where they were sold as grass-fattened cattle. The Scioto Valley was the center of the feed lot business in Ohio, and its proximity to eastern markets—it was closer than any other part of the corn belt—made it a dominant force in the industry. It remained so until the railroad changed marketing patterns. Improvement in the indifferent quality of Ohio cattle was slow in coming because farmers lacked capital to improve their herds, and they distrusted book learning. Some superior breeds, mainly from England, had been introduced by mid-century.

From early times Ohio was good hog country. The forests provided unlimited forage, and the tough animals thrived. It was not long, however, before care was taken to improve breeds and the quality of the animals. Efforts were concentrated in the Scioto and Miami valleys, where corn was abundant and transportation to market feasible. In many areas of the state, drovers shepherded huge herds to market; in southwestern Ohio the Cincinnati packing industry was absorbing large numbers by the 1820s. Among the improved breeds was the "Warren County hog" which ultimately came to be known as the Poland China. Agricultural historian Robert L. Jones called it "by far the most important breed in Ohio from mid-century till after the Civil War." By 1850 Ohio was the fifth largest producer of hogs in the U.S.

The sheep and wool industry suffered from the loss of animals to wolves. In time this menace lessened, and nearly every general farm had sheep whose wool was spun into yarn and woven into cloth. Ohio was early infected by the craze for imported Spanish Merino sheep, superior wool producers. Andrew Rotch, a wealthy Quaker, brought 400 Merinos with him in the 1820s to his new farm at Kendal (Massillon). Pureblooded stock was purchased at enormous prices by Ohio breeders, and while some animals remained pure-bred, many were crossed with local types. Like other livestock, sheep were driven to market, sometimes over enormous distances; in 1853, for example, 9,000 Ohio sheep were driven to the Santa Clara Valley of California. By 1850 Ohio was number one in sheep population and remained so for several decades. The eastern counties contained the largest sheep concentration throughout this period. Ohio was an important center of woolen manufacture with towns such as Steubenville and Cincinnati boasting woolen mills.

Ohio also led the nation in horses. Cincinnati was reputed to be the nation's largest horse-marketing center by 1850. People generally attached much sentiment to horses since nearly everyone needed at least one horse for transportation. Farmers prided themselves on improving their stock. Some horses were trained for racing, a favorite entertainment in rural areas. Mules were used principally as draft animals; it became even more profitable to raise them for export during the brief period when the army purchased animals for use in the Mexican War.

The general farmer in pioneer Ohio not only grew grains and raised livestock, but also planted fruit trees and grape vines and engaged in vegetable gardening. These were supplemental crops, and it was not until well after the Civil War that fruit and truck gardening became large industries. By 1840 farmers along Lake Erie already knew that their location was advantageous for growing fruit. Peaches were among the favorite fruits grown, possibly because they could be turned into peach brandy even as the wide variety of apples could be pressed into cider, either soft or hard. Apples were also used to fatten hogs and were the raw material of the vinegar works. Apples grown close to transportation arteries could be marketed at fair prices, bringing farmers a significant supplemental income. Dried apples were sent to distant markets.

Other crops grown in small quantities were occasionally profitable. The strawberry market was active in Cincinnati, where a distinguished local citizen, Nicholas Longworth, was credited with making the strawberry a popularly priced seasonal item in the local diet. Longworth also has claim to being the father of Ohio's winemaking industry; he introduced the Catawba grape to Ohio. Wine-grape growing was centered in the Cincinnati region; vintners sold their product profitably both locally and overseas. By the 1850s the growing of wine-grapes was taking hold on Kelleys Island in Lake Erie, making the Sandusky region the second-ranking wine-producing area in Ohio. When blight and root rot destroyed the industry around Cincinnati, the Erie Islands assumed the leading role.

Farmers grew other useful crops in small quantities during the pioneer period. Hemp for the manufacture of coarse cloth and for bags and rope was briefly grown along the Ohio. Flax also grew in small quantities; its chief use was in "linsey-woolsey" cloth, but cheap cotton goods soon drove this fabric out of the market. Flax seed, however, was processed into linseed oil. It was used locally and was exported to Ireland in small quantities. Tobacco was a crop in southern Ohio, although Ohio leaf was considered inferior to that raised elsewhere.

Before the pioneer period ended, farm machinery was beginning to appear on a limited number of Ohio farms. The gently rolling or flat lands of the western Till Plains were especially well suited to its use. By 1840 the cast iron plow had largely displaced the "bull plow," and Canton was an important center of its manufacture. Steel plows that cut a furrow six or seven inches deep were used in some sections of the state—especially in bottomlands—by the 1850s. Crude harrows and rollers were also used to prepare soil.

The invention of the reaper, almost simultaneously by Obed Hussey, who was from the Cincinnati area, and Cyrus McCormick of Virginia, was a major breakthrough which promised to end the back-breaking and time-consuming task of cutting grain by scythe or cradle. McCormick's machine was patented in 1831, shortly before Hussey's, and since McCormick proved the better businessman, his machines crowded Hussey's out of the market after mid-century. By the Civil War, the Buckeye mower and reaper and other farm machines were being manufactured in Ohio with Canton, Dayton, Springfield, Akron, and several other towns important production centers.

The threshing machine was yet another revolutionary development which changed agricultural practice. Originally threshers were powered by horses walking on treadmills or pulling sweeps. By the mid-1850s, however, portable steam engines mounted on wheels provided power for threshing machines. Threshers, like mowers and reapers, required a substantial labor gang to operate. Fears that farm laborers would be thrown out of work by machines were exaggerated at this time although clearly, over the succeeding decades, more sophisticated machines reduced the need for laborers.

Ohio's record in the development and use of early farm machinery is not especially noteworthy. In the words of Robert L. Jones, "Ohio farmers were . . . not notable among their contemporaries for the rapidity of their agricultural mechanization. They kept abreast of national trends and little more. In short, as far as the introduction of agricultural machinery prior to 1880 is concerned, Ohio's significance consisted not in the state's being exceptional but rather in its being typical."

Pioneer Industrial Development

The overwhelming majority of Ohioans lived on farms or in farm villages during the pioneer period. The more prosperous or fortunate of these farmers were sometimes engaged in emerging industrial activity as well, running mills of all sorts, blacksmith shops, harness shops, and so forth for their own benefit and that of their neighbors. It took capital to open and operate a business, and the large landowners most often had that capital. Thomas Worthington is a case in point. As previously noted, the sale of his Virginia lands gave him money to invest in Ohio land, and he acquired much additional real estate by buying veterans' land warrants and by taking land as payment for surveying and registering land for others. He bought mill sites and erected mills over a substantial area from the Paint Creek Valley in the west to the Hocking Valley in the east. The mills were operated by managers who not only ground Worthington's grain, distilled his whiskey, and sawed his lumber, but also paid him in kind. Thus in 1808–9 the manager of his Chillicothe mill paid him 100 barrels of flour, 1,000 gallons of whiskey, and many hogs for the privilege of operating the mill. Worthington started a cloth mill equipped to weave cotton, flax, and wool. Then he bought a purebred Merino ram to sire a flock of sheep to produce fine wool for his mill. He invested heavily in machinery, eliminated unprofitable procedures and products, and by 1820 was turning a profit of about 30 percent on his wool business. He also manufactured rope, which undoubtedly used locally grown flax and/or hemp, prospected for brick-clay, salt, iron ore, and coal, speculated in the fattening of Tennessee cattle (he didn't fare too well), contracted to build roads, and helped organize the Bank of Chillicothe. All of this, of course, was in addition to his chief business—farming—from which he derived substantial income from field, flock, and orchard. Since he was frequently away from his properties on public business, relatives, friends and hired managers looked after his personal affairs.

The spread of Worthington's activities was not unusual, mingling, as they did, agricultural, industrial, financial, and public service activities. Many an early Ohio "squire," like James Kilbourne of Worthington or Simon Perkins of Warren, was similarly engaged in the pioneer period; not till after the Civil War would increasing specialization tend to reduce their numbers, replacing them with entrepreneurs who focused their energies on developing the large-scale, complex industries which were emerging at that time.

Early Ohio industry was energized for the most part by water power. Large numbers of rivers and streams with sufficient "fall" provided ample mill sites. The dams, races, and mills were built of local stone and lumber. Initially fine millstones were imported, but it was not long before such excellent local stones as Berea sandstone were in use. Most milling machinery was imported during the state's formative years. A series of gears and belts transmitted power from the wheel-driven shaft upward to machines located on floors above the water level. By the end of the pioneer period, iron gears and shafts had replaced wooden ones. Some milling was powered by wheels mounted on barges moored in the Ohio and other large rivers where the current was strong enough to turn a water wheel. In periods of sustained drought, water flow was sometimes inadequate to turn mill wheels efficiently. During periods of low water, mill ponds stagnated; occasionally irate neighbors, blaming disease and illness on the stagnant water and the effusions of rotting vegetation, breached the mill dam, draining the pond and shutting down the mill. Ice closed mills in wintertime. It is hard to overemphasize the importance of the mills to farmers, who had their grain ground into meal or flour and distilled into whiskey, their timber sawed, and their wool and flax processed into cloth.

Great variety quickly characterized Ohio's industrial activity, which is not surprising in light of the fact that each group of newcomers brought familiar industrial skills with them even as they had brought agricultural practices. Ohioans simply adapted to the local scene the skills and crafts already well known to them.

Several stimuli contributed to the rapid growth of industrial activity. The high cost of transporting goods over the mountains in effect "protected" Ohio industries from the competition of established industries in neighboring states. In addition, Europe was preoccupied with the Napoleonic wars, giving American businesses a virtual monopoly in the domestic marketplace. And when those wars ended, Congress enacted the protective Tariff of 1816 behind which Ohio industries were shielded from the "dumping" of foreign goods. The War of 1812, as we have seen, provided a notable stimulus to Ohio commerce, agriculture, and industry, and after the war ended Ohio suppliers continued to send some goods to the military market. Immigrants to Ohio brought hard money (specie) which, while it lasted, stimulated every aspect of business. Finally, cheap, easily accessible raw materials were available across the state. Offsetting these stimuli were several deterrents to manufacturing in early Ohio: the difficulties of transporting goods to market, a lack of capital to underwrite large enterprises (too much of the available capital being channeled into land speculation and commerce), and a chronic shortage of skilled labor.

Far and away the industrial leader of Ohio in its early years was Cincinnati, as the traveller James Flint noted in 1819: "The manufactories of this new place are more diversified than extensive. An iron foundry, two breweries, several distilleries, a woolen manufactory, a cotton-mill, an oil-mill, a glasshouse, and a white lead factory, seem to be the principal ones." In this primitive industrial environment skilled laborers fared relatively well:

> But the more numerous part of the artisans are joiners, bricklayers, blacksmiths, plasterers, shoe-makers, tailors, hatters, bakers, tobacconists, cabinet makers, saddlers, etc. Journeymen mechanics earn from one and three-fourths to two dollars per day. Their board costs about three dollars per week. Most of them dress well on the days they are not at work, and some of them keep horses.

By 1820 only New York and Pennsylvania exceeded Ohio in the value of manufactured products, and Ohio ranked fifth in the nation in the amount of capital invested in factories. In twenty years' time a wilderness had become dotted with manufacturing establishments, most of which employed but a few workers. It was an impressive accomplishment, one destined to expand as Ohio more than held its own among the top manufacturing states in the nation.

Many of these early industries relied on the forests. Lumbering was a ubiquitous activity but too poorly recorded to chronicle with confidence. Pioneers used the varied hardwoods in building, furniture and cabinet making, and manufacturing wagons, barrels, and other goods. Some timber was exported. Black walnut and cherry were favorites of the furniture makers, but, ironically, when mahogany became fashionable before the Civil War, Ohio furniture makers imported it despite the high cost and an abundance of high-quality local woods.

The careful farmer saved his ashes when burning trees. He sold them to "asheries," where they were leached, boiled down, and baked into pearl ash (potassium carbonate) or potash (potassium hydroxide). These alkalies were used for making soap, glass, and hominy. Tanneries were also widely distributed throughout the state. Bark from chestnut, oak, and hickory trees provided the tannin essential to the processing of leather.

Even as the forest provided resources for industry, so did the farm, and the mills that sprang up to process the grain, pork, and wool were essential to Ohio's economy. They provided products consumed locally but also exported to more distant markets. One of the most impressive early Ohio industries was the woolen mill established by Bezaleel Wells and associates in 1815 at Steubenville. The building was a hundred feet long and three stories high and employed forty-eight men, twenty-seven women, and forty boys and girls. It fell victim to the depression of 1819 and to the fact that its product—broadcloth—was too extravagant for the needs of the local market.

Mineral resources provided the basis for many early Ohio industries. Salt had been processed in small quantities by the earliest settlers, who worked the same springs and "licks" the Indians used. After the War of 1812, demand made it necessary and profitable to develop larger quantities of salt, and wells were dug into rock salt strata. One such well at Zanesville reputedly reached several hundred feet in depth in 1817. Although much salt was processed in southern and eastern Ohio, a considerable quantity was still imported. Not until much later in the century would the huge resources of northeastern Ohio be tapped, making the state a large exporter of this valuable mineral. Meat packers were among the largest users of salt, yet Cincinnati's hog packers, for many years, imported sea salt all the way from New Orleans because Ohio salt was contaminated with mineral traces that affected the meat's taste.

Coal was abundant in Ohio, but coal mining as a business was slow to develop, probably because of the ready availability of cheap timber. About 1828 a Portage County businessman shipped coal via the newly opened Ohio and Erie Canal to Cleveland, where he finally succeeded in persuading the owners of lake vessels to use coal instead of wood to heat their boilers. Thus the large-scale commercial use of Ohio coal began modestly, but its growth was assured. Brier Hill in the Mahoning Valley was among Ohio's first well-developed industrial mining operations. By mid-century the widespread use of the steam engine created a demand for coal which was met by mines throughout eastern Ohio. This inexpensive energy source was a powerful industrial stimulus.

Clay and shale were staples of the clay products industry, in which Ohio would eventually assume national leadership. The early industry was localized around widely distributed clay deposits. Pottery could be made almost anywhere in the settled parts of Ohio, but high-quality dinnerware, stoneware, and pottery came to be associated with the eastern and south central regions, especially around East Liverpool and in the valleys of the Tuscarawas and Muskingum rivers. English potters supplied much of the skilled labor and artisanship that made this industry grow. These immigrant craftsmen produced goods that compared favorably with quality European pieces, but the lack of a substantial privileged class to purchase showy pieces encouraged production of more humble and utilitarian items. By the 1840s, there were so many operators in the clay products business that some producers joined together in "pools" whereby they tried to keep price levels up by dividing among themselves the markets for their finished products. This is an early Ohio example of those market forces which a few decades later would contribute to the rise of truly big business when "trusts" made it difficult for the small independent producer to compete.

Some fair-sized, surprisingly complex industries were developing in Ohio well before mid-century. One of the best known was Cincinnati's meat-packing industry. In the 1820s it was already processing up to 30,000 hogs annually for local and regional markets. Meat packing was literally a "stinking" business, as the stench of thousands of porkers, driven through the streets to the processing plants, permeated the air. The plants themselves, like the infamous Chicago stockyards of a later day, would appear to modern folk as a nightmare of squeals, blood, offal, and noxious substances in which over-worked laborers performed mind-numbing tasks over and over during a long work day.

Cincinnati's packing houses were true factories in which transient, un-skilled laborers could quickly learn a specialized task in one or another of the processing steps—slaughtering, cleaning, or cutting. Conveyor systems were used to move carcasses from one staging area to another. Thus an assembly line (or as one commentator called it, a "dis-assembly line") manned by workers performing a single, repetitive task made pork processing in Cincinnati the forerunner of the lines that dominate modern manufacturing. There was also an important by-product. Animal fats were salvaged for use in the soap and candle trade, a business which would assume major importance in Cincinnati's modern industrial history. By the 1850s more than 400,000 hogs were processed annually for local, national, and even international markets. Cincinnati had earned her sobriquet, "Porkopolis."

Iron manufacture was a second emerging industry that developed large-scale factory characteristics by mid-century. In 1804 the Hopewell Furnace was established near Youngstown in an area that would develop into Ohio's premier iron and steel center later in the century. Soon iron furnaces were operating throughout eastern and southern Ohio. The Hanging Rock region, centered in Lawrence, Scioto, Gallia, Jackson and Vinton counties, became famous for its concentration of iron "plantations," forerunners of the infa-mous company towns. These were communities located on thousands of acres of mineral and timber lands owned by an iron company. The iron ore, lime-

stone, and timber (for charcoal) essential to the smelting process were available close to one another and were easily accessible. Gangs of laborers cut
timber, "baked" it to make charcoal, mined and crushed the limestone, mined
iron ore, constructed the roads, drove the oxen, processed the appropriate
mix of materials in the furnace, and performed all the other varied tasks
required. They lived in isolated, relatively self-contained communities de-
void of comforts and diversity. There, too, lived company officials in "quality" housing. When local mineral resources were exhausted, the furnace was
abandoned. The company then moved operations to new land, built another
town and furnace, and continued operations. Generally these furnaces produced pig iron, which was forged into kitchen ware, machinery, accessories
for the building trades, and so on. Before the Civil War nearly every town
had its iron works, but in time the iron business concentrated in manufacturing towns and cities including Cleveland, Youngstown, Warren, Canton,
Massillon, Portsmouth, Ironton, and Zanesville; early in the century the latter
boasted an iron works employing 158 hands.

A chronic shortage of labor in Ohio was a problem during the first half of
the nineteenth century. Workers skilled in brewing, tanning, ship building,
pottery making, iron making, machine shop work, and all sorts of crafts had
their choice of jobs. In the metropolis of Cincinnati, a stream of immigrant
Irish and German workers provided cheap unskilled labor for growing industries and commercial activities. Free blacks and escaped slaves worked in
menial jobs. They were well represented among the dock workers and steve-
dores servicing the waterfront. Prior to 1830, Cincinnati employers paid average daily wages almost double those paid in the East; after 1830 the influx of
workers, coupled with the disappearance of cheap farmlands, served to keep
wages in line with those paid back east.

Life was grim for workers whose lack of skill kept them on the bottom
rungs of the economic ladder. No "safety net" of public support protected the
injured or unemployed. No retirement plans supported the worker once his
productive years were over. Only family and private charities provided assistance, and usually this help was minimal at best. Housing was poor, health
care unheard of, sanitation primitive. Even the most affluent members of
Cincinnati society had to maneuver the same filthy, pig-infested streets that
the poor traversed. When economic "panics" depressed the economy—as
they did with some frequency, but especially in the years after 1819 and
1837—real desperation and hardship was rampant among urban workers.

Early in the nineteenth century changes were occurring which affected the
worker-employer relationship. A skilled craftsman formerly worked for
himself or in close company with others of his trade. He tended to be involved
with every aspect of his craft, from securing raw materials, to training his
helpers, to making and marketing the finished product. The factory system

expanded this individually centered activity into large-scale enterprise in which the individual craftsman was but one of many persons whose interests had to be considered. Size and competition produced a group of merchant-capitalists who controlled more and more of the entire manufacturing process, from purchase of raw materials to marketing of the finished product. They controlled large enterprises because they had the financial resources to do so.

As his control over his own destiny weakened, the skilled laborer sought comfort and support in labor organizations. A Mechanic's Association, formed in Dayton in 1813, was perhaps Ohio's first organized labor group. Mechanics' associations soon sprang up elsewhere in the state, with Cincinnati leading the way since it had the greatest concentration of workers. By the 1830s every important trade had established an organization, but only a tiny percentage of the Queen City's workers were involved. Black artisans were barred from membership.

Organized craftsmen used work stoppages and strikes in an effort to protect wages, reduce hours, and fend off the employment of new artisans. Cincinnati tailors in 1836 demanded "more wages, fewer apprentices, no tailoresses" and the use of certain shops on Sundays "for beer and cards." Steubenville, Springfield, Cleveland, Columbus, and Dayton were among Ohio cities where labor organizations exerted modest influence in the 1830s. The severe and prolonged depression of 1837 weakened the mechanics' associations around the state, but by the 1840s they were making a modest comeback.

Ohio workers lagged behind their eastern brethren in developing workers' parties for political action. Abortive efforts to organize occurred as early as the 1820s, but nothing of substance came from them. Ohio workers occasionally resorted to mob violence to attain their objectives. The most explosive situation existed in Cincinnati, where both the mature, skilled workers and the young, unskilled workers protected their respective territory. An influx of blacks in the 1820s created tensions that led white Cincinnati workers to demand that Ohio's "black laws" restricting black immigration be enforced. In 1829 a mob of unskilled whites, fearful that this influx would force wages down, attacked black neighborhoods such as "Bucktown" and "Little Africa." An unanticipated sequel for white employers was the migration of hundreds of Cincinnati blacks to a new community—Wilberforce—which they founded as a refuge in Upper Canada. Blacks had organized through their ministers to develop this option; once white employers saw their cheap labor leaving town, they backed off demands for the enforcement of the restrictive black laws.

Tensions between worker and employer inevitably increased as industries grew in size and complexity. Not until after the Civil War, however, did a modern worker-employer relationship begin to develop. Even then the process was slow and cost society dearly.

Underlying all economic activity was the money question. How could the state manage currency? What roles should banks be encouraged—or allowed—to play? How was the money and banking situation in Ohio affected by decisions made elsewhere? These questions, in conjunction with the related question of how Ohio was to secure new markets to stimulate economic development, were vital to the state's continued economic growth. It is to these questions that we now turn.

7.

The Pioneer State

Money, Banking, Internal Improvements, and Politics

Ohio's economic development during the pioneer period depended in large part on the growth of a dependable currency and sound banking. But the state was unable to control its own destiny in these important areas. Rather, during much of this period it had to respond to initiatives of the Second Bank of the United States, a federally chartered institution which was beyond the control of state officials. The money and banking issue was important in the political realm as well as in the economic. Although neither of the major political alignments was a monolith, the emerging Whig party favored economic nationalism while the Democrats tended to favor state control of economic development.

These differences were also reflected in party attitudes toward federal support for internal improvements, yet another subject which stirred intense interest in Ohio. By mid-century, after several decades of political and economic conflict, Ohio had achieved reasonable stability in its money and banking practices, and it boasted an impressive new canal system and a national pike which helped to integrate the state's economy into the nation's.

Money and Banking Problems

During the frontier period, the social and economic levels of Ohio settlers ranged from the impoverished squatter to the man of means who brought his capital with him and invested it in his new home. More typical was the family that arrived in frontier Ohio with a small amount of cash that was soon spent for necessities. Unless they could sell produce in the marketplace, the new arrivals continued to be cash-poor. A traveller in the Western Reserve in 1820 described the absence of money and the barter system that functioned in its stead. "The nominal price of wheat and rye is 50¢ per bushel," he wrote, "but may be bought for a much less sum of money." In fact, "no one offers money for any article at any price unless it is tallow and the *black salts* or crude potash. A barrel of salt costs $6 in barter, but only $4.50 cash. . . . Money, (they say) is out of the question, as nothing they have to sell will bring money at any price."

This grim assessment notwithstanding, a dependable system of money and banking was essential to economic progress. Ohio, in common with other western states, was specie-poor because creditors in the East demanded that western borrowers repay them in specie (gold and silver coin), thus draining out hard money.

To meet the need for currency, state-chartered banks were granted the power to issue bank notes. Ohio's first banking charter was issued by the general assembly in April 1803 to the Miami Exporting Company of Cincinnati. This commercial company was allowed to issue notes payable to the bearer. The company maintained its character as a bank even after it ceased commercial operations. In 1808–9 the legislature chartered banks in Marietta, Chillicothe, and Steubenville, and between 1812 and 1814 added banks at Warren, Zanesville, Cincinnati, and Dayton.

Most early Ohio banks were capitalized at $100,000 although a few were capitalized at $500,000. If a bank was unable to raise its authorized capital, it was permitted to operate at a lesser level. Early bank charters commonly limited the amount of real estate a bank could own, limited interest charges, and permitted banks to issue notes with a proviso that the amount issued could not exceed three times the value of the bank's capital stock paid in.

The state banks performed well during the War of 1812. No alternative banking institutions operated at that time since the original Bank of the United States, a federally chartered institution, had expired in 1811. Ohio bank notes were redeemable in specie because the flow of government contracts to Ohio during the War of 1812 kept an adequate supply of specie available for bank reserves. Late in the war, however, specie payments were suspended by eastern banks, and Ohio bankers found themselves reluctantly following suit. Confidence in bank notes waned as specie redemption was halted; this led to inflationary pressures which plagued Ohio until 1825.

On February 23, 1816, the general assembly passed the "bonus law." This law extended the charters of existing banks until 1843, provided that one twenty-fifth of their bank stock would become the property of the state. Dividends from this stock would be used to purchase additional bank shares until the state owned one-sixth of the capital stock. In exchange for this "gift," the bank would be exempt from taxation. By January 1818, the state had a financial interest in twenty-five banks, and no interest in only three.

While twenty-eight banks were operating under state charter, many others were operating informally, with no corps of state bank examiners to control them. Some informal banks, such as the Bank of Xenia, had a good reputation while others, such as the Owl Creek Bank of Mount Vernon, were notorious for issuing worthless paper commonly called "shinplasters." Many commercial companies operated banks as a profitable sideline. Certain individuals printed paper notes and circulated them within their immediate neighborhood.

The proliferation of paper money created splendid opportunities for counterfeiters; indeed, counterfeiting was among Ohio's larger "businesses" in the pioneer period. Illegal banking operations existed throughout the West, but few counterfeiters moved with more elan and success than Jim Brown of Boston, Ohio. He and his confederates wholesaled "queer" (counterfeit money) to tavernkeepers, livery stable operators, and others who bought the artfully engraved paper at a discount (i.e., with $1,000 in legitimate bank notes they might purchase $5,000 of phony notes). The buyers then assumed the risk of discovery as they disposed of the counterfeit to their customers. Counterfeiters were seldom ostracized. Despite the fact that his surreptitious business was well known, Jim Brown's Cuyahoga Valley neighbors thought well of him even after he was jailed in New Orleans when a scheme for swindling merchants on an international scale went sour. Freed from jail, Brown returned to Boston, where his neighbors promptly elected him justice of the peace!

Another abuse of the money system was the "keg money" scam. Noteholders, skeptical of the bank's ability to back bank notes with specie, were shown money kegs apparently filled with gold and silver coin. The satisfied customer did not realize that the coin was but a thin layer atop a keg full of scrap metal.

While illegal practices victimized honest people, their impact was modest compared to the confusion inherent in a system where notes from unknown banks—some solid, some not—came routinely into the hands of farmers, manufacturers, and merchants. How were they to know whether various bank notes were passing at par or at a discount? People actively involved in business were likely to have a fair idea of the worth of various state bank notes, but the farmer who seldom got his hands on money had to rely on reports in the weekly newspaper or on conversation in the village marketplace to have some sense of which notes to trust and which to suspect. It is surprising that the economic system functioned as well as it did given the confusing and loose currency conditions.

Ohio's Struggle with the Bank of the United States

After the charter of the Bank of the United States expired in 1811, economic nationalists clamored for another financial institution of sufficient strength to give direction to the nation's banking and stability to its currency. In 1816, Congress chartered the Second Bank of the United States. Located in Philadelphia, the bank was capitalized at $35 million, one-fifth of which was subscribed by the United States government and four-fifths by private citizens. The bank could issue notes that were backed by United States Treasury deposits kept in the vaults of the bank in Philadelphia. A United States Bank note, therefore, was "as good as gold" in commercial transactions and in payment of government obligations.

The Bank of the United States was also the nation's largest lending agency. State banks, commercial companies, and speculators borrowed from it. It quickly established branches around the country, two of them in Ohio. Cincinnati businessmen secured a branch in March 1817, and the vigorous lobbying of Thomas Worthington won a Chillicothe branch in October. Leading citizens of these communities served as directors—Jacob Burnet, Martin Baum, John H. Piatt, Daniel Drake, and William Henry Harrison in Cincinnati; Edward Tiffin, William Creighton, George Renick, Duncan McArthur, and John Carlisle in Chillicothe.

Supported by a congressional resolution, and encouraged by the secretary of the treasury, the bank set out to restore sound currency by forcing state banks to redeem their notes in specie. Only specie or notes redeemable in specie would be received in payment of obligations due the United States government. The bank's president, William Jones, took the initiative by alerting western bankers that he intended to contract the paper of nonspecie-paying banks. The announcement brought consternation to Ohio bankers. Strong state banks held much paper from less secure banks. If forced to redeem this paper in specie, many banks would falter, bringing ruin to the western economy. Ohio bankers led by Simon Perkins of Warren, Charles Hammond of St. Clairsville, and Bezaleel Wells of Steubenville urged the directors of the Bank of the United States to recognize the special problems of western bankers before mandating the resumption of specie payment. Their efforts were in vain.

In June 1818, two Bank of the United States officials toured eastern Ohio to redeem paper notes. They visited the Farmer's Bank of Canton, the German

Bank of Wooster, and the Commercial Bank of Cleveland without securing any specie; indeed, in Cleveland young Alfred Kelley, president of the Commercial Bank and soon to be one of Ohio's outstanding business and political leaders, gave them a tongue-lashing for even trying. Finally, at Simon Perkins's Western Reserve Bank in Warren, they were able to redeem four-fifths of the paper which they held from that bank. This unsuccessful effort to contract unsupported paper currency was a portent of greater problems to come, among them, the overextension of credit.

Thousands of Ohioans had taken advantage of the credit provisions of federal land laws to buy more acreage than they could properly finance. When landowners were unable to make payments on time, they borrowed money to meet the payment schedule. By 1819 public land debtors nationally owed more than $20 million, and more than half that amount was for land purchased northwest of the Ohio River.

In 1819 a sharp recession hit the nation. Ohio and the West were unusually hard-hit, for, as the economic malaise deepened, the Bank of the United States demanded payment of outstanding obligations. That in turn resulted in other financial agencies calling in debts. Tens of thousands of debtors lost their property as the banks foreclosed on them. Congress saved some farmers and speculators when it enacted a bill permitting federal land purchasers to retain that portion of their property for which they had already made payment. If, for example, a farmer had contracted to purchase 320 acres, and he had already paid half of his obligation, he got to keep 160 acres but had to surrender the remainder. Tempers were short in the West, where it appeared the bank was attempting to save itself at the expense of debtors.

In 1818 the Ohio legislature proposed taxing the Cincinnati and Chillicothe branches of the Bank of the United States to secure revenue for the state. This proposal gained support with the deepening of the economic crisis and the election of Ethan Allen Brown, no friend of the bank, as governor. Brown believed that since state banks were taxed (or had equivalent obligations under the "bonus" law), the Bank of the United States branches should be similarly taxed. The general assembly concurred. Charles Hammond formulated a tax measure which included a provision calling for the annual collection of $50,000 from each of the two branch banks. The state's agent could take any steps necessary to collect; he could even conduct a search of vaults, cupboards, and closets to secure the appropriate sum. A bill levying this tax was passed on February 19, 1819, with only three dissenting votes in the House. This "crowbar law" was a punitive measure designed to drive the Bank of the United States from Ohio.

Ohio was not alone in its attempt to tax branches of the Bank of the United States. Five other western and southern states had already done so. Maryland's attempt to tax the Baltimore branch resulted in a federal case which was appealed to the Supreme Court. In March 1819, Chief Justice John Marshall handed down the majority decision in the case of *McCulloch v. Maryland,* in which he denied the right of a state to tax an agency of the federal government because "the power to tax is the power to destroy." Ohio reacted to this decision with less hostility than one might assume. Many citizens felt the decision did not apply to Ohio because the premises upon which the case rested were not descriptive of Ohio's situation. State officials, therefore, ignored the McCulloch decision.

Ohio's newly enacted bank tax was to be collected by the state auditor, Ralph Osborn. With the support of Governor Brown, Osborn hired John Harper and two other men to act as his agents. On September 17, 1819, Harper and his men entered the Chillicothe branch, showed officials a warrant signed by Osborn, entered the vault, scooped up notes and specie which they estimated at $100,000 and left the building. The next day, under guard, they took the money to Columbus and turned it over to the state treasurer who counted it and returned the excess of about $20,000 to the Chillicothe bank. The agents were paid $2,000 for their work.

The bank sued for the return of its money and charged Osborn with violating a court injunction forbidding collection of the tax. Osborn maintained he had not been properly served prior to the descent upon the Chillicothe branch. The bank won its case in federal circuit court; federal marshals took $98,000 from the state treasury and returned it to the bank. The suit was continued, however, over the $2,000 paid the agents and on the interest owed the bank during the time the state held its money. The case reached the Supreme Court in 1824 as *Osborn* v. *Bank of the United States.* The Court ruled that officers of the Bank of the United States were agents essential to the fiscal operations of the nation; as the Ohio law interfered with their ability to carry out their duties, it was, therefore, unconstitutional.

The struggle with the Bank of the United States would appear to be a clear example of Ohio asserting "states' rights." But it is well to reiterate the words of William Utter, a student of this period who wrote,

> It seems clear that the argument [of state sovereignty] was developed almost wholly to justify the State's course against the Bank. The very men who drafted the resolutions [asserting state sovereignty] were advocates of national aid in building the Cumberland Road, and in financing the Erie and Ohio canals. . . . Ohio's economic interests were best served by a nationalistic government; in the Bank matter only were economic interests aligned with an opposite theory of government.

Hence what appeared to be a states' rights position was really economic opportunism.

The money and banking crisis of 1819–25 took a terrible toll on thousands of Ohioans. Men of wealth were affected by the collapse of prices for land and for goods; the subsistence farmer survived because he could generally provide basic food for his family even if he lacked salt, coffee, tea, and other amenities. If he were among the thousands who lost their land, he could struggle along doing odd jobs for his neighbors or, as many did, he could pack up his family and belongings and head west for a new start. Some fell victim to despair: one Ohio farmer commented that "there are a great many farmers . . . who are becoming . . . habitual drunkards . . . destroying themselves, wasting their property, and leaving their families as poor and naked as when they came into the world."

While Ohio and other western states struggled with a faltering economy, the national economic issue which had most direct consequence in Ohio during the pioneer period was President Andrew Jackson's war on the Bank of the United States. Jackson had personally experienced the traumas of indebtedness. He distrusted banks, especially one run by eastern interests who seemed to victimize western debtors. He swore he would kill "the monster," an issue on which his political enemies tried to entrap him. They succeeded in getting a bill through Congress to extend the bank's charter beyond its expiration date in 1836. In effect, they were daring Jackson to veto the bill because such a move might cost him reelection in 1832. Jackson rose to the challenge; he vetoed the bill, was reelected, and then set out to hasten the bank's demise by ordering his secretary of the treasury to withdraw federal deposits from its vaults. In 1834 both houses of the Ohio General Assembly approved these measures. On March 1, 1836, the Second Bank of the United States ceased to function under its federal charter. Ohioans shed few tears.

Economic and other Crises

The severe Panic of 1837 followed the bank's demise; many observers connected the two events and blamed Andrew Jackson for the country's plight. Others claimed the depression resulted from Jackson's Specie Circular. Issued in 1836, it required that payment for federal land purchases be made in gold or silver. A case could be made for both of these charges, but the primary cause of the panic was, once again, uncontrolled speculation in lands and goods. In the crisis Ohio banks suspended specie payments as did banks everywhere.

From time to time during Jackson's presidency new banks were chartered in Ohio, except during the mid 1830s, when the anti-bank wing of the Democratic party (nicknamed the "locofocos") controlled Ohio's government. Some of the banks won political favor and were identified as "pet banks," eligible to receive in their vaults a portion of the federal deposits formerly kept in the Bank of the United States. Ohio had nine of Jackson's "pet banks"—two in Columbus, two in Cincinnati, two in Cleveland, and one each in Wooster, Zanesville, and Chillicothe.

Hard times remained in the state until well into the 1840s. Many manufacturing and business establishments went bankrupt. Poorly managed banks closed, costing depositors their life savings. Some Ohio bank notes were discounted between 10 and 90 percent. Unsecured "shinplaster" notes circulated as small change. "Red dog" and "wildcat" banks contributed to the mess by circulating unsecured notes. Barter returned as a means of exchange, even in some of the larger towns. Laborers were thrown out of work or had their wages reduced. In Cincinnati workers' strikes were ineffective in stemming unemployment, and mechanics' associations and other labor organizations were powerless to aid their members. A Toledo observer wrote in 1837: "Our only subject of interest—our only topic of conversation here is the hard times. Buildings are arrested in mid progress, laborers thrown out of employment and all public improvements suspended. . . . It is almost impossible to raise money anywhere even for the mere supply of subsistence."

Internal Improvements in the Pioneer State

On no issue were people of the West more united than on the need for improved roads, canals, harbors, bridges, and all forms of internal improvement. The rivers, lakes, and forest trails which had sufficed to bring the first settlers to Ohio were inadequate to meet the needs of a growing, increasingly complex state. What good was it to an ambitious farmer to settle in Ohio if he could not get his products out to market? How could the larger industrial enterprises flourish—Steubenville's woolen mill, Zanesville's iron furnace and forge, Cincinnati's pork packing—unless they had reasonable access to markets far beyond the state's confines? Something needed to be done—but what, and by whom?

In common with most westerners, pioneer Ohioans believed the federal government should help pay for internal improvements, since it needed roads for the postal service, the military, and access to areas where it was selling public lands. But efforts to secure federal help were seldom successful. The federals only supported occasional projects, like military roads cut into northern Ohio during the War of 1812, the National Pike, and land grants to assist the state to complete its canal system. If Ohio wanted roads, canals, and other improvements, either the state or private enterprise would have to provide them.

Roads

The Ohio Enabling Act of 1802, as amended, had provided that 3 percent of the proceeds of federal land sales in Ohio be used for building roads in the state; another two percent had been used to bring the National Pike to the borders of Ohio. This money, however, paid for laying out roads rather than for building them, and political jobbery undercut its effective use. Road building was encouraged by allowing men who did not pay taxes to earn the right to vote by working on road construction.

Early in the nineteenth century most Ohio roads were regionally focused around the population centers with only an occasional road connecting these centers. By 1820 Zane's Trace (1797), now somewhat improved, linked several growing centers in southeastern Ohio; Columbus was served by an east-west road and a north-south road each extending to the state's borders; Cincinnati had a northeasterly link and a road which followed the old army war trails to the north; and Cleveland was served by a lake shore road and by a long southern connection to Zanesville. The postal service favored these through routes as it moved mail across the state.

The overwhelming task of keeping roads open was largely a function of village, township, and county effort. Most roads were merely improved trails, pocked with mud holes in wet weather and dusty ruts in dry. Stumps tripped walkers and upset coaches, bridges were few and often treacherous. Many a rider drowned while attempting to swim his horse across a swollen stream.

Since public resources for road construction were so limited, the state chartered private turnpike companies to build and maintain roads. Such a company, comprising private investors, would secure a charter from the legislature to build or improve a road between two specified terminal points (e.g. Zanesville to Lancaster or Steubenville to Cadiz). The company sold shares to raise capital for construction.

The company's charter contained specifications dealing with construction, placement of toll booths, the rates it could charge users, and so forth. Eminent domain guaranteed the ability to purchase right-of-way. The charters also provided that local or state government could purchase the roads if they desired. Many turnpike companies failed in the Panic of 1819 and were taken over by counties and townships, but those more solidly financed endured for years before they were taken over by government. Bridges and ferries maintained by private enterprise charged tolls. The traveller who had to use turnpikes, toll bridges, and ferries, and who had to put up several nights at roadside inns, found himself paying out a considerable sum to traverse the state.

In time, passenger traffic and commerce flowed across Ohio roads. Stagecoaches vied with one another in advertising luxurious appointments and the speed with which they rushed passengers safely to their destinations. That they frequently overstated their case can be documented by the large number of travellers' narratives describing the dangers and discomforts of stagecoach travel. One exception might have been travel along the National Pike.

This great road had reached Wheeling by 1817 and was continued across Ohio between 1825 and 1838 via Cambridge, Zanesville, Columbus and Springfield. Carefully engineered, the road was well-paved with macadam: with its picturesque "S-shaped" stone bridges, its reassuring mile markers, and its comfortable inns, the National Pike likely offered the highest level of comfort available in the West for stagecoach passengers. Wagons, especially the high, canvas-topped Conestoga, hauled freight. By the 1830s freight travelled Ohio roads on a regular schedule. Teamsters had a well-deserved reputation as hard-driving, hard-drinking, hard-cussing characters, but they moved freight under conditions that would have tried the spirit of a saint.

Even when the roads were reasonably safe and passable, the traveller was hard-pressed in many areas to find suitable accommodations. Descriptions of unsanitary, raucous, and vile inns fill the travel literature of the time. Well-appointed inns could occasionally be found along the more heavily traveled roads, and by the 1830s and 1840s, weary travellers were welcome at Lebanon's Golden Lamb, Lafayette's Red Brick Tavern, Painesville's Rider's Tavern, and other comfortable establishments. Even well-managed inns were overcrowded periodically, the traveller frequently having to share with one or more bedfellows of varying degrees of cleanliness and sobriety.

Along lesser-travelled routes, farm wives earned a little extra money by putting up guests for the night. Henry Ellsworth, a young Yale graduate, and his companion found themselves in a predicament near Mantua in 1811. They were forced to take shelter in a house that was barely large enough to accommodate the owner's family. Dinner was abysmal and served in such a "sluttish manner" that the guests lost their appetite. "In all my life," said this well-bred easterner, "I never see so much dirt and filth in any human habitation." At bedtime the travellers were given a narrow bed so filled with fleas and bedbugs that they retreated to lie on the floor near the hearth. That was none-too pleasant since the man, his wife, the hired hand and four daughters were already crowded near the fire. In desperation the travellers retired to the barn, where they finished the night.

By mid-century Ohio's principal roads were much improved. Plank roads paved with boards had replaced many of the rougher "corduroy roads" paved with tree trunks laid across the roadway. Many miles had been paved with macadam—small stones pressed onto the roadbed and held together by stone dust which, when wet, cemented the stones in place. With improved roads, it became feasible to move freight overland from interior regions of Ohio to eastern markets.

River and Lake Shipping

From its earliest days, Ohio's principal commercial artery had been the Ohio River. It brought people and goods into the state and took them out. Traces and roads from the east and south led the traveller to its banks, from which he continued his journey by water. This vital lifeline was not without its drawbacks. Goods were shipped from October to May during periods of high water, for there were shallows which boats could not cross in low water. Hazards to navigation abounded—sand bars, embedded tree trunks and limbs called "sawyers," floating tree trunks which could puncture a lightly constructed vessel. Periodic floods caused extensive damage to loading docks, warehouses, and other support facilities. Most goods produced in Ohio before 1827 went to market in New Orleans, a river journey that required running the dangerous "falls" at Louisville, where many a boat capsized. As river traffic increased thieves preyed upon the unwary, sometimes changing channel markers to divert boats upon shoals where they could be plundered.

Even if all went well, the trip to New Orleans was arduous. The individual farmer could not afford the time and expense to take his own goods to market; thus exporting companies, stock companies that purchased goods from individual farmers and then transported consolidated loads to New Orleans, where the company made the best deal possible, were formed. If there was damage to the cargo, or a glut in the New Orleans market, the exporting company took a financial beating. In the early years of statehood, Ohio's economy suffered because there were too few exporting firms.

Shipping companies used special "barges" for upstream traffic. Usually wind-propelled, in difficult stretches the barges were moved by cordelling—towing with ropes—a backbreaking activity to be avoided if at all possible. These craft could be worked over the falls of the Ohio, and they unloaded their cargoes—tea, coffee, sugar, molasses, copperas, logwood, dry-goods—directly at Ohio ports.

Shipbuilding was an important business along the river in the first years of statehood. At Marietta ocean-going vessels were constructed. Some were small—fifty tons' burden, drawing six feet of water—yet they were loaded with local produce, sent downriver to the Gulf of Mexico and from there to eastern ports. A crew worked one 300-ton vessel built in Marietta over the falls of the Ohio in ballast; it then loaded hides, cotton and barrel staves at the mouth of the Cumberland, sailed to Norfolk, Virginia, and took cargo from that port to Liverpool, England. From Liverpool she took cargo to Trieste, where Italian officials found it hard to believe the ship had started its journey in Marietta, Ohio. From Trieste the ship returned to Liverpool, where she took on salt for Philadelphia. This sturdy vessel remained in the Atlantic trade for many years.

The Introduction of Steam

The first steamboat on the western waters, the *New Orleans,* made its way from Pittsburgh to New Orleans in 1811 to herald the age of steam on the Ohio. For the next several years various steamboat designs were tried out on the Ohio and the Mississippi. Building these craft required large amounts of capital, and the Robert Fulton–Robert Livingston syndicate of New York had the funds. With this advantage they virtually monopolized early steam traffic on the Ohio-Mississippi. However, a New Jersey native named Henry Miller Shreve not only built better vessels, but also broke the Fulton-Livingston hold on river traffic. At Wheeling in 1817, he launched the *Washington,* the first truly profitable steamboat on the western waters. In the 1820s he won a government contract for removing snags from the western rivers, and his success in clearing them reduced owners' risks substantially and encouraged a rapid expansion of the steamboat fleet. Shreve's pioneering designs also contributed to expansion of the steam fleets.

Between 1811 and 1825 twenty-six steamboats were launched in Cincinnati, second only to Pittsburgh's thirty-three, and in 1836 Cincinnati's five boatyards turned out twenty-nine vessels. The Queen City prospered in the steamboat era, consolidating its hold as the principal commercial center above New Orleans, as the steamship became the premier mode of travel in the West. River packets, some of them quite elegant, plied the Ohio and the Mississippi. With their great paddlewheels churning, decks crowded with passengers of exotic mix, and steam whistle blowing, they were a romantic and colorful sight long remembered by those who knew them.

Small Ohio towns along the river became ports during the steamboat era. Scarcely a hamlet was too small to be served by a freight hauler or by the small craft which carried coal and other cargo from place to place. The Muskingum was the only Ohio tributary which accommodated steamboats, thanks to a series of dams and locks that enabled boats to ascend from Marietta to Zanesville. With the coming of the rail systems of the 1850s, however, steamboat traffic languished, although the Ohio River would make a dramatic comeback as a freight hauler in the twentieth century. Still, the steamboat, once queen of the river, was replaced by inelegant though highly functional diesel towboats and steel barges.

Ohio's northern waterfront also welcomed the new age during the pioneer era. The 330-foot *Walk-in-the-Water,* constructed at Black Rock on the Niagara River, inaugurated steam travel on Lake Erie. On her maiden voyage in August 1818, she unloaded passengers off the bar blocking the Cuyahoga River's mouth while 400 incredulous Clevelanders looked on. The brave craft was destroyed three years later in a storm, one of literally scores of steamers which were to perish on Lake Erie's treacherous waters in the next few decades. Cleveland launched its first locally built steamship in 1826 and soon became an important shipbuilding center. Huron's pride was the *Great Western,* which entered service in 1838. Sandusky, Lorain, and Ashtabula were also in the race to dominate the shipbuilding industry on the lake. A lack of navigational aids and sand bars blocking Ohio ports to large ships hampered progress initially. Deepening the harbors and erecting lighthouses in the 1820s helped to remedy these problems.

Graceful sailing vessels continued to carry much Lake Erie cargo until the Civil War period, but passenger travel was monopolized by the "steamers" despite their appalling safety records. By the 1840s hordes of westward-moving immigrants crammed the lower decks of these vessels as they made their way to Ohio and beyond. After the opening of canals, Cleveland, and to a lesser extent Toledo, became thriving trans-shipment points for water-borne cargo. Those who had commercial interests in lake steamboats feared competition from the railroads, especially after a lakeshore line was opened in the early 1850s, but there was enough business to go around, and the steamboats continued to carry significant cargo and passenger loads until well into the twentieth century.

Canals

The stimulation of Ohio's economy during the War of 1812 revived speculation about the building of canals to connect the Ohio River with Lake Erie. Farmers and manufacturers needed an alternative to the distant New Orleans market; that alternative appeared in 1817, when New York State commenced construction of the Erie Canal connecting Lake Erie with the Hudson River and the markets of New York City. Once the Erie Canal was complete, Ohio producers who could get their goods to Lake Erie could move them by cheap water transportation to New York's national and international market. Suddenly the most expeditious way of moving goods within Ohio appeared to lie with canals.

Foremost among those now pressing for canals in Ohio was the new governor, Ethan Allen Brown of Cincinnati, who lobbied so effectively with the legislature during his two terms (1818–22) that he later acquired the nickname "Father of the Ohio Canals." In 1822, with the governor's support, the general assembly created an Ohio Board of Canal Commissioners. The distinguished reputation of each of its members—Benjamin Tappan, Alfred Kelley, Thomas Worthington, Ethan Allen Brown (now a senator), Jeremiah Morrow, Isaac Minor, and Ebenezer Buckingham, Jr.—shows the legislature's serious intent. The commission was charged with studying the feasibility of linking the Ohio River with Lake Erie by one or more canals.

Canals can go only where natural watercourses are available to keep the channels full. This reality limited the principal north-south routes to three main stems and two potential branches. In the west was the line defined by the Great Miami-Auglaize-Maumee; in the center the Scioto-Sandusky; and in the east the Muskingum-Tuscarawas-Cuyahoga. For the latter route there were two options north of Coshocton, the Killbuck Creek-Black River option and the Mahoning-Grand River option. Each of the three main routes followed ancient Indian pathways that crossed the continental divide separating the northward- from the southward-flowing rivers. For the canal builders it was essential that water be available at the high point where the canal crossed the divide. This was the principal concern of James Geddes, an experienced engineer from the Erie Canal whom the commissioners hired to survey the prospective routes.

Throughout the summer of 1822, Geddes ran his survey lines and discovered to the surprise of nearly everyone that there was insufficient water on the Scioto-Sandusky watershed to sustain a canal. Since that route was centrally located, served the state capital and accommodated the politically potent Scioto Valley, it had seemed the route most likely to be chosen. Adequate water was available, however, on the Portage Summit (Akron) between the Tuscarawas and the Cuyahoga where a natural spring-fed lake lay astride the route's highest elevation.

Revelation of these topographical facts led to a great deal of speculation over routes and stimulated political lobbying as each section of the state sought advantage. The contest was so bitter that it is somewhat surprising the legislators could pass any bill establishing a route; but they did. In February 1825, the general assembly authorized construction of the Ohio and Erie Canal. The route was a compromise. Commencing near Portsmouth on the Ohio, it ran northward up the Scioto Valley to a point eleven miles south of Columbus. There it bore northeast across the Licking Summit, passing through Newark on its way to the Muskingum, the Tuscarawas, the Cuyahoga, and Lake Erie.

The commissioners knew in February that the northern portion of the route was to cross Portage Summit and follow the Cuyahoga to Cleveland, but they kept people guessing about this portion of the route for three months in the hope that landowners would encourage the state to run the canal through their land by offering free right-of-way. The scheme worked. One such offer was made by Simon Perkins, the Warren banker and speculator who owned lands around the probable route across the Portage Summit. To assure that this route would be chosen, Perkins and an associate platted a proposed town which was to be called Akron (meaning "a high place"). In his town, Perkins deeded to the state the canal right-of-way, two turning basins, and one-third of the town lots. Perkins was a friend of Alfred Kelley and probably knew his offer would guarantee that the commissioners would select the Cuyahoga route. He was right. Perkins' Akron became a child of the canal; the state, the town, and the donor profited by it.

As routes were being chosen, political realities dictated several compromises. Southwestern Ohio, the state's most populous region, demanded and got a canal from Cincinnati to Dayton (the Miami Canal). Marietta and Zanesville, bypassed by the Ohio-Erie, were mollified with an assurance that the Muskingum River would be canalized, making it navigable the year around for commercial vessels. The state capital was served by an eleven-mile "feeder" canal connecting Columbus to the mainline of the Ohio-Erie near Lockbourne. However, nothing could placate citizens of Steubenville and Sandusky, and each of these regions harbored long-standing resentments toward the canal enterprise.

Even with these compromises the canal bill was in trouble in the legislature until critical votes from Washington County could be secured. In exchange for their canal votes, representatives from the Marietta region, led by Ephraim Cutler, demanded a new tax to support public education. Although the school tax was unpopular in many areas of the state, the bargain was struck—canal votes in return for school tax votes, and both issues were approved. By fixing canal routes and by establishing the precedent of tax-supported public education, the legislature had moved Ohio ahead in a progressive direction.

The canal project was so massive, and the state still so poor, that there was no real prospect that local capital could do the job. Nor was it likely that the federal government would underwrite the costs. And so once more Ohio followed New York State's example. The legislature established a Canal Fund Commission in 1825 to market state-backed canal bonds in eastern money markets. The fund commissioners decided to secure money as it was needed by floating bond issues sequentially. As work progressed and completed portions of the canals started to carry traffic and generate income, later bond issues would become attractive and sell on more favorable terms.

In 1825 fund commissioners Ethan Allen Brown, Ebenezer Buckingham, and Allen Trimble (soon to be replaced by Simon Perkins) sold the first bond issue for $400,000 to the New York financial house of Rathbone and Lord. Interest on these bonds was slightly more than 5 percent, payable semiannually. The Ohio bonds were attractive because New York investors had al-

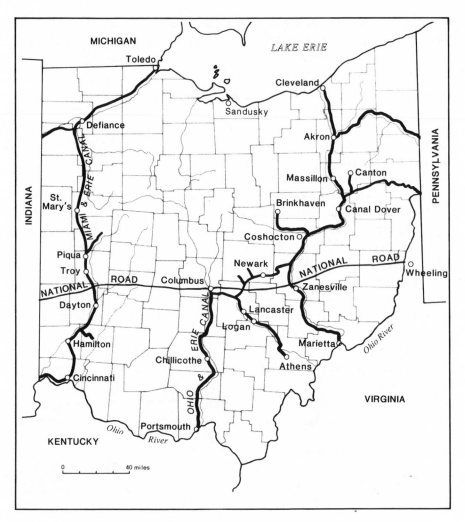

Map 10. Ohio Canals and the National Road

ready been profiting from Erie Canal bonds, for which there was a ready market. They were confident that New York would capture most western trade when transportation was improved, and the bonds were a safe investment since Ohio pledged its faith and credit (i.e., its taxing power) behind the bonds. The Ohio bonds, aggregating about $13.2 million, proved popular. Each new issue was subscribed promptly, usually at favorable terms for the state, and traded in both the domestic and the foreign securities market.

While bonds produced by far the largest share of capital, considerable help eventually came from the federal government. It was difficult for Ohio to secure assistance from Congress because eastern and southern congressmen were generally reluctant to see federal funds used for internal improvements. In the settled regions of the East, the transportation system was largely established and paid for. In the Lower South population was concentrated in seacoast cities or spread through the interior along navigable rivers, thus reducing their need for extensive canal projects.

After the War of 1812, population grew rapidly in the West, however, and the region's political influence increased. Ohioans of every persuasion tended to support federal aid for internal improvements. In 1828 Congress granted to Ohio 500,000 acres of federal land lying in its northwestern quadrant. The state was to use money from the sale of this land exclusively for canal building, specifically to support extension of the Miami Canal north from Dayton through the sparsely settled counties along the Auglaize and Maumee.

Construction started on the Ohio-Erie and the Miami canals as soon as the initial bond issue was sold. The first sections built were those which connected to Lake Erie or to the Ohio River. This was a prudent decision. The commissioners realized that should funds run out in the future the state would have at least some usable waterway in place. However, the ceremonial beginnings of construction took place near the center of the state, at Licking Summit south of Newark, where, on July 4, 1825, Gov. DeWitt Clinton, father of New York's Erie Canal, turned the first spadeful of earth. At the same time work commenced on the thirty-eight-mile northern section connecting the Portage Summit and Cleveland, and on the southern section of the Miami Canal between Cincinnati and Middletown.

Today, this construction project would be bid out to a single contractor who would hire such subcontractors as required. But in pioneer Ohio there were no contractors who could handle such a massive undertaking; thus the canal commissioners acted as prime contractors. Under their direction specifications and cost estimates were drawn up for each unit of work, a unit usually consisting of a half-mile stretch of channel or a single lock. Small contractors could handle units of this size and complexity. Ohio was lucky: just when it needed them, hundreds of skilled workmen who had recently completed work on the Erie Canal became available. At the beginning there were enough bids on each section of work that the commissioners could choose contractors with care. Most bids came in under estimate. Later, when competition for skilled labor came from Pennsylvania and other regions, Ohio was not so fortunate in its contractors, and it was required to pay much higher wages to canal laborers.

Specifications called for the main channel to be twenty-six feet wide on the bottom, forty feet wide at the waterline, with a minimum depth of four feet. Where conditions warranted, the channel could be wider and deeper. On each side of the channel, land was cleared for twenty feet to minimize the chance that deadfalls would block the passage. On the side nearest the ever-present river, a ten-foot towpath was to be built.

Supervision was essential if the state was to get its money's worth from the many contractors involved. In the first years of construction that supervision was supplied by Alfred Kelley and Micajah Williams, the "managing" commissioners. Kelley and Williams were remarkable public servants. They prepared for their task by spending months working with Erie Canal engineers until they knew every detail of canal construction and operation. Back in Ohio they literally got on their horses and rode the routes, checking to make certain that the work was up to specification. Kelley carried an iron rod with which he prodded suspicious spots, thus uncovering occasional shoddy workmanship. After 1837, the checking was done by regional engineers responsible to the Board of Public Works. Some of these engineers were skilled and dedicated, but others lacked the dedication which drove Kelley and Williams to neglect their own business concerns in order to see the task done properly.

While skilled masons, carpenters, and other craftsmen built locks, aqueducts, and the more complicated portions of the system, unskilled laborers dug the great ditches across the land. Some were local farmers who did the work in the off-season, but the majority were immigrant Irish and German workers. The Irish lived along the routes, concentrating in small "shanty towns" in places like Cleveland, Akron, and Cincinnati. Akron's shanty town was nicknamed "Dublin." Poor, uneducated, and passionate, the Irish were often social outcasts ridiculed by "people of quality." Yet it was their labor, often twelve hours a day in stinking ooze up to the waist, that built the canals. Thirty cents a day and a gill of whiskey was their usual wage until competition for their labor pushed wages up in the 1830s. Working conditions left them vulnerable to malaria, typhoid, and other scourges. Undernourished and overtired, living in squalor, they were an easy prey for epidemics such as a cholera epidemic of 1832 that killed hundreds. Alcohol, accidents, and murderous fights took many lives, and many a worker was placed in an unmarked grave along the ditch. Occasionally a worker, killed in mysterious circumstances, was buried in the canal bed.

The thirty-eight-mile section which connected the Portage Summit (966 feet above sea level) with the mouth of the Cuyahoga (573 feet above sea level) was completed first. In all, forty-four locks were required to raise or lower boats along this stretch. Many of these locks, seventeen of them in a mile and a half, were built at the Portage Summit. This complex section of the Ohio-Erie was completed in two years' time.

On July 3, 1827, Gov. Allen Trimble and the canal commissioners led a gala party aboard the canal boat the *State of Ohio,* built at Akron, and descended the canal to Cleveland, where the party arrived on the Glorious Fourth to a rousing reception of salutes, speeches, receptions, banquets, bonfires, and general celebration. The first canal in the West was in operation, and its impact on the region was immediate and beneficial. The remainder of the 308-mile Ohio-Erie Canal was completed to the Ohio River by 1832. In western Ohio, much of which was largely uninhabited, the 245-mile Miami and Erie was belatedly finished in 1845, giving the state two river-to-lake mainlines.

The arteries were not without trouble spots. Along the Ohio-Erie, the extreme southern connection to the Ohio River was never free from problems. Impounded waters from the Portage Lakes reservoirs south of Akron and from Buckeye Lake (the old Buffalo Swamp) in Licking County were required to keep the channel at proper depth during seasonal droughts. Similar problems also affected the Miami-Erie Canal. Maintenance was a nightmare. Annual spring floods and occasional "freshets" washed out sections of the canals. Locks and aqueducts required constant attention. Parts of the system froze in wintertime for four or five months. During this downtime, "state boats" (maintenance boats) repaired the canal banks and performed routine maintenance.

But when everything worked as intended, travel on a passenger packet boat could be pleasant. For five dollars a traveller could ride the Ohio-Erie at a stately four miles an hour, completing the 308 miles in eighty hours. In time the sheer popularity of canal travel caused problems, however, and passenger comfort suffered. One disgruntled passenger described his trip on a boat containing a gentlemen's cabin, a ladies' cabin and dressing room, a barroom, and a kitchen, all lighted by small windows and skylights. "Into this space were stowed thirty-five men, nineteen women, and ten children, seven of whom were at the breast." Beds were shelves attached to the walls in three tiers. "During the day the beds, consisting of mattresses, sheets, pillows, and cotton quilts, were piled one above another. . . . The smell of animal effluvia, when they were unpacked, was truly horrid . . . they were saturated with the perspiration of every individual who had used them since the commencement of the season."

Freight was the lifeblood of the system. Canal freighters were normally sixty feet long, fifteen feet wide, and could carry sixty tons of cargo. By 1840 canal freighters were carrying wheat, corn, oats, pork, bacon, lard, wool, butter, cheese, fish, iron ore, pig iron, coal, timber, clay products, stone, ashes, salt, whiskey, tobacco, and general merchandise. Occasionally some exotica—copper ore from Michigan or mahogany wood from Central America—appeared on the canals.

The dominance of water transport may be seen in a minor, but striking example. In 1837, Pierre Irving of Toledo received books a friend in Illinois had sent him. They came by way of the Illinois, Mississippi, and Ohio rivers, the Ohio-Erie Canal, and Lake Erie. This water transport covered a distance three times the direct land route from Illinois to Toledo, yet it was the expedient way to ship goods in an area where roads were virtually nonexistent.

State canal enterprise was not confined to the original plan of 1825. Through the years the canal system was constantly expanded with new "feeders" connecting additional areas to the main canals. Private enterprise also built canals, often with unhappy results. They were very costly to build and maintain, but Ohio was so eager for additional canals that the state legislature encouraged private builders by subscribing to stock in their companies. This was done under the Ohio Loan Law passed March 4, 1837 (its enemies called it the "Plunder Law"), which permitted the state or other political subdivisions to use public money to assist internal improvements. This costly and unwise act greatly increased state debt and did little to improve the canal system. On the contrary, it helped certain early railroad schemes to the detriment of the canals.

Nevertheless, for brief periods the privately owned, state-assisted Penn-Ohio (Mahoning) Canal succeeded in giving the underdeveloped Western Reserve a commercial boost. Its exports of dairy products increased so dramatically that the Reserve was referred to as "Cheesedom." In similar fashion state aid assisted the Whitewater Canal, which connected Cincinnati with Indiana. Another private canal connecting the farming center of Milan with the Huron River and Lake Erie made that town the nation's largest wheat exporter for a brief period in the 1830s. On the other hand, the Sandy and Beaver Canal, connecting Bolivar on the Ohio-Erie with Pennsylvania's Beaver River, was costly to build, impossible to maintain, and short-lived.

Construction of a canal system was Ohio's largest public effort of the early nineteenth century. And it worked, not only by providing faster and cheaper transport of goods and passengers, but also by boosting the state economy in other ways. Even before construction started, real estate prices rose sharply in regions through which the canals would run. Construction brought large sums into cash-starved regions. Workers had to spend what they earned for food, shelter, clothing, and other essentials; that money went to local merchants. Local producers furnished building supplies—stone, lumber, metal parts—giving work to hundreds of workers at good wages. State banks benefited from the deposit of funds from bond sales, which helped to strengthen and stabilize them.

The most dramatic evidence of the canals' utility is seen in their effect on the marketplace. This can best be explained by example. Prior to the opening of the canals farmers in the vicinity of modern Massillon sold their wheat in a local, glutted market where they were lucky to get twenty-five cents a bushel—even less if paid in cash. With the opening of the Ohio-Erie, they sold their wheat to a commission merchant or broker for about seventy-five cents a bushel, paid in money, not in goods. The merchant in turn paid a modest transportation fee to ship the wheat to New York, where it sold for well over a dollar a bushel. Even with the transportation charges taken into account, the merchant made a handsome profit. Soon local farmers no longer shipped bulk grain. They had it ground into flour at local mills which used excess canal water for power. The commission merchant then bought the flour and shipped it in barrels to the New York market. Reduced transportation costs also lowered the price Ohioans paid for goods imported from the East. For some time, until market forces balanced out, Ohio producers could sell dear and buy cheap.

Specialty trades tended to grow up around the peculiar trade patterns of each port area. Cleveland benefited immediately upon the canal's opening and became a growing commercial center dealing in a wide variety of exports and imports. Portsmouth specialized in corn, pork and bacon bound for southern markets. The canals enhanced Cincinnati's reputation as a pork-packing center and outlet for the rich Miami Valley.

New settlers poured into the canals' service areas. Population increased so rapidly in the 1820s and 1830s that it outdistanced growth rates elsewhere in the state. Vigorous towns—Akron, Massillon, Canal Dover, Coshocton, Newark, and Circleville—developed all along the Ohio-Erie. They were more than canal towns, however. Each had a manufacturing base which endured long after the canals fell into disrepair. They stand in contrast to towns like Boston, Peninsula, Clinton, Canal Fulton, Dresden, Lockbourne, and others that lacked the manufacturing base. As the canal languished, so did these towns, many of which remain pleasant villages to this day. On the Miami-Erie, the towns of Hamilton, Middletown, Dayton, Troy, Piqua, St. Mary's, Defiance, and Toledo owe much of their early growth to the canal.

Perhaps the canals' greatest service was their psychological impact. A state that had long felt isolated from the East, that had suffered serious economic disabilities by being forced to rely on the distant New Orleans market, was now part of the mainstream of developing American commerce. Confidence surged as people realized the fertile soils and rich resources of Ohio could produce a better lifestyle than was previously possible. It is more than happenstance that Ohio's emergence as a political power and a force on the national scene corresponds to this emergence from economic thralldom.

While the canals clearly put Ohio's modern economy into motion, their glory days were brief. The system did not pay for itself, and the state ultimately used public money to retire the debt. Undisciplined and expensive extensions and "improvements" in the 1840s enfeebled the state by greatly increasing debt and saddling it with costly maintenance and repairs for the benefit of marginal traffic. Moreover, after the mid-1830s, Ohio lacked the solid direction, planning, and oversight that the canal commission had

Ohio invested heavily in a network of canals as part of its internal improvements program. (Reprinted through the courtesy of the *Akron Beacon Journal*.)

brought to the early stages of development. The Board of Public Works, subject to considerable political pressures, succumbed to ill-advised schemes and became enmeshed in bureaucratic behavior that forestalled needed attention to the canals.

In 1861 the state leased the canals to a private operator who allowed the
system to deteriorate further. Large sections were inoperative and other sections abandoned. Adjoining landowners frequently preempted abandoned
canal lands, setting the stage for disputes which would last into the late twentieth century. The state reclaimed the system in the 1870s, but did nothing of
substance to rehabilitate it. Nearly every governor assuming office in the late
nineteenth and early twentieth centuries urged the legislature to restore the
canals as a vital link in Ohio's commerce. Their advice was ignored. The final
blow fell in March 1913, when a massive flood washed out nearly all remaining operative sections of the system. Only in a few limited places where
industries maintained the canal as an industrial water supply would remnants
of a once magnificent system remain.

Railroad Fever

Even under the best of conditions, the canals' lifespan was limited, because
a new, even faster and more flexible means of transportation—the railroad—
was on the rise.

Baltimore is usually credited with developing the first commercial railroad
in America in an effort to tap western trade in competition with New York
and Philadelphia. In 1830 the first few miles of the Baltimore and Ohio were
laid in Maryland. That same year, the Ohio legislature granted a charter to
the Ohio and Steubenville rail company, but no road was built. This railroad
activity, though aborted, demonstrates that Ohio was interested from the
start in this promising new form of passenger and freight transportation.

By 1836 Ohio had its first few miles of operating rail lines as the Michigan
venture known as the Erie and Kalamazoo connected Toledo with Adrian,
Michigan. The cars were drawn by horses and ran on oak rails. The following
year a steam locomotive was placed in service, and in time strap iron covered
the wooden rails.

Many early railroad schemes foundered before any track was laid. Charac-
teristically they engendered tremendous initial enthusiasm among optimistic
businessmen who rushed to get in on the ground floor of what could be a
profitable venture, but who also had no experience or direct knowledge of
what was involved in financing, building, maintaining, and operating a railroad. Typically, a group of local investors would secure a state charter incorporating their railroad company. Their own resources were seldom sufficient, so they sold stock to raise capital. After they had accumulated
construction money and secured right-of-way through eminent domain, road
gangs were hired, track was laid, stations built, rolling stock secured, and
personnel hired; ultimately the trains rolled.

That is how things were supposed to progress. However, it was difficult to raise capital, and enthusiastic state legislators tried to ease the railroad companies' plight. The "Plunder Law" permitted the state to invest in railroad companies of up to one-third of their capital requirement, provided the other two-thirds had been raised privately, but the law was repealed in 1840. Thereafter the state could not purchase shares in private companies, but it found other ways to aid the railroads, including selling canal lands to them at a fraction of the real cost. In addition, local political units continued to subsidize private railroad ventures. The Sandusky and Mad River Company secured help of this kind and opened its first sixteen miles of track, from Sandusky to Bellevue, in 1838. Ten years later it completed the line to Springfield, which subscribed $25,000 in company stock. The Little Miami, the first railroad to enter Cincinnati (1842), also received public assistance. By 1848 this line was completed to Springfield. Prior to the Plunder Law repeal, the state subscribed $150,000 in stock, Greene County $50,000, and Cincinnati $200,000.

The state chartered seventy-six railroad companies between 1841 and 1850, most of which never ran a train on company rails. But railroad fever increased in the 1850s, and 140 railroads were planned in that decade, with only twenty-five ever built. Nevertheless, Ohio's 299 miles of track in 1850 increased tenfold by 1860, when its 2,974 miles ranked the state first in track mileage in the nation.

These railroads, like turnpikes, tended at first to radiate out from the principal population centers, supported by businessmen anxious to enhance the economic climate of their town or region. Sandusky merchants, angry at being left out of the canal system, were especially quick to build rail lines. By 1851 they had a connection to Cincinnati via Springfield or Columbus, and their Sandusky City Railroad connected them with Mansfield and Newark. In other parts of the state numerous short lines joined to form long-distance systems. The earliest railroads had been oriented in a north-south line as had the canals, but the newly emerging systems tended more toward an east-west orientation. By 1860 four east-west lines crossed Ohio, and nearly every community of substantial size had at least one rail connection.

This new transportation nexus influenced the future development of Ohio cities and towns. Cleveland and Toledo, for example, both benefited because they were on the direct route between the east coast and the developing Midwest, while Cincinnati, on the other hand, would soon lose some of her preeminence. She remained queen of the river trade, and although her leading citizens tried mightily to make her a railroad center as well, it was now easier for some of her former suppliers and customers in the hinterlands to seek alternative markets for their agricultural products and competitive sources of supply for imported goods.

An irony of railroad building in Ohio is that this exciting new form of transportation was making its appearance while the extensive—and expensive—canal system was still under construction. Ohio's principal canals were state projects, yet the state also cooperated in bringing the railroad to Ohio. In doing so, it undercut its own investment, for the railroads quickly displayed advantages which the canals could not match. Railroads could be built almost anywhere. They were independent of the water sources which bound the canals. They were faster; early trains operated at fifteen to twenty miles per hour compared with a canal boat's four miles per hour. Rail lines could be joined into long-distance systems with a flexibility unmatched by the canals; this, in turn, allowed for flexibility in the location of manufacturing enterprises. Railroads ran year-round, not stopping as canal boats did during the four-or five-month winter freeze.

Public enthusiasm had been strongly supportive of the railroads in their early years, but it gave way to a growing skepticism, especially after the Panic of 1857 placed many projects in jeopardy. Railroad companies had oversold communities on the advantages they would reap. Many investors lost money in overly ambitious or poorly managed companies. In Akron, for example, Col. Simon Perkins, Jr., had to mortgage his extensive lands and holdings to bail out the Cleveland, Zanesville, and Cincinnati, of which he was president. He was one of the fortunate ones whose efforts succeeded. The Marietta and Cincinnati Railroad fell into receivership in 1857 after 157 miles of track had been laid. The historian of that line wrote: "As with many of the early railroads, an incurable optimism, buttressed to some extent by ignorance, contributed to the failure of the Miami and Cincinnati."

Railroad officials were sometimes arrogant in dealing with the public and with state officials. Landowners found them unsympathetic when employing their right of eminent domain to secure private lands for right-of-way. Farmers objected to engine stack sparks, which ignited dry grasses in their fields. Steam whistles scared livestock and startled people awake. Palls of smoke and soot settled on everything along the tracks and on the passengers, whose garments and luggage were often burned by sparks. Poorly maintained track resulted in frequent wrecks, many of them with fatal consequences. State officials resented the railroads' high-handed actions against their canal competitors, such as building a railroad bridge over a canal and leaving insufficient clearance for the boats and mules. In the early days certain Ohio railroads charged low freight rates on lines that served areas also served by the canals; they charged high rates where the railroad had a transportation monopoly.

On the balance, it is clear that the railroads' advantages outweighed their disadvantages by a wide margin. From its first introduction, the railroad was central to Ohio's growth and development. It sealed the state's emergence from the pioneer phase by thoroughly integrating it into the economic life of the East, the developing West and the Upper South. Ohio was now fully accessible. By 1853 Cleveland was connected by rail with Boston, New York, Philadelphia, Baltimore, Richmond, Wilmington, and Chicago, and soon would be linked with St. Louis, the Gulf of Mexico, and the Pacific, a connection completed in 1869. It took five hours and cost $4 to ride from Cleveland to Columbus; the trip to New York took only twenty-four hours and cost $10.

In addition to ease of transportation, Ohio derived many advantages from railroad capital invested in the state. Thousands of construction jobs were created. Local labor worked in train crews, as depot agents, maintenance workers, and supervisory officials. Further, the demand for ever-improved iron and steel rails was a boon to Ohio's basic metals industry as was the demand for engines and rolling stock. Even before the Civil War, the beginnings of the "railroad town" in which the railroad was the principal employer became apparent. Ohio was to have an extraordinary number of such towns by the end of the century.

But the impact of the railroad transcended economics. It was also a social phenomenon, a symbol. It was the link between small towns and the metropolis. It signified power, travel, speed, and adventure. It fed the imagination with the lure of distant places and exciting things yet to come. All across Ohio by the 1860s one could hear the beguiling whistle which represented these hopes and illusions.

Jacksonian Democracy and other Political Developments in Ohio

While money matters and internal improvements preempted the energies of many Ohioans, state and national politics vied for their attention. There was much support in Ohio for Henry Clay's "American Plan," whereby a protective tariff, favored in the manufacturing East, would provide income to be used for internal improvements, favored in the developing West. Ohio sentiments were also stirred by the Missouri Compromise, which introduced the slavery question into national politics in 1819–21. The general assembly instructed Ohio congressmen to vote against any extension of slavery. Of course, there was no unanimity on any of these questions, with the possible exception of internal improvements at federal expense; the plural character of Ohio's population militated against any uniformity of opinion.

Perhaps political sentiment can best be illustrated by the voters' response to candidates in the presidential election of 1824. For the first time in a national election, various states put forward favorite sons as presidential candidates. A congressional caucus nominated William Crawford of Georgia, the inheritor of the Virginia Dynasty's tradition. Then Tennessee put forward Andrew

Jackson, the Hero of New Orleans; Massachusetts nominated John Quincy Adams, son of the former president; Kentucky placed Henry Clay in nomination. South Carolina's John C. Calhoun was also nominated but withdrew from the race.

Henry Clay, exhibiting strength throughout Ohio except in the southwest, secured 19,255 votes. Andrew Jackson scored well among the Scots-Irish and Germans and won 18,489 votes. John Quincy Adams was strong in the New England enclaves and secured 12,280 votes. Crawford was not on the Ohio ballot. When none of the candidates received a majority of the electoral votes, the race among the three top vote-getters—Adams, Jackson, and Crawford—was decided in the House of Representatives, where each state had one vote. Ohio's congressmen were split; ten were for Adams, two for Jackson, and two for Crawford, so Ohio's vote went to Adams, contributing to the majority which made him president. It would appear Ohio's congressmen trusted Adams and his northern interests over the southern influences working on Jackson and Crawford. The voters of Ohio, however, had shown a decided preference for the Jackson or Clay style of leadership.

The old Republican party which had dominated national affairs during the so-called Era of Good Feelings now split apart with the National Republicans supporting Adams and Clay and the Democratic Republicans (soon to be known simply as Democrats) supporting Jackson. In 1828 Jackson got his revenge, winning the presidency from Adams and carrying Ohio by over 4,000 votes, with the Western Reserve again proving to be strong for Adams.

At this time America's first third party, the Anti-Masons, exerted modest influence in Ohio politics. The party grew out of charges that a New York man had been murdered by Masons for threatening to reveal secrets of the Masonic order. This revelation coincided with a rising tide of democratic sentiment in which the "common man" was increasingly the center of political attention. Secret organizations, of which Masonry was the strongest and most influential, came under attack as undemocratic and elitist, "sapping the very life's blood of our republican institutions." The Anti-Masonic party ran William Wirt as its presidential candidate in 1832. He received 509 votes in Ohio as contrasted to Henry Clay's 76,538 and the victorious Jackson's 81,146. In the state gubernatorial race, the National Republicans backed an Anti-Masonic leader, Darius Lyman of Portage County, who lost to the Democrat, Robert Lucas, by a substantial margin.

The Northern Boundary Dispute

The first Democrat to be governor of Ohio, Robert Lucas deserves much of the credit for securing to his state the disputed northern boundary region known as the Toledo Strip. The Ordinance of 1787 provided that the northern and southern tier of states to be created in the Northwest Territory would be divided by an east-west line drawn through the southernmost tip of Lake Michigan. Faulty maps led to the incorrect assumption that such a line would give Ohio the mouth of the Maumee and all of Maumee Bay, an assumption the Enabling Act of 1802 embraced. But it was discovered in Ohio's constitutional convention of 1802, thanks to information reputedly supplied by a beaver trapper, that Lake Michigan extended further south than supposed. Thus the framers of the state constitution asserted that, with Congress's assent, Ohio's northern boundary should be a line drawn directly from the southern extremity of Lake Michigan to the "most northerly cape of the Miami (Maumee) Bay"; this would then include the land north of the earlier, mistaken line.

Congress took no action on the matter, and in 1817 William Harris surveyed the line according to Ohio's claim. Michigan territorial officials countered by having the Fulton Line surveyed according to the language of the Northwest Ordinance. For many years Ohio and Michigan Territory were at a standoff on this issue; in the 1830s tempers heated up as the economic value of the Toledo region became ever more apparent. A comic-opera "Toledo War" ensued with each side threatening use of militia to secure its claim. Ohio authorities surreptitiously conducted a pseudo-court session in the region so as to claim jurisdiction over the disputed area. Steven Mason, the energetic twenty-one-year-old "boy governor" of the Michigan Territory, would not back down, nor would Ohio's Governor Lucas. Finally in 1835 President Andrew Jackson removed Mason and replaced him with John S. Horner of Virginia, who proved more amenable to working out an accommodation.

Once President Jackson and Congress became involved in the dispute, Ohio's chances for success improved. The political realities were obvious. Ohio, with two senators and several representatives in Congress, had much more political leverage than the Michigan Territory, which had but one nonvoting member in the House of Representatives. Furthermore, both Indiana (1816) and Illinois (1818) had been admitted to the Union with boundaries considerably north of the stipulated east-west dividing line and in both cases well north of the Harris line proposed by Ohio. It was in their interest to see Ohio's position upheld lest their own claims be challenged.

On June 15, 1836, President Jackson signed an act establishing Ohio's boundary along the Harris line and granting 9,000 square miles of Upper Peninsula land to Michigan, which was admitted to statehood the following year. In 1915 Ohio and Michigan cooperated in a resurvey of the Harris line which "satisfied" both parties.

Ohio secured about 400 square miles of valuable land plus the all-important mouth of the Maumee River. The legislature created Lucas County in the eastern portion of the Toledo Strip in recognition of the governor's significant role in securing it. However, one sore point remained to strain Ohio-Michigan relationships along the border. From the northwesternmost point of Maumee Bay, the boundary line ran northeastward through Lake Erie to the international boundary. Michigan claimed, from time to time, that it should run directly eastward and that she was the rightful owner of about 200 square miles of Lake Erie now within Ohio's borders. On this disputed point the United States Supreme Court ruled in Ohio's favor in 1973, presumably settling the issue.

Ohio's Response to National Issues

During Jackson's second administration, Ohio took rather predictable positions on issues of national importance. Ohio's general assembly and newspapers of all political persuasions strongly opposed South Carolina's claims that a state legislature could "nullify" unpopular federal legislation. A militant spirit inflamed some Ohioans at the prospect that South Carolina might subvert the Union. William Henry Harrison's son wrote to his congressman claiming "an indignation I cannot express against those who are for raising the standard of nullification, which I consider a decent term for rebellion and treason." Should the South rebel, he wrote, he would like to command a regiment of volunteers "from this part of the country" and "ride through the streets of Charleston." When Congress passed a Force Bill giving President Jackson extended powers to compel compliance with federal laws, Ohio's congressional delegation supported it completely.

Another inflammatory issue was the tariff, against which South Carolina's John C. Calhoun spoke out. The largely rural South would benefit little from such protection of American manufacturers while paying higher prices for manufactured goods. Ohio's congressional delegation overwhelmingly supported the Tariff of 1832 because it would shield Ohio manufactures, but also raise revenue that could be made available for aid to internal improvements. When Henry Clay proposed a compromise tariff to relieve southern anxieties, the Ohio delegation split, eight voting for the compromise and seven against, with economic nationalists opposing compromise and states' rights Democrats favoring it.

In other money matters, during Jackson's second term the federal treasury held a surplus which was returned to the states in proportion to their electoral votes, with Ohio's share an estimated $2,676,000. There was no lack of ideas as to how it should be used. The state legislature finally agreed to lend money to each county on the basis of population. County commissioners were to lend the money to private contractors who would use the funds on such projects of public benefit as internal improvements. Some of the money was to support the public schools. By 1850 the counties were to repay the principal to the state, which then would apply it against the canal debt. The counties conformed to this requirement although some delayed compliance until 1875.

The political consequences of the various economic crises during the Jackson presidency were predictable. Anti-Jackson economic nationalists had formed the Whig party early in the 1830s. Democrats blamed Whigs for the economic malaise and succeeded in gaining control of the legislature in 1839 only to be accused, in turn, of worsening the situation. In the election of 1838 the Democrat, Wilson Shannon, was elected governor over the Whig incumbent, Joseph Vance. Shannon, born in 1802 in Belmont County, was the first native son to become governor. A self-described "Jeffersonian," he distrusted the "high-toned" Whigs and sought new constraints on banks and bankers. He was ousted in 1840 by Lebanon native Thomas Corwin, a rising power in Whig politics who was to serve as secretary of the treasury (1850–53). Shannon was reelected in 1842, and so the characteristic tug and pull of partisan politics continued in Ohio.

While Whig battled Democrat in state contests, Ohio's political interests focused on the 1840 presidential race. The incumbent, New York Democrat Martin Van Buren, was again being challenged by William Henry Harrison, the Ohio Whig. While winning the presidency in 1836, Van Buren had lost Ohio to Harrison by an 8,000-vote margin. Harrison, born of a distinguished Virginia family, had come to the Northwest Territory to fight the Indians alongside Anthony Wayne. He served as governor of the Indiana Territory and commanded the western army in the War of 1812. From his home at North Bend just west of Cincinnati, he participated fully in the business and political life of the time. In 1840 Ohio's Whigs supported him in preference to Henry Clay, long a favorite of Ohio voters.

Historians have given much attention to the presidential campaign of 1840 because it embraced characteristics which were to become standard features of American political life. Harrison's enemies tried to picture him as an aging backwoods dunce and a log cabin rustic, but the Whigs turned this to their advantage by devising a "log cabin and hard cider" campaign that pictured Harrison as a man of the people. Torchlight parades, illuminations, and political rallies featured log cabins and hard cider. The candidate also made much of his military exploits, and his nickname—"Old Tippecanoe"—struck a popular chord. When the votes were counted, Harrison had won both the nation and the state by a comfortable margin.

At the time of his election, Harrison was the oldest man to be chosen president. Hair brushed forward over his brow concealed a retreating hairline. A long nose dominated a narrow face. The effect was not unpleasant. His age showed more noticeably in the stiffening of his attitudes and positions on political matters. Old friends were offended when he disregarded or failed to seek their counsel. Several Ohio men secured political preference, especially Thomas Ewing of Lancaster, who was appointed secretary of the treasury, yet Whigs, who had just gone through twelve years of Democratic dominance in the federal government, felt the rewards were not adequate.

We will never know what kind of president Harrison would have made, for just thirty-one days after his March 4 inauguration, he was dead of pneumonia, brought on, it is said, by standing through the damp cold of his inauguration festivities without a warm coat to protect him. His body was brought home to North Bend and buried in a grave overlooking a broad sweep of the river that was such an integral part of his life.

Meanwhile, through all of the political maneuvering on the state scene, the bank question remained a central issue. It caused disagreements within each party and between the parties. By 1839 a newly established state bank commission was attempting to bring order to the financial scene, but banking abuses continued. Finally, in 1845, with the Whigs controlling both houses of the legislature, and one of their own, Mordecai Bartley, in the governor's chair, the Kelley Bank Bill was enacted into law. Its principal sponsor was Alfred Kelley, Whig lawyer, banker, and entrepreneur, who had moved his base of operations from Cleveland to Columbus.

The Kelley Bill provided for the retention of specially chartered banks, but also provided for the establishment of the State Bank of Ohio, a consortium of independent banks with member banks located in each of twelve districts. The State Bank operated under a Board of Control made up of representatives from each member bank. By July 1845 the State Bank of Ohio was operating; it improved the stability of Ohio banking until, in 1863, the National Bank Act changed financial institutions once more.

The political and economic growing pains of this period were, perhaps, inevitable, as the young state hurried toward maturity. The lives of its people were changing in other ways, too, for as Ohioans became less concerned with mere survival, they became more concerned with establishing and nurturing those institutions that characterize and sustain a more advanced society.

✿

8.

The Pioneer State
Religion, Education, and Social Reform

Social change has long been characteristic of American life. This change does not proceed at an even pace; rather, it tends to cluster into periods of intense activity. In the decades following 1820, Americans experienced such a period. Much of the leadership for a whole spectrum of social change and reform came from the established eastern states. But the West, with its geographical and social mobility, contributed greatly to the new social thrusts. In Ohio one finds intense religious enthusiasm and diversification, the building of colleges, the emergence of public school systems, a proliferation of utopian ventures, and strong support for temperance, women's rights, antislavery, and other reforms. By mid-century Ohio's people had worked their way through the developmental stages of establishing churches and schools and had modified other social institutions, establishing patterns that would serve for years to come. Since its people came from many different social and cultural traditions, Ohio had as complex a mix of social practices as any state. Diversity in religion characterized it from the start. Public education evolved in response to pressures from conflicting traditions with regard to schooling and who should pay for it. Social reform sprang in considerable part from religious and educational stimuli. In Ohio as elsewhere, social movements were pushed forward by small minorities, but these dedicated few produced institutional patterns which had consequences far beyond what their numbers would suggest.

Religious, educational and social reform movements cannot be isolated from one another, nor from the economic and political context in which they develop. For clarity, we shall treat each of these themes independently, trusting the reader to remember that each is affected by the others.

The Church in the Wildwood

Religion has played a central role in American life from its earliest days: perhaps that fact has contributed to a popular misconception about the extent to which early Ohioans were affiliated with formal churches or religious bodies. This misconception permeates much writing about early Ohio, where coherent religious groups existed as islands in a sea of non-churched persons.

Certain clearly defined social groups conducted organized worship from the beginning of their settlement in the state. The German pietists—Mennonites, Amish, Dunkards, and Moravians—tended to settle in clusters, mainly in the Tuscarawas Valley and the "backbone" counties, and formed congregations. Quakers settled in the eastern and southwestern counties in groups large enough to support meeting houses. The early settlers from New England provide many examples of community worship; for example, the church was among the first structures built in Marietta, Hudson, Tallmadge, and other New England villages. Nevertheless, many Yankees who came to pioneer Ohio claimed no church affiliation. Some seemed to welcome the chance to escape the smothering embrace of church authority and payment of the church taxes collected in New England until the 1820s. Among them were moral people who lived in isolation or who simply chose to remain outside the church; some were indifferent to religion, others were scoffers and skeptics.

Squatters and "woodsies" who drifted into pioneer Ohio also remained outside the embrace of any organized religious body. They settled on the broken ridges and in the coves of the Allegheny Plateau where they were physically isolated from their neighbors. Some of these settlers were loners by temperament; others welcomed the circuit riders who sought them out and brought religious solace in time of need.

The fact that Ohio is the only state in which Congress set aside public land for the support of religion gave its first settlements a unique relationship to churches. One section in each township of the Ohio Company grant and the Symmes Purchase was reserved as "ministerial lands" for the support of organized religion. Income from these lands was doled out on a prorated basis to each religious body within the township. This limited and, on the whole, unsuccessful attempt to encourage religion and morality in the Northwest is of but modest lasting significance. Administration and disposal of these lands ultimately devolved upon state government.

Denominational Diversity in the Pioneer Period

Among the best-organized religious denominations in pioneer Ohio were Presbyterians. They were strong in the Miami Valley, in the Scots-Irish settlements of eastern and southern Ohio, and among New Englanders. The New England Presbyterians had formed a Plan of Union in 1801 with the Congregationalists by which they combined their resources in the thinly settled reaches of the Western Reserve. Here they shared churches and preachers and mutually supported the founding of schools. They also engaged in missionary work among the scattered Indians of the region and among their own New England brethren who had strayed from the fold. And many had. One early settler of the Reserve, Mrs. Betsey Austin, was so appalled at the "godlessness" she found there that she rode her horse nearly 600 miles back to Connecticut where she talked her former pastor—the Reverend Giles Cowles—into returning with her to redeem backsliders. Joseph Badger, the first missionary in the Western Reserve, found a fertile missionary field among unchurched New Englanders although his large family lived in abject poverty while he was about the business of saving souls.

As late as 1820 the Reserve was still undersupplied with churches, Presbyterian or otherwise. In that year the traveller Zerah Hawley reported that Ashtabula, containing about 750 inhabitants, had "no church belonging to any denomination." Missionaries, he said, "are . . . almost as much needed here as in the Islands of the Seas." A traveller touring the nominally Presbyterian Scots-Irish region of eastern Ohio about 1820 said there were few meeting houses, "and those for the most part wretched log buildings," except for the handsome Friends meeting house in Mt. Pleasant. "Religion and Learning, Churches and Schools," he wrote, "are all left at *loose ends.*"

In contrast to the underdevelopment found in some areas, handsome buildings and thriving congregations characterized Presbyterian efforts in Marietta, Cincinnati, Columbus, and other growing towns. In these places well-educated clergymen ministered to congregations which included many of the community's most substantial citizens.

Outside the cities, in the open environment of pioneer Ohio, the stubborn, self-righteous element within presbyterianism found fertile ground. The denomination split in Ohio, as elsewhere, into groups separated from one another by rather minor points of doctrine or practice. Each group nourished its particularisms even to the point of establishing colleges to train its young people in the "true" faith. Under their strict moral code, Presbyterians prohibited frivolous activities such as dancing and card playing. Sundays were reserved solely for rest and worship. A Connecticut youth who came to the Reserve in 1816 remembered his Presbyterian parents as "pretty rigid" because they would not let him "pick strawberries, hunt birds' nests, nor go swimming on Sunday." As an adult he regarded such strictures as "plain bigotry" and abandoned the church in which he had been raised.

Toward mid-century a more liberal element was gaining strength within presbyterianism. Many leaders of Cincinnati society attended the Second Church, where the distinguished Lyman Beecher preached. Beecher regarded himself as orthodox, but he and the Reverend Asa Mahan of the Queen City's Lane Theological Seminary were too liberal to suit the Reverend Joshua L. Wilson, longtime pastor of Cincinnati's First Presbyterian Church. Wilson brought heresy charges against both, though neither was convicted in the ensuing church trial.

Further strains within presbyterianism resulted from the growing antislavery controversy of the 1830s and 1840s. Nationally the church split into northern and southern branches over the slavery issue. Many Ohio churches were affected. In the Western Reserve, some of the more radical antislavery Presbyterians also followed a radical or "new light" theology. These beliefs led them away from orthodox presbyterianism toward congregationalism, fracturing the Plan of Union beyond repair.

Congregationalists, less numerous in Ohio than Presbyterians, were largely from New England. In 1809 Marietta's Congregationalists erected Ohio's first frame church building. Each of the state's principal cities had at least one Congregational church before mid-century.

Congregationalists were active in self-conscious efforts to create towns which would function as Christian communities. Among them were Oberlin, Berea, and Tallmadge, which was founded by the Reverend David Bacon, a former missionary to the Indians, who drew up a town plan featuring main roads radiating from the town center to the township lines. The town center was a large open circle in which, during the 1820s, local people erected a beautiful frame church which remains into the twentieth century as one of Ohio's architectural gems. Around the church Bacon hoped to establish a sacred community supported by a land tax paid annually to the church. With untaxed land available elsewhere, Bacon's scheme failed, but his community grew into a bastion of Congregationalism and a source of support for social reform movements.

The small number of Episcopalians in Ohio wielded influence disproportionate to their numbers because they attracted people of position and wealth. Virginians raised in the Episcopal, or Anglican, tradition formed the largest single group, but others of the faith came from various points in the East. One Episcopal priest, the accomplished James Kilbourne, left New England to make his fortune and his future in Ohio. As noted earlier, he was an inveterate town builder, and founded Worthington and helped develop Sandusky and Bucyrus. He speculated in land, ran a manufacturing operation, served in public office and still found time for his religious duties. His influence was eventually overshadowed by that of Bishop Philander Chase, perhaps the most prominent Episcopal clergyman in the state's early years. Under Chase's guidance, Kenyon College was chartered in 1824; a seminary was later erected nearby to train Episcopal priests.

The Methodists were the most aggressive of Ohio's early church groups. Zealously they sought converts, demonstrating an evangelical fervor and institutional flexibility unmatched at that time. Their Arminian theology (based on free will) won converts among some who had been raised in the predestinarian teachings of the Calvinist churches. Methodist emotionalism and informality appealed to pioneer people. Denominations which featured college-educated clergy often scoffed at the "illiterate Itinerant Methodists." One critic in the Western Reserve lamented that people were receiving instruction from "the most uninformed and fanatical Methodist Preachers." They are, he said, "the most extravagant Ranters . . . who bawl forth . . . their incoherent rhapsodies in one township in the morning, in another township in the afternoon, and . . . in a third place in the evening."

He might have been describing the work of a Methodist circuit rider. These clergymen or "exhorters" rode a regular circuit through the back country preaching and bringing religious services to isolated communities. James Finley, one of early Ohio's best-known circuit riders, rode the 475-mile Will's Creek circuit every four weeks. Many circuit riders were single men. The work was dangerous, exhausting, and poorly paid, $100 a year being a typical salary. Their reward was bringing solace to those in need and hope to those in despair. If their message appeared crude and unsophisticated to an educated elite, it rang true with those for whom it was intended.

Methodists made much use of the camp meeting, as did certain other denominations. Such meetings, held in forest clearings, attracted people from miles around, who encamped in groves around a clearing in which relays of exhorters preached "hellfire and brimstone" messages. Often the emotional intensity gave rise to hysterical excesses—fits, jerks, swooning, the "holy barks." Thus the camp meeting provided lonely people with emotional release, a release sometimes abetted by ample supplies of alcohol. The Methodists learned to control these conditions rather quickly, banning alcohol and discouraging emotional excesses.

Among the converts at one Methodist camp meeting was German-born Wilhelm Nast, a respected citizen of Cincinnati, whom the Ohio Methodist Conference appointed a missionary in 1835. He had little success among Cincinnati Germans, but he had better luck making converts on the 300-mile circuit which he rode every five weeks. He led the work which eventually brought 63,000 members to the German Methodist Church.

Methodist success in the rural areas was mirrored in the cities and towns. Methodism came to Cincinnati in 1804, where it gained strength rapidly.

Chillicothe Methodists claimed Thomas Worthington and Gov. Edward Tiffin within their fold. Tiffin was a Methodist preacher, but his high status did not protect him from church discipline. When he insisted on celebrating the birthday of a prominent Indian chief (doubtless in a "pagan" ceremony), he was charged with idolatry. A church court acquitted him, however, and he was restored to good standing in the church. By 1850 the Methodists had emerged as Ohio's largest denomination, claiming twice the numbers of the second-place Presbyterians.

Baptists were less successful in Ohio than they were in the southern states, but were an important influence from an early time. Like the Methodists, they permitted untrained exhorters to preach. A Baptist "called by the Spirit" could speak from the heart and testify to his faith. The Baptists' emotional, unsophisticated approach worked especially well in the raw regions of the state, but they also made inroads in the pioneer towns and cities, and by mid-century every sizable town had its Baptist church. Baptists organized a state association and founded Denison College (1831) as a training ground for their young people.

Lutherans in early Ohio owed their strength almost entirely to German immigrants although there was a small English Lutheran strain. While Lutherans were neither numerous nor especially influential in the state's early years, every Ohio town with a significant German population had its Lutheran church. Cincinnati, therefore, was a center of denominational activity, where sermons were often in German. Lutheran pastors were authority figures of central importance; they had great influence over parishioners. By 1850 the church was making important strides under the leadership of accomplished churchmen like Matthias Loy. Interest in education led the Lutherans to found Wittenberg College in Springfield (1845) and Capital College in Bexley (1850).

Like the Lutherans, the German Reformed Church traced its roots to German immigrants. This church was in the Calvinist tradition, however. By 1850 the denomination claimed seventy-four churches in Ohio. That same year members of this faith established Heidelberg College in Tiffin.

Germans of a different religious stamp left another imprint on pioneer Ohio. These were the Pennsylvania Germans (the "Pennsylvania Dutch") who had long been settled in Pennsylvania and elsewhere in the East. Mennonites and their spiritual offshoot—the Amish—established a presence in the first years of the nineteenth century. They settled in the "backbone" counties—Columbiana, Stark, Wayne, Holmes, Knox—and later spread into many additional areas, including Ashland, Putnam, Geauga, and Allen counties. Strict communicants, or "old order" Amish, adhered to a complex of social mores and rules which set them apart from the larger society. They persevered and remain today a living example of a pre-industrial agricultural society. Old order Amish have no regular clergy, eschew modern conveniences, maintain an archaic dress style, refuse to send their children to school beyond the upper elementary grades, believe in pacifism, and pursue self-sufficiency, rejecting government assistance.

Mennonites observe varying levels of strictness in their religious and social practices. The more "modern" among them are indistinguishable from their neighbors although in the middle of the nineteenth century they would have been much more distinct than they are today. Other groups which trace their origins to Pennsylvania Germans—the Dunkards (German Baptist Brethren) and the United Brethren—were present in small numbers before mid-century. Later immigration from Germany and Switzerland added to their numbers.

The pietistic Moravians had maintained a presence in the Ohio country since 1772, when they started Schoenbrunn, the first of several mission villages among the Delaware Indians. Although the Indian missions disappeared from Ohio, Moravian communities persisted, especially in the Tuscarawas Valley.

The Moravian and German pietists were pacifists, as were Ohio's most prominent "plain people" of the early nineteenth century, the Quakers (Society of Friends). During the first years of statehood entire communities came to Ohio from New Jersey, Pennsylvania, Maryland and the Carolinas. They settled Mt. Pleasant, Alliance, Salem, Lisbon, and other eastern towns, but located in other areas as well, especially in southwestern Ohio. As we shall see, their influence was far greater than their numbers, especially in the antebellum social reform movements. Mt. Pleasant in Jefferson County was of special importance to Ohio Quakers. Here was located a Yearly Meeting House, a large structure of unique interior design, which could seat up to 2,000 delegates who came annually to conduct sacred and secular business.

While trinitarian protestant churches dominated Ohio's religious scene in the early 1800s, nontrinitarian churches claimed the allegiance of small numbers. Universalists from New England came early to the state. They believed in only one manifestation of the deity, a view that orthodox trinitarians regarded as heretical. Especially strong in small towns and villages though not exclusively confined to them, the Universalists had fifty-three churches in Ohio by 1850. The Unitarians, who like the Universalists believed in a single manifestation of the deity, had even fewer. Unitarian churches were located in the larger towns and cities, and their parishioners, who were largely drawn from the upper socioeconomic level, appreciated their intellectualized approach to religion.

The Swedenborgians also had a presence in pioneer Ohio. These followers of the teachings of Emanuel Swedenborg, an eighteenth-century Swedish scientist and philosopher, called their communion the Church of the New

Jerusalem. Ohio's most famous Swedenborgian was John Chapman, the colorful "Johnny Appleseed" who roamed the frontier planting apple orchards, befriending isolated settlers and Indians, acquiring land, and earning a permanent niche in American folklore. Most Swedenborgians were conventional members of society. In 1850 they founded Urbana College to transmit their teachings to their young people.

Some people would classify Unitarians and Swedenborgians as "freethinkers." That term, however, relates primarily to certain Germans who immigrated after unsuccessful social upheavals in their homeland. Rejecting religious dogma of all sorts, they were often supporters of the "liberal" political and social causes of their time. There is no evidence that they had an impact on society comparable to that of the other religious bodies.

Outside the Protestant mainstream the most important religious body was the Roman Catholic Church. It was an immigrant church, its membership overwhelmingly drawn from Irish and German settlers, many of whom came to Ohio to work on the canals, the railroads, and in the emerging industries. Frequently these newcomers were stereotyped as ignorant, superstitious, and priest-ridden, useful only for menial labor or for the hard life of the army. They labored under a cloak of suspicion and rejection, thanks to long-standing Protestant fears that "popery" was a threat to free American institutions and that Catholics owed their primary allegiance to the Pope, a "foreign potentate," rather than to the United States of America. Through its first half-century in Ohio, therefore, the Catholic church was very much on the defensive.

St. Joseph's, Ohio's first Catholic church, was erected in 1818 just south of Somerset in Perry County. It was a log structure designed to serve the Irish who were settling the region. Elsewhere in the state Irish canal laborers, clustered in shanty towns near their work, had no resident priests. In Akron, for example, the local Irish were served by an itinerant priest who periodically made the long trip from Cincinnati to bring religious leadership to this and other northern Ohio communities. Not until 1844 were the Akron Irish numerous enough to form their own parish with a resident priest. Prior to that time Sts. Peter and Paul Church was erected in Doylestown (Wayne County) and was the first Catholic church in what later became the Cleveland diocese.

Cincinnati became the center of Catholic administration for Ohio when, in 1821, Father Edward D. Fenwick was installed as the first Bishop of Cincinnati. European nuns arrived in 1824 to assist in educational work, and by 1851 the magnificent cathedral church—St. Peter in Chains—was completed. Bishop John Baptist Purcell led the Ohio diocese as it developed rapidly, and native-born Ohioans joined the increasing flow of Irish and German immigrants to swell the church's ranks. Bishop Purcell defended the church's position on social issues, especially its desire to be relieved of support for public schools, with a vigor that alienated a growing number of non-Catholics. By mid-century Protestant alarm in Ohio over the growth in Catholic numbers and influence set the stage for political party action directed against the church.

Jews were present in pre-Civil War Ohio in very small numbers, mainly in Cincinnati. They were especially prominent in retail trades, many having acquired capital as peddlers, roaming the back roads to sell household items to isolated farm families. Some parlayed their capital into manufacturing, especially clothing. Cincinnati Jews formed a congregation in 1824, and by 1850 there were Jewish congregations in Akron, Cleveland, Columbus, and Dayton. Soon after the Civil War small but solid Jewish communities could be found in most substantial Ohio cities and towns.

Black churches have played a central role historically in marshalling sentiment and action within the black community. In pre-Civil War Ohio they were not well-enough organized or supported to provide more than a holding action against the injustices under which blacks labored. Cincinnati with Ohio's largest black population (about 3,500 in 1850) had the largest number of congregations, while Cleveland with its relatively small numbers had at least one black church well before mid-century. In the early 1800s, nearly all black clergymen were part-timers. Evidence is minimal, but it is likely that some of the efforts made by blacks working the underground railroad were church related. The African Methodist Episcopal Church emerged as the leading ecclesiastical organization among Ohio blacks, and in the 1860s it had acquired enough resources to take over and operate Wilberforce College.

One of the most interesting features of organized religion in pioneer Ohio was the presence of indigenous American religious movements. These religious bodies were, if you will, "made in America." Among the most influential was the Campbellite persuasion, founded in the 1820s by Thomas and Alexander Campbell, father and son, Scots-Irish ministers of the Presbyterian faith who discovered in western Pennsylvania and Virginia local practices which shut them out from their own denomination's sacraments. They were so disenchanted with this Scots-Irish Presbyterian particularism that they evolved a plea urging Christians of all denominations to give up the special doctrinal emphases that divided them, return to the simpler dogmas of the primitive church, and unite in the central truths to which all Christians subscribed. No denomination was eager to surrender its special corner on truth, however. The Campbells were attacked from all sides, and in order to defend themselves, they founded a new denomination. This group joined with the "Christians" led by Kentucky's Barton W. Stone to form the Disciples of Christ (popularly known as the Christian Church). The Disciples were considered to be radical, yet they won many converts from the Methodists, Presbyterians, and Baptists. They claimed ninety Ohio churches by mid-century, organized Hiram College (1850), and continued to thrive in Ohio.

The Mormons (Church of Jesus Christ of the Latter Day Saints) were invited to Ohio by Sidney Rigdon, a Campbellite convert and perennial religious seeker. He traveled to western New York State to visit Joseph Smith, the "prophet" whose visions involving golden spectacles, golden tablets, and the angel Moroni were the basis of this new faith. Rigdon persuaded Smith that Ohio was receptive ground for his doctrines. In 1831 Smith moved his community to the Western Reserve, and in 1833 the Mormons commenced construction of their unique tabernacle at Kirtland in Lake County; from this center the "prophet" acquired many followers, perhaps as many as 25,000. However, within a few years non-Mormons in the area became increasingly hostile. Communal land-holding practices alienated some; rumors of nontraditional sexual conduct affronted others; and those who held worthless paper notes from the Mormon "Anti-Bank of Kirtland" were aggrieved. By 1838, a year of terrible economic hardship in the West, most Mormons had followed Joseph Smith westward on the first leg of a long journey which ultimately would lead some to the State of Deseret, modern Utah. Joseph Smith and his brother Hyrum never reached this promised land, however; they were murdered by an Illinois mob. The small Mormon remnant in Ohio became affiliated with the Reorganized Church of Jesus Christ of the Latter Day Saints.

Possibly the most bizarre of Ohio's early religious enthusiasms was Millerism. The Millerites were followers of "Father" William Miller, a New England farmer who worked out a formula by which he purported to pinpoint the precise moment of Christ's Second Coming, at which time the world would stand in judgment. Thousands of people were caught up in the enthusiasm and abandoned their old denominations for the new. By 1842 Cleveland was the center of the movement in the West, and Cincinnati soon challenged its leadership. When Miller's targeted judgment day approached in April 1843, thousands of true believers wound up their earthly affairs. Some donned white "ascension robes" and got up on high places presumably to lessen the heavenward jump. The critical day came and went; disappointed believers had to pick up their lives again. Miller discovered that he had made an error in his calculations, and he advertised still another final day of judgment to occur six months later. Once again some true believers prepared to meet their maker, only to be disappointed once more. By this time Miller, who was utterly sincere, was becoming an object of ridicule as were his followers. In 1845 he helped found the Adventist movement. Although Adventists still believe in the Second Coming, they no longer set specific dates for the event.

Ohio's attractions for new religious enthusiasms were obvious. It was directly on the line of the westward movement, so that every eastern enthusiasm carried west through the state and affected it to some degree. In addition, pioneer Ohio was an open society, relatively free from traditional constraints on new ideas. No single sacred or secular belief was strong enough to dominate its people and enforce a particular form of orthodoxy on them. Furthermore, religious communities found that good land was still available at reasonable prices, a fact that people like the Mormons, seeking to establish new communities, found attractive. Finally, new and "peculiar" ideas did not press as hard on more traditional modes of thought and practice as would have been true in long-settled regions of the East. Even the Mormons who did incur suspicion and resentment were resented more for their social and economic practices than for their religious persuasions.

Utopian Experiments in Ohio

Ohio's receptive atmosphere attracted not only new religious persuasions, but also those special social units which historians call utopian societies. Such groups sought to separate themselves from what they regarded as a corrupt society by living in separate communities. Some were organized around a religious ethic while others were strictly secular. Most successful utopian groups tended to follow a charismatic leader, and when that leader was lost the ties which held them together weakened. Arthur Bestor, author of a classic study of American utopian societies, identified a hundred communitarian groups, three quarters of which were located in the Middle West. Ohio, with twenty-one groups, ranked far ahead of its neighbor Indiana, which had eleven. Wisconsin, Illinois, and Michigan followed in descending order. Although utopian groups located in Ohio, most sprang from roots that went back to the East and to Europe.

The Shakers (The United Society of Believers in Christ's Second Appearing) were among the most successful of communitarian groups. This movement, founded in England and nurtured under the leadership of "Mother Ann" Lee, spread to America late in the eighteenth century and appeared in Ohio early in the nineteenth. Strong communities were formed at Lebanon and North Union (Shaker Heights) and, briefly, at three other locations. Shakers were outstanding farmers, livestock breeders, herb gardeners, and fruit growers, as well as designers of furniture and implements noted for their grace and simplicity of line. They believed in the equality of men and women at the same time they practiced complete separation of the sexes. The peculiar shuffling "dance" which was part of their worship was a matter of wonder to outsiders and the source of the nickname, "Shaker." They took in orphans but apparently made no attempt to make them stay in the community as adults. As their numbers declined, these useful and productive people sold their Ohio lands and by century's end had largely disappeared from the state.

The Zoar settlement of German separatists in Tuscarawas County existed from 1817 to 1898, making it one of the longer-lived communitarian efforts. Under the leadership of Joseph Bimeler, the religious separatists from Wurtemberg made money to pay for the community's 5,000 acres of rich Tuscarawas Valley bottomland by contracting portions of the Ohio-Erie Canal. Everyone worked in this communal society, and property was held in common. The opening of the Ohio-Erie Canal ended Zoar's isolation, and outside influences pressed in. Following Bimeler's death in 1853 the community went into a long decline which ended in 1898 when remaining members of the community shared in a division of its assets. Other religiously oriented efforts to establish new social arrangements were made by Congregationalists at Tallmadge and Oberlin and, in 1836, by the Community of United Christians at Berea.

Efforts to establish secular communitarian groups in Ohio were unsuccessful. Owenite communities at Kendal (Massillon) and Yellow Springs had brief and stormy careers. Attempts to initiate French-inspired Fourier Phalanxes in a number of places failed, with only Phalanx Mills in Trumbull County actually emerging from the planning stage. Utopia, located upriver from Cincinnati, had a short lifespan. Invariably these secular efforts rose and fell quickly, probably because people attracted to unorthodox social schemes tended to be chronically dissatisfied with their lot and, when their new Eden failed to develop immediately, sabotaged the effort or withdrew. They had no faith in divine purpose to sustain them, as did the religion-based communities.

Social Reforms

Concurrent with the maturing of religious institutions in Ohio, support grew for certain social and philanthropic reforms. The initiative for these efforts came overwhelmingly from the Protestant churches. The rising social reformers shared the zeal for perfecting humankind that had characterized utopian communities, but instead of creating new societies, they remained within the existing society's mainstream, seeking to ameliorate certain of its conditions.

Social reform was not unique to Ohio although the state played an important role in furthering it. Much of the impetus and financial backing for reform activities came from the East, which in turn often drew support and inspiration from England. Participants in social reform movements included men and women, young and old, rich and poor, white and black, cleric and layman. Certain groups were, by their very nature, disproportionately involved. For example, though Quakers' numbers were few, their contribution was considerable. So was that of the Oberlin colony, which with its college was a Christian community infused with "New Light" reformist zeal, a magnet for all sorts of reformers who were looked upon askance by "Old Light" Calvinist traditionalists.

Reformers at work in Ohio between the 1820s and the Civil War were often involved in a spectrum of causes which they saw as interrelated. The span of activity was impressive. A score of national organizations, each with its state and local branches, addressed such causes as temperance, women's rights, peace, missionary work, and antislavery, the latter with extraordinary political consequences that will be examined at some length later in this book. At the same time, philanthropists were trying to improve the lot of the handicapped, orphaned, insane, and criminal. If the Kingdom of God were to come to earth, humanity must be perfected in all its parts.

Temperance

Alcohol lubricated work in frontier Ohio. The distillery was usually among the first buildings erected in a new settlement. While converting bulky grain into whiskey enabled farmers to move their product to market, and while much whiskey served as a kind of currency, the fact remained that much was also consumed locally. The traveller Zerah Hawley wrote that in 1820, Ashtabula's 750 inhabitants had "three very large whiskey distilleries and a number of smaller ones." That same year, Licking County boasted thirty-eight stills that produced 97,000 gallons of whiskey annually, of which 28,000 gallons were "exported," presumably in trade. Even if residents used some of the remaining 69,000 gallons in local trade, plenty of drinking whiskey was left to keep the county's 12,000 inhabitants well supplied.

One might say pioneer Ohio had its own kind of "high society." Residents consumed spirits at work sites, militia musters, social events, and even at religious camp meetings. Many stores kept an open keg of spirits, and a dipper, for the use of its customers. Whiskey not only encouraged social interaction, it was also believed to help ward off chills and fevers, and it temporarily dulled chronic aches and pains, as well as the loneliness of isolation.

Excessive drinking sometimes carried a social stigma. Public censure was directed at "town drunks," pitiful figures who were ridiculed more often than not and pointed out to young people as object lessons. Their peers played cruel pranks on them. Townspeople might dunk some of the drinkers under the town pump, or occasionally toss them into the shallow water along the canals, which, it was said, had "an instant sobering effect."

From an early time some individuals perceived alcohol's baneful effects on health, family, productivity, and public order. Some employers, including David Hudson and Simon Perkins, Jr. of the Western Reserve, stopped the practice of giving workmen partial pay in whiskey; the workers, the records show, were disgruntled. In 1829 Copley Township in Summit County (then still a part of Medina County) started a temperance society which claimed to be the first in Ohio organized under its own constitution. Putnam in Muskingum County organized a society the same year, and in 1830 Portage County claimed sixteen! By the 1840s well-organized temperance groups were active throughout the state. One such group, the Washingtonians, moved in from the East and secured a considerable following among church people and public-spirited citizens. Members wore cloth badges featuring George Washington standing beside a clear stream. A caption read, "If Health and Happiness you'd have, Drink only what th'Almighty gave." Other prominent groups were the Sons of Temperance and the Father Mathew Temperance Society, which worked among Irish Catholics. The societies circulated broadsides and pamphlets condemning alcohol, established small temperance newspapers, and supported lecturers, often reformed drinkers. Their efforts were directed as much toward the temperate use of alcohol as toward its total prohibition. Increasingly, however, reformers wanted Ohio to follow the lead of Neal Dow, who was moving Maine toward total prohibition. For years to come Ohio would debate whether or not to invoke "Dow laws."

Women were among the most active supporters of the temperance movement once it became institutionalized, as they and their children bore the brunt of excessive alcohol's effects. Old local histories make reference to mothers and children brutalized by a "ne'er-do-well" drunken husband and father. Many women temperance advocates were also involved in the concurrent women's and antislavery movements. The arena of social action was about the only place women could play a public role in the early nineteenth century.

Reformers always generate opposition. Resistance to the temperance movement was especially visible in towns with large German and Irish populations. Germans were primarily beer and wine drinkers while the Irish were partial to whiskey. In the back-country, Scots-Irish farmers traditionally kept their liquor jug handy. Naturally, those who owned and operated distilleries, breweries, and taverns were cool to temperance efforts. It frustrated travellers, looking forward to a drink, to encounter the occasional tavernkeeper who ran a temperance or "cold water" establishment. On his famous trip through Ohio in 1842, Charles Dickens had what he considered the misfortune to stop at a temperance hotel where "spirits are not to be had for love or money." His request for brandy was refused, whereupon he had nothing to drink but "tea and coffee . . . both very bad and the water is worse."

As Ohio emerged from frontier conditions toward a settled, mature society, the indiscriminate use of liquor abated. Not until well after the Civil War, however, would the temperance advocates succeed in securing the controls they sought.

Women's Rights

The women's movement in America grew hand-in-hand with other social reform efforts. Women who were finding their voice in the temperance, antislavery, and missionary movements were also directing their energies toward ameliorating their own condition in a society which relegated them to second-class status. They could not vote. They could not be guardians of their own minor children. The law made them dependent upon their husbands or their male relatives. The man was the head of the household and his wife had to obey his dictum.

Scarcely any occupations were open to women. Teaching was their most common vocational outlet, but here, as elsewhere, there was a double standard when it came to wages. Most women were paid far less than their male counterparts for the same work. For example, a pioneer township in Portage County paid its male teachers exactly twice what it paid its female teachers. Since many of the male teachers were single, there was little validity to the argument that men were supporting families on their pay.

Before the Civil War women were making a beginning in other careers. In journalism Josephine Bateham edited the ladies' department of the *Ohio Cultivator,* Amelia Bloomer wrote for the *Lily,* and Elizabeth Bisbee of Columbus edited the *Alliance.* (In the 1850s, Bloomer "scandalized the conservative citizens" of Zanesville by appearing on the City Hall stage in pantaloons and boots while delivering a lecture on "The Rights and Wrongs of Women.") A Female Medical Education Society, organized in 1852, promoted medical training for women. Most wage-earning women, however, held menial jobs in small manufacturing operations or worked as domestics.

America's first women's rights convention was held in 1848 in Seneca Falls, New York. The second, organized in part by Ohio women, was held in Salem in 1850. Ohio reformers were briefly invigorated by the idea that they might persuade the Ohio constitutional convention, then in the process of drafting a new state constitution, to include female suffrage; but that hope was soon dashed. The presence in Ohio of a substantial Quaker population and other supportive groups—Oberlin colony and college, for example—helped inspire the movement.

Frances Dana Gage of McConnelsville, "Aunt Fanny" to her admirers, was a leading spirit among Ohio women at this stage of the movement. She presided over an 1851 women's rights meeting in Akron during which local scoffers, including several ministers, heckled and badgered the speakers. Suddenly, uninvited, a tall black woman who called herself Sojourner Truth rose in the crowd and delivered a masterly rebuttal. As Mrs. Gage recorded the scene, Sojourner's talk "was pointed, and witty, and solemn; eliciting at almost every sentence deafening applause; and she ended by asserting; 'If de fust woman God ever made was strong enough to turn de world upside down all alone, dese women togedder . . . ought to be able to turn it back, and get it right side up again! And now they is asking to do it, de men better let 'em.' " Long-continued cheering greeted this. "I have never in my life," wrote Mrs. Gage, "seen anything like the magical influence that subdued the mobbish spirit of the day, and turned the sneers and jeers of an excited crowd into notes of respect and admiration." The simple eloquence of her remarks made Sojourner Truth's speech a classic of the women's movement in the late twentieth century. It is known by its refrain, "An Ain't I a Woman?"

Ohio's new state constitution of 1851 disappointed women's rights leaders. Neither women nor blacks received the franchise, but the women's movement did not fold. In 1852 the Ohio Women's Rights Association was formed in Massillon, but it accomplished little until the general assembly enacted laws in 1861 permitting women to own real estate and to make contracts in cases where husbands had deserted or neglected them, providing a court so authorized. An 1852 law to protect women in the workplace was the nation's first, but it was never effective. When the women's movement revived following the Civil War, Ohio women (and their male associates) would again press their cause on a state and national level.

Other Reform Activities

While some social reformers debated issues nationally and in Ohio, others directed new attention toward those citizens with special needs—the blind, deaf, mentally ill, orphaned, and imprisoned.

Two physicians serving in the state legislature, Marmaduke Wright and William Awl, persuaded their colleagues to provide state financing for care of the mentally ill and a state hospital eventually opened in Columbus in 1838 with Awl as superintendent. State money also helped support an institution in Cincinnati and, in the 1850s, new hospitals for the insane opened their doors in Dayton and Cleveland. In 1857 the state opened a small facility for educating "idiotic and imbecile youth." Care in these new state institutions was generally up to the level of the day, but most of Ohio's mentally ill were still held in county and local jails, where their treatment was indescribable. Ohio differed little from other states in this unenlightened practice.

The first facilities for the hearing and speech impaired opened in 1827 in Columbus, and in the 1850s they were expanded to accommodate 400 persons. A flourishing institution for the blind, conducted according to the best standards of the time, was established in 1837, also in the capital city. Orphans, for the most part, were cared for on county and local levels. Only those with handicaps or criminal records were apt to become wards of the state.

Humanitarians also urged prison reform. Jailers began to discard the extreme forms of punishment common to early prisons as solitary confinement replaced use of the lash or "cat" in disciplining hard cases. The Ohio Penitentiary in Columbus housed hundreds of prisoners who were employed in over forty shops within the walls, earning revenue for the state through their labors. Prison labor was a favorite target of the mechanics' associations and emerging labor unions, which saw the system as unfair competition to the free workingman and woman.

In 1857 the state established a reform farm near Lancaster, designed to take advantage of the best contemporary practices for holding and helping the juvenile offender. Legislators planned a girls' industrial home at the same time but it did not go into operation until 1869.

Ohio approached its responsibilities for the handicapped and unfortunate with humanitarian intent, yet it is uncertain whether this intent resulted in enlightened practice. Once the initial zeal of those concerned for social welfare faded and the humanitarians passed from the scene, public apathy allowed conditions to deteriorate in state institutions. Ohio faced then, and in decades to come, a continuing struggle to find the will and the money to keep its public charges in a healthy and humane environment.

The Rise of Public Schools

Local responsibility for public education is one of the great themes of American history although the country developed unevenly in this regard. While New England reformers and social uplifters led the way in establishing compulsory, free, tax-supported schools, more relaxed attitudes prevailed in the South and along the western frontiers, where physical and social distance made it more difficult to organize and sustain educational systems. Early Ohio embraced the New England, the southern, and the frontier traditions, which were in turn reflected in different parts of the state.

The celebrated provision in the Land Ordinance of 1785 reserving section 16 in each township for the support of public education indicates Congress's early interest in establishing an educated populace in the Northwest. The Northwest Ordinance of 1787 stated that "Religion, morality, and knowledge being necessary to good government and the happiness of mankind, schools and the means of education shall forever be encouraged." Congress passed subsequent laws extending the educational grants to newly surveyed federal lands in Ohio, the Virginia Military District, the Western Reserve, and private purchases. Ohio school lands ultimately amounted to 711,871 acres, or 1,112 square miles.

There was an enormous gap between the dream of an educated citizenry and the reality. Ohio's educational level actually declined in the first years of statehood. New settlers who had learned to read and write in the East saw their children growing up illiterate in the Ohio wilderness. Well-schooled easterners found no educational system to compare with what they had left, and well-educated immigrants despaired of their countrymen. For example, as late as 1846 a German traveller, Samuel Ludvigh, complained that in Cleveland only twelve children out of a German population of 1,500 were in school. He found a similar lack of enthusiasm elsewhere, partly because German parents resented having their children taught in the English language.

With few exceptions Ohio schools were primitive or nonexistent until population density was such that institutionalized educational practices could be organized. In the broken country of eastern and southern Ohio and in the back regions of the Western Reserve, schools remained inadequate until roads and canals opened up the areas and settlement became dense enough to support schools. Until then, as one traveller reported in 1818, schoolhouses were "very few" and for the most part "wretched." On the other hand, Marietta, Warren, Hudson, Cincinnati, Cleveland, Zanesville, and many other towns had schools which grew in quality as the towns grew. Here, however, it was local initiative which led the way, and such initiative was not present in isolated portions of rural Ohio.

The general assembly took its first steps toward organizing public support for schools in 1821 when it passed an act permitting locally organized school districts to levy taxes to build and maintain schools. State commissioners reported the next year that this permissive legislation was not effective. In addition, the reserved school lands were not producing sufficient income because township trustees all too often leased section 16 to favored persons for artificially low rates. A growing abuse, reported the commissioners, was awarding long-term leases to school lands so that income remained steady while surrounding land values skyrocketed.

Three men of New England background—Ephraim Cutler of Marietta, Caleb Atwater of Circleville, and Nathan Guilford of Cincinnati—led Ohio's next step toward a viable public school system. At their insistence, the legislature in 1825 *required* property owners to pay taxes to support schools. Opposition was intense from persons who believed the burden of education should continue to rest upon the individual rather than on the state. A good deal of lobbying was necessary, therefore, and the pro-education faction struck a deal with legislators who were trying to secure canal legislation. The school people promised to vote for the canal legislation, that was then before the legislature if canal supporters would vote for the tax bill in support of education. Both pieces of legislation passed, with the education bill receiving approval on February 5. The bill required county officials to collect and distribute a school tax not to exceed one-half mill. Township trustees were to set up school districts and employ teachers who had passed the scrutiny of a county board of examiners.

In 1838, newly appointed Superintendent of Common Schools Samuel Lewis, a self-educated New Englander who had migrated to Ohio, issued the "First Annual Report from this department for the State of Ohio," based on information he assembled while travelling about 1,200 miles across the state, mostly on horseback. Visiting 300 schools and conferring with officials in forty counties to gain an insight into the "practical operation of the system," he found much dissatisfaction with the system even though counties could now levy up to one-and-a-half mills in taxes. It would be unwise, he cautioned, to attempt to impose "internal regulations" on the schools. "It may take years," he wrote, "to secure a perfect uniformity in the system of teaching and conducting school business, with a people so varied in their origin, habits, and prejudices." When ill health forced Lewis to resign in 1839, the legislature abolished his position, but the responsibilities passed to the secretary of state. From 1844 to 1850 Samuel Galloway held that office and did much to strengthen Ohio's emerging system of public education.

During Galloway's tenure the Akron School Law (1847) was enacted by a local group of New Englanders. It brought together in a single package all the elements of a modern, graded school system such as we know it today. The entire village was constituted a school district within which there were to be common (elementary) school districts, each with its own building. All real property was taxed for support of the schools. An elected board of education oversaw the system's business and hired professionals to manage various operations. Classes were graded by level of achievement (i.e., first grade, fifth grade, etc.). A central "high school" could be established when appropriate. The general assembly recommended this model to other communities, and in 1849 adopted it as the Ohio School Law. In time, systems throughout the state converted to this model as did the school systems of many new western states. A new Ohio School Law enacted in 1853 simplified the school code, levied a uniform tax of two mills to be distributed to counties in proportion to the number of their school children, and established school libraries to be funded by a special tax.

Most students did not progress beyond the common (elementary) school level until private secondary schools, called academies or seminaries, began to proliferate in the 1830s. The first school in Ohio termed a "high school" was a private, stock-subscribed school in Elyria chartered in 1830. Soon thereafter the term "high school" came to represent the new level of free public education available in the larger communities. Such schools were few before the Civil War, and they attracted students from a considerable distance much as a college would. The 1830s also witnessed the beginnings of secondary-level education for girls; indeed, the origins of what later became the Western College for Women and the Lake Erie College for Women date to the secondary school offerings of that decade.

Ohio's schools varied greatly in quality. Nearly all township and county histories relate occasional horror stories about the local public schools while claiming that these schools were, on the whole, doing a good job. Until mid-century, schoolteaching was a part-time job. School terms lasted between six weeks and three months, but there might be more than one term in a year. While teaching was one of the few occupations open to women, the schoolmarm might be respected but was seldom accorded high status in the adult world. Young men (some as young as fourteen) often taught school for a brief period between their own student days and assumption of their lifetime vocation. Rutherford B. Hayes, James A. Garfield, and Warren G. Harding, for example, each taught briefly before moving on to broader fields of endeavor.

Considering the conditions under which teachers labored in pioneer Ohio and the miserable pay they received—a small cash stipend plus room and board in rural districts—it is remarkable how many of them brought skill and dedication to their work. Irene Hardy of rural Preble County was a case in point. She received excellent instruction in a one-room school from her father, a career teacher. She, in turn, became an unusually skillful and dedicated teacher, first in the rural schools of pre-Civil War Ohio, and later in California. She attended Antioch College soon after its opening in 1852 and later attended "teachers' institutes" to sharpen her professionalism. She found innumerable ways to challenge and attract her students, and her memoirs describe a lifetime love affair with her profession which resulted in excellent instruction for her pupils. In contrast are tales of "teachers" who were losers in life's battle, and who, through their ineptness and defeatism, were regarded with contempt or loathing by their charges. Some of them brutalized their students with the switch or with sadistic punishments. Misfits were most likely to be found in rural areas where there was little control over the schools. Progressive systems like Cleveland's or Cincinnati's monitored the quality of the teachers more closely. In the urban centers high schools were in operation before the Civil War, and the "professor" had emerged as a figure of respect.

The one-room schoolhouse—a log cabin with dirt floor, fireplace, benches, and writing shelves—prevailed in rural areas. There, children as young as five years old took lessons in the same room with adult young men and women. Irene Hardy was in school with "young men and young women, big boys and girls, and only two other little girls." Each recited lessons on his own level, sometimes aloud and simultaneously, creating a drone which could be heard a quarter-mile from the schoolhouse. The curriculum emphasized reading and spelling skills. Writing or penmanship was considered an art as well as a skill, and a "good hand" was valued. Ciphering (arithmetic) stressed rote memorization of rules as did most other subjects. There were no science courses although imaginative teachers often brought fossils, plants, insects, and other natural creatures to class for the edification of their pupils.

Ohio's substantial communities eventually replaced the primitive school-house with frame buildings with plastered rooms, heated by a centrally placed stove. Students wrote on paper instead of slates and sat at desks instead of standing at writing shelves. A growing selection of schoolbooks was available by mid-century, including Webster's *Spellers* and McGuffey's *Readers,* and maps were introduced for geography study.

The public schools did not serve all Ohioans, however. Blacks and mulattoes were not initially taxed in support of public education, nor could their children attend public schools. In Cincinnati well-disposed whites briefly operated a private school for black children; eventually black parents themselves were able to raise funds to operate their own schools in Cincinnati and Columbus. In Cleveland and Toledo, where blacks were few and posed no "threat" to the white community, black children attended public schools though technically in violation of state law.

A state law of 1848 established separate black schools in communities where there were twenty or more black children of school age. Their parents were to pay a property tax to support these schools. In communities where there were fewer than twenty, black children could attend white schools if local custom permitted. Just before the Civil War the state commissioner of public schools reported that "many of the colored schools are kept in mere sheds and basements; without decent furniture, or anything to render them cheerful and attractive. Their teachers, whether white or colored, are, with few exceptions, poorly qualified, and are employed because they can be had at small salaries." Very few black children attended these schools, only 4,888 out of 12,994 black youths enumerated; parents of school-aged children could not send their sons and daughters to public school even though they paid "heavy taxes" in that district. The commissioner reported that in Cleveland, where there were "perhaps no better public schools in our State," black children attended the schools "enjoying equal advantages with white children." Still, he lamented, "there are many places where the necessary instruction of the colored youth of the State is utterly neglected." In 1887 the legislature repealed laws requiring separate schools for blacks.

Another point of stress in maintaining a public school system centered on opposition from certain Catholic leaders, notably Bishop Purcell of Cincinnati. They resented having their people pay taxes to support a secular system of schools since their parishoners were also expected to bear the cost of sending their children to parochial schools. This issue flared in the 1840s and 50s and created deep resentment against the Catholic church. It provided additional fuel to those who maintained that devout Catholics who turned to the Vatican for leadership could not be totally loyal to the United States and to democratic government, thus fueling the nativist sentiments of the Know Nothing Party, which gained strength in the late 1840s and early 1850s.

The story of public education in Ohio would not be complete without reference to educators who produced textbooks that had profound impact on American life. Their influence was clearly as great as that of political, economic and military leaders since their work helped shape the minds of millions of citizens.

It would be difficult to overestimate the impact that McGuffey's *Readers* had on nineteenth century-America. William Holmes McGuffey, a Pennsylvania native, was turned down by school examiners as not sufficiently prepared when he first applied for an Ohio teaching job. Ultimately he qualified, taught in the grades and then in college, including teaching assignments at Miami University, Ohio University, where he served as president from 1839 to 1843, and at Cincinnati College and Woodward College in the Queen City. With some help from his family, he assembled material for the *McGuffey's Eclectic Readers,* the six readers progressing in difficulty and sophistication. The *Readers* stressed vocabulary, introduced students to selections from fine literature, and emphasized high moral and ethical standards. These *Readers,* frequently revised, sold more than 122 million copies. In the 1970s and 1980s would-be educational reformers insisted that McGuffey's readers be returned to the school curriculum. The movement failed to make any impact on Ohio schools.

Joseph Ray of Cincinnati won fame for his arithmetic texts, which systematized instruction in the subject, introduced "thought problems," and dominated the field for many years. New York native Platt Spencer taught in Geneva, Ohio, where he developed Spencerian script, a style of handwriting widely taught at a time when clear, attractive penmanship was prized. Painesville's Thomas W. Harvey wrote grammars. The works of these innovators, and others of their kind, were perhaps as instrumental in shaping American culture as any books of their time.

By 1850 Ohio had 11,661 public schools attended by nearly half-a-million students. If these figures are accurate (and it is prudent to suspect the accuracy of statistics from this period), then about one out of four Ohioans attended a public school in that year. Another 15,000 students attended one of the state's 206 academies. Clearly Ohio had come a long way in the twenty-nine years

Pioneer educator William Holmes McGuffey, whose "McGuffey Readers" were used by generations of schoolchildren.

since the first state tax support for education was approved. Yet at mid-century public education was a local responsibility, and the quality of its programs continued to vary with the capabilities and determination of local people.

Reading charts were part of the McGuffey instruction system.

Ohio's Early Colleges

Both the Ohio Company Purchase and the Symmes Purchase contained the requirement that townships be set aside for support of a college (two townships in Ohio Company lands, one township in the Symmes Purchase). The Ohio Company honored its commitment by setting aside two townships along the Hocking River and, in 1804, securing a state charter establishing Ohio University. It was located in the optimistically named town of Athens. Classes organized a few years later were more properly secondary than collegiate level, but by 1820 full collegiate instruction was available.

In southwestern Ohio, Judge Symmes ignored repeated efforts to make him comply with Congress's requirement. Nonetheless, Miami University, located on lands outside the Symmes Purchase, was finally chartered in 1809 and began instruction in 1823. The little town of Oxford—another great name in education—grew alongside the college. Both Ohio University and Miami University, Ohio's first colleges, received public assistance from the start.

Most private colleges were founded by religious denominations although the University of Cincinnati, which grew out of a medical school started in 1819, was nonsectarian. In the quarter century following Kenyon's founding (1824) by Episcopalians, more than twenty colleges were chartered. Presbyterians helped found Western Reserve in Hudson (1826), and Muskingum in New Concord (1837); Roman Catholics started The Athenaeum of Ohio and Xavier, both located in Cincinnati (1829 and 1831, respectively); Dayton was started by a Catholic order (1850); the Baptists organized Denison in Granville (1831); Congregationalists started Oberlin (1833), Marietta (1835), and Defiance (1850); Methodists founded Ohio Wesleyan in Delaware (1842), Baldwin College (later Baldwin-Wallace) in Berea (1845), and Mt. Union in modern Alliance (1846); Lutherans built Wittenberg in Springfield (1845), and Capital in Bexley (1850); Otterbein in Westerville (1847) was United Brethren; Heidelberg in Tiffin (1850) was Evangelical and Reformed; the Disciples of Christ had Hiram (1850); and the Swedenborgians founded Urbana (1850) initially as a two-year college.

Many other colleges which were vital places during this era have vanished. Franklin College, a Presbyterian school in New Athens, operated for over one hundred years before its remnants were absorbed into Muskingum. Farmer's College was once important in Cincinnati. Colleges failed at Scio and New Albany. Ripley College, opened in 1829 by the noted abolitionist, the Reverend John Rankin, once had 250 students, many of whom came from the South. The admission of a black student in 1831 split the college community and the town.

During their formative years early colleges were frequently little more than extended secondary schools. Some, however, could claim special distinction from the time of their founding. Congregational missionaries led by the Reverend John Shipherd started Oberlin in 1833 in a Lorain County wilderness as a "spiritual community" of town and gown. Its "New Light" theology set it apart from its Calvinist brethren elsewhere in the Western Reserve and gave it a radical reputation which it carried into the twentieth century. In 1835 Oberlin accepted the Reverend Asa Mahan and about thirty students who left Cincinnati's Lane Seminary in a dispute over antislavery activity. To secure these Lane emigres, Oberlin agreed to encourage black students to enroll. An occasional black student had enrolled in an Ohio college before this time, but Oberlin was the first college to seek blacks as a matter of policy. In 1837 Oberlin opened its doors to women, thus becoming the first coeducational college in America. The college also embraced manual training for students and pioneered in faculty governance and in virtually every social reform cause of the time. Otterbein, Mt. Union, and Antioch (1852) followed Oberlin's lead in coeducation.

In 1856 the Methodist Episcopal Church, whose membership was white, established Wilberforce College. The college was purchased in the 1860s by the African Methodist Episcopal Church, whose members were black. Located in rural Greene County near a sizable black population, Wilberforce was the first college in America established to serve black students.

Many additional institutions were established in the last half of the nineteenth century. By 1900 Ohio was noted for the number and variety of its colleges. College building continued in the twentieth century with much of the activity directed by the state, a phenomenon to be considered in a later context.

Except for the manners and mores of their time, nineteenth-century college students in Ohio were not appreciably different from college students of today. Prior to mid-century, all but a few were male. Some came from wealthy families and sought a "gentleman's education," but most scions of families with social pretensions went east to colleges with a long reputation for preparing the nation's elite. The majority of Ohio's students came from modest homes. Many worked part time to earn a portion of their fees. Job opportunities were limited, however, because colleges were often located in rural areas away from the temptations of corrupt and worldly cities. Students lived in dormitories and boarding houses. Some of the latter featured boarding clubs which gave members favorable prices on meals.

High spirits led to ingenious pranks and deviltry—assembling wagons on the roofs of college buildings, tethering a cow in the chapel, stuffing a professor's office with hay. This activity was a substitute for organized athletics, which appeared on campuses in the late nineteenth century. To minimize the damaging effects of pranks and to keep order, faculty bachelors were required to live in the men's dormitories where they served as monitors (and frequently as victims).

Social organizations were few and tended to be taken seriously. The fraternity system was obtaining a strong foothold on Ohio campuses before mid-century. Since the state had so many colleges at an early time, Ohio schools claim some of the oldest fraternity chapters extant. Miami University was the birthplace of three important national fraternities—Phi Delta Theta, Beta

Theta Pi, and Sigma Chi—the famous "Miami Triad." Literary societies were important extracurricular activities. Their members maintained small libraries, and they sponsored lectures, debates, and an occasional play. Students were devoted to these societies. In 1820 one dirt-poor student at Ohio University managed to scrape together $1.28. Instead of squandering it on himself, he purchased three books—*The New York Expositor, A Voyage Around the World,* and *The History of America*—for the library of the Athenian Literary Society.

In these early years of the nineteenth century, only an infinitesimal portion of the populace went to college. Parents, paying the bills, naturally expected that their sons and daughters would take advantage of their opportunities; it was not to be in all cases. Tom Corwin, the Whig political leader from Lebanon, sent his son to Denison College. The son wrote to inform his father that his health was suffering as a result of his studying. Tom Corwin's reply was terse. "I am informed that you are seriously injuring your health by study. Very few young men now-a-days are likely to be injured in this way and if you should kill yourself by overstudy, it will give me great pleasure to attend your funeral." How the son responded to this dash of cold water was not recorded.

Professional Education

Education in the professions—medicine, law, pharmacy, engineering, teaching—is now the responsibility of universities, but in pioneer Ohio qualifications for entering a profession were still minimal. Sometimes one merely told the world that he was a doctor and was accepted on his word, not on his credentials. Some early "doctors" evolved from caring for sick animals to caring for sick people and, in a day when medical science was little more than a name, it may not have made all that much difference. A brilliant exposition of the confused state of medical practice exists in the pages of R. Carlyle Buley's *The Old Northwest: The Pioneer Period.* Buley reminds us that the earnestness of the pioneer physician was no substitute for knowledge. Often he was not called until the patient was *in extremis,* so his arrival coincided with death. He was labeled, therefore, "death on a pale horse." It was said that "he healed slow, but he killed quick."

Transylvania College in Lexington, Kentucky, was the first medical college (1810) west of the Appalachians. Led by pioneer physicians, Ohio soon made efforts to emulate it by providing medical education. Daniel Drake, a distinguished Cincinnati physician, educator, historian, and philanthropist, was a leader in developing the Medical College of Ohio at Cincinnati in 1819. In its first fifteen years it graduated 239 doctors. Drake also helped establish

Cincinnati Medical College in 1835. Samuel D. Gross, professor of anatomy at that school, published the *Elements of Pathological Anatomy* (1839), the first systematic presentation of the subject in English. Another distinguished Ohio scientist, Jared Kirtland, helped found Cleveland Medical College (1843), an offshoot of the earlier Willoughby College. (Perhaps this was the college which Samuel Ludvigh described in 1846 as teaching "all branches of medicine and related sciences" in a single four-month term!) Also from Willoughby roots came the Starling Medical College (1847) in Columbus. Other medical schools, most of them short-lived, appeared elsewhere in the state.

One of the more bizarre impediments to effective medical education in pre–Civil War Ohio was the legal prohibition against dissecting human cadavers. Public repugnance against cutting up a dead body—the "temple of the soul"—had prompted states to pass laws prohibiting the act even while doctors were coming to understand the absolute necessity of dissection as part of their training. This conflict in perceptions led to a thriving "underground" trade in stolen bodies. Professional grave robbers (they preferred to call themselves resurrectionists), using special tools and techniques, extracted newly interred bodies and transported them to nearby medical schools, most of which contained cleverly concealed spaces in which to hide bodies from irate citizens. Cincinnati's most notorious resurrectionist, commonly known as "Old Cunny," moved cadavers in his carriage, propping them alongside himself so they would appear drunk. Upon his death, Old Cunny's unsentimental wife had his cadaver boiled down and sold the skeleton to the local medical college. Angry mobs descended upon medical schools when a new grave was disturbed. Professor Horace Ackley, who guarded the anatomy room with a small, loaded cannon, faced down one such mob at Willoughby Medical School. Convinced Ackley would use the weapon, the mob dispersed. The contempt for physicians and medical schools and the stealing of cadavers is evident in this bit of doggerel:

> Her body stolen by fiendish men,
> Her bones anatomized,
> Her soul, we trust, has risen to God
> Where few physicians rise.

The conflict between sentiment and science was partially reconciled in 1881 when the Ohio Legislature enacted an Anatomy Law permitting unclaimed bodies from public institutions to be used as anatomical subjects, but only under the supervision of a "Professor of Anatomy."

Dentistry was closely related to medicine, and training in dental surgery encountered some of the same frustrations and barriers faced by medical science. Dr. John Harris of Bainbridge (Ross County) was perhaps the pioneer educator in this field. In 1845 one of his students, John Allen, founded the Ohio College of Dental Surgery in Cincinnati.

Professional training for lawyers was similarly unstructured in pioneer Ohio. The casual manner in which men read law in the office of a practicing attorney, passed a cursory examination administered by a justice, and entered the state bar is well known. Essentially, young lawyers learned their trade as apprentices to older practitioners. Rules governing legal training in Ohio were lax in the early nineteenth century, but they were modestly better than those of some other states. In 1823, for example, a young Ohioan, travelling in the South, was admitted to the bar in Alabama after reading law for a few weeks with a practicing attorney. But upon his return to Ohio, he was required additional study before seeking admission to the Ohio bar.

Law schools had been functioning for some time in the East, and western lawyers, too, saw the advantage of formalizing legal instruction. In 1835 New Englander Timothy Walker, an author of legal treatises, moved his fledgling law school into a "handsome" new building in Cincinnati. A growing concentration of new legal talent, including Alphonso Taft, sire of a distinguished Ohio family, made the Queen City "a center for legal scholarship" in the pre-Civil War West. Other regions of the state boasted lawyers of distinction and influence—Elisha Whittlesey of Canfield, for example.

The science courses that were the basis for technical and engineering professions were not taught as discrete subjects in the pioneer period. If confronted at all, science subjects were part of an amalgam called Natural Philosophy. Not until late in the century did most colleges teach separate courses in geology, biology, physics, and chemistry.

Nonetheless, in pioneer Ohio a small number of skilled, largely self-taught investigators enlightened the West and the world through their work. Caleb Atwater, who revealed the wonder of Ohio's prehistoric mounds, wrote about them at length in 1820. The careful work of Ephraim Squier, a Chillicothe newspaper publisher, and Edwin Davis, a physician of that city, excited the scientific community. Their *Ancient Monuments of the Mississippi Valley* (1848) mapped and described scores of mounds, and their careful work is still interesting and useful.

Geology was represented in the southern part of the state by Dr. John Locke of Cincinnati, while Cleveland's Charles Whittlesey was an important contributor to the geological, ethnological, archeological, and agricultural knowledge of the northern regions. Whittlesey initiated the first geological survey of Ohio in 1839. Jared Kirtland, a Yale graduate, made numerous contributions to biological research as did the Columbus botanist, William Starling Sullivant. Ormsby McKnight Mitchel left the army for a professorship at Cincinnati College, where he led the development of the nation's first major observatory; in 1843 former president John Quincy Adams would cross

Ohio on a canal packet to Cincinnati to dedicate this observatory where, two years later, the nation's largest telescope was emplaced. Far to the north, in Hudson, Western Reserve College had earlier built the first collegiate observatory in the West, the second in the nation.

Hundreds of inspired amateurs emulated scientific activity on the professional level, collecting and classifying Indian artifacts, fossils, plants, insects, animals, indeed almost anything that stirred curiosity and imagination. Some collections eventually were given to colleges, museums, even to the Smithsonian museums where they contributed to a knowledge of the environment.

Educating the Public

Education involves far more than formal schooling. Once the pioneer Ohioan got beyond school years, he turned to newspapers, libraries, and lectures for his sources of information and opinion. One measure of a society's maturity is the degree to which it provides these resources.

It is not always clear what constitutes a library. If we assume it is a collection of reading materials which can be borrowed, then a number of Ohio towns have a claim to being among the first to operate one. Belpre, in Washington County, had a circulating collection in the late 1790s; Dayton and Cincinnati followed soon after. The famous "coonskin library" at Amesville, in Athens County, was assembled in 1803 from books donated by settlers. Additional volumes were purchased from funds secured by selling coonskins and other hides. To be eligible to borrow books, one had to pay annual dues of $2.50, a sum many paid in coonskins. This fine old collection is now on display at the Ohio Historical Center. By 1840 at least 140 libraries had been incorporated in Ohio although all but a handful were small and sporadically managed. Most were subscription libraries that loaned to paying members only rather than circulating libraries open to the public. Some special collections appeared at an early time, among them the State Library, established in 1817 to provide information to state officials.

Ohioans not only collected books, they also published them. Before mid-century nearly every sizable Ohio town contained publishing houses producing books, pamphlets, or maps. Cincinnati stood alone as the publishing center of the West, a large part of that business in schoolbooks. Dayton, Springfield, Canton, Akron, Columbus, and Cleveland had all taken steps which, after the Civil War, were to make them important publishing centers.

Another form of public education was the lyceum, an open forum where speakers informed the public about the ideas of the time. In the larger towns meeting halls provided a decorous setting for these programs focusing on culture and ideas. Arrangements were more casual in smaller towns, but popular response was no less enthusiastic, and many of the nation's great came to Ohio on the lecture circuit. Ralph Waldo Emerson was a favorite wherever he went although his liberal philosophy was none too palatable in areas where strong Calvinist orthodoxy flourished. Local communities formed literary societies and philosophical societies whose members read papers and discussed issues. In some towns blacks had their own debating societies. For one such group, meeting in Akron in 1851, the question before the house was, "Which have the greatest reason to complain of the treatment of the whites, the Indian or the African?" On a vote, the Africans were thought to have the greater reason.

Libraries and lyceums affected public attitudes, but newspapers were the main source of local, national, and international information. The first newspaper beyond the Ohio was *The Centinel of the North-Western Territory,* first published on November 9, 1793. The editor of this Cincinnati paper introduced himself to his readers by noting that the *Centinel* would not only "inform them of what is going on to the east of the Atlantic in arms, and in arts of peace—but what more particularly concerns us, the different transactions of the states in the union, and especially of our own territory." This was the model followed by most papers. Published weekly, they were bulletin boards of local happenings, but they also printed snippets from papers elsewhere, keeping Ohioans informed, albeit somewhat belatedly, of national and international events. In addition to news, early papers printed poetry, essays, and original stories; in short, they provided a vehicle for literary endeavors.

As business ventures, most newspapers were on shaky ground, hence the rapidity with which they rose and fell. Often the impetus for starting a newspaper was a transient political or moral issue, and the paper died with the issue. Papers were often absorbed by a competitor. Some, however, enjoyed a long period of continuous publication. By 1826 Ohio had at least sixty newspapers, a number that rose to approximately 145 in 1840. Cincinnati, with numerous papers, was the state leader and maintained its primacy until after the Civil War.

Early newspapers were especially influential as political beacons. Nearly all engaged in special pleading for the party of the editor's choice or vigorously pilloried the editor's political enemies. This sharp individualism gave editors visibility and importance in political affairs. Charles Hammond, the former St. Clairsville Federalist, became editor of the *Cincinnati Gazette,* whose columns he used to scourge Andrew Jackson and his Democratic followers. The *Cincinnati Enquirer* evolved out of several earlier ventures to become the state's leading Democratic paper in the 1840s. The *Ohio State Journal* in Columbus was Whig in sympathy while the city's *Ohio Statesman* was in the hands of a rabid Democrat, Samuel Medary, from 1837 to 1853. Before mid-century strong newspapers were established in each of Ohio's principal cities. From these roots sprang such distinguished and long-lived papers as the *Cleveland Plain Dealer*, the *Dayton Daily News*, the *Akron Beacon Journal*, the *Canton Repository*, the *Toledo Blade*, the *Youngstown Vindicator*, and the *Columbus Dispatch*.

Cultural Contributions of the Pioneer State

The preeminent fact of life in early Ohio, for all but a tiny fraction of her people, was the daily struggle to survive and to enhance one's material well being. Clearing the land, erecting buildings, paying off the mortgage, tending crops and livestock, protecting one's stake against the forces of man and nature—these were the overriding concerns. There was little leisure time for the cultivation of the arts. Until the state matured, until it had accumulated surplus wealth and some of its people had time left over from making a living, little artistic and literary activity could be expected.

Not until Ohio's lands had been open for a generation was there a locally written history to record the early days of trial. A young Cincinnati lawyer, Salmon P. Chase, published a "Preliminary Sketch of the History of Ohio" in 1833, perhaps the first attempt at a state history. Five years later, Caleb Atwater of Circleville published his *History of the State of Ohio*. Henry Howe, a Virginian, toured the pioneer state and recorded much of its history in his *Historical Collections of Ohio* in 1846, the first of many editions. Samuel P. Hildreth of Marietta published *Pioneer History* in 1848, and from it we still glean much of what we know about the beginnings of settlement in the Ohio Company lands.

Literary magazines made their appearance in Ohio by 1825. They provided an outlet for the work of westerners, whose efforts were seldom appreciated in eastern magazines. Cincinnati again led the way, as Judge James Hall established *The Western Monthly Magazine* in 1833. During its brief existence, the magazine published the literary efforts of a number of Cincinnatians, including Harriet Beecher, who, as Harriet Beecher Stowe, would become world famous as the author of *Uncle Tom's Cabin*. Other contributors to the magazine were Benjamin Drake, brother of the well-regarded Daniel Drake, along with Otway Curry, a poet of some distinction, and William D. Gallagher, a journalist who also wrote poetry. When Judge Hall defended Catholicism and opposed the immediate abolition of slavery he aroused opposition which resulted in his magazine's decline; it ceased operation in 1837. By the 1840s numerous periodicals provided Ohio writers outlets for novelettes, short stories, poems, and other occasional pieces. Inexpensive action novels became popular in that same decade. Emerson Bennett and Edward Z. C. Judson, both easterners who lived in Ohio, excelled in this genre. Bennett wrote *Prairie*

Flower, Forest Rose, and other bestsellers. Judson achieved fame in the West as
"Ned Buntline," his generation's most famous writer of "dime novels."

Popular ladies' magazines were published in Cincinnati, Ohio City (later a
part of Cleveland), Akron, and Zanesville from an early time. By 1827 a
magazine called *Social Circle* was published in Mt. Pleasant by Miss Rebecca
Bates. William Gallagher published *Minerva* in Cincinnati, and one of its most
popular writers was Ohio-born Mrs. Julia L. Dumont, whose stories rejected
cloying sentimentality in favor of greater realism. Cincinnati's *Ladies' Repository* was sponsored by the Methodist church and claimed a circulation of
31,000 by 1857. It featured religious, intellectual, and morally uplifting articles. The Methodists also published religious periodicals as did other strong
Ohio denominations. In cities where the German element was important, the
German-language press produced newspapers, religious tracts and other
timely pieces.

Poetry was a favorite preoccupation of the literate in early nineteenth-
century Ohio. Schools taught it, budding scholars wrote it, and newspapers,
periodicals, and books published it. Many western poets copied the subjects
and styles of their eastern counterparts, the result being an artificial and
stilted poetry dealing with themes unrelated to the Ohio experience. William
Gallagher was influential in helping overcome this devotion to eastern standards by writing poems about the landscapes and scenes of the new West.

Among western poets of this period were Alice and Phoebe Cary of Hamilton County, whose early work, published first in Cincinnati newspapers and
later in separate volumes, brought them a growing reputation. In common
with aspiring artists elsewhere in the United States, they relocated in New
York, where their reputations continued to grow. Much of their poetry is too
maudlin for present tastes, but it struck a responsive chord in its time.

Unlike the literary arts, the visual arts in pioneer Ohio were imitative, and
no Ohio "school" emerged. Itinerant portraitists painted in every part of the
state, nearly all of them born elsewhere and wandering to Ohio seeking commissions. A few had been brought to the new state by their families while still
very young and had learned their craft in the emerging towns and cities of
Ohio. Among those who displayed considerable talent were William Wat-
kins of Steubenville, Charles Soule, Jr. of Dayton, and Lily Martin, Sala Bos-
worth, and Charles Sullivan of Marietta.

Next to portraiture, landscapes or epic scenes seemed to appeal most to
Ohio's people. The list of those who contributed fine works in these genres is
too long to include here, but one must mention the English-born Thomas Cole
who, during his brief residence in Steubenville, painted the Ohio Valley in a
style later perfected when he moved east and became associated with the
famous Hudson River school. The native-born Alexander Helwig Wyant of
Tuscarawas County was another whose landscapes found favor. In Cincinnati

and Springfield, the Frankenstein family, German immigrants, added to the richness of the region's artistic life; Godfrey Frankenstein achieved acclaim for a huge panorama of Niagara Falls.

Cincinnati led the way in Ohio's artistic awareness even as it did in other fields. Indeed, the "Athens of the West," as enthusiasts called it, was the only western city to command an active artistic life of the sort found in Boston, Philadelphia and, increasingly, New York. One might characterize the Queen City as a cultural island in which a critical mass of artistic activity and consciousness had emerged. This was due to its cosmopolitan population (especially the German influence), its increasing wealth and sophistication, and the example set by some of its leading citizens. The estimable Nicholas Longworth was patron to many aspiring artists, among them painters Lily Martin, Thomas Read, and Alexander Wyant, and sculptors Shobal Vail Clevenger and Hiram Powers, the latter two receiving from him funds which enabled them to study in Italy. Powers, after developing his skills in his Cincinnati home, moved to the East, where he became the preeminent American sculptor of his time. His statuette, *The Greek Slave,* was among his best-known pieces and was widely copied even though the undraped female torso shocked moralists who had perhaps forgotten the great classic statues of the Greeks and Romans. John Quincy Adams Ward, born near Urbana, was another Ohio sculptor who, like Powers, would in later years achieve national prominence.

Architecture was another derivative artistic form in pioneer Ohio. From an early day the prosperous merchants of Marietta and Cincinnati erected imposing private residences. Among the most famous and enduring was the Cincinnati home of Martin Baum (1820) with its elegant furnishings and grand paintings reminding later generations that luxury and good taste were represented in the West. The vast influx of Germans in the 1840s gave certain Cincinnati buildings a distinct German flavor. The Virginia Military District, as one might expect, showed southern architectural influences. Since the southerners who came to Ohio were mainly from upland regions, there is little of the tidewater plantation influence although Thomas Worthington's home, Adena (1807), at Chillicothe, is in the genteel southern tradition, complete with outbuildings. On first arriving in Ohio the Worthingtons lived in a log cabin, then moved into an expanded cabin home, and finally moved into their grand new estate. For the fortunate, this progression up the scale was common as the crudities of the frontier period gave way to the comforts of an established society, so that the upland southern farmhouse, once quite common in the southern part of the state, has for the most part disappeared or been modified beyond recognition.

In portions of the Backbone counties and along the National Pike, Pennsylvania Germans built stone houses which gave a distinctive look to those regions. The Western Reserve was a bit of New England transplanted to Ohio. Towns such as Canfield, Poland, Hudson, Medina, Burton, and numerous others featured substantial frame houses and public buildings spaced on large lots around a commons. Many houses, churches, and public buildings in the New England regions of the state were built by master craftsmen like Samuel and Lemuel Porter, who did some of the finest work in the Reserve.

A distinct Western Reserve house style also evolved. It featured a two-story section with a one story extension to one side. Splendid examples of buildings in the Federal and the Greek Revival styles still grace the towns of the Reserve and New England enclaves such as Granville.

Among Ohio's architectural accomplishments was the Statehouse whose construction commenced in 1839 but was delayed by politics, disputes, and money shortages. When finally "completed" in the 1850s, it featured a truncated dome in place of the full dome originally planned. This fine Greek Revival building, built in part with convict labor, provided Ohio with an imposing capitol although detractors referred to it as a "cheese box on a raft."

Early Ohio structures were usually built of native materials, with locally quarried limestone and sandstone serving most needs. Ohio-made brick was a common material and local forests supplied outstanding timber for frames, siding, and shingles. Woodworkers made fine finishings and furniture from cherry, walnut, and other prized woods which were near at hand. Ohioans imported most fine furniture (including mahogany pieces) and the more elegant furnishings from the East until the state had matured to the point where local producers made these goods. Well before the Civil War Ohio craftsmen were turning out beautiful pianos, organs, and furniture of all sorts. The state's clay and glassworks were producing fashionable ware for the wealthy and functional ware for all. Thus the roots of flourishing businesses which would make Ohio a leader, later in the nineteenth century, in the manufacture of fine products for the home began to take hold in the pioneer period.

While architectural and craft artifacts remain to tell the story of these arts in Ohio, it is more difficult to assess the role of music. Old letters and journals seem to indicate that familiar folk songs were sung wherever a country fiddler could be found. Settlers sang hymns in the home and in most churches; some churches would permit vocal music only, with no organ or other instrumental accompaniment allowed. One does not read of pioneer farmers whistling while they worked, but it would seem likely that some did, just as the housewife probably hummed to herself while doing chores. For organized musical performances, however, the Germans were the most active. Each German community had its singing societies, bands, and orchestras, and since Cincinnati had the largest German contingent, it took the lead in providing these cultural outlets. Welsh immigrants also made notable contributions to early Ohio music, especially vocal music, and in time their singing festivals rivaled the Germans' in size and excellence.

One substantial Ohio contribution to musical entertainment was the minstrel show. Early in the 1840s, Tom Rice and Edwin Forrest presented the first show of this kind in Cincinnati. However, it was Daniel Decatur Emmett of Mt. Vernon who devised and popularized the classic formula for these shows in 1843. White men in blackface parodied the Negro in song and dance. Ironically, Emmett's composition, "In Dixie's Land," adapted from a song composed by the Snowdens, a Knox County African-American family of musicians, later known simply as "Dixie," was adopted by the Confederacy as its rallying song during the Civil War years. Songs that Stephen Foster wrote for minstrel shows made him famous. He composed some while working as a Cincinnati bookkeeper, but most were written after he returned to his Pennsylvania home.

Professional theater as an entertainment medium was growing with Ohio, and as with the other arts, Cincinnati led the way. It boasted the biggest and busiest theaters and early became an important stop for national touring companies. By the 1830s Columbus had two theater buildings although one was soon shut down as a public nuisance. By mid-century nearly every town of size had a "hall" or an "opera house" to accommodate travelling companies of actors who journeyed by every mode available—wagon, stagecoach, canal boat, steamship, and railroad. Well before mid-century showboats had appeared on the Ohio. These gaudy and dazzling vessels brought glamour and escape to drab river towns, creating a romantic aura that persists to this day. On occasion plays were presented from barges on the canals.

In some localities the idea that the theater was sinful lingered on, but increasingly plays came to be accepted as entertainment. Ohio made little original contribution to the theater in the first decades of the nineteenth century, but after the Civil War contributed important innovators and a seemingly unending supply of theatrical talent to the American stage.

Thus in its formative years Ohio participated in the cultural activities common to America. Much of the talent and much of the taste of pioneer Ohio was derivative. But by mid-century, a mature and confident state was ready to assume a new level of leadership in all aspects of American life.

9

Antislavery and Antebellum Politics in Ohio

 **In the decades preceding** the Civil War, the Ohio political scene shifted in response to both internal and external currents. Internally, state politics responded to economic and ethnocultural conditions, and, as the nation moved toward separation, all the diverse currents in national affairs buffeted the state. Ohio's free blacks, many of them fugitives from slavery, were "kept in their place," but in some sections lived under fewer restraints than blacks commonly endured in free states.

Of the western states, Ohio was most heavily involved in the great issues and events that surrounded the institution of slavery and its possible extension into the territories. Antislavery sentiment played a major part in determining the state's political realignments in the 1840s and 1850s, and in 1860, when the political battle lines were clear, Ohio supported the newly elected president, Abraham Lincoln, and his determination to preserve the Union.

The Black Experience in Pioneer Ohio

From the earliest days of statehood, Ohio blacks were relegated to an inferior position. While often serving as pawns in political contests, they were denied the vote, deprived of certain basic civil liberties (e.g., they could not serve on juries or testify against whites), banned from the militia, excluded from some public services such as the "poor house," and prevented from sending their children to the public schools. The attitude of whites toward blacks was what later generations would label "racist." The general assembly epitomized "racist" sentiment in 1804 by enacting laws designed to slow black migration to Ohio. Upon entering the state, a black had to post bond for $500 (presumably so he would not become a public charge) and had to file evidence of his free status with local authorities. These and other restrictive acts were referred to as "black laws." These provisions were generally ignored.

Even well-disposed whites perceived blacks as an inferior race, incapable of developing the full equivalent of white accomplishments and virtue. Ohioans were determined to keep the state "white man's country." From today's vantage point it seems clear that fears of a massive black migration to Ohio were exaggerated, but for forty years prior to the Civil War those fears motivated many whites.

In the 1820s only a few thousand blacks lived in the state. Though technically free, small numbers still served in de facto slavery in scattered regions of the southern counties. Forty years later, on the eve of the Civil War, Ohio was home to just 36,700 blacks, slightly more than 2 percent of the population. By 1850 blacks were unevenly distributed throughout the state, with the largest concentrations in Hamilton, Ross, Gallia, and Franklin counties. Hamilton County, with 3,600 persons, accounted for 10 percent of the total black population. The southwestern quadrant outside Hamilton County, plus the eastern counties of Muskingum, Belmont, and Jefferson also contained heavy concentrations.

Many of their white neighbors had slave-state origins and retained strong negative perceptions of blacks. An economic consideration also perpetuated racist attitudes. In Cincinnati especially, and to some extent in other southern Ohio towns, poor whites had to compete with blacks for unskilled jobs. Furthermore, commercial connections with slaveholding states predisposed southern Ohio businessmen to assert the same attitudes on racial matters as their southern trading partners.

This climate lent itself to racial paranoia. In 1829, as earlier noted, hundreds of blacks left Cincinnati for Canada following riots caused in part by job competition from Irish immigrants. In 1830 citizens of Portsmouth drove about eighty black residents from their town. Even in rural areas blacks were not necessarily secure: in the Scioto Valley hostile white neighbors drove black settlers from their farms.

Fears of a black influx into Ohio were intensified by the colonization movement. The American Colonization Society (1816) proposed to raise funds from public and private sources to send blacks "back to Africa," the presumed land of their forefathers. The society secured Liberia on the west African coast as a place for the relocation. This prospect for a black haven in Africa encouraged a small number of southern idealists to free their slaves, but funds were never adequate to send free blacks and recently freed slaves to

Africa. Furthermore, why should blacks "return to Africa"? Most had never been there! Since free blacks were unwelcome in the slaveholding South, northerners feared that colonization efforts would cause a great flood of blacks to flow into their states.

Ohio shared these fears. Gov. Allen Trimble warned in 1827 that the state was experiencing a "rapid increase" in "this unfortunate and degraded race." A committee of the Ohio House of Representatives added its voice, indicating that blacks tended to degrade white labor and furnished a disproportionate number of convicts for the penitentiary. Since territorial days southern slaveholders migrating to the Ohio Country had freed their chattels and brought them along as free persons. Since jobs were difficult to find, these largely unskilled blacks often continued to work for their former masters under conditions little changed from those they had known in the South. Sometimes slaves, freed in their deceased master's will, were located on Ohio lands purchased for them by the estate's executor.

Fears of a massive influx of blacks heightened in the 1840s when, upon the death of John Randolph of Virginia, his 518 freed slaves were to be resettled on forty-acre farms near Carthagena in Mercer County. Carthagena was already the site of a functioning black community. Established in 1835 by Augustus Wattles, an eastern Quaker, it was described as the "most successful negro settlement in the state . . . a thriving, self-sufficient and self-governing community of blacksmiths, tinsmiths, shopkeepers, school teachers, church leaders, grist and sawmill operators and farmers." However, when Randolph's freedmen attempted to take up their land, white settlers drove them out. Some finally relocated in the vicinity of Troy, Piqua, Sidney, and Xenia. Despite all the restrictions and prejudices against them, a few black businessmen and real estate owners prospered in Cincinnati, Columbus, Zanesville, Dayton, and smaller cities in the southern half of the state.

Few blacks lived in the northern counties. Lorain and Erie counties contained between 200 and 400 each in 1850; Cuyahoga (Cleveland) led with 1,277. But thirty-four northern counties had fewer than 100 black residents, and some counties, especially in the northwestern quadrant, had none at all. Blacks were so rare in this region that whites did not perceive them as a threat. In the Western Reserve, the New England conscience smoothed the way for the free blacks of Cleveland, Akron, and other towns to enjoy a somewhat more open opportunity than was available generally throughout the state. Although the overwhelming majority of blacks worked as menial laborers or practiced such trades as barbering, horseshoeing, carpentry, and metal-smithing, some held higher status positions, as did John Malvin, an escaped slave who made his way to Cleveland, where he became captain of a canal boat. A few black teachers, lawyers, and businessmen lived in the Reserve, and some of the first black doctors graduated from a Cleveland homeopathic medical school. Fragmentary records reveal that some northern Ohio blacks owned considerable real property, especially in Cleveland.

While some blacks were able to settle in Ohio successfully, they still had to contend with the racial discrimination that permeated all areas of social contact between the races. John Malvin described his efforts to integrate the Baptist church in Cleveland and the strain which it caused. He employed the "sit-in" tactic which was used effectively over a century later by civil rights activists. He sat quietly in a regular pew and politely declined to leave when requested to do so. He returned to the pew for several weeks until he had made his point about the supposed brotherhood of man. Similarly, John Brown, the famous abolitionist, was criticized in Franklin Mills (Kent) for bringing blacks to his church pew rather than having them sit in the accustomed place in the rear of the hall.

Some of the most flagrant discrimination existed in education, where state law prevented black youngsters from attending public schools except in unusual circumstances (see chapter 8, p. 188). A law enacted in 1853 modifying the segregation law of 1848 required boards of education to provide schools for black children, but only if there were more than thirty in the district. When there were fewer, township boards were responsible for determining how to accommodate them. By 1859, some 517 school districts contained resident black children, but 416 of that total provided no public schooling for them. An Ohio Supreme Court decision in that year ruled that children who were distinctly black were not entitled to attend white schools.

Despite these difficulties a small percentage of black children secured schooling either at private schools, at black schools supported by tax money, or, in a few cases, in integrated schools where local sentiment permitted it. For the handful of blacks who sought higher education, Ohio provided some options. Ohio University and Western Reserve had black students in the 1820s. As noted earlier, in 1835 Oberlin welcomed black students as a matter of policy, being the first college in the nation to do so. (New York's Oneida Institute also welcomed blacks, but it closed years before the Civil War.) Several other Ohio colleges were among the early co-racial institutions, especially Otterbein, Albany Manual Labor University, and Antioch, which was founded on liberal social principles similar to those that Oberlin endorsed. Wilberforce was designed for black students' needs, and after 1863 was operated by the African Methodist Episcopal Church.

Growth of Antislavery Sentiment in Ohio

While Ohio relegated blacks to an inferior status and guarded its borders against a large influx of black newcomers, a kernel of antislavery sentiment was developing into a movement of major significance. In 1815 Benjamin Lundy, a Quaker, formed the first western antislavery society in St. Clairsville. Two years later Charles Osborn started to publish the antislavery paper, the *Philanthropist,* in the Quaker community of Mt. Pleasant. Another small antislavery newspaper, Lundy's *Genius of Universal Emancipation,* soon appeared. These early papers were local, transient efforts which reached few readers, but they were seeds which would grow to make Ohio a strong center of opposition to the South's "peculiar institution." In the 1820s, however, many Ohioans who thought about it at all would probably have agreed with Charles Hammond, the influential Cincinnati newspaper editor, who opposed slavery but cautioned that there was no way the institution could be touched except by action of the slave states themselves.

The American Colonization Society appeared to provide one solution to the vexing racial problem. Its program was conservative, according to historian Merton Dillon, because "it made no effort whatever to alter the racial prejudices of white Americans, accepting these as unchangeable." Indeed, it may have intensified racist attitudes by "incessantly emphasizing the degradation of free Blacks."

Colonization, therefore, was not an adequate answer for those who wanted an immediate end to slavery and who hoped to ameliorate the condition of free blacks. In the 1830s, some former colonizationists were converted to the more radical cause of freeing slaves in America and providing for them in this nation. These abolitionists formed the radical fringe or "hard-core" opposition to slavery. Different levels of intensity existed among antislavery advocates. Most wished to proceed gradually and constitutionally against the slave power, but others, especially William Lloyd Garrison and his followers in the East, were for "gradual emancipation immediately begun." The easterners formed the American Antislavery Society in 1833 with financial backing from the New York merchants, Arthur and Lewis Tappan. The Tappans also funded Lane Seminary, a new Presbyterian college in Cincinnati. In doing so they followed the advice of Theodore Dwight Weld, a former colonizationist turned abolitionist. Weld, a man of great persuasive power, had an electric effect in Ohio where he made converts to abolitionism. Among them were President Charles Storrs and professors Elizur Wright, Jr. and Beriah Green at Western Reserve College. Their abolitionist zeal spread among the students and faculty, creating ideological strains which split the college and the Hudson community.

In 1833, Lane Seminary students, some of them from the South, were smitten with antislavery zeal and a desire to assist the dispossessed blacks of Cincinnati. They held antislavery meetings and performed charitable work in the black community, thereby alienating many whites, including merchants who feared that their southern commercial customers would retaliate economically against the agitation. Fifty-three Lane students took voluntary dismissal from the school rather than surrender their principles and their work among blacks. In 1835 about thirty of them responded to an invitation from the Reverend John J. Shipherd, founder of Oberlin College, to enroll in that new institution. The Lane students accepted Shipherd's invitation after securing assurance that Oberlin would welcome black students, that a Lane professor—the Reverend Asa Mahan—would become president of the college, and that Theodore Dwight Weld and John Morgan of the Lane faculty would receive professorships. These conditions were met. Weld refused the professorship, but he had much to do with bringing to Oberlin America's foremost revivalist, the Reverend Charles Grandison Finney of New York.

Finney and Weld converted many to abolitionism. With missionary zeal, "Finney's band" of young zealots spread the gospel of abolitionism throughout the state and adjoining areas. They were barred from halls and lecture platforms and frequently harassed. When the abolitionists persisted, they were insulted, physically manhandled, and pelted with rotten eggs. In one incident Theodore Weld, speaking in Putnam, was seized by Virginians from across the Muskingum in Zanesville, "dragged to the street and attacked with stones and clubs before his rescue by Putnam abolitionists."

Out of this affray emerged plans for a state abolition convention which was held at Putnam in April 1835. Weld and two other prominent Ohio abolitionists, James G. Birney and Henry B. Stanton, attended, although taunted by rowdies. Antislavery sentiment grew rapidly, and by 1836 there were 250 antislavery society members in Muskingum County.

Local chapters of the American Antislavery Society (1833) and its state affiliate, the Ohio Antislavery Society (1835), multiplied but in many areas of the state—including the Western Reserve, where abolition sentiment was strongest—anti-antislavery societies were formed to counteract abolitionist efforts. Zealous abolitionists persisted, however, and by the late 1830s Ohio had more than 200 antislavery societies: one Portage County society claimed more than 900 members and was purported to be the largest in the country.

In addition to local efforts, Ohioans were much involved in certain national aspects of the antislavery movement. One effective tactic used by antislavery societies after 1836 was to persuade sympathetic legislators in Congress to introduce petitions opposing slavery. Among the first of these in the Senate were petitions presented by Sen. Thomas Morris of Brown County, a Democrat and staunch antislavery man. Slave-state senators resented the reading of these attacks on the institution. Ultimately the Senate prevented a crisis by allowing the petitions to be presented and then tabled. At the same time there was trouble in the House, where former president John Quincy Adams fought to maintain the "right to petition." The House enacted a "gag rule" in 1836 whereby antislavery petitions were tabled without a reading. Opponents of the rule included those who resented this limit on the constitutional guarantees of free speech and the right to petition.

Adams's chief supporter in the fight against the "gag rule" was Ohio's Joshua Giddings, an Ashtabula County lawyer whose confrontational tactics and sense of self-importance did not prevent him from being an effective partisan of antislavery and of the right to petition. He defied Whig party discipline to present antislavery resolutions, and for this temerity he was censured by the party. Nevertheless, in 1842 he won reelection to the House of Representatives despite lack of party support. He continued to work against restraints on free speech and the right of petition, and, in 1844, the House revoked the "gag rule."

The Antislavery Element in Ohio Politics

American reform movements, sooner or later, tend to seek support from the major political parties and, failing that, often form third-party movements. So with the antislavery people. Although both Democrats and Whigs numbered antislavery people in their ranks, the reformers did not come close to having a controlling interest in either party. In 1840, therefore, antislavery enthusiasts, including Gamaliel Bailey of Cincinnati, formed the Liberty Party and ran candidates in the national presidential election and in some state elections. This party was concerned with more than the moral issue of slavery. It also spoke to slavery's impact on economic and political institutions.

James G. Birney was the party's presidential candidate in 1840. A former slaveholder, Birney had freed his slaves and then moved to Cincinnati, where he edited the antislavery *Philanthropist;* an angry Cincinnati mob destroyed his press in 1836. Birney secured but a handful of votes in Ohio in 1840, while the favorite son, William Henry Harrison of the Whig party, was carrying the day. In 1844 Birney ran again, but Liberty Party votes were still few in number; their impact in crucial districts denied the presidency to Henry Clay, however. In Ohio contests, Leicester King in 1842 and Samuel Lewis in 1844 were gubernatorial candidates on an abolition platform, but neither garnered more than 1 percent of the vote.

In addition to those local defeats, the election of James K. Polk to the presidency in 1844 had implications for antislavery enthusiasts since it was a victory for expansionist sentiment. Just before Polk's inauguration, Texas was admitted to the Union as a slave state, much to the chagrin of antislavery advocates. They were further alarmed when President Polk's pressures on Mexico ignited a war in 1846. Distressed when it appeared that territory won from Mexico could become slave territory, Ohio's antislavery people supported Rep. David Wilmot of Pennsylvania, who tried to amend a House bill to the effect that any land received from Mexico should be forever free from slavery. (Some historians maintain that the Wilmot Proviso was borrowed from a proposal drawn originally by Jacob Brinkerhoff, an Ohio Democrat.) The Wilmot Proviso failed in Congress, but its intent, no extension of slavery, remained a rallying point for antislavery people.

Ohioans in Congress expressed strong opposition to the Mexican war. Five Ohio Whigs voted against the declaration of war, and the Whig press was solidly against Polk's desire to acquire territory for what it called "the use, benefit, and extension of Southern Slavery and the augmentation of the Slave power." Thomas Corwin, a Whig senator from Lebanon, urged withdrawal of American troops from Mexico and refused to vote for appropriations to sustain the war. His famous peroration while addressing the Senate is often quoted: "If I were a Mexican, I would tell you: Have you not room in your own country to bury your dead men? If you come into mine, we will greet you with bloody hands, and welcome you to hospitable graves."

In contrast to the antiwar faction, about 7,000 Ohio men enlisted to do battle in Mexico. Some served in Gen. Winfield Scott's expedition against Mexico City, but the larger part campaigned in Mexico's northern provinces with "Old Rough and Ready," Zachary Taylor. Both Scott and Taylor overcame stiff Mexican resistance to secure their objectives and, along with American victories in California, sealed Mexico's fate. The Treaty of Guadalupe Hidalgo (1848) confirmed the fears of antislavery people by securing to the United States a huge expanse stretching westward from Texas to the Pacific, a region which appeared to be in the direct line of slavery's westward advance.

Liberty Party members were especially distressed by the potential for slavery's extension. Now they joined anti-expansionist Whigs and Democrats who left their parties to form the Free Soil Party, dedicated to keeping slavery within its present bounds. The presidential contest of 1848 exacerbated the fears of those opposed to the further extension of slavery. The Democrats nominated Lewis Cass, onetime Ohio lawyer and military leader now identified with Michigan and with questionable views on the extension of slavery, while the Whigs chose Zachary Taylor, war hero and southern slaveholder. The only viable alternative for strong antislavery people was Martin Van Buren, the Free Soil candidate. Saddled with an unacceptable candidate, Western Reserve Whigs abandoned their party. Five Reserve counties gave a plurality to Van Buren, and these votes were enough to give the state to Cass. Taylor won the presidency, but Ohio had given clear signs that its political loyalties were in flux, and that old party alignments might break under the strain.

The Free Soilers ran no gubernatorial candidate in the state elections of 1848. In the Western Reserve they supported the Whig, Seabury Ford, who was elected by an exceedingly thin margin over his Democratic opponent, John B. Weller. Whigs and Democrats were evenly divided in the Ohio Senate and nearly so in the House. This gave a handful of newly elected Free Soil legislators the balance of power, and they used this leverage to advantage. Whigs and Democrats now competed to secure Free Soil support, and with it the ability to organize the general assembly. The Democrats proved the more responsive to Free Soil demands and pledged that, in return for Free Soil votes in organizing the legislature, they would support a repeal of the "black laws." Repeal was the *sine qua non* of the Free Soilers, but an additional political plum was theirs when Salmon P. Chase of Cincinnati, a Liberty Party man in '41 and a Free Soiler in '48, was elected to the United States Senate as a reward for his maneuvering to bring the Free Soilers and Democrats together.

Students of Ohio politics mark the emergence of the Free Soil Party as a turning point in state political alignments. For the moment, the Free Soilers were triumphant. With Democratic support, the "black laws" were partially repealed in 1849, much to the chagrin of those southern counties which continued to fear a large influx of blacks. No longer would blacks coming into the state be required to post bond, register their "freedom papers," and secure the endorsement of responsible whites—even though these strictures were rarely enforced. Though still denied the vote and many other rights, blacks secured the right to testify in court, but these gains do not represent any lessening of the conviction among the white population that blacks were an inferior race.

Many Free Soilers had concerns beyond the spread of slavery. Some joined with Democrats and Whigs who believed that corporations—turnpike, canal, bridge, and railroad companies—must be more closely monitored, that banks must be controlled and limited, and that the state must revise its constitution to effect these changes. To this end, the general assembly placed the constitutional issue on the ballot and, in February 1849, Ohio voters approved calling a constitutional convention by nearly a three-to-one margin.

The Ohio Constitution of 1851

The Constitution of 1802 gave the Ohio voter ample opportunity to express his opinion on the performance of those representatives he had sent to the general assembly. The legislature was supreme, bolstered by its power to appoint state officers except for the essentially powerless governor. Without a veto, the governor lacked the restraining capacity the U.S. Constitution delegated to the president. The state legislature also chose judges, which clearly limited the judges' independence and had on occasion led to abuse. The requirement that the supreme court meet once each year in each county proved totally unworkable as the number of counties increased. Indeed, the issue of creating new counties was yet another concern the convention must address.

Election of delegates to the state's constitutional convention produced a substantial majority for the Democrats. Among their number was William Medill of Fairfield County, soon to be elected governor, who was chosen president of the convention. The delegates were, on the whole, men of substance. Among the more aggressive was Charles Reemelin, who represented the anti-establishment sentiments of Cincinnati's mixed working class and immigrant population. There were enough conservative Democrats to join with Whigs in blocking radical economic proposals, but there were also enough reform-minded Whigs to join with Democrats in advancing some of the convention's more "liberal" objectives. Late in 1850 the convention assembled in the state capital, but before the delegates were well into their deliberations, a cholera epidemic swept Columbus, forcing adjournment until December, when the delegates reassembled in Cincinnati.

The new constitution made important changes in the structure of government, but the legislature remained the most powerful branch despite new limits on its authority. Its members were to be elected biennially. They could enact no special laws of incorporation, only general ones; new counties must contain at least 400 square miles, and the voters affected by their creation must approve the change. (No new county has been formed under this constitution. Noble County, established April 1, 1851, was the last county created in Ohio.) Commissioners were to create a capital fund to extinguish the debt; taxation was to be on the "uniform rule" that all classes of property would be taxed at the same rate; and lotteries and poll taxes were banned.

The governor was still denied the veto. The principal executive officers were now to be elected by popular vote, however. New district courts were created on a level between the county common pleas courts and the state supreme court. All judges were to be elected by popular vote.

The new constitution dashed the hopes of certain social reformers. Only adult white males of one year's residence could vote. Blacks were denied the franchise by a vote of 66 to 12. Women's suffrage failed by a 72 to 7 margin. The liquor issue was sidetracked from the constitution by providing that a popular vote on licensing be held at the same time the constitution was submitted to the voters for ratification.

The constitution could be amended by the voters after each house of the general assembly had approved the proposal by a three-fifths vote. In 1871 and every twenty years thereafter, the voters were to decide whether or not to call a constitutional convention. Before adjourning on March 10, 1851, the delegates adopted the new Constitution by a vote of 79 to 14. Thirteen conservative Whigs and one Free Soiler refused to sign.

Although the document failed to address many issues, the delegates saw it as distinctly superior to the old constitution. Yet, as a student of this period has written, the new constitution failed to take account of "the changing economic life of the State, and made no provisions for the transformations

that railroads, factories and financial institutions were to make in the generation to come. In a sense, it was the last effort of the Jacksonians to strengthen
the bulwarks of agrarianism against the onset of the new economic order."

On June 17 the voters ratified the constitution by a 16,288-vote margin,
with opposition strongest in the conservative southern and southeastern counties. The new constitution took effect September 1, 1851. Twice in coming
years Ohio voters would call another constitutional convention into being.
The 1873 effort came to naught, but the 1912 convention produced numerous
amendments of great importance. Still, the 1851 constitution, now liberally
amended, remains the fundamental law of Ohio.

The Discordant Decade, 1850-60

By mid-century, Ohio was a mature state very much in the heart of national affairs. Her internal dynamics reflected national issues, her resources
contributed a large portion of the nation's wealth, and her leaders were becoming ever more intimately entwined in positions of influence. One can
view these developments from the inside out—projecting Ohio developments
on to their national setting—or from the outside in—describing how Ohio's
own concerns and experiences reflected those of the nation. This brief review
of the 1850s will follow the latter approach.

The five national laws known collectively as the Compromise of 1850 carried implications for the future of slavery in the United States. Of special
interest to Ohio's antislavery advocates were the act admitting California as a
free state and the new fugitive slave law.

California's emergence as a state was precipitous. In 1848 the discovery of
gold at Sutter's Mill set off a mass movement of gold-seekers from around the
world, but especially from the East. The saga of the "Forty-Niners" is a
colorful and well-known episode in American history. Their heroic—or
foolhardy—journeys across the western plains, mountains, and deserts are the
stuff of high adventure and human endurance. Equally trying were the dangerous sea voyages by which many an Argonaut made his way around the
Horn or across the Isthmus of Panama. What is imperfectly understood is the
impact which the sudden loss of thousands of people had on the economy and
the life of Ohio and other regions abandoned for the Golden West.

Between 1849 and 1853 a veritable flood of Ohioans joined the search for
instant wealth. Summit County, far from Ohio's most populous, sent more
than 400 men and women to the gold fields. Among them, said a local chron-
icler, were "a large proportion . . . of our most useful citizens—chiefly
mechanics." In March 1850, a cavalcade of nearly 200 people left Massillon

for the Golden West. In Lorain County an emigrant society chartered a ship for the water voyage to California; so it went throughout Ohio and the western states generally. Few of these seekers struck it rich; most returned home poorer but wiser, treasuring little more than memories of a great adventure.

California's burgeoning new population was in need of orderly government. The lack of evidence to the contrary suggests that Ohioans generally approved admitting California to the Union as a free state. Certainly antislavery people supported it, for now the westward march of slavery would stop short of the Pacific coast.

Another proviso of the Compromise of 1850, the fugitive slave law, was made as a sop to the South. Slave owners decried the loss of valuable property; they were infuriated that free-state people assisted runaways. The recapturing of fugitives was presumably covered by the federal fugitive slave law of 1793, but that law had been widely ignored by northerners who were developing ever more substantial ways of aiding escaping slaves. There is evidence as early as 1815 that Ohioans were assisting runaways. Two decades later, as antislavery enthusiasm matured into a virtual crusade, this assistance became better organized until outraged slave owners claimed that a conspiracy existed to spirit their property to freedom in Canada or to free-state havens where pursuit was unlikely.

This organized aid was the famous "underground railroad." Its history is somewhat murky and indistinct, for its operations were, by their very nature, surreptitious and covert. On the well-established routes through Ohio "conductors" moved fugitives from one "station" to another. Levi Coffin, a Cincinnati Quaker, was possibly the best-known conductor, claiming responsibility for moving hundreds of fugitives toward freedom. The Reverend John Rankin, a Presbyterian, kept a lantern shining in the window of his house, located high above the Ohio River at Ripley, as a beacon to slaves escaping across the river. But hundreds of less visible men, women, and occasionally children, both white and black, participated in secreting and forwarding fugitives. Quakers, Methodists, Presbyterians, and Congregationalists were especially involved in this activity, and areas where they were concentrated, such as Congregationalist Oberlin, were well known centers of the movement.

As a major contributor to the underground railroad, Ohio came to be called the "trunk line" of the passage north. For every person who assisted runaways on a regular basis, there were others who helped occasionally as circumstances dictated. For instance, while still a boy the arch-abolitionist, John Brown, led slaves from Wellsville on the Ohio to his home area of Hudson, where residents hid them until it was safe to move on to Cleveland (reputed to have had the code name "Hope"), where passage to Canada could be arranged. Conductors hid escapees in wagons, under loads of hay, in canal boats, even on trains. Generally the fugitives moved at night to reduce chance encounters with suspicious whites. Disguises were used, a favorite ploy being to dress a man in woman's clothing and vice versa.

It is now impossible to separate fact from fancy in reporting this romantic theme. Nearly every Ohio town boasts an old house or building which, the locals will insist, once concealed fugitives. Still, exaggerations notwithstanding, Ohio was a major route to Canada. In Muskingum County alone, according to historian Norris Schneider, at least twenty-five families "operated stations on the underground railroad" while many of the county's 631 blacks helped escapees.

In 1839 the general assembly responded to southern pressure to halt this traffic by passing a state fugitive slave law which charged state authorities with the apprehension of escapees. The law was repealed in 1843 after the United States Supreme Court ruled (*Prigg* v. *Pennsylvania,* 1842) that enforcement of the fugitive slave law of 1793 was a federal responsibility in which the states had no role. Thus matters stood when Congress enacted new legislation.

The fugitive slave law of 1850 made it a federal offense, under threat of severe penalty, for any person to interfere in the capture and return of fugitive slaves. Citizens were required to assist federal marshals and their deputies when called upon. Blacks apprehended as escaped slaves were taken before federal magistrates or commissioners, where they were denied a jury trial, nor could they testify on their own behalf. Abolitionists were outraged at what they branded the "Kidnap Law" which required citizens to assist slave catchers who cruised the free states looking for runaways. In the Western Reserve, leading citizens and newspapers called for defiance of the law. The *Ashtabula Sentinel* would have fugitives meet slave catchers with "powder and ball, with dirk and bowie-knife. . . . Slay the miscreant," it advised the black man, "if he comes to re-enslave you or your wife or child." A former mayor of Akron spoke against the law; as late as 1859 he told an audience to disobey this "immoral" law: "I say resist it." Conservatives, fearful that radical antislavery people would be tempted to consider nullification of the federal law, urged caution and prudence. For the moment this position prevailed. The critical testing of the new law did not come until toward the end of the decade, by which time many fugitives who had temporarily settled in Ohio had made their way to Canada where they were beyond pursuit.

Antislavery forces enjoyed a surge of popular support from quite an unexpected quarter. In 1852 Harriet Beecher Stowe published *Uncle Tom's Cabin,* a novel that originally appeared as a serial in Gamaliel Bailey's antislavery newspaper. The daughter of Lyman Beecher, a Cincinnati preacher and head of Lane Seminary, she was a Massachusetts woman who lived in Cincinnati for seventeen years. She was married to Calvin Stowe, a Lane professor. In the river city Harriet Stowe knew many black women from whom she heard true stories of the tribulations of slavery and efforts to escape from it. These stories formed the background of her novel, which featured powerful characterizations of kindly and wise Uncle Tom and the malicious slave driver, Simon Legree, both of whose names have passed into our language. Eliza, carrying her baby across Ohio River ice floes while pursued by bloodhounds and slave catchers, evoked the sympathy of persons never before touched by the slaves' plight.

The book was an instant success. Over 300,000 copies sold in America within a year; in England, 1.5 million; ultimately the book was translated into thirty-seven languages. Scoffers challenged Stowe's sentimental and melodramatic account, so in 1853 she published her sources in the *Key to Uncle Tom's Cabin*. It has been said that she made more converts to antislavery than all the earnest preachers and lecturers combined, and that she contributed to that firming of opinion which led to the Civil War. During the war Stowe met President Lincoln, whom she felt was not moving fast enough against slavery. As the six-foot-four-inch Lincoln bent down to shake the hand of this "little bit of a woman, about as thin and dry as a pinch of snuff," he is reported to have said, "So this is the little woman who made this big war."

In 1854, Sen. Stephen A. Douglas of Illinois, a leader of the Democratic Party, introduced a bill which Congress passed as the Kansas-Nebraska Act. The bill created the new territories of Kansas and Nebraska in regions of the Louisiana Purchase which, according to the Missouri Compromise, were to remain forever free from slavery. Douglas's bill allowed the slavery issue to be decided by "popular sovereignty." Those who controlled the territorial legislature would decide whether or not to permit slavery. The act repealed the Missouri Compromise and reawakened northern fears that territories once protected from slavery would be vulnerable to its spread. Douglas managed to split his own party: anti-Nebraska Democrats now sought new political alliances. The Whig party was already in final disarray. Clearly new political alignments were imminent.

Led by Free Soilers Chase and Giddings, anti-Nebraska protests were mounted throughout Ohio. Chase was the principal author of an "Appeal of the Independent Democrats" to arouse the North against the proposed repeal of the Missouri Compromise. The "Appeal" called upon all to "protest . . . against this enormous crime"—the extension of slavery into the territories. The protest meetings attracted men from all political camps, and generated enough enthusiasm to support a call for a state convention which assembled July 13, 1854. Radical antislavery delegates attempted unsuccessfully to make the fugitive slave law an issue in this convention. Instead moderates succeeded in making the principal issue the extension of slavery in the territories. They also asserted that there should be no more slave states admitted to the Union. Unlike similar gatherings in Wisconsin and Michigan, the

UNCLE TOM'S CABIN;

OR,

LIFE AMONG THE LOWLY.

BY

HARRIET BEECHER STOWE.

VOL. I.

BOSTON:

JOHN P. JEWETT & COMPANY.

CLEVELAND, OHIO:

JEWETT, PROCTOR & WORTHINGTON.

1852.

Title page of Harriet Beecher Stowe's famous novel. (From *Uncle Tom's Cabin* . . . , Boston, 1852.)

Ohioans failed to adopt the name "Republican" at this time. For the moment they were known by the name which their opponents assigned them—the Fusion Party.

To the Free Soilers, anti-Nebraska Democrats, "conscience" Whigs, and other members of the emerging coalition, a new, and to some a disturbing element, was added. A virulently anti-Catholic secret society, the Know-Nothings, expanded from their eastern strongholds into Ohio in 1854. They attracted support from a variety of sources, including conservatives who had left the Whigs and the now-fragmented Democrats. The Know-Nothings advocated a strong Union, and they remained largely neutral on the slavery issue. The growing presence of a Catholic minority, continued prejudice against the Irish, boasts from Catholic clerics about their growing numerical strength, and Bishop Purcell's opposition to tax-supported public schools, which had led to rioting in Cincinnati, added impetus to the movement in Ohio.

Though Fusion leaders feared they might lose German votes, they quietly accepted the Know-Nothings into their camp. But since many Germans were protestant and others were free thinkers, fears of alienating Germans failed to develop into much of a problem.

The Fusionists won their first test of strength in a landslide victory over the Democrats in the 1854 state elections. The Democrats were punished for being the party which had repealed the Missouri Compromise and the party that wanted to tax businesses.

Fusionist leaders now had to find ways to consolidate their new political power. At their 1855 convention in Columbus, they adopted the name "Republican Party." For governor, the Republicans nominated Salmon P. Chase, who had failed in reelection to his Senate seat because the legislature was Democratically controlled. To placate the large Know-Nothing element, the Republicans promised certain state offices to their men. The Democrats chose the incumbent, William Medill. When the ballots were counted, the Republicans had the governor's chair, many state executive offices, and control of the general assembly.

In their next test—the presidential election of 1856—the new party did not fare so well. Two Ohioans—Chase and John McLean—were Republican hopefuls, but the nomination went to John C. Frémont, the "Pathfinder of the West," who was a hero to Ohioans; admirers in Lower Sandusky had changed the name of their town to Fremont in 1849 in his honor. Fremont lost to James Buchanan, whose popular vote was less than the combined vote for Fremont and the Know-Nothing candidate, Millard Fillmore. Ohio supported Fremont, giving him 17,000 more votes than Buchanan. This election marked the decline of the Know-Nothings, whose conservative platform and anti-Catholic bigotry were not widely attractive. Ohio was again a two-party state where future political contests would be Republican vs. Democrat.

While political realignment was under way in Ohio, a mini civil war was raging in Kansas, where both proslavery and antislavery forces were attempting to control the territorial legislature and determine the future of slavery in the region. Proslavery Missourians crossed into Kansas with their slave property. Eastern and midwestern abolitionists organized "emigrant trains" of antislavery settlers. Included in their baggage were antislavery tracts and "Beecher's Bibles" (Sharps rifles).

"Bleeding Kansas" attracted extremists like John Brown. Brown, born in Connecticut, grew up in Summit County and later lived elsewhere in Ohio, Pennsylvania, and New York. He was a religious zealot who failed as a farmer and as a wool merchant. He moved west to join his sons and took with him a determination to save Kansas from the slave power. One dark night in 1856, in retaliation for proslavery atrocities, Brown led a small band along Osawatomie Creek in eastern Kansas. Five times they stopped at proslavery cabins, took the man of the house, and killed him in cold blood. Moderates of all stripes disavowed this murderous deed, but it was condoned by radical abolitionists, including some in the Western Reserve who bragged that they had supplied Brown with weapons. "Old Brown of Osawatomie" now became the embodiment of southerners' worst fears.

Troubles in Kansas strained Democratic party solidarity, and in 1857 party unity was totally ruptured. The occasion was the Supreme Court decision in the case of *Dred Scott* v. *Sandford*, which rejected the popular sovereignty principle. The Court ruled that Negroes were not citizens and that Congress could not prohibit slave owners from taking their property into the territories; indeed Congress had the duty to protect property, including slave property, wherever it existed. Justice John McLean of Ohio wrote a spirited dissent to the majority decision, but this had no effect on events. Southern Democrats rejoiced at the decision while northern Democrats were aghast at the scope of the ruling, which made the Missouri Compromise unconstitutional and destroyed Douglas's popular sovereignty. While debating Abraham Lincoln in 1858 in a campaign to retain his Senate seat, Douglas, put on the defensive by Lincoln's questions, claimed that the Dred Scott decision would have no effect unless supported by local police authorities. This doctrine, which appeared to deny the South its victory, split the Democrats into northern and southern branches, opening the door for a Republican triumph in the 1860 presidential elections.

Economic malaise added to political conflict: the American economy was depressed. The Ohio Life Insurance and Trust Company of Cincinnati failed, triggering a national recession—the Panic of 1857. Again Ohio suffered business failures. Banks were threatened but managed, on the whole, to survive the crisis. Bad news on the economic front was bad news politically for the Republicans in control of state government. Governor Chase won reelection in 1857 (after the adoption of the Constitution of 1851, governors were elected in odd-numbered years), but the statewide vote was almost evenly divided between Democrats and Republicans. In fact, the Democrats carried the general assembly. The American Party (formerly the Know-Nothings) failed in its efforts to defeat Chase and vanished as a political organization.

Ohio Democrats supported Stephen A. Douglas. They denounced the Lecompton Constitution (a proslavery scheme to control Kansas) as a fraud and denounced President Buchanan for playing into the hands of the southerners. Samuel S. "Sunset" Cox, a brilliant young legislator from Columbus, was making a name for himself in the federal House as an anti-Lecompton leader. Some Ohio Democrats continued to support Buchanan, among them former governor Reuben Wood and the Columbus newspaper editor, Samuel Medary, both of whom held federal patronage appointments. Yet, despite cooperation between Democratic groups in the 1858 congressional elections, the party won only six of twenty-one districts. It was, for the Democrats, an unhappy portent of troubles to come.

While growing polarization over the slavery issue affected the Democratic party, the abolitionists remained active in Ohio, where fugitive slave cases had long stirred emotions. In 1836 James G. Birney was found guilty under an 1804 Ohio law of "secreting" a runaway mulatto named Matilda. Her defense lawyer, Salmon P. Chase, later got the decision reversed on appeal to the state supreme court. In 1847 Chase defended John Van Zandt, an old antislavery enthusiast sued for harboring and concealing fugitive slaves. On appeal to the United States Supreme Court, Chase lost the case.

Now a new series of fugitive slave cases revealed the abolitionists' determination to challenge federal policies which they felt protected the South. In 1856 a fugitive named Margaret Garner, living in southwest Ohio, was seized by federal authorities, but not until she had been indicted for murder by an Ohio grand jury. She had killed one of her children with a butcher knife while in agony over the prospect of being returned to slavery. Federal authorities succeeded in sending Margaret and her family back to Kentucky before state authorities could interfere, and later efforts by Governor Chase to have her returned for trial on the state charge failed. Conflict between state and federal authorities also erupted in the Champaign County rescue cases when a federal marshal and his agents arrested four county residents for assisting a fugitive to escape. While the federals were taking the prisoners to Cincinnati, local officials tried to stop them. The Greene County sheriff, on a writ of *habeas corpus,* took the prisoners from the marshal after a minor gun battle, and also arrested the deputy marshals on the charge of assault with intent to kill. It took a personal conference between Governor Chase and President Buchanan to settle the issue, with both sides agreeing to drop charges.

Local residents frustrated many attempts by slave owners and their agents to take fugitives from Ohio. In several Western Reserve settlements slave catchers, even when they appeared to carry valid papers, were run out of town by angry citizens. Rutherford B. Hayes, a young Cincinnati lawyer, was but one of several attorneys who defended fugitives, free of charge, from efforts to return them to bondage.

Ohio's classic fugitive case was the "Oberlin-Wellington Rescue Case." In September 1858 John Price, a fugitive slave, was identified by a slave catcher and seized by a federal marshal in Oberlin. He was rushed secretly to nearby Wellington. Abolitionist Oberlin was outraged. A group of its citizens pursued the marshal to Wellington and there cooperated with local people to free Price and send him to safety. A federal grand jury indicted thirty-seven of the Oberlin and Wellington people for violating the fugitive slave law. Of the thirty-seven, Simeon Bushnell (white) and Charles Langston (black) were tried in April 1859, found guilty in federal court, and jailed. However, the Ohio Supreme Court heard their cases and those of the others charged so that the court could determine if the prisoners were legally held. At issue was the question, was the fugitive slave law of 1850 constitutional? The federal courts had ruled that it was, but radical abolitionists were unwilling to accept this verdict and sought through the state courts to overturn it. Some went so far as to suggest that Calhoun's discredited nullification doctrine be applied. This would have allowed the Ohio legislature to block enforcement of obnoxious federal laws within the state. In Cleveland, thousands rallied against the federal fugitive slave law and its workings within the state.

The state supreme court finally ruled in the cases. They found the federal fugitive slave law to be constitutional (by a 3 to 2 vote) and refused to block proceedings in the federal court. However, Bushnell and Langston served but short sentences during which they were eulogized as martyrs for the cause. Charges were dropped against the other defendants and the antislavery forces paraded and celebrated their "victory."

In the political arena, the Republican state convention, meeting in 1859, chose a Columbus banker and railroad man, William Dennison, as gubernatorial candidate. He was acceptable to moderates as well as to the more radical elements in the party, whose platform called for repeal of the fugitive slave law of 1850 while remaining silent on the nullification issue. The Democratic convention, hoping to cast their opponents as dangerous radicals whose extreme actions threatened the Union, chose for their candidate Judge Rufus P. Ranney, whose antislavery views kept the Democrats free of charges of proslavery.

Both parties imported talent to assist in the campaign. Abraham Lincoln came from Illinois to support Dennison and the Republicans even though he disapproved the party's stand on the fugitive slave law. He was countered by Sen. Stephen A. Douglas, who had triumphed over Lincoln the previous year in the Illinois contest. These powerful spokesmen thus reenacted their famous stands of 1858 in an Ohio setting. Both Dennison and Ranney campaigned vigorously, engaging in face-to-face debates. When the ballots were counted, Dennison and the Republicans had won a handsome victory, successfully holding together the party's radical and more moderate elements.

The discordant decade ended with high drama. Once more John Brown flamed across the national consciousness. "Old Osawatomie" had spent time since leaving Kansas collecting equipment and support for a vaguely conceived blow at the slave power. In October 1859, Brown led eighteen men, including five blacks, into Harpers Ferry, Virginia, where he seized the federal arsenal, presumably to secure arms with which to stock a sanctuary for escaped slaves. His troops killed the town's mayor and seized prisoners before barricading themselves in the arsenal where they defended themselves against state and federal troops, the latter led by Col. Robert E. Lee. One of Brown's sons lay dead, another wounded, and the zealot himself was wounded when Lee's marines forced an entrance and seized the defenders.

While imprisoned, Brown was interrogated by Governor Wise of Virginia and by others who sought to understand his motives. Though they abhorred his acts, some of his jailers developed a grudging respect for the poised and wounded Brown. His trial was widely reported. He rejected advice to plead insanity: he knew what he was about. Found guilty on charges which included treason against the State of Virginia, he was sentenced to hang. On December 2, 1859, at Charles Town, Virginia, seated on his own coffin, he was taken in a cart to the gallows. He died with dignity and composure. Sympathizers, fearing his body would be desecrated, spirited it away, switched coffins, and ultimately carried the body to his farm in North Elba, New York, where he was buried.

Back in Ohio Brown's activities were followed with intense interest. Democrats condemned him; Republican newspapers hastily disassociated the party from his actions. On the day of his hanging, however, some Western Reserve towns shut down public and private businesses and held public exercises to honor "our old friend and neighbor, John Brown." In Cincinnati, far removed from the radical abolition element in the northern counties, blacks and German freethinkers held a sympathy meeting for the "new saint." The South viewed Brown's raid as confirmation of its worst fears—that murderous Yankees would stop at nothing in their vindictiveness toward southern society and its slave-labor system. And so it seemed in some radical quarters. In the little canal town of Akron, a former mayor, Lucius Bierce, praised Brown: "It has been said that old Brown is crazy. Would to God there were millions of such crazy men at the North." Then came a warning to supporters of slavery: "Let the South and her servile minions of the North know that [the South] sleeps on a magazine that a spark from the North can at any moment explode." So passed John Brown, but in the radicals of Ohio his soul went marching on.

The presidential election of 1860 was one of the most critical in American history. The Republicans entered it with vigor and purpose. They rejected the extension of slavery in the territories, but took no stand that threatened that institution where it already existed. The party supported economic nationalism, including a protective tariff and federal support for internal improvements, and called for free land under homestead laws. The Republican delegates, meeting in Chicago's Wigwam, had numerous candidates to choose from, including Ohio's Salmon Chase, John McLean, and Benjamin Wade. William H. Seward of New York and Edward Bates of Missouri were prominent candidates with Seward much better known nationally than Chase and the other Ohioans. On the third ballot, Abraham Lincoln of Illinois won the nomination. Ohio Republicans were well pleased with the outcome, having shifted their vote from Chase to Lincoln, thereby providing the votes which put Lincoln over the top.

The Democrats, on the other hand, were in disarray. Ohio's delegates to the party's convention in Charleston, South Carolina, were solidly for Sen. Stephen A. Douglas. They supported popular sovereignty on the slavery issue. The Charleston convention collapsed when northern and southern positions could not be reconciled, and at a succeeding convention of northern Democrats, Ohio supported Douglas again as he won nomination. The southern Democrats, at a separate convention, nominated John C. Breckinridge of Kentucky, who received support from a conservative minority of Ohio Democrats. A Constitutional Union Party composed largely of conservative ex-Whigs nominated John Bell of Tennessee, and he appeared on the Ohio ballot.

Lincoln won handily, despite getting only about 40 percent of the popular vote. In Ohio Lincoln had 231,610 votes to Douglas's 187,232, with another 23,600 votes evenly split between Breckinridge and Bell. The Western Reserve was strongly for Lincoln, who also carried southwestern Whig strongholds and, in a surprising reversal, Hamilton County, where the German wards of Cincinnati went for him.

Southerners made their position clear. No "Black Republican" could be *their* president. Lincoln did not secure a single electoral vote in the slaveholding states. He was a minority president, a northern sectional president. For four agonizing months, Lincoln had to sit by helplessly as President Buchanan allowed the sectional crisis to worsen. Following South Carolina's secession in December, seven southern states met at Montgomery, Alabama, in February 1861 and established the Confederate States of America. Others soon joined. Shortly after Lincoln's inauguration, Virginia, Arkansas, Tennessee, and North Carolina rounded out the Confederacy at its full strength of eleven states.

Although the signs were ominous, it is unlikely that many people, North or South, realized they were witnessing the opening moves in the bloodiest and most threatening crisis which they or their progeny would face.

ojos

10.

Ohio for the Union

The Civil War was America's supreme test. For four bloody, traumatic years the struggle affected every facet of American life. By war's end the Union had been preserved, and American ideals, including concepts of individual worth and democratic precepts, were shaken but intact.

The Confederacy's defeat left it in dire distress. The war had severely damaged much southern land and destroyed buildings, transportation systems, and institutions. The emancipation of 3.9 million slaves represented a great capital loss to former slaveowners, but much more significant was the need, somehow, to integrate these largely unskilled persons into their new role as free men and women. That process began by war's end, but it did not progress far before southern whites, regaining control of their reconstructed states, relegated their former chattels to an inferior status that endured for another century. North and South alike shared the heaviest price the war exacted: the more than 600,000 men who died in military service, the hundreds of thousands of men and women who carried wounds—physical, mental, or emotional—for the rest of their days, and the innumerable victims whose lives forever changed.

Ohio on the Eve of Civil War

By 1860 Ohio was well beyond her pioneer days except for isolated, primitive pockets. With 2,339,500 people, Ohio trailed only New York and Pennsylvania in population. Native whites accounted for 86 percent of its people; 2 percent were black.

Ohio was still largely rural, with 83 percent of its inhabitants living on farms or in rural areas. The best agricultural lands had long since been preempted, except for Black Swamp lands still being drained. Thriving farms placed the state at or near the top in production of crops and livestock. It ranked first in horses, sheep and wool; second in corn; third in oats, and fourth in wheat. It was a major producer of beef cattle and dairy products, especially cheese, and of tobacco, fruit, and many small-volume farm products. Sixty-two percent of its farmland was classified as improved. It is clear that Ohio would be part of the Union's "breadbasket" in the coming conflict.

Important urban industrial centers had emerged by the eve of the Civil War. Cincinnati, with 161,044 people, was the state's preeminent city in 1860, a cosmopolitan city, the intellectual and cultural capital of the West. The war would bring adjustments to its historic trade patterns in the Ohio Valley. Its merchants could no longer deal with southern customers, but thanks to canals, the river, and east-west rail connections, it retained its share of the vigorous commerce stimulated by wartime demands. Cincinnati was a major processor of foods, soaps, candles, clothing, leather goods, and dozens of other products. During the war its foundries produced armaments, its shipyards iron-clad warships.

Cleveland was Ohio's second leading city. Thanks to trade stimulated by the Ohio-Erie Canal, lake traffic, railroads, and highways, Cleveland boasted 43,417 persons and was starting to fulfill the long-predicted promise of growth. Its Erie waterfront, once lauded for its beauty, already displayed the ugliness of the industrial age. Small industries and large warehouses lined the "flats" alongside the Cuyahoga River. A varied manufacturing base was developing, and workers of diverse background were coming to take jobs in businesses still largely owned and managed by Yankees. A small community of blacks found as much freedom of opportunity in Cleveland as was then available to them anywhere in the nation.

Columbus was still a mid-sized city of 18,554 inhabitants. The newly finished statehouse was its principal ornament. The Neil House, which burned in the war years and was later rebuilt, along with other hostelries enjoyed a steady trade from the many visitors whom a state capital inevitably draws. City streets were less obstructed than formerly, when hogs roamed them at will. Perhaps the hogs contributed to the city's reputation for unhealthiness, but it is more likely that poorly drained land nearby was the prime culprit. Although commerce and manufacturing were important to the city's life, politics was its most visible business.

Dayton with 20,081 people and Toledo with 13,768 were also important urban centers. Scores of lesser towns claimed several thousand persons each.

The largest of these was Zanesville (9,229) which, forty years earlier, had been Ohio's second leading city. Chillicothe (7,626) and Marietta (4,323) once ranked with Cincinnati as Ohio's most important towns. Although these historic communities remained significant regional centers, the future appeared to belong to others.

City growth was related to industrial growth. Ohio ranked fourth in the nation in the value of its industrial products in 1860. Iron production was widely distributed, with the Hanging Rock region of south central Ohio and the Mahoning Valley leading the way in the production of pig iron. This material was processed in foundries and rolling mills located all around the state. Each of the larger towns had its "iron works," making Ohio second only to Pennsylvania in the production of this basic industrial material.

After a lull during the war's first year or two, industrial growth accelerated as the insatiable demands of the military provided a huge new market. Loss of manpower to the armies initially slowed industrial growth, but the labor void was filled in time by immigrants and in some instances by women who assumed jobs formerly reserved for men.

Whole new industries received an artificial boost from wartime demand. Oil had been discovered accidentally in 1859 in Washington County; unlike the oil produced in northwestern Pennsylvania by the new drilling techniques of Edwin L. Drake, Ohio oil was not exploited at first. Petroleum products were useful as lubricants and illuminants, and wartime usage caused this young industry to grow. In Akron a German immigrant, Ferdinand Schumacher, developed America's first oatmeal cereal. The inexpensive, nutritious, easily stored cereal became a favorite of Union soldiers, and large army contracts put Schumacher on the road toward becoming America's "oatmeal king." New product lines such as uniforms and tents enhanced Ohio's strong woolens industry. The war also stimulated the farm machinery industry then still in its infancy in Springfield, Canton, and many other locations. Manufactures came out with improved mowers and reapers. In spite of some farm laborers' hostility toward and resistance to new-fangled ways, the machines were indispensable during the Civil War, when manpower was reduced on the home front. Ohio manufacturing growth in the war years kept pace with northern industrial growth generally, rising by 122 percent in the 1860s.

As with the farms and the factories, Ohio's mineral and timber resources developed under wartime conditions. The rapid expansion of steam power created a growing market for Ohio coal, with railroads and steamships as major customers. Ohio's abundant clay supported an ever-growing clay products industry. Salt was yet another essential resource, much of it used to preserve meat. Timber served local shipbuilding activity along the Ohio River and on Erie's shore; bark provided tannin for the leather goods industry. Although local iron ores were still heavily mined, a canal at Sault Ste.

Marie, Michigan, had already opened the prospect that these inferior ores would be supplanted in time by high quality ores from the Upper Peninsula and eventually from Minnesota.

Transportation was one of Ohio's special strengths during the war years. In 1860 it had more miles of railroad tracks than any other state, serving nearly every region. The Ohio lines were vital links in systems which bound the east coast with the Mississippi Valley. Railroads also connected Ohio's river and lake ports, carrying large numbers of passengers and great quantities of freight. The canal system continued to function, moving bulk goods at low cost. Water and rail traffic remained vital, since only the National Pike and a few other highways were properly maintained, and most road traffic remained local.

While it is evident that Ohio's farms, factories, mines, natural resources, and transportation network were to contribute mightily to the Union's war effort, the state also enjoyed a growing political centrality in national affairs. The impressive success of the Republican party brought Ohio to the attention of those who had political preferment to dole out during Lincoln's administration. As the third most populous state, Ohio had the third largest representation in Congress and the third largest number of electoral votes. This gave the state great political influence, especially after southern representatives abandoned Congress and left a vacuum of power and experience that could be filled by relative newcomers. Ohio politicians made the most of these opportunities and played a central role in the nation's political life during the war years.

While the Buckeye State's Republicans (and pro-war Democrats) secured influence with the Lincoln administration, it earned a political distinction of another sort during the war years. Its antiwar Peace Democrats (Copperheads) were as visible and outspoken as any in the North. They assumed a leading role in criticizing Lincoln, his party and his policies, and in obstructing officials who were trying to implement wartime objectives such as recruiting.

Politically Ohio was in the limelight during the war years. No party or leader could afford to ignore it.

It's War!: Organizing an Army

At 4:30 on the morning of April 12, 1861, batteries commanded by General P. G. T. Beauregard opened fire on Fort Sumter, a federal stronghold in the harbor of Charleston, South Carolina. After enduring a day and a half of bombardment, Maj. Robert Anderson surrendered the fort. In succeeding

WAR WITH THE SOUTH

A HISTORY OF THE

GREAT AMERICAN REBELLION

BY
ROBERT TOMES M. D.
ILLUSTRATED
WITH NUMEROUS ENGRAVINGS

The Civil War aroused patriotic fervor among many Ohio citizens, a popular reaction as illustrated by this vignette title page. (From Robert Tomes, *The War With the South: A History of the Late Rebellion* . . . , vol. 1, New York, 1862.

days the Confederacy took other belligerent actions, and on April 15 President Lincoln issued a call for 75,000 volunteers to serve for three months. They were to put down a series of actions "too powerful to be suppressed by the ordinary course of judicial proceedings"; the troops, said Lincoln, were needed to see that the laws were "duly executed." The language reflects his view that the Union was indissoluble and that the seceded states were in rebellion against legally constituted authority as provided in the Constitution. The Confederate viewpoint rested on the Constitution as a compact among sovereign states. These sovereign states, they claimed, could disassociate themselves, if they wished, from a union which they had voluntarily joined.

Initial reactions to the war news varied. Some citizens, like the young state senator Jacob D. Cox (who was to render distinguished military service during the war), felt "the shame, the outrage, the folly" which "seemed too great to believe." But for a much larger group, the news of Fort Sumter brought a patriotic thrill. Enthusiasts turned out at the first reports, not waiting for the president's call. Private military companies such as the sporty Cleveland Grays sped to Columbus by every means available. Gov. William Dennison was swamped with offers. Within days Ohio was struggling to accommodate more than 30,000 volunteers who far exceeded the 13,000 men that Lincoln's call required of Ohio.

Cincinnati alone could have filled Ohio's quota: her Irish formed a regiment, the Germans were enthusiastic, and French, Poles, and other European minorities enlisted. Most volunteers sat around makeshift Camp Jackson in Columbus. Their crude, temporary quarters were depressing, and inactivity was galling. By April 18, however, the First and Second Regiments of Ohio Volunteers had been formed from members of existing military companies, most of whom were from the southern part of the state. These regiments headed by rail for Washington to protect the capital city. They were poorly uniformed and equipped; order and discipline were minimal; the trains were delayed and halted along the way. Finally, however, the Ohio boys reached the capital, where they joined confused and undersupplied units from other states.

In Ohio the situation was chaotic. Governor Dennison was a suave, competent businessman with but limited experience in managing a volatile public. He and his assistants in state government were overwhelmed by the unprecedented demands made upon them. Volunteers, bored with being cooped up in hotels and encampments, complained of their inaction. State agents scoured Ohio and the East to find uniforms, arms, field equipment and the thousand-and-one things which military units require. The government authorized new camps, principal among them Camp Dennison on the Little Miami northeast of Cincinnati, which, along with Camp Chase in Columbus, served as a mar-shalling center for troops in federal service. State military units were distrib-uted among nine other encampments spread around the state.

Neither Ohio nor any state could be expected to meet this outpouring of excited fervor in an orderly manner. Improvisation was inevitable, but disap-pointed and disgusted volunteers were not receptive to excuses. Many three-month men vented their unhappiness on anyone who would listen when they again reached home. Their stories had a deleterious effect both upon later enlistments and popular support of the war. It is not surprising that utter confusion marked these first days of martial activity; the surprising thing is that within a matter of months, state government was handling its complex new responsibilities quite satisfactorily. Irritating problems, endemic in war-time, continued, but Ohio was among the first states to make its presence felt on the battlefield.

"Ohio Must Lead"

Organizing enlisted men was a chore, but accommodating *prima donna* of-ficers was politically sensitive. The tradition of allowing the men to choose their own officers up to the rank of colonel continued in the new volunteer units and caused Dennison much grief when he attempted to modify it. The governor did appoint officers of the higher ranks, however, often men with political influence who could be counted on to raise volunteers. Typical was the young college professor and state legislator, James A. Garfield, who par-layed these opportunities into a colonelcy in the Forty-second Ohio Volun-teer Infantry. Many of his Hiram College students volunteered for his com-mand and, with a regiment recruited, he marched off to learn the art of war, largely from manuals from which he instructed himself.

Among Dennison's first appointments was the brilliant but brittle West Point graduate, George Brinton McClellan, a native Pennsylvanian employed in Cincinnati as an officer of the Ohio and Mississippi Railroad. Dennison wanted Ohioan Irvin McDowell to command the state's first volunteer troops, but powerful Cincinnati interests prevailed upon him to choose McClellan. It was "Little Mac" who would lead Ohio's first troops in the field.

Dennison, learning that plans were afoot in Washington to call volunteers for a three-year term of service, requested Salmon P. Chase, secretary of the treasury in Lincoln's cabinet, to use his influence to secure a three-year ap-pointment for McClellan because, said Dennison, "Ohio must lead through-out the war." To the amazement of all, including McClellan, who was not normally a modest man, McClellan was appointed major general in the regular army, quite a step for one who, but a few weeks earlier, had been a captain. That politics dictated most appointments to state units was evident in Dennison's choice of brigadier generals. The appointments went to Newton Schleich, a Democratic leader in the Senate, Jacob Dolson Cox, a Republican leader in the Senate, and J. H. Bates, an officer of the old state militia. Only Cox would play an important role in the war.

Governor Dennison's assertion that "Ohio must lead" was not mere rhetoric. He cooperated energetically with the governors of Indiana and Illinois to arrange protection of the Ohio River border with Kentucky. These precautions were prudent for, although Kentucky remained in the Union, it was a slaveholding state with large numbers of aggressive Confederate sympathizers. Defensive emplacements were erected along the river, especially around Cincinnati, which was too valuable a prize to risk. Federal authorities turned down the governor's request to seize vital points south of the river, and Kentucky went through the war as a "border" state, contributing to both the Union and Confederate causes.

While holding the line on Kentucky, Dennison was equally concerned about neighboring Virginia, whose panhandle thrust a narrow strip of land northward between Pennsylvania and Ohio, its tip lying less than 100 miles from Lake Erie. Dennison saw clearly, however, that Ohio's best defensive line was not the Ohio River, but rather the mountains of Virginia's western counties. McClellan, apprised of the governor's view, advised caution and delay. As Dennison was later to say, from that time on he had "doubts as to McClellan's being . . . a man of action."

By May 1861 McClellan had his troops—mostly Ohioans with some Indianans—in motion. He posted men along the Ohio at Bellaire and Marietta to guard vital rail connections. Col. James B. Steedman crossed the Ohio, seized Parkersburg and surrounding area, and repaired its important rail line. Col. William Irvine did much the same thing at Wheeling with help from Virginians loyal to the old Union. With these initial objectives accomplished, McClellan moved to secure the vital Baltimore and Ohio rail line through western Virginia. The Ohio troops drove hostile forces from the region and encouraged loyal local people to come forward. The troops were bloodied in engagements at Phillipi, Rich's Mountain, and Carrick's Ford, but, for the most part, Ohio boys spent endless hours in boring, uncomfortable camps wondering if this was what war was all about. In September 1861, western Virginia was cleared of Confederate troops in the Kanawha campaign directed by Delaware County's Maj. Gen. William S. Rosecrans. McClellan took credit for these initial successes and in November 1861, Lincoln gave him overall command of the Union armies.

Political Repercussions

Partisan politics flourished in the disorder and confusion of the war's early months. Republicans were solidly prowar, and they were joined much of the time by Fusion Democrats and War Democrats. On September 5, 1861, Republicans and Fusion Democrats met in convention in Columbus and formed the Union Party, pledged to support the war to preserve the Union and defend the Constitution. Their platform did not mention slavery.

The Union convention made a difficult decision in selecting its gubernatorial candidate. Governor Dennison had performed heroically in trying circumstances, but he had made powerful enemies and was considered a political liability. The party dumped him, therefore, in favor of a Fusion Democrat, David Tod of Youngstown, a successful businessman in iron, coal, and railroads. It was imperative to the Unionists that the War Democrats remain united with the Republicans, and Tod's nomination seemed the best way to accomplish this end.

Peace Democrats—those opposed to the war—anticipated success in the fall elections, arguing that northerners would repudiate Lincoln's party, which was responsible for the embarrassing Union defeat in the first large-scale battle of the war. At Bull Run (Manassas Junction), just thirty miles southwest of Washington, Maj. Gen. Irvin McDowell's green troops were beaten by equally inexperienced Confederates on July 21, 1861. With a longer war in prospect, Lincoln issued a call for 500,000 volunteers to serve three-year terms. Once more Ohio oversubscribed her quota (67,000) by enlisting more than 77,000 volunteers. Although the handling of new recruits had improved, there was still enough disgruntlement among the soldiers and their families to encourage the antiwar party.

The War Democrats nominated Hugh J. Jewett, a respected and experienced leader of the party, on a platform that called for peaceful reconciliation with the South but stopped short of taking a strong antiwar stance. Tod won easily with 206,997 votes to Jewett's 151,774. Unionists rejoiced in victory but worried that the Democrats were still capable of making so strong a showing.

The Critical Year, 1862

Governor Tod moved swiftly to consolidate the gains Dennison had made. Tod was fortunate to be assisted by an able staff and a cooperative state legislature, for shortly after assuming office he had to deal with the highly emotional aftermath of the battle of Shiloh. Until that battle, Ohio troops had suffered modest losses. But Ohioans were numerous in the western armies led by Maj. Gen. Ulysses S. Grant, who was pushing south along the Tennessee and Cumberland rivers. Unionists cheered his brilliant moves against Fort Henry and Fort Donelson. In late March and early April Grant attempted to consolidate his forces at Pittsburg Landing on the Tennessee River. With his mind set on offensive maneuvers, and with a confidence born of his recent victories, Grant failed to fortify his encampment or to place proper pickets. Albert Sidney Johnston took advantage of these egregious errors and on April 6, 1862, his "butternuts" smashed into and nearly through the unprepared federals in the vicinity of Shiloh Church. Northern troops recovered from the bitter and bloody fighting and won the field on April 7; Grant was supported in the effort by the generalship of William Tecumseh Sherman and by the arrival of relief columns under Don Carlos Buell, both Ohioans. Union losses were enormous; Ohio alone suffered approximately 2,000 men killed and wounded.

Governor Tod and private citizens responded to the crisis by organizing emergency aid. Eleven steamboats rushed scores of doctors, a large group of nurses, and hundreds of cartons of medical supplies to the battlefield. Some supplies were paid for by the Sanitary Commission (a soldier-relief organization), some by the federal government, but most of the cost was borne by the state government. This precedent persisted after most major battles for the remainder of the war. Among the Ohio nurses at Shiloh was one who ranked with the famous Clara Barton in effectiveness. She was Mary Ann (Ball) Bickerdyke of Knox County. Throughout the war "Mother Bickerdyke" compiled an enviable record, battling official red tape to bring care and comfort to thousands of Ohio soldiers.

The most prominent commanders at Shiloh were Ohioans, and they had to bear the brunt of the public's wrath. Grant was a proper target for their anger; yet he had won, he was a fighter, and he learned from his mistakes. Grant's career went into temporary eclipse after Shiloh but emerged with new luster in the Vicksburg campaign of 1863. Sherman had also proved his fighting qualities at Shiloh, where he demonstrated that he was a talented commander. Bloody Shiloh doomed Memphis and opened routes into the Mississippi heartland.

During the spring and summer of 1862, McClellan led massive Union armies to the James-York Peninsula in Virginia, expecting to seize Richmond and end the war. Although some of his men got near enough Richmond to hear its church bells, Confederate forces under Gen. Robert E. Lee blocked them from the city. McClellan's army fought a number of sharp engagements (the Seven Days' Battles) before withdrawing from the peninsula and returning to Washington. Meanwhile, Maj. Gen. John Pope, who had won fame along the Mississippi, mismanaged an army in northern Virginia allowing Lee, Thomas "Stonewall" Jackson, and James Longstreet to inflict another disheartening defeat upon the Union in the Second Battle of Bull Run.

Lee now led his Army of Northern Virginia across the Potomac into Maryland, thus threatening Washington. McClellan, once more commanding the Army of the Potomac, finally met Lee's challenge at Antietam (Sharpsburg) in September. A tactical draw, Antietam was the bloodiest single day of the war. McClellan had not committed his entire army, and his failure to prevent Lee from escaping back into Virginia ended his career as a leading Union officer.

This Federal "victory" provided Lincoln with a setting he felt appropriate for issuing his famous Emancipation Proclamation, declaring that, as of January 1, 1863, slaves in those areas still in rebellion against the United States would be free. The proclamation freed no slaves in the Union border states nor in Union-occupied areas, but Lincoln's act converted the war into a "war to free the slaves." Antislavery Unionists (often called radicals), including Sen. Benjamin "Bluff Ben" Wade of Ohio, were pleased; conservatives were concerned. Ohio Democrats, especially Irish and German immigrants, feared that a flood of former slaves would now descend upon the state, competing for jobs and, in their view, lowering the social tone.

Many other military events of 1862 had little impact on Ohio, but in December, at Fredericksburg, Virginia, Maj. Gen. Ambrose Burnside sent wave after wave of valiant men, including Ohioans, into the face of Confederates entrenched on Marye's Heights. Once more casualties were unacceptably high, and morale plummeted in the Army of the Potomac.

Peace Democrat or Copperhead?

Antiwar protest, while unpopular in "patriotic" circles, has been an American privilege and practice since "Patriot" and "Loyalist" espoused differing visions of America's role in the British Empire. The nation was divided by the War of 1812 and, during the Mexican War, antiwar protest had risen to an art form. The emotional impact of the Civil War exceeded that of any previous American conflict, and those who opposed the prosecution of it were understandably targets of abuse and censure. The traditional peace churches—Quakers, Moravians, German pietists—were well represented in Ohio. Though many individual members of these denominations fought to preserve the Union, these pacifists traditionally sought peaceful reconciliation. Similarly opposed were thousands of northerners who believed in "states' rights" and the protection of slavery where it already existed. To them, emancipation was but a prelude to social chaos. Among this latter group, sentiment on effective tactics to be used ranged from passive resistance to rioting and, in some instances, armed resistance to recruiting efforts.

Antiwar advocates, especially Peace Democrats, were labeled "Copperheads" by pro-war advocates who said that these protesters, like the venomous reptile, would strike a lethal blow, without warning, to the Union cause. In no state was Copperhead activity more visible or led by abler men than in Ohio. And these leaders found fertile soil for protest in the emotional malaise that accompanied the growing casualty lists and the partial but incomplete victories of Union armies.

Ohio, it will be recalled, oversubscribed Lincoln's first calls for volunteers in 1861. A year later, however, enlistments had slowed due in part to discouraging war news and in part to speeches made by antiwar protesters. One of these, Dr. Edson B. Olds of Lancaster, was so outspoken that Governor Tod asked federal authorities to arrest him under the terms of the president's proclamation suspending *habeas corpus*. That suspension was yet another cause for protest. All told, eleven Ohioans suffered Dr. Olds's fate, most being imprisoned for several months on charges of obstructing recruiting efforts. One who escaped imprisonment was Samuel Medary, the Democratic editor of the *Columbus Crisis*. He argued that the South could not be defeated militarily, and he attacked the policies of the Unionists throughout the war despite the burning of his office in 1863 by angry soldiers from nearby Camp Chase. The most widely known and fervently admired Peace Democrat was the arch-Copperhead, Clement Laird Vallandigham. Of southern heritage, he was born in New Lisbon (now Lisbon, Columbiana County), the son of a Presbyterian minister. He was serving the Dayton district in the United States House of Representatives when the war broke out. From the beginning he won a following for his position that the Confederacy could not be conquered, that states had a right to secede, and that slavery was protected under the Constitution. Through an immediate peace he hoped to see the Union restored under a constitution which would protect slavery. He rejected using force to accomplish these ends. Courageous and bold, articulate and impassioned, Vallandigham became more and more conspicuous as the voice of dissent through 1862.

As the Union war effort struggled through that summer and fall, southern Ohio girded for possible invasion. Maj. Gen. Kirby Smith's Confederates seized Lexington, Kentucky, on September 1 and dispatched patrols to the Ohio River. In response to these probes, Maj. Gen. Lew Wallace led Union volunteers in organizing the defense of Cincinnati and surrounding areas. They built entrenchments in the hills above Covington, Kentucky, hastily assembled supplies, and erected a pontoon bridge across the Ohio to move men and materiel to the new emplacements.

The mayors of Cincinnati, Covington, and Newport were anxious to cooperate with the military in defense of their cities and supported a declaration of martial law issued by General Wallace. "Patriotism, duty, honor, self-preservation," said the order, required that business be suspended and that everyone gather at public places for assignment to defense duties. The necessary labor "must be performed equally by all classes," and it ought to be a labor of love; "anyhow, it must be done." Wallace then stated, "The principle adopted is: Citizens for the labor, soldiers for the battle." All of Cincinnati responded with alacrity. For the moment there were no divisions, only concerned citizens intent upon protecting their city.

Governor Tod responded to the crisis with characteristic force. He authorized arms and ammunition for the city's defenders. Who was to pay could be settled later. On September 2 the governor urged armed men from regions close to Cincinnati (except those from the river counties) to converge upon the city, promising that the state would pay their rail fare. His appeal, and similar calls throughout Ohio, created a flood of volunteers who quickly outnumbered army men. Looking as if they were out for an afternoon shoot in the woods, these volunteers were called "squirrel hunters."

Some confusion was inevitable. On September 10, Tod asked Cleveland to send men, but just three days later he called a halt to the volunteer effort throughout the state. On September 12 confirmation reached Cincinnati that Kirby Smith had been recalled south to assist in the defense of eastern Tennessee, then threatened by advancing Union troops. Cincinnati and its suburbs were safe! Local people returned to civilian pursuits, and the "squirrel hunters" were sent home with special certificates commemorating their volunteer service. Perhaps the most significant fact to emerge from Cincinnati's scare was that Ohioans would rise as one to meet a threat to their own soil. For a brief moment they united in a common purpose. But immediately after that danger abated, they were ready to return to their partisan ways.

Politics and Protest, 1862–63

The Democrats approached the fall elections of 1862 with confidence. The Peace faction was led by Vallandigham, ex-Senator George Pugh, George Pendleton, and William Allen, and they were joined by certain War Democrats who left the Union Party and returned to their old allegiance. These fugitives from the Union Party had many reasons for changing allegiances; prominent among them were the gloomy reports that continued to flow from the war fronts, the perception that Lincoln could not be persuaded to change the direction of his policy, and the fear that a flood of blacks would descend upon Ohio as the Emancipation Proclamation started to take effect. The legislature had recently redistricted the state, expecting to enhance Republican (Union) chances, but by and large the maneuver failed. Democrats won fourteen of Ohio's nineteen congressional seats. The victory at the polls excited Ohio-born R. G. Dun, a New York businessman, who wrote to his cousin: "I must congratulate you on [Ohio's] glorious Democratic victory. . . . Good for Ohio! I am not ashamed to own her now as my native State."

The Unionists made a special effort to beat Clement Vallandigham, persuading the popular and able Maj. Gen. Robert C. Schenck to leave his military post and challenge the Democrat. Vallandigham campaigned with great vigor but lost, thanks largely to Republican strength in Warren County, which had been added to his district in a recent gerrymandering. Proud and self-righteous, Vallandigham did not take his loss gracefully. He stepped up the ardor of his protest, assuming an increasingly shrill tone during the lame duck session of Congress. "Traitor" was one of the milder epithets Republicans and Fusion Democrats applied to him, but he had the courage of his convictions and prejudices, and seemed to revel in conflict.

The Union and the Confederacy as well were finding it increasingly difficult to fill manpower quotas. It was a matter of pride in most counties to fill local quotas with volunteers, but repeated calls for troops in 1862 drained the pool. Most Ohio counties found it necessary to stimulate enlistments with bounty money. Bounties were raised locally, and by war's end bounty payments amounted to hundreds of dollars in some communities. Bounty jumping was common. A man would enlist and collect his bounty payment, then he would desert, enlist again elsewhere, and collect another bounty. One enterprising Ohioan enlisted, collected, and jumped eighteen times before being caught.

In 1863 the federal Conscription Act went into effect. Any recruiting unit failing to fill its quota with volunteers had to draft enough men to make up the difference. If drafted, a man could avoid service by paying a $300 commutation fee or by hiring a substitute. Some thought that commutation and substitution converted the war into "a rich man's war and a poor man's fight," but the fee helped many a poor man financially.

By 1863 Ohio started to enroll blacks in its volunteer units. At Lincoln's first call for volunteers, hundreds of Ohio blacks offered their services but were refused, as they were in all other northern states. Massachusetts broke the color line by enrolling blacks in state units in 1862, and hundreds of Ohio blacks went to the Bay State to enroll in their black regiments. A year later, blacks were enrolled in Ohio. They were formed in all-black units, normally under white officers, with their pay half that of white volunteers. Despite these impediments, more than 5,000 Ohio blacks ultimately served in state or federal units, and others served in the units of other states.

Antiwar extremists made a bad situation worse for recruiters by encouraging draft resistance and desertion. In one instance a group of about a hundred armed men, many of them antiwar Scots-Irish "uplanders," tried to protect a deserter from a deputy marshal at Hoskinville, Noble County. The marshal received troop support, and the demonstration was broken up. Several men were fined and imprisoned by federal court order. In June 1863, a much larger group organized in Holmes County, a Democratic, antiwar stronghold. Nine hundred armed men with four howitzers fortified themselves against 450 troops sent to enforce the draft. A desultory exchange of gunfire resulted in two wounded; the protesters fled to the woods, and thus ended the "battle of Fort Fizzle." On other occasions, troops directed by the adjutant general's office in Columbus went by train to Morrow County and to other disaffected parts of the state to break up protest groups, sequester arms, or assist local authorities to carry out the draft.

There were no antiwar protests in Ohio to compare with the vicious draft riots that rocked New York City in 1863. Disaffection in the Buckeye State was most common in sparsely settled, rural, or semi-rural areas, and in areas of heavy German and Irish settlement in the northern half of the state. Some urban areas, notably Cincinnati and Toledo, also experienced anti-black riots. Ironically, the southern counties, where many settlers were of southern origin, outperformed the northern counties in filling their quotas with volunteers. The Western Reserve, so strong for the Union and containing a radical antislavery element, had to resort to the draft in each of its counties. Why should this be? Were Yankees less patriotic than Ohioans of southern origins? Were the city and townspeople of the Reserve less likely than the farmers in the southern counties to retain vestiges of individualism and direct action? Did those of southern origin retain an enthusiasm for combat reputedly a part of their culture? It is easy to challenge each of these contentions: so far no wholly satisfying explanation has been forthcoming.

Muddled recruitment practices played into the protesters' hands. Vallandigham had both national and gubernatorial ambitions and, while professing loyalty to the Union, he seized every opportunity to put himself forward as leader of the opposition. This especially irritated Maj. Gen. Ambrose Burnside. Fresh from his disastrous defeat at Fredericksburg, Burnside commanded the Department of the Ohio with headquarters at Cincinnati. On April 13, 1863, he issued General Order No. 38, directed at two classes of "enemies of our country." Those who committed overt acts "for the benefit of the enemies of our country," were to be tried as spies and traitors and, if found guilty, "will suffer death." The second category included those with "the habit of declaring sympathies for the enemy." Persons arrested for this offense would be tried "as above stated" (meaning they could be tried as spies and traitors) or they might be "sent beyond our lines into the lines of their friends."

If Burnside intended to test the mettle of the protesters, he certainly succeeded. Such responsible men and long-time leaders of the Democracy as
George Pugh and George Pendleton attacked the measure as a limitation on
free speech, a further erosion of traditional civil liberties. Vallandigham, con-
scious that martyrdom could further his political ambitions, rose to the bait as
Burnside suspected he would. On May 1 Vallandigham and others addressed a
Democratic rally in Mount Vernon. Burnside had officers in the audience
recording their words. Vallandigham denounced General Order No. 38. His
right to speak, he said, was protected by "General Order No. 1," the Constitution of the United States. Although his remarks were somewhat intemperate, they were no more so than those of a leading Democrat, Samuel S.
"Sunset" Cox, with whom he shared the platform.

When apprised of Vallandigham's comments, General Burnside ordered
his arrest. A special train carried 150 soldiers to Dayton where, in the early
morning hours, Vallandigham was seized at his home and rushed to Cincinnati before his admirers could organize resistance. Confined to Kemper Barracks, Vallandigham was brought before a military tribunal which found him
guilty of violating the terms of General Order No. 38 and sentenced him to
confinement. His counsel's protest that no military court held jurisdiction
over a civilian while civil courts were available was ignored. In 1866, in the
case *ex parte Milligan,* the United States Supreme Court declared that civilians
could not be tried by a military court when the civil courts were functioning.
It came too late to help Vallandigham. Burnside ordered the prisoner transferred to Fort Warren in Boston, but, upon reviewing the case, President
Lincoln countermanded the sentence and decreed that Vallandigham be sent
through southern lines into the Confederacy. Late in May he was taken to
Maj. Gen. William Rosecrans' headquarters at Murfreesboro, Tennessee, and
from there sent into southern lines, but only after considerable discussion by
Confederates who were not too sure they wanted him.

Reaction to the arrest was severe. In Dayton a mob roamed the streets
intimidating Union men and burning the office of a Republican newspaper.
Responsible Democrats like George Pugh condemned the proceedings and
tried every legal tactic to free Vallandigham. Some state officials agreed with
Lincoln that Burnside had put Vallandigham in position to become a martyr,
and they approved Lincoln's solution.

As for Vallandigham, he received a cool reception in the South. To accept
him would indict the Peace Democrats as being pro-Confederate. Since his
views coincided so nicely with those of the Confederates, Vallandigham lost
his voice. Removing him from the object of his scorn left him unfulfilled; he
itched to regain contact with his friends and admirers. With the assistance of
Confederate authorities, he boarded a blockade runner for Bermuda. He then
sailed to Canada where, early in the summer of 1863, he established himself on

the Canadian side of the Niagara River, across whose waters he could see the soil of the United States.

Meanwhile, Union fortunes were improving on wide-flung battle fronts. In the West, Grant's armies successfully executed one of the war's great military feats. From a position on the Mississippi northwest of Vicksburg, Grant passed his troops southward around that citadel and crossed to the east side of the Mississippi below the town. Cutting himself off from his base, he moved eastward, defeating Confederate forces in the vicinity. He then be-sieged Vicksburg for six weeks, pounding it with artillery until the gallant defenders collapsed of malnutrition, disease, and loss of fighting strength. On July 4 General John C. Pemberton surrendered the city and 30,000 soldiers. On July 8 Port Hudson fell; the entire length of the Mississippi River was now in Union hands, and the Confederacy was split into eastern and western en-claves. Abraham Lincoln said it best: "Once more the Father of Waters flows unvexed to the sea."

In Virginia, meanwhile, "Fighting Joe" Hooker led a huge Union army in May 1863 against Lee at Chancellorsville, where the South won a costly vic-tory. Afterward Lee once again sent his columns north of the Potomac. At the end of June, several Confederate columns converged upon the Pennsylvania market town of Gettysburg. Federal troops under Maj. Gen. George Gordon Meade moved to intercept them. After three days of some of the hottest and most gallant action of the war, Meade's army prevailed. Lee retreated south of the Potomac, saved only by the inability of the Union forces to follow and press him at this critical point.

These major victories at Gettysburg and Vicksburg—one east, one west—coming while the Union was celebrating Independence Day, appeared to be a promising omen for the Northern cause. Historians mark Gettysburg and Vicksburg as a turning point in the war. Ohio troops were involved in both of these campaigns, and once more casualty lists brought grief to many homes. In November, a new military cemetery was dedicated at Gettysburg to those who had given "the last full measure of devotion." A large Ohio delegation including the past, present, and future governors, went by train to listen to the immortal words spoken on that occasion by President Lincoln, who exhorted his divided nation: "It is for us the living . . . to be dedicated here to the unfinished work which they who fought here have thus far so nobly advanced."

Ohio authorities had sent thousands of men into distant fields, but what could they do to defend their own soil? The hastily improvised defense of Cincinnati in 1862 had revealed the state's lack of preparedness. Governor Tod, therefore, supported a bill that the legislature enacted in 1863, establish-ing the "Ohio Volunteer Militia" and calling for the enrollment and training of all able-bodied men between the ages of eighteen and forty-five. By summer approximately 345,000 men had registered, but they were not yet organized, supplied, and trained. They were not ready, therefore, when the state needed them to repel rebel raiders in July 1863.

Ohio Invaded

Col. John Hunt Morgan, a Confederate cavalry leader from Kentucky, had threatened Cincinnati in 1862. In June 1863, he led 2,460 mounted men into Indiana, where he scourged the countryside while federal cavalry and state militia pursued. Ohio authorities feared he intended an assault upon Cincinnati. General Burnside declared martial law in the city and hastily provided for its defense. On July 12, Governor Tod called out the old state militia, but even before they heard the order, Morgan was on the Ohio border. Feinting toward Cincinnati, Morgan drove his men ninety miles in thirty-six hours before resting them within sight of Camp Dennison, Ohio's major staging area for federal troops. After brief refreshment, Morgan's men dashed off eastward on a convoluted, exhausting ride across Ohio's southern counties. David Hulse, a Sharonville farmer, was glad to see them leave his part of the state. "The Morgan raid created the greatest excitement that I ever seen," he wrote to his brother. "Citizens in every direction, were running off their horses into back hollows and thick woods. . . . There was much loss by the train of thieves, which always follows Armies in the disguise of soldiers."

Morgan's objective was to disrupt Yankee affairs, demonstrate the Union's vulnerability, and create panic and confusion. He certainly succeeded in part. One observer said that Morgan's men had a "disposition for wholesale plunder." They seemed "actuated by a desire to pay off, in the enemy's country, all scores that the Union army had chalked up in the South." Basil Duke, Morgan's second in command, said:

> They did not pillage with any sort of method or reason; it seemed to be a mania; senseless and purposeless. One man carried a bird-cage, with three canaries in it, for two days. Another rode with a chafing dish . . . on the pommel of his saddle until an officer forced him to throw it away. . . . Another slung seven pairs of skates around his neck, and chuckled over the acquisition. I saw very few articles of real value taken; they pillaged like boys robbing an orchard. . . . They would, with few exceptions, throw away their plunder after a while, like children tired of their toys.

Some plunder was useful: Farmer Hulse reports the raiders taking food, coffee, sugar, clothing, tobacco, and especially the best horses.

Morgan outdistanced his pursuers through Piketon, Jackson, Vinton, and Berlin, but just before reaching Pomeroy he ran into stiff resistance from

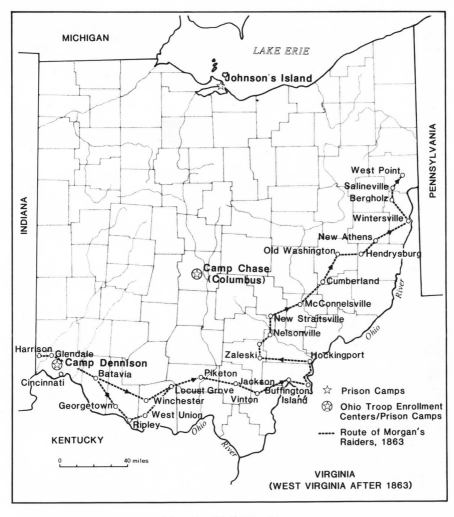

Map 11. Civil War Sites

militia. Pressing on he reached Chester, and on the evening of July 18 arrived at the Buffington Island ford on the Ohio River. Here he fought a sharp skirmish with federal troops and Ohio militia. More than 700 of his men were captured and sent by steamer to Cincinnati: Morgan and the 1,200 or so remaining troopers escaped entrapment and moved twenty miles upriver, where about 300 crossed safely before a gunboat blocked that escape route. Now seriously depleted in strength and spirit, Morgan's raiders turned northward, hard pressed at every step by their pursuers. They crossed the Muskingum near McConnelsville, rode through the streets of Old Washington, and finally were brought to bay at Salineville in Columbiana County.

Morgan surrendered at West Point, ten miles northwest of East Liverpool. No other Confederate unit had operated so far to the north.

Maj. Gen. Henry Halleck, then in command of all Union forces, ordered that, in retaliation for the treatment accorded certain Union prisoners held in the South, Morgan and his officers be placed in the Ohio Penitentiary as common criminals. Morgan had the last laugh, however. He and six officers tunneled their way out in the only successful nineteenth-century escape from that Columbus bastille. After making his way back to the Confederacy, Morgan was killed in 1864 in Tennessee.

The cost to Ohio from this hectic two-week period was modest. There was little loss of life. The state reimbursed property claims to the amount of nearly half a million dollars, and it expended about the same amount to put its militia in the field. Disrupted communications were reestablished, and the country-side returned to its placid ways. But the memory of sudden terror endured for a generation.

Politics Again

While issues were settled on the battlefield in the summer of 1863, Ohio's political parties were girding for a gubernatorial election. Moderate prowar men within the Democratic party wished to nominate Hugh Jewett. But their voices were soon drowned by an almost hysterical excitement among the party rank-and-file to nominate Vallandigham. So vehement were they that many peace men expressed a determination, should Vallandigham win election, of arming 100,000 men if need be to escort their man to the statehouse. Although much of that enthusiasm was mere braggadoccio, it revealed the depths of discontent among a large segment of the party. Urged on by the implacable editor of the *Columbus Crisis,* Samuel Medary, who wanted the Lincoln administration rebuked, the convention voted by acclamation to nominate Vallandigham. Medary, who presided at the convention, appointed a committee to approach Lincoln in the hope that he would "return Clement L. Vallandigham to his home in Ohio." The effort was unsuccessful.

The vehemence of the Democrats alarmed Ohio Unionists, who now strengthened their party position. They dumped incumbent David Tod because he was soft on emancipation, and many malcontents held a grievance against him. Their nominee was John Brough, a War Democrat and successful businessman. The gubernatorial contest intensified in August when Vallandigham moved his operations to Windsor on the Canadian side of the Detroit River, where he was more readily available to his supporters. Unionists stepped up their charges that Vallandigham's activities were treasonous and that his supporters would be cursed as were the Tories of the Revolution.

Through their control of the legislature, Unionists also arranged for Ohio soldiers in the field to vote. Some soldiers were granted leave to come home to cast their ballots and to encourage the folks at home to support the Union Party. Almost in panic at the possibility that Vallandigham might win, Lincoln and Union party leaders sent Senator Wade, Sen. John Sherman, and Secretary Chase home to Ohio to help Brough campaign.

On October 13 the voters decided the issue. Brough received 288,374 votes to Vallandigham's 187,492. Brough carried the soldier vote by a 19-to-1 margin. Obviously men in the field did not want to vote for a man who claimed their service was misplaced. There is some evidence that pro-Union soldiers on occasion intimidated comrades from voting for Vallandigham, but Brough would have won the election handily even without the soldier vote. Though Vallandigham was trounced, the size of his vote revealed a large amount of disaffection with the conduct of the war. Lincoln was aware of this even as he reputedly sent a telegram to Brough: "Glory to God in the highest: Ohio has saved the Union."

Despite his rejection at the polls, Vallandigham was not ready to fade away. He was later permitted to drift back into Ohio, unmolested, where he played an important but losing role in the presidential election of 1864. He was also reputed to command the Sons of Liberty, a secret society opposed to the war, but the Sons were ineffectual and wielded no real influence.

Relief on the Home Front and in the Camps

Soon after his inauguration in January 1864, Brough urged the legislature to increase the state tax for support of soldiers' families. This tax had been enacted early in the war; Governor Tod had been anxious to increase it. Now the legislature did so, raising the tax to two mills, permitting county commissioners to add another mill and local officials to add a half-mill. Shortly after the new legislation took effect, it was apparent that officials in disaffected areas of the state were not collecting the tax or were misappropriating the funds raised. Brough attempted, with what success is not known, to police tax collections by asking the chairmen of county military committees to supervise and to report any misuse of the tax funds.

This assistance to soldiers' families was urgently needed. One of the poorly told stories of the war years is the degree to which families, left without their men, struggled to keep going. Frequently a woman alone had to raise the children and care for the farm and livestock, though she needed male help for tasks like plowing, threshing, or mending fences. Many readers are familiar with poignant letters from men in the field describing their fear and loneliness, but some letters from home were every bit as sad—a child dead of "milk sick," the cow going dry, fences crumbling, the mortgage payment unmet. Men receiving such news sometimes deserted and headed home, especially when they seemed to be accomplishing little in camp and field.

According to the adjutant general's figures, Ohio's manpower shortage was not as acute in 1863 as one might suppose. Immigration into northern states continued through the war years and helped to fill empty slots in the labor force. The vitality of business and manufacturing activity, however, assured positions for women which they ordinarily would not have held. Jobs involving sewing skills expanded greatly thanks to the demand for uniforms, tents, and all sorts of cloth and canvas products. As younger women filled these jobs, older women took on ever more responsibility for child care and maintenance of the home. Left to cope with new and enlarged challenges, women needed all the help they could get. The state tax money for relief of soldiers' families was supplemented by locally raised money; these funds, whatever their source, were often the margin by which families survived intact on their own property.

Assistance to soldiers in the field came from several sources. Early in the war, Ohio established state agencies—relief posts of sorts—wherever significant numbers of Ohio troops were stationed. To these posts the state rushed supplies of many kinds. Following battles, the state sent doctors, nurses, and medical supplies for the immediate care of the wounded. The medical personnel who travelled with the armies were overwhelmed after a battle. It was a relief to them, and a mercy to the wounded, to move the injured to hospitals in rear areas where care could continue as long as necessary.

For female nurses service in field hospitals was a new experience. We have mentioned "Mother" Bickerdyke's work at Shiloh, but many other Ohio women earned a reputation for their work in military hospitals. Among them were Sister Anthony O'Connell of Cincinnati and Lucy Webb Hayes, who went to hospitals to care for her thrice-wounded husband and while attending him also assisted others. This work was performed, it must be remembered, when society at large was still somewhat shocked at the idea of gentle ladies working amidst the horrors of military hospitals.

While the state provided assistance to men in the field, so did voluntary agencies. Foremost among them was the United States Sanitary Commission, the forerunner of the Red Cross. Its first Ohio branch was established by the men and women of Cleveland on April 20, 1861, as the "Soldiers' Aid Society of Northern Ohio." The Commission's Cincinnati branch became one of the most productive in the nation, sending tremendous amounts of material goods—everything from handkerchiefs to horseradish, from socks and shirts to sauerkraut—to relief centers, establishing hospitals, and extending their work in a hundred useful directions. Women had the central role in this work. It was of major importance to the Union war effort. The Sanitary Commission carried on to war's end, and, at its close, invested surplus funds in government bonds, the income from which was used to relieve needy veterans.

Yet another group providing soldiers' relief was the clergy. From the conflict's first days, a majority of Ohio's clergymen supported the war. Some Protestant denominations officially announced their support of the effort, as did Roman Catholics. Bishop Purcell of Cincinnati displayed his support by flying the American flag above his cathedral. Individual Jews served the Union, but there was no official Jewish position on the conflict. Not all Ohio clergy approved. Those from the traditional peace churches, those with southern sympathies, and those who supported the Peace Democrats largely avoided support.

At first clergymen directed their energies toward supplying troops with Bibles and religious tracts, but the clergy's aid to troops soon broadened. In addition to religious literature they supplied material support through an organization called the Christian Commission, which has been likened to the YMCA. It appears that this activity overlapped substantially with that of the Sanitary Commission and other relief groups. However, grateful troops in the field probably cared not at all about overlapping jurisdictions. Like soldiers from time immemorial, they eagerly awaited good things from family and friends; the folks back home who supplied them made army life more endurable.

Holding on Course, 1864

The excitement Unionists felt following the victories of Vicksburg and Gettysburg led to unrealistic expectations. The fighting was far from over; bitter and prolonged struggle marked the last months of 1863 and all of 1864.

In September 1863, Bragg's Confederates checked Rosecrans's Army of the Cumberland, containing many Ohio men, at Chickamauga, Georgia. Confederates holding the heights that commanded Chattanooga, Tennessee, then imperiled the Union base there. In brilliant moves, U. S. Grant, now in command, captured the heights, relieved Chattanooga, and seriously injured Confederate hopes. President Lincoln ordered Grant to Washington, and on March 9, 1864, the president promoted him to lieutenant general and named him general-in-chief. Command of the western armies devolved upon William Tecumseh Sherman.

Under Grant, Union strategy was to keep simultaneous pressure on the eastern and western Confederate armies so as to use the North's superior manpower and materiel to wear down southern forces. Acting on this plan, in the spring of 1864 Sherman's men won hard-fought engagements in the campaign against Atlanta and stopped short of the city while the general pondered ways of regaining his army's forward momentum.

In northern Virginia, already well soaked with Yankee and Confederate blood, a costly new campaign was under way in 1864. The Army of the Potomac, now led by Grant, moved from the terrible fields of the Wilderness to Spotsylvania, Cold Harbor, and by midsummer to Petersburg. Grant understood what Lincoln had intuitively known, that Lee could be worn down by superior Union numbers and equipment. Lee's army was the proper target, not Richmond. Grant's army ground away at Lee, suffering many casualties, but fatally weakening the opponent. Back home, however, Grant's casualty lists were considered shocking; he was called "Butcher" Grant by unfriendly newspapers. Now Grant settled in before Petersburg. Again Northern enthusiasm ebbed: once more war weariness blanketed the land.

Against this backdrop, Governor John Brough attempted to deal with the unending trials of office. Complaints came to him from every side. Convalescent soldiers were not receiving proper food; equipment was not up to standard; railroads wanted adjustments to the policy governing soldiers' fares; officers of state regiments clamored for promotion and favors. Brough met these problems with energy and stubborn competence. As one admiring historian put it, "The state has never had a more honest, conscientious, and fearless executive."

Brough also knew when to take the initiative, and in April 1864, he persuaded the governors of Indiana, Illinois, Iowa, and Wisconsin to join in offering the War Department 85,000 state troops to serve for 100 days in defense of Washington; veteran troops could then be withdrawn to serve in the field with Grant's armies. These 100-day men would be treated as United States Infantry volunteers, paid by the federal government, with no bounty or excuse from the draft involved. President Lincoln accepted the offer within two days, and Brough immediately made arrangements to send the 30,000 men Ohio had promised. On Monday, May 2, more than the required number of state militia (called at this time the National Guard) assembled in various encampments. Among their number were substantial businessmen and citizens of status who had to make a substantial sacrifice to leave on short notice; their response was gratifying.

The driving spirit behind the movement was clearly Brough's. Ohio oversubscribed its 30,000 quota and the governor offered the extra men to the War Department. Secretary Stanton accepted, telegraphing Brough that "The other states will be deficient and behind time. . . . Let us have all your regiments within the next week. *They may decide the war.*" Within eleven days 35,982 men were organized, mustered, clothed, armed, equipped, and turned over to the United States military authorities for transportation and assignment. In September they were dismissed from federal service after serving effectively at several critical points from western Virginia to the seaboard.

The Hundred Days Men were an adjunct to other troops required of Ohio under four calls in 1864. Ohio met its share of 148,979 men although the draft had to be applied to accomplish it. Local patriots continued to encourage volunteer enlistments by raising bounty money. Their methods of getting contributions were often peremptory. In one instance, a Summit County farmer, unsympathetic to the war and constant calls for funds, shot and killed a member of the local solicitation committee. He served time in the penitentiary for his deed, but was pardoned shortly after the war since he had acted in "an excited state" brought on by the tensions of the time.

Tension also surrounded the guarding of important prison camps in Ohio. Confederate officers were incarcerated on Johnson's Island in Sandusky Bay. Other Confederate prisoners were held at Camp Chase and a small number at Camp Dennison. Resourceful rebel agents, from time to time, schemed to release the Johnson's Island prisoners. From their base in Canada they planned to seize lake vessels, storm the island, and carry off the freed prisoners to Canada. In 1864 one such plot came close to success, but the war ended with the prisoners secure in their camps. The Ohio prisons had their problems, but none were an affront to humankind as was Andersonville in Georgia. Wounds, disease, and poor nutrition took their toll of the Ohio-based prisoners, and to this day there are Confederate cemeteries on Johnson's Island and at the site of Camp Chase in southwest Columbus.

The War Moves to a Close

Even in the midst of a civil war American presidential politics ran their course. In 1864 President Lincoln, determined that the election proceed, indicated that he would seek reelection, but he faced formidable obstacles. Salmon P. Chase and his doting daughter, Kate, both inveterate political manipulators with eyes fixed on the main prize, allowed their circle of friends and admirers to encourage Chase to challenge Lincoln. Sen. John Sherman and financier Jay Cooke were among those urging their fellow Ohioan on, but as support grew for Lincoln, the Ohio cabal prudently withdrew and supported his nomination.

The Democrats were in disarray. Hard-core Peace Democrats were unhappy when the party named Maj. Gen. George B. McClellan as its presidential candidate. As a sop to the peace faction, "Gentleman George" Pendleton, a leader of Cincinnati's Copperheads, was the vice-presidential nominee.

The summer military stalemate and an acute case of war weariness threatened Lincoln's chances. He was "saved" in September when Mobile fell, Sherman's army finally seized Atlanta, and Union cavalry units led by Maj. Gen. Philip Sheridan of Somerset (Perry County)—ably served by a pugnacious young Ohio-born brigadier, George Custer—gained control of the Valley of Virginia. These significant victories rekindled hope that the war was winding down to its final stages.

Lincoln won the electoral vote easily: his popular margin was 400,000 votes. He carried Ohio by 60,055 votes, losing some Ohio counties which he had carried in 1860, but capturing nearly the whole of the soldier vote. Seventeen of Ohio's nineteen seats in the House of Representatives went to the party of Lincoln. It was clear from the vote that the Union intended to pursue the war to what many war-weary Unionists expected would be its imminent conclusion.

The western armies controlled Tennessee and northern Georgia, allowing Sherman to consolidate his hold on the Atlanta region. In November, he led 62,000 troops across Georgia, cutting a swath of devastation sixty miles wide through the heart of the Confederacy. He undercut Confederate morale by bringing war home to civilians in a manner they would neither forget nor forgive. Arriving at Savannah in December, Sherman moved northward early in 1865 through South Carolina, leaving Columbia, the capital of this "Cradle of the Confederacy," in smoking ruins. April found him well into North Carolina, where he was confronted by southern forces under Joseph E. Johnston.

It was apparent in the spring of 1865 that the Confederacy had played out its options. Courage was no substitute for men and materiel. Petersburg fell, followed quickly by Richmond. Lee led a final desperate dash toward the west, but Sheridan's cavalry headed him off. On April 9, Lee surrendered to Grant at brief ceremonies in the McLean house at Appomattox Court House. Grant's simple and generous terms—allowing the Confederates to return home, taking their mules or horses with them—set a pattern for the additional capitulations still remaining.

The deadliest war in American history was over. Throughout Ohio and the Union spontaneous celebrations—bonfires, speeches, salutes, toasts—greeted news of Lee's surrender. It was the greatest outpouring of sentiment since January, when Congress had passed the Thirteenth Amendment, freeing the slaves, once and for all. The Ohio General Assembly ratified the amendment in February by large margins in both houses.

Joy was not unalloyed in the spring of 1865. Hundreds of thousands had died for the Union cause, and suddenly the president himself was dead of an assassin's bullet just as his cause became triumphant. Holiday Ames, a lieutenant in the 102d Ohio Volunteer Infantry, expressed a common soldier's reaction to the news in a letter to his wife: "I have not felt as bad since I have been in the army as I have today. I heard of the death of A. Lincoln on last evening it made me feel so bad that I went to bed and have not felt like getting up since. I feel now like staying in the army three years more and fighting for reveng, yes fighting until every cursed Rebble is exterminated." Throughout the war

Lincoln had endured criticism from those who objected to his war policies. He also endured personal attacks from ambitious, malicious, or short-sighted men who were unable or unwilling to see beyond certain superficial characteristics. Lincoln's amazing popularity with the common man had grown through the war years. The funeral train carrying his body to Springfield, Illinois, stopped at Cleveland, where an estimated 100,000 viewed the coffin, and at Columbus, where for six-and-a-half hours mourners filed past his coffin in the Statehouse rotunda. Through the countryside and small towns sorrowing people lined the track to see the train pass. It was a fitting farewell from Ohio, which had given so much support to the man and to his cause.

Ohio's Contributions: A Summing Up

For two days in May 1865, Union troops paraded in the streets of Washington in a Grand Review, their final moment of glory before demobilization. On the first day the eastern armies marched. Their military bearing, their "spit and polish" impressed the crowds. On the second day the western armies marched, many Ohio units among them. They swung down Pennsylvania Avenue with an insouciance and elan that reflected their confidence and their accomplishments. For hundreds of thousands of soldiers, it was the "last hurrah."

It took little time for veterans to settle into civilian life again, but they never forgot their experiences. Both individually and as members of their veterans' organization, the Grand Army of the Republic (GAR), they were a force to be reckoned with. Politically they supported veterans' bonuses, and many wished to see stern measures applied to the defeated South. The great majority would support only those political candidates who had taken the "right" stance on the war issues. For decades to come they cast their ballots for men who, like themselves, had served on the battlefield.

The price of the Civil War was astonishing. No fewer than 630,000 Americans died in the conflict, either from battle wounds or from disease. In human life it was indisputedly the costliest war the U.S. ever fought, and Ohio contributed its fair share to these numbers. Civil War statistics must be used cautiously, but the Ohio adjutant general credited the state with a total of 346,326 men in military service as of December 1, 1864. The war was still in progress, with four-and-a-half months to go in the major theaters, so it is possible that some additional men were taken into the service during that period even though no more presidential calls for troops went out.

By whatever standard used, Ohio provided the third largest number of troops to the Union, exceeded only by the more populous states of New York and Pennsylvania. However, in proportion to state population, Ohio's contribution ranked number one. A considerable number of Ohioans also served in the Confederate armies. Seven became Confederate generals, and hundreds, perhaps thousands of Ohio boys served in Confederate units. Given the strong southern element in the state, this is not surprising. Both Indiana and Illinois, which shared Ohio's southern legacy, had the same experience.

Confusion about numbers carries over to casualty figures, but it is commonly accepted that 34,591 Ohioans died in the service. Of these 11,237 died of battle wounds and 23,354 died of disease. Approximately 30,000 Ohio veterans bore severe wounds for the remainder of their lives. Another unhappy statistic credits Ohio with 18,354 deserters, without any discussion as to what constituted desertion. No reliable figures exist for the number of draftees who failed to report. We do know that draftees were often sworn into the service on the spot, once their number was called, so as to minimize their opportunity to disappear or flee to Canada.

Military and Civilian Leaders from Ohio

No state of the Union produced as many first-rate general officers as did Ohio. Those who were Ohio-born or who spent their formative years in the state include the great Union triumvirate—Grant, Sherman, and Sheridan. By war's end, they were more than a match for their Confederate counterparts.

Hiram Ulysses Grant, born in 1822 in Point Pleasant (Clermont County), was a tanner's son who spent his boyhood in Georgetown (Brown County) before receiving an appointment to West Point at age seventeen. A mixup on his papers caused him to be known as Ulysses Simpson Grant, an error he never bothered to correct. His initials led to such nicknames as "Unconditional Surrender" or "Uncle Sam" Grant. Married to Julia Dent, a Missouri slaveholder's daughter, Grant remained devoted to his wife, and she to him, throughout a far more exciting life than either could have imagined upon betrothal.

Young "Sam" Grant learned the soldier's trade in the Mexican War, following which he was stationed in boring, isolated western posts. He became a problem drinker, resulting in his resignation from the service. For the next several years he was unsuccessful at various enterprises until, at age forty, he was rescued from obscurity and near poverty by the Civil War. Troops had confidence in him although he did not cut an imposing military figure. He was disheveled; he slouched; he smoked twenty strong cigars a day; but he knew what to do with an army.

Early in the war Grant led Illinois troops. He grew rapidly in ability and by 1864 was general-in-chief of Union forces. He worked well with Lincoln, who recognized Grant's strategic sense, and when the general's enemies tried to undercut him, the president said, "I can't spare that man; he fights!" Grant grasped the brutal reality which underlay the contest—he could afford large losses, but his enemy could not—and he had the fortitude to operate on that reality. By war's end, he was a lieutenant general, America's highest-ranking officer since George Washington.

Tecumseh "Cump" Sherman of Lancaster, one of thirteen children, was raised by the distinguished Ewing family, neighbors to the fatherless Sherman children. Mrs. Ewing insisted upon a new Christian name for the boy, who thus became William Tecumseh Sherman. He married Ellen Ewing and vacillated between the military career he had trained for at West Point and various civilian attractions. In 1862, apparently unnerved by the stress of command, Sherman was relieved of duties until he recovered his emotional equilibrium. He did so with such success that he became the vigorous, resourceful, and implacable leader considered by some observers to have been the most interesting officer of the war. He was, said Whitelaw Reid, "either vehemently right, or vehemently wrong." His western armies were the scourge of the South.

Maj. Gen. Philip Sheridan was also associated with devastating raids against southern property. "Fighting Phil" was, by war's end, the preeminent cavalry leader in the north. For all his fierce reputation in battle, he was physically unprepossessing—short, stocky, and normally of calm demeanor. Admired and liked by his men, who called him "Little Phil," he was a fighter. "The first smell of powder arouses him, and he rushes to the front of the field," wrote an admirer. His bold dash up the Valley Pike near Winchester, Virginia, standing in the stirrups of his black war horse Rienzi shouting "follow me, follow me" to rally his troops, was immortalized in the poem "Sheridan's Ride."

Another Ohio officer who might have earned a larger public reputation had he not been killed before Atlanta was Maj. Gen. James B. McPherson of Clyde. Universally liked and admired, he was the highest-ranking Union officer to die in battle. He was thirty-seven.

The list goes on: Major generals Irwin McDowell, Don Carlos Buell, William Rosecrans, Robert Schenck, Ormsby Mitchel, and many others, including Rutherford B. Hayes and James A. Garfield, whose distinguished war records would be eclipsed in the public mind by later political activity. George McClellan, leader of Ohio's first field troops, properly belongs to Pennsylvania since his Ohio residence was brief.

One cannot leave the military without taking notice of an extraordinary family, the "Fighting McCooks" of Carroll and Columbiana counties. The "Tribe of Dan" included the ten sons of Daniel McCook; the "Tribe of John" was composed of the seven sons of his brother John McCook. The fathers and their sons fought in the Union armies. Twelve of them were officers, including three who reached the rank of general. Two were killed in action, including Dan McCook, shot down in a skirmish with Morgan's raiders.

On the civilian side of the ledger were numerous Ohioans who served prominently in Lincoln's cabinet, in Congress, and in other posts. Lincoln appointed his political rival, Salmon P. Chase, as secretary of the treasury, a post in which the Ohioan chafed but performed acceptably. Chase worked with John Sherman, an Ohio senator, to secure tax money to prosecute the war. In his long political career, Chase had been a foe of slavery and its extension into the territories. He was prominent among those Republicans who urged Lincoln forward toward an emancipation policy. While tempted to challenge Lincoln's renomination in 1864, he refrained and instead continued to serve loyally. Lincoln rewarded Chase by appointing him Chief Justice of the United States (December 1864).

An indispensable cog in the northern war effort, indeed one of its prime movers, was Edwin M. Stanton of Steubenville, the secretary of war, who replaced the ineffective and corrupt Simon Cameron and brought order out of chaos. He was a difficult man, abrupt, arbitrary, and abrasive even with the president, whom he often patronized and even insulted. Slowly he learned to appreciate Lincoln, and upon the president's death said of him, "Now he belongs to the ages."

Ohio-born Jay Cooke was the nation's foremost banker. His sponsorship of war bond sales brought large sums into the treasury. He has been called the "financier of the Union," and in harness with Chase and John Sherman gave Ohio three of the leaders essential to the financing of the war.

John Sherman was a cautious man, not especially impressed with Lincoln's leadership. He performed notably in Congress and, after a brief fling in the Chase camp during the presidential election preliminaries in 1864, he supported the administration's conduct of the war's late stages. His fellow Republican senator was Benjamin "Bluff Ben" Wade, an Ashtabula County lawyer and rabid abolitionist who proved to be a thorn in Lincoln's side. Wade used his considerable ability to demand that the president make the war a crusade to free the slaves. He also led the charge to keep control of Reconstruction in the hands of Congress. He never forgave the president for his pocket veto of the Wade-Davis Bill, through which Wade hoped to achieve some of those objectives. His support of the Union cannot be faulted, whatever the grief he laid on President Lincoln.

Is there any significance beyond state pride in listing some of Ohio's "stars" from the Civil War period? Possibly: it is evident that Ohio provided the Union with an uncommon number of key leaders during the nation's greatest crisis. That fact brought the state much visibility and was important in keeping Ohio men before the nation for decades to come. Ohio was a powerful state during and after the war. It had economic, political, and perhaps moral influence (from its central role in the antislavery movement). Where better to look for leadership in the postwar years than to the state which had done so much to lead the Union to victory?

Reconstruction

The Civil War and Reconstruction marked a watershed in Amercan politics and in Ohio politics as well. Few periods in American history reveal so much political turmoil, so many false starts, as do the years of reconstruction. Ohio men played central roles on the national scene and, concurrently, on the state scene as well. Seldom have state and national politics been so intertwined. To sort out events in brief scope, we will first describe Ohio's involvement in national affairs, and then relate how state politics were affected by circumstances surrounding reconstruction.

Ohio and the National Scene

Following the Civil War the old political leadership, which had reached its apogee of influence during the sectional crisis, was passing from the scene. Chase, Wade, and Stanton were among the prominent Republicans playing out their final moments on the national stage, struggling to maintain influence while younger men—John Sherman, Rutherford Hayes, James Garfield, and Jacob Cox—challenged them. Among the Democrats David Tod, John Brough, and Samuel Medary were finished; William Allen and Lewis Campbell had one final grasp at office in the early 1870s; but the future of the party in Ohio was in the hands of Clement Vallandigham, Allen Thurman, George Pendleton, Hugh Jewett, George Hoadley (a former Republican), and other younger men.

John Wilkes Booth's brutal act deprived the nation of its leader at his moment of triumph. Perhaps it is well for Lincoln's reputation that he did not have to see Reconstruction through to completion. Instead, the confusion and bitterness of that period swirled around his successor, Andrew Johnson. With some changes, Johnson continued Lincoln's liberal policies for returning the southern states to their rightful place in the Union. Early in the process, in 1865, Ohio legislators generally supported this "presidential plan," but the Republican majority in Congress was already having second thoughts about it.

In Congress the radical Republicans—including senators Ben Wade of Ohio, Zachariah Chandler of Michigan, Charles Sumner of Massachusetts, and Rep. Thaddeus Stevens of Pennsylvania—were gaining allies among moderates in their efforts to seize control of Reconstruction from the president. These legislators viewed the southern states as having truly seceded: they were now conquered provinces which, like the territories, were to be administered under congressional direction. The radicals wanted ex-Confederates to suffer for their folly. They also hoped to assure the freedmen their civil rights, including the vote, and expected, in the process, that grateful blacks would cast their ballots for those who had liberated them—the Republicans.

President Johnson attempted to block such congressional measures. The Republican leadership struck back by refusing to seat representatives elected to Congress by state governments reconstructed under the presidential plan. Congress then set up its own plans for reconstructing the South. It passed laws, over Johnson's veto, dictating new terms which the ex-Confederate states must meet before their representatives could be seated in Congress. Congress imposed military rule on the South to assure that control of state and local governments would be in accordance with its dictates, and passed the Fourteenth Amendment to the Constitution which, among other things, defined citizenship to include blacks. Southern states were required to ratify this amendment as a condition of readmission to the Union. Seven states did so, and in June 1868, Congress seated their representatives. The three remaining unreconstructed states were required to ratify the Fifteenth Amendment, which Congress passed in 1869 to extend the franchise to blacks, without regard to previous condition of servitude. These states did so and were readmitted. The Fifteenth Amendment took effect in 1870.

In all these maneuvers, Ohioans were centrally involved, especially in a direct challenge to the president. Congress passed, over Johnson's veto, the Command of the Army Act (March 2, 1867), which required that the president issue all military orders through the general of the army (U. S. Grant), and the Tenure of Office Act (March 2, 1867), which required the president to get Senate approval before removing an appointee from office. Johnson claimed these acts were unconstitutional, and they were, but the ruling came far too late to help him. Through the Tenure of Office Act, Congress was protecting Edwin Stanton from Johnson's efforts to remove him as secretary of war. Stanton was in the radical camp and hence opposed the president's policies. Johnson removed Stanton from office anyway, and the radicals seized upon this as one of several reasons for impeaching the president.

It was the idealistic James Ashley, representative from the Toledo area, who introduced an impeachment resolution in the House. He proposed that the House Judiciary Committee "inquire if any officer of the United States" had been guilty of high crimes and misdemeanors while in office. Ashley hoped to discredit General Grant, whom he felt had been too obliging to President Johnson; in the process, Ashley expected to clear the presidential field for his own preferred candidate, Ben Butler of Massachusetts. Ashley's maneuverings were exposed by a fellow Ohioan, John Bingham of Cadiz, who called Ashley a "fool," and the impeachment resolution failed to pass. In January 1868, Ashley tried again with an impeachment resolution aimed specifically at the conduct of President Johnson, charging him with willful violation of the Tenure of Office Act.

This time it worked, and the House of Representatives impeached the president. A House committee, including John Bingham, prosecuted Johnson before the Senate, which sat as a court. Chief Justice Salmon P. Chase (appointed to the Supreme Court by Lincoln in 1864), presided over the trial in an even-handed manner. A two-thirds majority vote was required to convict the president; when an uncommitted Kansas senator, Edmund Ross, voted to acquit, Johnson's enemies realized they had lost by the margin of a single vote. That was the margin by which Ben Wade, president *pro tempore* of the Senate, missed becoming president of the United States. Perhaps his bitterness over this near miss caused his increasingly erratic political behavior in succeeding months. Despite acquittal, Johnson was finished as a political force; friend and foe alike turned their attention to the 1868 presidential race.

The Republican presidential contest of 1868 revealed the least attractive qualities of those old political antagonists, Chase and Wade. Both let ambition overrule good judgment. Both were willing to sell out long-time supporters if necessary in order to win the presidential prize. Wade backed off his earlier vociferous support of black rights and shifted position on economic matters. Chase campaigned for the Republican nomination even though his friends questioned the propriety of a Supreme Court justice engaging in partisan politics. In a final desperate bid, Chase abandoned the Republican camp and sought the Democratic nomination. In the final analysis, however, neither Chase, nor Wade, nor Ashley's friend Ben Butler had a chance. Ohio Republicans, deeply hurt by state Democratic victories in 1867, needed new faces without links to the party factions that had brought on hard times for the faithful. Among the newcomers was perhaps the best-known man in America—Ulysses S. Grant.

Grant received the support of Ohio Republicans at the party convention in Chicago. Indeed, support for Grant was so well orchestrated that he won nomination on the first ballot. Though Grant was essentially apolitical, he was captured by the radicals, who also had the allegiance of Grant's running mate, Schuyler Colfax of Indiana. The Republican platform endorsed congressional reconstruction and supported sound money, but was ambiguous on the tariff and rights for blacks. The Democrats chose Horatio Seymour, former governor of New York, a hard-money Democrat. When the votes were counted, Grant had a 306,000 popular vote margin; his majority in the electoral college was a comfortable 214 to 80.

Aside from his vote-getting ability, there was little to recommend Grant for political office. The strategic thinking, decisive command, and penchant for direct action which had served him so well in the military were not transferable to the political arena. Presidents cannot command; they encounter opposition from the other party and from dissident elements within their own. They must persuade and use political leverage to secure their goals. Grant never adapted to these realities. He left too much discretionary power in the hands of his appointees. He made poor appointments and then, with misplaced loyalty, stood behind them even after they had demonstrated their unworthiness. Scholars of the presidency invariably rank Grant at or near the bottom of the list when assessing presidential performance.

Grant, the "simple soldier," and his wife Julia, grew to like and depend on the attention and adulation accorded them in the presidency, and he was anxious to hold on to the perquisites through another term. But corruption and venality permeated all levels of political life, much to the dismay of reformers who vowed to unseat Grant and clean up presidential government. Reform Republicans bolted the party in 1872 and held their own nominating convention in Cincinnati, naming Horace Greeley, editor of the *New York Tribune* and a long-time political gadfly, as their candidate. The demoralized Democrats also picked Greeley though he was a Republican and a high-tariff man, but they hoped that by joining with the reform Republicans they stood a chance of unseating Grant. Greeley was not a popular candidate, however, and Grant beat him handily, increasing his popular vote margin and winning 286 to 66 in the electoral college.

The details of Grant's eight presidential years are not germane here. Possibly he was more representative of his times than his critics have admitted. Certainly politics on the state and local levels tended to be uninspired when they were not downright crooked. Ohio had no more success than her sister states in making its way through the political and economic quicksands of the immediate postwar period.

Reconstruction Politics in Ohio

During Reconstruction both parties in Ohio were involved in restructuring and in seeking new directions. The chief political issues—reconstruction policies in the South, civil rights for blacks, and sound money versus paper money (gold versus greenbacks) created factions within each party although the Republicans were the harder hit. Third parties and independent parties flourished, drawing adherents from the major parties. The foremost student of Ohio's reconstruction politics emphasizes the "grass roots disintegration" of party in postwar Ohio. At the district, county, and local levels no rigid line divided Republican and Democrat. The Union Party survived in name only as Fusion and War Democrats returned to their old party. That left only Republicans, and the Republican party from its birth comprised factions held together by the critical concerns of the prewar and war eras. Now, within Ohio, Republicans were struggling to find identity.

Ohio Democrats were a bit more fortunate although they too had to cope with party stress. The roots of Democratic strength—Irish and German immigrants and conservative farmers of the "Backbone" and northwestern counties—remained largely intact. Their biggest challenge was to throw off the Copperhead label, the charge that they were the party of treason. They were ready to play racial politics even as they had before and during the war, preying upon popular fears that freed blacks would innundate Ohio and the North.

The elections of 1865 provided a test of Ohio's political climate. The Republicans chose Gen. Jacob D. Cox of the Western Reserve, a man with a fine war record and strong antislavery convictions that dated to before the war. The Democratic candidate, Gen. George W. Morgan, also had a substantial military record. The Republican platform said nothing about suffrage for blacks; the Democratic platform opposed it outright.

Cox had shifted his attitude on racial issues as a result of his wartime experiences. During the campaign, a group of Oberlin blacks requested his views on race, and Cox answered them with a long, thoughtful analysis that revolved around his conviction that blacks and whites could never live as equals in the same area; racial prejudice was too fundamental and too strong to combat. His proposal was to give blacks their own contiguous territory in the American south where they would be organized into "a dependency of the Union analogous to the western territories." This view was out of step with that held by such Republicans as Wade, Garfield, and Hayes, who proposed leaving blacks where they were and guaranteeing them the vote. Cox won a narrow victory, and during his administration the general assembly ratified the Fourteenth Amendment on the governor's recommendation. The new Republican leadership now pressed to amend the Ohio Constitution to delete the word "white" in describing who should have the right to vote.

By 1867 the radicals and their allies controlled the Republican party in Ohio. Governor Cox was tolerated for his good administrative record, but he was not the party's choice for renomination. Rep. Rutherford B. Hayes of Cincinnati, who voted with the radicals, was their choice for governor. Voters were also to decide whether or not to amend the state constitution to permit blacks to vote. There was no doubt in Hayes's mind as to the proper

course for Ohio and the nation: "The plain and monstrous inconsistency and
injustice of excluding one seventh of our population from all participation in a
Government founded on the consent of the governed in this land of free discussion is simply impossible. No such absurdity and wrong can be permanent.
Impartial suffrage will carry the day."

Allen G. Thurman of Chillicothe, a "safe" candidate, was the Democrats'
choice for governor. He was not so tainted with Copperheadism as were
Vallandigham and Pendleton, each of whom had ambitions of his own. The
Democrats' position on the voting issue was blatantly racial; they urged
Ohio's voters to save the state from "niggerism." Hayes attacked their tactics
in vigorous language. "In Ohio the leaders of the peace Democracy intend to
carry on one more campaign on the old and rotten platform of prejudice
against colored people," he said. "The principles of the fathers, reason, religion, and the spirit of the age are against them." But the voters were with
them. Though Hayes squeaked through to victory by a 3,000-vote margin, the
black suffrage issue lost by 50,000 votes, and Democrats won control of the
state legislature. The Democrats were thus able to replace Wade in the Senate. Their choice was Allen Thurman, whose conservative style would help
the party live down the image that Vallandigham and other assertive Peace
Democrats had created for the party during the war.

Party leadership now devolved on Cincinnati's George Pendleton, who had
presidential ambitions and who sought to rally Democrats around a fiscal plan
that came to be called the "Ohio Idea." This plan provided that government
bondholders who had purchased their bonds with greenbacks (now worth
considerably less than gold-backed dollars) should have such bonds redeemed
in greenbacks and not in gold as many had anticipated. New greenback issues,
used to redeem the bonds, would inflate the currency, but Pendleton argued
that national bank notes could be taken out of circulation, thus minimizing the
inflationary effect. Bondholders would thus be paid in currency as good as
that they had used to purchase the bonds, but no better.

There was considerable support for the "Ohio Idea." Even Republican
leaders such as John Sherman saw merit in it, although he wanted all forms of
money to carry the same value, thus putting issues of this sort to rest. Ohio had
been following Pendleton's principle with its debt holders and would continue to do so until 1879. However, eastern conservatives undermined Pendleton's plan. Pendleton's presidential ambitions were destroyed in Ohio by
fellow Democrats who were supporting the ambitions of Chief Justice Chase.
As a result, no Ohioan figured prominently in the final balloting at the national convention. The nomination went to Horatio Seymour who, as we
have seen, lost to Grant.

In 1869 Pendleton was again in the race for office, this time opposing Gov-

ernor Hayes in his bid for reelection. Once more Democrats supported the
"Ohio Idea" and once more played racial politics. While Republicans endorsed ratification of the Fifteenth Amendment, which would give the franchise to blacks, Democrats opposed it. Hayes won a narrow victory and the
new general assembly ratified the Fifteenth Amendment by a majority of one
vote in the Senate and two votes in the House. The vote was not as close as one
might assume since approval required a two-thirds majority in each house.

In 1870 the amendment was declared ratified and in effect, and that same
year black delegates attended the state Republican convention in Ohio for the
first time. Blacks could now vote in the state except in rare instances where
local pressures kept them from the polls. Nevertheless, Ohio stubbornly refused to amend the language of its own constitution on the suffrage issue until
well into the twentieth century, although that resistance had no practical
effect on black voting rights.

The Democrats now reached out, hoping to attract Republicans disgusted
with the inefficiencies and corruption of the Grant era. Clement Vallandigham played a leading role in this effort, as the state convention adopted his
ideas, called the "New Departure." In effect his policy stated, "Let bygones
be bygones." He invited Republicans to join in accepting "the natural and
legitimate results of the war so far as waged for its ostensible purpose to
maintain the Union and the Constitutional rights and powers of the Federal
Government," including the three amendments recently adopted. He was
ready to accept reconstruction and "all questions as to the means by which it
was accomplished." It was a remarkable about-face for the contentious Vallandigham and won respectful attention from many political quarters. Hard-
line Republicans, of course, scoffed, reveling at the sight of their old antagonist knuckling under to the new political realities.

Enthusiasm for the "New Departure" was brief, and it died with its author
in 1871. Vallandigham had resumed lawyering and was defending a client
charged with shooting another man. While demonstrating to a friend how his
client's pistol could have discharged accidentally, Vallandigham pulled a
loaded pistol from his pocket; the firing mechanism caught on his pocket; the
gun fired and Vallandigham was killed.

Within Ohio the attempt to wed Liberal Republicans and Democrats to
defeat Grantism was a failure. Republicans continued to control state politics
in the early 1870s, sending John Sherman back to the Senate for another six-
year term and generally dominating the political scene. The issues were
changing, however. Bitter wartime divisions were finally subsiding, although
an occasional Republican orator still waved the "bloody shirt," and safe candidates were those who had served the Union effectively.

Ohio, along with the rest of the North and Midwest, was increasingly affected by a massive transformation which was moving the state away from its rural, agricultural past toward an urban and industrial future. As is always true of such massive shifts, the pace was uneven and the results were mixed, some individuals benefiting and some suffering from the new alignments in society. Both political and economic practices adjusted to the new realities. We turn first to the political forces which characterized that transformation.

1 Hayes
2 McKinley - killed
3 Garfield - shot
4 Cleveland
5 Harrison
6
7

11

Ohio Leads the Nation

Politics from Hayes to McKinley

As they had done during the great crisis of the Union, Ohioans played a leading role in the federal government in the post–Civil War era, a success that masked bitter party in-fighting on their home grounds. Nonetheless, a number of Buckeye State natives would overcome party struggles to ascend to high office—including the highest office in the land.

Mother of Presidents?

Ohio and Virginia each claim the title "Mother of Presidents," with the implications of this term a focus of pride in each of these states. Four of the nation's first five presidents were Virginians, and that state's great triumvirate—Washington, Jefferson, and Wilson—ranks at or near the top of effective presidential leadership. No Ohio-born president enjoys such a strong reputation as custodian of the executive office. Of the seven Ohio-born presidents, only Hayes and McKinley (and occasionally Taft) are rated "average" or slightly better by students of the presidency; indeed, the Ohio presidents are often perceived as a rather dull and colorless lot. But such comparisons are pointless. Presidents should be rated only in relation to their times and what was required of them.

The late nineteenth century was a time of transition. Small businesses grew to giant size, new industries proliferated, urban centers grew at a phenomenal

rate, mass immigration enlarged and changed the population. In short, the old
agriculturally based society was giving way to industrial forces. Political
leaders and party bosses who controlled the choice of candidates were, more
often than not, sympathetic to this transition and selected men who would
support rather than impede it. They found the candidates they needed in
Ohio, where changes within the state reflected those generally present in the
industrial North and Midwest. The politician who learned his trade in Ohio's
hard school encountered nearly every interest and condition he might encounter in the national arena.

The "Ohio Dynasty" was a remarkable phenomenon. Seven native-born
sons occupied the White House in a fifty-four-year period. Ulysses S. Grant
was a political aberration, quintessentially the successful general whom
kingmakers coveted, the respected front behind whom they hoped to maneuver the levers of power. Rutherford Hayes, James Garfield, Benjamin
Harrison, and William McKinley, on the other hand, had all served political
apprenticeships in Congress, and Hayes and McKinley had been governor.
Ohio's two twentieth-century presidents—William Howard Taft and
Warren G. Harding—also completed political apprenticeships, Taft in administrative appointments, Harding in the Senate. They were "safe" candidates
to whom conservative business interests could entrust presidential power.
But the conditions under which they gained and held presidential power
differ enough from those of the nineteenth century that they will be considered separately.

Ohio Men in the White House, 1877–1901

Rutherford Birchard Hayes (1822–93) was well qualified for presidential
office. Born in Delaware, Ohio, Hayes was raised by his widowed mother
and his maternal uncle, Sardis Birchard, a highly successful businessman. After leading his class at Kenyon College, he graduated from Harvard Law
School, was admitted to the Ohio bar, set up practice in Cincinnati, and was
elected City Solicitor. During the Civil War he rose from major to major
general of Ohio volunteers. He fought in many battles and sustained several
battle wounds. After Appomattox his impeccable war record contributed to
his election as a member of Congress, where he supported radical reconstruction. Hayes was elected governor of Ohio three times between 1868 and 1876.
While serving his third term he was chosen to be the Republican presidential
nominee. His personal rectitude, outstanding war record, and concern for
good government offset his somewhat bland personality. The Republicans
found him a likely candidate in 1876 because he had been reelected governor
of a major state in an election otherwise dominated by the Democrats.

The presidential election of 1876 was one of the most dramatic in American history. It has been called the "stolen election," or, more kindly, the "disputed election." When the ballots were counted, the Democrat, Samuel Tilden of New York, had received a quarter-million more popular votes than Hayes and appeared to have the necessary electoral votes as well. But Republican strategists challenged the electoral counts from Florida, South Carolina, and Louisiana, states that had remnants of "carpetbag" government controlled by Republicans and their black supporters. Each of these states submitted a Republican slate of electors in competition with the Democratic slates. In addition to these contests, the party challenged one electoral vote from Oregon. In all, twenty-one electoral votes were disputed.

To sort out the mess, Congress established an electoral commission of fifteen members composed of senators, representatives, and Supreme Court justices. Seven were Republicans, seven were Democrats, and the swing vote was to belong to David Davis, a Supreme Court justice whom both sides trusted. But the Illinois legislature had placed Davis in a different public service role by this time, electing him as their U.S. senator, and so another justice, a Republican, was chosen for the electoral commission. In each disputed case, by an 8 to 7 party vote, the commission certified the Republican elector. This gave Hayes 185 electoral votes to Tilden's 184. Outraged Democrats were partially mollified by assurances that the Republicans would address their agenda of wants, including Democratic control of the internal affairs of southern states, the removal of remaining federal troops in the South, and the appointment of a southerner to a cabinet position.

Grant's term was to expire at noon on March 4, but that was a Sunday and public ceremonies were to be held on Monday. Fearful of risking a twenty-four-hour period without a president, Hayes took the oath of office on the evening of March 3 in a private ceremony and publicly on March 5. This upright and honorable man came into office under a cloud not of his own making. He did promptly withdraw the last federal troops stationed in the South, and he appointed a southerner, David M. Key of Tennessee, to be postmaster general. With federal protection now withdrawn from southern Republicans, the former Confederate states returned to the Democratic column and the "solid south" emerged as the most obvious political legacy of the Civil War.

Hayes had precisely those personal qualities so much needed to retrieve the reputation of the presidency from the nadir to which it had fallen during Grant's two scandal-ridden terms. In the words of biographer Kenneth Davison, Hayes had great strength of character and moral purpose. He "epitomized the best middle-class, moderate Victorian standards" of his time. He was "not brilliant or colorful, but he was kind, high-principled, public-spirited, unaffected, loyal, and singularly decent and honest, a man without pretense, without egotism."

Hayes was an able administrator and caretaker. He attempted to maintain sound money policies by vetoing the Bland-Allison Act (1878), although Congress passed it over his veto. This act, supported by inflationists and by the new silver interests in the West, was contrary to orthodox Republican monetary policy. More to Hayes's liking was the careful management of the treasury under Ohioan John Sherman, who brought the nation's currency such stability that on January 1, 1879, greenbacks became redeemable in gold. In addition, Hayes struck a blow for clean government by dismissing men charged with irregularities in their stewardship of the New York customs office even though he alienated powerful New York Republicans in the process. His secretary of the interior, Carl Schurz, employed a merit system in his department, and "launched a new era in Indian affairs by treating the native Americans with human dignity."

LUCY

Throughout his career Hayes had the support of his charming and vivacious wife Lucy. Lucy Ware Webb of Chillicothe was the first president's wife to be called "First Lady," and also the first to be a college graduate, a rarity for a female in those days. Although she stayed within the conventional role which Victorian society assigned women, she did not sublimate her personality or intelligence to convention. A devout Methodist, she was an arch-foe of alcohol and refused to serve it in the White House, some say at her husband's request. But she was far from being the humorless puritan that her nickname, "Lemonade Lucy,"—a name that apparently was not used while the Hayeses occupied the White House—would imply. Declining to serve alcohol, the Hayeses nevertheless gave the most splendid entertainments the White House had seen in many a year.

Having served their term in Washington, the former president, his First Lady, and their five children returned to Spiegel Grove, the family estate in Fremont. This beautiful property with its giant oaks named for prominent associates of the president was the Hayes family home until well into the twentieth century, when a museum and the nation's first presidential library were added, and the whole opened to the public. Both Hayeses are buried on the property. Their enduring monument was the reestablishment of decency and credibility at the heart of the national government.

The Republican nominating convention of 1880 was overburdened with candidates. The "halfbreed" faction of the party backed that perennial hopeful, James G. Blaine of Maine. The old guard "stalwart" faction, led by Roscoe Conkling of New York, supported a third term for U. S. Grant, who proved to be willing to break the unwritten precedent against a third term. These factions cancelled out one another. Meanwhile, Rep. James A. Garfield had gone to the convention to plead the case for his fellow Ohioan, John Sherman, but when the convention deadlocked, Garfield emerged as the delegates' choice. As a sop to the stalwarts, Chester A. Arthur, whom Hayes had dismissed from the New York customs office for his lax stewardship, was nominated for the vice-presidency. In November, Garfield defeated his Democratic opponent, Winfield Scott Hancock of Pennsylvania, by 7,018 votes out of more than 9.2 million cast.

James Abram Garfield (1831–81) was the last American president born in a log cabin. Born in Orange Township, Cuyahoga County in the Western Reserve, Garfield worked from an early age to help his widowed mother and later was to make political capital out of the few weeks he spent as a mule driver on the Ohio canals. After attending the Western Reserve Eclectic Institute, he graduated from Williams College, then returned to the institute as professor of ancient languages and literature. He became principal (president) of the school, which later became Hiram College. After years of rigorous work, he abandoned teaching, read law, and was admitted to the Ohio bar. During Garfield's youth, the Western Reserve was a hotbed of religious enthusiasm stoked by the evangelical preaching of the Campbellites (Disciples of Christ) and by the millennial claims of the Millerites. The Disciples claimed his allegiance, and he became a popular lay minister of that denomination. He was large, physically attractive, and outgoing, a friendly bear of a man.

Garfield served in the Ohio Senate before leading Civil War units in Kentucky and Tennessee. He distinguished himself both in the field and as a staff officer before resigning his commission in 1863 to take a seat in the House of Representatives. The Garfields left "Lawnfield," their Mentor home, for Washington, where Garfield became a staunch supporter of radical reconstruction. As a leader in the House, his verbal skills helped him weather an attempt to tie him to the Credit Mobilier scandal, one of many that marked the Grant administration.

After his inauguration on March 4, 1881, Garfield had an active presidency of but four months, too brief a time for reliable judgments about his performance in office. He supported sound money, a flexible tariff policy, and business interests. He showed mettle in opposing Conkling and the stalwarts in their efforts to maintain influence over appointments.

On July 2, 1881, while walking through a Washington railroad station on his way to the New Jersey shore and a trip to his alma mater, he was shot in the back by Charles J. Guiteau, a deranged office-seeker and stalwart supporter whom the *New York Times* called "a half-crazed pettifogging lawyer." Garfield was physically strong and remained optimistic about recovering from his wounds. However, blood clots formed around the .44-caliber bullet lodged near his spine; slowly infection sapped his energy. Washington's humid heat was unbearable. To ease the patient, the Navy fashioned what may have been the first crude air conditioning (air fanned across ice), but it was ineffective and Garfield asked to be removed to the seaside at Elberon, New Jersey. A special train was fitted out, but despite elaborate precautions and high hopes, the president failed to benefit from the sea air. On September 19, he died. His body was carried home to Ohio by special train and once more, as they had sixteen years before, mourners lined the track to honor a president cut down by an assassin's bullet. Throngs of people wended their way past Garfield's coffin which rested on an ornate catafalque in Cleveland's Public Square. Ultimately the president and his wife Lucretia (whom he called "Crete") were interred in a towering mausoleum in Cleveland's Lakeview Cemetery. As for the assassin, Guiteau was eventually hanged for his crime.

Public outrage over the assassination helped pressure legislators into dealing with civil service reform. In 1883, Congress passed the Pendleton Act introduced by Sen. George Pendleton of Cincinnati; it is the basic civil service legislation upon which the superstructure of federal civil service law rests.

Ohio's primacy on the national political scene had been closely contested by New York. Grant had defeated New Yorkers Horatio Seymour and Horace Greeley (a liberal Republican supported in 1872 by the Democrats). Hayes had nipped Tilden of the Empire State. Now it was New York's turn as Chester A. Arthur succeeded Garfield and served out his term. Arthur was followed in the presidential office by the Democratic Grover Cleveland, a former governor of New York. In 1884 Cleveland defeated Blaine in the only presidential contest of the era in which Ohio was not represented. (It was also the only one in which the Republican candidate was not a Union veteran.) Though honorable and courageous, Cleveland thoroughly alienated powerful veterans' groups by vetoing the Veteran's Pension Bill and by recommending that northern states return captured Confederate battleflags.

These actions worked against Cleveland when he ran for reelection in 1888. His running mate was Ohio's "Noble Roman," Sen. Allen Thurman, a Jeffersonian and former Peace Democrat. Challenging Cleveland was the Ohio-born Republican, Benjamin Harrison, then a citizen of Indiana. Neither candidate had personal magnetism, and their campaigns were not instructive. Cleveland had a margin of about 96,000 popular votes, but lost to Harrison by 233 to 168 electoral votes. "Providence has given us the victory," cried Harrison, to which a hard-bitten Republican boss replied, "he ought to know that Providence hasn't a damn thing to do with it."

Benjamin Harrison (1833–1901) was born on the farm established by his grandfather, former President William Henry Harrison, at North Bend, just downstream from Cincinnati. Benjamin graduated from Miami University, read law in Cincinnati, and then at age twenty-one moved to Indianapolis to begin his practice. He was involved in Republican politics both before and after service in the Civil War, from which he emerged as a brigadier general of volunteers. He lost a bid for the Indiana governor's chair, but was elected to a Senate seat.

Harrison was physically unprepossessing. He was short and seemed overbalanced by a large head which was the delight of caricaturists. He was an intellectual and a Republican loyalist who in his undramatic way could be counted on to support sound money, high tariffs, and policies favorable to business. Among the most important acts of his administration were several bills Ohio legislators presented to the Senate and the House. In the Senate, John Sherman gave his name to the Sherman Antitrust Act (1890), designed to thwart monopolies that were thought to be strangling competition in many industries. Initially the act was not effective although it set the precedent of federal intervention in antitrust suits. The Sherman Silver Purchase Act (1890) was a compromise measure which pleased neither the silverites, who wanted more silver cast into coin, nor sound money men, who distrusted the monetization of silver. The McKinley Tariff (1890), sponsored by Rep. William McKinley of the Canton district, established very high tariff schedules and was bitterly attacked by free traders. Harrison's support of this tariff may have cost him reelection.

Harrison made a strong bid to retain the presidency in 1892. His running mate was a friend of big business, the former Ohio newspaperman and distinguished Civil War reporter, Whitelaw Reid, at the time editor of the *New York Tribune* and a resident of New York. His opponent was again the New Yorker, Grover Cleveland, who won a narrow victory. Harrison retired to his Indianapolis home and resumed his law practice. His first wife, Caroline Lavinia Scott Harrison, daughter of a Miami University professor, died while the Harrisons occupied the White House. She had served as the first president of the Daughters of the American Revolution, a patriotic organization dedicated to preserving the nation's heritage.

Perhaps Harrison was fortunate to leave the presidency when he did. Cleveland returned to the presidential office just in time to inherit the nation's first industrial depression, the terrible Panic of 1893 in which, within a year, 15,000 businesses failed and unemployment reached 4 million. While Cleveland was struggling with the ensuing problems on the national level, William McKinley, governor of Ohio, was attempting to address the severe problems which the depression brought to the Buckeye State.

William McKinley (1843–1901) was born in Niles, a Mahoning Valley iron-making town. His father was in iron, a chancy business, and the family's financial fortunes vacillated. McKinley worked from an early age and contributed to the family income. A combination of illness and lack of funds terminated a brief stay at Allegheny College. At the outbreak of war, he enlisted in a volunteer regiment (Hayes's 23rd Ohio Volunteer Infantry) and demonstrated unusual initiative and courage. His leadership talents recognized, he rose to the rank of major, serving for a time on Hayes's staff. A lifelong mutual regard marked the relationship of these two men, each of whom was to preside over his state and his nation. After the war McKinley practiced law in the thriving industrial city of Canton, winning the regard of his associates and the hand of Ida Saxton, a banker's daughter. The young couple suffered a terrible blow when both of their daughters died in infancy. This trauma helped push Ida, once a spirited and lively girl, over an emotional threshold. She was also epileptic, and the combination of her burdens made her a semi-invalid through the rest of her life. During her periods of distress, only her husband could calm and console her, and he did so with devoted attention. Despite this condition, the McKinleys maintained the active social life required of their political station.

In his first try for national office McKinley was elected to Congress from the Canton district despite his defense of high protective tariffs in a district largely populated by wage earners. McKinley reminded workers that, were it not for tariffs, many American companies could not compete successfully against better-entrenched European companies. It was preferable, said McKinley, to have a job and pay slightly higher prices than not have a job at all. He was reelected until his district was gerrymandered in 1890, stripping him of much support.

Meanwhile, the young Ohio congressman had come to the attention of a wealthy Cleveland industrialist and Republican boss, Marcus Hanna, who decided that McKinley was just the kind of man he could groom for high office. Using his impressive organizational and fund-raising skills, Hanna helped McKinley win the governorship in 1891 and reelection in 1893. Hanna had a genuine liking and respect for McKinley; "I love McKinley! He is the best man I ever knew," he once said, and he worked to groom his man for the presidency, guiding him to victory in the Republican nominating convention of 1896. The Democrats selected young, vigorous William Jennings Bryan of Nebraska, the "Boy Orator of the Platte." Bryan went on a whirlwind whistle-stop tour preaching the gospel of free silver as an inflationary measure to aid debt-burdened farmers and end the depression, and condemning trusts and high tariffs. In marked contrast, McKinley stayed home. Excursion trains brought organized groups to Canton from all parts of the nation. The faithful marched behind banners, their bands blaring martial music, to McKinley's home. The candidate would then make a dignified appearance on his front porch, speaking in support of high tariffs, sound money (his own private bimetallic views had changed), and promising a return of prosperity. It was exciting, noisy, and hard on the lawns, but if McKinley's neighbors complained history has failed to record it. Ohio gave its favorite son a victory margin of 50,000 votes, and the nation put him in the White House. The voters also sent Republican majorities to both houses of Congress.

The Republican platform called for a vigorous foreign policy, but no one could have known that the United States would be at war barely a year after McKinley's inauguration. The trouble spot was Cuba. For years Spain had been trying to suppress Cuban rebels, using harsh methods which were reported in extravagant prose by the new, mass-circulation, sensationalist "yellow press." Since 1895, when the latest crisis in the long-standing contest flared anew, jingoists, militarists, and the "yellow press" brought pressure upon the government to take action in support of the rebels. President McKinley, who believed that differences with Spain could be negotiated, was reluctant. McKinley has "no more backbone than a chocolate eclair," said the disgusted jingoist, Teddy Roosevelt. An emotional crisis flared in February 1898, when the American battleship *Maine* was destroyed in Havana harbor with the loss of 260 lives. No one knew who was responsible—it probably was an accident—but war fever intensified, and increasing numbers of Americans were chanting "Remember the *Maine,* to hell with Spain." McKinley finally gave in to the clamor and on April 11 sent a war message to Congress, which responded by a joint resolution declaring that Cuba should be free and granting the president war powers. Spain declared war on the United States on April 24, and Congress declared war on Spain the next day.

Fighting in Cuba lasted but six weeks. The "splendid little war," as John Hay, McKinley's secretary of state called it, had little impact on Ohio, although Gov. Asa Bushnell promptly ordered out state troops to supplement the regular army. Ohio's three regiments saw virtually no action, arriving in Cuba and Puerto Rico as the shooting stopped. Ohio furnished 15,345 militia and volunteers, of whom 230 died, all but a handful from disease. The Peace of Paris (1898) gave the United States new island possessions—Puerto Rico, Guam, and the Philippines. Anti-imperialists protested loudly that it was a betrayal of America's tradition to join the ranks of the colonial powers. But America was already becoming a Pacific power; her new island possessions joined Hawaii, which McKinley had persuaded Congress to annex as a territory.

President McKinley presided over this transitional period in American life with considerable skill. Possessed of an organized, methodical mind, he helped develop modern administrative methods in the presidency. To a much greater degree than tradition holds, McKinley was his own man. He led more than he followed. Though he valued and relied on Hanna's judgment, he was in no way a "puppet" of the Republican boss.

The Major, as his friends called him, was a popular figure at the end of his first administration. While economic recovery, sound money (the Gold Standard Act of 1900 assured the sound money position), and effective tariff levels contributed to his popularity, resurgent patriotism resulting from the easy victory over Spain assured it. In 1900 he again faced Bryan. McKinley's running mate was the ebullient New York war hero, Teddy Roosevelt, who was on the ticket despite Hanna's reservations. Stressing "four years more of the full dinner pail," a prosperity they attributed to their economic policies, the

The Eighth Ohio Volunteers board the USS *St. Paul* en route to Cuba during the Spanish-American War. (Courtesy of Frank Klein, The Bookseller, Akron.)

Republicans won convincingly, carrying both houses of Congress as well as the presidency.

McKinley was inaugurated for the second time on March 4, 1901. Just six months later, while attending the Pan American Exposition in Buffalo, he consented to shake hands with well-wishers. Among those in line to see the president was a twenty-eight-year-old anarchist named Leon Czolgosz. Czolgosz concealed a small-caliber pistol in his hand, wrapped it with a handkerchief, held the wrapped hand across his chest and calmly walked through a double line of security guards. As the president reached to shake his hand, Czolgosz pumped two bullets into McKinley's ample mid-section, knocking him to the floor. The president did not respond to treatment. On September 14, he died, and Teddy Roosevelt was sworn in as president. Czolgosz was quickly tried and executed. His body was placed in an unmarked grave in New York's Auburn State Prison yard and sulphuric acid was poured on it to dissolve the assassin's mortal remains.

Ohio and the nation mourned their president. A southern blues song expressed how some felt: "Czolgosz, Czolgosz, you done him wrong, shot po' McKinley when he was walking along. . . ." In 1904, the Ohio General Assembly made McKinley's political good luck piece, the scarlet carnation, the official state flower. Levi Lamborn of Alliance had developed the flower and had introduced McKinley to it when they were political opponents in the 1876 congressional race. Ida McKinley spent the six years remaining to her among memorabilia of happier times. Soon after the president's death, popular subscription raised money for an appropriate tomb. Pennies from schoolchildren helped build the large mausoleum in Canton where the bodies of William, Ida, and their infant daughters are entombed.

Did these four Ohioans, who each held the presidency during the last quarter of the nineteenth century, possess common traits or experiences that the American voter responded to? Perhaps so. In late twentieth-century parlance, the Ohioans were WASPs (white, Anglo-Saxon protestants). Each had a protestant religious heritage although personal commitment to organized religion varied from Hayes's indifference to Garfield's and McKinley's devotion. Each had a superior education. Only McKinley was not a college graduate, but he finished his preparatory work and successfully completed the course at Albany Law School. Their family origins show no consistency. Harrison was born into a high-status family; Hayes was middle class; McKinley, at best, was middle class; and the Garfields were lower on the socioeconomic ladder. Each was a lawyer by training, but Garfield did not earn his living from the law. Each of the Ohioans had a distinguished military record; it could hardly have been otherwise for a successful Republican in the postwar years. All supported sound money with McKinley a belated convert; the protective tariff, although on this issue they swung from McKinley's high extreme to Garfield's ambivalence on protective tariffs; and policies that minimized restraints upon business. Finally, they were all "low-profile" leaders. None had the flamboyance of a Teddy Roosevelt. Garfield was perhaps the most personable, while Harrison was the most reserved. They were low-profile also in the sense that they did not promise to achieve extensive political agendas; Congress assumed as much leadership in that regard as the president did. The claims of each of the four were more modest than those of contemporary presidents, who work under a spotlight much more intense than their nineteenth-century counterparts. All in all, their images come to us today as somewhat restrained and stuffy. For example, McKinley refused to be photographed holding a cigar: "The youth of America must not see their president smoking," he is reported to have said. Yet they were in tune with their contemporaries and their times.

Presidents frequently look to their home state for persons to appoint to federal office. There they find colleagues and cronies, people they can trust, or persons to whom they owe a political debt. It is not surprising, therefore, that many Ohioans received appointments to federal office in the late nineteenth century. Five Ohio-born men served on the Supreme Court during the period—Salmon P. Chase, Noah H. Swayne, Morrison R. Waite, William B. Woods (born in Ohio but resident in Georgia), and Stanley Matthews. Chase was chief justice until his death in 1873, at which time Waite succeeded him, serving fourteen years. Grant appointed Edwin Stanton to the court, but he died before serving.

Those holding cabinet positions were John Sherman, William R. Day, and John Hay, each of whom served briefly in McKinley's cabinet as secretary of state. Sherman was also secretary of the treasury under Hayes; Charles Foster held that office under Harrison. Stanton, William T. Sherman, Alphonso Taft, and Ohio-born Russell Alger served as secretary of war. Henry Stanbery, Alphonso Taft, and Judson Harmon were attorneys general. Finally, Jacob D. Cox and Columbus Delano served as secretary of the interior under Grant.

Also prominent in national affairs were two Ohio military heroes. From 1869 until his retirement in 1883, William Tecumseh Sherman served as commanding general of the army. His successor was Somerset's Philip Sheridan.

Why Ohio?

It is clear that Ohio men exerted an uncommon amount of leadership and influence in late nineteenth-century America. This extraordinary concentration of political influence from a single state is based on several factors. First was the visibility earned during the war years. Ohio's contribution to the Union cause was so substantial that the state may have become associated in the public mind with a likely place to look for continued leadership. No state produced more high-level leaders in support of the Republican administration. The military triumvirate of Grant, Sherman, and Sheridan plus civilian leaders Stanton, Chase, John Sherman, Wade, and Cooke continued to influence the Republican-dominated Reconstruction period and beyond. These men had name recognition, an invaluable political asset.

Second, Ohio was strategically located; the main east-west economic and social currents of that time passed through the state. It was constantly in tune with developments elsewhere in the nation. Ohio has been described as the easternmost of the western states and the westernmost of the eastern states. It is true that it shared the characteristics of the settled East while identifying with the experiences and aspirations of the emerging West. It also maintained strong commercial ties to the South and the North.

Third, in 1850 Ohio was already the nation's third most populous state. By the end of the nineteenth century it ranked fourth, Illinois having passed it. This gave Ohio either the third or fourth largest delegation in Congress and in the electoral college. Such political influence could not be ignored. Furthermore, Ohio had a history of close electoral contests. And in an era (1876–96) when no presidential candidate received more than 51 percent of the vote, the Republican party, in order to assure Ohio's critical electoral votes, was more prone than it might otherwise have been to select a favorite son from the Buckeye State. Those selected were "sound" on political and economic issues; they would not rock the ship of state.

Fourth, the make-up of Ohio's population was perhaps a more representative cross-section of the nation's people than any state in the Union. Ohio embraced significant numbers of people from three of the four older settled regions of the East—New England, the Middle States, and the Upper South, the only exception being the Tidewater South. Nearly every immigrant group was well represented in Ohio. Each group of newcomers brought with them traditional cultural and political outlooks which any aspiring politician had to learn to recognize and accommodate. Blacks were a small percentage of the population and had virtually no political influence.

Fifth, Ohio's economic profile made it an area to be reckoned with. Ohio remained a major farm state while embracing the new industrialism and urbanism of the Age of Big Business. It was centrally involved in nearly every growth industry of the period. During much of the late nineteenth century, Ohio trailed only New York and Pennsylvania in the production of industrial goods. Newly rich industrialists like Mark Hanna supported the political ambitions of conservative, safe candidates who cherished the capitalistic goose and would protect its golden eggs—sound money, the protective tariff, support for business growth, and a proper nod to the farmer.

In summary, Ohio was as near a microcosm of America as one could find in the late nineteenth century. Candidates who learned to deal with its political, economic, and cultural complexities had learned what they needed to perform on a national stage.

State Politics, 1873–1901

Presidential politics were intimately related to politics on the state level. By the end of Reconstruction the divisive issues of bringing southern states back into the Union and dealing with the black franchise in Ohio were largely resolved. Political contests now focused on money issues, tariff schedules, business regulation, social issues, and an unsuccessful attempt to revise Ohio's constitution.

The Constitution of 1851 fell short of reorganizing state government to accommodate an accelerating change from an agriculturally dominant to an industrially dominant economy. The strain of the war years and the turmoil of Reconstruction led both Republican and Democratic leaders to endorse calling a new constitutional convention, and voters authorized it in October 1871. Of the convention's 105 delegates elected in 1873, fifty were Republicans, forty-six Democrats, and nine Liberals or Independents, a balance that reflects the competitiveness of Ohio's party politics. The delegates gathered under the chairmanship of Morrison R. Waite and completed their work in May 1874. They presented the voters with a new constitution that called for annual sessions of the legislature, a veto for the governor which could be over-ridden by a three-fifths vote of each house, establishment of state circuit courts, eligibility of women for election to school boards, and restrictions on municipal debt. As a separate issue, a licensing system for control of intoxicating beverages was to be introduced.

Voters in the August election soundly defeated both the proposed constitution (102,885 to 250,169), and the liquor licensing proposition. While organized opposition came from special interest groups whose activities would be curtailed, a general lack of enthusiasm contributed to the outcome. One disenchanted newspaper editor referred to the delegates as "public men who fritter away great opportunities in hair-splitting debates . . . to accomplish doubtful purposes." An important lesson emerged from this effort: it is difficult to secure voter approval for an entirely new instrument of government. Delegates to Ohio's next constitutional convention would keep that very much in mind.

It is hard to say what effect economic conditions may have had on the voters. Congress, in 1873, demonetized silver in what came to be called the "Crime of '73." That same year the nation plunged into depression. Bad economic news and growing disgust with the inept and corrupt Grant administration contributed to a malaise that infected state politics. Gov. Edward F. Noyes, a Republican war veteran, was trying for a second term in 1873. The Democrats, torn between liberal and conservative factions, sought and found a compromise candidate in veteran political warhorse William Allen. By an 817-vote margin, the septuagenarian Allen became the first Democrat to win the governorship since William Medill left office in 1856. For the remainder of the century (with one exception) Republican and Democrat would alternate as governor although the Democratic governors served single terms while the Republicans served two.

State politics in this period were affected by the new militancy of temperance reformers. A determined minority of Ohioans supported the Prohibition Party in every state and national campaign from 1869 to 1914. Their candidates received a mere handful of votes, but that does not begin to tell the story of the political impact that temperance issues had. A distinguished Ohio historian was not exaggerating when he described temperance as "that perennial football of Ohio politics." The earlier temperance movement, which had faded during the war years, was quickly reenergized after Appomattox.

In 1873 a group of Hillsboro church women led by Mrs. Eliza Jane Trimble Thompson, daughter of a former governor and wife of a local judge, rekindled the Ohio women's crusade. Churchwomen marched to local saloons where they knelt in prayer to embarrass the saloonkeeper and his customers. The tactic worked in Hillsboro, for the time being, and was quickly adopted WCTU in Washington Court House and other Ohio communities.

The ladies' success was due in part to the deference most men still showed "women of quality" in the Victorian Era. Saloonkeepers and their patrons took a lot of shaming from the crusaders, but civility cracked in some cases. In one notable instance, an irate saloonkeeper poured a bucket of beer on the heads of the praying women; female barkeepers would sometimes curse or punch their tormentors, but such lack of decorum was exceptional.

It was difficult for the ladies to sustain their physical presence at the saloons once the novelty wore off. The number and frequency of the demonstrations declined, but they had planted a powerful seed that bloomed into a permanent agency through which women fought "the liquor interests." In 1874, church women met in Cleveland and founded the Women's Christian Temperance Union (WCTU). It became a mighty crusader against alcohol, adapting the tactics of the Washingtonians and other early reformers to the needs of a new time. No Ohio election of the late nineteenth or early twentieth centuries was fought without reference to the temperance issue.

In 1893 the temperance interests secured another powerful proponent when the Ohio Anti-Saloon League was formed in Oberlin. The backbone of its support came from protestant churches, notably the Methodists, which has led some interpreters of the temperance reform initiative to say that it was a device by which protestant America tried to keep immigrants, especially Catholics, in their place. Under the intellectual leadership of Ernest Cherrington and the administrative leadership of Wayne Wheeler, an Oberlin graduate, the league became a powerful national organization headquartered in Westerville in Franklin County. It used all the tactics long familiar to lobbyists and devised some new ones. It aggressively forced political candidates to state publicly their position on the liquor issue. They were sure to be asked, "Are you wet or dry?" The League's successes stemmed from its solid organization, professional management, and its well-focused program.

Short of outright prohibition, alcoholic beverages could be controlled by licensing or taxation or both. The more extreme temperance advocates—the prohibitionists—opposed licensing since it represented tacit recognition of the legitimacy of the liquor business. On the other hand, taxes, if high enough, could put the liquor interests out of business. Organized opposition came primarily from persons who made their living from the production, distribution, and sale of alcoholic beverages. Certain ethnic groups, especially the large and influential German population, to whom the use of alcoholic drinks was an ingrained part of social custom, also opposed the "drys." In Ohio's larger cities, notably Cincinnati, Cleveland, and Columbus, these people were strong enough to provide stiff opposition to would-be reformers. The contest over liquor control remained central in Ohio politics through the World War I era.

Meanwhile, the political wheels continued to turn. In 1875 the Republicans called Rutherford Hayes out of political retirement as their best gubernatorial hope for defeating the Democrats' Allen Thurman. Although the liquor issue was present, the candidates fought this campaign primarily on the issue of sound money (gold) versus inflationary money (greenbacks). Hayes and the Republicans were obviously the sound money men while the Democrats were proclaiming that "Greenbacks saved the Union . . . [now] let them avert starvation," a reference to widespread unemployment and distress brought on by the panic of '73. A remnant of the old Know Nothing bigotry emerged in the campaign when Democrats were charged with support of the recently passed Geghan Bill, which provided that equal facilities for worship and religious instruction be provided in state custodial institutions for persons of all denominations. Republicans represented this as a dangerous concession to Catholics, who, they feared, would become strong enough through rapidly rising numbers to alter fundamentally the core beliefs of Protestant America. The Geghan Bill was repealed during Hayes's term.

In the largest vote yet cast in Ohio, Hayes defeated Thurman by 5,544 votes. Hayes felt right at home in Columbus. He wrote his son, "It is like getting into old slippers to take my seat in the Governor's office once more." He noted that there was more business to address than formerly. Before resigning to run for the presidency, he tried to reinvigorate state institutions, and he sent the state militia to Massillon to maintain order during a coal miners' strike.

As earlier noted, Hayes's victory in a key state brought him to the attention of national Republican leaders looking for someone to bind the wounds of their factionalized party. And so he plunged into presidential politics, leaving the remainder of his term to be filled by Lt. Gov. Thomas L. Young of Hamilton County.

The Gilded Age and the years immediately following were fraught with economic problems and deep division on the proper course to rectify them. The resumption of specie payments for greenbacks, the re-monetization of silver, decreases in farm prices, and poor pay generally for Ohio's miners and industrial workers created so many competing interests and intraparty factions that full party regularity was seldom accomplished. In 1877 Bellefontaine's Judge William H. West, a Republican, lost his bid for the governorship to the Democrat Richard M. Bishop, a former mayor of Cincinnati. Governor Bishop watched his party's strength undermined when hard core inflationists and pro-labor factions defected for a third-party movement called the National Greenback Party, which cut into the Democratic vote in the congressional elections of 1878. Nevertheless, the Democrats won eleven of Ohio's twenty seats in the House.

By 1879 Samuel F. Cary, a former vice-presidential candidate on the Greenback ticket, Isaac Sherwood of Toledo, and several other influential National Greenback leaders returned to the Democratic Party and supported its gubernatorial candidate, Thomas Ewing, Jr. of Lancaster, an avowed inflationist. One wonders how Ewing's father, the distinguished Whig leader and former secretary of the treasury, would have regarded his son's pro-Greenback policies.

The Republicans chose Charles Foster. Growing up in Fostoria (named for his father), the young Foster embarked on a lucrative business career. He served four terms in the United States House of Representatives and was later to be secretary of the treasury under Harrison. In the 1879 campaign, his opponents played up his nickname, "Calico Charlie," which was a derisive thrust at Foster for staying home during the Civil War to work in the family's dry goods business. Whatever effect that charge might have had was more than offset by a return of prosperity. The Republicans claimed credit for it, and it helped give their candidate a 17,000-vote victory margin over Ewing. Two years later, Foster won by a slightly larger margin over John W. Bookwalter, a Springfield manufacturer.

Foster's administrations were characterized by efficiency. He modernized some procedures, including the establishment of bipartisan boards to oversee public institutions and to keep a protective eye on Ohio's mines and forests, but the dominant issue of Foster's governorship was control of the liquor traffic.

Foster was a staunch advocate of controlling the liquor trade, urging the voters and the legislature to support measures to lessen liquor's "devastating" effect on hearth and home. With his support the legislature, strongly Republican, passed two proposed constitutional amendments which were to be submitted to the voters in 1883. These amendments would allow local choice in liquor regulation, permit taxing the liquor traffic, and open the possibility of prohibition on a statewide basis. If total prohibition were adopted, of course, the other options would be unneeded. While the vote on these amendments was pending, the legislature passed the Pond Bill, taxing alcoholic beverages. German-language newspapers said this bill would make criminals out of honest German saloonkeepers. The Cincinnati *Commercial* asked, "What are those pot-bellied lobbyists doing at Columbus, with jugs of whisky and boxes of cigars, and the best rooms at the hotels?" The Pond Law was promptly challenged in Crawford County, and the Ohio Supreme Court ruled it violated the constitutional ban on licensing the liquor traffic. The legislature also passed the Scott Law, taxing retail sales of liquor and banning its sale on Sunday. The Ohio Supreme Court eventually declared this law unconstitutional in 1884.

This Republican attack on the liquor traffic engendered growing resentment which the Democrats hoped to channel to their advantage. They were encouraged by the defeat of the proposed constitutional amendments in October 1883. Not even the WCTU's vigorous campaign, during which they "sowed Ohio streets knee deep" with temperance tracts, could save the amendments, although the vote was close. ꝫ4ȣ

In 1883 the Republicans paid a price for alienating the large German and Irish vote on the temperance issue. To minimize the German reaction, they nominated a popular Cincinnatian, thirty-seven-year-old Joseph Benson Foraker, Civil War veteran and prominent local judge. Rutherford Hayes described him as witty and handsome, but he feared Foraker's tendency to say "sharp things." The Republican platform endorsed civil service reform, a high protective tariff, and regulation of the liquor traffic through taxation.

The Democratic candidate was George Hoadly, also of Cincinnati. Judge Hoadly was a former Republican and was not enthusiastically received by all segments of his new party. His former Republican associate, Hayes, called him a "reckless chatterbox." The Democratic platform approved tariffs for revenue only and favored a licensing system to control the liquor business.

The election was a smashing repudiation of recent Republican stewardship. Hoadly received 359,793 votes to Foraker's 347,164, but Democrats won the Ohio Senate by a two-to-one margin and the House by a four-to-three margin. This election attracted national attention, as both parties sought to identify future political trends. Ohio did supply a clue to the political drift, for in one more year the Democrats would elect a president for the first time since 1856.

During Hoadly's term attention focused on a bitter intraparty fight. Sen. George H. Pendleton of Cincinnati, fresh from his sponsorship of the 1883 Pendleton Act (the legislation that created a federal civil service), was opposed for reelection by strong elements within his own party. Among them were Cincinnati Democrats who felt he had not dispensed patronage to their advantage. Pendleton's challenger was Henry B. Payne of Cleveland. Once politically active, Payne had left politics to make his fortune in business. Opponents claimed, though later investigation proved inconclusive, that Payne received help from his son Oliver, who used Standard Oil money to assure his election. The affair left a bitter taste in Ohio politics.

In 1885 Hoadly and Foraker, both of whom aspired to national office, engaged in a rematch. This time Foraker won by 17,000 votes, almost precisely the margin by which he had lost two years earlier. Republicans controlled both houses of the legislature. However, the wider significance of this election is that it marked a transition in Ohio politics. Up to this point local and state issues dominated; after 1885 both parties ordered their state campaigns around broader national issues resulting from industrialization, urbanization, immigration, monetary considerations, business practices, and immersion in world affairs. Most of these issues surfaced on the state as well as the national level. In addition, the temperance issue kept state political waters roiled.

The last fifteen years of the nineteenth century found Ohio's major parties consolidating their positions on the currency, tariffs, and the appropriate posture toward big business growth. Republicans continued to favor a high protective tariff, sound money (although some favored bi-metalism) and a supportive attitude toward big business growth and development. Democrats gave up on greenbacks and endorsed "free silver." They opposed high protective tariffs and were more skeptical than Republicans about the *laissez faire* posture toward big business. Of course gradations of orthodoxy existed within these broad parameters.

Joseph Foraker owed his election in considerable degree to the Grand Army of the Republic. While campaigning he waved the "bloody shirt of the rebellion" with the best of them. Indeed, his oratorical style was so vigorous and pointed that he earned the sobriquet "Fire Alarm" Foraker. He won increased popularity with veterans when he castigated Grover Cleveland for vetoing the pension bill and for urging return of captured Confederate battle flags. No rebel flags would leave Ohio, said Foraker to the applause of appreciative veterans. In 1888 (the centennial of the first legal white settlement in Ohio) the G.A.R. held its national encampment in Columbus. Seventy thousand old soldiers marched through the capital's streets with such notables in attendance as Gen. William Tecumseh Sherman and the former president and war hero, Rutherford B. Hayes.

Hayes may have loved the parade, but he was not particularly enamored of Governor Foraker. He believed, along with the Hanna group of Republicans from the northern part of the state, that Foraker was too much for himself and not enough for the party. Dissidents were unable to block Foraker's nomination for a third term. He pointed to his record: his support of the 1886 law taxing the liquor business, as well as the establishment with his blessing of the Ohio State Board of Health, a commission to recapture illegally occupied state canal lands, and a board of pardons. He also urged that discriminatory laws still on the statute books be "swept away." He said that "our coloured fellow-citizens" have the same rights and opportunities for education and self-advancement that others have. "This is due them—they have earned it. They are a loyal people, and always have been." The Democrats countered with James E. Campbell, a veteran congressman from the Dayton district and an accomplished orator. He proved a good match for Foraker, who had only halfhearted support from his own party.

Campbell won office by nearly 11,000 votes and, more importantly, the Democrats won control of both houses of the legislature. The new regime enacted no seminal legislation, but the secret, Australian ballot was adopted (1891) in the expectation that it would reduce election fraud. An effort to allow cities a modicum of home rule was not successful. As six years previously, the party was wracked by a senatorial contest. The legislature elected Calvin S. Brice to succeed Payne. Like Payne, Brice, a champion of business interests, represented the conservative rather than the liberal sentiment in the party.

Governor Campbell and his party had but one term to enjoy their hegemony. New forces were about to usurp the stage, with Marcus Hanna as the organizing genius and William McKinley the instrument of its fulfillment. Much has been made of Hanna being the "closest thing to a national 'boss' in American history." He was conspicuously successful because he was able to harness the interests, hence the wealth, of rising industrialists, bankers, and other businessmen to the election of Republican candidates, notably McKinley.

In 1891 McKinley was available. He had recently lost his congressional seat through gerrymandering and through popular reaction to the high-rate McKinley Tariff of 1890. Hanna now set out to make him governor. The first step was successful when the state convention nominated McKinley by acclamation, a tribute to Hanna's groundwork. In the ensuing election McKinley defeated Campbell, and the Republicans regained control of the legislature. The Hanna-McKinley team further demonstrated its power when it succeeded in reelecting John Sherman to the Senate over the vigorous efforts of Joseph Foraker.

Battle lines were now clearly drawn in Republican circles. Hanna dominated the party organization in the north and Foraker (who was a respectable front for Cincinnati's "Boss" George Cox) dominated it in the south. For the moment, the Hanna faction rode high and, in 1893, succeeded in reelecting McKinley, this time by a larger margin over the Democrat Lawrence T. Neal.

McKinley was not one to rock a boat sailing on predictable seas. No vigorous reforms marked his first administration. His second term in the statehouse was most difficult, for he had to deal with the results of the deep depression of

1893. Hundreds of thousands were unemployed, especially in Ohio's rapidly growing industrial cities and in the coal mines of the southeastern counties. Social turmoil and lawlessness prompted McKinley to send troops to keep peace during labor unrest in the coal mining districts, yet he also responded to humanitarian appeals. In January 1895, he helped organize a relief expedition that brought food to more than 10,000 impoverished persons in the Nelson-ville (Athens County) area.

During this troubled period a voice was calling for radical reform, but it was neither Republican nor Democratic. In the 1880s and 1890s distressed farmers in the South and Middle West formed Farmers' Alliances, out of which grew third-party political activity organized as the People's Party, but better known as the Populist Party. The Populists advocated cooperatives, regulation of railroads, banks, and other private corporations, a sub-treasury system, the secret ballot, free silver, and a tariff for revenue only. In 1891, John J. Seitz, their candidate for governor of Ohio garnered 23,472 votes, just 0.03 percent of the total. James B. Weaver, the Populist candidate for president in 1892, received only 10,000 votes in Ohio. Obviously Populist strength was minimal, although Populist arguments did have modest impact on the Democratic platform.

The People's Party candidate in the 1895 governor's race was such an original that he was briefly the focus of national attention. Jacob Sechler Coxey, a successful Massillon businessman, was convinced that the way out of the depression was for the federal government to put the unemployed to work on public projects, paying them with money raised by new bond issues. The unemployed would gain purchasing power, and the sale of bonds would stimulate business by infusing the economy with new money.

Coxey's ideas were too radical for mainstream America. In 1894, to dramatize his plan, he led a caravan of followers from Massillon to Washington, D.C. Thousands of Coxeyites from the far West also set out for Washington. "Coxey's Army" was a motley group that fluctuated in size and character as the march progressed. It was even infused with a mystical religious motif symbolized by Coxey's beautiful blond daughter, on horseback, dressed all in white to symbolize purity. His son, Legal Tender Coxey, was still a babe in his mother's arms. When the army, about 500 strong, arrived in Washington, panicky authorities arrested the leaders for walking on the Capitol's lawn. Coxey was unable to present his plea to the legislators, and the army eventually dispersed.

Throughout the nineties, Coxey was a perennial political candidate. In 1895 he garnered an impressive 52,000 votes as the People's Party gubernatorial candidate. Clearly it was a momentary protest vote; when he ran again two years later, he received only 6,276 votes. However, Coxey had the last laugh on his detractors. Forty years later, in the throes of an even greater economic crisis, the federal government adopted his scheme of public works for the unemployed. And early in the depressed 1930s, Coxey's own neighbors turned for leadership to the old crusader, now ninety-two, and elected him mayor of Massillon.

In the 1895 gubernatorial race Asa Bushnell, a wealthy Springfield manufacturer, beat the Democrat, James Campbell, by 22,000 votes. Bushnell was Foraker's candidate; the Hanna faction was not especially enamored of him. Conflict between the Republican factions was intense. It was time to select a United States Senator, and both factions coveted the prize. With the governor's help, the state Republican convention endorsed Foraker and chose him for the seat vacated by Calvin Brice. Once more big business money seemed to influence the outcome, and Senator Foraker repeatedly denied charges that he had received money improperly from corporate interests.

The same year in which Foraker assumed his Senate seat his rival, Mark Hanna, joined him in that august body through some shrewd political manipulation. To clear the decks for Hanna, President McKinley appointed Sen. John Sherman secretary of state. Bowing to great pressure from influential party contributors, Governor Bushnell appointed Hanna to fill the Senate vacancy. The Hanna machine then succeeded in securing a full term for their leader despite opposition within the party. Hanna served in the Senate until his death in 1904, when he was succeeded by his lieutenant, Charles Dick of Akron.

In his second term as governor, Bushnell had to deal with organizational problems brought on by the war with Spain. Temporary barracks were fitted out at Camp Bushnell in Columbus. The war was so brief, small, and contained, that the war effort disrupted normal state operations but briefly. Ohio troops returned home to outpourings of patriotic fervor. For the moment, the country felt good about itself. As the nineteenth century wound to a close Republicans maintained their hold on the governor's office, electing George K. Nash over the wealthy Cincinnati newspaperman, John McLean. Not until 1910 would the Democrats again succeed in capturing the governorship.

In significant ways Republicans dominated the state's political life during the late nineteenth century. Between 1865 and 1900 Republicans were in the governor's chair twenty-seven years, Democrats eight; obviously the governor was influential, although Ohio did not grant the governor real power in the form of a veto until 1903. More importantly, Republicans controlled the state legislature more than twice as long as the Democrats. Still they found it difficult to maintain their hold, for periodically the voters sided with the Democrats to "throw the rascals out."

Despite these differences in numbers, the major parties were not radically different, one from the other, in philosophy. Each contained factions which advocated special interests whose historic roots we have already traced. By far the most visible and significant factionalism was the split between the

Cox-Foraker group of Cincinnati and the Hanna-McKinley group of Cleveland; each sought to dominate state Republican politics and control the patronage. Both served the interests of the rising business class, and when forced to cooperate with one another created what historian Randolph Downes described as "the mirage of Ohio Republican unity."

But old party alignments were soon to be tested by a rising spirit of reform which would bring a "progressive" faction to the fore in the first decades of the new century. Before treating that development, however, we must first understand the issues underlying the reform effort; that leads us directly to Ohio's significant role in the Age of Big Business.

12

Ohio's Economy and the Growth of Big Business, 1865–1900

The growth of Ohio's economic base both during and after the Civil War propelled its rapid rise to national leadership. The insatiable demands of Union armies for all sorts of goods and services stimulated agriculture, commerce, mining, and manufacturing, and Ohio's economy was mature enough to respond. The postwar era witnessed the rapid transition of American business, and by the end of the century Ohio led the way in nearly every new growth industry—automobiles, aircraft, electrical equipment, business machines and scores of others—even as it remained an important farming state.

Agriculture

In 1860, 83 percent of Ohioans lived in rural areas. Though their numbers rose slightly in the next twenty years, rural dwellers comprised but 68 percent of the population by 1880. The value of processed agricultural goods had more than doubled, but they accounted for just 19 percent of all Ohio manufactured products by value. These figures do not include the value of processed dairy products, wines, tobacco, hemp, and a few other smaller items. Ohio farmers provided virtually all the food consumed in the state in addition to exporting food to other states and overseas. Processed meats and grains accounted for 26 percent of all Ohio manufactured products by value in 1860. It is safe to say, however, that while in 1860 Ohio was at or near the top of the states in the value of its agricultural products, twenty years later the state was losing position relative to the rapidly developing prairie states.

By the end of the Civil War the pioneer stage of Ohio farming was over except for the northwest quadrant, especially the Black Swamp, where land was still being drained and cleared. Meanwhile some unproductive farms in the Allegheny Plateau had already been abandoned and the fields allowed to return to their natural state. This was especially true of Lawrence, Vinton, Scioto, and Adams counties, where much farmland was valued at only $16 to $18 an acre in 1880. In contrast, farms producing market products for Cincinnati, Cleveland, and other growing urban areas were valued much higher. Hamilton County land averaged $100 an acre, more than twice the state average of $46. In fifty of Ohio's eighty-eight counties in 1880 at least 75 percent of the land was classified as "improved." The state had 247,189 farms, averaging ninety-nine acres in size.

The pioneer farm was giving way to modernization throughout most of the state. Large, new barns replaced the log and pole barns of the early period. Farmhouses were enlarged or new ones built incorporating refinements such as cast iron stoves, kerosene lamps, and finished furniture. Despite improvements in lifestyle the farm family was still commonly isolated by poor roads. They lacked the options of farm families living in more accessible regions where roads were leveled, drained, gravelled, macadamized, or otherwise improved to the point where farm families could join with one another at church gatherings, socials, Fourth of July celebrations, and the like.

Even for the fortunate, agriculture remained a chancy business subject to forces, both natural and manmade, beyond the farmer's control. The widespread introduction of farm machinery was one of those forces. Mowers, reapers, seed drills, rakes and threshing machines proliferated after the Civil War. The hired hand viewed farm machinery as a threat to his job, and some farmers saw it as a threat to a way of life. The tractor, introduced early in the twentieth century, became a special threat. As one farmer put it, "What you can't do with horses isn't worth doing." But nothing could stop the modernizing process. The machine prevailed in agriculture just as it did in manufacturing, and in both locales it changed traditional work patterns. Though Ohio agriculture mechanized and increased in productivity, so did the competition, especially gently rolling Illinois and Iowa, which were quickly outproducing the Ohioans.

During the late nineteenth and early twentieth centuries, most Ohio farms were worked by their owners; only some 6 percent of Ohio farmers worked land owned by others. Tenants usually worked on shares, paying the owner from two-fifths to one-half of the produce raised. Farmers raised a variety of crops although some in the corn-hog belt of the western counties tended to specialize. Diversity insulated the Ohio farmer from disaster; if prices sagged for one crop, he usually got reasonable prices for another. He seldom experienced a bonanza, but he could weather poor market conditions with the eternal hope that next year things would be better.

The farmer was coming of age organizationally. In 1864 the general assembly began the practice of voting an annual appropriation to the Board of Agriculture (established 1846). The board met annually to hear reports on conditions around the state, and they used this information to advise the legislature. The board's main activity, however, was to manage the state fair. For many years local agricultural societies had held fairs, and in 1850 the first state fair was held in Cincinnati. After moving about from site to site, it took up permanent residence in Columbus in 1874. Fairs were valuable laboratories where farmers and their wives saw the best work of their neighbors and learned improved ways of carrying on their own activities. But fairs also meant fun, as "side shows" and other attractions provided entertainment for the whole family.

More formal educational avenues were opening to farm families, among them the land grant college. In July 1862, Congress passed the Morrill Act, authorizing states to receive allocations of federal land to be used to support colleges of agriculture and the mechanical arts. Late in 1862 Ohio was offered 630,000 acres, an allocation based on the size of the state's representation in Congress. The general assembly accepted the offer in 1864 and in March 1870, the Ohio Agricultural and Mechanical College received its charter. Governor Hayes appointed a board of trustees which selected the Neil farm north of Columbus for the new campus, and there University Hall was erected. Classes commenced in 1873. From the first, controversy raged over the curriculum, which included the liberal arts. Norton S. Townshend, secretary of the Board of Agriculture and later professor of agriculture at the college, criticized the curriculum, saying it was not focused enough toward farmers' needs. Indeed the school made little impact on agriculture in its first years. In 1878 the college was renamed The Ohio State University and shortly thereafter its college of agriculture commenced to make significant progress including development of an experimental station. This activity was later moved to Wooster, where the university continues to operate the Ohio Agricultural Experiment Station. To assure that farmers were served by a vigorous agricultural school, the state initiated a tax subsidy in 1891.

By the 1870s and 1880s Ohio farmers had access to farm journals. Among them were *Ohio Farmer, Farm and Fireside,* and the *Christian Farmer,* published by Waldo F. Brown, a Butler County agrarian. He described Ohio's tillers of the soil in colorful terms. The poor shiftless farmer who neglected his property was "Peter Poverty." One who exploited several farms for short-range profits and then moved on to new lands was "Sam Skinsoil." The prudent, hardworking farmer who treated his family and possessions with respect, and made money in the process, was "William Wealthy." Brown urged his readers to become well-rounded individuals by getting involved in cultural and intellectual activities.

The social and intellectual side of farm life was also a concern of the Grange. Founded in 1867 as the Patrons of Husbandry, the Grange had more than 900 local organizations in Ohio by 1875. A secret organization open to both men and women, it sponsored cooperatives for buying and selling goods. To serve its growing army of members, Montgomery Ward and Company of Chicago organized to provide mail order service to Grangers. Nationally the Grange led the fight for fair railroad rates and practices. In Ohio, however, the Grange's political influence was somewhat weaker. There was less farmer militancy than in the West, partly because the diversity in Ohio farming meant that farmers did not all face the same problems. Although they remained a powerful influence in the state's political life, they shared attention with industrialists, who had their own special issues to plead. By the twentieth century the Grange was increasingly a social organization and remains so to this day.

By the end of the nineteenth century Ohio's farm population was declining although the pace would be slow for several decades to come. In 1900 some 52 percent of the population lived in rural areas. Agriculture was still Ohio's largest industry by a substantial margin, both in value of goods produced and the number of persons employed. But manufacturing was advancing rapidly, threatening to displace agriculture as the dominant force in Ohio's economy.

Stimulating Industrial Growth

A number of elements combined to spur Ohio's development from an agriculturally dominant society into an industrially dominant society. This process can be effectively described by examining how each of the principal elements of industrial growth related to Ohio conditions.

Location

Post–Civil War Ohio was a bridge between the populous industrial centers of the East and the rapidly expanding West, where agriculture and manufacturing were both blossoming. With few exceptions the nation's principal east-west transportation arteries crossed the state; in addition Ohio maintained some of its historic connections with the Upper South. The goods, the people, and the ideas and intellectual currents of America passed through Ohio and influenced it. But the state was much more than a receiver; it was a transmitter sending economic, political, and social initiatives across the land.

The historic center of Ohio manufacturing, Cincinnati, had long enjoyed a locational advantage to mediate trade along the Ohio River Valley. Following the Civil War Cincinnati had to struggle to maintain business connections with the Upper South with increasing competition from Louisville and St. Louis.

As the industrial age advanced, other cities found their locations advantageous. Cleveland was 400 to 600 miles closer to growing western markets than were industrial rivals in the East. Since transportation costs were a large part of the cost of doing business, Cleveland prospered. In 1870, Dr. B. F. Goodrich relocated a small New York rubber factory to Akron, partly because it was west of the Appalachians while all of his many competitors were located in the East. Although other competitors arose in Chicago, Goodrich found itself, by a stroke of serendipity, in the heart of the region where the automotive industry was developing. Even after the auto industry focused around Detroit, Akron remained just 180 miles away.

Location also helped Ohio achieve a dominant position in the early growth of the oil refining business. Cleveland, where most activity centered, was well served by rail lines that brought crude from nearby western Pennsylvania and the western Ohio fields and then distributed the finished product to other states. Location benefited the developing iron and steel industry. Iron ore from the Lake Superior region could be carried by cheap water transportation—in ships owned for the most part by Clevelanders—to Cleveland mills and to Lake Erie ports from which it was but a short rail haul to the Mahoning Valley and other Ohio steel centers. Limestone used in the smelting process arrived by water from western Ohio, and later from Michigan. Coking coal came by rail from nearby mines in Ohio, Pennsylvania, and West Virginia. An 1899 observer aptly summed up Ohio's locational advantage: "Ohio . . . perceived the advantages of its location at the gateway of the Middle West, and, adding industry to industry, became one vast resounding workshop."

Natural Resources   *salt, oil, natural gas*
coal

Ohio was blessed with a variety of essential resources that settlers had used in the primitive industrial processes of the early nineteenth century. The new manufacturers quickly took advantage of the abundance of easily and cheaply accessible materials.

By the end of the nineteenth century the commercial extraction of salt was concentrated in the state's northeastern quadrant, as mines at Cleveland and Painesville extended deep under Lake Erie. At Akron and Rittman superheated water was forced into salt strata and the resulting brine was pumped to the surface, where the salt was extracted by drying. Once an importer of salt,

Ohio became a major exporter, ranking second only to Michigan in this industry.

As the clay products industry matured following the Civil War, production of chinaware focused around East Liverpool, Roseville, Crooksville, and other towns where skilled English craftsmen added the necessary talents to the fashioning of local clay. Stoneware (jugs, crocks, and the like) was widely made throughout the state. Brick and tile clays were abundant in the Tuscarawas and Muskingum valleys and elsewhere, and Ohio consistently ranked either first or second in the nation in brick manufacture. Zanesville claimed to be the largest producer of brick in America and the largest producer of tile in the world. Akron area clay products manufacturers developed a process for making vitrified (glazed) clay pipe and tile, a superior product that gave them an advantage over their competitors at a time when growing cities were installing new water and sewage systems and creating a huge demand for pipe. Briefly Summit County would be the "sewer pipe capital" of the world. After World War I the clay products industry shifted locales as local clay pits were exhausted, yet some Ohio regions remain important producers of clay products.

Ohio iron ore, timbers, and limestone once supplied iron makers with their resources. However, as the iron and steel business developed technologically, it demanded higher grade materials. Ore now came from the rich iron ore ranges of the Lake Superior region. Charcoal from local timber gave way to coke made from high quality coking coal, much of which was imported from nearby states. Even Ohio limestone from Kelleys Island and the Marblehead Peninsula would be replaced in large part by stone from Michigan. In short, Ohio's large iron and steel industry no longer operated with local resources, yet it continued to prosper since the cost of importing raw material was but a small part of the cost of the finished product.

A great new resource emerged in the 1880s. Oil in commercially significant quantities was discovered in the Lima-Findlay area. This became the nation's second major commercial field, and its development brought in its wake all of the color and corruption characteristic of America's oil booms. Cleveland's Standard Oil Company had interests in the region, but numerous smaller operators started oil companies, most of which disappeared within a few years. The Ohio Oil Company (originally controlled by Standard) endured well into the twentieth century, becoming in time part of the Marathon Oil Company of Findlay.

The burgeoning oil industry would make Toledo an important refining and shipping center in the 1890s. The city was close to the Lima-Findlay fields, and in 1895 the Klondike well blew in at East Toledo, creating a new surge of enthusiasm. Other oil fields of modest size were spotted around Ohio: Cow

Run near Marietta and the Mecca Field in Trumbull County, for example. Ohio's oil glory was brief. Early in the twentieth century massive new oil fields in California, Texas, and Oklahoma completely overshadowed the dwindling Ohio fields, where only a modest production survived.

Concurrent with the oil excitement, northwestern Ohio experienced a natural gas boom in the 1880s. The action centered around Findlay, which grew from a town of about 4,000 to a city of about 18,000 during the decade. The city's historian wrote, "It was a wild, mad, exciting, exhilarating, spectacular town." The Chamber of Commerce advertised "Free Fuel! Free Sites! For the Manufacturer Who Will Locate in Findlay, Ohio." With natural gas in abundance Findlay "must become . . . the greatest manufacturing center of a mighty republic. The only city in the world having 60,000,000 cubic feet of gas per day, equal to 3,260,000 pounds of coal, which is furnished—free—as the air, to every inhabitant that settles within her borders." The entire town was converted to gas heat, light, and power. Gas jets burned day and night. Lesser wells were left uncapped or were ignited and burned until exhausted. Officials warned the people that their extravagance would lead to no good end. Dr. Edward Orton, the state geologist, reminded them that "these stocks of buried light and heat and power are small at the best and demand the most careful husbandry." But no one listened, and within twenty years the boom ended with a whimper.

Some lasting good was accomplished, however, as companies started during the boom period endured and prospered. In 1888 Edward Libbey moved his glass plant from East Cambridge, Massachusetts, to Toledo to take advantage of cheap fuel. He brought 100 workers with him and established the first of Toledo's great glass-making companies.

Other Ohio resources continued to support important industries. Limestone, in addition to its role in smelting iron ore, is a building stone, soil "sweetener," and source of industrial chemicals, and substantial businesses grew up around Ohio limestone. Gypsum, a special kind of lime used in plaster and plasterboard, has long been quarried in Ohio, notably on the Marblehead Peninsula. Sandstone provides building stone and high-grade silicas for specialized use in the glass, foundry, and abrasives industries. For a time Ohio's Berea sandstone was the source of over 80 percent of American grindstones; every farmer had one. Millstones were made of Berea sandstone also. Shale was important to the clay products industry, sand and gravel essential to the construction industry.

Coal, which began to replace wood as a fuel before the Civil War, was still another vital element in Ohio's industrial growth. Coal powered the steam age, and mining was a major source of employment within the state. Despite the admonition that "the natural market of Ohio coal is Ohio," this resource was exported by rail to the West, and by lake vessel from Toledo, Huron, and

Sandusky to ports on the Great Lakes. Ohio coal was of mixed quality, but the clean-burning variety was quickly mined out. Inhabitants of the nineteenth century paid little attention to pollution resulting from high sulphur content, but manufacturers did recognize that some Ohio coal was inferior in quality to coal from neighboring states.

Capital

Industrial development cannot occur without funding, and most of the capital required to underwrite the growth of Ohio business came from within the state, although some exceptionally costly enterprises such as canals and railroads required infusions of capital from eastern financiers. In addition, some railroads received public funds, often from a 5 percent township tax. For a brief period cities, counties, and the state itself subscribed shares in transportation companies. In 1873 Cincinnati businessmen, determined to recapture their hold on the Upper South, persuaded the city to finance a 336-mile railroad that was completed to Chattanooga, Tennessee, in 1881. Their daring and foresight paid off with gross earnings in the millions of dollars soon after the line went into operation.

At the beginning of the postwar period, most Ohio industries were still capitalized at a modest level. Money could be raised locally; John D. Rockefeller's experience is instructive although hardly typical. As a young bookkeeper in a Cleveland produce commission house, he saved a fraction of each paycheck until he had accumulated a small amount of capital which, in combination with a partner and loans from a local bank, enabled him to go into business for himself. Using his enhanced worth, he moved into the fledgling oil-refining business. Once more, using partners and his good credit with lending institutions, he secured the capital necessary for acquiring an ever larger share of the local refining business, which in turn gave him leverage with railroads, suppliers, and every other element in the industry. In 1870, just eleven years after going into business for himself, he and his three partners formed the Standard Oil Company of Ohio, capitalized at $1 million. By the end of the century the business, now reorganized, was capitalized at $110 million.

Rockefeller's spectacular parlaying of capital into a gigantic enterprise was extraordinary, but his early reliance on local capital resources was fairly typical. Local business pledges of $13,600 clinched B. F. Goodrich's decision to locate in Akron. Although modest compared to the resources of Goodrich and his brother-in-law, the Akron contribution provided the essential margin required for the move. It also demonstrated the support the entrepreneur might expect from the local business community. There is a story to the effect that Goodrich first approached Cleveland businessmen, but they were preoccupied with the prospects of iron and steel, lake shipping, and oil and showed no enthusiasm for a relative unknown—rubber.

In addition to the oil men—Rockefeller, Stephen V. Harkness, Samuel Andrews, Henry M. Flagler—Cleveland capitalists including Samuel L. Mather, Marcus Hanna, and David Rhodes were investing in iron and steel, iron ore and coal mines, and lake shipping. They also invested in railroads, banks, real estate, and other commercial ventures. Every Ohio city had its counterparts. In Dayton in 1884 John Patterson needed but $6,500 to purchase James Ritty's "mechanical money drawer," which became the basis of the National Cash Register empire. Two years later local capital enabled him to build a remarkable factory and enter into large-scale production. In 1898 Frank Seiberling secured $43,000 in cash from Akron friends to start his new Goodyear Tire and Rubber Company, which was soon capitalized in the amount of $100,000. Similar stories abound all over the state.

While most Ohio manufacturers sought capital locally, nearly every industrial community hoped to attract new business ventures and capital. As early as the 1830s Cincinnati boasted a board of trade; Cleveland established its board in 1848. Other industrial centers followed, especially after the Civil War. Zanesville's board, established in 1868, published a pamphlet and a book extolling the city's virtues as a business site and seeking "to induce Eastern capitalists to come here and aid us in developing our resources"; the appeal had limited success. As already noted, extreme boosterism also accompanied the oil and gas strikes in northwestern Ohio with Toledo, Findlay, and other communities trying to outstrip one another in trumpeting their advantages. Their message was "invest in our area."

Although local sources provided adequate capital for the start-up costs of small industries, rapid growth and expansion caused most to broaden their search for resources through sales of stocks and bonds and through ever larger bank loans. Although modest amounts of capital were sufficient to establish Cincinnati's Procter and Gamble, Dayton's National Cash Register, Toledo's Libbey Glass Company, Springfield's Champion Works, Cleveland's Standard Oil Company, Akron's Goodyear Tire and Rubber, and any number of other Ohio companies, the industries developed an insatiable appetite for capital infusions as they grew to giant size early in the twentieth century, and increasingly they sought this capital outside the state. Ohio banks were not large enough to meet all their needs; Ohio companies turned to Chicago and New York financial centers to float new securities and obtain loans.

Energy

Throughout the Age of Big Business, Ohio industry had access to plentiful and cheap energy, primarily produced, either directly or indirectly, from the state's coal supply. Abundant water power had served early industrial establishments well, but by mid-century more than half of Ohio's manufacturers were using steam power. At first, wood fired the steam boilers, but the more common fuel was coal, and the wide availability of water near coal deposits added to its advantages. By 1900 over 90 percent of Ohio's factories ran on steam from coal-fired boilers. Only a few industries—glass and ceramics, for example—used natural gas as an energy source, and oil-fired boilers were still in the future. By the 1890s electricity generated by coal-fired steam propelled trolleys and interurbans, lighted streets, and powered a growing number of other activities, all on energy produced at reasonable cost.

Thirty counties mined Ohio coal. The northern coal fields in Mahoning, Portage, Summit, Stark, and Wayne counties dominated the early stages of the mining industry, but eastern and southern counties became prominent by the 1860s. Before mine regulation and mechanization it cost as little as $2,000 to open a shaft mine. Even less was required for a small, family operated drift mine, a mine that sloped into the side of a bank or hill. Thousands of such operations were scattered around Ohio's hills. Marginal operators tended to disappear as mining became big business requiring large amounts of capital and extensive labor forces. In 1880 more than 6 million tons of coal were mined at an average cost to the consumer of $2.25 per ton. By 1900 more than 16 million tons were extracted by 19,000 miners. Capital invested in the mines was about $13.5 million.

Ohio cities vied for access to this cheap energy source. Dayton business leaders spent an inordinate amount of time and effort organizing a rail line (later known as the Detroit, Toledo and Ironton) to the high quality coal fields in Jackson County. This led to lower energy costs and gave them an edge on their industrial competitors. Columbus likewise recognized the advantages of direct rail connection with southern Ohio fields. The Columbus, Hocking Valley and Athens Railroad Company brought coal at reasonable cost directly to the capital city and its expanding industries.

Transportation

During Ohio's great industrial surge, a comprehensive transportation network was one of its main assets. Few states could rival its combination of transport via water, road, railroad, and interurban systems. Of these, only the canals failed to grow in importance in the twentieth century. As noted earlier, canal transport fell on hard times during and after the Civil War as rail promoters purchased canal right-of-way at a fraction of its value. Throughout the late nineteenth century canal proponents tried repeatedly to generate support in the legislature for modernizing the system. Each governor of the period urged action, but the state did little to help the ailing system. "Stateboats" maintained short stretches on which bulk goods continued to move, but this was clearly a secondary traffic in the total scheme of things. After the great flood of 1913 washed out the last viable stretches, canals ceased to function except as sources of industrial water.

On the Ohio River, steamboats continued to carry much freight and some passengers. Removal of navigational hazards improved the channel yet the river was still subject to alternating periods of flood and low water. The river trade boomed in importance during World War I when it took on much of the overload that railroads could not handle. This helped convince the federal government to "canalize" the river by creating a series of forty-six dams and locks which the Army Corps of Engineers completed in 1929, making the river into a series of pools with a channel of predictable depth. Modernization of the river traffic after World War II resulted in new dams and locks that created a nine-foot channel. Barges could carry large loads through all seasons, propelled by powerful diesel "towboats" that had replaced the old steamers. Industries grew along the river as the efficiency and accessibility of cheap water transportation increased. Clearly river transport was a continuing asset to Ohio's economy.

Water transport also flourished on Lake Erie during the late nineteenth and early twentieth centuries. As the period progressed, passenger service, once available at several Ohio lake ports, centered in Cleveland, from which regular service was available to Buffalo and Detroit. Sailing on a well-appointed ship could be a pleasant, even glamorous way to travel. The scenery was appealing by day, the staterooms comfortable by night. But Lake Erie is notional; when the wind rises suddenly to whip its shallow waters into a frenzy it is no place for the faint-hearted. Shipwrecks were certainly not everyday occurrences, but they were common enough to give pause to cautious travelers. Passenger service declined rapidly after World War I, doomed by the automobile and by the 1930s depression. Later efforts to revive it were futile.

Although passenger transport languished, Cleveland continued to hold its leading role as a center of lake shipping. The Lake Carrier's Association, dedicated to the improvement of lake navigation, was organized in the city in 1892. Pickands, Mather and Company, Oglebay, Norton and Company, and the Cleveland-Cliffs Iron Company were among those that made Cleveland supreme in the transport of iron ore from the Lake Superior mines. Their great ore boats—"freshwater whales"—grew ever larger as locks and docks were extended to accommodate them. Lorain, Fairport Harbor, Ashtabula, and Conneaut got their share of the ore trade while Sandusky and Toledo became ever more important coal shipping ports. Ohio companies not only operated lake fleets, they built them. In the twentieth century Lorain's American Shipbuilding Company would build some of the largest ore boats on the lakes.

The Age of Big Business was also the railroad age. While waterborne traffic remained important, the spectacular growth of railroad systems overshadowed all other means of moving goods and passengers. Furthermore, railroads were among the largest employers of the time, providing jobs for tens of thousands of construction, maintenance, and operating workers. The 2,946 miles of track that ranked Ohio first in the nation in 1860 had expanded to 8,951 miles by the end of the century. Mileage peaked in 1908 at 9,581.

Ohio was uncommonly well served by rail lines. All of the consolidated east-west rail systems developed by eastern capitalists served Ohio—the New York Central, Pennsylvania, Baltimore and Ohio, Erie, and others that developed in the twentieth century. These powerful companies also controlled such secondary lines as the Nickel Plate (New York, Chicago and St. Louis) or the Big Four (Cleveland, Cincinnati, Chicago and St. Louis). While the great railroad systems were being formed, local entrepreneurs continued to develop intrastate lines such as the Hocking Valley, the Northern Ohio, and the Toledo and Ohio Central. In the eastern part of the state the Wheeling and Lake Erie became an important coal carrier. The steam trunk roads handled Ohio's needs in large part although on occasion a short line such as the Akron and Barberton Belt Railroad connected the main lines with local industry.

While railroads increased in track mileage, they also sought to improve the quality of service on their "crack" trains. Elaborate coaches, Pullman cars, and dining cars now graced the most important passenger trains. Indeed, the "Broadway Limited," "Erie Limited," and "Cleveland Express" became household words for luxury travel. Gentlemen could retire to a parlor car to lounge in comfortable chairs, read the newspaper, smoke, drink, and use the ubiquitous spittoons which were a necessary accoutrement in that day of tobacco chewers. Obviously, ladies were not welcome in this male refuge. Although a layer of fine soot might still cover one's clothes, the damaging sparks which formerly blew in through open windows were now controlled. The new railway cars were equipped with sanitary facilities, to the inestimable relief of the passengers.

All in all, a trip on a fine train was an adventure, allowing the rider to move in comfort toward a distant destination. The romance of the rails was especially felt in small rural towns, where the world's business passed through the local depot. Nothing quite matched the distant train whistle for evoking a wanderlust among small-town people whose world was circumscribed. Sherwood Anderson, recalling his boyhood in Clyde (a junction point of the Lake Shore and Michigan Southern and the Cincinnati, Sandusky and Cleveland) wrote in his *Memoirs:* "There was a passenger train going away into the mysterious West at some twenty minutes after seven in the evening and . . . we all congregated at the station to see the train arrive, we boys gathering far down the station platform to gape with hungry eyes at the locomotive."

The railroads brought tremendous rewards to Ohio cities and towns by contributing a vital link with national and world markets and by keeping this part of America's hinterland in touch with world events. News flashed over telegraph lines that paralleled the rail lines and allowed the rural county seat to know what was happening as soon as it was known in the metropolis. This kind of connection was an important step in ending rural isolation, a process which would not be complete until automobiles, telephones, radios, mass circulation magazines, movies, and television completed the job well into the twentieth century.

Certain spin-off benefits came to Ohio from the growth of railroading. The iron and steel industry, second only to Pennsylvania's, profited from the manufacture of rails and rolling stock. The mills of Cleveland and Youngstown made steel rails, trestles, and railroad equipment. Dayton's Barney & Smith Car Company was an important producer of both passenger and freight cars, and later of electric trolleys. The elegance of fine passenger cars made it necessary for Barney to hire workers skilled in wood carving, inlay work, and other crafts. In 1880 the company employed 900 workers; just three years later it had a work force of 1,500. A combination of absentee ownership, management for short-term profits, failure to keep abreast of technological change, and the Panic of 1893 contributed to its decline, however.

The growth of railroads was not without its negative by-products. Hundreds of railroad schemes drained capital needed elsewhere, and all too often the promotions collapsed, taking their investors down with them. In their eagerness to secure rail connections, many cities and towns made unwise concessions to the rail companies, sometimes allowing them to dictate where the lines would run; the railroads would respond by preempting property which could more appropriately have been used for other purposes. Railroads were often involved in unfair practices such as pooling, rebates, drawbacks, and long-haul, short-haul rate discrepancies. Stock watering, free passes, and outright bribes to legislators were other abuses. The Ohio commissioner of railroads complained that the rail companies largely ignored his department even though they were required to submit regular reports on their operations. Fears of monopolistic railroad consolidation led Attorney General George K. Nash to bring suit in the Ohio Supreme Court in 1881 against William Vanderbilt and associates who were seeking to combine two important lines into a single corporation. Even though Ohio was a most competitive railroad environment, the supreme court upheld Nash's contention that this was a dangerous precedent leading toward monopoly of a vital economic resource. It may have slowed, but it did not stop future consolidations.

Farmers, especially the Grangers, led opposition to the railroads' monopolistic practices in Ohio. Though not as militant as the Farmers' Alliance in some western states, the Ohio Grange organized pressure on the state legislature, which responded by regulating railroad practices. An 1872 act required

Sprawling steel mills such as this Republic Steel plant in Youngstown were part of Ohio's big business era.

railroads to charge the same price to all shippers and set a maximum rate of five cents per mile per ton on lines thirty or more miles in length. Another act limited passenger fares to three cents per mile. By 1881 the legislature passed a package of laws regulating the handling of freight, but the rail companies frequently ignored or circumvented these laws.

Another charge against the railroads was their reputed lack of concern for safety. In 1899 about 400 persons were killed and more than 6,000 injured in Ohio railroad accidents. The next year the number of deaths increased 25 percent and the injured by about 15 percent. Ohio's most spectacular rail tragedy occurred in December 1876 when the Pacific Express crashed through a trestle near Ashtabula and fell sixty feet into a ravine. Although warned about the trestle's condition, the railroad had done nothing to improve it. Eighty-three people were killed outright and others died later. More than sixty sustained serious injury.

Despite all of its inadequacies, the railroad provided the most vital link in Ohio's economic chain. Railroad operators have been fairly charged with the dear price that people paid in lost investments, unfair rates, uncomfortable and unsanitary facilities, even death or dismemberment; still, when balanced against the economic and social benefit to the state, the railroads must be accorded a success. It is impossible to conceive how modern Ohio could have emerged without them.

trolly

Important competition with the railroads developed during the last decade of the nineteenth century, when the electric trolley began to replace horse- and mule-drawn cars in Ohio cities, and electric traction lines connected cities. America's pioneer experiment in intercity traction was the short Newark-Granville line, but it was the ABC Line (Akron, Bedford, Cleveland) opened in 1895 that demonstrated the advantages of this new transportation form, the interurban. Interurbans were cheaper to build than steam railroads, and the cars served local areas, were fast, and ran frequently. They carried passengers primarily but also hauled considerable freight.

Early in the twentieth century Ohio was swept by "interurban madness." Roger Grant, a historian of Ohio transportation, remarks that Ohio held "the indisputable claim as the heartland" of the interurban by World War I: "Interurbans linked all sections of the state; no town of 10,000 population lacked traction service." Ohio's 2,798 miles of track exceeded by a thousand miles that of any other state. The interurban extended the effective market area of the larger towns and cities, and in the process helped reduce rural isolation. Real estate values rose along right-of-ways much as they had seventy years earlier along the canals. Excess power distributed along the traction lines provided electricity to farmers.

The rise of the interurban was spectacular, but so was its fall. As with steam railroads, many schemes flopped for every one that succeeded. The advent of the motor car and truck effectively undercut the local advantages which interurbans had enjoyed. By the 1920s many companies were in trouble financially and the depression of the 1930s dealt most of them a death blow. "No major American industry collapsed so totally and so quickly as did electric traction," Grant writes.

Ohio's roads and highways at the beginning of this period were largely unimproved. Few had been paved, and Ohioans mostly struggled through the mud. Plank roads (roads paved with boards) built by private investors were popular until after the Civil War; by 1873 Ohio had 1,502 miles of toll roads and 4,327 miles of free highway. The bicycle craze of the "gay nineties" and especially the introduction of automobiles at the turn of the century gave strong impetus toward good roads. The Ohio Good Roads Federation, organized in 1909, won considerable support for improved roads as did the Lincoln Highway Association a few years later.

Ohio stood to profit from the upgrading of highways in ways other than ease of transportation. In the early twentieth century Ohio made cement; in fact, the nation's first cement pavement was laid around Bellefontaine's courthouse square in 1891, proving highly successful. The state also ranked either first or second in the manufacture of brick paving blocks. In addition, Ohio produced road building equipment, and had a large stake in the manufacture of autos, trucks, and their parts. Akron-based tire companies were especially aggressive in furthering the good roads movement; the B. F. Goodrich Company published tour guides and posted directional signs to assist travelers venturing far from home on America's new highways. Ultimately Ohio had a highway network to match its rail network.

In aviation, Ohio's pioneering efforts were unexcelled. Much experimental work was done in the state and it was a center of aircraft manufacture. Dayton, home of Wilbur and Orville Wright, was heavily involved as were Sandusky, Niles, Alliance, Akron, Cleveland, Piqua, and Cincinnati. U.S. airmail routes crossed the state. America's first air freight was flown from Dayton to Columbus in 1910. Ohio cities were among the nation's first to have regularly scheduled commercial passenger flights, with Cleveland boasting connections with Detroit as early as 1922. Pioneering experiments in crop dusting (near Troy, 1921) and cloud seeding (Dayton, 1923) kept the state in the forefront of aviation development.

Meanwhile, World War I created a demand for dirigibles that brought Akron rubber companies into the lighter-than-air business. Goodyear parlayed its experience into world leadership in building lighter-than-airships. The future of passenger dirigibles was shaken when the *Shenandoah* crashed near Ava, Ohio, in 1925; what had seemed a promising venture literally collapsed as first the *Akron* and then the *Macon* crashed in the 1930s. The future of the large, rigid, passenger-carrying dirigible ended with the burning of the German ship *Hindenburg* in 1937. Non-rigid "blimps" used for promotional purposes and for wartime service continued to be manufactured in Akron.

Labor

To add still more impetus to Ohio's economic growth, its labor forces expanded rapidly in the late nineteenth and early twentieth centuries. Two sources fed this growth: young men and women leaving rural areas for new opportunities in the cities, and immigrants seeking jobs and a new life in America. Ohio was not unique in this regard, for every industrial state drew labor from the same sources. The unskilled labor supply varied with economic conditions. In prosperous periods of rapid industrial expansion, plenty of jobs were available and some employers experienced temporary shortages of workers. In periods of depression, such as the prolonged traumas of 1873–78 and 1893–97, great numbers of unskilled workers lacked employment. Skilled workers enjoyed a more stable environment until machines started to eliminate many of the jobs they had performed.

Although average wages increased over this period of rapid industrial growth, the cost of labor was proportionately a much smaller part of the cost of production than would be the case after World War II. Unskilled men worked long hours for very modest wages; women and blacks earned less than half the wages paid to white men for similar work; children earned less still. Benefits were nonexistent in all but a few progressive companies. Without effective union protection workers were vulnerable to wage fluctuations. For example, in 1901 machine cutters in Athens County coal mines averaged $1,045 per year in wages while men doing the same work in Belmont County averaged $770. By 1910, however, a surfeit of operators had reduced the average Athens County wage to $468 annually while wages remained stable in Belmont. Such fluctuations and disparities were not uncommon in other Ohio industries.

Wage instability makes it somewhat meaningless to generalize about whether Ohio was a high labor-cost state or a low labor-cost state. In the 1880s, for instance, Akron's B. F. Goodrich Company paid its workers less than their counterparts in most eastern rubber shops. By World War I, however, Goodrich and other Akron rubber companies paid the top wages in the industry. When John Patterson started to build cash registers in Dayton in the 1880s he attracted good workmen by paying premium wages. Since he had little competition, he could afford this luxury. In 1894 young Tom Johnson (later a reform mayor of Cleveland) moved his steel-making operations from Pennsylvania to Lorain. He paid unskilled native-born workers 50 percent more than the prevailing wage rate in the industry. Not enough were willing to do the grueling work for $1.50 per day, so Johnson recruited immigrants—Italians, Poles, Hungarians, Slovaks—to work for wages native-born workers rejected.

By modern standards wages during the industrial boom years seem incredibly low. Yet wages increased faster than the cost of living. Ohio workers' real wages rose by 50 percent between 1860 and 1890. They continued to rise at a slower rate until World War I, when wartime conditions skewed both wages and prices. No special conditions appear to distinguish Ohio labor.

What happened to working men and women in the Buckeye State was similar to the fate of laborers generally in the industrial states of the Union.

As industrial enterprises grew rapidly in size, so did the need for industrial workers to organize in their own behalf. They sought "strength through union." Mass production industries grew spectacularly in the late nineteenth and early twentieth centuries, and numbers of employees grew correspondingly. Between 1880 and 1910 the average number of workers in iron and steel companies rose from about 300 to 849, in rubber from 94 to 663, in glass from 109 to 249, and in other industries accordingly. In 1887 Dayton's Barney Car Works employed over 2,000 workers. Akron's Goodyear Tire and Rubber Company started business in 1898, but just twelve years later it had a payroll of 2,500 with "more coming in daily."

The impersonal environment of the large factory, where the foreman generally had the power to fire any worker he disliked, fostered worker unrest and dissatisfaction. Some of Ohio's more progressive companies tried to deal with new conditions through extensive worker welfare programs. Procter and Gamble of Cincinnati, following a series of labor disturbances, was one of the first. In 1887 the company introduced a profit-sharing plan (later rescinded) and followed with other benefits. John Patterson's National Cash Register also experienced labor problems and responded constructively. He hired experts to build attractive "daylight" factory buildings on a landscaped "campus." The company addressed all areas of employee welfare—health, recreation, leisure-time activities, personal hygiene, and education. When challenged for spending so much on employee welfare Patterson stated simply, "It pays." Other industrial cities had companies committed to improving the worker's lot. The Acme Sucker Rod Company of Toledo, operated by the idealistic Samuel "Golden Rule" Jones, provided employees with picnics, a company band, and a library, and allowed workers to keep track of their own working time. In Akron, Firestone Tire and Rubber and Goodyear vied for leadership in developing employee benefits, while Columbus's Buckeye Steel Castings Company led the move toward worker benefits in the capital city. Cleveland boasted several companies with employee welfare plans, among them Arthur L. Garford's Cleveland Automotive Company and the Joseph & Feiss Company, whose female garment workers had benefits that included company outings featuring athletic contests. Some manufacturers provided single-family housing for their workers, among them Youngstown Sheet and Tube, which had distinct housing groups for American workers, foreign-born workers, and "colored" workers. In Akron both Goodyear and Firestone sponsored real estate developments—Goodyear Heights and Firestone Park—where attractive housing was available at favorable rates. Thus the more progressive Ohio industrialists tried to ameliorate the effects of size and depersonalization on the worker's relationship to his company. They also

Patterson

hoped to lessen worker militancy and to head off unionization. This aspect of
industrial paternalism was to reach its height in the 1920s.

One should not assume from this recital of enlightened management practices that such efforts were common; the majority of Ohio manufacturers did
little to humanize working conditions. Among the worst conditions were
those faced by women working in the "sweatshop" environment of the garment industry. A state official, gathering labor statistics in 1879, described a
rather "typical" situation. A Cleveland widow, with a child to support, made
vests in her tenement room; if she worked "steadily all day, and quite late at
night" she could turn out enough vests to earn almost two dollars a week. Her
room rent was two dollars a month and she paid three dollars a month on her
sewing machine. This left her about three dollars a month to live on. "I am
ashamed," she said, "to tell you how little we spend for food. I would never
. . . have believed that anyone could exist on what I have had to this
winter."In 1890 the *Cincinnati Enquirer* examined the condition of working
women in Cincinnati, focusing on those engaged in tailoring, shoe-fitting,
laundry and housework, cloak and vest making, sewing, and restaurant work.
The newspaper account concluded that, had the destitution uncovered in its
investigations been caused by some sudden catastrophe, it "would call forth
the sympathy of the world," but, coming as it did, "gradually, year by year,
through the natural operation of business systems, it has been systematically
ignored and its existence even denied."

As women suffered from poor pay and abominable working conditions, so
did children. In the 1880s, "girls can be found in the factories, and in the
planing-mills running planers, and in the potteries doing men's work, receiving from 50 to 75 cents a day, while men working beside them get from $1.50
to $2.00 for the same kind and quantity of work." Children entered the work-
shops at age twelve, "and at fifteen they are able to do a man's work. They are
given work at meager wages until they reach the years of manhood, when
they are thrown out of employment to make room for some other boys who
will work cheaper. . . ."

Low pay and dreadful working conditions kept the cost of production
down. So did new equipment that replaced highly paid skilled craftsmen with
low-paid, unskilled workers. Cigar-making machines allowed Cincinnati
cigar makers to replace veteran male workers with girls and boys who could
operate the machines satisfactorily, and for much lower wages. Machinery
replaced workers in the coal mines and the potteries. In Toledo, Michael
Owens invented a machine that made bottles automatically. His work was
hailed by everybody except the glassmakers who lost their jobs. A technological revolution in the iron and steel industry increased efficiency at the expense of skilled craftsmen who were replaced by less skilled machine operators. Early in the twentieth century the industrial production line was

perfected. Now workers with low skills could be assigned a single task which they repeated endlessly through the long work day. Such workers were easy to secure and train so they had little bargaining power. Eager immigrants were waiting to take production line jobs at prevailing wages under prevailing working conditions. In every way, industrial workers were vulnerable.

In the words of historians Raymond Boryczka and Lorin Lee Cary, "Regardless of the industry in which they toiled . . . Ohio workers in manufacturing came to share certain similarities in their jobs. Not until the 1930s would that commonality form a sufficiently strong base for trade unionism in the mass-production industries." And yet, strong efforts were being made in the late nineteenth century to initiate an effective labor movement. The Knights of Labor (founded in 1869 by Uriah Stevens of Philadelphia) pursued an idealistic dream of uniting all workers in one big union. Its influence faded after 1886 when Terence Powderly, leader of the Knights, undercut efforts by other nascent unions to cooperate in striking for a universal eight-hour day. This not only created unrest within the Knights, but it also alienated the independent trade unions. An assembly of these dissidents was held in Columbus in December 1886, where, under the leadership of Samuel Gompers, a cigar maker, a new American Federation of Labor (AFL) was formed with Gompers as president. Each craft (e.g., carpenters, typographers) was to have a single trade union, but these unions were federated together for collective action. By the 1890s the AFL's craft union model prevailed over the Knight's industrial union model. With their new sense of direction, the craft unions survived the devastating depression of 1893–98 while the Knights did not. The revival of business at the end of the century brought a corresponding revival of union activity and influence.

Meanwhile, the roots of another strong labor organization had been growing in the coal fields of Ohio and its sister states. Workers in the coal industry were militant, and with good cause. The industry was characterized by abysmal and dangerous working conditions, long hours in the bowels of the earth, job competition from immigrants, technological unemployment, and a volatile wage scale manipulated to the miner's disadvantage. Many Ohio miners lived in a company house, in a company town and traded at the company store, using company scrip. Even well-motivated mine owners and operators laid a heavy burden on their employees. John R. Buchtel of Akron, for example, tried to make Buchtel, Ohio (a company town founded in Hocking County by the Akron Iron and Rolling Mill Company) into a model of good management, yet found that his employees were most disgruntled at what they considered to be abuses in the company store.

To combat the unfavorable and sometimes atrocious conditions in their workplace, the coal miners of the Tuscarawas, Mahoning, and Hocking valleys affiliated in 1863 with the American Miners' Association, the first national miners' union. A broader group within the state emerged in 1882 as the Ohio Miners' Amalgamated Association.

But as the miners organized, so did the operators. In the Hocking Valley they formed an association popularly known as "the Syndicate," and in 1884 they slashed wages to provoke a strike that would afford them the opportunity to break the union and introduce new labor-saving equipment. They got their strike; indeed, a bitter conflict ensued in which lives were lost and much property destroyed as idle miners battled the "scabs" (strikebreakers) brought into the valley by the operators. Pinkerton guards protected the scabs, but violence continued. Strikers set several mines on fire, the most flamboyant case occurring near New Straitsville (Perry County) when miners pushed cars of burning coal deep into the shaft, where they ignited the coal seams. A century later the underground fire still raged, and the coal consumed was conservatively valued at over $50 million. Ultimately the operators prevailed as state militia and Pinkertons brought a modicum of normality to the valley, but the emotional scars endured.

Miners increasingly realized that local associations could not combat the combined power of the operators. In 1890 representatives of miners groups met in Columbus, where they formed the United Mine Workers of America (UMW). Severe economic conditions and the continuing introduction of mechanical aids offset the union's effectiveness during its early years. Late in the 1890s, however, its fortunes started to improve and, despite a very checkered history, the UMW was on its way toward becoming one of the most important labor organizations in the country.

Organizing activity also marked the state's other growing industries. In every case—potters, glassmakers, iron and steel workers, railroaders, rubber workers, seamen—organizing efforts ran into strong opposition from management. Many Americans still regarded union activity as foreign to a free society. Employers saw it as a conspiracy and, ironically, so did certain courts which ruled that unions were combinations in restraint of trade as prohibited under the Sherman Antitrust Act of 1890.

In 1901 a dispute between management and a small number of union molders led to a strike against the National Cash Register Company. The union lost but the employees benefited since John Patterson established the first modern personnel department in American industry to win the allegiance of his workers. Akron rubber barons strongly reflected anti-union attitudes when workers struck their explosively growing industry in 1913. The strikers received support from the radical Industrial Workers of the World (IWW or "Wobblies") and their crack organizer, "Big Bill" Haywood. But the "substantial" people of the city rallied around a local Episcopal priest to form a large and visible citizen's group which openly demonstrated against the strikers. Without widespread support the strike collapsed, but here too industry responded by introducing a variety of employee services designed to keep workers isolated from the allure of unionism.

In 1877 the Ohio legislature established a Bureau of Labor Statistics to gather data on the condition of working men and women and report to the legislature and the public at large. The bureau claimed that Ohio workers, as of 1870, were as organized as those of any state in the union. In the nineties, Ohio was one of fifteen states permitting workers to organize and bargain collectively. In 1900 Ohio's 956 trade unions, representing 123 occupations, claimed 79,884 members. Although those figures would increase in the next three decades, the next great forward thrust for organized labor did not emerge until the old economic order broke in the 1930s, presenting labor with a spectrum of new opportunities to organize and bargain collectively.

Scientific and Technological Innovation

Scientific initiatives in the early period of Ohio statehood came from a small but distinguished group of men—Daniel Drake, Jared Kirtland, Ormsby Mitchel, Asa Gray, Lucas Sullivant, Charles Whittlesey—who had been born and educated in the East. They brought their training and their skills with them to the new west of Ohio. By the late nineteenth century, however, Ohio-born researchers were making scientific and technological advances of great variety and significance. Many, if not all, of these advances led to processes that kept Ohio in the vanguard of industrial development.

Support for scientific and technical work was becoming institutionalized. Ohio colleges and universities developed strong laboratory courses in the physical and natural sciences and organized colleges of engineering. Ohio State's college of agriculture helped introduce new principles and techniques to the state's farmers. Certain forward-looking industrial companies established their own research laboratories before the turn of the century. At B. F. Goodrich, for example, the founder's son, Charles Goodrich, put his eastern college education to practical use in 1895 by establishing a company research laboratory. Other rubber companies quickly followed suit, and thus began an impressive stream of industry-generated scientific and technical advances which continues to this day. Similar developments were under way in other important Ohio industries from soap to steel.

Some scientific breakthroughs created new industries or completely changed the primitive character of existing ones. Such was the result of Charles M. Hall's work. While a student at Oberlin College, Hall carried on experiments in a backyard laboratory of his own devising. He found an electrolytic process for reducing aluminum ore, thus opening the way for a great new industry. Unlike many innovators who did not profit materially from their inventions, Hall became an officer of the Aluminum Company of America and a wealthy man. Even more significant, perhaps, was the work of Indiana-born Wilbur and Ohio-born Orville Wright, Dayton bicycle mechanics who built and flew the world's first successful airplane. Their December 1903 flight along the sands of Kitty Hawk, North Carolina, was followed by years of additional developmental work until a skeptical public was ready to endorse the practicality of flight. The Wrights also manufactured aircraft and set Ohio on course as a leading state in the aircraft industry.

Ohio inventors and technicians were at work in other fields of the greatest significance. The harnessing of electric power is a case in point. Ohio's greatest name in electricity is Thomas Alva Edison (1847–1931), though his ties with the state were minimal. He moved from his Milan birthplace when just seven years old. He returned years later as a successful and much-honored man to marry Mina Miller, daughter of Lewis Miller, an inventive genius in Akron's farm machinery business. Edison's great work was done at his Menlo Park, New Jersey, laboratories. Charles F. Brush of Cleveland was also important in developing practical applications of electric power. He invented arc lighting, which he successfully demonstrated in Cleveland in 1879; within years arc lighting illuminated the streets of America's growing metropolises. Brush also perfected the dynamo, thus opening new fields to the application of electric power. Benjamin G. Lamme, born near Springfield, added over a hundred improvements to applications of electric power. His work also led to whole new industries. The electrical equipment and appliance field was an explosive area of industrial development. Once more Ohio was in the forefront of an important growth industry.

Hundreds of inventors helped Ohio keep pace with America's growing industrial economy in the Age of Big Business, but one cannot leave this subject without noting some contributors to the most phenomenal of all the new businesses, the automotive industry. Many Ohioans contributed to the development of the internal combustion engine and its use in the "horseless carriage." Among the early builders of practical automobiles were Alexander Winton and Frank Stearns of Cleveland and the Packard brothers of Warren, whose vehicles incorporated important refinements. The Ohioan who contributed most to the auto industry was probably Charles F. Kettering of Loudonville and Dayton, who perfected some of his inventions in the Dayton Engineering Laboratories Company ("Delco"). He is best known for inventing the self-starter which, it was said, put ladies in the driver's seat since it eliminated dirty and dangerous hand cranking. Each new automotive feature led to a new supplier industry, and parts manufacturers soon operated in virtually every Ohio town of size. The entire automotive industry grew in Ohio at an extraordinary pace. Between 1910 and 1920 it increased by 878 percent while the tire industry increased by 923 percent. Even after the industry focused around Detroit, Ohio suppliers were well situated to serve the market.

Inventive minds are found among all races and classes of people. Many of Ohio's best were raised in homes which a later generation would describe as "deprived." Two of the Buckeye State's most productive inventors were black. Granville T. Woods of Columbus made basic contributions to the development of electrical equipment, air brakes, and steam boilers. Each of his contributions had profitable industrial applications. Cleveland's Garrett Morgan invented a smoke inhalator and demonstrated its usefulness when he led in the heroic rescue of miners trapped in a shaft under Lake Erie. A special adaptation of the inhalator was the gas mask; in World War I Morgan's mask was standard equipment along the Western Front. He also invented the automatic traffic signal, so essential to America's vehicular traffic, and sold the patents to General Electric.

Entrepreneurship

The growth of Big Business following the Civil War brought businessmen to public attention as never before. Before the rise of great national and international enterprises, business leaders were seldom known outside their home areas. By the late nineteenth century, however, the men who built the great rail systems, Wall Street banks, and prominent industrial trusts were notorious. Cornelius Vanderbilt, Andrew Carnegie, Jay Gould, J. P. Morgan, and John D. Rockefeller were names to be reckoned with; their power reached across America.

On a level slightly below that of the Rockefellers, Morgans, *et al.* were to be found hundreds of impressive builders in every industrial state. These leaders were frequently true risk capitalists who had their assets tied up in the business. For them it was make or break; many had no financial cushion to tide them over in case their business failed. They tended to maintain close personal supervision over business operations until size, complexity, and the managerial revolution caused them to decentralize authority and responsibility and to hire specialists to oversee discrete parts of the operation. Although there were similarities in the ways industrialists handled their business affairs in an age when many were moving toward monopolistic combinations, some entrepreneurs come across the decades as "captains of industry" while others are perceived as "robber barons." Ohio had examples of both types.

The quintessential entrepreneur of late nineteenth century America was John Davison Rockefeller, born in New York but from boyhood a resident of the Cleveland area. After attending business school Rockefeller took a bookkeeping job. Through disciplined saving he accumulated modest capital which in combination with a partner was enough to start him in his own business. He soon moved into the newly developing oil refining business, parlaying his capital and credit shrewdly into an ever more powerful position. He was an organizational genius, a secretive man, and a stickler for cost savings through vertical integration. His chief advantage over rivals was his own farsightedness and acumen. In 1870 he incorporated the Standard Oil Company under the laws of Ohio. Within the next several years Standard forced most of its competitors to sell out to it or absorbed them. The company took full advantage of the lax business practices of the time, using railroad rebates and drawbacks to special advantage. Rockefeller organized his now large and diverse company into a "trust," through which stock in member companies was held and voted by a small board of trustees. This gave Standard an advantage of scale unmatched in American business.

Standard's aggressive tactics created many enemies. Among them was the attorney general of Ohio, David K. Watson, who brought suit in 1890 against the Standard Oil Company of Ohio, a key unit in the Standard trust. In March 1892 the Ohio Supreme Court ruled that the Standard trust was a monopoly in violation of the common law and ordered Standard of Ohio to withdraw from it. Standard of Ohio did not comply immediately, and further actions were directed against it without immediate result. Meanwhile the Standard was reorganized as a holding company under the laws of New Jersey. It controlled an estimated 90 percent of the refining business. Ultimately, in 1911 the United States Supreme Court found Standard of New Jersey in violation of the Sherman Antitrust Act and upheld an order for its dissolution.

Long before the final resolution of Standard's court cases, Rockefeller abandoned Cleveland for New York, where he moved both his residence and the Standard offices. He needed to be in closer touch with his worldwide empire and his New York financial resources, but it is said he also felt somewhat unappreciated in Ohio, the state in which his enterprise was born and flourished. He and his wife Laura returned each summer to Forest Hill, their East Cleveland estate. They are buried in Cleveland's Lakeview Cemetery.

Trusts and other forms of business combination cut both ways for Ohio. Locally controlled combines such as O. C. Barber's Diamond Match Company (1881) of Barberton worked to the state's advantage. Other trusts, controlled elsewhere, absorbed Ohio companies, which then lost their character and ultimately went out of business. For instance, several strong Ohio farm machinery manufacturers sold out to the McCormick interests of Chicago and later emerged as units of the International Harvester combination. In similar fashion some Ohio millers and cereal makers, weakened by shifting markets and supply sources, became units of the American Cereal Company (1891) based in Chicago. American Cereal in turn became Quaker Oats; the company continued to operate Ohio plants for some years before ultimately phasing them out.

Political and Social Climate

The political and social climate of the period is all important in assessing its business climate. In the late nineteenth and early twentieth centuries, the public's acceptance of latitudinarian business practices shifted toward a cry for regulation of business in the public interest.

Shortly after the Civil War corruption was rife in some segments of the American business community. Hard-driving profiteers worked in collusion with members of state legislatures or of the United States Congress to achieve selfish ends. An attitude prevailed rather widely that what was good for business was good for America, and Ohio had its share of that sentiment. Business leaders saw their task as a benevolent one, since they created jobs. Some, borrowing from the views of Charles Darwin and Herbert Spencer, rationalized their success at any price by claiming that it was in the natural order of things; it was a case of survival of the fittest. "God gave me my money," John D. Rockefeller is reputed to have said. While he was a good steward of his wealth, giving enormous sums to worthwhile causes, his company had earned that money through some fast-and-loose practices that shaded the laws and business ethics of that time.

Given the great disparity between the lifestyles of wealthy owners and managers on the one hand and laboring people on the other, it is remarkable that there was not more social unrest. There are several explanations, among them that American workers had not formed a working class in the sense that they self-consciously banded together for their common benefit. There was no "workers' party" directing political action. If a particularly effective leader rose among men and women in a factory work force, management could co-opt him by "promoting" him to the management team. If this tactic failed, he could be fired. Another factor controlling unrest was the fact that just enough social mobility existed in America to keep alive the dream that with pluck and luck a poor kid could grow up to become rich and famous. Most of Akron's late nineteenth-century industrial leaders started life on the lower rungs of the economic ladder. Ferdinand Schumacher, the "Oatmeal King," was a poor immigrant from Germany; John R. Buchtel, head of the Buckeye Mower and Reaper Company, was the son of a debt-ridden farmer; O. C. Barber, the "Match King" and head of the Diamond Match trust, was the son of an itinerant matchmaker who peddled his own product. These men took pride in being "graduates of the school of hard knocks." Countless American workers fantasized about emulating them, and these workers seemed under no compulsion to upset the system which held out that hope.

One area of industrial life which did come under attack was the monopoly. Giant companies, most significantly the railroads, had gained a stranglehold on important segments of the American economy. State legislatures in Illinois and Massachusetts led the move to regulate railroads, and the Supreme Court upheld the principles of regulation in the Granger Cases of the 1870s. In 1887, Congress passed the Interstate Commerce Act. Ohio's legislature was not in the vanguard of regulatory legislation. Still, Ohio had a state commissioner of railroads and telegraphs acting under an 1867 law. Among the commissioner's duties was reporting on rates, but he had no power to act, only to recommend.

Antitrust legislation was another attack on monopoly. In 1898 the general assembly passed the Valentine Anti-trust Law with the backing and blessing of Attorney General Frank S. Monnett. This law was enacted after an extensive investigation revealed monopolistic practices in coal, railroads, oil, insurance, and other businesses. The law prohibited combinations in restraint of trade by limiting production, restraining competition, controlling sales, or fixing prices. Not everyone was in favor of this action. Many Findlay and Toledo businessmen feared it might have a pernicious effect on the oil boom. Though well intended, this law was hard to enforce as businesses found loopholes. Ohio could not well stand alone when large monopolistic companies were under little restraint in neighboring states. Although Congress passed the Sherman Antitrust Act in 1890, it was not until the presidential administration of Theodore Roosevelt that antitrust efforts shift to the federal arena.

Summary

From the end of the Civil War to the end of World War I Ohio was one of the chief players in America's industrial growth. Location, natural resources, cheap energy, unrivaled transportation, and a plentiful labor supply made Ohio industry competitive. There was scarcely a growth industry in which Ohio did not have a major interest. In 1880 the state produced 6.5 percent of United States manufactures by book value. In 1920 it produced 8 percent. Though remaining an important agricultural state, Ohio's shift toward industrialization was pronounced, resulting in enlarged cities whose swelling populations included large numbers of immigrants.

13.

Society in Transition
Progressivism and World War I

Industrial growth changed the face of Ohio. Coupled with immigration, it stimulated urbanization, a process which created within the state an unusual number of large and medium-sized industrial cities that were fraught with all the problems of modernization. The state's political structure proved ineffective in dealing with these problems until the reform initiatives of the Progressive Era succeeded in bringing government somewhat closer to the service of its constituents. The reform spirit persisted through World War I. At war's end, Ohio had become a mature urban and industrial state, a transition that was successful, on the whole, although progress was uneven and beset with frustration.

Emergent Cities

Ohio's shift toward industrialism had profound effects upon how and where people lived. Factories clustered in urban centers, and so did workers, most of whom lived within walking distance of their place of employment, so that Ohio cities grew dramatically during the late nineteenth and early twentieth centuries. Cleveland, Youngstown, Akron, and Canton dominated the northeastern region; Cincinnati, Dayton, Springfield, and Hamilton dominated the southwest. Columbus anchored the central region and Toledo the northwest. A string of small industrial cities along the Ohio River—East

Liverpool and Steubenville, for example—gave a modest urban presence to what was otherwise a rural area, as did Portsmouth and Chillicothe in the south central region. Lima and Findlay were emerging urban centers in the agricultural lands of the northwestern farm belt.

By 1900 Ohio's urban clusters were becoming well-defined. Cleveland, with 381,768 people surpassed Cincinnati (325,902) as Ohio's largest city. Toledo (131,822) had spurted ahead of Columbus (125,560). Then followed Dayton (85,333), Youngstown (44,885), and Akron (42,728).

These cities varied considerably in their population mix. Cleveland was Ohio's most ethnic city, "ethnic" being defined as first- and second-generation non-native-born Americans, most of whom were of central, eastern, and southern European descent. Seventy-five percent of its people fell into that classification. In 1900 more than forty languages could be commonly heard on the streets of Cleveland. Its steel mills, clothing firms, and heavy industry attracted large numbers of Italians, Hungarians, Poles, Czechs (Bohemians), Jews (mostly Polish and Russian), Slovenes, Greeks, Austrians, and others who established ethnic neighborhoods throughout the city. Their efforts to find living space brought pressure on existing ethnic and black residential enclaves and tightened residential patterns, with well-defined neighborhoods focused around the church, social clubs, neighborhood saloons, the foreign language press, and stores stocking food specialties from the old country. A Cleveland Federation Survey made about 1915 revealed that the city had many ethnic coffee houses where men met for conversation, cards, and music. They found fifteen to twenty Greek meeting places, ten Bulgarian, three Romanian, three Croatian, and at least fifty sandwich and coffee houses, mostly Jewish.

Protestants who dominated early Cleveland were especially visible in board rooms of banks and big businesses, in the professions, and in Cleveland society. The numerical balance shifted sharply, however, as the mostly Catholic newcomers—Roman, Eastern Rite, or Orthodox—established strong parish churches and parochial schools, often organized along ethnic lines. When the Cleveland diocese was established in 1847, its new bishop, the Reverend Amadeus Rappe, presided over the northern third of Ohio in which an estimated 10,000 Catholics lived. When he resigned as bishop in 1870, the Cleveland diocese boasted St. John's Cathedral, 137 parish churches, many parochial schools, four Catholic colleges, and a variety of church-related social institutions. In the next thirty years Cleveland's position as one of America's strongest Catholic communities was assured.

Cleveland's first Jewish congregation was organized in 1846. By the end of the century congregations in the Orthodox, Conservative, and Reformed traditions served the growing Jewish community. One of the most "liberal" congregations, the Temple, dedicated its new house of worship in 1894, inviting clergymen of other faiths to participate in the ceremonies. This was recognized as the first "open temple"—one that cooperated with members of other congregations and faiths—established by Jews anywhere in the world.

The influx of newcomers created competition for jobs and living space, which in turn created strains among the city's more vulnerable groups. Blacks were especially affected. In 1900 Cleveland's 6,000 blacks constituted 1.6 percent of the population. They lived in every one of the city's forty-two wards although 70 percent were concentrated in just eight wards southeast of the city center. The squeeze on urban living space intensified as employers recruited thousands of southern blacks to work in Cleveland industry in the first two decades of the new century. Some of the recruits had no place to live initially; they ate and slept in shanties and in box cars on railroad sidings. However, some of Cleveland's better-established blacks moved into new residential subdivisions. A black realtor, Welcome T. Blue, advertised the Mount Pleasant area in 1907 as a place where "100 Negroes own choice lots" with others buying daily. There they were free from "the crowded, smoky city." They had a church and had room to raise vegetables, fruit, chickens, hogs, and cows. During this same period a small black elite, represented by the distinguished writer, Charles Chesnutt, lived elegantly in a style like that of wealthy whites.

Though the majority of black citizens worked as unskilled laborers, Cleveland had a substantial black middle class of skilled workers, shop owners, real estate agents, and professional people. After 1890 Cleveland blacks, Republicans all, served regularly in the Ohio General Assembly, where they made important contributions such as supporting anti-lynching legislation and helping to defeat a bill which would have prohibited "mixed" marriages. David Gerber, a student of black Ohio, has written that "it was in Ohio, in response to a rash of lynchings in the early 1890s, that the nation's first serious attempt to legislate lynching out of existence was made" through collaboration between Harry C. Smith, a black state legislator and newspaper publisher from Cleveland, and Albion Tourgée, a well-known white proponent of racial equality. The ensuing 1896 anti-lynch law was known as the Smith Act. Also in 1896, Smith introduced the bill which became the Ohio Civil Rights Law. It made racial discrimination in public places subject to civil or criminal prosecution. A black legislator from Cleveland made another initiative in this period. Rep. John P. Green's bill (1890) made Labor Day a legal holiday in Ohio. Four years later Congress established it as a national holiday.

Cincinnati also received many immigrants around the turn of the century, but its population mix differed from Cleveland's. Germans and Irish dominated this flow, adding to their already disproportionate presence in the city. In 1900 Cincinnati was 60.7 percent ethnic and 4.4 percent black. Various racial and ethnic groups lived side-by-side in residential portions of the Circle, the old central city which historians call the "walking city." Here one might find in a single block native-born whites, Hungarians, Italians, Germans, Greeks, and Irish. Irish and blacks shared some neighborhoods although they viewed one another with suspicion and hostility.

The Circle was the most crowded section. Here tenements and apartments were so concentrated that Cincinnati had the unenviable distinction of being the nation's most crowded city. In 1870 the city averaged 37,143 people per square mile, the densest population cluster in America. Poverty, crime and vice, poor sanitation, and miserable health conditions were endemic in these circumstances.

Extending beyond the Circle was the Zone, a mixed business-industrial-residential district. Here were located several German enclaves, the best known of which was "Over the Rhine" just north of the Miami and Erie Canal. Housing was crowded in the Zone's inner reaches, but tended to be superior to that of the Circle. Toward the thinly populated outer reaches of the Zone, single-family dwellings dominated, and population density declined perceptibly. While Germans dominated the Zone, some Italians, Jews, and blacks had penetrated into parts of it.

Upward social mobility was very difficult for Cincinnati blacks to achieve for the city maintained much of its old, southern-oriented racial attitude. Qualified blacks were excluded from a fair share of public jobs. The black middle class was small and encountered more opposition in housing, schooling, and employment than was true in Cleveland. Despite difficulties, some blacks moved into better neighborhoods, notably Walnut Hills, where their numbers increased to 3,611 by 1910.

The Zone was the most Catholic section of Cincinnati. In 1910, some 70 percent of the city's church members were Catholic, distributed in seventy-two parishes. As in Cleveland, parochial schools, colleges, and social institutions grew apace, with church authority centered in the bishop who ruled from his cathedral, St. Peter in Chains. Despite strong church influence the Zone had its share of worldly distractions. The saloon, the "workingman's club," flourished as a place of bonhomie and socializing and as a center of political influence. Commercial amusements—movies, dance halls—were available to all but blacks, who encountered discrimination there as elsewhere in the city's life.

Beyond the Zone were the Hilltops, centers of middle- and upper-middle-class affluence. Ultimately the area was linked with the Zone and Circle by electric transit lines and incline railways. Most Hilltop communities were dominated by a white, Anglo-Saxon Protestant elite, but upwardly mobile Catholics and Jews also migrated to these desirable residential regions, where their acceptance rested upon their general deportment. Cincinnati's influential Jewish leadership had been enhanced in the 1870s when Rabbi Isaac Wise founded Hebrew Union College and Seminary and made it the heart of "Reformed" Judaism. The growing city absorbed many Hilltop communities through annexation; others, including some of the nation's finest residential communities, remained independent.

Columbus was Ohio's least ethnic city; in 1900 only 33.7 percent of its people were so classified. The capital city had the largest percentage of blacks (6.5) among the state's principal urban areas. Both ethnics and blacks were concentrated in working-class districts close to places of employment. The least fortunate huddled in slum housing alongside railroad tracks or close by the Scioto's muddy banks. On the near south side German workers dominated a large neighborhood whose brick cottages, houses, and stores would become, a hundred years later, "German Village," an attractive residential area.

Toledo's and Youngstown's heavy industries also attracted new immigrants; only Cleveland had a higher percentage of ethnics in 1900 than Youngstown, and Toledo received large numbers of Hungarians and Poles. Both cities had small black populations: Toledo's was 1.3 percent and Youngstown's was 2 percent.

Of the major cities, Dayton and Akron attracted fewest new immigrants from eastern Europe and the Mediterranean. The great industrial growth of these cities was tied to the automotive business rather than to iron and steel. Dayton grew at a steady pace between 1880 and 1920, giving it time to absorb its new residents. In contrast, Akron exploded. Between 1910 and 1920 it grew 201.1 percent, making it the fastest growing city in America. Tensions in Europe during the World War I era slowed immigration, so Akron's labor recruiters toured Appalachia, seeking workers for the city's burgeoning factories. Dayton also secured workers in the southern hills. Although the vast majority of these newcomers were white, enough blacks came to increase Akron's black population to about 5,000 in 1920 (2.4 percent) while Dayton blacks comprised 5.9 percent of the population in that year.

Ohio's smaller industrial cities and its mining regions also attracted new immigrants. Poles, Italians, and Russians were among those seeking work in eastern Ohio coal fields. Czechs ultimately concentrated near the little mining center of Dillonvale. Immigrants gave a special flavor to many towns. In Ashtabula, for example, Finns and Swedes settled around the harbor and observed their own customs, adding a unique texture to the town after their late nineteenth-century arrival.

Modernization

The concurrent need to assimilate into Ohio cities tens of thousands of newcomers, many of whom spoke no English and had no concept of local laws and customs, complicated the modernization of urban areas. The new arrivals were largely peasants unacquainted with industrial work and with craftsmanship. They learned on the job, acquiring not only job skills but also rudimentary English. Most were determined to succeed in America and worked hard toward that end.

Formal methods for easing the immigrant's transition were in place by the late nineteenth and early twentieth centuries. Schools, churches, YM and YWCAs, and other agencies sponsored Americanization classes designed to teach English and enough civics to pass the citizenship examination. Settlement houses in the larger cities helped immigrants cope with the myriad problems of joblessness and substandard housing. Cleveland's Hiram House, founded in 1896 by Hiram College students, secured the support of wealthy patrons, enabling it to build a substantial hall and maintain programs to benefit inner-city residents. Goodrich House, sponsored by Mrs. Samuel Mather and friends, performed social services. It led the drive to secure legal aid for the indigent, campaigned for clean streets, encouraged formation of a consumer's league, conducted a school for crippled children, and supported a "boy's farm" in the country so young offenders could be kept separate from hardened criminals.

Columbus's First Neighborhood Guild opened in 1898 in "Flytown," a working-class district northwest of the central city. This project had the support of civic-minded people like Washington Gladden, minister of the First Congregational Church. Gladden advocated the "social gospel" which urged Christians to put the social teachings of Jesus into practice by fighting graft and corruption and assisting the needy.

Concurrent with private efforts directed at easing the burden of individual citizens, cities were trying to cope with a host of pressing problems, among them transportation. The crowding of central cities had resulted in part from the workers' need to live within walking distance of their place of employment. The electric trolley liberated them from this bond. New residential districts could be developed, especially for white-collar workers who could now reach their jobs within reasonable time. Blue-collar workers would also gravitate away from the factories as economic factors allowed. Promotional literature published by cities always mentioned the street railways. For example, Columbus in 1900 boasted of its 100 miles of track. The lines ran to outlying parks and dance pavilions which the traction companies maintained as a means of stimulating business, especially on weekends and holidays. Electric trolleys also reached out to connect the central city with nearby communities: Lakewood on Cleveland's west side, Bexley on Columbus's east side, Norwood northeast of Cincinnati, and Cuyahoga Falls northeast of Akron, for example. The electrified rail line—the interurban—reached even further into the countryside and brought rural villages into the market sphere of the larger cities.

Street railway franchises were often lucrative, and there lay the basis for an inordinate amount of skullduggery as businessmen and their political allies vied to monopolize city rail systems. Scarcely an Ohio city of size escaped these bitter contests. Cleveland provided the classic struggle, pitting Marcus Hanna and his "little consolidated" against the influential Tom Johnson and his "big consolidated" traction company. Johnson failed to break Hanna's grip on the business, and he also failed, as mayor, to institute the three-cent fare on a continuing basis. This struggle, as we shall see, had important political consequences.

Coincident with the development of electric traction lines, indeed leading it by a few years, was electric lighting for city streets. In 1879 Cleveland's Charles Brush successfully demonstrated his new arc lights on the streets of his home town. Shortly thereafter, Cleveland became the first city in the world to be lighted electrically, and other Ohio cities followed. Cincinnati installed electric street lights in 1882. They worked well, but some other efforts failed. Akron enthusiasts placed arc lights atop high masts, two of which were supposed to light the entire downtown area. They didn't. Total darkness reigned a short distance from the masts while people living close by them complained that their chickens would not roost. This ill-advised experiment was abandoned.

Gas and oil interests had monopolized urban street lighting, and they now fought electric lighting company franchises. As with street railways, battles for street lighting franchises proved yet another incubator for municipal corruption.

Streets required paving as well as lighting. It is difficult today to imagine that as late as the 1880s, pigs rooted in city streets in some Ohio communities. Unpaved city thoroughfares, liberally covered with horse manure, were unsanitary and unsafe. Prior to the late nineteenth century only a few principal city streets were paved, many with Nicholson Blocks (wooden bricks) or with macadam. By 1890 Columbus was paving its principal streets, and ten years later boasted of its 150 miles of "improved" streets, more than any city its size in the country. Dayton claimed 58 miles of pavement by 1908. Cleveland speeded its street paving program and in 1903 inaugurated one of the nation's first clean-street programs.

Early in the twentieth century, as the automobile became commonplace, city streets were paved with ceramic brick and with concrete. Ohio was an important producer of these building materials, and local industry benefited from their use. The state also profited as road-building machinery became more sophisticated; ultimately Lima, Galion, Marion, Lorain, and Bucyrus built much of it.

Paving was extended into rural areas by the World War I era; the National Pike, for example, was partially paved in 1916. Frequently just one lane was paved. Since traffic was light, everyone tended to drive on that lane, and

Tom Johnson

when cars encountered one another the driver lacking right-of-way had to get off onto the dirt lane until passing was completed. Growth of automobile and truck traffic also required better bridges, and steel replaced wood, stone, and brick as the favored structural material.

Sewage disposal and clean water supply were interrelated concerns that affected everyone, especially those living in Ohio's crowded cities. The systems that had served cities through their early growth were inadequate to handle the enormous increase in water use and sewage disposal, a need brought on by rapidly growing populations and the proliferation of large industrial plants. In the 1870s, for example, hundreds of Cincinnati's inner-city dwellings were without water or privies. Mill Creek was a "noxious mess." Much local drinking water came from contaminated sources. Cincinnati modernized its water system late in the century, but the new system was constantly overtaxed by the need to extend it into newly annexed areas. Expensive pumping equipment was required to keep the hilltop reservoirs filled.

Cleveland suffered similar growing pains. Its health department, directed by medical men, constantly expressed concern about the health hazards posed by pollution. Cleveland built its first sewer line in 1858; thirty years later, twenty-five sewers poured effluent directly into the Cuyahoga River which was already surfeited with industrial waste; the river was literally an open sewer. Cleveland garbage was loaded on scows where it festered for days before being dumped in Lake Erie, from which the city drew its water supply. In 1895 the city started work on interceptor sewer lines that carried effluent to regional treatment and disposal plants. Meanwhile, to find clean water the city extended intake cribs and connecting tunnels ever farther into Lake Erie.

Small cities, too, wrestled with these problems. Dayton inaugurated its publicly financed water system in 1870. In Akron, however, the water company was owned by influential men who fought to keep their franchise even though tests revealed that the water they supplied from Summit Lake was polluted. Only after a typhoid epidemic killed forty people in 1911 did public opinion mobilize to overcome private interest. Even then, city officials faced one roadblock after another before setting up a successful water system using the resources of the upper Cuyahoga. Meanwhile the city dumped untreated sewage into the same river system from which it drew its drinking water, although downstream from the water plant, and refused to build a disposal plant until ordered to do so by the state courts in 1914. Although it complied, Akron's skyrocketing growth made the new disposal plant obsolete from the beginning.

Poor water and sewage systems were responsible for certain serious health problems, such as typhoid fever. But other threats to public health, cholera and typhus, for example, existed in the crowded cities. Smallpox struck

Cleveland in 1902, killing more than 220 people; the city paid for 195,000 vaccinations in a successful effort to stem the epidemic. Tuberculosis was endemic in the nineteenth and early twentieth centuries, and many Ohio cities erected sanatoriums and "fresh air camps" for victims whose care became a public charge.

City slums posed the most threatening health conditions. A Cleveland newspaperman reported one typical case of human misery. He found a hovel in which "a man and his wife lay on some of the filthiest beds ever spread and a dog lay beneath it. . . . Vermin was everywhere and the place was literally alive [with vermin]. In an inner room, smaller and nastier, one little girl and two small boys lay on a bundle of rags. They were almost entirely naked and looked thin and pale. All the air they could receive . . . by the time it reached the children . . . had lost every particle of health giving power and purity." Cleveland and Cincinnati had thousands of such dwellings, the smaller cities proportionately fewer.

Modernization of health care was closely tied to the rise of scientific medicine and the growing sophistication of hospitals. Medical schools were now concentrated in the larger cities; Cleveland retained its School of Medicine at Western Reserve University, Columbus had the Ohio State College of Medicine, and Cincinnati had the medical college of the University of Cincinnati. Ohio physicians and surgeons like Cleveland's George W. Crile, a pioneer in blood transfusions and nerve-blocking anesthesia, made original contributions to medical knowledge and also helped to develop new hospitals and clinics encompassing the latest in medical science. Crile himself founded the world-famous Cleveland Clinic, and every substantial Ohio city developed new hospital facilities in the late nineteenth century and expanded them in the twentieth. In 1916 the Cleveland Hospital Council was established to coordinate the city's health institutions, the first such health-care organization in the country.

Disease was an ever-present problem, but fire was the great scourge of the American city. None escaped. Over the years, Cleveland lost hotels, schools, churches, opera houses, hundreds of dwellings, and any number of businesses. Akron lost its largest mill, its Academy of Music, and its college. Cincinnati watched three courthouses succumb to fire, and so it went throughout the state.

The larger cities led the move toward modernization of fire equipment and service. Horse-drawn steam pumpers were becoming increasingly efficient, and Ohio-made "White Anchor" fire hose solved the old problem of leather hose cracks and breakage. Between 1889 and 1896 Cincinnati added twelve new fire companies and adopted chemical equipment, a fire alarm telegraph system, and direct telephone connections among station houses. Every city added hook-and-ladder equipment to reach upper floors of tall buildings.

Programs to educate the public were introduced; Cleveland developed Fire Prevention Week, one of the first cities in America to do so.

City police departments also modernized late in the nineteenth century. In most cities police collusion with gamblers, saloonkeepers, prostitutes, and politicians undermined public confidence. In Cincinnati public disgust over lax sentences meted out to murderers exploded into action in March 1884, when concerned citizens objected to what they saw as yet another miscarriage of justice. A civic gathering to determine what course of action to take got out of hand and a mob descended upon the jail to seize a young man whom mob members believed guilty of murder. He had been given a reduced sentence for manslaughter. Police resisted the mob, firing a shot and killing a man. The rioters then stormed the cell blocks, and militia was hastily called to quell the melee. For the next two days outraged citizens, joined by local toughs, erected barricades and battled the soldiers in open warfare. The troops even used a Gatling gun on the rioters. Fifty-four persons died and more than 200 were wounded. Perhaps some good came from it, for it stimulated the city's efforts to improve law enforcement machinery. To that end, in 1885 the governor (George Hoadley, a Hamilton County Democrat) appointed a Cincinnati Board of Police Commissioners. This bipartisan board tried to remove political favoritism from the department. The force was enlarged to about 500 men, and paramilitary discipline was introduced. Officers were trained to be more than "mere clubbers." The Queen City continued to have law enforcement problems—small race riots, anti-Catholic and anti-Jewish disturbances—but it had made a healthy start toward meeting these problems in a more professional manner.

Education was also affected by rapidly evolving conditions within the cities. In 1889 the state legislature enacted a compulsory school attendance law to be enforced by truant officers in each locality. Some employers who wanted to use child labor opposed the law; schooling interfered with their plans. Farmers, on the other hand, could adjust since school terms were short, leaving sons and daughters free for work on the farm during the busiest seasons. Modern standards of attendance were enacted in the Bing Law of 1921, which required school attendance between the ages of six and eighteen unless the student had finished high school. Provisions were made to release children for farm work at age sixteen and completion of the seventh grade.

Before the school reforms of the twentieth century were enacted, city schools were far in advance of most rural schools. The rapidly expanding cities had tax resources to erect modern buildings incorporating electric lighting, fireproofing, sanitary plumbing, and other up-to-date features. The school systems modernized and expanded the curriculum, placing more emphasis on both the earlier and later grades. Kindergartens were established in Cincinnati (1905) and in other Ohio cities, and high schools proliferated. Until well after the Civil War only substantial towns had boasted high schools (often called the "central" high school), but by 1880 there were 567 in the state with the larger cities each having several. The public high school spelled the doom of the private academies and seminaries that had dominated secondary education since the state's founding. By World War I only a few private academies remained.

Subjects taught in the public high schools multiplied rapidly. In addition to standard courses such as algebra, geometry, philosophy, history, geography, and "natural philosophy" (science), new offerings appeared: Latin, Greek, German, botany, zoology, chemistry, and rhetoric. Some schools introduced "practical" courses. Manual training for boys and home economics and secretarial work for girls helped placate those citizens who felt that schools should prepare a person to earn a living. By 1902 the state board of examiners had established some uniformity in length of school terms, number of grades and subjects of instruction for the high schools, thus clearly differentiating them from elementary schools.

New standards of teacher training evolved in response to the increased scope and specialization of the curriculum. Private normal schools (teacher training institutions) were available in at least seven locations before 1875. Among them was the successful National Normal University at Lebanon, a school organized largely by teachers themselves. In rapidly growing urban school districts, city-operated normal schools appeared late in the nineteenth century. The legislature finally heeded pressure for public aid for teacher training in 1902 and started state-subsidized programs at Ohio University in Athens and Miami University in Oxford. These did not meet the demand, and in 1910 additional normal schools were authorized in Bowling Green and Kent, giving each quadrant of the state a publicly supported teacher-training institution. Central State University, which offered teacher training primarily to black students, was established in 1887 at Wilberforce despite opposition from those who feared it would undercut its neighbor, private Wilberforce College.

The formalization of teacher training protected the interests of women, who outnumbered men in normal school programs, but once employed, all too often received less money for their services than their male counterparts. Except in a few districts, the "school mar'm" had not yet achieved parity with the schoolmaster and would not until the last half of the twentieth century.

Collegiate training to prepare young people for jobs in industry was another emphasis of the time. The University of Cincinnati received municipal tax assistance and developed a close working relationship with local business people. This was especially true during the administration of President Charles Dabney, who supported Dean Herman Schneider in developing an engineering cooperative education program that placed students in practical work situations during a portion of their undergraduate program. The University of Toledo provided the Glass Capital with a municipally supported college which, at its founding in 1872, emphasized the training of young people for practical tasks. In 1913 the city of Akron assumed the assets and operation of Buchtel College, founded in 1870 as a venture of the Ohio Universalist Convention, and patterned the Municipal University of Akron's programs of community service on Cincinnati's successful model. Clevelanders rejected efforts to establish a municipal university partly because they were already served by Case School of Applied Science, founded in 1880 through the generosity of local businessman Leonard Case. It had been only the fourth college established in America, and the first west of the Appalachians, devoted to higher technical education. In 1882 Western Reserve University moved from Hudson to a new campus adjacent to Case. Its first unit was Adelbert College, named for the deceased son of Amasa Stone, the local businessman who lured the college to Cleveland with a donation of $500,000. In 1967 Case and Western Reserve merged to become Case Western Reserve University.

Columbus's needs in higher education were met by several colleges, but The Ohio State University dominated. Chartered in 1870, it underwent several decades of growing pains until finding its niche as the dominant public institution in the state. The private, Catholic-related University of Dayton, founded in 1850, had not yet extended its curriculum to serve community needs as it would in later years.

The late nineteenth century push for "practical" courses and programs persisted into the twentieth century, triggering an ongoing debate with those who believed schools should confine themselves to basic "liberal" education, leaving the practical work to proprietary or "trade" schools. The debate continues to this day.

A Growing Discontent: Industrial and Political Malaise

The panic of 1893–97 was America's first industrial depression. Not all Ohio cities suffered from it as Cleveland experienced a boom in the electrical equipment business and Cincinnati's diverse industrial base protected it from some of the extremes rampant elsewhere. Still, as a state increasingly dominated by "smokestack" industries, Ohio as a whole was hard-hit by this economic crisis.

Many key industries were clearly in transition. New technologies made old plants obsolete, and as new plants were built, they were located close to new markets and new sources of raw material. This was especially true in the farm machinery business. In the early nineteenth century Ohio supplied much of the nation's grain and the state was a manufacturing center for the machines that planted, cultivated, and harvested it. By century's end, however, the vast productive fields of the trans-Mississippi West had become the nation's breadbasket, luring farm machinery manufacture westward to Illinois and beyond. This move decimated much of Ohio's production. Akron, for example, had two important companies until the 1890s. The Excelsior Works folded outright; the Buckeye Mower and Reaper reduced its work force by half and then sold out to the McCormick interests of Chicago. Plants in Dayton, Springfield, Canton, and Columbus also felt the pinch brought on by shifting markets, by business consolidation and by the depression. When farm machinery manufacturers moved, a host of supplier industries—foundries, knife works, binder twine makers, chain drive manufacturers—followed them to their new locations.

During the depression unemployment figures in some of Ohio's major industrial centers were sobering, running above 50 percent of the industrial work force for brief periods. There was as yet no safety net of government support and benefits to aid the unemployed, but private charities, churches, and family friends provided help to desperate people. Some communities made land and seed available to unemployed workers who planted "potato patches"; in Youngstown an enlightened city administration put the unemployed to work on a public works project out of which grew the city's handsome Mill Creek Park. In Ohio's mining centers unemployment ran deep. Even those who retained jobs found wages reduced and family income severely restricted. Desperate miners responded to their frustrations with strikes and sabotage, and Governor McKinley sent troops to the coal fields to protect property and maintain order.

Miners and other workers increasingly turned to labor unions in the hope that, through concerted action, they could influence employers to improve wages and working conditions. For the first time, union membership did not drop precipitously as the result of hard times. Immediately after economic recovery in 1897, union membership grew for a period of about six years, then stagnated prior to World War I.

Popular discontent during the depression reached beyond concern for the unemployed. Powerful new trusts and business monopolies gouged consumers. The great business entrepreneurs and their allies in the banks and law firms were wielding disproportionate influence in local and state legislative chambers. Privilege, supported by an inequitable tax structure and by a lack of regulatory controls, triumphed over the public interest. An unprecedented gap separated the very rich from the very poor; when Ohio was still largely an agricultural society, the rich farmer had rubbed shoulders with the poor farmer, but the new industrial baron was physically isolated from his workers and from people on the lowest rungs of the economic ladder.

Domination of economic and political affairs by "big business" was a source of discontent to men of accomplishment who saw themselves cut out of their share of influence and material success. Small businessmen were hard-pressed to compete against monopolistic trusts. Local and state legislators to whom they looked for relief were frequently controlled by political bosses working with big business.

These political machines had a corrupting influence on American life. As we have seen, two powerful machines dominated Republican politics in Ohio, the Hanna group out of Cleveland and the Foraker-Cox group out of Cincinnati. Each controlled its own sphere around the turn of the century, and competed for control of state politics. Votes were bought and sold with impunity. Hanna lieutenants openly boasted of buying votes in Toledo, just one of the many places where they were determined to retain influence.

For thirty years Cincinnati Republicans were controlled by the state's most effective local machine, the handiwork of George B. Cox, a saloonkeeper and former city councilman. Cox was an organizer, influence peddler, and manipulator who worked behind the scenes to dispense favors for his friends and cronies while enhancing his own power. From time to time some of Cincinnati's foremost citizens, including William Howard Taft, Nicholas Longworth, and Bernhard Bettmann, supported him because they admired his ability to bring order to local affairs. Joseph B. Foraker, twice governor of Ohio and a United States senator, worked closely with him. Cox lived well but denied that he condoned graft. After temporary "retirement" in 1905 he reentered the political fray and survived unscathed from efforts to convict him of misusing city and state funds.

Cincinnati also had a Democratic machine of sorts controlled by the politically ambitious publisher of the *Cincinnati Enquirer,* John McLean. The McLean influence was possibly more effective in statewide Democratic councils than in Cincinnati, where the Cox partisans were supreme.

Although cities were the principal locus of political manipulation and corruption, rural areas did not escape it. Early in the twentieth century *McClure's,* a muckraking magazine of wide influence, featured an exposé of vote buying in Adams County. In this county, "populated by as old and excellent American stock as any in the United States," political bosses bought and sold votes openly. Before the advent of the Australian ballot (the secret ballot adopted in Ohio in 1891), vote buying was "a matter-of-fact transaction." One participant claimed he stood in front of the West Union courthouse and saw "a voter auctioned off to the highest bidder of two precinct leaders, like a horse or hog." The winning bid, he said, "was thirty-odd dollars." The successful bidder "took his man to the polls, cast his vote, brought him back, and stood him up again on the auction block. Then he peeled the money from his bank roll and paid him." One must suspect this story. The "going rate" for a vote was about one-tenth the thirty dollars quoted, and vote buying was generally handled more discreetly.

Progressivism in Ohio

The Progressive Movement was a multifaceted reform effort which affected to some degree all sections of the United States from the turn of the century until World War I. Most progressive reforms were established on the state and local level although some key federal legislation of the period was also in the progressive spirit.

Who were the reformers? This question is the subject of an ongoing debate among historians. In Ohio the reform initiative was led by people who fit the description of progressive leadership which the historian Richard Hofstadter draws in his influential book, *The Age of Reform*. They were in large part educated, white, middle-class Protestant professionals and businessmen who felt that their traditional leadership roles had been usurped by newly rich industrial magnates and their banking and legislative allies. These business barons used their money and influence for selfish interests detrimental to consumer interests and corrupted the political process. Ohio progressives, therefore, wanted to restore economic competition, eliminate favored treatment for monopolies, and widen popular participation in government. Many Ohio progressives also sought to restore a sense of order to economic and social worlds that had become disjointed during recent periods of industrial and urban growth. These reformers were looking for efficiency in business and governmental processes. Reform transcended party lines although Democratic activists outnumbered Republicans by a two-to-one margin.

Ohio's major contribution to progressive reform lay in the realm of municipal government. Such reform was much needed, for urban communities labored under a substantial handicap in that they were completely subordinate to state law. Time after time the general assembly undercut urban leaders by enacting so-called "ripper" bills designed to shift power and patronage from city to state officials. Every city initiative was at the mercy of the state legislature and the party which controlled it. It was common for the legislature to reconstitute urban boards and commissions to keep city officials in line, a widely used practice intended to keep city government from interfering in franchises held by the businessmen who had influence with the party controlling the legislature. Thus "home rule" for the cities became a goal of progressive reformers, and since four states had enacted home rule provisions by 1900, Ohio reformers were encouraged to seek it for the Buckeye State.

However, before they achieved their goal, reform mayors in Toledo and Cleveland were pointing the way toward clean, effective city government.

Municipal Reform

Jones
Reelected 3 x's

The pacesetter in municipal government reform was the extraordinary mayor of Toledo, Samuel "Golden Rule" Jones. Born in Wales, his early years as a common laborer were capped by a successful business career. Ultimately he achieved wealth as owner of the Acme Sucker Rod Company, a manufacturer of oil well–drilling equipment. He applied the principles of the Golden Rule to his workers, making his business one of the most enlightened operations of its kind in America. Politically an independent, his favorable reputation catapulted him into municipal politics in 1897 when the fractured Republican party chose him as its mayoral candidate. The politically unsophisticated Jones overcame opposition from the utilities and from saloon-keepers, who misread him as a moral reformer, to win the election. He was reelected three times.

Jones had been influenced by the books of Henry George, a self-taught economist who argued that a "single tax" on land would cover all costs of government, leave a surplus, and unburden labor and capital of taxes on their output. Jones was also sympathetic to the social gospel. Despite these influences, Jones was an original, and he now set about applying his unorthodox views to the city.

A first step in trying to make Toledo "a model co-operative commonwealth" was to establish the eight-hour day for police, water department employees, and all labor privately contracted by the city. Kindergartens (first introduced in America by Ohio's German immigrants) were established in the schools, and the city provided its citizens with playgrounds, parks, free concerts, and a municipal golf course (the second in America). Some of Jones's initiatives failed, notably an attempt to persuade Toledo voters to endorse municipally owned utilities. Ohio law frustrated his interest in city ownership of the electric railway, but he led a successful move to reduce fares.

Some of the mayor's enthusiasms and convictions were too idealistic, too out of touch with harsh realities, to win approval. He urged Toledo policemen to surrender their billy clubs for canes so as to reduce the brutality with which the police treated the city's down-and-outers. More effective was improving the quality of policemen through use of the merit system. He alienated his church support by opposing moral reformers' attempts to implement "blue laws" closing saloons on Sunday; he opposed limiting the poor man's recreation on his one day off. From time to time he presided at police court and usually dismissed charges brought against street people. He even dis-

Police

missed two burglary suspects on the theory that incarceration would do them no good.

This radical extension of Christian idealism was too much for practical men. The Republicans dropped Jones after his first term, and from that time forward he ran as a political independent. This was consistent with his belief in the nonpartisan principle, which he tried to extend to statewide politics in 1899–1900, when he became an independent candidate for the governor's chair. His platform urged direct primaries, public ownership of all utilities, the nonpartisan principle, direct legislation, and various labor reforms. He came in a poor third behind the Republican victor, George K. Nash, and the Democrat, John McLean. Jones's ideas, which seemed so radical at the time, were adopted in large part within a decade and a half as reform initiatives took hold statewide. When Jones died in 1904, Brand Whitlock, also reform-minded though more conventional than Jones, succeeded as mayor and gave Toledo another eight years of conscientious municipal leadership.

An important associate of Jones in statewide affairs was Washington Gladden, pastor of Columbus's First Congregational Church, located on Broad Street across from the state capitol. A man of "quiet energy and strength in reserve," he came to Columbus in 1882 with his reputation as a proponent of practical Christianity already established. He found city government at best inept, and at worst corrupt. He was particularly distressed by open defiance of laws requiring Sunday closing of saloons; he viewed intemperance as the root of much city vice and crime. His sermons and writings, exposing the weakness and corruption of city government, attracted favorable attention but did little to persuade those in power to mend their ways. In 1900, therefore, he ran for and was elected to the city council. Hoping to put his progressive theories into practice he found his time monopolized by efforts to secure an equitable fare on the street railways and by a successful campaign to secure municipal ownership of a power plant of sufficient size to provide electric lighting for the city. The press of his professional responsibilities kept him from seeking reelection in 1902, yet he continued to preach and write in support of such favorite causes as settlement houses for the needy and the right of labor to organize and bargain collectively. Like his friend Samuel Jones, Gladden recognized the necessity of reforming state government as a means toward securing effective municipal government in Ohio.

Possibly the most influential Ohio municipal reformer was Tom L. Johnson of Cleveland. Certainly he had great impact on both state and local government. Like Jones, he was a self-made business tycoon, achieving wealth at an early age from investments in street railways and steel. His control of the "big consolidated" street railway network in Cleveland brought him into conflict with Marcus Hanna's "little consolidated" in the business arena. Ultimately he and Hanna would become bitter political rivals as well.

In 1900 Johnson, a former United States Representative, returned to Cleveland to enter municipal politics; he was already well known. He had imbibed with enthusiasm the ideas of Henry George and his single tax, principles of humanitarianism and tax redistribution that struck a responsive chord; young Tom Johnson sold some of his street railways and steel mills in order to devote himself to good government and the implementation of George's theories.

Upon reemerging in Cleveland, Johnson was approached by Democrats eager to persuade him to campaign for mayor. They thought Johnson had the experience and the resources to head off a renewal of Mark Hanna's street railway franchise. Johnson entered the fray willingly although recognizing that Hanna was a tough opponent. His platform called for home rule, a three-cent street railway fare, tax equalization, and the single tax. Supported by the *Plain Dealer,* the city's morning newspaper, Johnson won a narrow victory and assumed his duties in 1901. He was reelected three times.

Johnson's considerable success was due in part to his choice of able associates. His vibrant personality attracted bright young idealists: Newton D. Baker, temperamentally more conservative than his mentor, became Johnson's chief lieutenant. Baker's political creed was simple and consistent: "I am a follower of Tom Johnson," he said. Johnson's pastor, Harris Cooley of the Cedar Avenue Disciples Church, was an innovative director of the department of charities and corrections. His humane and enlightened treatment of prisoners and wards of the city brought him a national reputation and made Cleveland a leader in these endeavors. The fiery Peter Witt became the gadfly of the administration and one of its most effective spokesmen. Frederic C. Howe, Edward W. Bemis, Carl Friebolin, and several other idealistic young college graduates rounded out this extraordinary group. It is unlikely that any city administration to that time had attracted such a high-minded and talented crew. All were Johnson loyalists and most shared his passion for the theories of Henry George.

Though Johnson's motives were admirable and his administration proved to be healthy for Cleveland, he was no secular saint. His critics claimed he created lasting enmities in the city through the vigor of his attacks on "Privilege." They charged him with duplicity and self-serving tactics. While condemning political bosses, he and his associates created an effective political apparatus that dominated Cleveland politics for fifteen years. Nonetheless, by the time Johnson and his successor, Newton D. Baker, completed their mayoral terms, Cleveland had been transformed into one of America's most progressive cities, with an enviable record in clean government, social services, citizen participation in civic reform, cultural and recreational amenities, and the growth of civic pride.

The Johnson administration can claim a striking list of accomplishments. The mayor's office weeded corruption out of the water department and instituted a huge new intake tunnel that reached out to purer Lake Erie waters. The sewage system was undergoing modernization. The city assumed the task of collecting garbage and performed the task efficiently. Strong new building standards reduced substandard housing. The Department of Public Works paved, drained, lighted, and cleaned the streets. A businesslike purchasing department saved money through quantity buying. The city enforced strict new sanitary regulations for public markets. Chief Fred Kohler led efforts to restructure Cleveland's police force, minimize graft and corruption within the force, shut down gambling and drinking halls, and close houses of prostitution. Ironically, Kohler was later ousted from office for "conduct unbecoming an officer." The humane reforms instituted by Harris Cooley included the purchase of extensive acreage in Warrensville Heights where a "campus" of buildings sheltering public institutions was erected in a healthy country environment.

While trying to make the city work, the Johnson people were also interested in restoring its handsome appearance of the Civil War era. Its tree-shaded streets, including Euclid Avenue, called "millionaires' row" and at one time one of the handsomest boulevards in America, were rapidly disappearing in the face of urban expansion. Industrial growth had ravaged Cleveland's river and lake shores. Johnson encouraged implementation of the Cleveland Group Plan to which Daniel Burnham and other distinguished architects contributed. This plan called for monumental public buildings to be placed around a tree-shaded mall extending from the lake escarpment almost to Public Square. Later administrations carried out the plan giving Cleveland an impressive urban focus and providing a model for other American cities. Also for the public's benefit, city government expanded parks and built new ones; playgrounds proliferated and the people were encouraged to use public spaces. It is symbolic of Johnson's outlook that he ordered "Keep off the Grass" signs removed from city parks.

Municipal reform in Toledo, Columbus, and Cleveland did not take place in a vacuum. Jones, Gladden, and Johnson were catalysts for reform sentiment that was rising across the state, a sentiment that was increasingly directed against the old way of doing business in the Statehouse.

In 1897 Marcus Hanna had won a bitter battle with the Foraker group to take a seat in the United States Senate. He did not enjoy it long. By 1904 he was dead and leadership of the Hanna Republicans (called by some the "regulars") devolved upon Hanna's choice, Charles F. W. Dick of Akron. Dick, basking in the favorable publicity he had earned as an officer in the Spanish-American War, had served four terms in Congress where, in 1902, he wrote the influential "Dick Bill" reorganizing the national army reserve force. The party now chose Dick to succeed Hanna in the Senate, and he also worked out an accommodation with the Foraker-Cox Republicans to become leader of

Ohio's Republican "stand patters," those satisfied with current political and economic practices.

While the Republicans were restructuring their political leadership, the Democrats were struggling. John McLean continued to wield disproportionate influence until he departed for Washington, D.C. to look after his extensive business interests. From that distance he attempted to influence Ohio affairs, but in 1903 he severed his connections with state politics.

The Republicans and Democrats each had a progressive wing that was rapidly growing in visibility and influence. Progressive Republicans looked to President Theodore Roosevelt for inspiration. The ebullient president swept Ohio in the 1904 election and established himself as spokesman for the new look in Republican affairs. In both the major parties political alignments were flexible enough that a "progressive" on one issue might be a "stand patter" on another. Ohio's Socialists, like their brothers nationally, were visible beyond their numbers. They had little influence, partly because their program was not too dissimilar from that of the progressive Democrats.

Political reformers scored significant triumphs in 1905 state and local elections. The Roosevelt wing of the Republican party asserted itself. In an Akron address, William Howard Taft, then secretary of war in Roosevelt's cabinet, blasted the Cox machine and boss control of urban politics, much to the discomfiture of Charles Dick and Gov. Myron T. Herrick, his political ally. The Democrats, gaining confidence from divisions in the Republican camp, increased their assault against "bossism." The tactic seemed to work as their gubernatorial candidate, John M. Pattison of Clermont County, carried fifty-seven of Ohio's eighty-eight counties, far outdistancing Herrick. Pattison thus became the first Democrat to occupy the governor's chair in fourteen years, but he died before serving his entire term and was succeeded by Lieutenant Governor Andrew L. Harris of Preble County.

In the principal municipal races, reformers virtually swept the field. Tom Johnson won reelection by a large margin in Cleveland. Brand Whitlock carried on Samuel Jones's tradition in Toledo. Dayton and Columbus voters defeated the bosses and elected reform Democrats. Most striking, however, was a Democratic sweep in Cincinnati and Hamilton County that prompted Boss Cox to announce his retirement from active politics. In rural and small-town Ohio, conservative Democrats and Republican "stand patters" maintained influence.

Some important adjustments occurred in the political process early in the twentieth century. In 1903, by constitutional amendment, the legislature and voters granted veto power to the governor; two years later a constitutional amendment took effect placing election of state and local officials in the even-numbered years; in 1906 a new law made mandatory the direct primary election as the nominating device for members of the general assembly and most judges, plus county, township, and municipal officials, and local school board members. Instrumental in the success of the latter bill was a Cincinnati minister, the Reverend Herbert Bigelow. Yet another of Henry George's disciples, Bigelow was allied with the Johnson Democrats and ultimately was perceived as being among the most radical of that group, his political enemies calling him socialist or communist. He played a leading part in Ohio's progressive reform effort.

The 1912 Constitutional Convention

Every twenty years Ohio voters could choose whether or not to call a state constitutional convention. In 1911 this opportunity coincided with a pent-up demand for reform. The demand was rather broad-based, supported by backers of municipal home rule, woman suffrage, court procedural reforms, and legislative regulation of improved working conditions. In addition, Herbert Bigelow's Direct Legislation League pressed for adoption of the initiative and the referendum, the Ohio Chamber of Commerce lobbied to abolish the uniform rule in taxation, and the liquor interests wanted licensing of saloons.

Interest in these issues was not the only sign that voters were reform-minded. The Socialists, although never a major voice in Ohio politics, were very active at this time, going beyond radical Democrats by urging state ownership and operation of the means of production (utilities, industries, and so on). Among their leading spokesmen were Max Hayes and Charles Ruthenberg of Cleveland. The party brought Eugene Debs and other national Socialist leaders to the state, but progressives had already preempted too much of the Socialist platform to give the latter broad voter appeal. Nevertheless, Socialists were highly visible in municipal races in 1911. They won mayoralties in Canton, Lima, Barberton, Lorain, and ten smaller cities, nearly all of which had sizable numbers of recent immigrants, and in larger cities Socialists won some council seats. But the Socialists found it difficult to live down the taint of being a "foreign" element in American politics. Further discredited in World War I, they disappeared as a viable political force.

Ohio voters elected 120 delegates to a constitutional convention which met on January 9, 1912. The delegates were young, able, and progressive to a marked degree. Among them were twenty-five farmers, fourteen bankers and businessmen, ten laborers, six educators, four ministers, four physicians, two newspaper editors, and a large bloc of lawyers. Sixty-five were Democrats, forty-eight Republicans, three Socialists, and three Independents. It was perhaps the ablest group ever assembled in Ohio to consider state affairs.

It was also a practical group. Remembering the overwhelming defeat which voters administered to the constitutional convention's work in 1873, these delegates decided to avoid rewriting the existing constitution; rather, they would submit amendments, each of which the voters would consider separately. Herbert Bigelow was elected president of the convention despite misgivings from conservatives, but his conduct of business was even-handed. Each of nineteen committees was assigned topics to research and present— i.e., good roads, initiative, and referendum.

The convention was an excellent educational forum for Ohioans. National leaders, among them President William Howard Taft, addressed the convention and their views were widely reported. Theodore Roosevelt, who was gearing up for another run at the presidency, also appeared, as did three-time Democratic presidential candidate William Jennings Bryan, Hiram Johnson the progressive from California, and Ohio's own governor, Judson Harmon, a Democrat who had won office in 1909 with the support of reformers.

The convention accomplished a great deal. Among the forty-one amendments proposed to the voters in a special election in September 1912 were several that expanded or interpreted the Bill of Rights in regard to trial by jury, the right to confront witnesses, and the right to seek redress and extend damages in a wrongful death suit. The legislature's powers were amended. Initiative and referendum, devices which set procedures whereby voters can circumvent the legislature, were adopted although Ohio lagged behind other states in doing so. This emotional issue prompted Cincinnati representative Herbert Bigelow to a bit of ministerial hyperbole: "Oh my friends," he said, "we are forging the greatest tool democracy ever had." The recall of public officials, regarded as a truly radical step, was strictly limited on the state level although cities could institute it under home rule charters. Other political changes assured the direct primary, established civil service protections, and granted the governor a line item veto in appropriation bills.

Working men and women received new protections. The legislature could fix the hours of labor, establish a minimum wage, and provide for "the comfort, health, safety, and general welfare of all employees." Pay for contract labor could be secured by a "mechanic's lien" against the property on which men had worked. The eight-hour day was to be the standard in public work "except in cases of extraordinary emergency." The optional workman's compensation established in 1911 could now become mandatory, making Ohio a leader in framing this provision.

Under general welfare, amendments assured state control over public education but gave cities discretionary power to operate their own school systems. Other amendments permitted public financing of good roads and gave the legislature power to control the use of timber, water, and mineral resources for the public benefit, a provision that met the demands of conservationists.

Important in bringing the state into the modern world was the adoption of a home rule amendment permitting Ohio cities of 5,000 or more population to adopt charters under which they would govern themselves, provided that such charters conformed to the state constitution and limitations imposed by the general assembly. In securing this amendment the Johnson Democrats and the Ohio Municipal League managed to overcome the suspicions of rural delegates, as well as objections from both sides of the liquor question and from public service corporations who saw it as a device permitting municipal ownership of utilities.

The proposed amendments were published and widely circulated during the summer of 1912. Debate was particularly strong on the issues of woman suffrage, liquor licensing, initiative and referendum, employee welfare, primary elections, judicial changes, good roads, and municipal home rule. On September 3 the voters approved thirty-three proposed amendments in spite of such obstructionists as the Ohio State Board of Commerce, which advised, "When in doubt, vote no." Many counties were strongly supportive. Columbiana, Lucas, and Summit counties approved all forty-one amendments. Only woman suffrage and the use of voting machines failed in urban counties. The northern half of the state was more supportive than the southern half, possibly because of its different population makeup, its highly ethnicized cities (there was much ethnic support for social programs), and possibly because Johnson democracy was stronger in the north than in the south.

Among the eight losing amendments were woman suffrage, the use of voting machines, regulation of outdoor advertising and abolition of the death penalty. The voters also rejected an amendment which would have removed the word "white" in that section of the constitution defining eligibility for voting. Blacks had voted in Ohio since implementation of the fifteenth Amendment to the federal Constitution in 1870, yet they were to wait another eleven years for Ohio to delete color as a voting criterion from its state constitution.

On balance, Ohio voters chose reform. Although conservatives railed against "socialism," that was standard political bluster. The liberal swing of Ohio springs from other sources: from the growing political strength of cities reacting against rural conservatism, from voter reaction against the strength of selfish business interests, from a perception that the voter was manipulated by laws and rules that perpetuated boss control, from effective leadership by responsible reformers in both major parties, and from "the spirit of the time." Bigelow, Whitlock, Baker, and other reformers rejoiced in the triumph of principles which Tom Johnson, Samuel Jones, and Washington Gladden had

Ohio women show support for the women's suffrage movement, Columbus, 1914.

espoused. On the national scene, meanwhile, progressivism had tougher going.

Taft and Presidential Tensions *ßot* 955

William Howard Taft, scion of a prominent Cincinnati family, became the sixth Ohio-born president in 1909 by defeating William Jennings Bryan, marking the third time the Nebraska crusader had lost to an Ohio moderate. Young William ("Willie" or "Will" to family and friends) graduated from Yale and the Cincinnati Law School. Of a judicial temperament, he found early assignments on the bench congenial to his nature. In 1900 McKinley appointed him president of the Philippine Commission and later he performed admirably as civil governor there. In 1904 Theodore Roosevelt appointed Taft secretary of war, using him as a troubleshooter in a variety of hotspots. Increasingly the amiable and able Taft became regarded as a spokesman for the Roosevelt wing of the Republican party, but the appearance was deceiving; it concealed his innate conservatism. In 1908, at the urging of his wife, Helen Herron Taft, and of his many friends, he somewhat reluctantly became the Republican presidential candidate.

Scholars assessing Taft's administration usually picture the president as a conservative who betrayed the expectations of the Republican party's progressive wing. While that is true in certain instances—in his support of a continuing high tariff policy, for example—Taft either supported, or at least did not interfere with a number of progressive developments, including passage of the Sixteenth and Seventeenth amendments (for a graduated income tax and direct election of senators, respectively), establishment of a postal savings plan, vigorous "trust busting" activity, establishment of a Department of Labor, and other changes in the progressive spirit.

Throughout his term Taft was caught in the tension between conservative and progressive. He tended to eat when nervous; he must have been quite nervous as president, for his weight ballooned to more than 300 pounds. In addition to being the largest president, he was also the first to play golf, throw out the first pitch of the professional baseball season, and drive to his inauguration in an automobile. Despite these humanizing considerations, Taft appeared lackluster when contrasted with Teddy Roosevelt, and when TR attempted a comeback and challenged Taft for the 1912 presidential nomination, the contrast in styles was apparent; it was said that Teddy Roosevelt made law, Taft quoted it.

Roosevelt, unable to pry control of the party away from Taft, bolted to the Progressive "Bull Moose" party. By splitting the Republicans, Roosevelt assured the election of Woodrow Wilson, who carried Ohio and the nation by a

comfortable margin. Taft retired to teach law at Yale. In 1921 President Warren G. Harding appointed him Chief Justice of the United States, a post he
held until near death in 1931. He is the only person to hold both of the
nation's most prestigious offices, and of the two he regarded the court position as by far the better job. The Taft legacy of public service continued,
assuring his accomplished family a continuing place in the political life of the
state and nation.

James M. Cox and the Progressive Initiative

While Taft presided in the White House, the Cincinnati Democrat, Judson
Harmon, presided in the Statehouse. A tall, distinguished man of military
bearing, Harmon had served as United States attorney general under Grover
Cleveland and had performed various services for President Roosevelt, though
not of his party. Politically, Harmon was caught between the conservative and
the Johnson wings of his party, and could not please the one without disap-
pointing the other. Still, he was able to give the state responsible leadership
during his two terms as governor (1909–13).

The state elections of 1912 were critical. The constitutional convention
was in session, and reformers knew their success would ultimately depend
upon the governor and the legislature putting into effect the new constitutional provisions. They found their gubernatorial candidate in the person of
Rep. James M. Cox of Dayton.

Like Sam Jones and Tom Johnson, Cox was a poor boy who made good. He
bought the *Dayton Daily News* and used it as the nucleus of a modest newspaper empire. Looking for new challenges, he put his talent for management to
the service of politics. While sympathetic to most progressive reforms, he was
essentially a moderate and rejected such extremes as the single tax. He was the
workers' friend, interested in improving working conditions. In the 1912 election, Cox defeated the Republican, Robert B. Brown, and the Progressive,
Arthur Garford. Nineteen of the twenty-two representatives elected to Congress were Democrats. The party also secured large majorities in both houses
of the general assembly.

In his inaugural address Cox told his audience, "We are entering upon a
new day," and he immediately undertook to make that a reality, bringing great
energy and administrative ability to the task. Cox proved a master at using
patronage and careful organization of legislative committees as instruments for
achieving his goals. He sought inspiration wherever it could be found. Wisconsin, widely regarded as the most progressive of states, was the inspiration
for a number of Ohio programs including formation of a legislative reference
bureau charged with the careful drafting of legislative bills.

With his organization in place, Governor Cox directed the legislature to enact laws that would flesh out the new constitutional amendments. The general assembly adopted the direct primary for all state and local elective offices, with minor exceptions, and rewrote initiative and referendum laws to safeguard against fraudulent use. Such precautions were necessary; Ohio Attorney General Timothy Hogan had already brought suits against the fraudulent practices of the Ohio Equity Association, the instrument that Cleveland's Daniel R. Hanna used to fight tax reforms. The association, said Hogan, had secured referendum petition signatures representing "dead men, livery stables, empty houses, children, public parks, churches, stores, convicts, brick yards, public playgrounds, factories, vacant lots, flop houses, houses of ill repute and non-residents."

In other business the legislature put into effect the limited recall provisions passed as a constitutional amendment and resubmitted to the voters an amendment which would permit women to hold official positions in institutions for the care of women and children. It passed handily. The assembly addressed municipal home-rule problems, but with mixed success. Home-rule partisans saw the legislature undercut their hopes for fiscal reform and broad-based powers to finance city-owned utilities. The governor rewarded labor for its strong support by pushing a strong workman's compensation bill through the legislature. Accomplishments in the realm of minimum wage and maximum hour legislation were not so appreciable, but with Cox's hearty endorsement, Ohio led the nation in enacting a comprehensive Children's Code that revamped laws affecting minors in their work, their education, and their treatment for delinquency. Legislation established a Bureau of Juvenile Research to employ scientific knowledge and methods in dealing with the needs of minors.

Penal reform was yet another concern of reformers. Cox rejected his predecessor's conviction that imprisonment was for punishment only. He believed in rehabilitation, and his recommendations that convicts be used in healthful labor, that they be paid for this work, that intermediate sentences be adopted and a parole board established were all adopted. Schools also caught the governor's attention. With his blessing a Rural School Code established consolidated rural schools under county supervision; the schools were to be graded, with prescribed offerings for each grade, and teachers were to be college or normal school graduates. The basis of state financial support to local systems was also revised. Congruent with school consolidations was an attempt to secure good roads. New legislation appropriated state funds for main highways and permitted local governments to appropriate money for road improvement in counties, townships, and cities.

James Cox had grown up on a farm in southwestern Ohio, and he never forgot the farmers' interests. The governor formed an agricultural commission as an umbrella under which to regulate various special concerns. The state increased support for agricultural experiments and the advancement of scientific farming, and rural and village schools were required to offer courses in agriculture. By making farm life more profitable and attractive, Cox hoped to stem the rush of young people from the farms to the industrial cities.

The 1913 Flood and Conservancy

Ohioans knew about floods. Each spring, with few exceptions, the mighty Ohio and its tributaries spilled over their banks. Ice blockages created floods in northern rivers flowing into Lake Erie. But the great flood of 1913 was extraordinary; it was Ohio's greatest natural disaster.

During Easter week, March 1913, torrential rains fell for three days over much of the state. Nearly every riverside city had flooding; even Akron, set in apparent safety on hills above the Little Cuyahoga, had problems. To eliminate flooding from backed-up waters, city officials dynamited Ohio Canal locks at Akron; similar actions elsewhere ended, once and for all, commercial boating on the once-impressive canal system.

The heaviest rains fell in the Great Miami Valley north of Dayton. The Gem City had suffered floods previously, but this time raging floodwaters inundated residential areas and broke through protective levees depositing up to twenty feet of water in the downtown section. Fires fed by ruptured gas mains destroyed the upper reaches of many flood-encircled buildings. City government was helpless in the emergency. At this juncture, John Patterson took charge, turning his National Cash Register plants into emergency shelters where refugees were provided food and medical care. His employees built evacuation boats and rescued hundreds of stranded persons from housetops and trees. Patterson thought of everything, including an emergency telegram to the governor in Columbus. Informed of Dayton's desperate plight, Governor Cox placed the state's resources, including the National Guard, at Patterson's disposal. The state as a whole suffered 428 known deaths, destruction of more than 20,000 houses with perhaps twice that many seriously damaged, and severe losses to industries and railroads exceeding $300 million. Dayton claimed a major share of these grim statistics.

Once the clean-up started, Patterson and Col. Edward A. Deeds, a National Cash Register vice-president, raised $2 million to finance a thorough study of conditions. Deeds and his associates hired Arthur Morgan, a distinguished hydrological engineer who would later be president of Antioch College, to survey the flood problem and make recommendations. Morgan proposed that six earthen dams be constructed on waters upstream from Dayton. Gates in the dams could be shut to impound water in an emergency. Morgan also suggested that the river channel through Dayton be straightened and improved levees constructed.

New legislation was required to implement these recommendations. Governor Cox pushed vigorously to help his fellow Daytonians, and with his support the legislature passed the Vonderheide Act (Ohio Conservancy Law) in 1914. It permitted formation of watershed districts administered by boards which could issue bonds to secure construction money, employ eminent domain to secure land, and levy taxes for operating funds. The taxes were to be levied on those who benefited from the improvements. This feature of the law, plus the threat of losing land through eminent domain, created substantial opposition. The law was challenged in the Ohio courts, but the Ohio Supreme Court upheld its constitutionality in 1915. The United States Supreme Court did likewise four years later in *Orr* v. *Allen.*

The Miami Conservancy District (1915) was the first major watershed district formed in the United States. By 1922 the dams and other improvements had been completed at a cost of $39 million. This model was followed in 1933 for the establishment of the much larger and more complex Muskingum Conservancy District. Nationally, the Tennessee Valley Authority project of 1933, a key element in the New Deal recovery program, relied on precedents established by the Miami project, and Arthur Morgan was a key mover in the massive project, which embraced portions of seven states.

While Governor Cox and the Democratic legislature pursued state issues, home-rule advocates were pushing the adoption of city charters. Mayor Newton D. Baker lost no time securing election of a commission to draft a charter for Cleveland, and in July 1913, the city's residents approved the charter in a light vote by a two-to-one margin. It called for an elected mayor, appointed executive officers, and a large elected council chosen by wards. It was appropriate that Cleveland, with its history of concern for home rule, led the way. Columbus experienced far more division in securing a satisfactory instrument. In May 1914 her citizens narrowly approved a charter establishing a small council of seven members elected at large. Toledo, too, adopted a federal form of government. Dayton, meanwhile, became the first large American city to experiment with the city manager plan of municipal government, by which an elected council would hire a non-partisan manager to run city business. Springfield, Ashtabula, and Sandusky also chose city managers. In years to come more than thirty other Ohio cities tried the city manager scheme; several, notably Cleveland and Akron, abandoned it after a brief experience. The commission plan of city government did not catch on in Ohio; only Middletown and Salem tried it.

Some early efforts to adopt home-rule charters faltered, although renewed efforts were successful years later. Cincinnati was one conspicuous home-rule failure; nevertheless, the historian of Ohio progressivism, Landon Warner, claimed that home rule allowed reform to spread beyond Cleveland, Columbus, and Toledo. Other Ohio cities that had been on the periphery of reform activity now saw prospects for more efficient and enlightened municipal government, and most took advantage of the opportunity.

Republican Interlude

Governor Cox's aggressive leadership aroused opposition in a number of constituencies. The public, coached by special interests, ultimately tired of reform, a factor that contributed to the governor's defeat in 1914 by old guard Republican Frank B. Willis of Delaware County, a highly regarded professor of history and law at Ohio Northern University with a long record of involvement in public issues. The unsuccessful Progressive candidate was James R. Garfield, son of the martyred president.

In this election Ohioans also rejected woman suffrage and statewide prohibition. They approved establishment of the local option for alcohol regulation on the township or municipal level, a move the "drys" used as a fall-back position in the likelihood that statewide prohibition would fail. Willis's administration was essentially a stand-pat period in which little new legislation was proposed. Half-hearted efforts to undo some of the recent reform legislation were largely unsuccessful, perhaps because the European war preempted the public's attention.

Prelude to War

Ohio's reaction to the European war which began in August 1914 was as complex as its population. While most Ohioans ultimately supported the Allies (Britain, France, Russia, and Italy) a substantial and influential portion of its population was of recent German or Austro-Hungarian extraction; the German-language press was strong and expressed sympathy for the German nation and the Central Powers (Germany, Austria-Hungary, and Turkey). People from these lands did not believe that family, friends, and neighbors in the old country were vicious and sadistic as pictured in Allied propaganda. The Irish were also well represented in Ohio, and they still nurtured hatred for the English.

The presidential election of 1916 took place in an atmosphere of growing tension. German attacks on neutral shipping had resulted in American deaths.

Allied propaganda made it increasingly difficult for Americans to remain neutral in spirit and deed as advised by President Wilson, who ran for reelection under the slogan, "He kept us out of war." Wilson defeated Charles Evans Hughes, but by such a slim margin in the electoral college that, had Ohio gone for Hughes, he would have won; only Ohio, of all the populous states of the northeast and the Great Lakes region, gave its votes to Wilson. Within the state, all major urban counties except Hamilton went Democratic. Efforts to explain Ohio's seemingly abberational conduct center on the peoples' genuine response to Wilson's efforts to maintain neutrality, to labor's support in gratitude for Wilson's pro-labor legislation, and to the return of many progressives to the Democratic party.

Having supported the Democratic president, Ohio voters in turn elected James Cox to another term as governor. Riding Wilson's coattails, Cox beat the incumbent Willis by fewer than 7,000 votes. A Johnson Democrat from Canton, Atlee Pomerene, won reelection to the United States Senate, defeating former governor Myron T. Herrick. Ohio's other senator during the war years was Warren G. Harding, a Republican. The Democrats also won thirteen of Ohio's twenty-two House seats.

Departing from the policies of his previous term, Governor Cox did not ask the legislature for an ambitious legislative program. He chose, instead, to concentrate on efficiency in government. Among the accomplishments of this legislative session were improvements in the workmen's compensation laws, separation of ballots for state and national elections, absentee voting procedures, and a nine-hour workday for women. The legislators also appropriated matching funds for federally sponsored highway improvement and for vocational education. Consistent with his centralizing tendencies, Cox focused control of public health in a state health commissioner and a four-member Public Health Council; he also established two new offices, the superintendent of public instruction (a restructuring of an existing function), and the commissioner of securities.

Ohio and World War I

Before adjourning from its short session, the legislature appropriated a war emergency fund, a precursor of things to come. By April 1917, the United States was a belligerent in World War I, and the Statehouse referred the complexities of dealing with the resulting problems to the Ohio Branch of the Council of National Defense. The council, created by Congress, was used by Secretary of War Newton D. Baker as an instrument for coordinating the civilian war effort. The Ohio Council advised Cox's administration on criti-

cal matters ranging from finding adequate labor for the fall harvest to building good roads. In the latter case, vagrants, "slackers," and convicts were put
to work on the highways.

The council's most impressive work was in the area of labor and industrial
relations. The Ohio Industrial Commission tied government, industry, and
labor into a network to assure efficient use of the labor supply. Men who were
out of work in one locale were directed to another. During the commission's
existence, employment offices matched 564,570 jobs with applicants, and responded to such emergency needs as providing 3,000 workers within forty-
eight hours to build housing at the enormous Camp Sherman complex outside
Chillicothe.

The role of this organization was vital, for Ohio was a leading producer of
basic metals, heavy machinery, automotive and truck assemblies, electrical
equipment, rubber products, road construction equipment, and other products most in demand in wartime, and many industrial plants expanded as fast
as materials and workers could be found. This expansion was most dramatic
in the rubber center of Akron. Between 1910 and 1920 the city added 144,000
new residents, most of them attracted by high wages in the giant plants that
built tires and tubes, gas masks, balloons, and other wartime products. The
Industrial Commission was unable to provide the tens of thousands of new
workers required, so company recruiters ran ads in newspapers and scoured
the hills and valleys of Appalachia seeking hardscrabble farmers, unemployed
miners, and other available workers to send to the "gum mills" of Akron. Key
industries elsewhere in Ohio had similar problems, notably the steel centers,
which were affected by the constriction on immigration brought on by the
war. By 1918 the situation improved slightly as Ohio's labor recruitment
practices were coordinated with the federal employment service.

The War Council and various state agencies undertook other essential
initiatives, many of them in cooperation with federal coordinating agencies.
Farm prices soared during the war years, but farm labor was in short supply.
To meet the critical shortages, factories gave workers short-term leaves for
plowing and planting. College and high school students were organized into a
volunteer labor pool tapped by farmers during critical periods. They were
excused from classes to help with the spring planting and the fall harvest.
Low-interest loans allowed farmers to purchase new tractors: "We must replace by machinery what we have lost by having our boys go to the front,"
said Governor Cox. City dwellers contributed to the food supply by planting
gardens in backyards and vacant lots. Service organizations distributed seeds
and tools. Citizens conserved food by observing "wheatless" and "meatless"
days.

Officials sought increased efficiency in the transportation network by controlling the use of railroad cars and increasing the amount of freight that the state's extensive electric interurban system hauled. At the governor's urging, the state made improvements to the Lincoln Highway (U.S. 30) to stimulate the use of trucks. Essential (and long-neglected) repairs to the National Road (U.S. 40) speeded the removal of 40,000 trucks from Detroit to the port of Baltimore.

Cox vigorously supported efforts to enlighten the public on war aims. As part of a larger national effort, public information was organized on a state-wide basis, led by President William Oxley Thompson of Ohio State University. Governor Cox also supported Americanization programs designed to assist aliens to learn English and American values in preparation for becoming citizens. Western Reserve Professor Raymond Moley was placed in charge. The Americanization Committee went beyond its initial task and served as a censorship bureau, publishing reading lists of approved books and urging libraries to "withdraw temporarily" from circulation books which appeared on a list of "pro-German" writings.

This was but a small manifestation of anti-German action, to which Ohio was especially susceptible because of its large and visible German population. To later generations, Ohioans seemed to have an unreasonable hysteria about rooting out all things German, but the governor's vigorous anti-German pronouncements helped set the tone. Towns renamed streets that had German names; New Berlin became North Canton; sauerkraut was now "liberty cabbage."

Citizens treated persons suspected of German sympathies roughly. The Cincinnati press characterized Herbert Bigelow, so prominent in recent reform efforts, as a traitor for opposing both the American entrance into the war and conscription. He was kidnapped, driven to a remote area of northern Kentucky, beaten, and left to find his way back. President Wilson and Newton Baker vigorously condemned the assault. Governor Cox ordered an investigation, which proved abortive. Cincinnati's mayor probably expressed a common opinion when he said Bigelow got "what's coming to him."

Anti-German sentiment was especially prevalent among those who would censor school curricula. Many colleges stopped teaching German language and literature or imposed restraints upon it. Baldwin-Wallace College students succeeded in removing their president for failure to condemn alleged German crimes. Even after war's end the legislature, at Cox's insistence, passed the Ake Law (1919) banning the teaching of German below the eighth grade in any school, public or private. The Supreme Court later found laws of this type unconstitutional so far as they extended to private and parochial schools. All teachers in public, private and parochial schools had to take loyalty oaths, swearing to support the constitutions of the United States and

Ohio and to show exemplary respect for the flag, adherence to law and order, and allegiance to the nation.

Ohioans Go to War

Unlike the Civil War, in which state regiments were well-identified, one cannot trace Ohio's soldiers so satisfactorily in World War I. Ohio men were well represented in several units, and they dominated the famous Thirty-seventh Division, the state's National Guard unit. The Thirty-seventh was called to service and assembled at Camp Sheridan, Alabama, in August 1917. The following June its commanding officer, Maj. Gen. Charles F. Farnsworth, led the unit overseas. The division was in the lines along the western front for only a few months in the summer and fall of 1918, but it performed gallantly and with great success at Verdun, along the St. Mihiel Salient, and in Belgium.

While the National Guard was gone, Ohio protected vital areas with a Home Guard, whose members patrolled waterworks, power sources, railroad bridges, dams, and docks where enemy sabotage could damage the war effort. Reported cases of sabotage had been sufficient to make this precaution seem reasonable.

In addition to her National Guard unit, Ohio provided the military forces with volunteers, although they were never very numerous. Under the Conscription Act, which took effect in May 1917, 1,389,474 Ohio men between the ages of eighteen and forty-five were registered for service. Of these, 154,236 were drafted. Many conscripts were trained at Camp Sherman, an enormous facility on the outskirts of Chillicothe. At one time the camp held 40,000 men.

The draft was an emotional issue. Rep. Isaac Sherwood of Toledo voted against it. An old man who had been a Civil War hero, he was convinced that the European war was no concern of the United States. "As I love my country," he said, "I would use every honorable means to keep the young manhood of America out of this horrid holocaust of European slaughter. My experience in the Civil War has saddened me all my life." Conscription created a special problem for thousands of young men who were raised in the traditional peace churches—Mennonite, Amish, Quaker, and others. Some fulfilled service obligations by working in hospitals, in the ambulance corps, on farms, and other noncombatant assignments. Some conscientious objectors like Evan Thomas, brother of the Socialist Norman Thomas, refused to make any concession to their convictions. Thomas served time in the federal prison stockade at Fort Leavenworth; Ammon Hennacy, a Socialist who refused to register for the draft, was incarcerated in the federal prison at Atlanta. America's most prominent Socialist, Eugene V. Debs, was jailed in Canton for speaking against America's war policies.

Many Ohio draftees served in the Eighty-third Division, where they outnumbered men from other states. A former Ohio Guard unit, the Fourth Regiment, was part of the famous Forty-second "Rainbow" Division, which had a distinguished fighting record in France. In all, Ohio sent about 225,000 volunteers, draftees, and national guardsmen to the military. With 5.1 percent of the nation's population, Ohio supplied 5.3 percent of its military manpower. Approximately 6,500 Ohioans died from battle wounds and disease. No figures exist for those who suffered permanent injury or the debilitating effects of gas poisoning.

Unlike the Civil War, which spawned a host of well-known Ohio heroes, World War I heroism focused on units instead of individuals. An exception was the fame accorded America's "Ace of Aces" in air combat over France, Capt. Edward V. "Eddie" Rickenbacker, a Columbus native. Rickenbacker returned to his city in February 1919 to a tumultuous reception. A few days later black soldiers of the 372nd Infantry, the "Fighting Tigers," were welcomed in the capital city. Soon the bulk of Ohio's fighting men were receiving similar welcomes around the state. They may not have realized it, but the Ohio to which they returned was in the throes of reconciling important social issues which would bear upon their lives for years to come.

14.

Between the Wars

Several social issues which had long engaged Ohio politics were resolved, at least temporarily, at war's end. Proponents of prohibition and woman suffrage fought campaigns on both state and national levels. Reformers had made halting progress toward their goals over a seventy-year span, but World War I, the struggle "to make the world safe for democracy," had spawned an idealism that provided the emotional setting for what appeared to be final victory. That "victory," apparently secured by amendments to the United States Constitution, proved to be only a temporary one for the prohibitionists and a partial one for women's rights advocates.

Prohibition

Ohio had led the nation in the post–Civil War crusade against "demon rum" (see chapter 11, p. 277 ff.). The Women's Christian Temperance Union was the best-organized lobbying group in the temperance crusade until the emergence in 1893 of the Anti-Saloon League. Howard Hyde Russell, the first superintendent of the Ohio organization, also headed the national group. But Wayne B. Wheeler, who personified the League's aggressive tactics, supplied much of the League's lobbying skill. He helped develop a strong bureaucratic organization that overwhelmed its targets with publicity barrages. No political campaign fought in Ohio in the late nineteenth and early twentieth century was free from the "wet" versus "dry" conflict. In local, state, and national elections, the liquor question obscured other issues.

Constitutional amendments the state adopted in 1912 posed problems for the "drys." Populous urban counties where "wets" were strongest used the referendum to offset some of the advantage held in the legislature by the small rural counties, where prohibition sentiment was strongest. The initiative and referendum could be used by the "drys" as readily as against them, however. In a related development, home rule for cities began to circumvent the Rose Law (1908), which established local option on a county-wide basis; under home-rule authority, Cleveland could remain "wet" no matter what Cuyahoga County chose to do.

Rural Ohio was more prone to be sympathetic to prohibition than urban Ohio. Rural people were conservative, and Methodism, which along with other evangelical Protestant denominations supported temperance, was strong throughout the agricultural areas of the state. Rural areas lacked the concentrated "wet" sentiment found in cities with large immigrant populations. In addition, producers and distributors of alcoholic beverages were apt to be more numerous in urban areas. And the cities in general assumed a more liberal posture on social issues than did rural areas.

The "drys" were tireless in their efforts to secure statewide prohibition. In 1914, 1915, and 1917 the issue was on the ballot, and each year the "dry" vote crept closer to a majority. In 1918 prohibitionists got their wish; by a 25,759-vote margin the state went dry.

The legislature passed the Crabbe Act in 1919 to enforce prohibition, but in referendum votes, Ohioans repealed the Crabbe Act and also overturned the legislature's ratification vote on the proposed eighteenth Amendment to the federal Constitution. The latter use of the referendum was later ruled unconstitutional by the United States Supreme Court in *Hawke* v. *Smith* (1920).

A second Crabbe Act was enacted by the legislature in 1920. It defined enforcement machinery for statewide prohibition, and in 1921 a state agency was established to enforce the law. Meanwhile, the Eighteenth Amendment went into effect in January 1920, and Congress passed the National Prohibition Enforcement Act, better known as the Volstead Act, late in 1919. It invoked penalties for the manufacture, sale, and transportation of alcoholic beverages. The Bureau of Internal Revenue was entrusted with its enforcement; like other states, Ohio experienced a two-tiered assault—state and federal—on the liquor traffic.

During the early twenties, the Anti-Saloon League maintained its vigorous political lobbying and through its widely circulated paper, *American Issue,* endorsed candidates for state and national office. In 1924, nineteen of the state's twenty-two congressmen were "drys," as were the overwhelming majority of state legislators. This was perhaps the high-water mark of Anti-Saloon League success. In 1927, in a referendum vote, Ohio voters soundly defeated a law that gave fees to local magistrates when enforcing liquor laws. In 1930 they elected Robert J. Bulkley, a "dripping wet" Cleveland Democrat, to the United States Senate. Two years later the "drys" were dealt substantial reverses in national and state elections.

The inauguration of Franklin Delano Roosevelt in March 1933, brought to power a new political alignment, less responsive to American traditionalism. The liquor issue was overshadowed by the dreadful plight into which the nation had plunged with the onset of the Great Depression. New federal legislation in March 1933 allowed states to initiate sales of beer that had 3.2 percent alcoholic content by weight. Within a month Ohio legalized the sale of such beer subject to license and tax limitations. At the same time the Twenty-first Amendment, repealing the Eighteenth, was before the states. It was ratified in Ohio by a popularly elected convention whose delegates favored repeal two-to-one. On December 5, 1933, the Twenty-first Amendment was declared ratified. Ohio voters also repealed the prohibition amendment in the state constitution, but the supportive legislation remained to be dealt with by a later legislature. In 1933 the general assembly passed the State Liquor Control Act establishing a Department of Liquor Control; it managed the state monopoly on the sale of hard liquor which was to be dispensed through state stores. By 1985 sales in state liquor stores produced income for the general fund in excess of $100 million annually.

Women's Rights

Ohio, along with New York, led the nation in pre-Civil War efforts to secure the suffrage and other rights for women, but the effort sagged through the war years and immediately thereafter. One bright but highly controversial spot during the post-war regrouping focused on a Homer (Licking County) woman, Victoria Claflin Woodhull. Raised in a somewhat unorthodox environment (her mother was a spirit-rapping seer and her father a ne'er-do-well), Woodhull and her sister, Tennessee, stepped beyond traditional bounds of propriety by advocating (and practicing) a liberated lifestyle that shocked Victorian America. With the financial support of their patron, Cornelius Vanderbilt, the young women built a successful brokerage business in New York City and used the proceeds to publish *Woodhull and Claflin's Weekly,* in which Victoria argued for the suffrage and equal rights for women, and for abolition of the double sexual standard. She challenged election laws by running as the presidential candidate of the Equal Rights Party in 1872. She received only a handful of votes and her outspoken views outraged and perhaps titillated audiences who repeatedly invited her to defend them. In a speech called "The Principles of Freedom," delivered in New York's Steinway Hall in 1871, Woodhull proclaimed her unorthodox views on love: "Yes, I am a Free Lover. I have an *inalienable, constitutional* and *natural* right to love whom I may, to love as *long* or as *short* a period as I can; to *change* that love every *day* if I please, and with that right neither *you* nor any *law* you can frame have *any* right to interfere."

Woodhull—"Mrs. Satan" to her enemies—overreached herself when she charged Henry Ward Beecher, America's most prominent preacher, with having an adulterous affair with a member of his church choir. A divided jury found Beecher innocent; it was "Vickie" who went to jail under New York's ultra-Puritanical Comstock laws.

Leaders of the women's movement were divided on the issue of Woodhull. Some saw her as an embarrassment while others, such as Elizabeth Cady Stanton, saw her usefulness. To the latter she was a lightning rod attracting the wrath of traditionalists and making the moderate objectives of mainstream reformers more acceptable by contrast. Both sisters married Englishmen, became "proper ladies," and lived discreetly in their later years.

In a quieter vein the Ohio Women's Rights Association (organized in 1852) continued to press for reform, lobbying with considerable success between 1887 and 1894. During this time the legislature granted married women control over their own property, gave women power to act as guardians, executors or administrators, and allowed them to sue and be sued. An 1894 law allowed women to vote in school elections.

While leaders of the women's movement took heart from these developments, their efforts increasingly centered on securing the franchise. Twelve states, all in the West, had given women the vote by 1913, but Ohio voters turned down the proposed constitutional amendment in 1912 that would have extended this right to its women. The voters, of course, were males, many of whom still held traditional views of women's roles. But there was also an organized and well-financed opposition to woman suffrage from Ohio brewers and liquor interests who feared that women would vote to dry up the state if given the chance.

Suffragists—women who believed in direct action or confrontational tactics—increased their activities after this rebuff. They helped secure modest victories in Columbus, Lakewood, and East Cleveland, which all granted women voting rights through home-rule charters. But a 1917 effort to secure presidential voting rights for Ohio women was turned down in a referendum vote.

World War I was again a catalyst to reform. Women had assumed many new jobs as men were called into the military, and their patriotic service in industry, soldier relief work, and nursing argued for full political participation. When in 1919 Congress passed a constitutional amendment giving women the vote, Ohio became the fifth state to ratify; the nineteenth Amendment took effect in 1920.

Women hastened to consolidate their gain, as the amendment was ratified in time for them to vote in the all-Ohio presidential contest of 1920. By 1922 the first women were elected to the general assembly, two to the Senate and four to the House. In 1923 the legislature voted to extend full civil rights to women, making twenty-one years the age of majority. Meanwhile women moved forward in other political realms. Fairport Harbor voters made Amy Kankonen Ohio's first female mayor in 1921. Florence Allen, a Cleveland lawyer, became the first woman in America to sit on a state's highest tribunal when, in 1922, she won election to the Ohio Supreme Court. In 1934 President Roosevelt appointed her the first woman judge to serve on the United States Circuit Court of Appeals.

Despite these gains, it would be a mistake to assume that women made continuous progress in securing their share of political leadership roles. Instead, once the initial enthusiasm wore off, women did not fare especially well in electoral contests. Nor did they receive many appointive offices. For decades to come, local, county, and state government in Ohio continued to be overwhelmingly male-dominated.

Child Labor Reforms

Yet another carry-over from the progressive era was the desire to protect children from exploitation in Ohio mines and factories. An 1852 law had sought to limit working hours for twelve-year-olds in mines but, like the law of the same year affording protection to women workers, it was largely unenforced. By the late nineteenth century, the factory system, with its demand for cheap labor, had contributed to the exploitation of children. Employers of child labor led the fight against compulsory school attendance laws, and court decisions undercut federal efforts to protect children from exploitation. In 1905 the general assembly enacted a law prohibiting employment for wages of boys under age fifteen and girls under sixteen while public schools were in session. The Bing Act of 1921 required students to stay in school until they received a diploma or until age eighteen, and barred young people below age sixteen from employment in most industries.

Opposition to these restrictions came from manufacturers' associations and from the Ohio Farm Bureau and the Ohio State Grange. Farmers resented and resisted any threat to their traditional source of cheap labor, and decried legislation which they felt deprived parents of control over their children.

Congress passed an amendment restricting child labor in 1924 but it failed of ratification; Ohio's congressional delegation voted overwhelmingly for a similar proposal in 1933 and the state legislature ratified it, but the proposal failed to receive final ratification nationally.

Presidential Politics: The Harding Years

In the first two decades of the twentieth century, Ohio Democrats enjoyed their longest run of political success since pre–Civil War days. After defeating Frank Willis in two close gubernatorial races (1916, 1918), Gov. James M. Cox emerged as a national figure, a promising presidential candidate from a key state. The progressivism Cox displayed in his first term (1913–15) had given way to a more conservative, middle-of-the-road leadership that focused on making government orderly and efficient. This emphasis appealed to businessmen somewhat more than did Cox's interest in economic planning. Among his dreams was a St. Lawrence seaway that would stimulate Ohio trade. The project was completed in 1959 through federal initiatives.

Cox attended the 1920 Democratic convention in San Francisco as a dark-horse candidate for the presidential nomination and won on the forty-fourth ballot. His vice-presidential running mate was an attractive young New Yorker, Franklin Delano Roosevelt. Cox pledged support for Wilson's League of Nations; he urged reconciliation and understanding between capital and labor.

Cox was handicapped by voter reaction against Wilson's conduct of the war, but even more so by Wilson's moralizing and preaching. Cox's vitriolic anti-German rhetoric of the war years also cost him, especially in his home state. Italian-Americans opposed the League of Nations because Italian territorial claims went unsatisfied in the peace negotiations. Irish-Americans remained hostile to Britain and to cooperation with her in a League of Nations. The Anti-Saloon League opposed Cox; Wayne Wheeler said Cox was "the last hope of the wets" for staving off prohibition.

The Republican convention in Chicago also had difficulty finding a candidate to please its various factions. Party leaders finally broke a complete deadlock by choosing the "available man," Sen. Warren Gamaliel Harding of Marion. Harding was the quintessential accommodating politician. Born in Blooming Grove (Morrow County) and a graduate of Ohio Central College in Iberia (little more than a secondary school), young Harding became owner of the *Marion Star*. It remained a small operation until his wife, Florence Kling Harding, put her considerable business energies into it and helped make it a profitable enterprise. Harding's Ohio political career was marked mainly by his ability to get along with various Republican factions. They rewarded him with a senatorship in 1915; in typical fashion, Harding was unusually passive in this role. He was a faithful party wheelhorse who, in order to "get along" would "go along." In a moment of self-realization, Harding apparently knew he was not equipped for the presidency, but he accepted the nomination extended to him after a hopeless deadlock in the famous "smoke-filled room" in Chicago's Blackstone Hotel had eliminated the prime candidates. His running mate was the dour New Englander, Calvin Coolidge.

The Republican platform was broad enough to avoid alienating important segments of the electorate. Harding initially had no objection to some sort of international league of nations, but he attacked "Wilson's League." His bland oratory was soothing. A call for "a return to normalcy" struck a responsive chord in a war-weary populace.

The 1920 presidential race, pitting two Ohio newspaper publishers against one another, was the first in which women voted. Turnouts were large with the Ohio vote total nearly double that of any previous presidential election. Harding won more than 60 percent of the popular vote, and in the electoral college his winning margin was 404 to 127. In Ohio he had an impressive 400,000-vote edge over Cox.

Harding was friendly, amiable, companionable. He was well liked, but he was not a distinguished president. In the Progressive Era, and especially during World War I, Americans had come to expect personal leadership from their president, but Harding lacked the intellectual capacity and the drive to be a true leader. Revisionist historians have claimed with some justice that Harding should not be judged as harshly as he has by president watchers. As evidence they point to his support of the Washington Arms Conference, to programs which he initiated but did not live to carry out, to his concern for labor and agriculture, and to a few strong cabinet appointments, notably Herbert Hoover at the Commerce Department and Charles Evans Hughes at State.

Harding's critics counter by emphasizing his poor appointments, among them Albert Fall, who was convicted of corruption as secretary of the interior, and Harry Daugherty, attorney general and chief figure in the "Ohio Gang," a group of political placemen and sycophants notorious for securing favors for themselves and their friends.

Harding also displayed moral obtuseness. As President, he was sworn to uphold the Constitution and the laws of the land, yet he flouted prohibition by entertaining his cronies at frequent poker and drinking sessions in "the little green house on K Street." He had long-running extramarital affairs with Carrie Phillips, the wife of his close friend, and with Nan Britton, an infatuated neighbor. The latter bore him an illegitimate daughter to whose care he made generous contributions. Harding continued to see his paramour while in the White House, revealing a self-indulgence that does not square with the popular image (often sadly at variance with reality) of how a president should comport himself.

While touring the West in 1923, Harding suffered an attack of apoplexy and died within twenty-four hours in a San Francisco hotel. The public mourned their president because they did not yet know what Harding had discovered just before leaving on his journey; there was deep corruption in his administration. Harding was outraged to discover that people he had trusted had betrayed him. The ensuing scandals in the Interior Department, the Veterans Administration, and elsewhere were the worst since the Grant presidency. As with Grant, Harding was not personally involved in any graft. His burden was that people he appointed were not called to account until it was too late. Revelation of the scandals and of the President's personal lifestyle shocked the public. His reputation plummeted. His wife did not long outlive him, and in 1931 both were interred in a handsome new mausoleum in Marion.

Calvin Coolidge served out Harding's unexpired term, and the 1924 Republican nominating convention in Cleveland selected him for a full term of his own. The Progressives, also meeting in Cleveland, selected Robert La-Follette of Wisconsin, while John W. Davis of West Virginia was the Democratic standard-bearer. Coolidge won by a large margin, carrying Ohio with ease. Perhaps some of his popularity in the Buckeye State could be traced to the new vice-president, Charles Gates Dawes, born in Marietta but a resident of Illinois. His Dawes Plan, dealing with the war debts problem, won for him the Nobel Peace Prize in 1925.

After four years of Coolidge prosperity, Herbert Hoover swept to victory over the Democrat Al Smith with all but two Ohio counties (Mercer and Putnam) going for Hoover. Only Pennsylvania gave Hoover more popular votes than Ohio did. Republicans captured all but three Ohio seats in the House of Representatives, and both senators—Frank Willis and Simeon D. Fess, a former president of Antioch College—were also Republicans. National affairs were securely in the hands of the Grand Old Party.

State Politics in the Twenties

While Republicans were riding high in national affairs, they also controlled most state offices, and throughout the decade outnumbered Democrats in the state legislature. They elected Harry L. Davis governor in 1920 by a margin of 121,000 votes over the Democrat Vic Donahey. Socialism, which some observers in this era of the "Red Scare" equated with "bolshevism, communism and anarchism," was fast disappearing as even a marginal threat to conservative ways. The Socialist candidate, Frank B. Hamilton, got but 43,000 votes.

Governor Davis was a self-made man who worked himself up from the steel rolling mills to become mayor of Cleveland, administering that city during the difficult war years. His single term in the Statehouse was unexciting, but it produced a basic reorganization of executive authority in state government. A plan worked out by a joint committee of the legislature, chaired by state senator Frank E. Whittemore, focused more power in the hands of department heads, who could now appoint their division chiefs. The governor retained appointive power in the division of banking and had complete control over his own department heads. This clarification of the chain of command was supposed to lead to efficiencies in the conduct of public business. It made Ohio a leader among the states in securing executive efficiency, at least on paper.

Davis stepped down after one term, and Democrat Vic Donahey of Tuscarawas County defeated Carmi A. Thompson in 1922 by a slim margin. Donahey proved to be a popular governor, successfully bucking a Republican tide. As auditor, he had won attention for his careful husbanding of state funds, and he continued to keep tight control of the purse strings as governor. Donahey was in constant conflict with Republicans in the legislature, frequently vetoing their measures and earning the nickname "Veto Vic." In his first term he returned seventy-four bills to the legislature and in his second term forty-three. In addition he vetoed line items in appropriation bills. The Republican-dominated legislature passed many bills over his veto, but Donahey was a restraining force on their ambitions to determine Ohio's future.

Little dramatic legislation passed during Donahey's three terms. It was more a time for assimilating the substantial changes brought about during the progressive era and World War I. To improve the court system—a chronic concern in Ohio—a judicial council of nine justices headed by the chief justice recommended means of making the system more responsive and equitable. An effort to amend the constitution to permit use of voting machines failed because people still distrusted them and believed they would increase election costs. During Donahey's administrations substantial progress was made in improving and paving roads. A dramatic increase in motor vehicles made this imperative; support for a gasoline tax to pay the bills came from both rural and urban regions. It was said that this 1925 tax "lifted Ohio out of the mud."

Vic Donahey picked an auspicious time to retire from the statehouse. His successor in 1928 was a Republican businessman from Cincinnati, Myers Y. Cooper, who had run unsuccessfully against Donahey in the previous election. Cooper's victory margin over Democrat Martin L. Davey was in excess of a quarter million votes. The state legislature was overwhelmingly Republican, and for the moment the new administration and legislature continued to seek governmental efficiencies, especially in financial administration. Ohio attained an important new direction in taxation policy in 1929 when it abandoned the uniform rule of taxation, which had not accounted adequately for newly popular forms of personal property, especially intangible property like stocks and other investments. The new tax procedures allowed intangible property to be taxed at a lower rate than real estate, thus improving chances that intangible property would be reported and the tax actually collected. The same amendment limited taxes on real property to fifteen mills but permitted taxing districts to exceed this limit under special conditions.

Governor Cooper confronted serious economic problems whose full impact would be borne by his successors. The great stock market crash of October 1929 was the prelude to America's most serious economic crisis. As economic conditions worsened across the state, the public blamed Cooper and his fellow Republicans in the legislature, even as voters blamed President Hoover on the national scene, for the problems which ensued.

Ohio's Economy in the Postwar Decade

The economy rather than politics preempted public attention in the postwar decade. The wartime boom continued for some Ohio industries through 1919 and on into 1920. For example, employment in Akron tire factories reached a peak in excess of 70,000 workers in 1919–20. The conversion back to civilian goods traumatized some other industries, as did termination of government contracts, a dramatic fall-off in product demand, and labor unrest and militancy. The latter was true in Toledo where Willys-Overland and other major employers were caught in labor conflict as were the steel-making cities on the Cuyahoga, Mahoning, and Ohio.

The industrial record was uneven in the months following the Armistice, but the wartime boom definitely ended in mid-1920 when the nation was rocked by a short but sharp depression. Cities with a balanced economy— Columbus and Cincinnati, for example—were less affected than the steel centers and the automotive centers. Production dropped so fast in the tire plants that about 50,000 blue-collar and white-collar workers were dismissed from their Akron jobs in 1921. Roads leading south from the Rubber City were crowded with folks "going home" to the overworked farms and mines of southern Ohio, West Virginia, and Kentucky.

The postwar economic shakeout brought a temporary end to the successes enjoyed by labor organizers during the war. A large segment of Ohio's work force consisted of immigrants from European nations where syndicalism and radical labor movements were commonplace. Some of these workers were attracted by socialist political philosophies. When they supported union organizing efforts and liberal political candidates, traditionalists—mostly the urban middle class and the farmers—found them threatening to American values and traditions. As a result, they stereotyped many aliens as anarchists, "bolsheviks," communists, and socialists, terms that they used in the most pejorative sense. Violent labor conflicts in the steel and automotive centers where this segment of the labor force concentrated confirmed critics in their belief that foreign ideologies were undermining the American Way.

In 1919 in Toledo the unions struck Willys-Overland. With 15 percent of its industrial work force unemployed, and with returning veterans clamoring for jobs, workers struck to shorten hours, maintain wage levels, and distribute work evenly. They were also angered by Willys's effort to establish a company union. The strike collapsed from company intransigence, adverse court rulings, and hostile public opinion. During a national steel strike that same year, brought on by AFL organizing efforts, an estimated 100,000 workers walked off their jobs in Youngstown, Niles, Warren, Cleveland, Alliance, Canton, Massillon, and Steubenville. In all but a few cases government authorities cooperated with company officers to limit strike activities and protect "scabs" brought in to replace strikers. Many of these recruits were desperate for jobs and willing to run the risk of injury involved in taking jobs in the mills. Among the strikebreakers were unemployed blacks, and racial hostility became another element in the ensuing confusion. The strike collapsed in January 1920 without the strikers achieving any of their goals.

Through the remainder of the twenties, labor was comparatively quiescent. In some plants employers had co-opted the unions by improving working conditions, thus keeping workers loyal. Many Ohio companies were in the forefront nationally of corporate paternalism. National Cash Register was a model employer in the early twentieth century, extending an impressive array of benefits and amenities to its employees. Health care, shower rooms, rest periods, exercise periods, clean and attractive factory buildings, savings plans, athletic teams, a library, a cafeteria, and other attractions helped keep employees loyal to the company. Procter and Gamble, Firestone, Goodyear, Youngstown Sheet and Tube, Willys-Overland, and scores of other important Ohio industrial firms had comprehensive employee benefit plans. Goodyear brought the industrial assembly, a form of worker self-government, to a new level of influence and led the way in constructing high quality housing which employees could buy under favorable terms.

Company paternalism and company unions succeeded in holding the line against major union breakthroughs during the 1920s, but signs of future strain were apparent. The rapid growth of technology threatened to bring a permanent loss of jobs in key industries—steel, heavy machinery, autos, rubber, glass—as labor-saving machines reduced the number of workers required for production. Brute strength was becoming less a prerequisite for factory labor while manual dexterity in synchronization with machines was becoming more important. Between 1920 and 1930, Ohio's industrial work force declined by 4 percent in relation to the total work force. Another ominous shadow on the workers' horizon was the start of a decentralizing process that saw Ohio-based industries begin to build plants in other parts of the country. In its early phases decentralization was a response to market conditions, but it was later used as a weapon against union organizers in the labor-management conflicts of the 1930s.

During the war, wage increases had outpaced cost of living increases by a substantial margin, but workers lost this favorable edge in the late twenties. And the character of the industrial work force was changing as foreign immigration was severely curtailed by the quota acts of the early twenties. The percentage of foreign-born workers fell off substantially while the percentage of native-born whites and blacks increased. Blacks, primarily from the rural South, came to Ohio's industrial cities during the war years, and the flow continued at a modest level through the postwar decade. Blacks represented only 3 percent of the state's population in 1920 and 5 percent in 1930. Few black workers held industrial production line jobs; most of those working in factories did janitorial work or labored on the loading docks.

Like the industrial worker, the farmer also experienced postwar difficulties. Farmers enjoyed high prices throughout the war years, and farm land doubled in value, tempting many farmers to buy additional acreage in what appeared to be a rising market. Shortly after the war, however, farm prices fell; farmers who had bought expensive land on credit and could not meet their payments lost their farms. By 1930 land values had fallen to their lowest levels since 1910. The farm problem was national in scope, and Ohio's problems reflected the wider scene. In Ohio the farm population held its own in absolute numbers during the decade, but as a percentage of the total populace rural population declined from 36 to 32 percent.

The Cities Mature

By 1930 Ohio's major cities had matured into the form they would keep for the next generation. Prosperity had returned to the industrial cities under the benevolent, pro-business policies of the Coolidge and Hoover administrations, and one striking manifestation of urban maturity was the construction of new skyscrapers and commercial buildings. Ohio cities started to take on an appearance that would hold until another building boom changed skylines in the post–World War II era.

Cleveland's population swelled to 900,400 by 1930, making it America's fifth largest city, and predictions were that its residents would soon pass the one million mark. The Forest City's new landmark was the fifty-two-story Terminal Tower, the tallest building between New York and Chicago. The

Tower and its companion buildings were constructed over the tracks of Cleveland's railroad terminal through the efforts of Oris and Mantis Van Sweringen, bachelor brothers who were also developing Shaker Heights into the nation's finest planned residential suburb. The Tower fronted on Public Square, a four-acre space dominated by the Soldiers and Sailors Monument, a massive, busy piece of stonework and sculpture that had been erected in 1894.

Close by Public Square was the Cleveland Public Library, second only to New York's in size and prestige. Other impressive public buildings flanked the library and stretched northward toward the lake along the landscaped Mall. Large new department stores were nearby as was a Cleveland landmark, the Arcade, a multi-storied shopping mall whose open interior was illuminated by great skylights. Several miles to the east of the central business area was University Circle, a handsomely landscaped region featuring Case Institute, Western Reserve University, Severance Hall (the home of the Cleveland Orchestra), the Art Museum, the Western Reserve Historical Society, and other cultural institutions. Running northward from University Circle to the lake, a landscaped parkway featured monuments and "cultural gardens" dedicated to Cleveland's ethnic groups.

A massive new stadium was erected along the lake shoreline, and in the 1940s the Cleveland Indians moved from their old haunts, League Park, into this cavernous structure. Those seeking other kinds of recreation could find it to the east along the lakeshore. Euclid Beach Park was a mecca for thousands who came by trolley, bus, and auto to swim, picnic and enjoy the rides at the city's popular amusement park.

The industrial "flats" along the twisting Cuyahoga River were spanned by monumental new bridges from which one could look down on the steel plants, oil refineries, and other sources of Cleveland's wealth. And Cleveland was a wealthy city despite the maldistribution characteristic of America. Affluent residents were moving to the suburbs. Lakewood, Bay Village, and Rocky River to the west, Bratenahl, Shaker Heights, Pepper Pike, Hunting Valley, and others to the east, were among America's finest residential suburbs. Blue-collar workers also moved to modest, well-kept homes in suburban Garfield Heights, Maple Heights, Brooklyn, and Parma.

Cleveland was a national leader in trying to meet modern problems of poverty, illiteracy, disease, and family trauma. To this end it started the Community Fund in 1919 to secure support for institutions ministering to the needy. From this beginning grew the standard fundraising efforts copied by other cities. For at least the next sixty-five years, Clevelanders gave more per capita to the Community Fund than did residents of any other major city in the country.

At the opposite end of the state, Cincinnati was growing out of its late nineteenth-century civic doldrums. Reform administrations addressed city problems and ameliorated many of them. Like her rival to the north, Cincinnati built a landmark structure. The Carew Tower gave new substance to the city's skyline. Fountain Square was the city's heart, and the unique Tyler-Davidson Fountain (1874) gave it character. Museums and civic structures erected in Eden Park on Mount Adams enhanced the city's well-earned reputation as a cultural center. The art museum, museum of natural history, historical society, and a conservatory graced the area. They shared the neighborhood with workers' houses and the Rookwood Pottery, still producing some of America's finest ceramics. Closer to the city center, the Cincinnati Symphony Orchestra played in the Music Hall. The Hall was close by Central Parkway, a boulevard constructed over the abandoned Miami-Erie Canal. A short distance to the west was Crosley Field, where the National League Cincinnati Reds played. By the early 1930s an enormous new Union Terminal, one of the nation's finest, would rise nearby.

When seeking a day of good fun, Cincinnatians boarded a boat for Coney Island, an amusement park on the city's eastern outskirts. The zoo and the trails of the Mt. Airy preserve attracted others. A model suburban community, Mariemont, rose in the eastern suburbs. As in Cleveland, the very wealthy often migrated some distance into the country, to Indian Hills, for example, where they built estates.

Downtown Columbus was dominated by the Statehouse and its landscaped square. An annex, built in 1914, spoiled the building's symmetry. Monuments on the Statehouse lawn included "My Jewels," a tribute to important Ohio Civil War figures. Across High Street the Neil House accommodated visitors; nearby rose the new Lincoln-Leveque Tower, Columbus's tallest. Improvements along the Scioto River bank held promise for the future attractiveness of the downtown area. Columbus in this era was patronizingly referred to as an "overgrown county seat town," but it had attractions including the Ohio State University, which had recently erected a giant horseshoe-shaped stadium to accommodate the football frenzy associated with the school and the city. A continuing irritation to the city was the Ohio Penitentiary, whose massive walls blocked out twenty-four acres in the near downtown area. Fire in 1930 killed 318 of the 4,000 prisoners, but a call for new quarters went unheeded and half a century later the outmoded structure would still be in partial use.

In Columbus the well-to-do were moving to the suburbs. Bexley to the east remained a favored residential enclave even after it was completely surrounded by Columbus. Upper Arlington and Worthington were outlying areas just on the verge of becoming fashionable.

Toledo, one of the nation's busiest rail centers, dominated the northwestern corner of the state, giving it a considerable market area. Important in lake shipping, oil refining, steel, and the automobile industry, the city boasted a strong industrial base. Glass making had assumed such importance that Toledo became identified as the Glass Capital. The municipal university moved after 1928 into handsome new quarters on the west side of town, and its football stadium in later years briefly hosted the "Glass Bowl." Like Columbus, Toledo's baseball team was minor league, but locals loved their Mud Hens, surely one of the most distinctive names in professional sports. Glass magnates underwrote construction of a superb art gallery and museum which remains a first-class cultural institution. Toledo also won national attention for its zoo. In common with every other Ohio city, Toledo ignored its waterfront, allowing the Maumee to be lined with railroads, power plants, and aging, unsightly commercial structures. Just beyond the waterfront, however, new construction created a substantial skyline. Ottawa Hills was a developing western suburb of distinction, and some Toledoans built fine homes along both sides of the Maumee River toward Perrysburg and the city of Maumee.

Akron, too, experienced a building boom at the end of the twenties. Developed along the old Ohio-Erie Canal, the business district was too long and too narrow for its own good. Its businesses were strung out, making it difficult for them to be mutually supporting and creating a severe problem some thirty years later. The First Central Tower, a skyscraper YMCA building, and other structures gave Akron some impressive buildings, but the downtown was so hemmed in by surrounding hills that its skyline did not show to advantage.

Post–World War I interest in the German zeppelin, plus the industrial surge of the late twenties, brought the zeppelin industry to Akron. To manufacture the world's largest rigid dirigibles, the *Akron* and the *Macon,* the Goodyear Zeppelin Company erected an enormous airdock, once the world's largest structure without internal supports. This engineering wonder covered more than eight acres (about ten football fields) and was so huge that occasionally moisture condensed and it "rained" inside the structure. Akron needed paving, sewers, parks; it was still trying to catch up with capital requirements remaining from the superheated growth between 1910 and 1920. Its wealthy families moved to the west side where Frank Seiberling's authentic, Tudor-style manor house, Stan Hywet, outshone the mansions of the other rubber barons. Seiberling also backed the development of Fairlawn Heights, soon to become a fashionable address.

Akron shared with Cleveland some of the nation's finest parks. Organized in 1919 in Cleveland and 1922 in Akron, the Metropolitan Parks system of the two cities grew along the Cuyahoga and met in later years, preserving splendid scenic portions of the Cuyahoga Valley and surrounding land. For Cleveland the parks were an "emerald necklace" surrounding the city; for Akron they provided welcome escape from a city with too few urban parks. In the

1970s, many of these parks were incorporated into the newly established Cuyahoga Valley National Recreation Area.

Dayton recovered from its 1913 flood with dispatch. Behind new protective levees, the city built an enlarged and improved business center appropriate to a world leader in business machines, electrical equipment, publishing, paper, automotive products, refrigerators, and scores of other manufactured goods. A fine new art institute was built on a commanding site overlooking the city. E. A. Deeds's Carillon Park was becoming a focus of pride. A growing military air complex was developing on Dayton's northeast side, presaging the time when Wright-Patterson Air Force Base would be among the nation's most important facilities. While ethnic neighborhoods dominated the east side and blacks congregated on the west side, Dayton's well-to-do were moving south to Oakwood and Kettering.

Youngstown lived and died with steel, as the city was the hub of the nation's second-largest concentration of steel-making capacity. Fortunes made in the business were reflected in homes which spread out Wick Avenue. Youngstown experienced a building boom in the Twenties, and among its amenities none exceeded Mill Creek Park, which brought natural beauty close to the heart of downtown and provided an appealing play area as well as a setting for some of the city's best residential streets. Nearby, Idora Park provided the commercial pleasures of an amusement park and dance hall.

Canton, which also had a population exceeding 100,000, had faded from the national spotlight since McKinley's death, but the city grew as World War I increased the demand for its steel products. New buildings gave substance to Canton's downtown, and a small central plaza gave it focus. The Timken family contributed to many Canton projects; among early gifts was support for Canton Timken vocational high school. For recreation Cantonians could watch their professional Bulldogs play the Massillon Tigers, the Akron Indians, the Shelby Blues, and other teams in the National Football League, founded in that city in 1922. Meyers Lake amusement park and its dance pavilion attracted thousands who arrived by trolley and by automobile.

Each of Ohio's smaller but substantial cities had some special distinction which made the locals proud. Sometimes it was the heroics of their professional football teams as in Shelby, Ironton, and Portsmouth. Sometimes it was an industrial product with which the city had a special identification. Earth-moving machines of many varieties carried the names of Marion, Lima, Galion, Lorain, and Bucyrus around the world. Specialty steel was made in Middletown, and one of the nation's largest paper manufacturers was located in Hamilton. Springfield boasted one of the largest publishing companies in the country. Lorain, Elyria, Warren, Steubenville, Lancaster, Troy, Sidney, and scores of others grew around their important industries as did Mansfield, which rode the boom in electrical equipment. Nicknames gave distinction to some: Alliance was the Carnation City, Van Wert the Peony City, and Barberton the Magic City. Sandusky was the gateway to the Erie Islands, to the Chautauqua-like summer community at Lakeside, and to Cedar Point, one of America's finest amusement parks. And so it went as Ohio cities large and small sought identity.

Society in Transition

The 1920s have been indelibly fixed in the American mind as the "Roaring Twenties," the "Jazz Age," the "Flapper Era," appellations that suggest an exciting social transition. For a small segment of the American public—the social pace-setters and fashion leaders—it was indeed a period of rapid change, of liberalized sexual mores, of emancipated women, of broadened social horizons. For the vast majority, however, social constraints remained virtually intact. The sons and daughters of middle-class and working-class Americans were expected to conform to the familiar ethical and behavioral standards of their parents—and they did.

But all Americans were influenced by new social forces. Throughout the twenties, educational levels were rising. Mass media first became a significant phenomenon in American life as mass-circulation newspapers and magazines proliferated. Radios, little more than exotic toys at the beginning of the decade, were home fixtures by decade's end—at least in the cities, where electricity was available. Movie theaters proliferated in city and small town alike. The "movies" became "talkies" and extended their influence on the nation's self-image. Henry Ford's Model T put an automobile within the financial range of a vast consuming public, but Ford's competitors were gaining market share by the moment. Automobile ownership gave Americans unparalleled mobility and influenced everything from shopping patterns to courtship practices. Ohioans were exceptionally car-conscious ranking at or near the top of the list in car ownership; Akron vied with Detroit and Los Angeles for the most car registrations per capita in American cities.

Health

In 1918 an epidemic of unprecedented proportion in the industrial age—Spanish influenza—scourged the world, resulting in millions of deaths. In America it hit military installations with special force. At Camp Sherman more than 1,000 soldiers died; volunteer embalmers from throughout the state could scarcely keep up with their morbid task of preparing bodies for burial.

By conservative estimates, some 1.5 million Ohioans contracted the disease and more than 22,000 died, nearly four times the number of Ohioans who died serving in World War I. Schools, churches, and businesses closed; saloons stayed open.

Poliomyelitis was another dread disease which took its yearly toll in the postwar world. Often called infantile paralysis, it struck the young with crippling force. Some Ohio health care facilities, among them the Gates Hospital for Crippled Children in Elyria and Children's Hospital in Akron, earned reputations for excellence in the treatment of this puzzling and devastating disease. In 1962, an oral vaccine developed by Dr. Albert B. Sabin of the University of Cincinnati Medical College advanced the struggle to eradicate polio, building on Dr. Jonas Salk's pioneering 1950s breakthrough toward controlling polio. Tuberculosis continued to affect thousands. Sanatoriums and fresh air camps were standards in the battle against the "white plague." During the 1930s depression, malnutrition increased vulnerability to the disease. Meanwhile the war against two long-time killers was nearly over. Typhoid fever diminished as sanitary water and sewage systems developed, and compulsory inoculation of school children virtually eradicated smallpox.

Social and Political Reactionism

Postwar extremes in social behavior had an impact on Ohio as on the nation. Wartime intolerance carried over into the postwar years as the anti-German emphasis was replaced by anti-radical rhetoric directed against "reds" of all stripes—socialists, communists, anarchists, bolsheviks. From time to time violence supplanted rhetoric. In a "Red May Day" demonstration in Cleveland in 1919, 1 person was killed, 40 injured, and 125 arrested. There was much support in Ohio for A. Mitchell Palmer, attorney general of the United States, who was leading a sweep of aliens which resulted in the deportation of thousands as "undesirables." This anti-foreign thrust was one manifestation of what historian Richard Hofstadter has called "the paranoid style" in American politics.

Another manifestation of that paranoia was in the activities of the Ku Klux Klan, a secret society which spread north from its southern roots and found congenial soil in several of Ohio's urban areas. Klansmen and Klanswomen, noted for their arcane terminology (Kleagles, Klaverns, Kluds, and so forth) and their hooded robes and burning crosses, meant to preserve Americanism as they understood it. To that end they intimidated Catholics, Jews, and blacks, who, in their view, were undermining one hundred percent Americanism.

The Klan enjoyed spectacular success in a few Ohio locales during the

1920s. Klan activity was especially visible in Dayton, Columbus, Springfield, and Akron, where support came from southern whites who were unusually susceptible to the Klan's message. Klansmen in Summit County boasted that its 50,000 members comprised the nation's largest chapter, but the numbers are unverifiable. Whatever their number, they elected an Akron mayor, several judges, the county sheriff, county commissioners, and controlled the Akron school board. As a local judge, once a Klan member, later put it, "If you wanted to get elected in Summit County you had to join the Klan just like you joined the Moose or the Masons." The Klan was opposed by Catholic, Jewish, and black leaders and by many Protestants who regarded it as an aberration in American society. Eventually the Klan overreached itself; local chapters quarreled over dues and the stewardship of money. The organization lost its waning support when an Indiana court convicted a national officer of assault which led to the death of a young woman. During the hard times of the thirties the Klan made a modest comeback in Ohio, but its influence disappeared with the return of prosperity at decade's end.

The kinds of fundamental Christian precepts that groups like the Klan supposedly adhered to were being challenged in the twenties by a strong modernist trend in American Protestantism. The classic confrontation of fundamentalism and modernism took place at the Scopes "Monkey Trial" in 1925 in Dayton, Tennessee. There, Ohioan Clarence Darrow, a nationally prominent criminal lawyer born in Kinsman, lost the battle but won the war. His client, John Scopes, was found guilty of violating a Tennessee law forbidding the teaching of Darwinian evolution, but Darrow's probing questions and sarcasm destroyed the arguments of his adversary, William Jennings Bryan, the defender of the concept of special creation. On a less dramatic level fundamentalism and modernism were in conflict across the land, with Ohio religious leaders very much involved, a struggle that continued through the thirties and into the World War II era. By the war's end, however, most old-line Protestant denominations had adopted the modernist position, including relaxed standards of personal conduct, and fundamentalism became identified with "Bible preaching" focused on the scriptures rather than on social concerns.

Response to Prohibition

Though undertaken with the best of motives, national prohibition quickly became a source of social conflict, a "noble experiment" that did not work nearly so well as its advocates anticipated. Later generations would point to it as a prime example of the futility of trying to legislate morality. Nonetheless, alcohol consumption dropped during prohibition and then remained low after 1933, although those people denied legal access to liquor found extra-legal means of securing it. Some made their own "bathtub gin"; others patronized speakeasies and roadhouses where illegal booze flowed. Immigrants from countries where beer and wine were staples sometimes brewed or distilled their own drinks. On the other hand, other immigrants from the same cultural background were anxious to live within the laws of the United States, even at the sacrifice of their traditional beverages.

Both federal and state enforcement agents were in the field, but they were too few to deal with the magnitude of the problem. They found it impossible to interdict all of the illegal alcohol both professional and amateur bootleggers were trafficking. Along Lake Erie's shore, for example, both amateurs and professionals ran boatloads of illegal liquor from Canada into isolated beaches or into safe harbors where locals conspired to allow the illicit traffic. Gangs who controlled lucrative markets could make huge sums of money, and competition for such markets led to widespread gang warfare. Bootlegging and gambling went hand-in-hand and financed new crime empires. Gang leaders corrupted local law enforcement officers and a fair number of revenue agents. Officers "on the take" made it difficult for the "honest cop" to do his duty, and when prosecutors and judges were involved in payoffs, the criminal justice system broke down.

Nearly every Ohio city and many rural areas had law enforcement problems. A Cleveland newspaper story described Canton as "a lurid little city" having all the vices of Chicago, but on a smaller scale. In 1926 a crusading Canton newspaperman, Don R. Mellet, was killed while conducting a vigorous campaign against local crime. Cincinnati was the operating base for big-time bootleggers, much of whose business was with the notorious, wide-open towns across the Ohio River in northern Kentucky, towns which drew many patrons from the Ohio side. Near Cleveland, roadhouses lured patrons beyond the city limits, where law enforcement was minimal. Cleveland mobsters, financed by liquor sales and gambling, would in time become major crime lords with ties to powerful criminal interests elsewhere.

In some areas the corruption was notable. Gambling flourished in urban centers. The openness with which it operated was directly related to lack of police pressure. Prostitution was also an urban problem. When police efforts proved ineffective a popular Akron evangelist toured the red-light district in his "gospel bus," seeking to convert the girls and shame their clients. Toledo was reputed to be safe for gangsters who were lying low while the "heat" was on in Chicago or Detroit. It took a brave police officer to do his duty in Youngstown, Steubenville, and other eastern Ohio steel towns which were, for the time being, strongholds of bootleggers, gamblers, "white slavers," and other crime figures.

Still, this recitation of crime and corruption should not create the false impression that corruption reigned supreme and that honest, law-abiding citizens were intimidated. A more accurate reading of the times would be that law-abiding citizens were a "silent majority" frustrated by the inability (or unwillingness) of the criminal justice system to shut down bootlegging, gambling, and prostitution. The end of prohibition in 1933 failed to end the influence of organized crime, as the hard times and desperation of the thirties provided the criminal element with further opportunity to maintain its activities.

Ohio During the Great Depression

The economic boom of the late twenties came to a dramatic end presaged by the great stock market crash of October 1929. With the exception of the Civil War, nothing in American history could match the economic and social dislocations brought on by the Great Depression.

As a leading industrial state, Ohio was particularly vulnerable to massive unemployment as companies fought to stay in business by slashing payrolls. Each slash placed more persons among the jobless, thus creating a snowball effect. In 1930 an estimated 13.3 percent of all Ohio workers were unemployed; by 1932 the total reached 37.3 percent, a figure which included 67 percent of Ohio's construction workers and 44 percent of its factory workers. Industrial unemployment was highest in cities tied to steel and auto manufacturing. Cleveland experienced 50 percent industrial unemployment, Youngstown and Akron 60 percent, and Toledo staggered briefly with a reputed 80 percent. Although unemployment did not remain at this level, it was an economic crisis of unparalleled severity.

Factory workers who kept their jobs frequently had their hours reduced, which cut their income by a third or a half. Some manufacturers, notably Akron's tire makers, introduced the six-hour shift in an effort to distribute employment among more workers. Wage reductions averaging 30 percent were common in all segments of the work force. Tax delinquency rose as unemployed and underemployed people could not pay their taxes. Such public employees as school teachers and government workers, whose pay rested on tax collections, suffered severe salary cuts; some were paid in scrip (paper notes to be redeemed by future tax collections).

Desperate people coped as best they could. Some urban workers returned to the farms and small towns from which they had come. Blacks, far removed from their southern origins, tended to remain. Cleveland, Toledo, Akron, Youngstown, Portsmouth, Hamilton, and Lorain lost population during the 1930s. Columbus, however, grew by 15.5 percent, possibly due to the influx of government workers required to administer extensive new social and economic programs. Dayton, Cincinnati, Canton, Warren, Steubenville, and

Lima grew modestly. Statewide, population increased by 260,000 during this decade, which produced the lowest birthrate in United States history.

One must look behind statistics to appreciate the social effect of such widespread economic malaise. Schools opened late in the fall and closed early in the spring. Many banks failed, taking with them the life savings of their depositors. A few bankers, facing hate and social obloquy, committed suicide. Some men of wealth and status were reduced to menial tasks such as selling pencils or apples on street corners. Families foraged about neighborhoods for scraps of food and fuel. "Hoovervilles," small shanty towns built by the poor, sprang up along Cleveland's lake front and elsewhere in the state's larger cities. Shoeless children were kept from school; health needs went unattended. In 1931 Cleveland's Hiram House reported the plight of one working-class neighborhood. Of 234 families, 44 had no visible means of support; 22 lived on garbage; 11 supported themselves through gambling, bootlegging, theft, or prostitution; 9 depended entirely on relatives; 26 relied solely on females for support; and 37 lived on the earnings of delivery boys.

Ohio in common with other states was overwhelmed by the magnitude of its citizens' needs. Gov. George White, a Marietta Democrat, faced enormous problems when assuming office in 1931: voters had unrealistic expectations, and White faced a legislature and other top state officials who were Republicans, which meant he could anticipate a minimum of cooperation. Initially the new governor said that relief for the unemployed and destitute was a local problem. But cities, villages, townships, and counties were overwhelmed, and relief funds were quickly exhausted. The governor responded by recommending state relief allotments.

In March 1931 the legislature authorized local taxing units to borrow and to issue bonds to make up revenue deficiencies caused by a fall-off in tax collections. Shortly thereafter the general assembly permitted counties to issue bonds for relief purposes, increased excise taxes on public utilities to redeem the county bonds, authorized boards of education to supply shoes, clothing, and medical aid to school children, diverted some of the gas tax to local relief, and, in 1932, established the State Relief Commission to coordinate relief activities. A lack of funds hampered the commission's efforts.

Housing and schooling were among the problems the legislature addressed. In August 1933, amendments to the Federal Housing Act permitted the creation of metropolitan housing; that same month Cleveland and Cincinnati officials secured from the general assembly the nation's first enabling legislation for forming metropolitan housing authorities which were to use federal grants to improve housing and clear slums. Although a lack of funds restricted activity, projects were completed under this program in Cleveland, Cincinnati, and, somewhat later, in other cities. Ohio's most interesting housing development of that period was a federal Resettlement Administration proj-

Ohio nativism on parade. The Ku Klux Klan in Springfield, 1923.

Clevelanders wait in a relief line during the Great Depression.

ect near Cincinnati called Greenhills—a new, self-contained model town of
670 family units set in an attractive environment.

Ohio's school crisis was too severe for partial measures to alleviate. The
depression was reducing revenues while interest and debt retirement ate up
between 20 and 30 percent of the budget of many school districts. School
administrators shortened terms and reduced teachers' salaries, but operating
funds remained insufficient. In November 1932, Dr. Paul R. Mort of Columbia University submitted a report to state educators which stated that Ohio
relied too heavily on real property taxes to support its schools. It also argued
that too much responsibility rested in the hands of local school boards. Although legislators were unwilling to adopt the Mort Plan, some of its recommendations had influence, as the state made help available to troubled districts
under the School Foundation Program Law in 1935. This act funneled state
subsidies to school districts according to a formula designed "to enable the
school to operate at a reasonable level of educational efficiency." Enacted as an
emergency measure, the School Foundation Program endured, and for the
next sixty years would be subject to repeated scrutiny and change.

During his second term, Governor White worked with the legislature,
which by now had shifted from Republican to Democratic control, to develop
the most important new tax source in Ohio's recent history. The governor
recommended and the legislature enacted a 3 percent sales tax. The Ohio
Retail Sales Tax Law took effect on January 1, 1935, producing in its first year
$47,848,866, which was distributed for use in schools, local governments, poor
relief, old-age pensions, administration and collections, and county treasuries.

The political shift in Ohio's Statehouse was mirrored nationally, as voters
blamed Republicans for the economic crisis and elected Democrats who promised solutions to the country's woes. In the 1932 presidential election Franklin
Delano Roosevelt defeated the Republican incumbent, Herbert Hoover. FDR's
victory margin in Ohio was 74,000 votes. Norman Thomas of Marion, who
once delivered the *Marion Star* for Warren Harding, ran as the Socialist candidate and was far back in the pack. This was his second presidential race; he was
to run four more times.

A strong Democratic majority swept into the Senate and the House, giving
Roosevelt and congressional leaders the opportunity to enact their "New
Deal." Broad new social and economic programs affected every area of American life. These programs, which extended federal power in areas previously
administered by state and local governments or ignored completely, offended
conservatives. Two of Ohio's depression-era governors, Democrat Martin Davey
and Republican John Bricker, fought these federal intrusions into what they
regarded as the state's preserve.

The new federal recovery programs were numerous and all-pervasive;
many had a profound impact upon Ohio. One of FDR's first acts after his

March 4, 1933, inauguration was to declare a national bank holiday, closing all banks until examiners authorized them to reopen their doors. Many never did, or reopened under new management. This initiative brought some order to the chaotic banking situation. The nation was taken off the gold standard; it was illegal to hoard gold. The federal government printed paper money unsecured by bullion, a move which alarmed fiscal conservatives.

Among those suffering most were the farmers. In the early thirties Ohio experienced severe droughts and erratic weather which, when coupled with weak market prices, pushed thousands of farmers toward economic disaster. Under the Agricultural Adjustment Act (AAA) of 1933, Ohio farmers participated in programs designed to reduce inventories by withholding produce and livestock from the market. Although it was declared unconstitutional in 1936, the AAA benefited Ohio farmers, as farm cash income rose from $157,138,000 in 1932 to $355,553,000 in 1937, an increase of 126 percent. In this same period, farm real estate values climbed by 27 percent while taxes on farm real property declined. Ohio farmers also cooperated with the Soil Conservation and Domestic Allotment Act of 1936 by replacing soil-depleting crops like tobacco with soil-enriching crops like alfalfa. For their participation they received nearly $10 million in payments from the federal government.

The farmer also benefited from electrification, now widely available under the Rural Electrification Act. In some sections of the state, local cooperatives had already brought power to rural areas. But the representative from Ohio's Eleventh Congressional District (southcentral Ohio) reported in 1937 that only about 10 percent of the farms in his district were electrified before the new program went into effect. Now, he said, the REA, working through farmer's cooperatives, was rapidly spreading electric power throughout his district, bringing "much comfort and happiness to the people." Despite these and many other forms of federal assistance, farmers weren't out of economic trouble until World War II sent farm prices soaring.

Among the most dramatic federal programs were those designed to bring economic relief to the needy and the unemployed. Pre–New Deal relief was direct relief—payments in the form of outright grants—to the needy, the old-age pensioner, and the unemployable. Direct relief relied on state and local money, and the State Relief Commission and local agencies administered the programs.

Other types of relief required the recipient to work for a wage. Work relief plans or, as their opponents called them, "make-work" programs, became the largest conduit for funneling federal money into the pockets of the unemployed. These programs showed a startling variety as the government experimented to find the most effective and least costly—or the most politically expedient—program. Among the first work relief programs was the

Civilian Conservation Corps (CCC), established in 1933 to employ needy young men in healthy body- and character-building outdoor work. Billeted in quasimilitary barracks and directed by army personnel, these young men built parks and flood control projects, fought forest fires, planted seedlings, cleared forest lands, and generally upgraded the physical environment. Among their many projects was erosion control and reforestation in the Muskingum Conservancy District and the building of roads, shelters, playing fields, bridle paths, and other improvements in metropolitan and state parks. Between 12,000 and 14,000 men per year were enrolled in Ohio camps. They were paid $30 per month and had to send $25 back home, where it helped hard-pressed relatives to survive.

The CCC was widely applauded and thus spared the hostility directed at other federal work relief programs. The Civil Works Administration, Federal Employment Relief Administration, Public Works Administration, National Youth Administration, and Works Progress Administration, all put unemployed persons on federal payrolls. Conservatives feared recipients of federal money would not really earn wages. They believed people who really wanted to work would keep looking until they found jobs, and that being on a government payroll would lessen both the moral fiber and the will to work. On the other hand, desperate people securing these jobs saw them as short-term salvation until the return of good times made jobs available in the private sector.

Of these various programs the Works Progress Administration (WPA) was the largest and most far-reaching, hence the most controversial. The WPA was authorized by the Emergency Relief Appropriation Act of 1935. Harry Hopkins, former director of the Federal Employment Relief Administration (FERA), was named program director and enrollment of workers began in July 1935. All WPA projects had to be approved by Washington. The state had little control, which caused serious friction between federal and state officials. Despite these differences WPA got off to a fast start in Ohio; within eight months 187,000 persons were working in both skilled and unskilled positions. In addition to construction, the program created jobs for unemployed writers, artists, musicians, actors, and other professionals. In September 1938 there were twelve Ohio counties in which more than 25 percent of the families had at least one family member on WPA. In October of that year 287,000 Ohioans were on the payroll, the largest contingent in the nation.

No final tally of WPA work in Ohio is available, but a small inkling of what the program accomplished can be garnered by looking at Summit County (Akron) alone. There workers constructed 40 miles of sewers and water mains; paved or reconditioned 600 miles of streets and roads; reconditioned 381 public buildings, including every school building; built 17 new public structures; constructed a classroom building and reconditioned the campus of the municipal university; paved and extended runways at the municipal airport; built the 35,000-seat stadium that came to be known as the Akron Rubber Bowl; built 46 playgrounds and parks, including Cuyahoga Falls' Waterworks Park and its mammoth swimming pool; and constructed Mogadore and Nimisila Reservoirs to guarantee Akron's industrial water supply. In addition to these permanent improvements, WPA workers gave public concerts and plays, conducted sewing classes, indexed the local newspaper, made school lunches, and performed other useful services.

Since relief projects were designed to keep people employed, there were times when a work force was put on a non-productive job. Critics seized upon occasional leaf raking to stereotype the entire program as specious and worthless. Indeed, among its many worthy projects Summit County did have at least one massive boondoggle: a huge, elaborate cut-stone staircase, estimated to cost many thousands of dollars, which ran up unpopulated Glendale Hill, from nowhere, to nowhere.

Ohio's largest depression-era public works project was the development of the Muskingum Conservancy District. The drainage basin of the Muskingum and its tributaries cover one fifth of the state. Floods were endemic in this watershed, especially around Zanesville, whose citizens organized in 1933 and secured authority under the Ohio Conservancy Act to proceed with flood control measures. The Army Corps of Engineers designed and operated impoundment dams, most of which created permanent reservoirs, but CCC and WPA workers handled soil erosion control, reforestation, and related projects. The original project plans were fulfilled in 1938 at a cost of $43,500,000; since that time many new reservoirs and recreational areas have been added, especially during the administrations of Gov. James A. Rhodes.

The constructive work accomplished under federal programs was accompanied by political wrangling and bitterness. Generally Ohio fared well because the Roosevelt administration, for political purposes, directed a great deal of federal funding to it. During the administrations of governors Davey and Bricker, however, it appeared that Ohio was being punished by the federal administration for the barely concealed hostility which these governors directed at Washington's programs.

Martin L. Davey, a Kent tree surgeon, won the governor's chair in 1934 by a modest margin over his Republican opponent, Clarence J. Brown. Two years later Davey defeated John W. Bricker in the Democratic landslide which swept Franklin D. Roosevelt back into office. FDR carried Ohio by 600,000 votes and piled up similar margins in other states. The magnitude of the Democratic victory appeared to be a strong endorsement of the New Deal program, including work relief.

Davey appeared unimpressed by the New Deal's popularity and kept up a running feud with federal authorities over what he felt was their interference in state affairs and their wasteful mismanagement of federal programs. Federal employees, he claimed, were preempting jobs traditionally carried out by county, township, and local officials. Davey was especially aggrieved when federal case workers were sent into the Ohio countryside to check on eligibility for relief. "This [federal] policy of sending strangers into most of the counties of Ohio as administrators and case workers is responsible for many conditions that give rise to complaint," he said. One federal official "had frequent drinking parties in the office at night." Another "required the girls in the office to go out on parties with him in order to keep their jobs." No doubt certain inadequate persons were employed in these federal programs, but could the governor be sure that similar practices did not go on when local officials ran things? Davey did not comment.

The governor's attacks on federal programs had serious consequences. Washington officials charged Davey with corruption (although the charges were never proved), and temporarily stopped relief money from coming into the state. When the money flow resumed, federal supervision was tighter than before.

Davey was succeeded as governor by the Republican John W. Bricker, a Columbus lawyer. Bricker's conservative Republican values were out of tune with those of the federal administration, and he was highly critical of the New Deal. He charged the Roosevelt administration with allowing "public assistance in Ohio to become a football of disgraceful partisan politics in Washington."

Bricker was pledged to economy in government (always a potent appeal to Ohio voters) and took pride in paring expenses; indeed, he created a surplus. He claimed the support of the general assembly in this effort, but state authorities were hard-pressed to meet relief needs in 1939 when wholesale layoffs in the state's WPA programs occurred. Some observers claimed the layoffs were a means by which federal administrators punished Ohio for its intransigence regarding administration of federal programs.

The governor's tight money policies faced opposition from certain strong men of his own party. Cleveland's Republican mayor, Harold H. Burton (later a senator and Supreme Court justice), led a delegation to Columbus seeking money from the state surplus to help his city meet urgent relief needs. Bricker suggested alternative means of securing funds, but newspapers played up Cleveland's problems until it appeared there was actually starvation in the city, and the story went out over the news wires, to the embarrassment of the city and state. Bricker released some state aid, Cleveland officials checked certain abuses that had drained relief funds, and the crisis passed. Bricker survived many such crises and was reelected to two additional terms. By the time he left office his political success in a Democratic era had made him a national figure in Republican circles.

Throughout the troubled thirties disenchantment with America's capitalist economy was unprecedented. Although most citizens were willing to stick with the existing system, its apparent inability to cope with political and social problems radicalized many others. They were visible beyond their numbers. Most were on the political left; many were Communists. The rise of fascist dictatorships in Europe during the decade enhanced their legitimacy by allowing them to pose as defenders of freedom against the tyranny of fascist governments.

Ohio was not a particular hotbed of leftist activity although cells existed in every city and on many college campuses, where their influence was noisy but never strong. Many students and professors who joined communist front organizations for what seemed at the time to be compelling reasons, found themselves suspect when McCarthyism and the loyalty mania hit the nation following World War II. One interesting manifestation of idealistic action, supported by the political left, was the effort on several Ohio campuses to ban the Reserve Officers Training Corps (ROTC). The Communists may have had a hidden agenda for condemning ROTC, but many students were simply against any form of compulsory military training. As warlike tensions increased throughout the world, peace activists increased their organizing efforts directed at eliminating all vestiges of support for the military. In Ohio they were again led by members of the traditional peace churches and by campus activists.

Organized Labor on the March

Union organizing efforts languished during the late 1920s, but the severe economic problems of the thirties gave organizers a fertile field of discontent in which to work, and the New Deal created a climate in which labor unions would reach their full potential. Federal planners responsible for labor's new opportunities were motivated by sympathy for the workers' plight, by their powerlessness against management, and by evidence that revolutionaries were finding a hearing among the unemployed. Political strategists also saw a chance to make organized labor part of a newly emerging Democratic coalition.

In 1933 Congress enacted the National Industrial Recovery Act (NIRA), under which hundreds of industries formulated codes of fair competition. Cooperating businesses displayed the "blue eagle" logo in their windows. Section 7(a) of the law was of special importance for labor: it guaranteed workers the right to organize and bargain collectively with their employers.

By placing its blessing on union organizing, the federal government set off a spurt of activity as workers flooded AFL offices seeking to join a union.

Many of these workers had no specific craft. They were production-line workers, and the AFL was not geared toward their needs. Although AFL leaders tried their hand at organizing industrial workers, their efforts appeared half-hearted and inefficient.

During this formative period, impatient workers conducted scores of wild-cat strikes, though without experienced leadership, their efforts usually floundered. Some manufacturers used strong company unions to fight off organizing efforts. Goodyear, for example, fragmented workers' loyalty by playing off the company union against the AFL's bumbling organizing efforts. Meanwhile certain other manufacturing companies were stockpiling tear gas and weapons in anticipation of industrial warfare.

Two landmark strikes in 1934 gave evidence of things to come. Toledo had suffered as severely as any American city during the Depression's early years, and its masses of unemployed workers were in a rebellious mood. Communists and other political radicals played on their desperation, encouraging them to strike for their rights under the benevolent protection of the federal government. Workers struck the Auto-Lite plants in the spring; the company reacted by hiring 1,800 strikebreakers, setting the stage for violence. In the desperate weeks which followed, Governor White sent the National Guard to protect people and property, but unionists claimed the guardsmen were there as strikebreakers. Although the strikers won some concessions, they returned to work dissatisfied with their lot and nursing grievances against their employer.

Meanwhile, seventy miles to the south in rural Hardin County, labor violence erupted in the onion fields. The onion growers were all-powerful in the region, supported by local residents whose well-being was in large part dependent upon the onion crop. Migrant laborers from Kentucky and Tennessee worked the fields and increasingly were staying the year round in Hardin County, where most lived in squalor and existed on relief. To the locals they were undesirables.

In June the Agricultural Workers Union, representing these migrants, struck for higher wages, and in the ensuing violence, Okey Odell, the union president, was badly beaten. The growers hired strikebreakers and ultimately, as historian Bernard Sternsher wrote, "vigilantes loaded insurgents into trucks and dumped them across the state line." This bitter struggle had elements of class struggle, of locals versus outsiders, that set it apart from most Ohio labor confrontations. It was also one of the nation's first strikes involving a union of agricultural workers.

The momentum organizers received from the NIRA appeared to be lost in May 1935 when the Supreme Court ruled the act unconstitutional, but that same month Congress passed the Wagner-Connery Act, known as "labor's magna carta," which reenacted the provisions of section 7(a) of the NIRA, in effect making the federal government labor's ally. The act established the National Labor Relations Board to referee labor elections and disputes. The board seldom ruled against labor's larger interests, but when it did fail to provide the support unionists wanted, direct appeals were made to the Department of Labor and its influential secretary, Frances Perkins.

The inability, or unwillingness, of the AFL to organize industrial workers created a schism in labor's ranks in the mid-thirties. In 1935 John L. Lewis, the aggressive and effective head of the United Mine Workers, led a faction which by 1938 had severed its ties with the AFL and had formed the CIO (Committee—later Congress—of Industrial Organizations). More susceptible than the AFL to the influence of radicals, and prone to violence in strikes, the CIO won the battle with management in industry after industry.

The union's first major success in heavy industry was its organizing effort among rubber workers, heavily concentrated in Akron. In 1936–37, more than a quarter million workers struck Ohio employers, and setting the tone for many of these strikes was the rubber industry strike of 1936, which focused on the contest at Goodyear. Rubber workers in the Akron plants rebelled against speed-ups and reduced wages for piece work. Determined to win the right to organize, Goodyear workers shut down production lines and sat down at their work stations. This "sit-down" strike technique had proved effective two years before at a General Tire strike. Employers could not risk bringing in strikebreakers for fear of sabotage and bloody conflict; strikers could maintain strike discipline and morale, at least in instances where the work stoppage was authorized. Although Akron Mayor Lee D. Schroy opposed the strikers, he was none too successful in persuading his police to keep picket lines open so that "loyal" workers could enter the plants. When the police massed forces to carry out the mayor's wish, 500 law officers marching toward the Goodyear plants on East Market Street were faced down by thousands of strikers and their allies from other local rubber companies, hastily assembled to forestall them. The lawmen stopped in their tracks, and the picketing continued.

In the fall of 1941, on the eve of America's entry into World War II, Goodyear signed a contract with the United Rubber Workers (CIO), the last of the major Akron firms to do so. This victory for the CIO is said to mark the first successful effort to organize a major heavy industry under the banner of industrial unionism.

Bitter strikes were occurring in many other industries, some relatively small like the Ohio Insulator Company strike in Barberton, some of major scope, like the strike against Cleveland's Fisher Body plant. The 1937 "Little Steel" strike in which the CIO attempted to organize plants of Bethlehem, Inland, Republic, and Youngstown Sheet and Tube was a classic organizing conflict. Union organizers, flush with success in organizing the giant of the industry, United States Steel, encountered intense anti-union sentiment among leaders of little steel, especially Tom Girdler of Republic, which had plants in Cleveland, Massillon, Canton, and Youngstown. Much of the violence associated with the strike occurred in the Mahoning Valley where Youngstown Sheet and Tube, one of the more benevolent, paternalistic employers in the steel business, was set to do battle. Industrial police were hired to reinforce company guards. The strikers used mass picketing; sympathizers were brought from a distance to support local men and women on the picket lines. When bloodshed ensued, Governor Davey sent the National Guard to maintain order, but in effect this move broke the strike. The CIO ("Collapsed in Ohio," according to its enemies) was temporarily derailed but, four years later, in elections supervised by the National Labor Relations Board, the union won recognition and signed contracts with Little Steel.

Organized labor learned important lessons during the turmoil of the late 1930s. First, industries heavily concentrated in a single geographic region (as was tire and tube manufacturing in Akron and steel making in the Mahoning Valley) made good targets since organizers could concentrate their efforts effectively, and strikers at one company got support from their counterparts at other company plants in the vicinity. Second, the sit-down was a two-edged sword. A handful of malcontents could shut down an entire production line at any time to frustrate management, but wildcat work stoppages also frustrated union leaders who were trying to establish discipline in the ranks. Third, harsh action by the police and company guards played into the strikers' hands. Public sympathy was aroused when strikers suffered physical beatings. Considerate response to organizing strikers undercut their effectiveness. During the rubber strikes, for example, Firestone nearly killed its local with reasonableness. Fourth, local union leaders were essential tacticians for carrying out the broad strategies formulated in concert with organizers from national headquarters.

Under the protection of the Wagner Act and the National Labor Relations Board, organized labor scored spectacular gains despite the depressed economy. In the thirties Ohio's industrial growth rate sagged by a negative 24 percent (the national average dipped 19 percent), and the state lost 20 percent of its industrial workers. Nevertheless, union membership more than tripled. More importantly, workers' attitudes were affected. There is much evidence that employees no longer felt powerless, and this in turn contributed to a growing sense of self-worth. To the extent that the worker had a voice in his union, he had a voice in his future welfare.

Labor's gains were not without a price. In the short run, men and women who retained jobs earned higher wages, but other workers were let go. While Goodyear was increasing the wages of its newly unionized workers, it was dismissing some 15,000 tire builders. Many of these were ultimately rehired when war contracts brought a business recovery in the early 1940s.

The surge of war-related industry concealed momentarily a condition that had substantial long-range consequences for Ohio. Manufacturers in steel, rubber, and other heavy products saw how vulnerable their geographic concentration made them. They determined to disperse manufacturing operations, to build new plants in states where the unions were not welcome. This was just one of many considerations which resulted in the relocation of industrial production facilities outside Ohio, but it was an important one. It might be said that Ohio's reputation as a high-cost labor state, and as a state prone to militant union activity, had its origins in the organizing struggles of the 1930s.

꧁꧂

15.

World War II and Its Aftermath

 **As the 1930s** drew to a close, Americans were increasingly aware of the threat posed by deteriorating conditions in Europe and Asia. Aggressive authoritarian regimes in Germany, Italy, and the Soviet Union, coupled with the determination of Japanese warlords to extend their Greater East Asia Co-Prosperity Sphere, boded ill for the ultimate peace and security of the United States.

Despite the ominous implications of this aggression, Americans were seriously divided on how to respond. Isolationists claimed that no vital United States interests were at stake. Among those calling on the president to show restraint was Sen. Robert A. Taft. This Cincinnati Republican, son of the former president, had served in the state legislature before defeating Robert Bulkley in the Ohio Republican landslide of 1938. Tall, scholarly, somewhat abrupt in manner, Taft soon mastered the intricacies of domestic legislative matters. His touch was less sure in foreign affairs, but there too he learned how to achieve through accommodation what he could not achieve through stubborn independence. In the process, he became a highly visible Republican leader in Congress and a force in world affairs.

With presidential urging, Congress moved closer to a war footing by enacting a "cash and carry" policy in 1939. Without relinquishing its claim to neutral status, America could now supply goods to any nation which would pay cash and carry the goods away. There was little doubt that this policy would be of greatest assistance to Great Britain; she and her allies desperately needed it, for on September 1, 1939, Hitler unleashed his blitzkrieg against Poland. He was soon joined by his momentary ally, Joseph Stalin, in the dismemberment of that country. Hitler's attack caused Great Britain and France to declare war on the Axis powers. By late summer, 1940, German armies had overrun Norway, Denmark, the Low Countries, and much of France. Great Britain stood alone against the Nazi juggernaut.

In September 1940, Congress passed the Burke-Wadsworth Act establishing America's first peacetime draft. The Ohio National Guard was called into federal service in 1940 under its historic designation, the 37th Division, and commenced training at Camp Shelby, Mississippi. Guard units from other states were called as well. In 1941 Congress stepped up aid to embattled Britain and her allies through a liberal "lend-lease" policy designed to provide them with war materiel; Senator Taft, at that time an isolationist, said, "Lending war equipment is . . . like lending chewing gum. You don't want it back." Congress also passed, by a single vote, an extension of the draft.

Each of these moves to place America in a state of preparedness stimulated isolationists to new protests. They charged President Roosevelt with rushing the nation toward war. However, all substantial opposition vanished on December 7, 1941, a "date which will live in infamy," when Japan unleashed a devastating surprise attack on the American naval base at Pearl Harbor, Hawaii. The nation was now united in its determination to defeat the "evil" regimes that had plunged the world into conflict.

Ohio on the Eve of War

As the nation moved toward war, a residue of the New Deal work relief programs remained in place, but they were not needed for long. Soaring employment in war-related industries brought jobs to nearly every able-bodied man or woman. Full employment temporarily solved the nation's most pressing economic problem, but wartime conditions brought myriad new problems to be addressed by political leaders.

In January 1939, state government in Ohio was firmly in Republican hands. Gov. John W. Bricker's economic austerity proved popular with the voters and with the Republican-dominated legislature. In 1940 Bricker campaigned for reelection, calling attention to his "firing" of 2,000 state employees (many of them Davey appointees) and his maintenance of a balanced budget without the help of new taxes. His opponent, Martin L. Davey, was haunted by his reputation for controversy and lost by 365,000 votes. The legislature remained in Republican control. The popular mayor of Cleveland, Republican Harold H. Burton, now joined Taft in the United States Senate.

Some Ohio Republicans had put Taft forward as a possible presidential candidate in 1940, but the nomination went to a political newcomer, Wendell L. Willkie. A native of Indiana, Willkie was a Wall Street lawyer and businessman who had practiced law in Akron in the 1920s. His only chance of defeating Roosevelt lay in popular opposition to FDR's attempt to secure a third term. Though many chastised Roosevelt for violating the long-standing two-term limit, he won handily, securing Ohio's electoral votes by a comfortable margin.

Though Democrats controlled the federal administration during the war years, Republicans were in charge in Ohio. Governor Bricker did not wait for actual hostilities before putting Ohio in a proper defense posture. The administration recruited and trained an Ohio State Guard for protection during the absence of the National Guard. Bricker established a Defense Council to coordinate industrial planning with national defense needs. The state Manpower Council in 1940 made one of the first state studies of employment needs under conditions of full wartime employment.

Bricker's handling of affairs received strong voter endorsement in 1942 when the governor easily defeated John McSweeney of Wooster, thus becoming the first Republican governor to serve three consecutive terms. This election revealed the basic conservatism that runs so deep in Ohio politics. The voters sent no fewer than fourteen Republicans of isolationist bent to Congress, where, with Senator Taft, they were critical of administration policies not only in domestic affairs, but also in the conduct of the war.

Wartime Industry and Labor

In the American "boom and bust" economy, war promotes prosperity. This truth was especially evident in World War II, when the contrast between high wartime employment and wages contrasted sharply with the depressed conditions immediately preceding it.

Prosperity came first to the farm, Ohio's largest industry, as the enormous demand for foodstuffs created by the armed forces and America's allies sent prices up. By 1945 farm income had risen 191 percent over the 1939 level. Since many farm workers joined the military or took jobs in the cities, the number of farm workers actually declined as did the number of acres under cultivation. Nevertheless, farm production rose by 30 percent during the war years. The farmers' real income rose substantially since what they made on sales ran well ahead of general increases in the cost of living.

Migrant workers, mostly Mexicans and West Indians, eased the labor shortage during critical periods. In addition, by 1943 more than 8,000 German and

Italian prisoners of war were billeted in Ohio, where they worked on farms and in food-processing plants in Bowling Green, Celina, Defiance, and other points. Some prisoners worked in hospitals and in manufacturing concerns.

Food shortages were common despite the heroic farm effort. To supplement the food supply a massive "victory garden" movement was initiated. Individuals, organizations, businesses, and communities mobilized to sponsor garden plots. Many businesses provided land, tools, fertilizer, and seeds to their employees. Ohioans responded enthusiastically, planting more than a million gardens with produce valued at $150 million.

Before the war Ohio was the nation's fourth largest producer of industrial products, a statistic disproportionately skewed toward heavy manufacturing—iron and steel, heavy machinery, automotive products, tires—the very products upon which the wartime economy would rest. Through the war years, about a million workers served 933 key war industries within Ohio. Cleveland was Ohio's largest producer of war goods with contracts totalling $5 billion; Cincinnati ($3.4 billion), Akron ($2.1 billion), and Dayton ($1.7 billion) followed. Then came Youngstown, Toledo, and Columbus with over $1 billion each in contracts.

Among hundreds of key industries Ohio was strongest in aircraft, ordnance, and shipbuilding. A spectacular development occurred in Akron where Goodyear Aircraft, a subsidiary of Goodyear Tire and Rubber Company, manufactured airplanes without having prior experience. In less than two years, the company built massive plants and staffed them with more than 30,000 workers, most of whom had to be newly trained. By war's end they had produced 4,000 Corsair fighters for the Navy and Marine Corps plus component parts for twenty-one other aircraft. Achievements of this sort were commonplace nationally, although few were of this magnitude.

While Ohio industries produced huge quantities of war materiel, the federal government established large armaments operations in the state. Near Ravenna the United States government cleared more than 30 square miles of Portage County farmland for a massive arsenal that specialized in artillery shells, in the process forcing about 300 families, mostly farmers, off their land. Four thousand workmen knocked down homes and other buildings and built the installations. One local woman, among those dispossessed, recalled years later, "They paid us and gave us ninety days to get out. We all went friendly," she said, though consternation at the suddenness of the move was understandable. To accommodate the 15,000 new workers, federal housing was erected at Windham and other nearby communities. Another large arsenal was located at Rossford in suburban Toledo, and Marion, Lima, Columbus, and other Ohio locations maintained federal ordnance plants and activities. Federally operated tank plants at Lima, Brook Park, and elsewhere were a natu-

ral in a state long associated with the production of heavy vehicles. But the
G.I.'s favorite vehicle was anything but heavy. It was the omnipresent Jeep,
manufactured by Toledo's Willys-Overland Company.

Ohio played a central role in the development of what some have called the
second most important scientific breakthrough of the war. America's development of synthetic rubber on a commercially feasible basis was only overshadowed by the advent of atomic power later in the war. The Allies desperately needed an alternative material for tires and other wartime uses because
Japanese control of the Pacific meant they also held the sources of natural
rubber. In Akron the tire companies, in cooperation with government and
other industrial personnel, perfected a product that was an essential rubber
substitute, and Akron became the site of the nation's first pilot plant to produce these synthetics.

Industrial expansion opened more job opportunities than the Ohio labor
force could handle. As in the first world war, industrial recruiters scoured the
countryside for workers. Skilled labor was in such short supply that retirees
were called back to work. Men physically disqualified for the draft had their
choice of jobs. For example, in Akron a large number of hearing-impaired
employees took over positions in the rubber factories.

Women poured into the labor market, taking on jobs of nearly every description, ranging from heavy production-line work to high-precision tasks.
Some manufacturing plants were "manned" entirely by women. By 1944, 40
percent of Dayton's industrial workers were women; Columbus and Akron
also approached this figure. Statewide, women comprised about 30 percent of
the wartime work force.

The presence of women in the workplace in such numbers led to adjustments. Resentment on both sides often made relationships with male co-
workers difficult at the beginning. Women were paid far less than their male
counterparts, and many unions spurned them. On the other hand, many males
held the old prejudices about women in the workplace. Even practical matters as mundane as modification of washrooms and other physical facilities
had to receive attention as women entered previously male-dominated work
environments. By war's end, however, "Rosie the Riveter" of production-
line fame was accepted as part of the industrial environment. Like the woman
bus driver, she had convinced the skeptics that she could handle the job.

Southern blacks provided another industrial labor source. Booming northern industries attracted an unprecedented northward flow of largely poor,
rural blacks who found jobs in northern cities but who also faced discrimination there. Even though workers were in short supply, many blacks were
confined to menial jobs until the need was so acute that the more fortunate
moved into semi-skilled and skilled positions. By 1945 blacks constituted 8
percent of Ohio's skilled work force. As a result of this influx, 513,000 blacks
lived in Ohio in 1950, comprising 6.5 percent of the total population.

Another source of new workers was the surplus population of Appalachia; as in World War I, white upland southerners flocked to Ohio. This mass movement was not carefully tracked, so that no accurate measure of its magnitude is possible. Jack T. Kirby, a student of this migration, estimates that by 1950 about 568,000, or 7.2 percent of the state's population, came from the southern highlands. This figure does not include native Ohioans who migrated to the industrial cities from the worn-out farming and mining sections in Ohio's segment of Appalachia. In Hamilton, Middletown, Cincinnati, Dayton, and Columbus, southern white Appalachians constituted a significant population grouping. The northeastern Ohio cities attracted people largely from southern Ohio and West Virginia, where a considerable number had kinfolk who had made a similar northward trek in the World War I era.

Newcomers from whatever source, many of them ill-equipped for urban life, placed a burden on the cities, contributing to a shortage of housing, fuel, transportation, food, and clothing. Cities built temporary housing in "projects" or tracts and devised makeshift transportation systems to move thousands of workers to distant workplaces at all hours of the day and night. Newly crowded schools erected temporary additions or used church facilities and other buildings to accommodate swelling enrollments.

On the whole, throughout Ohio and the entire nation, war affected every facet of life. Nearly everyone had a family member, relative, or close friend in the military service. Civilian morale rose and fell with news from the war fronts. Shortages of consumer goods required rationing of familiar products like gas, tires, meat, and dairy products. People were urged to conserve fuel and energy, some observing "brownouts" when electric companies reduced current. Scrap metal drives cleaned the junk out of farm yards and city lots. Male enrollment on college campuses dropped dramatically, except on those campuses that hosted military training units. Such schools maintained intercollegiate athletics while less-favored schools cancelled them for the duration. In professional sports the absence of front-line players who had left to serve in the military was noticeable in the low level of play, but most programs continued to operate as a contribution to morale.

Unions Find New Strength

The war period was one of confusion for organized labor. While many industrial unions experienced great growth, some were too new to have developed effective leadership and discipline in the ranks before the war changed the texture and the tenor of the work force. New workers who were unfamiliar with the cooperation required for effective operation swamped production lines. Women and blacks were discriminated against although the CIO unions were more receptive to them than were the AFL craft unions.

Workers were often under great tension. Some worked seven days a week and put in long hours of overtime. Production lines moved at an unrelenting pace; work environments were frequently unsanitary and unsafe. After finishing a hard day's (or night's) work, men and women had to deal with shortages, long waits in lines, inadequate housing and services, family problems, and occasional bad news from the fighting fronts. It is little wonder that emotions became strained and tempers flared.

Labor had pledged a no-strike policy in war-related industries, but growing discontent led workers to disregard their own union leaders. By 1943 more than 300,000 Ohio workers were involved in 467 work stoppages. There was no improvement the next year as rank-and-filers defied efforts by union leaders to keep production lines moving. Toledo, Cleveland, and Cincinnati were storm centers of discontent. On a few occasions wildcat strikers defied their local and national leaders, the company officials, and public opinion in strikes so critical that military officers were sent to get production moving again.

Strikers found little sympathy from many quarters. Local newspapers often criticized them, writing that while things might be bad on the job, they were a whole lot worse on the fighting fronts. Soldiers and sailors earning $21 a month (the initial pay level of new draftees in 1940) often resented striking civilians earning many times that amount and having the freedom and safety to spend it as civilians; a common sentiment among the troops was, "If they don't want to work, draft them!" Despite organized labor's problems, negative image, and setbacks during the war years, it made great strides in membership, which rose nationally by about 60 percent, and in Ohio, which emerged from the war as a strong union state.

Military Units

In the second world war, as in the first, few military units comprised men from a single state. Ohio men and women served all over the globe, and seldom were they in units with a distinctly Ohio flavor.

An exception was the Thirty-seventh Division, commanded by Major General Robert Beightler. During its Camp Shelby training period, its strength was doubled with newcomers from other states. Soon after Pearl Harbor the division sailed for the Fiji Islands, where it helped protect Australia and New Zealand. Later it fought well in the Southwest Pacific campaign in New Georgia, Bougainville, and on Luzon in the Philippine Islands. Other Ohio units included Company C of the 192nd Tank Battalion. These northwestern Ohio men attempted to repel Japanese landings on Luzon in 1941, but were captured along with other American soldiers. Remnants of the unit partici-

The 37th Division, comprised mainly of Ohioans, on duty in the South Pacific.

pated in the infamous Bataan Death March to Japanese prison camps. The
112th Engineer Combat Battalion, originally part of "Cleveland's Own"
112th Engineer Combat Regiment, arrived in Great Britain soon after America entered the war and later fought in Normandy and in the sweep across
France. The 174th Field Artillery Battalion fought at the siege of Brest in
France and in the Battle of the Bulge.

Conscientious objectors, mostly from Ohio's traditional peace churches,
provided a little-known aspect of wartime service. Hundreds of them accepted alternative service by working on farms, in hospitals, and other services depleted of male workers. Some worked out of Civilian Public Service
Camps, including one operated by the Friends Service Committee and the
Soil Conservation Service at Coshocton, which operated for four years beginning in 1942. Designed for 150 men, it received its first contingent early
in 1942; the camp closed four years later. The Mennonites maintained small
camps at Tiffin and Marietta. Hard-core war resisters, those who refused to
render any support service as a matter of conscience, were incarcerated for
the duration, many of them in the Chillicothe Federal Correctional Institution.

It is difficult to get an accurate total of Ohio men and women who served
in military units. The number depends on what is counted as military service.
Roughly 12 percent of Ohio's population, an estimated 839,000 men and
women, served in some military capacity. Of these about 23,000 were killed
or missing in action.

World War II ended on a somber note. In August 1945, Paul Tibbets of
Columbus piloted the *Enola Gay* on a mission over Japan, delivering an atomic
bomb that devastated Hiroshima and ushered in the atomic age. At the time,
the use of this fearsome instrument was widely regarded as a justifiable and
necessary means of forcing Japanese surrender without an invasion, a move
which military planners estimated might cost a million American casualties.
Later, as the magnitude of this new threat to life became evident, many people
had second thoughts; its use represented the ultimate rejection of the old
tribal concept that war was glorious and that honor was to be won on the field
of battle.

Perhaps that recognition had something to do with the rapidity with which
the many legitimate heroes of World War II faded from public memory. One
whose heroism remained in the public consciousness was Pvt. Rodger Young
of Clyde, possibly because he was memorialized in a song, "The Ballad of
Rodger Young," that commemorated his feats in the South Pacific. It is a
truism that every sizable Ohio community has, or once had, a monument to
its Civil War veterans. Many also displayed statues, artillery field pieces, or
other reminders commemorating those who served in World War I. But few
Ohio towns boast monumental tributes to veterans of the second world war.

Most commonly they are remembered on plaques, modest memorials, or on public buildings in lists of names of those who died in their country's service.

At War's End; A Return to Civilian Life

Twelve million American men and women had to be re-absorbed into the civilian economy at war's end. Fearing the same kind of widespread unemployment that had followed rapid World War I demobilization, the federal government eased veterans into the job market by spreading their entry over a period of several years. This was achieved by enacting assistance programs such as the G.I. Bill, a program that paid veterans a modest stipend if they enrolled in some form of approved schooling. About 3 million service men and women took advantage of this program; college enrollments rose to unparalleled levels. The resulting "G.I. Bulge" required colleges to erect temporary buildings and expand physical plants. Qualified faculty were in short supply. As colleges prospered, so did technical and proprietary schools, which taught an amazing variety of skills from aircraft maintenance to mortuary science.

The demand for housing blossomed as veterans began to have families. New subdivisions sprouted on the outskirts of every city. These modest houses were within the reach of veterans eligible for federally backed loans. Veterans who could not find employment could enroll in the "52-20 Program," which provided unemployment checks of $20 a week for up to fifty-two weeks. A state bonus enhanced Ohio veterans' purchasing power by paying up to $400 depending on length of service. In retrospect, it is clear that these programs achieved their broad goals, smoothing the transition to civilian life, stimulating the economy with federal funds and the spending of state bonus money, and avoiding the sharp economic recession that followed the first world war. The economic growth of the 1950s absorbed the costs of these programs.

As male veterans reentered the job market, considerable social pressure supported their claim to jobs which had been held by women. Millions of women nationwide were happy to exchange the production line for a domestic role, but others were not at all anxious to surrender their jobs. The latter had little support from labor unions. In the terminology of a later day, unions were still sexist.

Blacks and Hispanics also faced pressure to relinquish well-paying wartime jobs, especially those skilled and semi-skilled jobs which had opened for them due to wartime pressures. They, too, found little support from unions, though to a considerable degree blacks succeeded in retaining gains made during the war years. Hispanics were largely agricultural workers, migrants who were

unusually vulnerable to arbitrary employers and a developing technology
which threatened to replace them with labor-saving machines. In the 1960s
some joined the Farm Labor Organizing Committee, which was trying to
unionize migrant workers. An effective agricultural workers' union would
not appear in Ohio until the 1980s, however.

Ohio in an Age of Affluence

By 1950, World War II veterans were well integrated into the civilian
population. Pent-up consumer demand stimulated the economy, and a "baby
boom" created a continuing demand for products and services associated with
raising children. These conditions, plus the economic stimulation of the Korean War, contributed to what economist John Kenneth Galbraith was to
label the "affluent society."

Ohio's population continued to swell, adding 1,760,500 persons in the 1950s,
a 22 percent increase, the state's largest of the twentieth century. In 1960
Ohioans were overwhelmingly native-born whites. Blacks constituted 8.1
percent of the population, a 23.8 percent increase in the fifties that resulted
from a continuation of the northward trek, as relatives and friends from the
rural south came north to join those who had found employment in Ohio.

And employment remained high. The state's productive economy did more
than its proportionate share in supplying the nation and the world with goods
and services. Throughout the 1950s, Ohio, with 5.3 percent of the nation's
population, produced about 6 percent of the Gross National Product. Depending on the standard used, Ohio ranked either fourth or fifth in industrial
production and was second only to Michigan in the value of its exports.

Political Affairs, 1944–60

As World War II entered its late stages, President Roosevelt won a fourth
term, defeating the Republican ticket of Dewey and Bricker. The popularity
of the Ohio governor may have been enough to swing Ohio into the Republican column, for the party carried the state by a narrow margin.

Several strong candidates hoped to succeed Bricker as governor in the 1944
election. Cincinnati's mayor, James G. Stewart, won the Republican primary
but lost the election to Cleveland's popular mayor, Frank J. Lausche. Meanwhile, Robert A. Taft retained his Senate seat, and for the next several years
was a dominant voice among Republicans because of his skills and his leadership of the Republican policy committee. Taft was well known for his cautious approach to international commitments and for his sponsorship of the
Taft-Hartley Labor Management Act of 1947. This act outlawed closed

shops, provided for mandatory cooling-off periods during labor strife, and required labor union officers to sign affidavits disavowing any communist connections. The law passed over President Truman's veto, and it made Taft anathema to union leaders.

Republicans fared well in the 1946 state elections as former Attorney General Thomas J. Herbert defeated Lausche's bid for reelection. The party retained strength in the general assembly as all but four seats in the Ohio house went to Republicans; the gains were short-lived, however. In 1948 Lausche returned to the governor's office while Democrats picked up twelve congressional seats and won control of the general assembly. On the national scene, the party sacrificed Taft's presidential ambitions to Thomas Dewey. In a major upset, President Truman defeated Dewey, carrying the nation and Ohio. Analysts attributed Truman's victory to high farm prices and industrial wages, but two years later, his "Fair Deal" domestic program drew criticism and may have influenced Ohio voters to reject the Democrats in the 1950 state elections. The popular Lausche was reelected governor, but Republicans picked up other state offices, sent a strong delegation to Congress, and reelected Taft to the Senate.

The Republican surge continued in 1952. Again Taft's presidential ambitions were thwarted, this time by the immensely popular Dwight D. Eisenhower, who won the Republican nomination and carried the party to victory over Adlai Stevenson. His campaign supporters claimed "We like Ike," and Ohio responded by giving him nearly a half-million-vote victory margin. Taft died in July 1953, just six months after Eisenhower's inauguration.

Elsewhere on the national political scene, John Bricker was reelected to the United States Senate, which he had first entered in 1947. At the close of the Korean struggle (1953), he led a fight for the so-called Bricker Amendment to the Constitution. Concerned by President Truman's unilateral commitment of American troops, Bricker would have limited the president's power to conclude executive agreements with foreign nations. The proposal was a rallying point for many Republicans and for peace groups, but it failed by a single vote in the Senate. Bricker's political career ended with his retirement from the Senate in 1959.

Republicans continued to dominate the Ohio congressional delegation in 1952, capturing sixteen of the twenty-three House seats. Among the Republican victors were Frances P. Bolton and Oliver O. Bolton, the first mother-and-son team in House history. The Ohio General Assembly was also overwhelmingly Republican.

One aberration in the flow of Republican victories was the reelection of Governor Lausche by a record margin. Political analysts have been intrigued by his success during a period when Ohio Democrats generally were not faring well. There are a number of reasons for Lausche's popularity. He had attractive personal qualities. His Slovenian roots contributed to his appeal in northern Ohio steel towns. Plain-living, plain-speaking, with a shock of hair crowning what one might describe as an "honest face," Lausche was the sort of understated politician that Ohioans tended to trust. He was a conservative Democrat of the kind most successful in early twentieth-century Ohio politics: Judson Harmon, Vic Donahey, George White, and Martin Davey were all conservative. Even James M. Cox trimmed his sails considerably to recapture and hold the governorship against a conservative Republican resurgence by keeping a tight rein on spending. Economy in government has always been attractive to Ohio voters whether practiced by Republican or Democrat.

Lausche's reelection in 1954 made him Ohio's only five-term governor. A constitutional amendment (1954) extended the governor's term of office to four years, effective January 1959, and limited a governor to two consecutive four-year terms, clearly a Republican device for stopping Lausche. The strategy backfired in 1971 when, after serving two terms, Gov. James A. Rhodes, a Republican, had to sit out four years before winning two more terms as governor, then had to wait four more years before again seeking the governor's chair in 1986. Lausche resigned before completing his 1954 term to take the Senate seat he won in the 1956 election. A Medina County Republican, John W. Brown, the lieutenant governor, served the remaining eleven days of Lausche's final term.

Korea and Loyalty

While Lausche was still governor, the nation was again at war. In June 1950 North Korean forces invaded South Korea. To counter this aggression, President Truman ordered American troops into service in what was described as a "police action." Though hundreds of thousands of Americans ultimately participated in the fighting, Congress never formally declared war. United States troops comprised the major part of a United Nations command led by Gen. Douglas MacArthur. The war expanded into a major conflict when, in response to UN efforts to gain control of North Korea, soldiers from the communist Peoples Republic of China came to the aid of their North Korean allies. Once more in America the military draft swung into action. Reserve units were called up. Orders for military hardware and supplies poured into American factories, and once again Ohio responded to the national need. By the summer of 1951 an uneasy truce was arranged, but sporadic fighting continued until an armistice was signed in 1953. Ohio casualties in this brief but bloody war were 1,777 dead and 4,837 wounded.

The Korean conflict added fuel to a debate which had been raging in America since the 1940s. To some it appeared that the government was infiltrated with security risks—Communists and Communist sympathizers ("Comsymps"). The fall of nationalist China to the "red Chinese," Soviet treachery in its development of an A-bomb, and other traumas led many to conclude that Communists were subverting American governmental and social institutions. On the national scene, investigations of this supposed condition ranged from the responsible reviews of sincerely concerned legislators to the totally irresponsible and damaging work of Sen. Joseph McCarthy of Wisconsin.

These national investigations had their counterpart on the state level. In 1951 the Ohio General Assembly created the Ohio Un-American Activities Commission, which held hearings around the state examining, under oath, numerous persons charged with aiding and abetting Communist causes. The Commission reported in 1952 that labor and youth were special targets for organizers.

It proved impossible for the commission to determine Communist party membership since records had been destroyed, but using what it called the "best figures available," the commission claimed there were 1,300 party members in Ohio in 1952. About half were located in the Cleveland area, another 400 in the other northern industrial cities, and 200 in southern and central Ohio.

The Ohio investigation mirrored the national investigations of the House Un-American Activities Committee in identifying some professed Communists, charging some persons who had only tangential relationships to the Party, and smearing some innocent parties by implication. Among the latter were persons who, in the despair of the thirties, had joined college groups later identified as Communist front organizations. Though they had long since renounced any part in the group's activities, they were still called to account, casting doubt on their loyalty.

State Politics Again

The 1956 state elections belonged to the Republicans as Ohio again supported the victorious Eisenhower and sent a Republican-dominated delegation to Congress. Marietta's C. William O'Neill, former Speaker of the House and attorney general, easily defeated Toledo's Michael V. DiSalle for governor. The state legislature was heavily Republican. Although O'Neill had progressive plans for the state, several things conspired to limit his success.

Nationally, a sharp business recession in 1957 was blamed on Republican policies. That same year the Soviet Union successfully launched Sputnik, the world's first earth orbiting satellite, and the Republicans in control of the national administration also took the blame for America's failure to compete in the so-called "space race." Much more central to Ohio, however, was

Republican sponsorship of a right-to-work constitutional amendment that would have banned the union shop. This proposal brought an unprecedented response from organized labor which put together a massive opposition campaign. The amendment lost by about a million votes. While the issue revealed how much political force organized labor could muster in Ohio when all elements pulled together, labor's strong showing proved to be an aberration. Seldom since has labor been so united on any issue.

As so often happens in Ohio politics, the outs became the ins when DiSalle won his rematch with O'Neill in 1958 by a margin of more than 400,000 votes. O'Neill would later be appointed chief justice of the Ohio Supreme Court, thus becoming the only person to serve at the head of the three branches of state government. While O'Neill's defeat was predictable once labor focused its attention against him, the defeat of Senator Bricker by Stephen A. Young was a surprise. Democratic voters carried the Clevelander into the Senate, where his propensity for responding to critical letters with irreverent missives of his own made this peppery septuagenarian a media favorite. To one complainer he replied, "I think you should know that some idiot wrote me a stupid letter and signed your name to it."

Michael DiSalle was the first Ohio governor to serve a four-year term. A veteran of the federal bureaucracy, he knew the frustration of trying to move the governing machinery. Though not a classic liberal, he had progressive ideas for improving state services, especially in education and in state custodial institutions. Ohio lagged seriously in its state-supported services. Some of its mental-health, child-care, and penal institutions were so underfinanced and poorly run that the governor emerged from tours of the facilities with tears of compassion and chagrin on his face.

DiSalle's concern, translated into dollars, was opposed by Republican legislators. He overcame their objections, however, and secured a half-billion dollars in new expenditures which were to be paid for by a variety of tax increases. Two years later the governor tried a similar but more modest package for the 1961-63 biennium budget, and the legislature blocked it. In frustration, DiSalle vetoed all appropriations for the biennium's second half, and in time a smaller appropriations bill and capital improvements bill passed without the governor's signature. This was symptomatic of the conflict which was to limit legislative and administrative accomplishment in DiSalle's last two years in office.

One modest success which did not cost anything was adoption on October 1, 1959, of a new state motto: "With God all things are possible." It was suggested by a twelve-year-old Cincinnati boy, James Mastronardo. The old motto, "Imperium in Imperio" (an empire within an empire) had been abandoned in 1867 because it was "too royal."

Though DiSalle had two years of his term remaining in 1960, his party was in trouble. Economic conditions caused many small farmers who had long supported the Democrats to switch to Republican ranks in 1960. Inflation was causing middle-class urban and suburban voters to support conservative fiscal policies. National issues were also affecting Ohio voters. Foremost among them was the presidential candidacy of John F. Kennedy, a Massachusetts Democrat and a Roman Catholic. Kennedy's Catholicism was significant in that political analysts purported to find some latent anti-Catholic bias among Ohio voters. Kennedy carried the nation by a slim margin, but Ohio gave its vote to Richard M. Nixon, then completing eight years as Eisenhower's vice-president. Nixon's plurality was larger in Ohio than in any other state, and one suspects the reason can be traced to the state's political conservatism rather than to religious bias.

The decade-and-a-half following World War II found Ohio in what might be described as its typically cautious political posture. Although Democrats controlled the governor's office during much of that period, thanks largely to Lausche's five terms, other state elective offices and the general assembly were predominantly Republican. The State's congressional delegation was heavily Republican throughout the period: indeed, Ohio sent the largest Republican delegation to Congress during much of this period.

Ohio's electoral votes went to the GOP in 1944, 1948, 1952, 1956, and 1960, a loyalty that was rewarded with high-level patronage. Harold Burton of Cleveland and Potter Stewart of Cincinnati were appointed to the Supreme Court. Cleveland industrialist George M. Humphrey was Eisenhower's secretary of the treasury (1953–57). Ohio-born (but Michigan resident) Charles E. Wilson was secretary of defense (1953–57), and Neil McElroy of Cincinnati succeeded him (1957–59). Arthur E. Fleming, former president of Ohio Wesleyan University, served Eisenhower as secretary of health, education, and welfare (1958). Even a Democrat made cabinet rank as Cincinnati's Charles W. Sawyer served Truman as secretary of commerce (1948–53).

Ohio's Republicanism is surprising because the Buckeye State appears at first glance to fit the mold of the heavily industrial state with generally Democratic-voting population groups like labor union members, blacks, and ethnics. Why such a state should keep so many Republicans in office will be explored further in chapter 17.

New Population Patterns Emerge

As previously noted, Ohio's population reached 9,707,100 by 1960. Though closely pursued by Texas, Ohio was still the nation's fourth most populous state. The press of additional people coupled with changing concepts of the "good life" caused substantial demographic changes. These changes were not unlike those occurring elsewhere, but the unusual number of large cities in the state coupled with its citizens' traditional mobility had a pronounced effect upon living patterns. In Ohio the most significant population shift was a move outward, away from the central cities.

Beyond the inner-city areas of Cleveland, Cincinnati, and other urban centers, old residential neighborhoods struggled for survival. Population shifts were draining them of their former vitality. These tired neighborhoods did not attract returning veterans, who looked instead to the new and thriving suburbs to settle their young families. Thanks to G.I. loans that provided low-interest mortgages many veterans had enough purchasing power for a new house in one of the rapidly proliferating residential subdivisions. These appeared in every city and sizable town where there was open land on the outskirts. Most subdivisions featured tract housing, monotonous but suitable for the young families that monopolized them. Seven or eight thousand dollars would buy an adequate house in a new residential area in the late 1940s.

The new subdivisions brought substantial changes in lifestyle, wedded as they were to the automobile, which was essential transportation because few new areas were adequately served by public transportation. The two-car family became common in these outlying neighborhoods, as the breadwinner took one car to work while the other served for running errands, taking children to their far-flung activities, and making trips to the neighborhood shopping centers. Offering easy suburban access and free and convenient parking, shopping centers thrived early in Ohio. The Town and Country Shopping Center on Columbus's East Broad Street claimed to be the first of its kind in the nation, although this claim has often been challenged.

New residential patterns also required new schools. They were funded largely through local property taxes, and it was a struggle for young families with extensive claims upon their income to vote to tax themselves for new and improved schools. Local funding was inadequate to meet the need, and the state floated bond issues in the fifties and later to provide much-needed capital improvements. The Ohio School Foundation helped local schools meet operating expenses, but in this rapid growth period school needs always outran available funds.

Churches were another social feature of the new subdivisions. Old congregations tended to locate new church buildings in the suburbs to capture the vitality of young families. Any number of old, central city congregations faced a wrenching decision: should they stay in their historic site and serve people different from those traditionally served, or abandon their roots, move to the newer sections of town, avoid the inner-city problems, and revive the vitality of the congregation with the young families there? Each answered in its own way. Among those that remained in their traditional location were churches which opened their facilities to their neighbors, providing them with counseling, day care and pre-school services, and other forms of assistance.

The 1950s also brought a large movement of city dwellers to former farmlands lying just outside the city limits. Here people hoped to acquire a few acres, a little elbow room where perhaps they could keep a horse and a garden. As this movement progressed, rural areas became suburbanized. Township government was no longer adequate to address the needs of a burgeoning population, and so new cities were formed, often reaching out to the old township borders to define their limits. Aurora in Portage County and Strongsville in Cuyahoga County developed in this manner. Occasionally the rural location of a large industrial plant keyed new community development as at Lordstown in Trumbull County and Streetsboro in Portage County.

The intrusion of new residents and businesses into the townships threatened to strangle the core cities with a ring of small satellite communities. Incorporated communities already thoroughly boxed in Cleveland and Cincinnati. Columbus, however, grew spectacularly by annexing much surrounding township land. Its colorful mayor, Jack Sensenbrenner, traded land for municipal services, giving the capital city room to grow. Toledo followed this lead and added large areas. A direct connection existed between annexation and the growth of these two cities; during the fifties and sixties, when most new development was taking place outside the older city limits, both Columbus and Toledo flourished because developers found open land within the city limits.

While the cities coveted surrounding township land, the townships were in constant danger of losing land, and annexation controversies became endemic. Frequently the land annexed by an adjoining municipality was the most highly developed in the township. Its loss deprived townships of much of their limited tax base, making it difficult to maintain adequate local services in the remaining area. Sometimes township residents reacted by facing the inevitable and at least choosing their city. In 1985, for example, after years of speculation, Northampton Township, which lies north of Akron in Summit County, voted to join the city of Cuyahoga Falls rather than face annexation by Akron. The merger created an enlarged Cuyahoga Falls, more than doubling its area. Only time will tell whether Northampton's rural character will disappear once city water, sewers, and other services are extended into its further reaches.

Annexationists also had their eye on the new industrial parks which were developed just outside the limits of nearly every Ohio city, large or small. Land was at a premium in the city, and taxes were generally higher than in the townships. It was less costly to build a new plant on open land than to redevelop urban property that was already crisscrossed with utility lines, streets, and other impediments. Initially the industrial parks attracted "clean" industries, but as the concept matured large manufacturing operations relocated in semirural areas as well. In the 1960s, for example, General Motors built an enormous manufacturing complex at Lordstown, in a rural Trumbull County township, and in 1979 a Honda plant opened in countryside west of Marysville.

Another decentralizing move saw many giant corporations move their headquarters into nicely landscaped suburban or rural settings. The pattern of dispersal from the old central city was now complete: residential housing, retail trade, business and industry, professional offices, and central headquarters had all abandoned the city. With them, of course, went much of the city's tax base. The cities fought back through annexation and through massive new efforts to retain the businesses they had and to attract new ones within the incorporated limits.

Ironically, the cities' attempts to retain residents and businesses by improving transportation actually hastened the dispersal beyond the city limits. Rail and bus transportation had lost favor as the freedom brought by the automobile made it the preferred mode of travel. That preference had an unpleasant side effect: city streets became choked with cars. To ease traffic flow, the major cities constructed expressways, cutting through settled urban areas and displacing older housing and businesses in the process. These very arteries made living in the suburbs and commuting to a city job much easier than before. They also encouraged the use of private automobiles at the expense of public transportation, thus creating massive traffic and parking problems.

Outside the cities Ohio's principal highways had been in place for nearly half a century. Built to accommodate the traffic of an earlier time, they were sadly out of date by the 1950s. Ohio did much to help itself by authorizing several highway construction bond issues and increasing the gasoline tax for highway construction and improvements. Its most dramatic step, however, was the creation of the Ohio Turnpike Commission in 1954, which was to construct and operate a toll road across northern Ohio, connecting in the east with the Pennsylvania Turnpike and in the west with a similar road proposed for Indiana. The guiding spirit of this venture was James W. Shocknessey, chairman of the Ohio Turnpike Commission, for whom the turnpike was later named. Completed in 1955 at a cost of $325 million, the tollway generated so much income that its bonded indebtedness was retired early.

Another success story of the period was the interstate highway system. Authorized by the federal Interstate Highway Act of 1956, this national network of high-speed highways proved invaluable for moving goods and people over long distances. It took decades to complete some parts of this complex system, but interstates linking major Ohio cities were operating in the 1960s and were completed in the 1970s.

These interstates changed traffic patterns around the cities and affected smaller towns along their paths. During rush hours, local traffic overloaded such routes as I-75 in Cincinnati and Dayton and I-70 and I-71 in Columbus.

To alleviate this condition and provide feeders into the interstates, ring or belt highways were built around Toledo, Columbus, and Cincinnati. Bypasses funneled traffic around other urban centers. These developments hastened the growth of new residential and business complexes where belt roads intersected main highways. Some interstates created new population centers, new suburban satellites, far from the central city. Interstate 71, for example, made rural Medina County an exurb of Cleveland. The city of Medina changed from its old county seat character into a fashionable upscale residential community, while Brunswick emerged from country crossroads status into a city approaching 30,000 people by 1986. Westerville, a quiet college town northeast of Columbus, became an expanding, upscale community with completion of the I-270 loop.

While tens of thousands moved from older city residential areas to the outskirts of town, the old neighborhoods remained home to rather dense populations. In what had once been pleasant neighborhoods of single-family houses—Cleveland's Hough district or Cincinnati's Zone—the poor and underprivileged moved in, frequently filling the houses to overflowing with relatives, friends, or those simply needing a place to stay. Disproportionately these people were blacks, white Appalachians, or old-age pensioners. Such neighborhoods never seemed to have enough police or fire protection; schools and playgrounds were inadequate; public services such as garbage collection and street cleaning were erratic. City officials regarded them, with reason, as problem areas.

It is ironic that efforts to improve inner-city living conditions sometimes resulted in relocating the problems to other neighborhoods. Federal urban renewal programs provided funds to cities for clearing and redeveloping slums and substandard housing and moving residents to better-grade housing. Old business and industrial areas could be leveled to make way for new enterprise which would enhance the city's tax revenues. When properly done, it was argued, urban renewal would benefit the relocated resident and the city's finances, and would physically improve portions of the inner city. While urban renewal did accomplish these goals, the displaced residents moved to other neighborhoods, where often their resources were too limited to maintain their new properties, thus creating new problem areas in the city.

Most sizable Ohio cities had at least one urban renewal program, and the large cities often had several. Cleveland's Erieview project was one early program as was Cincinnati's waterfront development, which made possible the building of Riverfront Stadium and other dramatic improvements. Even small cities like Crestline used urban renewal to upgrade properties in the business district. Akron had more urban renewal acreage than any city of its size in the nation.

Even as urban renewal affected urban living patterns, so did public housing. The modest start on public housing made during the Great Depression had been further extended during World War II. Since 1916 the Cincinnati Better Housing League had worked to alleviate slum housing problems. Leaders of this movement joined Cleveland's Ernest J. Bohn to secure the nation's first state-enabling legislation for forming metropolitan housing authorities. After 1933 the Cincinnati Metropolitan Housing Authority used federal funds for slum clearance and public housing, and other Ohio cities soon followed this lead.

In the fifties, public housing became a staple of urban life. Many early efforts resulted in "projects" consisting of low-rise apartment complexes. Later the emphasis shifted to high-rise apartments, especially for the elderly, as longer life expectancy was making them a population group whose needs cities had to consider. By the 1970s the state was dotted with housing for the elderly, most of it built with federal funds.

Beginnings of the Rhodes Era

During the postwar years of Republican hegemony, James Allen Rhodes, former mayor of Columbus and popular state auditor, was a rising star. In 1962 he won the governorship in a Republican sweep that gave his party firm control of both houses of the state legislature. He knew what to do with this politically auspicious situation.

Born in Coalton, a tiny Jackson County community, Rhodes was a hardworking young man who dropped out of Ohio State to enter business. He found his true vocation in politics, where he rose rapidly as an effective votegetter. Part of his political appeal lay in his rise from humble origins. He was the self-made man whom Americans have found appealing in political life. Although he became wealthy through private business ventures and had the support of people of power and wealth, the so-called "little man" still responded to his seemingly unsophisticated ways and down-to-earth speech. A super-salesman in the tradition of the medicine show peddler of rural America, Rhodes plugged his product hard; his vigor and enthusiasm helped listeners overlook occasional lapses in grammar. He made no effort to be candid; he emphasized the positive and kept quiet about the negative.

When Rhodes assumed office, Ohio was still growing in population and industrial strength. Nevertheless, it had its share of unemployment, and population projections predicted the need for thousands of new jobs to provide work for the emerging work force. The governor made jobs the cornerstone of his program. He and his staff utilized marketing techniques; whole-page ads in the *New York Times* and other key newspapers proclaimed that "Profit is not a dirty word in Ohio." From time to time in his sixteen years as governor,

Rhodes led teams of Ohio promoters, dubbed "Rhodes' Raiders," into other states and to Europe, Latin America, and Asia, where they sought to promote Ohio products and lure manufacturers to the Buckeye State. When foreign dignitaries visited Ohio, the governor, with a folksy touch, would treat them to Ohio hamburgers instead of fancy luncheons.

These promotional efforts, buttressed by support from the Ohio Department of Development and other state and local agencies, resulted in some successes. Huge new investments were made in Ohio, especially by the automotive industry, which located foundries, stamping plants, engine plants, and assembly plants across the state. The Lordstown complex, opened by General Motors in 1966 in Trumbull County, dramatically illustrates the kind of development that made Ohio second only to Michigan in the automotive industry.

According to Rhodes, an important element in promoting new business was the state's low tax base. He resurrected the old Ohio political chant, "No new taxes," and made it his own. To keep the cost of government down, Rhodes, like Bricker and Lausche before him, sought to pare state payrolls. While there is virtue in eliminating unnecessary expenditures, the governor's policy caused havoc among already poorly funded public institutions, especially in Ohio's beleaguered mental health facilities, where professional salaries and working conditions compared unfavorably with other states. This was a side of the "no new taxes" policy that Rhodes never talked about; rather he insisted that all would be well if the state increased jobs, which, he claimed, would reduce crime, divorce, delinquency, mental illness and similar problems. The governor's solution appeared simplistic to professionals working in these fields.

It seemed almost a paradox that at the same time he was pressing for economy in government, Rhodes asked the legislature to appropriate a record budget. He believed that higher revenues from existing taxes would cover the increased costs. Republicans also approved a variety of minor, largely inconspicuous tax increases to cover the budget, in what one historian calls a "rubber-bands-and-glue" approach. Rhodes also succeeded in securing a $250 million capital improvements bond issue from the voters in 1963, only the beginning of his continuing effort to secure funds for construction. Rhodes won voter approval for a $500 million highways bond issue in 1964, a development issue of $290 million in 1965, and a $759 million capital improvements issue in 1968. There was certainly a need for such funds.

It was no secret that the governor's favorite activity was a groundbreaking, a ribbon-cutting, or building dedication. During the Rhodes years scores of new structures, most of them sorely needed, were built. Among them were a forty-story state office tower located across Broad Street from the Statehouse, prison structures including the maximum security Lucasville prison in Scioto County, a striking if austerely modern Ohio Historical Center in Columbus, airports for every county lacking one, and many college and university buildings. A development close to the governor's heart was a super highway running eastward from Cincinnati across southern Ohio into an area the federal government had recently identified as Appalachia, a depressed farm and mining area eligible for federal funding. Though federal funds were used, Rhodes expedited the project. Yet another of his pet projects was the development of fine lodges, cabins, and recreational facilities at state parks. As the governor frequently pointed out, people living in depressed areas near these parks needed jobs and income; in addition, the new facilities would enhance tourism in Ohio, and they did.

New Initiatives in Education

His strong leadership and a solidly Republican legislature enabled Rhodes to set his own priorities during his first terms in office. Among them was an upgrading of Ohio's system of higher education. Historically Ohio lagged behind similar industrial states in funding state colleges and universities. Some claimed that was due to resistance from and loyalty to the state's many fine liberal arts colleges, which, it was argued, would lose students if the state system expanded. Nor were existing state schools anxious to share limited funds for higher education with new state universities. It also seems likely that inertia resulted from the legislature's traditional conservatism, especially when it came to spending.

Whatever the cause, Ohio's poor showing in higher education became an embarrassment at a time when Wisconsin, Michigan, Indiana, New York, California, and many other states were pumping large amounts of new money into their colleges. On every scale measuring state support to higher education, Ohio ranked close to the bottom. Only New Hampshire and Vermont students paid more than Ohio students did to attend their state institutions. The least expensive public higher education was in the municipal universities—Cincinnati, Akron, Toledo—and in the few recently started community colleges. One of the more optimistic reports, issued in 1958 by the Ohio Commission on Education Beyond the High School, showed Ohio ranking eleventh in personal income per capita, but only thirty-sixth in per capita expenditures on higher education. This was well below the national average.

Governor Rhodes saw support of higher education as consistent with his push for jobs and economic advancement. When he assumed office there were six state universities. By the end of his second term (1971) there were twelve. Existing state universities were Ohio, Miami, Bowling Green, Kent, Ohio State, and Central State. New additions were Akron and Toledo, Cleveland

State (formed from Fenn College), Youngstown State (formerly a YMCA college), and Wright State (formerly a branch of Miami). Cincinnati remained essentially municipal until coming fully within the state system in the 1980s. The legislature authorized Shawnee State in 1986. A new Medical College of Ohio was created in Toledo and the medical schools of Cincinnati and Case Western Reserve received state subsidies. Later, new medical schools were established at Rootstown by an Akron-Kent-Youngstown consortium, at Wright State, and at Ohio University.

The larger universities operated numerous branches. State monies also helped organize new two-year technical colleges and encouraged locally assisted community colleges. The state-assisted institutions were governed by their own boards of trustees, but the Rhodes administration formed a new Ohio Board of Regents in 1963 to provide oversight for the entire system. Before the governor finished his final years in office, he had reached his goal: a public college of some kind was located within thirty miles of every Ohioan.

While higher education received its share of attention and resources, public elementary and secondary education also took a new direction. In addition to its traditional focus, the public school system expanded its mission in the realm of vocational education. Most large cities had long operated vocational high schools for a few selected students, but Governor Rhodes and his advisors argued that practical, job-oriented courses would serve a large part of the school population better than traditional academic courses. Expanding Ohio industries and service occupations would welcome trained young people to the work force. At the governor's urging, new state legislation created joint vocational school districts throughout the state. Impressive new facilities, often equipped with fine machinery donated by local industries, appeared across Ohio. The concept did not reach its full realization, undermined in part by a reversal in the state's economic fortunes in the 1970s. The new jobs failed to materialize; instead Ohio suffered tremendous job loss. Only students trained for the service sector had jobs waiting upon graduation.

Civil Rights

Two significant events mark the birth of the modern civil rights movement. In 1954 the United States Supreme Court ruled in the case of *Brown v. Board of Education of Topeka, Kansas* that the old doctrine of "separate but equal" educational programs and facilities was no longer a valid basis on which to conduct schools. The court said that segregated schools were unequal by their very nature, and in 1955 ordered desegregation "with all deliberate speed." This landmark decision opened an intense legal assault on all forms of racial discrimination. The second event keying the black civil rights movement was the Montgomery, Alabama, bus boycott of 1955, which represented the beginning of concerted, sustained direct action by blacks seeking their rights. It also marked the emergence of Dr. Martin Luther King, Jr. as the movement's preeminent leader.

Through his Southern Christian Leadership Conference, King tried to keep the movement nonviolent. Young blacks staged "pray-ins," "sit-ins," and "wade-ins" to dramatize their exclusion from various activities. Social discrimination was as much an issue in Ohio and the North as it was in the South, although most of the great, dramatic confrontations which captured a nationwide television audience took place in the South.

It was clear that racial segregation was widely practiced in Ohio. The Ohio Public Accommodations Law of 1884, banning discrimination by race in public facilities, was still in effect in the 1950s, but it was ineffectively enforced. In 1959 the general assembly enacted a new civil rights law "to prevent and eliminate the practice of discrimination in employment against persons because of their race, color, religion, national origin, or ancestry," and created the Ohio Civil Rights Commission to monitor and enforce these provisions. The commission's first report to the governor detailed discriminatory practices around the state, which included denying blacks access to hotels, restaurants, dance halls, roller skating rinks, swimming pools, bowling alleys, cemeteries, and even commercial fishing ponds. Some recreational establishments circumvented the law by converting their facilities into private clubs for members only. The commission recommended that new legislation be passed which would put teeth into antidiscrimination laws, and in ensuing years such legislation eliminated the most egregious practices.

But perhaps the most emotion-laden arena for desegregation action was the public school system. Although Ohio had long abandoned its nineteenth-century discriminatory laws, residents of some sections of the state functioned as though they were still in vogue. Hillsboro, the county seat of Highland County, operated into the 1950s under local ordinances that created a segregated school system. The major school desegregation problem, however, existed in all of Ohio's major cities, where de facto segregation was less a matter of formal school board policy than a result of segregation in residential housing. Where whole neighborhoods were black or white, the school population reflected that condition. Court challenges seeking to prove that realtors were involved in a conspiracy to deny housing to blacks outside certain well-defined areas were time consuming and expensive. School desegregation could not wait upon racial realignment in housing.

Prodded by federal courts, Ohio cities were forced to address the problem. In every case busing was required to achieve racial balance. Large numbers of parents, black and white, objected to busing since it undercut the virtues traditionally associated with neighborhood schools. Children resented being forced into uncomfortable new social contacts. Violence erupted sporadically as busing was implemented. In Dayton, Columbus, and Cleveland, blacks were locked in confrontation with school boards over plans to achieve racial balance. Cleveland faced an especially difficult problem since so much of its white population had moved out of the city and much that remained was located in ethnic neighborhoods traditionally protective of their own customs. To achieve balance, children, both black and white, had to be bused long distances from home. Mechanical problems with the equipment and attitudinal problems with some drivers caused tempers to flare. The school board did not move fast enough to satisfy Frank J. Battisti, the federal judge monitoring Cleveland's compliance with federal directives. So the judge assumed control over Cleveland schools and put his own administrator in place to monitor compliance. A chronic shortage of funds, the rapid turnover of professional leadership, and infighting among school board members contributed to the Cleveland system's difficulties. In 1986 Judge Battisti ordered the State Board of Education to monitor integration of the system, thus removing control still further from local authorities. Though Cleveland continued to have problems, all but a handful of Ohio school systems were in compliance with the intent of the Brown decision thirty years after it was rendered.

Most social reform movements have an irrational side which can, on occasion, flare into violence. So it was with the civil rights movement. The NAACP's legal maneuverings and Dr. King's nonviolent restraint did not impress certain street people and militants. In the 1960s many American cities suffered "long hot summers" of burning, looting, and vandalism as ghetto blacks vented their frustration and rage. The prototype was Los Angeles' Watts riot, but Detroit, Newark, and other cities were also affected. In Ohio, Dayton and Cincinnati had trouble in the streets, but the most severe problems erupted in the Hough district on Cleveland's east side. There in June 1966, four black citizens were killed and many injured during several days of rioting. Fire levelled blocks of houses and commercial structures. The police were overwhelmed, and city officials called in 2,200 National Guard troops to restore order.

A grand jury investigation into the causes of the rioting placed the blame on outside agitators and Communists, a simplistic and comfortable conclusion the city administration accepted. A later report, issued by a biracial review board comprising neighborhood citizens, dismissed the influence of outsiders. Neglect and disregard had created frustration and desperation in the neighborhood. "The underlying causes of the rioting," said the board, "are to be found in the social conditions that exist in the ghetto areas of Cleveland."

In the 1967 Cleveland mayoral race Carl B. Stokes, a lawyer and former state legislator, won 95 percent of the black vote and 19.3 percent of the vote in essentially white wards to become the first black to preside over a major American city. (Ohio's first black mayor, Robert Henry, had been appointed mayor of Springfield under its commission form of government.) Both blacks and whites looked to the handsome, articulate, and personable Stokes to cool racial tensions. He did so during the tense period following the assassination of Martin Luther King in 1968 by personally walking the streets, accompanied by other black leaders. But violence again erupted in July 1968 as militant blacks and the police fought one another in the "Glenville shootout" on the troubled east side. In one hour, three policemen and four civilians were killed; twelve police and a number of civilians were injured. General violence spread from this core, and two days and nights of burning, beatings, and looting followed.

The focus of black anger was the police force, which had a reputation for crude racism and insensitivity to the needs of law-abiding blacks. The racial imbalance of the force—only 165 of the force's 2,200 officers were black—contributed to blacks' resentment. The Glenville incident did not end Cleveland's racial troubles, but the extremes of violence tended to die out in time partly because of improved city policies and partly through exhaustion.

In addition some blacks were encouraged by increasingly visible leadership roles in national, state, and local affairs during the 1960s. Mayor Stokes appointed blacks to many important city posts. His brother, Louis Stokes, was elected congressman, beginning a long and increasingly influential career in the House of Representatives. In 1963 Governor Rhodes appointed William O. Walker as his director of industrial relations, the first black to serve in an Ohio governor's cabinet. Arthur C. Elliott of Cincinnati was appointed a federal marshal; Clevelander Lillian Burke was seated on the Ohio Industrial Commission; Mae Stewart became president of the City Commission of East Cleveland. These accomplishments were important as visible symbols of black advancement, but a more important and lasting benefit to the social progress of black Americans were the thousands of new college students, teachers, lawyers, doctors, businessmen, and others of accomplishment who were assuming their rightful place in society. In Cleveland, Cincinnati, Columbus, and smaller communities, a black middle class was finding an ever larger field for personal advancement and for service.

Antiwar and Social Protest

As the civil rights movement progressed in Ohio, another element of change was at work, especially among the young people on college campuses. America's involvement in Southeast Asia had been slowly building during the Truman, Eisenhower, and Kennedy administrations. In 1964 Congress overwhelmingly approved the Gulf of Tonkin Resolution, giving President Lyndon Johnson virtually a free hand in defending American interests. He promptly escalated the American presence in the Far East, ordering North

Vietnam bombed and increasing U.S. troop strength to more than 500,000 soldiers plus extensive air force and naval contingents in the war zones.

As the war intensified, so did the distance between the "hawks," who supported the president's escalation of the war, and the "doves," who opposed American involvement. Ohio's two Republican senators, Robert Taft, Jr. and William B. Saxbe, were hawks at this time, while college students in Ohio and elsewhere were especially prominent among the doves. To an unprecedented extent these young people were anti-establishment, disillusioned with authority in all of its forms. The feeling that America had been led into an immoral war was widespread. Thousands of men eligible for the draft enrolled in college to obtain deferment while other thousands slipped across the Canadian border or found some other haven for their self-imposed exile. In avoiding the draft some were advised by sympathetic counselors, many of whom were associated with churches.

The war protesters viewed themselves as taking a stand against an immoral war, but they also believed they were fighting a corrupt social system, one which was co-opting the rights of the individual. Their idealism tended to make them self-righteous, and they were clearly present-minded, having little knowledge of or tolerance for historical facts and forces. Parents and traditionalists found the young protesters' attitudes confusing and threatening. They were repelled by the scruffy and often purposefully outrageous dress, customs, and lifestyle of those who followed drug culture guru Timothy Leary's suggestion to "turn on, tune in, and drop out." Equally threatening was a sexual environment turned promiscuous by easy access to birth control, and social rebellion characterized by slovenly hygiene, mind-numbing music, and mind-altering substances like marijuana and LSD.

Ohio's many large cities and college campuses provided gathering points for those protesting the war and other social conditions. From little Wilmington College in Clinton County to sprawling Ohio State there were vigils, "teach-ins," and demonstrations. Nationally, antiwar protests were strong enough to dissuade President Johnson from seeking another term in 1968. His vice-president, Hubert H. Humphrey, became the Democratic presidential candidate, but his support of Johnson's Vietnam policies cost him liberal support and his support of black civil rights cost him blue-collar votes. He lost by the narrowest of margins to Richard Nixon, who won the presidency with only 43.4 percent of the vote and carried Ohio with 45 percent. George C. Wallace, a conservative independent whose running mate was Maj. Gen. Curtis E. LeMay, an Ohio State ROTC graduate, got nearly a half million Ohio votes.

Despite the negative reaction to Johnson's war policies, President Nixon continued a tough line on Vietnam. The war dragged on inconclusively despite more bombing, the mining of Haiphong harbor, and other escalations.

As American disenchantment grew, large numbers of adults, formerly hawks, now joined the doves. Public opinion polls revealed that during the war's early years, two-thirds of Americans supported the government's policies, but support shrank rapidly and soon two-thirds would oppose continued American involvement. In the spring of 1970 President Nixon ordered American forces into Cambodia to interdict Vietnamese supply routes. This action triggered the most violent student protest to date. National Guardsmen were ordered to seal off the Ohio State campus as authorities tried to deal with widespread acts of violence and vandalism, and other Ohio campuses suffered unrest and destruction as well.

But it was at Kent State University where protest had the most tragic consequences. In that small Portage County city, roving bands of students and non-student protesters smashed downtown store windows and confronted and defied police. On May 3 a mob burned the ROTC building on campus; firemen and police trying to control the fire were obstructed and jeered. Governor Rhodes, determined to restore order in Kent, ordered National Guard troops to the campus. On Monday, May 4 the guardsmen maneuvered on "Blanket Hill" on the Kent campus. They were confronted by a group of cursing, jeering, rock-throwing demonstrators while a much larger group of uninvolved students looked on from a distance. Suddenly, shots rang out. It has never been determined on whose orders, if any, the troops fired, but for many seconds guardsmen fired over and into the crowd. Four students were killed—Allison Krause, Jeffrey Miller, Sandra Scheuer, and William Schroeder. Nine others were wounded.

The shock was profound. Campuses across the state shut down, some for a few days, others for the remainder of the term. Charges and countercharges flew as efforts were made to fix responsibility for the tragedy. Some citizens applauded the killings. Eventually Governor Rhodes, the National Guard, and its commander, Sylvester Del Corso, were cleared in federal court of charges that they had deprived the slain students of their civil rights; nevertheless, the troops were responsible for the deaths and injuries, and in the eyes of many they would forever stand accused. The emotional wounds remained open for years; not until 1986 was it possible for the Kent State campus community to agree on a suitable memorial, and even then the Ohio American Legion protested what it said was the memorializing of war protest. Kent State would forever signify the tragic tensions of the Vietnam era.

Three years after the Kent shootings, the Vietnam War came to an end. Promising an end to the war, Nixon had won an electoral mandate in 1972 by securing 60 percent of the vote in his victory over George McGovern. His Ohio plurality was over 900,000 votes. The president sent Secretary of State Henry Kissinger to negotiate an armistice with North Vietnam, and early in 1973 American troops were withdrawn.

Hundreds of thousands of Ohioans served at some time during the twelve years of the Vietnam War. Of these, 2,997 were killed and more than 20,000 wounded. Little Bealsville in Monroe County had the sad distinction of having more of its young men killed, per capita, than any community in America. Sparsely populated Vinton County also suffered disproportionately. Many veterans who did return felt frustrated and unappreciated. They suffered insults and neglect as if the nation was embarrassed by what it had asked them to do. Many found it hard to adjust to civilian life; ten years after war's end, Vietnam veterans in Ohio had an unemployment rate twice the average, and nationwide, veterans suffered other emotional and psychological symptoms that came to be recognized—and treated—during the 1980s.

While the protests, riots, and social malaise of the sixties were both highly visible and deeply disturbing, America achieved significant progress in other areas. One of the most notable was in the U.S. space program. After a series of humiliating setbacks, America finally succeeded in 1962 in putting a man in space in a brief suborbital flight. This was followed on February 20, 1962, by the three-orbit flight of *Friendship 7*, a capsule carrying Lt. Col. John H. Glenn, Jr., of New Concord, Ohio. Glenn's achievement as the first American to orbit the earth exhilarated the nation and restored its confidence in its scientific abilities. President Kennedy was so encouraged that he pledged America would put a man on the moon before the end of the decade. Skepticism greeted this announcement, but on July 20, 1969, as television viewers around the world watched in fascination, they heard the startling transmission, "Houston, Houston . . . the *Eagle* has landed." Astronaut Neil Armstrong of Wapakoneta, Ohio, emerged from the lunar module *Eagle* and took man's first step on the moon. In fulfilling mankind's ancient dream, Armstrong and his crew were pioneers just as surely as any lone explorer who had once crossed the Ohio River into Indian country.

Many other Ohioans were involved in the space program as crew members and as technical and support personnel. The state's considerable scientific establishment, including NASA's Lewis Research Center in Cleveland and the Air Force's Wright-Patterson complex at Dayton, contributed to the program as did various industrial firms that fabricated parts and equipment.

As Ohio shared in the triumphs of the space program, so it shared in its tragedies. In 1986 the space shuttle *Challenger* exploded shortly after lift-off from Cape Canaveral, killing its crew of seven. Among them was Judith Resnick of Akron, an accomplished engineer and veteran of a previous space flight.

Political Adjustments

In *Baker v. Carr* (1962), the United States Supreme Court enunciated the "one man, one vote" doctrine which required that legislative districts contain

equal populations. It had a profound effect on Ohio politics. Since 1903 Ohio
had labored under the Hanna Amendment, which required that each of the
state's eighty-eight counties have at least one representative in the Ohio
House. This created a serious imbalance. In the early sixties, the 11,000 people
in Vinton County, for example, had as much representation as more than
400,000 had in heavily urban districts. Rural Ohio was traditionally more
conservative than the populous northern urban areas. Some political observers attributed the slowness with which Ohio addressed many of its urban
problems following World War II to rural domination of the legislature.

Conforming to the Supreme Court mandate, Ohio voters approved a state
constitutional amendment in 1967 calling for a thirty-three-seat Senate and a
ninety-nine-seat House. Electoral districts were to be reapportioned on the
"one man, one vote" basis, and congressional boundaries redistricted.

Other legislative concerns of the late sixties included strict new controls on
strip mining. Though reluctant to put barriers in the way of Ohio's troubled
coal industry, the general assembly realized that the ravaging of the land and
pollution of streams caused by stripping called for attention. Mine owners and
operators now had to post bond pending recontouring and reseeding of
stripped-over land. The salubrious impact of the new controls was dramatic.
The healing of nature's scars became apparent to anyone travelling the back
roads of Ohio's eastern counties.

In other action the last Rhodes legislature, in response to federal regulations, banned billboards within 600 feet of interstate highways. State development officials hoped that Ohio highways could be made more attractive to
tourists, but the sign industry erected huge new signs easily visible from the
interstates. The legislature also liberalized the sale of birth control devices,
allowed Sunday sale of alcoholic beverages by local option, and restricted the
sale of hallucinogenic drugs.

The Gilligan Administration

The 1954 constitutional amendment which Republicans had fostered to
keep another Frank Lausche from dominating the governor's office now
barred their own James Rhodes from seeking a third consecutive term. Thus
in 1970 the Republicans chose the state auditor, Roger Cloud, as their gubernatorial candidate. His opponent was a young, attractive Democrat, John J.
Gilligan, a former college professor, city councilman, and congressman from
Cincinnati.

Each candidate faced difficulties. Although Cloud was competent and experienced, he lacked charisma. Republicans were also charged with responsibility for alleged misuse of state funds in the so-called Crofters loan scandal.

Gilligan's problem was of his own making: he proposed a new state income tax on individuals and businesses. While Ohio was the only major industrial state without such a tax, it seemed like political suicide for a candidate to promise new taxes. Still, Gilligan's act of political courage paid off, at least in part. He won 54 percent of the vote, but he was confronted by a Republican-dominated state legislature; Ohio's delegation in Washington remained largely Republican.

Shortly after assuming office, Governor Gilligan received a report from his thirty-four-member "Citizens Task Force on Tax Reform." The report proposed a new graduated income tax that would yield up to $500 million per year, this to be accompanied by property tax relief, homestead exemptions for older residents, and repeal of the intangible (personal property) tax. Gilligan submitted the proposed legislation to the general assembly along with a new budget that would increase spending in state operations that had long been underfunded.

Gilligan's first budget was based on revenues anticipated from the new income tax. It took nine months of bitter fighting to work the budget and the income tax, which was Ohio's first major new tax source since the 1935 sales tax, through the general assembly. Within a year an effort to repeal the income tax was solidly defeated in a referendum vote. For many years to come, the state sales tax would remain Ohio's largest source of state revenue, but by the mid-1980s the general revenue fund was receiving more money from the income tax than from the sales tax. Despite cries that Ohio had become a high-tax state, comparative figures showed that it still ranked well below the national average in the level of state and local taxes paid by its citizens.

Another new source of income was approved by constitutional amendment. In 1974 a state lottery went into effect despite the opposition of Governor Gilligan and of those persons who objected to state sponsorship of gambling. Its proceeds were to be used for public education. In its early years of operation the lottery was poorly managed and produced little income. Ten years after its inception it had overcome its early problems and was returning a substantial revenue, only a portion of which went to education.

State revenues and expenditures, as always, preempted much of the legislature's and governor's time, yet other measures, including lowering the age of majority, did become law. On July 25, 1973, the legislature lowered the age of adulthood from twenty-one to eighteen. Eighteen-year-olds could now vote and were eligible for all other rights except drinking high-proof alcoholic beverages and service on police and state highway patrol forces. The Gilligan administration also organized a new Department of Transportation (1972), incorporating responsibilities formerly spread among various agencies. A grave concern for the department was the effect on Ohio business of the erosion of rail service. Railroad companies had abandoned hundreds of miles of track in the 1960s, 1970s, and 1980s in moves to consolidate into a handful of super carriers. Although Ohio had strong resources in trucking and air traffic, it had historically relied upon the railroads, and the state retained the highest rail density in the nation.

During this period two court rulings had wide effects in Ohio. In one case in 1973 a federal district judge ruled that Ohio's anti-abortion laws were unconstitutional, since they were in conflict with recent Supreme Court decisions. Anti-abortionists organized immediately to support new legislation. An Akron law placing restrictions on abortions seemed promising to them, but it was ultimately rejected by the courts. As of 1988 no new restrictive legislation had succeeded. The other court ruling, sent down by the United States Supreme Court, awarded to Ohio some 200 square miles of western Lake Erie, thus ending a border dispute with Michigan of some 138 years' standing.

Environmental Concerns

Environmental pollution is as old as humankind, but, in the post-World War II period, a growing number of Americans resented and resisted the continued defilement of air, water, and land. For convenience we lump many different types of concerned citizens together under the label "environmentalists." As in every movement one finds the whole range of commitment. By the 1970s it was clear that Ohio had serious pollution problems. Indeed, the state was often singled out as harboring some particularly gross offenses against nature. Steubenville and the surrounding upper Ohio Valley were said to have the nation's most polluted air. Despite emission stacks 800 feet tall, local power plants, along with the steel industry, contributed to that pollution, especially when air inversions trapped pollutants near ground level. Conditions were so bad that West Virginia—although producing its own plentiful supply of polluted air—threatened to take court action unless Ohio cleaned up.

Lake Erie was perhaps the nation's favorite example of a lake dying from mistreatment. Doom-sayers predicted that it was turning into a swamp while admitting, of course, that it would take thousands of years to do so. The rivers feeding into Lake Erie were sorely troubled. Governor Rhodes blamed Detroit industrial wastes for Erie's problems, conveniently overlooking the contributions of Ohio's rivers, some of which carried phosphates from fertilizers spread on farmers' fields and from commercial detergents. The phosphates stimulated algae growth, which starved the lake for oxygen. Every Ohio river carried sewage and/or industrial wastes. When the Cuyahoga River, covered with floating, volatile wastes, caught fire in Cleveland's flats, the once-proud city became the butt of poor jokes—the city whose river caught on fire, the "mistake on the lake."

Other forms of pollution preempted attention in the 1980s. Toxic waste disposal was a national as well as a state problem. Ohio was identified as having especially lethal dumps in Ashtabula, Portage, Hamilton, and several other counties. Some were eligible for federal "Superfund" clean-up monies. Disposal of nuclear wastes concerned Ohio as nuclear power plants and industries located there and as its highways and railroads were used to transport the dangerous material. Disposal of the brine produced in drilling for oil was yet another environmental problem.

While the public at large was being sensitized to environmental concerns some groups had a history of involvement in preserving the natural balance. Money from hunting and fishing licenses had long been used to extend and protect fish and wildlife habitats. Well-motivated youth groups from the Scouts to the 4-H clubs were involved in useful environmental projects.

It takes enormous funding and political courage to counter the power of corporate giants or to stimulate recalcitrant cities and towns into taking proper measures to protect the environment. Ohio demonstrated such commitment by contributing to one of the earliest successful regional consortiums fighting pollution. In 1948 the eight states of the Ohio River basin formed the Ohio River Valley Sanitary Commission (ORSANCO). Headquartered in Cincinnati, this commission monitors environmental conditions in the watershed and establishes controls and programs which are designed to satisfy industry's needs while making the river system safe and attractive for other uses. This model program has been widely copied. More recently the Great Lakes states joined to explore means of protecting the world's greatest fresh water resource through concerted action. In 1972 the Ohio Environmental Protection Agency was established to direct state control of its land, air, and water resources. Critics claimed it was inadequately funded to police polluting activities, and said it was subject to political pressure. Nevertheless it provided a structure for organizing the multifaceted attack on pollution.

The federal government did more to fund clean-up projects than did the state. Ohio received hundreds of millions of dollars to build and modernize sewage treatment plants, monitor industrial wastes, check shore erosion along Lake Erie, and generally support the interrelated tasks required to protect the environment. Federal money also protected the Little Miami River, Ohio's first national scenic river. A striking development was the creation in 1974 of Ohio's first national park. Thanks to efforts by representatives John Seiberling of Akron and Ralph Regula of Navarre, approximately 32,000 acres of scenic land were set aside as the Cuyahoga Valley National Recreation Area. Incorporating units of the Cleveland and Akron Metropolitan parks systems, it brings outdoor recreation resources to the 4 million people who live within an hour's drive.

While federal monies have been most helpful, the state has also spent large sums on environmental control and the setting aside of new natural preserves. Since its pathfinding work with the Miami Conservancy District (1915) Ohio has expanded its concern for watersheds. In 1985 there were thirty-eight conservancy districts and subdistricts in Ohio. The state maintained seventy-two parks and numerous game and wildlife refuges.

The struggle to maintain a healthy and pleasing natural environment is a never-ending one. Overly strict environmental controls can cost jobs; in the 1970s and 1980s that was a prime concern. While Ohio was slow to throw its resources wholeheartedly into environmental control, it made great strides after mid-century. But it was clear that there could be no slackening of effort if Ohio was to maintain an attractive quality of life.

16.

The Arts and Leisure-time Activities

 **In 1891,** James Ford Rhodes of Cleveland moved to Cambridge, Massachusetts. There, close by Harvard Yard, he found a congenial environment in which to write and socialize. He was already a recognized historian, scion of the newly rich iron and coal family to whom Mark Hanna was related by marriage. But Cleveland was too absorbed in mundane affairs for his taste. "A writer of books walking down Euclid Avenue would have been stared at as a somewhat remarkable personage," he wrote. In Cambridge and neighboring Boston, about as old a seat of culture as one could find in America, Rhodes observed that "the work of the mind was appreciated." Here he finished his monumental seven-volume *History of the United States From the Compromise of 1850* (1893–1906), which assured him a secure place in national and Bay State intellectual circles.

Even as Rhodes with his polished skills and manners was accepted into greater Boston society, so too was another Ohio expatriate, William Dean Howells. Born in Martins Ferry, young Howells followed his father, an itinerant printer and newspaperman, to Hamilton, Dayton, Columbus, Jefferson, and other Ohio towns. A successful campaign biography of Abraham Lincoln brought Howells an appointment as American consul to Venice during the Civil War. Returning to the United States in 1866, Howells took up residence in Boston and New York, where he entered fully into the literary life about him. A prolific writer, his novels, including perhaps his best-known work, *The Rise of Silas Lapham* (1885), were noted for their realism, their humanitarian spirit, and increasingly, for their socialist sympathies. His great fame sprang from editing the *Atlantic Monthly* and from commentaries and essays written for *Harper's Magazine*. He became the champion of young writers and, as the leading literary figure of his day, earned the sobriquet, "Dean of American Letters."

In peopling his imaginary world, Howells was certainly influenced by his Ohio childhood. In the socialist novel *A Traveler from Altruria* (1894), Howells may have patterned Alturia after the rural villages of pre–Civil War Ohio, which he nostalgically identified with "simplicity, equality [and] cooperative spirit," though he remained aware of their "monotony, boredom, isolation." Yet Howells's world view had an eastern coloration. Historian Gregory Crider writes that Howells was "a city dweller who enjoyed above all the material comforts and sparkling conversation of the best society," yet he "pined for the simplicity and equality, the plain living and high thinking, of the country village. . . . In his own words, he was resigned to the position of theoretical socialist and practical aristocrat."

Not all writers and artists whose beginnings were in Ohio acknowledged their connections and debts to the Buckeye State, but many did. Clearly there was no "Ohio school" of literature or art. Diversity and eclecticism mark Ohio culture in the same way they characterize Ohio politics, economics, or social orientation.

Literary Figures

When Abraham Lincoln needed a moment's relief from wartime burdens, he enjoyed the writings of Petroleum V. Nasby, whom literary historian David Anderson has called "our only authentic Civil War anti-hero." Nasby was the fictional creation of David Ross Locke, a New Yorker who edited northwestern Ohio newspapers in the Civil War era. Nasby's humorous comments made him the "self-styled spokesman of the midwestern Peace Democrats." He was portrayed, said Anderson, as "a patriot, a Democrat, a Jeffersonian, and finally a clergyman"; but he was also "a lazy, illiterate, cowardly, alcoholic seeker of political patronage and booty, a racist, an unscrupulous opportunist." Though Locke had but transient Ohio connections, his fictional character represented the viewpoint of large segments of the state's people during the troubled war years.

The Civil War also inspired much of Ambrose Bierce's writing. Born in Horse Cave (Meigs County), Bierce rejected his none-too-successful father and looked to his accomplished uncle, Lucius Bierce of Akron, for inspiration. He had his uncle's penchant for direct action and served admirably in an Indiana regiment during the Civil War. He won fame and attention for macabre war stories such as those collected in *Tales of Soldiers and Civilians* (1891). Moving to California, Bierce became the literary arbiter of the West coast. His savage, cynical style, developed perhaps during his hardscrabble youth, was apparent in his popular *Devil's Dictionary* (1911). In 1913 he disappeared in Mexico; no trace of him has ever been found.

Mary Hartwell Catherwood, born along the National Pike at Luray (Licking County), would become what critic Robert Price calls "the first American woman novelist of any significance born west of the Appalachians." The first well-known woman writer to earn a college degree and the first to get that degree from a non-eastern school (she graduated from Granville Female College), Catherwood displayed in her early work what Price describes as "critically realistic reporting of life as she knew it in . . . communities in Ohio, Indiana, and Illinois." This phase culminated in *Craque-O'Doom* (1881), which Price says is based on "the provincial barrenness of the Ohio town of Hebron, where she spent her girlhood." Price calls the novel "the forerunner of all the later *Winesburgs*." Catherwood's book for juveniles, *Rocky Fork* (1882), was an excellent account of a central Ohio school district in the 1860s. Catherwood was best known for historical romances set in French America, and she helped pioneer the genre in such works as *Romance of Dollard* (1889), *Lady of Fort St. John* (1891), and *Old Kaskaskia* (1893).

Other early writers of historical fiction who used Ohio themes included Mary Stanbery Watts of Cincinnati, Burton Stevenson of Chillicothe, and James Ball Naylor of Malta (Morgan County). Naylor, a physician, wrote in his spare time; his historical novels such as *Under Mad Anthony's Banner* (1899) had Ohio settings and captured a large reading audience.

Brand Whitlock of Urbana was one of several turn-of-the-century Ohio writers to picture small-town life realistically. His early work, such as *The 13th District* (1902), focused on politics. For Whitlock, it was a case of art immitating life, for he was caught up in practical politics during much of his life, especially during his stint as reform mayor of Toledo, where he became an effective practitioner of good government and a proponent of social justice. His best-known work, *J. Hardin & Sons* (1923), was published after his public career ended. According to one commentator, its excellence "was lost sight of in the sophistication-saturated decade" of the 1920s.

The most famous Ohio writer of adventure stories was Zane Grey. A dentist in his home town of Zanesville, he was a direct descendent of the influential Zane family, which had played so central a part in settling pioneer Ohio. His novel *Betty Zane* (1933) was based on the authentic heroism of his great-great-aunt, who helped save Fort Henry (Wheeling, West Virginia) from Indian attack during the Revolutionary War. It did not become the great American novel he hoped it would; he published it at his own expense. However, his westerns—*Riders of the Purple Sage* (1912), *The Thundering Herd* (1925), and many others—made him the world's best-selling author with over 28 million copies in print. These stories had no Ohio connections, nor did Grey himself after moving to California and Arizona to be close to the land he wrote about.

Ohio's premier poet at century's end was Xenia's Ridgely Torrence. Though he spent his active literary career in New York, his collected poems, *The House of a Hundred Lights* (1900) and *Hesperides* (1925), show the influence of his Ohio years. Poetic plays sprang from Torrence's childhood memories of Xenia's black community, for that town and surrounding Greene county had long been home to a substantial black population.

Ohio boasts several early black writers of distinction. Though his reputation has been in eclipse for many years, Cincinnati's George Washington Williams published *History of the Negro Race in America* (1883), which became a starting point for those who later wrote on this subject. Another influential writer around the turn of the century was Charles Chesnutt, born of free black parents in Cleveland. While Chesnutt was very young, the family moved to Oberlin, a hotbed of antislavery agitation, and there his father may have participated in the famous Oberlin-Wellington rescue case. A student of his career wrote that "long after, Chesnutt was to recall these formative years and . . . realize how they had impressed him and molded his character and career." After fighting in the Civil War, the elder Chesnutt took his family to North Carolina, where Charles became virtually self-taught in history and mathematics, and, with a tutor's help, learned Latin, German, and French. As an adult, Chesnutt returned to Cleveland, earned his living as a court reporter, and commenced writing. Among his best-known works were *The Conjure Woman* (1899), a collection of black dialect stories, and *The House Behind the Cedars* (1900), his most popular novel, which treated interracial marriage, an untouchable theme for the time. His writing helped lay the groundwork for the Black Renaissance of the 1920s.

Paul Laurence Dunbar, another accomplished black writer of the period, was born in Dayton and lived there except for a seven-year period spent in New York and Washington, D.C. His father, a Civil War veteran, died while the boy was very young, and his mother worked as a laundress to support her son and herself. Dunbar was a good student who held several leadership positions at Central High School even though he was virtually alone as a black student. His white classmates scattered to jobs upon graduation while Paul could find work only as an elevator operator in a local department store. He composed rhymes in his head while riding the car up and down.

Dunbar was twenty-four years old when a collection of his poems, *Majors and Minors* (1896), was published, the second of more than twenty volumes he would publish in his short life. William Dean Howells praised the poems, and with Howells's support, Dunbar's fame expanded and he was much sought after for readings in America and overseas. His black dialect verse as represented in *When Malindy Sings* (1903) and *Candle-Lightin' Time* (1901) won people's attention and affection. But Dunbar also had an excellent prose style and used it to protest the racial conventions of his day. Critic Gossie Harold Hudson has called Dunbar's work "a representative document of black thought, one in which both the old and the new mental attitudes of black Americans are focused sharply and artistically. It reflects changing attitudes of mind in every sphere: social, political, spiritual and intellectual." Plagued by personal problems and poor health in his last years, Dunbar died of tuberculosis at age thirty-three. In the cemetery of his native Dayton, the citizens have honored him by placing a monument affixed with a plaque inscribed with Dunbar's poem "A Death Song":

> Lay me down beneaf de willers in de grass,
> Whah de branch'll go a'singin' as it pass.
> An' w'en I's a-layin' low,
> I kin hyeah it as it go
> Singin,' "Sleep, my honey, tek yo' res' at las'."

The Ohio Historical Society preserves his Dayton home as a state memorial.

Ohio was in the blood of Sherwood Anderson. Born in Camden, he grew up in Clyde and worked in Cleveland before finding his writer's vocation and moving, first to Chicago and then to the East. Anderson's professional reputation has received mixed reviews. Most favorable attention centers on his contribution to realism, especially in his classic *Winesburg, Ohio* (1919), a collection of vignettes about lonely and inarticulate people, presumably based on his Clyde neighbors. The neighbors didn't appreciate the often unflattering portraits, but the critics did. Anderson's Ohio connections remained clear throughout his lifetime as indicated in his well-known assertion, "I have always thought of myself as an Ohioan, and no doubt shall always remain, inside myself, an Ohioan."

Another Ohio writer whose roots pulled upon him was Mansfield's Louis Bromfield. An early novel, *The Green Bay Tree* (1924), reputedly earned the author $1.5 million and *Early Autumn* (1926) won a Pulitzer Prize. For years Bromfield lived in France, returning to America shortly before World War II. He purchased four soil-depleted farms in Richland County, merged them, and restored the land using natural fertilizers. One of his interpreters believes Bromfield was thus rejecting the industrial age's rape of the land by restoring a portion of it to its proper condition.

His restoration efforts worked, but the expense was such that ordinary farmers would be hard-pressed to emulate them. Malabar Farm attracted soil conservationists from around the world. Many of Bromfield's books dealt with agricultural society. In *The Farm* (1933), he follows the course of his great-grandfathers into early nineteenth-century Ohio, creating in the process what literary historian David Anderson labeled "a myth of nineteenth-century Ohio, a myth of the Ohio frontier" involving the farm as a self-sustaining unit in a pastoral world of Jeffersonian virtue. Later books—*Pleasant Valley* (1945) and *Malabar Farm* (1948)—were based on his own agricultural work. Years after Bromfield's death, Malabar Farm became a state park operated by the Department of Natural Resources.

Hart Crane was as alienated from his native Ohio as Bromfield was attracted to it. Born in Garretsville (Portage County), young Crane reluctantly worked in his father's candy stores in Cleveland and Akron. Ultimately he succeeded in escaping what was for him a stultifying environment, made more difficult by his parents' divorce. His mood can be sensed in "Porphyro in Akron."

> Greeting the dawn
> A shift of rubber workers presses down
> South Main
> With the stubbornness of muddy water
> It dwindles at each cross-line
> Until you feel the weight of many cars
> North-bound, and East and West,
> Absorbing and conveying weariness,—
> Rumbling over the hills.
>
> —
>
> Akron, "high place,"—
> A bunch of smoke-ridden hills.
> Among rolling Ohio hills.

Crane's early poems attracted financial support that enabled him to produce *The Bridge* (1930), his most promising work. Described as "highly obscure" and "filled with vivid images," it is no longer as well regarded as it once was. Disappointed in his work, distressed by homosexuality and alcoholism, Crane leaped from a ship taking him from Mexico to New York. He was thirty-three.

James Thurber wished to be known as a serious writer of consequence, and so he has been. But his larger fame rests upon his skill as a humorist. He added a new name to the language—Walter Mitty, the perennial dreamer featured in *The Secret Life of Walter Mitty* (1942). Thurber's own early life and that of his family appear in *My Life and Hard Times* (1933), *The Thurber Carnival* (1945), and other pieces. Columbus born and bred, a student at Ohio State—which he and Elliott Nugent satirized in a play, *The Male Animal* (1939), spoofing the excesses of Ohio State football—Thurber was thoroughly Ohio even though New York was the center of his professional career. In 1959 he wrote to the mayor of Columbus, "I have always waved banners and blown horns for

Good Old Columbus Town." And it was Thurber who said "the clocks that strike in my dreams are often the clocks of Columbus."

Those who admire Ohio themes in literature have long appreciated the contributions of Harlan Hatcher and Walter Havighurst. Hatcher, born in Ironton, achieved a full career as a writer and an Ohio State University administrator before he was lured north to become president of the University of Michigan. His significance as an interpreter of Ohio rests not so much on his fiction as on such gracefully written popular histories as *Buckeye Country* (1940) and *The Western Reserve* (1949). One of his great services to the state was his work with the *Ohio Guide* (1940), a depression-era project that preserved much of a rapidly vanishing story, a book that is indispensable to those interpreting the Ohio scene.

Walter Havighurst was born in Wisconsin, but his long-time home was the Ohio college town of Oxford. An early novel, *The Quiet Shore* (1937), was set along Lake Erie, but the Ohio settings for which he is best known are those found in his absorbing regional studies such as *The Long Ships Passing* (1942), *Land of Promise* (1946), and *Wilderness for Sale* (1956). A romantic aura hangs over his scenes, adding to a sense of time and place without seriously detracting from reality.

Late in the twentieth century, Ohio writers continued to find inspiration in their native or adopted soil. No better example could be found than Xenia's Helen Hooven Santmyer. Her tour de force, entitled . . . *And Ladies of the Club* (1982), details the lives of several generations of families from the Civil War until the 1930s as they unfold in fictional Waynesboro, an Ohio town based on real-life Xenia. Rich in authentic detail and true to its historical setting, the novel compares favorably with any attempt to describe small-town America.

Another writer who mined Ohio lore for material was Allan Eckert. His choice of subject was eclectic; his most popular book in an Ohio setting is *The Frontiersmen* (1967), a work which graphically explores the Revolutionary War period through the experiences of the scout, Simon Kenton, and the Shawnee leader, Tecumseh. Eckert gave his "histories" a dramatic punch through his use of realistic contemporary dialogue. William Donohue Ellis is another writer who provided insights into Ohio's pioneer period. Money and banking, law, and pioneer medicine are subjects treated in *The Bounty Lands* (1952), *Jonathan Blair, Bountylands Lawyer* (1954), and *The Brooks Legend* (1958). An evocation of a disappearing lifestyle can be found in John Baskin's *New Burlington: The Life and Death of an Ohio Town* (1976), which reveals the feelings and experiences of people in a small rural community soon to be inundated under the waters of a new reservoir.

Should anyone question the vitality of Ohio's literary world as the state approaches its bicentennial, he would do well to read the *Ohioana Quarterly*.

This publication of the Ohioana Library Association, founded by Martha Kinney Cooper, wife of the former governor, keeps track of contemporary Ohio authors and their works. The list is impressive.

In the 1980s two talented black women with Ohio origins won Pulitzer prizes: Rita Dove of Akron for her poems *Thomas and Beulah* (1987) based on her grandparents' experiences as they moved from the South to Akron, and Toni Morrison of Lorain for her novel *Beloved* (1988), describing the haunting memories of an escaped slave in post-Civil War Ohio. And so the tradition continued.

The Visual Arts

The clear evocation of a sense of place is not so easily demonstrated in the works of Ohio visual artists. While Cincinnati remained a focus of artistic life in the post-Civil War years, its importance was not as great as it had once been. Ohio-born painters and sculptors, like their peers from other parts of America, gravitated toward the East and Europe. The leading spirit in Cincinnati's art world was Frank Duveneck, a native Kentuckian who had studied and painted in Europe. In 1888 he returned to the Queen City and exerted great influence in his position as dean of the faculty of the Cincinnati Art Academy and as an advisor to the art museum. Duveneck was an accomplished artist in his own right, working in oils, sculpting, and etching. His subjects were not Ohio-oriented. An important contemporary of Duveneck's was Joseph Twachtman, an impressionist who was also based in Cincinnati. Still another member of that group, L. H. Meakin, painted Ohio River scenes.

Next to Duveneck the best-known Cincinnati painter was Robert Henri, who, after a long sojourn in Europe, returned to America to become a powerful influence on young painters, directing them toward American themes. He and his students, especially Columbus-born George Bellows, contributed to a style which critics dubbed the "ashcan school." This school emphasized realism and truth in art; Bellows's *Stag at Sharkey's*, depicting boxers battering each other in a smoke-filled arena, was perhaps the best-known work of this genre. Another Ohio artist noted for realism was Ashtabula's Charles Burchfield, who often depicted scenes of small-town streets and of people on everyday errands.

In the early twentieth century, Cleveland's art community was led by Archibald Willard of Wellington. Willard's *The Spirit of '76* is the most familiar patriotic painting in the nation. He practically made a career of that work, painting at least six "originals," each with slight variations. Grace V. Kelley was a well-recognized member of the Cleveland art community. Other prominent artists included Alice Schille of Columbus and Josephine Klippart, a Columbus art teacher, who founded the Ohio Water Color Society early in the twentieth century, and served as its long-time president.

That the visual arts were claiming attention in rapidly industrializing Ohio was evident in the emergence of the great museums that make the state a mecca for art lovers. As usual, Cincinnati led the way with the establishment of the Cincinnati Museum Association (1881). This museum represented all of the visual arts and cooperated with art-related local industries like the Rookwood Pottery, whose ceramics were among the world's finest. Today the Cincinnati Art Museum, atop scenic Mt. Adams, spreads its impressive collections through scores of galleries and serves as a major national cultural resource. Down the hill from the Art Museum is the Taft Art Gallery of fine paintings, housed in the Greek Revival Martin Baum house later owned by Charles P. Taft; the family later donated house and collections to the public.

Cleveland, bursting with new wealth, housed its new Museum of Art (1916) in a classical temple set amid landscaped grounds. Through the generosity of many donors, including the Hanna family, it developed into one of the world's great art institutions. By the last half of the twentieth century, it was well financed and was, in every sense, a major force in the art world. Edward Libbey's new wealth helped make Toledo still another first-class center for the arts. From his original donation, the Toledo Museum emerged as an eminent institution housing many treasures including an outstanding collection of art glass.

Late in the twentieth century, Ohio's other cities were enhancing their position in support of the arts. The Columbus Museum of Art traces its origins to the nineteenth century, but its impressive growth was post-World War II. The Dayton Art Institute is housed in a grand renaissance-style building, and maintains its reputation for public service; the Butler Art Institute has provided Youngstown with a fine collection of Americana; Akron's Art Museum is housed in a beautifully restored nineteenth-century post office building and features contemporary art and photography; Canton's Timken Cultural Center houses an art gallery as part of one of America's finest small-city arts complexes. Small galleries such as the Johnson-Humrickson gallery at Roscoe Village (Coshocton), combining art objects with more general museum displays, are found throughout the state. The Ohio Historical Society, the Western Reserve Historical Society, and the Cincinnati Historical Society are custodians of impressive museum-grade pieces. The Ohio Statehouse contains delightful murals and oil portraits of each Ohio governor.

Ohio's unusually large number of colleges and its many comprehensive state universities give it yet another strong place in the art world. Oberlin's Allen Art Museum, founded in 1908, was one of the first college museums in the trans-Appalachian west. Ohio State University has a strong reputation in the visual arts, especially in ceramics-related productions. Each of the large

state universitites has painters, sculptors, etchers, engravers, weavers, potters, jewelers, photographers, and other specialists. Most are practicing
craftsmen displaying their work in faculty shows and in galleries and festivals
around the country. Some museums which once had art schools have abandoned them since training is widely available elsewhere, but the strong proprietary schools in Cincinnati and Cleveland continue to produce talented
artists.

Interest in and financial support for the arts is an attribute of a mature
society. By the last quarter of the twentieth century, there could be no doubt
about art's place in Ohio, from its great permanent institutions to the vitality
of its local art scenes.

From Saengerfest to Symphony

Ohio's musical heritage is long-standing. The German and Welsh singing
societies so important in the musical life of early Ohio continued to be influential well into the twentieth century. From their 1848 founding in Cincinnati, the German *saengerfeste* were held on at least ten occasions before 1900.
Similarly the Welsh festival, the *Eisteddfod,* was held in the Welsh stronghold
of Jackson, and in Cleveland and Columbus in the twentieth century. These
choral societies were joined by others organized by the new ethnic groups
crowding Ohio's industrial cities before World War I. Such societies helped
keep diverse musical traditions alive.

English-speaking choral societies also had an impact. They were influential
in starting Cincinnati's May Festival (1873), the most famous of its day. People travelled hundreds of miles to attend this festival that also served as a focus
and stimulant for other kinds of musical activity. By 1895 Cincinnati had a
symphony orchestra which, after a rude start, achieved respectability under
the direction of Leopold Stokowski. Liberally endowed by patrons, the orchestra continued to grow under the direction of Fritz Reiner, Eugene Goos-
ens, Thor Johnson, and other conductors. It remains today a world-renowned
ensemble.

Cleveland's orchestra also had a checkered beginning, but it survived early
traumas to achieve permanence in 1918 under the direction of Nikolai Soko-
loff. Cleveland had no music hall to match Cincinnati's until John L. Severance, a wealthy industrialist, donated funds to underwrite the cost of a new
building named in his honor. Encouraging Severance in his philanthropy was
Adella Prentiss Hughes, whose role as impresario eventually bore fruit in the
founding and managing of the Cleveland Orchestra. Artur Rodzinski developed the orchestra during a critical growth period, but it was George Szell, in
the years following World War II, who polished the orchestra until many
critics considered it the world's finest symphonic ensemble.

Symphony orchestras matured and proliferated across the state after the second world war. Columbus and Toledo developed regional orchestras while Akron, Canton, Dayton, and Youngstown supported strong local groups. Smaller cities, too, created their own orchestras, among them Ashland, Hamilton, Lima, Mansfield, Middletown, Newark, and Springfield, and many colleges and universities have symphony orchestras which enrich the musical life of surrounding areas.

Ohio boasts outstanding facilities in which to showcase its musical talent. In addition to Cincinnati's Music Hall and Cleveland's Severance Hall, fine facilities for performance exist in nearly every Ohio city. Once more we can look to the colleges and universities, where the facilities range from starkly contemporary halls to the timeless auditoriums that have served generations of music lovers. Superb outdoor facilities can be found at the Cleveland Orchestra's Blossom Music Center, located in rolling countryside south of the city, and Cincinnati's Riverbend, located eastward along the Ohio River.

Symphony orchestras are but one manifestation of the musical life of a state that has supported everything from sitar groups to steel drum bands. It was a nineteenth-century Ohioan turned New York impressario—Akron's Henry Abbey—who introduced Italian and other European opera stars to the American musical scene. For many years, Cleveland was the opera capital of the midwest, hosting the Metropolitan Opera Company of New York in annual appearances. Opera week in Cleveland was a sellout and remained so until discontinued in the 1980s due to high costs and scheduling problems. Other Ohio cities and universities maintain strong opera programs.

The recent proliferation of ballet and modern dance groups in Ohio provides further evidence of a maturing artistic taste in a state once skeptical of the more esoteric art forms. Dayton boasts one of the state's oldest ballet companies, Cleveland one of the newest. Columbus has Ballet Metropolitan and Cincinnati shares a company with New Orleans. Akron-based Ohio Ballet, organized in the 1960s, won national acclaim under the direction of Heinz Poll. As with other art forms, Ohio's universities have given a substantial boost to ballet; in a few institutions it is possible to secure a college major in the subject.

While Ohio scored well on most types of music-related activity, it has not yet produced a classical composer of unqualified world-class stature. Most Ohio-born composers sought the larger centers of the music world in which to exercise their talents. In the late twentieth century, however, Cleveland retained a group of significant composers, including Donald Erb and Marcel Dick, who found support in the Cleveland Composers' Guild. Another much-admired figure of recent times was Arthur Loesser of the Cleveland Institute of Music, a noted teacher, critic, and pianist.

Ohio composers have historically achieved more recognition in the realm of popular music, including folk songs, hymns, band music, and concert pieces. These were the tunes people sang and whistled, tunes which were central to American culture in an age when group singing was a feature of family life, church, school, and social activity. Earlier we noted some of these contributions—Daniel Decatur Emmett's "Dixie," for example—but we might add to the list of folksongs such favorites as "Darling Nellie Gray" and "Up On the Housetops," both written by Benjamin Hanby (Rushville and Westerville), "Down By the Old Mill Stream," Tell Taylor's evocation of the one-time charms of Findlay's Blanchard River, "Lorena," a plaintive Civil War song written by H. D. L. Webster (Zanesville), and in more recent times, "When Irish Eyes Are Smiling" and "Let the Rest of the World Go By," both by Cleveland's Ernest Ball. Ohio composers wrote many famous concert pieces. Among the favorites were "Sylvia" and "On the Road to Mandalay," works by Oley Speaks (Canal Winchester).

Those raised in the evangelical Protestant tradition would recognize many hymns written by Ohio composers. Some of the best known are: "Brighten the Corner Where You Are," by Homer Rodeheaver, once a music leader for the Billy Sunday revivals and later a successful publisher of religious music; "The Old Rugged Cross," by George Bernard; "Softly and Tenderly Jesus Is Calling" and "Bringing In the Sheaves," by William Thompson; and "Jesus Lover of My Soul," by R. E. Hudson.

Band music was especially important to small-town Ohio in the late nineteenth and early twentieth centuries. Seldom was a town without a local contingent playing in the town bandstand, marching in parades, and performing on holidays and other special occasions. As the automobile, radio, and other social forces changed traditions, the town band gave way to the local high school band. Eventually most high schools and colleges had a marching band that performed at football games. Uniforms, equipment, and formations became ever more elaborate. In the 1930s the band director at Massillon High School, "Red" Bird, popularized a revolutionary new style by introducing a swing band that accompanied its jazzy music with a double-time march step. It attracted national attention and thousands of imitators. Eugene J. Weigle, band director at Ohio State, introduced the all-brass marching band and made his organization one of the best college bands in the nation.

There is no corpus of Ohio-centered music. The official state song, adopted by the legislature in 1969, is "Beautiful Ohio," a pleasant piece which alludes to the river, but says nothing about Ohio scenes and sentiments.

Theater

As a popular recreational activity, the theater has had a substantial impact on the state's people. Cincinnati was the earliest center of theater activity. In

1801 the Thespians of Fort Washington presented a comic opera, *The Poor Soldier,* and for the remainder of the early nineteenth century the Queen City dominated the theater scene. Conservative residents often shunned early theater, believing it encouraged sloth and sin and fearing its corrupting influence on young minds. In Ohio's capital city, for example, the new Columbus Theater, opened in 1835, was soon closed as "a public nuisance," possibly because its most popular feature was a bar in the rear of the building.

Ohio's most exciting theater settings were the showboats, which made one-night stands at small ports and held week-long engagements at larger cities along the Ohio River. With its bright lights, aura of adventure, and steam calliope tooting an engaging tune, the showboat appealed to saint as well as sinner. "It was irresistable," wrote an observer. "Local church elders, Sunday School superintendents, and their families, usually denied such luxuries, found their way to its moorings, so that the children might have an opportunity to hear the 'music.' "

Vying in popularity with the showboats were minstrel shows. Mt. Vernon's Daniel Decatur Emmett was an important creative figure in this entertainment medium. Somewhat akin were the tent shows, simple carnivals with barkers enticing the credulous to see their wonders, including animals, sideshows, freaks, music, and other attractions. In time Ohio became home to several of the nation's leading carnivals, tent shows, minstrel troupes, and circuses. Most famous of the latter was the Sells Brothers Circus headquartered in Columbus.

The late nineteenth and early twentieth century produced a golden age of live theater, as great performers of the day—Sarah Bernhardt, Maude Adams, Anna Held, Edwin Booth, the Barrymores—performed before Ohio audiences. Great new theaters opened across the state. Their success was short-lived, however, as the growth of the motion picture industry undermined the theater's central role in American entertainment. The excitement and scope of screen fare, coupled with low prices and ready availability to a mass market, quickly made the movies America's most popular form of entertainment.

Perhaps the most important features of Ohio's recent theatrical history have been efforts to support local repertory companies and the tremendous swelling of little theater activity. Repertory theater got a boost in the depressed 1930s from the Federal Theater Project, which supported companies in Cleveland and Cincinnati. Cleveland had a Repertory Theater, a marionette unit, and a Negro unit which performed plays including *Conjure Man Dies* and *Noah.* The Cleveland unit produced 87 performances and the Cincinnati unit 191 before the program was phased out in 1939.

Among Ohio's little theater groups and repertory companies, a few stand out. The Cleveland Playhouse, organized in 1915, specialized in experimental work and the revival of old plays. The Karamu Theater, which was associated with Karamu House, a black settlement activity center in Cleveland, became a pacesetter in regional black theater. Yet another Cleveland initiative, Cain Park Theater, was a successful early attempt at the staging of outdoor drama, and Cincinnati's Playhouse-in-the-Park was also an important force in local theater. By the mid-twentieth century, every sizable Ohio community had its own "little theater" groups. Some of these, like the Canton Playhouse—one of the oldest and largest community theaters in the nation in terms of budget—developed a regional reputation for excellence. The number of productions staged by schools, colleges, industries, churches, and countless local associations provides ample evidence that amateur theater has been and remains a flourishing leisure-time activity.

Ohio and the Arts: An Interpretation

Several generations ago it was commonplace to hear Ohio referred to as a culturally deprived region, and at one time that charge may have had some validity. As was true of the rest of America, talented Ohio men and women left the state to find more congenial surroundings in the major eastern cultural centers and in Europe. But the fact remains that Ohio could claim more accomplishments in the arts than most of her neighbors thanks to the cultural leadership of Cincinnati both before and after the Civil War. Furthermore, by the early twentieth century the newly rich were underwriting great new art galleries, music halls, and other cultural amenities, and few states could boast a larger group of such philanthropists. Finally, Ohio was better served than most states by its uncommon number of culturally aware colleges and universities.

The contemporary vitality of the arts in Ohio could be characterized as explosive. The weekly entertainment sections of major newspapers are crammed with an astonishing array of public cultural events ranging from symphony concerts and art shows featuring the world's treasures, to Broadway musicals, experimental theater, dance ensembles, recitals, art fests, and more. The art enthusiast has neither the time nor, in most cases, the money to take it all in. Contemporary Ohio remains a major producer and consumer of the arts, serious and popular, on all levels and for all tastes.

Recreation

A society reveals much about itself in the way its people spend their surplus time and money once they have provided themselves the necessities of life. Though limited by isolation, poverty, illness, and other circumstances, most

Ohio pioneers found some way to pursue recreational activities, often through a cooperative work effort. Husking and quilting bees, barn raisings, and other group work activities brought people together for the social and emotional release they needed. Similar release came from occasional militia musters or religious camp meetings, where copious amounts of raw whiskey often accelerated conviviality to the detriment of the serious purpose at hand.

Sporting contests involved tests of strength and skill in activities that were essential to the development of a pioneer society. Shooting at a mark, log-chopping contests, foot races, wrestling, and horse racing were outlets for competitive spirits that also provided the chance to make a wager. Hunting and fishing were practical necessities for supplementing the pioneer diet, but they often doubled as sporting or recreational activities. The great community hunts, organized to reduce the population of varmints that destroyed crops and livestock, were as much social as practical. Indeed, from a practical point of view they were almost too effective since such mass slaughters hastened the premature disappearance from Ohio of several wildlife species.

The earthiness associated with activities of the earliest period gave way to a more constrained and sedate type of leisure activity later in the nineteenth century, at least for a middle- and upper-class population influenced by the formality and delicacy that represented good manners during the Victorian era. The constraint of this part of society should not be confused with the more relaxed attitudes prevailing in the larger society. Nevertheless, since the class most influenced by Victorian mores tended to control much of the business and political life of the state, the sedate and genteel element sometimes succeeded—as with the introduction of Sunday blue laws restraining business and entertainment operations—in limiting the options of those who did not share their sense of propriety.

But people still had fun. Among the organized activities popular in the mid-nineteenth century were dances, with folk or square dances much more common and popular than ballroom dancing. Also popular were picnics, church and Sunday school outings, boating, excursions to picnic groves or amusement parks, festivals, and parades. Ohio communities organized mass sleigh rides during which scores of sleighs would drive to and through a nearby town. It was then a matter of pride for the town thus visited to organize an even larger return visitation. The crisp air created hearty appetites, and a sumptuous spread of food and drink was a perfect way to end the trip. In March 1856, Cuyahoga, Medina, and Summit counties competed in a grand contest in Richfield. Only four- and six-horse teams counted, and on the big day 462 sleighs came into Richfield "with horses prancing, bells ringing, and horns blowing." Some 12,000 persons witnessed the gaiety and color of the day's events. The victory banner went to Summit County, which had 171 teams, but a few days later Summit relinquished the banner to Medina when that county made a surprise descent on Summit with 182 teams.

Similar competitions flourished in later years, except that horses and sleighs gave way to bicycles, or still later, to automobiles. In 1916 some 1,100 Zanesville residents motored to Newark to celebrate the paving of the National Pike, and the next year nearly 1,500 Newark residents rode in 500 automobiles to Zanesville to return the visit.

The picnic grove, the lakeside pavilion, and the amusement park were to be found nearly everywhere in Ohio by the late nineteenth century. An extended transportation system was partly responsible for the proliferation of these recreational spots. People arrived by boat or power launch at river and lake locations, by railroad excursion train, by horse and buggy, but above all by trolley and interurban car. Street railway and traction companies promoted recreation areas to stimulate business. A ride to the park on the "cars" was nearly as big a thrill for youngsters as the allurements of the park itself. Many picnic groves and amusement parks were transient, flourishing for a few years and then disappearing as housing or commercial developments encroached upon them or as economic difficulties pressed them.

The small, informal parks of earlier days gave way to much larger, diverse, and commercially oriented parks. One could not begin to name even the famous amusement centers in Ohio without the risk of leaving out some that were much loved by generations of youngsters who, now grown considerably older, still associate them with halcyon days. Some of the more representative amusement parks of note were Cedar Point outside Sandusky, Coney Island on the Ohio just east of Cincinnati, Cleveland's Euclid Beach Park, Idora Park in Youngstown, Meyers Lake in Canton, Olentangy Park in Columbus, Summit Beach in Akron, Chippewa Lake in Medina County, Russell's Point on Indian Lake, and Buckeye Lake just south of Newark.

In the post–World War II era, only a small number of amusement parks still flourished. Increased costs of operation, competition for the entertainment dollar, the rise of television, and other social changes help explain their demise. The parks that flourished later tended to be much more comprehensive and elaborate than earlier ones. Families would drive long distances to spend the day at modern and attractive parks like King's Island north of Cincinnati; Cedar Point; Geauga Lake and Sea World, both near Aurora southeast of Cleveland; Fun 'N Sun near Hillsboro; Le Sourdsville Lake in Butler County; and Gooding Amusement Park north of Columbus. Some commercial enterprises, including those at Port Clinton, Sandusky, Cedar Point, Kings Mills, and Aurora, featured wild animals or aquatic shows as their central attraction.

People who enjoy the entertainment or instructional value of zoos are well served in Ohio. The Toledo Zoological Park and the Cincinnati Zoo are among the country's best, and Cleveland, Columbus, Akron, and Mansfield have smaller parks.

Sandusky's Cedar Point amusement park, a favorite for leisure-time enjoyment.

For the outdoor lover, Ohio has always offered a variety of seasonal attractions. The development of artificial snow and ice greatly extended the season for skiing and ice skating. Ice boating attracts a limited number of enthusiasts, as does ice fishing. In the warmer months outdoor activities proliferate, stimulated by the ready availability of recreational facilities whose origins extend well back into the nineteenth century. The creation of Mill Creek Park in Youngstown during the 1890s affords an early example of government recognition of the need to support recreational areas. As earlier noted, in 1919 a magnificent system of metropolitan parks was begun near Cleveland, surrounding the Forest City with an "emerald necklace" of inestimable value. A similar development led to the Akron Metropolitan Park District (1922), and other districts were established in Columbus and Toledo. These districts had the power to generate tax support to finance their facilities, and other park systems were put into good operating conditions through the work of the Civilian Conservation Corps during the 1930s.

Ohio's best example of governmental responsibility for recreation is its impressive state park system. The pace of this development has accelerated as population pressures, coupled with diminishing amounts of open land, spur recognition that there is never a better time than the present to secure land. By 1988 Ohio had seventy-two state parks, most of which offered camping, swimming, boating, hunting, and hiking. Some, like Crane Creek and Headlands Beach on Lake Erie, were started as swimming beaches; others, like Hocking Hills and Nelson's Ledges, evolved around interesting and scenic natural sites. Finley, near Wellington, is an example of a park developed around an artificial lake in a region where there is no outstanding natural attraction.

During the postwar era, the state built beautiful rustic lodges at Punderson, Mohican, Salt Fork, Burr Oak, Lake Hope, Shawnee Forest, Deer Creek, and Hueston Woods, and the Muskingum Conservancy District maintains a popular lodge at Atwood Lake. These facilities are well patronized in every season. Families also find attractive, functional cabins available at these sites for modest rents.

Another leisure-time activity which Ohioans have always enjoyed is the excitement and socializing associated with fairs, festivals, and parades. The Ohio State Fair, started in large part to encourage better agricultural practices, became the nation's largest in the 1970s as big-name entertainment became as much a feature as displays and contests. Every Ohio county developed an annual fair, generally held in the late summer or early fall. Throughout the year various localities sponsor festivals to celebrate some local product and to bring money into the community, with galas that feature grapes at Geneva, pumpkins at Circleville, bratwurst at Bucyrus, poultry at Versailles, sweet corn at Millersport, maple products at Chardon, apples at Jackson, apple butter at Burton, tomatoes at Reynoldsburg, and honey at Lebanon. Others celebrate a theme: the Ohio Hills Folk Festival at Quaker City, the Flax-Scutching Festival at Winona, pottery at Crooksville, clay at Urichsville, canal days at Canal Fulton, cherry blossoms at Barberton, an International Festival at Toledo, an Antique Festival at Millersburg, and the Wonderful World of Ohio Mart at Akron.

Parades are a feature of every festival, and Ohioans have always loved them since they were first a feature of early Fourth of July celebrations and of political campaigns. But their great surge in popularity can be traced to the post-Civil War era when parades featured units of the Grand Army of the Republic (GAR), as in 1888 when some 70,000 veterans marched through Columbus streets. Every town brought forth its local band and marching groups on every suitable occasion. When the cornerstone was laid at Akron's Buchtel College in 1872, the parade included among its twenty-two units the GAR, Masons, Odd Fellows, Knights of Pythias, city officials, clergy, citizens, many bands, and even the Father Matthew Temperance Society, a group which must have felt needed when two drunken men crashed their carriage through the parade lines.

The large urban parades of recent years appear to have fewer lodges, military, and veterans' units among the marchers while attracting more floats, bands, and special drill units. Cleveland must hold the record for parades, since its many ethnic and other special communities favor this activity. In ethnic communities a parade would be but part of a daylong celebration which often included a High Mass, speeches by community leaders, sumptuous food, drink, and dancing.

Organized Sports

The advance of the industrial age with its clustering of people in cities and towns gave impetus to the development of team sports, and Ohio has made notable contributions. Perhaps the emergence of baseball as the national pastime best illustrates the state's role in this process.

Baseball evolved from cricket and rounders, and was played before the Civil War. Not until war veterans popularized the sport, however, did it enjoy wide acceptance. Local communities then formed clubs in which they took great pride. A Cincinnati team was the focus of such pride, and so players and fans alike were humiliated when their team was defeated by the barnstorming Washington Nationals, who operated on what appeared to be a semiprofessional basis. As a result, in the summer of 1869, Harry Wright, a jeweler who headed the amateur Cincinnati club, established America's first professional baseball team. Supporters paid him $12,000 to organize, manage, and play centerfield for the Cincinnati Red Stockings. Wright recruited talent so successfully that his professional players won fifty-seven games without defeat in the 1869–70 season. Not until the Red Stockings lost 8–7 to a Brooklyn team were the escalating salaries and other team procedures questioned.

The Red Stockings temporarily disbanded in 1870, but eleven years later they joined the Cleveland Forest City team and several other squads to form the National Association of Professional Baseball. In 1886 this association became the National League, the first of the modern leagues. The second major league also had Cincinnati origins when, in 1892, Bancroft "Ban" Johnson and Charles Comiskey, manager of the Cincinnati Reds, formed the Western Association, which evolved into the American League.

In recent decades, the National League Reds and the American League Cleveland Indians have had their ups and downs. In the pennant-winning years of 1948 and 1954, the Indians set attendance records thanks to winning teams and the huge seating capacity of Cleveland Municipal Stadium. Cincinnati's glory years came after leaving comfortable Crosley Field for the more spacious Riverfront Stadium. In 1961, 1970, 1972–73, 1975–76, and 1979 the Reds won the National League pennant and came to be called the "Big Red Machine," which featured outstanding players like Johnny Bench, Joe Morgan, and Pete Rose.

Cleveland has a special claim to attention for pioneering the employment of blacks in the American League. Shortly after Jackie Robinson of the National League's Brooklyn Dodgers broke the modern color barrier in baseball, the Indians hired Larry Doby, the American League's first black player. Others soon followed, including one-of-a-kind Leroy "Satchel" Paige, veteran of the Negro leagues, who was still an effective pitcher at an age rumored to be in the fifties. Paige was almost as well known for his folksy observations ("Don't look back; something might be gaining on you") as for his pitching. Another Cleveland breakthrough came with the hiring of Frank Robinson as manager in 1975. This distinguished black player, the only man to win most valuable player awards in each league, led the Indians through 1977.

Coincident with the rise of professional baseball was the development of football, an outgrowth of English rugby. By the late nineteenth century, Ohio colleges were playing one another, often using non-student "ringers" to uphold the school's honor on the field of play. Shortly after the turn of the century, semiprofessional football proliferated across the state. Famous teams like the Columbus Panhandlers, Akron Indians, Dayton Triangles, Toledo Maroons, Massillon Tigers and Canton Bulldogs attracted large crowds. The teams recruited famous college players; Canton got the recruiting prize in 1915 by signing Jim Thorpe, "the Carlisle Indian," once voted the outstanding American athlete of the first half of the twentieth century.

In 1920 the American Professional Football Association was formed in Canton, and an effort was made to bring order and respectability to the game. Canton's founding role was later recognized as the Professional Football Hall of Fame was located there. The professional game of recent decades produced the Cleveland Rams, who ultimately moved to Los Angeles. The Cleveland Browns of the All-America Conference took up the slack with championship teams coached by the peerless Paul Brown, who had a reputation from outstanding seasons at Massillon High School and Ohio State University. The Browns reintroduced black players to the professional leagues in 1946 when they hired Bill Willis and Marion Motley, both of whom were later voted into the Hall of Fame. The Browns (until 1996) and the Cincinnati Bengals (led for a time by Paul Brown after he left Cleveland), represented the state in the Central Division of the National Football League.

On the collegiate scene, football became the principal spectator sport, and Ohio colleges were among the first west of the Appalachians to organize teams. From student-managed club efforts, the sport grew phenomenally.

Among major college powers, Ohio State's Buckeyes have been perennial contenders for conference and national honors. Another major football conference—the Mid-American—includes Kent State, Toledo, Bowling Green, Ohio University, Akron, and Miami, which earned a well-deserved reputation as the "cradle of coaches," having given an extraordinary number of them to the football world. The former Ohio Athletic Conference, dating from pre–World War I days, involved many of the state's fine small colleges. On the high school level, such teams as the Canton McKinley Bulldogs, Massillon Tigers, and Cincinnati Moeller Crusaders have received nationwide attention for their prolonged success.

Basketball is another team sport long popular in the Buckeye State. Both Cleveland and Cincinnati fielded teams in the professional leagues although by the 1980s only Cleveland's Cavaliers were still active. Among colleges and universities, Cincinnati, Xavier, Dayton, and Ohio State have won major national titles, and for many years Wittenberg was a national small-college power.

Contrary to the predictions of some social commentators, America has not become a nation of spectators who satisfy their athletic interests vicariously through television viewing. If anything, the popularizing of sports through extensive television coverage brought thousands out to participate and enjoy sports suited to their skills, pocketbooks, and physical condition.

Golf and tennis, once associated in the public's mind with the country club set, became extraordinarily popular, and major golf tournaments have been staged on the state's numerous courses. Annually Akron hosts the World Series of Golf, bringing the season's professional tournament winners together in a head-to-head meeting. Major professional tennis tournaments have been held in Cincinnati, Columbus, and Cleveland. And the Rubber City also became a mecca for another popular sport. The Professional Bowlers Association was founded and maintains its headquarters there. Many Ohio cities stage top-flight tournaments each year.

Track and field has remained a sport dominated by amateurs. Few track stars achieve more than transient fame, but among the immortals one must surely rank Cleveland's Jesse Owens. He won four gold medals in the 1936 Berlin Olympics, where his brilliant performance flew in the face of Adolph Hitler's claims of Aryan racial supremacy. Many sports historians rate Owens the premier American athlete of the twentieth century.

Ohio has also been home to all forms of professional racing. A top breeder of championship race horses, the state has popular tracks in Cleveland, where the Thistledown track hosts the annual Ohio Derby, and in Columbus, Cincinnati and other cities, where devoted thousands watch their favorites run through a long racing season. One of the state's best-known races is the Little

Brown Jug for trotters, held yearly at Delaware. And Ohio is also well represented in automobile racing with an outstanding course at Lexington (Morrow County).

A different kind of racing is Ohio's Soap Box Derby. Billed as the "world's greatest amateur racing event" the derby was started in Dayton in the 1930s by an enterprising newspaperman. In 1935 it relocated to Akron where, each August, local champions from across the country meet at Derby Downs to compete for college scholarships and other prizes.

Boxing, wrestling, ice hockey, field hockey, soccer, cross country, riflery, and gymnastics are represented, most on both the professional and scholastic levels. Shooting scarcely seems a sport to some people, but for those thousands of target shooters who attend meets at Camp Perry or Vandalia, it is a passion. And Ohio can claim the greatest shooter of her time, Darke County's Annie Oakley, "Little Miss Sure Shot," who was known on both sides of the Atlantic for her remarkable skills.

Traditionally American women led a physically active life on the farm, in the factory and in the home, but there was popular ambivalence about their participation in competitive team sports. Early in the twentieth century team sports developed for women in certain schools and factories, but by midcentury this modest initiative had vanished. Not until social values changed during the women's movement of the 1960s and 1970s were competitive team sports once again prevalent. Today, on all levels—professional, collegiate, scholastic, and little league—girls and women are involved.

It is not possible in these pages to do justice to all the accomplished Ohio athletes who have excelled in their sports. Every golfer knows of Jack Nicklaus, perhaps the best competitive player to date; tennis buffs recognize Tony Trabert and Shirley Fry for their accomplishments; every baseball buff is aware of the heroics of Denton "Cy" Young and George Sisler. There are too many outstanding performers to list here. What can be noted, however, is that in athletics, as in the arts and letters, Ohioans have distinguished themselves on every level and have enriched their own lives while enhancing the quality of life in their state.

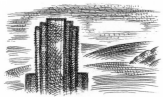

17.

Ohio in the Post-Industrial Age

Ohio has been in the throes of tremendous change since the early 1970s, and the state that is emerging as a result of these changes promises to differ in important ways from the industrial colossus of the early twentieth century. While recounting the history of the recent past, one is aware that the era of heavy, basic industry has faded as the service economy and the "information age" have gathered strength in the 1970s and 1980s. Politically, meanwhile, some familiar Ohio themes were played out.

The Election of 1974

As his term drew to a close, Gov. John J. Gilligan had good reason to believe that Ohio voters would return him to office. The income tax he had shepherded through the legislature was producing funds for enhanced state services and for new state initiatives. Ohio still lagged behind its sister industrial states, but it was beginning to catch up in providing a suitable level of support for essential services and for state institutions, and Gilligan had attracted national attention for his efforts. Organized labor was but one of the special interest groups supporting his reelection. The governor was confident.

Gilligan's opponent was former governor James A. Rhodes who, at age sixty-five, was eager for political battle. In the four years since leaving office, Rhodes had run a profitable development firm. Now he was back seeking public office and working his fund-raising magic. He held most of his political war chest in reserve for an effective last-minute television barrage in which he pinned the "high tax" label on Gilligan.

The election was close. Rhodes won with 48.6 percent of the vote to Gilligan's 48.25 percent. Gilligan's unexpected loss sprang from several roots. Overconfidence kept him from campaigning as vigorously as he should, especially in Cuyahoga County, whose large Democratic majority he badly needed. In addition, he underestimated Rhodes's appeal to voters and the force of his last-minute television assault. Finally, some Democratic leaders who perceived Gilligan as aloof and arrogant failed to work hard on his behalf. Gilligan's own assessment was terse: "I blew it!" At any rate, the loss cut a promising political career short. Gilligan worked for awhile in the federal bureaucracy and then left politics for an academic position at the University of Notre Dame.

Rhodes Returns

On January 13, 1975, James A. Rhodes began a third term as governor. He announced the same program that had served him well during his previous tenure: economic development, highway improvement, support for education and for state institutions, and the revitalization of the inner cities. Despite the fact that Ohio lagged behind progressive states in its support of public services and institutions, Rhodes assured Ohioans that their state was in fine shape compared to others, and they apparently believed him.

As in his previous terms, Rhodes benefited from following a Democratic administration that had raised substantial new revenue. He had sufficient funds to work with initially, so that he could afford to raise the "no new taxes" cry. The slogan was a sham, however, for as new revenue was required he secured increases in existing sales and gasoline taxes.

Fate was not so kind to the governor this time around. Although he won reelection in 1978, even some of his loyal supporters were later to admit that Rhodes did not have a distinguished record during his second eight years in office. Possibly the most important reason for his drop-off in effectiveness was the Democratic majority in the legislature. Unlike his first eight years in office, when a Republican-controlled legislature seemed anxious to endorse the governor's initiatives, he now encountered opposition at every turn. Toward the end of his tenure the Democrats had a "veto proof" majority and the resulting stand-off between a stubborn governor and an intransigent legislature cost the state the quality of political leadership it had a right to expect and desperately needed. Even without this political stand-off the governor and the legislature would have been hard-pressed to match the Rhodes record of ten years earlier, for, as we shall see, Ohio's slide into economic malaise accelerated during the 1970s. Although the governor attempted to stem the slide with his once-successful formulas for selling the state, conditions had changed so rapidly in industrial America that the old approaches no longer worked. The governor seemed unable to adjust to the new thinking required to deal effectively with this phenomenon.

An early indication of Rhodes's problems with the legislature came as he unveiled a master plan for the state. This plan, which would have addressed urban problems, transportation, health, and other pressing concerns, was to be financed with increases in the sales and gasoline taxes. The legislature rejected the plan, so Rhodes initiated a petition drive which succeeded in placing on the ballot a bond issue that he now termed a "Blueprint for Ohio." Despite a massive media campaign, the initiative failed. Opposition came from both rural and urban sections of the state. After this defeat, the governor tried to secure capital funds through regular legislative channels. He was still promising massive convention centers and similar amenities to cities and state university campuses where he was trying to build support. It was clear the governor had not lost his "edifice complex."

Despite the stand-off between the executive and the legislature, some useful legislation did pass. Limits were placed on medical malpractice awards, and a 55-mile-per-hour speed limit was established in conformity with a national effort to conserve fuel in the wake of high prices and gas shortages. The legislature, influenced by the national Watergate scandals, passed a "sunshine law" in 1975 which required public bodies to hold open meetings. Business as usual behind closed doors was outlawed, but only the vigilance of newspapers, especially the *Akron Beacon Journal,* kept officials from violating the law with impunity.

The legislature also addressed certain critical problems dealing with school finance. Compared to many industrial states, Ohio schools were supported disproportionately by local property taxes enacted by voters who were all too often reluctant to fund their local systems adequately. A wide disparity existed between the "rich" and the "poor" districts in facilities, programs, teacher pay, and other fundamentals. The legislature could not, or would not, come to grips with the fundamental changes required to put school finances on a fully equitable and rational basis, however. In the meantime many school systems were in serious financial difficulty. Cleveland gained most of the attention because of the size of its problem. Erosion of the city's tax base combined with political gamesmanship both within and without the school board forced the system to the brink of closure in the seventies. An emergency loan from the state in 1978 kept the schools open, but no one seemed to know how the Cleveland school board could secure funds to repay that loan.

Another burden on public education stemmed from strike actions. Teachers who despaired of attaining adequate salaries defied Ohio's Ferguson Act, which ostensibly prohibited public employees from striking. In the 1970s Ravenna teachers stayed out so long that they established a national record, an unenviable distinction which they probably wished to avoid. Negative publicity surrounding teachers' strikes and school closings had an adverse effect on Ohio's reputation as a good place to live and work.

From Ford to Reagan

On the national political scene, Ohio continued to be a critical state for the ambitions of both major parties. As had happened so often in the past, the state gave its electoral votes to a presidential candidate by the slimmest of margins. In 1976, President Gerald Ford, who had calmed stormy waters following the Watergate scandals and the resignation of President Nixon, needed Ohio's twenty-five electoral votes. But he didn't get them. By only 10,401 votes Ohio gave its support to the Democratic challenger, James Earl "Jimmy" Carter of Georgia. Political pundits made much of the narrow Ohio margin which, some claimed, put Carter in the White House.

In the 1976 Senate race, Cleveland businessman Howard Metzenbaum unseated Robert Taft, Jr., thus joining a fellow Democrat, John Glenn, in the upper house. Metzenbaum was to build a reputation as an aggressive liberal on social and economic issues. Glenn maintained a more moderate, middle-of-the-road posture.

Four years later, Ohio was again supporting a Republican presidential candidate. Ronald Reagan, a former movie actor, conservative ideologue, and ex-governor of California, defeated President Carter, who was laboring under a number of handicaps, not the least of which was his inability to resolve the highly emotional Iranian hostage crisis. Ohio gave its electoral votes to Reagan, as it had done with every successful Republican presidential candidate. For the next four years President Reagan enjoyed a swell of popularity as he personally led a resurgence of American confidence and patriotism. The accompanying costs, including a growing trade deficit and an alarming budget deficit based partly on greatly increased defense expenditures, appeared to be acceptable to the voters.

In 1984 Reagan sought reelection. His Democratic challenger, Walter Mondale of Minnesota, chose as his running mate Geraldine Ferraro of New York, the first woman to run on the presidential ticket of a major party. Reagan's victory was total; he lost only Minnesota and the District of Columbia. Seldom had a candidate so dominated the votes of the electoral college. He won all but six counties in Ohio—Cuyahoga and five eastern border counties in the depressed steel and coal centers of the state.

A Democratic Resurgence in State Politics

Ironically, while Ohio was pledging its support to the popular Republican president, it was placing Democrats in the highest state offices and giving them a majority in the legislature. This Democratic control only added to the dreary and unproductive nature of the last years of the Rhodes regime. The governor appeared to have lost heart: he refused to push for the long-term policies and revenue sources which would help Ohio meet its critical needs. Although he had a major role in securing additional new industry for the state, especially a large Honda manufacturing complex at Marysville, his successes were limited. He gave the impression of merely holding on, of trying to avoid responsibility for securing the new revenue which the state urgently required.

The general assembly was equally guilty of placing personal political interests ahead of the public's needs. Democratic legislators were no more inclined to risk heroic deeds than was the governor. In 1982, when financial exigencies became too great to be ignored, the governor proposed, and the legislature adopted, a 50 percent increase in the income tax rates, but this increase was to be temporary, designed to expire in the spring of 1983.

Under Ohio law James Rhodes could not seek a third consecutive term in 1982. Republicans chose U. S. Representative Clarence "Bud" Brown of Urbana as their gubernatorial candidate. He was handicapped by a growing public perception that it was "time for a change" in Columbus.

The Democratic candidate for governor was Richard J. Celeste, son of a former mayor of Lakewood, a Rhodes scholar, and an unsuccessful candidate for the governor's post in 1978. Using the rhetoric of John F. Kennedy, Celeste promised to get Ohio moving again, and the voters responded by giving him a substantial victory margin. Democrats also controlled both houses of the legislature although their margin in the Senate was paper-thin.

As with DiSalle and Gilligan before him, Celeste felt it was urgent for the state to provide better support for its institutions and services. Neil Peirce, a contemporary observer of political life in the fifty states, once wrote that:

> In the measure of what a state does for its people—in education, health, welfare, mental care, environmental control—Ohio remained near the bottom of the 50-state rankings and in the absolute cellar among the great industrial states throughout the 1960s. . . . Ohio just plowed through history, turning out immense amounts of manufactured goods, shortchanging its own people, practicing a politics of indifference.

Although support levels improved somewhat after this unhappy assessment was written, Ohio continued to lag in its financial commitment to good government.

Governor Celeste promised to improve this commitment. Immediately following his inauguration he pressed the legislature to support new taxes, claiming that Governor Rhodes had left the state with a $500 million deficit. Without a single Republican vote, the legislature approved a 90 percent increase in the personal income tax. Fifty percent of the increase came from making permanent the temporary tax enacted by the outgoing administration; the remaining 40 percent was an add-on. The new tax was immediately challenged in a referendum vote, and, by a surprising two-to-one margin, the voters retained it. Later, when it brought in more revenue than anticipated, a modest portion of the tax take was refunded; this was a political gesture of small immediate consequence, but one which accentuated later budgetary problems.

The impact of the new tax revenues was soon apparent. Elementary and secondary education, higher education, welfare, mental health, and other state services received much-needed assistance. During this period of budgetary expansion, welfare joined elementary and secondary education as the largest consumers of the state's general revenue fund.

In retrospect, it was fortunate for Governor Celeste that he acted promptly to secure new funding despite charges that he should have taken time to educate the public about the need for new taxes. In the mid-term elections of 1984, Republicans won control of the Senate by an 18 to 15 margin. Given their party discipline in opposition to tax measures, it is hard to see how the governor could have prevailed against a Republican-dominated Senate.

Other new initiatives were soon apparent. Governor Celeste appointed more women and blacks to state boards and commissions than had his predecessors. The governor's wife, Dagmar, was outspoken in her support of such appointments. However, the governor left himself vulnerable to criticism when a number of positions went to persons whose chief claim to office appeared to be party loyalty. A more serious charge against Celeste and his advisors was that those who would do business with the state had to pass a political test of party loyalty and had to contribute to party coffers.

In his first term Governor Celeste was caught up in a banking crisis triggered by the failure of Cincinnati's Home State Savings Bank, owned by Marvin L. Warner, a major supporter of the governor. Home State Savings, along with some seventy other Ohio savings and loan companies, lacked federal deposit insurance: their depositors were insured by an inadequate, underfinanced Ohio Deposit Guarantee Fund. Celeste met rising panic and a depositors' run on the bank in the wake of Home State's troubles with firm action: he ordered all of the underinsured institutions closed. They were to remain closed until they agreed to secure federal deposit insurance or until they were bought or combined with other financial institutions. This firm action, coupled with a state-funded bail-out, cooled the panic, and within a year all of the affected savings and loan banks were reopened or reorganized. A trial court found Warner and other Home State officers guilty of mishandling depositors' money. As of 1988 some vestiges of the Home State Savings case were still in the courts.

The state elections of 1986 provided a referendum of sorts on Celeste's stewardship. The governor ran on his record, citing new funding for schools, welfare, state institutions, and state services. He also took credit for a surge in new jobs although many of them were low-paying jobs in the service sector. His opponent was former governor James A. Rhodes, now seventy-seven years old but still influential enough to beat out several younger candidates in the Republican primary. Rhodes expected to ride back into office by pinning the high-tax label on Celeste just as he had done years earlier to DiSalle and to Gilligan.

Early in the campaign it appeared Rhodes might still have his old zest and political magic, but as the lackluster contest wore on, the public seemed to lose interest in his tired cliches and outmoded formulas for economic recovery. Sensing this loss, Rhodes attacked Celeste's character and stewardship, but to no avail. Celeste won an easy victory and brought the entire Democratic slate of state officials back into office with him. The Republicans salvaged two victories: they retained control of the state senate, and they defeated Frank Celebrezze, the controversial chief justice of the Ohio Supreme Court.

Ohio Politics: An Assessment

A number of historically significant conditions have shaped Ohio politics, some of them traceable back to early statehood. Among the more distinguishing characteristics is the fact that *politically, Ohio is several states.* There is no unity of political purpose in the voting behavior of its citizens. In the nineteenth century one could predict voting behavior by region—the Western Reserve, the Virginia Military District, the "backbone counties," the German enclaves, and so on. But social intermingling has largely eliminated the early character of these regions, so that no single population cohort dominates Ohio politics. Unlike Michigan or Illinois, where one massive urban complex dominates state politics, Ohio's people are distributed across the state, and each area except the southeast has its own major urban center. No one running for a statewide office can focus solely on Cleveland, or Cincinnati, or Columbus and hope to carry the state. Cleveland's voting behavior is markedly different from Cincinnati's, and Columbus's is different still. Even within sections of the state there are differences. In northeast Ohio, for example, highly ethnic Cleveland and Youngstown may respond differently from Akron, whose population base traces heavily toward rural southern origins. Marketing experts recognize eight media markets within the state, which means that candidates must tailor their appeals to meet expectations within each of these markets. Appeals to voters must be broad, for it is too expensive to fashion TV and news spots aimed specifically at each media market.

Another political characteristic of twentieth-century Ohio is the *conservative bias* of its voters. Only on rare occasions, and then for brief periods, have the voters placed their destiny in the hands of reform-minded or liberal governors or legislators. Only during the reform era before the first world war did progressive Republicans and Democrats join forces to enact a significant package of reform legislation. But as H. Landon Warner, the historian of Ohio's progressive period, reminds us, this reform spirit was transient; it was effective only because of a happy combination of events which one could not expect to recur with any frequency. The reform initiatives of the New Deal era preceding World War II sprang from sheer desperation. It seems unlikely that the state sales tax and the school foundation formula could have been enacted had it not been for the undeniable need which forced reluctant conservatives to support them. Indeed, the sales tax was also opposed by certain liberals who thought it placed an unfair burden on the poor.

Political conservatism in Ohio has had a strong rural flavor. As we have noted, the 1903 Hanna Amendment required that each of the state's eighty-eight counties have at least one representative in the Ohio House. Because of Ohio's largely agrarian base, that pattern of representation assured rural control of state politics until the 1960s, when Ohio complied with federally ordered reapportionment, which for the first time gave the cities equal representation. But the rural influence went deeper. With the possible exception of Cleveland and Cincinnati, Ohio's major cities lived in immediate juxtaposition to the rural areas surrounding them. Some political observers claim that awareness of rural interests predisposed urban political leaders to temper their stance on issues, taking a more conservative direction. County chairmen, for example, were aware of their rural constituents and their expectations, and county commissioners were often powerful enough to influence politics within the cities. By 1996 only Summit County was organized under a county charter, which replaced the county commissioners with an elected county executive and an elected county council. Several other counties tried, but failed to adopt charter governments.

In addition, among Ohio's twentieth-century governors, the conservative bias again prevails. This is not surprising when dealing with Republicans, for they had lost much of the creative thrust which had marked the party's early years. What does seem strange is the frequency with which Democrats followed the Republican lead in avoiding risks and in keeping a tight hold on the

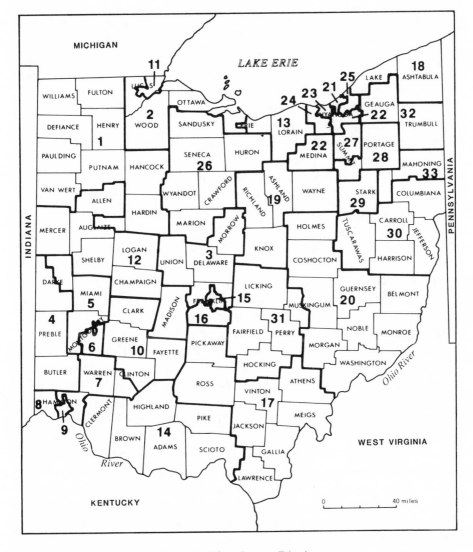

Map 12. Ohio Senate Districts

public purse strings. Democratic governors Vic Donahey, Martin Davey, and Frank Lausche were as tight-fisted as any Republican. Indeed, during the crisis of the Great Depression, Governor Davey was one of the nation's chief defenders of states' rights against the intrusions of the federal government, a stance which seemed more likely to be taken by a southern governor than by the executive of a would-be progressive northern industrial state.

Democratic leaders who were truly progressive or liberal have been relatively rare, at least in the governor's chair. James M. Cox, who helped usher into law many progressive reforms, was not a political liberal. He was motivated by a search for order and efficiency, and he trimmed his sails when challenged by reactionary Republicans. Forty years later, in 1959, Michael DiSalle emerged as a Democrat espousing rather traditional liberal Democratic policies, but the legislature frustrated him at every turn when he attempted to raise the level of funding for state enterprises. Both John J. Gilligan and Richard Celeste were viewed as "classic" Democrats, supported by labor, ethnics, and minorities, and securing new revenue with which to upgrade state services and programs.

If there is one theme beyond all others which has appealed to Ohio voters over the generations, it is economy in government. Both Republicans and Democrats have played to that theme with success. It is significant that Cox, DiSalle, and Gilligan, each perceived by the voters as big spenders, served but one term before being rejected. Cox made a successful comeback after being out of office for one term. But he had learned his lesson; after reelection he pursued a more cautious spending policy.

Another characteristic of twentieth-century Ohio politics was *fragmentation within the Democratic party*. David Larson, an admiring biographer of John Gilligan, refers to "the organizational incapacity of the Ohio Democratic Party" which led, in part, to the 1966 Republican landslide. Ohio Democrats sought to develop elements "vital to . . . the ideological struggle that was occurring in other states," but were hampered by local conditions. The state's industry was decentralized, and there was no powerful labor union to rally working people as the United Auto Workers had done in Michigan and other large industrial states. Furthermore, lower-middle-class Ohioans "failed to identify politically with a working class or other liberal political groups." Finally, the Democratic party in Ohio was divided into many factions. Powerful county chairmen ran their territories like feudal fiefdoms, putting their local interests ahead of those pursued by their state leaders. In Cuyahoga County, for example, party chairmen were often a power unto themselves. Maintaining the local power base took precedence over larger party interests across the state.

Since the 1930s when the Democratic coalition of blacks, ethnics, and working-class people brought power to Franklin Roosevelt and the New Deal, popular knowledge has held that northern industrial cities where these groups are prominent should vote Democratic. And often they did, as in Cleveland and the steel cities of Ohio. But the population makeup of Ohio cities varied. One expert on Ohio politics, Thomas Flinn, found that only about 30 percent of white, gentile Ohioans in 1968 could be classified as "Democratic nationality groups." In Cincinnati and certain other cities, the population base slants toward the more conservative nationality groups (e.g.,

Germans) or toward those persons whose "native American roots" went back many generations.

Another phenomenon which bedeviled Democratic strategists was the frequency with which cities with overwhelming Democratic voter registration saddled their Democratically controlled city councils with a Republican mayor. Both Akron and Canton had long runs of Republican leadership in the mayor's office after World War II. The quintessential Democratic strongholds—Cleveland and Youngstown—occasionally elected a Republican mayor. In Cleveland's case, election of a Republican mayor may have been voter reaction against Dennis Kucinich, a brash and contentious young Democratic mayor who had loaded his administration with very young, inexperienced loyalists, and then took on the establishment in public battles that alienated the very people whose support he needed. Bankers refused to renegotiate loans, forcing the city into default. In 1978 Kucinich barely survived a recall vote, but once his term was up, the voters wanted no more of his style.

Ohio politics are also affected by what contemporary political historians call the *ethnocultural bases of political behavior*. How one votes, they maintain, is a function of one's ethnicity, religion, and cultural identity. There was evidence to that effect in Ohio prior to the first world war when many clusters of voters followed ethnocultural political lines. The German farmers of north central and northwestern Ohio, for example, retained their Democratic loyalties, which traced back to their support of Civil War-era Copperheads and beyond. Until late in the nineteenth century, one could almost depend upon a New England Presbyterian living in the Western Reserve, to vote Republican. One observer of Ohio politics claims that there was a "moralistic impulse" in the state's nineteenth-century politics, and that this impulse was the influence of evangelical Protestantism.

Even today certain rural regions and urban wards which have an ethnocultural homogeneity behave politically with a high degree of predictability. The ever-increasing amalgamation of peoples and traditions in modern society blurs once-clean lines, however. Whole segments of the voting public, especially those who moved from cities to suburbs, changed voting behavior as their interests changed. In short, the ethnocultural makeup of Ohio's people is now too complex to serve as a secure base on which to base political predictions except in a very selective way.

An additional feature of Ohio politics was what political scientist William Fenton labeled its *"issueless" character*. Strong, ideologically oriented interests that influenced political life in certain other states were missing in Ohio. Issueless politics made for a bland, uninspired political climate. Fenton may have a point; one can identify a few statewide campaigns in which unusual excitement was generated precisely because there *was* an important issue at stake: the 1958 right-to-work initiative, for example, captured public attention and aroused vigorous partisanship. On the local level, of course, issues such as school levies, liquor permits, and public improvements were routinely fought with passion.

Despite the relative absence of issues in statewide elections, partisanship was visible. The Democratic fragmentation notwithstanding, some observers have noted what Fenton called the "strong and persistent political loyalties" which they claim characterized Ohio voting behavior. Yet those loyalties could be shaken, not only by intraparty feuding, but especially "by persuasive evidence that canons of personal morality have been violated." Perhaps that was one reason why candidates so often appeared to smear the opposition, to campaign *against* the competition. An influential Ohio newspaperman referred to that tendency and the corrupting influence of the special interests as the "grungy" politics of Ohio.

Yet another striking feature of twentieth-century Ohio politics was the *narrow margin which often separated Republicans and Democrats.* Political operatives cannot afford to take anything for granted in statewide and national elections. The costs of departing from the middle of the road outweighed the benefits. In presidential elections Ohio's considerable number of electoral votes was a significant prize to be won: early in the twentieth century, the state had the fourth largest number of electoral votes, and by 1980 it had the sixth largest number. Candidates have always campaigned hard in the many different sections of the state to assure those votes.

For the past half-century, Democrats have enjoyed a large advantage in the number of registered voters. In the state's northern industrial cities, the ratio of registered Democrats to registered Republicans has been about three to one. Given this margin it is surprising that Republicans often scored victories that would appear to have been beyond their reach. In part this phenomenon was due to the fragmentation within the Democratic party, which we noted earlier. But in part it was due to the large group of "independents," uncommitted voters who often seemed to vote against—rather than for—a candidate or issue.

Republican success can also be traced to superior party discipline and organization. These were in large part the handiwork of an Akron insurance broker, Ray C. Bliss, who made the Ohio party one of the nation's most effective in the post-World War II period by avoiding extreme partisanship and concentrating on grass-roots organization to elect GOP candidates. Bliss later served as national party chairman during the Nixon administration. Republicans also were bolstered by the Ohio Chamber of Commerce and the Ohio Manufacturers Association, whose members contributed support and funds. In several major urban centers, influential newspapers supported Republicans. Finally, Republicans tended to vote in proportionately higher numbers than did Democrats. For all of these reasons, what appeared to be a minority party continued to fare well in Ohio's political life.

New Directions for Ohio's Economy

As the 1970s began, Ohio appeared to be at a peak of economic well-being. Agricultural production was strong, and the exodus of population from the farms had slowed. The state's industrial base had been expanding since World War II, creating new jobs that steadily attracted new residents. Ohio's population grew from 7,946,600 in 1950 to 9,707,100 in 1960, an increase of 22 percent. By 1970 it had increased another 9.7 percent to 10,652,000. There was every reason to assume that Ohio would maintain its position as a leader of America's economy. Few could guess how rapidly this picture would tarnish, how radical were the changes in store for the state's economy. But warning signs were already visible.

Agriculture

Ohio's character derives in part from the fact that although it is urban and industrial, it is still an important agricultural state with three-quarters of its area in cropland, pastureland, and woodland. Until recently one could drive from the center of the major cities and within twenty minutes be in a rural environment.

As of 1980, fifty-seven counties were classified as rural; of these, twenty-five were concentrated in the hilly, economically troubled southeast. During President Johnson's administration, these counties were classified as part of a multistate region called Appalachia, which made them eligible for federal development funds. Much land in this region is pasture and woods, but the river bottoms sustain profitable crops. In the Scioto, Muskingum, and Tuscarawas valleys, cornfields stretch for miles. Mining is still carried on in this region as is logging, especially in the Wayne National Forest, which covers approximately 170,000 acres.

Northwestern Ohio was essentially a farming region from the time of its first settlement, although that part of it which was once the Black Swamp has required continual draining to this day. Properly prepared, however, its clay soils support profitable, diversified farming, and a drive through this area strongly confirms the assertion that the state is still agricultural.

Scattered throughout the northern and western two-thirds of Ohio are fifteen counties which have been rapidly changing character from rural to urban. They lie just beyond the reach of large cities, but interstate highways have enabled city dwellers to move into them. Here farms have given way to residential subdivisions, shopping malls, and industrial parks. In the 1980s, however, farming continued to be important in these transitional counties.

Farming changed radically in the last half of the twentieth century, not only in technology, but also in crops grown. Corn,traditionally Ohio's main income-producing crop, retained its importance, but the state's largest cash crops in 1980 were soybeans, corn, and dairy products, in that order. Hogs, cattle, wheat, poultry, and eggs were also major income producers. The state is still known for its tomatoes, pickle cucumbers, sugar beets, white burley tobacco, and its greenhouse products, but they play a lesser role than in the past. Some products which once figured large in Ohio's rural economy—sheep and orchard products, for example—play minor roles.

Although Ohio lost position in the twentieth century, it remained among the largest producers of agricultural goods, ranking between ninth and twelfth in the value of its farm products in the 1970s. Farm production remained high, but fewer people were required to sustain that level of production. In 1980 about 27 percent of the state's people were defined as rural dwellers, but only 3 percent lived in full-time farm families. By far the larger part of the rural dwellers were part-time farmers, supplementing farm income with wages from jobs in nearby communities.

Paralleling the decline in full-time farm dwellers came a decline in the number of farms. There were 221,000 farms in 1945, but only 89,000 forty years later. The farms that remained were much larger on the average, increasing during those four decades from 100 to about 178 acres. This was part of a national trend in no way unique to Ohio.

The capital investment required for profitable farming became too heavy for the traditional family farmer to carry during the post–World War II era. "Agribusiness" replaced the family farm with large investor-financial agricultural companies using hired hands and costly equipment to farm thousands of acres. New hybrid seeds and chemical fertilizers increased yields. Waste was minimized by breeding plants of uniform size so they could be processed mechanically.

For generations Ohio farmers used seasonal or migrant labor to process labor-intensive crops such as tomatoes, onions, pickle cucumbers, and fruit. Often the farmers maintained barracks or cottages to house the workers, the quality of the facilities varying with the resources and the conscience of the individual farmer. Even under the best of conditions, migrants lacked schools for their children, health care, and other benefits. In the postwar years, poor white migrants from the rural South gave way increasingly to rural southern blacks and to Hispanics from Mexico and the Gulf of Mexico region. Their plight was dramatized during the civil rights struggles of the sixties, and shortly thereafter migrants in Ohio tried to organize and bargain collectively.

Some of the bitterness that had marked the Hardin County onion-field conflicts in the 1930s also marked attitudes in northwestern Ohio tomato fields in the 1970s and 1980s. In February 1986, an eight-year dispute between migrant workers and the Campbell Soup Company ended when the Farm Labor Organizing Committee reached an agreement with the company. The new contract covered 150 migrant workers on twenty Ohio tomato farms and 400 workers on twelve Michigan cucumber farms. The pact brought workers a wage increase, medical insurance, a paid holiday, and grievance resolution procedures. Except for California farm workers, this was the only farm labor agreement in the country.

One special group of Ohio farmers—the Amish—successfully bucked trends in the farm economy during the 1970s and 1980s. They made the family farm profitable. The Amish continued to plant, cultivate, harvest and process farm products in the age-old fashion. Where others relied on machinery, they used manpower and horsepower, which minimized costs. Horses required no expensive fuel or repairs. They reproduced themselves, helped produce their own food, and their manure saved the farmer the cost of commercial fertilizers. Plain living kept food, clothing, transportation, and household entertainment costs at a minimum. The Amish made purchases in cash, thereby eliminating interest charges. Sophisticated Americans soon discovered the "quaint" Amish, and produced a demand for their foodstuffs and handicrafts.

Except for the Amish, by the 1980s farmers were no longer as independent as they had been through most of American history. Massive federal and state aid programs affected farm life in many ways, from paying the farmer not to grow certain crops to subsidizing his "tree farm" or the construction of his farm pond. However, the same government that financed subsidies also wrote regulations that hedged in the farmer as tightly as they did the industrial employer. Government restraints, the high cost of land, indebtedness for capital goods, and that ancient antagonist, the weather, made farming a risky proposition. It was a tribute to those who continued farming as a way of life that they were able to persevere. Agriculture continued to constitute the largest single unit in Ohio's economy.

Industrial Ohio on the Defensive

Social change has a way of sneaking up on people. Despite warning signs and rumblings of impending change, few are prepared when the time comes. And so it was for Ohioans who sensed a turning point in the state's industrial life, but who continued to get mixed signals as late as the 1970s.

Early in that decade Ohio alternated between fourth and fifth nationally in value added by manufacturing. It was second only to Michigan in the value of its industrial exports, and was a national leader in new plant investment, much of it in the automotive industry. Employment levels were still high, and workers in the state's primary industries received top wages and benefits.

Beneath this promising surface, and almost unnoticed, dry rot had crept into key sectors of the state's economy. The fat days of rising employment, wage and benefits increases, job security, and affluence were nearly over for many great industries. Ohio had become a high-cost state in which to do business. As part of a newly emerging world economy where foreign competitors undersold American products, it fell victim to the greatest economic crisis since the Great Depression.

For years to come historians will be arguing about where to place the beginnings of what appeared to be a shift in American economic life from the industrial to the post-industrial age. A date of convenience might be 1973, the year in which the Organization of Petroleum Exporting Countries (OPEC), an international cartel dominated by Middle Eastern oil producers, more than tripled the price of crude oil, ultimately settling the price above $30 per barrel. This price increase had devastating effects on the industrial nations of the world and on third-world nations that lacked their own energy resources. American industry generally, and Ohio industry specifically, depended heavily on imported oil, and price increases affected the cost of everything from gasoline to pharmaceuticals. Furthermore, Americans now realized the necessity of conserving fuel, and the public scurried to adopt small, fuel-efficient automobiles, a change with far-reaching consequences for the automotive industry.

The OPEC price increase compounded Ohio's economic plight. The state's major industries—steel, automobiles, machine tools, rubber, basic metals—were already suffering from competition, both from southern and western states, where the costs of doing business were less, and from Europe and Japan. The effect of domestic competition is apparent in Ohio's falling share of the Gross National Product (GNP), which is the value of all goods and services produced in a year. In the 1950s, Ohio's economy accounted for over 6 percent of the GNP. Thereafter this percentage fell, slowly but steadily, to little more than 5 percent in the 1970s, even though the value of goods produced in the state increased during that period.

The harsh reality of Ohio's growing economic plight was most apparent in unemployment statistics. The closing of non-competitive plants threw tens of thousands out of work. Between 1972 and 1982, Ohio lost 246,553 manufacturing jobs, an 18.3 percent decline. The job drain continued after 1982 at a slower pace, but throughout this period unemployment in Ohio exceeded 11 percent, well above the national average.

Job losses were concentrated in industries with the highest labor costs. An unemployed steel, automotive, or rubber worker might eventually get another job, possibly in the so-called service sector, but such jobs seldom paid the premium wages and benefits of manufacturing. By 1980 the Mahoning

Valley made little steel; Cleveland made few metal fasteners; Akron built just a few specialty tires; Dayton manufactured few business machines; and so it went across the industrial heart of Ohio.

The Buckeye State shared this misfortune with other states of the old industrial belt which stretched westward from New York and New Jersey to Michigan, Illinois, Wisconsin, and Missouri. Throughout this area population growth slowed as jobs were lost. Ohio's population, which had grown by almost 10 percent during the 1960s, showed only a 1.4 percent increase—to some 10,797,600 Ohioans—by 1980. Negative publicity bedeviled the region. Television and the other media dubbed it the "rustbelt" and contrasted it unfavorably with the more prosperous "sunbelt" of southern and western states that were riding a population surge based on relatively cheap energy and labor. The sunbelt also benefited from large infusions of federal funds, from mild winter climates, and from the mystique that draws people to rapidly developing areas. By the early 1970s the movement was clearly toward the sunbelt region, which took positive steps to insure its continuance. States and local communities made land and new plants available there at reduced cost to new industries, and gave tax abatements and preferential treatment to attract newcomers. Some southern states had right-to-work laws that restricted the power and influence of organized labor. In due time northern industrial states would take similar measures (except for right-to-work laws) to keep the industries they had and to attract others, but by then much industry had already flown south.

In addition to the pull of the sunbelt location, northern industries felt the push of negative conditions where they were. Underlying many of these conditions was the fact that much northern industrial plant capacity was old-fashioned and obsolescent. Ironically, Ohio and its sister states suffered because they had been in the industrial race for such a long time. Too much of their industrial plant had been built fifty or sixty years earlier, when industries were first reaching giant size, and too little had been done to modernize these plants or to replace them with more efficient, competitive facilities. By 1976 more than 25 percent of the Mahoning Valley's steel-making facilities had become outmoded. Even a casual observer could see that Akron's five-, six-, and seven-story tire plants could not accommodate modern, efficient production lines. Cleveland's old Standard Number One refinery was just that—old!

In retrospect it would appear that industrial America had been living in a fool's paradise during the affluent postwar decades. Its owners and managers had failed to modernize as they should, preferring to put much of the company's profits into shareholders' pockets. The nation's economy got away with that until confronted with the harsh new competitive realities of the early seventies, and by then it was too late for some industries to recoup.

If new plants and new capital investment were needed to keep pace in the newly competitive environment, where were Ohio companies to locate them? Expensive urban property hemmed in most existing factory complexes, surrounding them with city streets, houses, utility lines, and other business establishments. Taxes were comparatively high on urban property. Clearly it would be costly to build new plants in that setting. Then why not build the new plants in the Ohio countryside? Indeed, some companies did just that. But the lure of cheaper labor, inexpensive energy, access to growing markets, an attractive lifestyle, and the blandishments of state and local governments caused Ohio manufacturers to look to the south and west for new plant locations. Some long-time Ohio manufacturing concerns—Cleveland's Diamond Shamrock Company and the Harris Business Machines Company, for example—moved not only their plants, but also their executive headquarters to the new locations.

Economic Elements in a New Era

In discussing Ohio's remarkable industrial growth during the late nineteenth and early twentieth centuries (see chapter 12), we examined the impact of several distinct economic elements. The same approach toward the period of the 1970s and 1980s allows comparisons with the earlier era and reveals how historical forces can be a function of time and place.

Location

Much of Ohio's booming economic growth a century ago could be attributed to her central location, which was almost ideal for serving growing markets to the east and the west, the north and the south. Location remains an advantage in the 1980s. About two-thirds of the people of North America north of Mexico live within 600 miles of Columbus (approximately a twenty-four-hour truck haul), constituting perhaps the world's greatest market. Ohio is conveniently connected by transportation facilities to all parts of this market, and yet locational advantage is not as important to industrial prosperity as it had once been, because transportation expenses as part of the cost of the finished product were less in 1980 than they had been in 1880. Nevertheless it is advantageous for a parts supplier to be located near the assembly plant, for the short haul of materials is cheaper than the long haul.

While location is not the advantage it had once been in manufacturing, it is still a major consideration for distributors of merchandise. For example, in the 1960s and 1970s several major retail store chains opened distribution centers in Columbus to take advantage of its central location and accessible transportation. Similarly, air freight companies used Ohio cities as distribution centers.

Natural and Mineral Resources

The ready availability and cheap cost of diverse natural and mineral resources fueled Ohio's early industries, but as they matured, some of these industries required resources of better grade than Ohio could provide. For example, the charcoal, iron ore, and limestone which supported the early iron industry was available locally at many spots around the state. But as iron gave way to steel, higher-grade ores were imported from the Lake Superior region and charcoal was replaced by coking coal, much of it from Pennsylvania and West Virginia. Today raw materials for the blast furnaces are all imported, even limestone, although much of Ohio is underlain with that material. In similar fashion, Ohio oil and natural gas once supported substantial industries within the state. Today all but a small part of those energy resources are imported from the American southwest, and local production is largely supplementary in nature.

Coal was, and still is, the state's most abundant mineral resource, but the limited supplies of high quality coal have long since been exhausted. What remains is a bituminous coal with a high sulfur content which, when burned, creates severe pollution problems. Although the coal can be strip-mined at reasonable cost, the pollution control equipment needed to burn it within clean air standards proved prohibitively expensive for many industries. Modern electric power generating plants using Ohio coal found that more than a third of their operating costs resulted from pollution control.

Just as Ohio's best-quality coal was used up years ago, so too were its high-quality clays, and fine chinaware and pottery are no longer made in the state. Ohio does have abundant sources of clays and related minerals suitable for the manufacture of bricks, tiles, drain tile, and other clay products, however. In a related industry, Ohio still has sources of silica and other minerals used in its once-flourishing glass industry. But the natural gas which fueled that industry is no longer available locally at an acceptable price.

In addition to its coal and clay, Ohio had other resources which under-girded important industries. The state ranked second in the nation in the production of salt, a commodity that has many more uses than the early pioneers could have imagined while they were boiling down the salt water secured from springs and salt licks. Limestone is still employed in many traditional ways, but over the years it has become an important component in the chemical industry. Gypsum has increased in value, thanks to its all-pervasive use in the building trades. Sandstone, silicas, and sand and gravel remain significant mineral resources.

Even oil and natural gas made a modest comeback after the fuel shortages of the 1970s convinced Ohioans that they needed reserves of their own. Until the price of oil dropped on world markets in the early 1980s, thousands of new wells were drilled annually, and many businesses, schools, private individuals, and communities around the state enhanced their income by selling surplus oil and natural gas to the major suppliers.

As earlier noted, controlled logging in state and national forests, plus the timbering-off of farm lots has revived another old Ohio industry. Systematic reforestation and planned management of timber resources promise continued growth in this industry's future.

Possibly the most critical resource affecting Ohio's economic development is water. Except for occasional droughts, the climate assures that the state will continue to have abundant surface and subsurface water supplies, provided that residents do not abuse them. Some observers believe that in the 1980s the semi-arid states of the southwest are approaching the limit of their water resources, and that as pressure for new water supplies becomes acute, water-dependent industry might return to the Great Lakes states. Since the 1970s the Great Lakes states have cooperated with one another to see that the thirsty southwestern states are not allowed to raid the Midwest of perhaps its greatest asset.

The Ohio Department of Natural Resources supervises the state's natural heritage. Its many subdivisions oversee everything from soil conservation and control of strip mining to the preservation of wildlife habitat. In common with other populous states, Ohio came to realize that the natural environment is its most precious asset and that short-range, selfish interests must not be allowed to threaten it.

Capital

One hundred years ago many important Ohio industries were started on the proverbial shoestring. John D. Rockefeller, John Patterson, Frank Seiberling, and hundreds of other entrepreneurs founded their businesses on capital secured from their own savings, from friends and neighbors, and from local bankers. But as Standard Oil, National Cash Register, Goodyear Tire and Rubber, and other industries grew to giant size, their capital needs were too great for local sources to accommodate.

Indeed, no financial institution within the state was large enough to service their growing capital requirements. Ultimately many Ohio industries turned for capital resources to New York's Wall Street, where financiers exacted a stiff price for their aid. They demanded a strong voice in company affairs which, in effect, placed control in the hands of outsiders. These absentee influences seldom served Ohio's best interests. In the vernacular of the 1980s, the absentee managers focused on the bottom line, and the impact of their policies on the workers and the home communities were of little concern.

Not only were Ohio banks too small to handle the major capital infusions needed by growing companies, but even in cases where they could accommodate the need, they seemed, as a group, to be unusually cautious. Some attribute this caution to the conservative ambience of Ohio society, while others attribute it to the economic shocks—the recessions or depressions of 1907, 1920–21, 1929–1940, and 1957—which gave bankers a depression psychology that made them unusually hesitant to participate in high-risk ventures. For example, during the post–World War II period the redevelopment of Ohio's cities languished, partly due to the reluctance of local bankers to take a chance on lending the funds required. Not until some key projects financed by out-of-state institutions demonstrated solid profits did Ohio bankers change this conservative view. Paradoxically, such caution contributed to Ohio banks' reputation for soundness and profitability in the 1980s.

By the 1970s Ohio banking was well into a new phase. Statewide bank holding companies, most headquartered in Columbus, Cincinnati, and Cleveland, were becoming dominant in the industry. New laws enacted in the 1980s permitted Ohio banks to purchase financial institutions in certain neighboring states, and the bank holding companies rushed to do so, partly because they hoped to become too large to be targets for takeover attempts by still stronger banks in other states.

The growth of Ohio banks did little, however, to ameliorate a pressing need for new industrial seed money and venture capital. Local entrepreneurs found it difficult to find financial backing. Unlike California and a handful of other states, few venture capital firms operated in Ohio, and those that did frequently invested in out-of-state enterprises. This lack of confidence in Ohio business ventures was one discouraging by-product of the economic malaise which the state endured from the 1970s to the 1990s.

Energy

Ohio's rise to industrial leadership rested to a considerable degree on abundant and cheap energy sources. When coal was king, Ohio could compete with any state. Ohio coal suffered no disadvantage in the pre–World War II era when air pollution had not yet become a national concern, but once clean air did become a priority, costly antipollution measures greatly decreased coal use. As the nation switched to oil and natural gas, prices soared in Ohio, as local industries and other consumers had to pay transmission costs from southwestern fields as well as severance taxes levied by the states of origin. When oil and natural gas were in short supply during parts of the 1970s, some Ohio consumers reconverted to coal.

Nuclear power appeared to have a promising future in the 1960s, and Ohio utilities entered the field. Yet, by 1986 only the Davis-Besse plant near Port Clinton and the Perry plant along the lakeshore east of Cleveland were operating, and both plants experienced frequent shutdowns from one problem or another. A third nuclear plant was started on the river east of Cincinnati, but this trouble-plagued Zimmer plant was converted to conventional energy sources. Fears engendered by the Three Mile Island fiasco in Pennsylvania (1979) and the Chernobyl disaster in the USSR (1986) stimulated protests against the use of nuclear power. Public opposition, coupled with the extraordinary cost of building nuclear power plants, impelled utility companies to scrap or delay plans for new reactors.

Once the beneficiary of cheap fuel, Ohio had become a high-cost energy state by the 1970s. This fact was a severe blow to the state's competitive position.

Transportation

The state's comprehensive transportation network remains a great asset to industry as the twentieth century draws toward its close, but the transportation business itself is in flux. Several rail companies have been absorbed into other railroad systems, including the federally subsidized networks—Amtrak for passenger service and Conrail for freight. Loss of trackage forced some manufacturing companies to find alternative ways of moving goods. Nevertheless, the railroads continue to serve the state well, and Ohio still had the nation's highest rail density in the 1980s.

Although shipping tonnage on Lake Erie declined as the steel industry languished in the seventies and eighties, that waterway remained an essential link in the state's transportation network. Lake Erie still carries diverse cargo, and the St. Lawrence Seaway is an important link to world shipping routes. Toledo was the first Ohio port to flourish as a result of Seaway traffic, since it was the first to organize an effective port authority to run operations in a businesslike fashion. The Seaway also stimulated waterborne commerce in Cleveland and Ashtabula.

But the Seaway has proved less productive than originally projected. The locks limit ships to an inefficient size; tolls are high; weather shortens the shipping season; and maintenance problems occasionally shut down the system at critical times. Some Ohio exporters who use the Seaway can cope with those problems, but are frustrated by federal trade policies that deal a blow to their competitive position in world markets. Nonetheless, Seaway boosters, citing the cost advantages to users, claimed in 1987 that the system was maturing and that it would flourish in coming years.

The Ohio River continues to be invaluable for the inexpensive movement of coal, chemicals, oil, sand and gravel, and other bulk cargoes. A new system of dams and locks was completed in the 1970s, assuring a nine-foot-deep channel for the diesel towboats and their enormous loads; one tow of fifteen steel barges can haul as much coal as ninety of the largest railroad hopper cars or hundreds of semi-trailer trucks. By the early 1980s, more than 100 million tons of cargo moved on the river annually.

While discussing the importance of Ohio's location we noted the importance of the interstate highway network to the state's economy. These roads carry an unending flow of trucks as does the James W. Shocknessey Turnpike, with traffic volume much greater than had been anticipated. These highways have been a boon to the trucking industry, and many major trucking companies made their headquarters in the state.

The state is also well served by airlines, including the ever-expanding air freight business, which uses several Ohio airports as distribution hubs. In short, ready access to transportation at reasonable cost is still one of the state's principal attractions to business.

Labor

One of the most dramatic changes in the cost of doing business over the past century has been the rising cost of labor. Few persons would advocate a return to the days when the employer's control over workers was absolute, and yet the very success of workers in organizing for their own benefit became a heavy burden late in the twentieth century. High wages and benefits greatly increased the cost of doing business in America and placed the country at a disadvantage when it found itself in a worldwide competition for markets. Not even the domestic market was secure from imports made by foreign workers who earned but a tiny fraction of the pay common to U.S. workers in the same industry.

Ohio suffered from this phenomenon more than most other states, for it was precisely in those industries where Ohio was a leader—steel, automobiles, rubber, heavy machinery, machine tools—that organized labor had its strongest hold and foreign competition was most acute. By 1980 it was common for top-of-the-line wages and benefits in steel, autos, and rubber to cost the company more than $20 per hour per worker. Additional expenses resulted from restrictive union work rules that protected unnecessary jobs and reduced flexibility in job assignments. Federal, state, and local health and safety regulations further increased labor costs.

To compensate for these higher expenditures, manufacturers in Ohio as elsewhere automated production lines, produced goods in low-labor-cost countries, moved manufacturing plants to states where organized labor had little influence, and negotiated wage and benefit concessions from workers. In an attempt to remain competitive by automating facilities, for example, the Timken Company of Canton opened its Faircrest plant, a state-of-the-art steel mill so automated that a few hundred workers could produce more and better steel than many times that number had previously produced. In automobile plants robots performed repetitive tasks; they did not stop for rest periods or coffee breaks.

But America's competitors were also using the newest technology and labor-saving devices, so to achieve even more favorable labor costs, many industries moved operations to foreign countries or bought from foreign suppliers. In the early 1980s General Motors and Ford, both with huge investments in Ohio, opened plants in Mexico, where automotive workers earned about $17 *a week* in contrast to the more than $20 *an hour* paid in wages and benefits in Ohio. American workers felt betrayed by such moves, but the companies claimed these measures were necessary to remain competitive. If the company went out of business, no employee would have a job.

Not all relocation was international in nature. Some Ohio manufacturing companies started as early as the 1920s to locate plants in the American south and west, where they hoped to reach developing markets. After the bitterness engendered by the labor union organizing strikes of the 1930s this decentralization accelerated. The labor climate in certain southern states was anti-union, and the new plants established in those states escaped the restrictive union work rules found in Ohio. The Mead Corporation of Dayton acquired or built paper mills in Tennessee, Georgia, and Michigan's upper peninsula before World War II. In perhaps the most dramatic example of this decentralization, Akron's tire plants, which had accounted for nearly 60 percent of America's production in the early thirties, produced only a few specialty tires by the late seventies. For a variety of reasons, including cheaper labor costs, the new center of tire production had shifted to the southern and southwestern states by 1980.

In addition to relocation, Ohio companies tried still another tactic for reducing labor costs. In negotiating new contracts, some companies in steel, automobiles, and other commodities asked their workers for concessions— lower wages and fewer benefits—in exchange for job guarantees. The workers were in a dilemma: either they agreed to reduce their scale of living or they would face the prospect of unemployment. On occasion workers called the company's bluff, only to discover that management meant what it said, as jobs were eliminated and plants closed. Sometimes union members approved concessions only to find that a short time later plants closed anyway.

Whether justified or not, organized labor in Ohio had a reputation for militancy, perhaps a result of the bitterness between labor and management engendered by the CIO organizing strikes of the 1930s. The reputation was enhanced during World War II when certain undisciplined workers in key industries defied their own leadership to stage walkouts and shutdowns. Unions lost considerable popular support when they proved unable to curb these "unpatriotic" actions. That same militancy paid off in the prosperous post-war years when American industry still ruled world markets; wage and benefits levels increased substantially with every renegotiated contract, and unions invoked ever more restrictive work rules. Rather than lose competitive position in the domestic market, manufacturers acceded to labor's demands and passed the increased costs along to the consumer.

One example of labor militancy which received national attention occurred at General Motors' Lordstown manufacturing complex, where state-of-the-art facilities for automobile production were opened in 1966. The plants were designed to enhance worker efficiency. But the new production lines proved too efficient; "speed-ups" angered the militant young workers who manned them. Influenced perhaps by the anti-establishment rhetoric of the day and bored by repetitive, mind-numbing tasks performed in what they called a dehumanizing environment, the workers reacted with repeated work stoppages. Although this condition was not unique to Lordstown, the media coverage that stretched on for months focused national attention on Ohio's labor problems.

Until 1980 Ohio was a center of union strength, in the forefront of industrial unionism since the inception of the CIO. The percentage of the state's industrial workers belonging to unions had always exceeded the national average. In the late thirties, Akron was called the most unionized city in America. By 1969 more than 36 percent of the state's industrial workers were union members, and in the basic industries—steel, automobiles, rubber—the figure was closer to 100 percent.

The growing economic malaise of the seventies eroded union strength dramatically, however. The fall-off in membership resulted from loss of production-line jobs in those industries where unions were strongest, from the lack of enthusiasm which many young workers had for unions, and from the emergence of small, new manufacturing operations which were nonunion from the start. In 1986 a major new manufacturing complex near Marysville, making Honda automobiles, successfully resisted the organizing efforts of the United Auto Workers.

Although organized labor was on the defensive among industrial workers, it moved forward aggressively to organize public employees, most of whom held white-collar jobs. Until the Celeste administration led the way in repeal-

ing the Ferguson Act in 1983, it had been illegal for Ohio's public employees
to organize and bargain collectively. In the main, the prohibition was observed, but occasionally teachers, fire fighters, and police went out on strike
in defiance of the law. Efforts to enforce it were mild and ineffective. With
repeal, a sizable new field opened to union organizers. Especially active in
seeking new recruits was the American Federation of State and Municipal
Employees, which quickly succeeded in organizing large groups of public
employees. The scene of action has shifted from industrial blue-collar worker
to public white-collar worker, but clearly the union principle is still very
much alive in Ohio.

Science and Technology

America's great industrial growth has always been closely tied to scientific
and technological advancement. Fundamental scientific breakthroughs—the
vulcanization of rubber, the harnessing of electricity, the development of
flight—gave rise to new industries. An endless line of technological improvements led directly to ever more sophisticated manufacturing processes
and products.

Leaders in a number of key Ohio industries—paint, soap, oil, rubber, electric power—recognized early that company research laboratories could pay
big dividends. Late in the nineteenth century, some Ohio companies had established laboratories, but following World War II, every important industry
in the state developed sophisticated new research capabilities. Cleveland and
Cincinnati with their diverse industrial bases had research facilities of many
different sorts. Among the Forest City's laboratories were those in paints,
steel, and petroleum products, while Cincinnati's Procter and Gamble had
extensive research capabilities. Akron, disproportionately focused on rubber,
claimed more Ph.D. chemists than any American city except Wilmington,
Delaware. Columbus was the home base of the Battelle Institute, the largest
independent research organization in the nation. The federal government
maintained advanced research activity at the NASA Lewis Research Center
in Cleveland and at the Wright-Patterson air force complex in Dayton.

In 1985 the state legislature, at the urging of Governor Celeste, enacted a
number of programs through which the state subsidized research activities
carried out through cooperative efforts between universities and private industry. One such effort, for example, combined the research capabilities of
The University of Akron, Case Western Reserve University, and northeast
Ohio industry in a program designed to make the Cuyahoga Valley a "Polymer Valley" which would attract productive new industries to the region.
Similar cooperative efforts were in place elsewhere around the state. Such

Ohio's contribution to the history of flight. *At top,* Orville Wright and one of his early flying machines, Dayton, ca. 1912. *At Bottom,* the lunar landing module carrying Wapakoneta's Neil Armstrong, first man on the moon. (Courtesy of the National Aeronautics and Space Administration.)

imaginative initiatives provide a clear example of the importance of scientific research in the evolving industrial scene.

Entrepreneurship

In the post–World War II era, American industry was long past the stage when individual entrepreneurs could operate as free-wheeling risk capitalists, almost single-handedly building their tiny enterprises into giant industries. Economic, political, and social constraints now hedged in the business leader. It was rare for an industrial leader to become a household name in the manner of Henry Ford, John D. Rockefeller, or Andrew Carnegie. Industry was in the hands of corporate managers, themselves employees who seldom spent their entire careers in one company; hence they lacked the total identification with the company that had characterized the true entrepreneur. The new breed of executives could place their personal stamp on a company only to the extent that they could persuade stockholders, powerful boards of directors, unions, and their own complex companies to follow their lead. They dealt daily with a maze of federal, state, and local constraints which would have dismayed their predecessors.

A different personality type emerged to lead large, modern business combinations. Dubbed the "organization man" in a 1950s book by William Whyte, these executives were bureaucrats operating in the depersonalized ambience of the modern corporation. Unlike their swashbuckling predecessors, many of whom came to corporate leadership through production or sales, they were more often trained in accounting, finance, or law. Some observers claimed that this training predisposed them to be cautious and detail-oriented, unlikely to show the boldness and take the risks of their predecessors. Another tendency attributed to the new corporate leaders was their propensity to believe that they were being judged by their ability to generate suitable profits, not over the long haul, but short-term. Indeed, by the late seventies it was apparent that prudent corporate leaders who had diversified their companies and had invested profits in the company's future growth had made their companies vulnerable to corporate raiders who, by taking advantage of undervalued stock, seized control of lucrative industrial properties for their own enrichment. A number of strong Ohio corporations suffered this fate in the seventies and eighties. Perhaps the best-publicized case was the successful defense which the Goodyear Tire and Rubber Company made in 1986 to escape the international corporate raider, Sir James Goldsmith. It was a costly victory for Goodyear, which incurred debts by buying Goldsmith's stock at a stiff price. It then was forced to sell off important auxiliary enterprises to reduce debt, and also the company reduced its labor force and office staff to cut costs.

Political and Social Climate

The new corporate managers operated in a social and political milieu strikingly different from that of a hundred years ago. Most were imbued with some sense of social responsibility for the policies and practices of their companies, many of which tried to be good corporate citizens of the communities in which they were located. Charitable activities such as the United Way counted on corporate donations for much of their money, and companies contributed to local colleges and hospitals, supported school levies, raised money for disaster relief, and helped bankroll local cultural groups. Such use of company funds would have been thought inappropriate in earlier years.

While the company had a stake in its community, the community also had a stake in the company's continued profitability. A growing public recognition of the degree to which the health of an important business and the health of the community are intertwined provided a more supportive environment than industry had enjoyed historically.

It is easy to overstate the case for this rapprochement, but one need look only to the 1960s to see a time when it was fashionable for large segments of the public to regard American industry as oppressive, part of America's problem. With the ending of the Vietnam war and its accompanying discontents, and with the onset of Ohio's economic malaise, public perceptions changed. Communities began to see industry as the solution to their needs. It is safe to say that, as of 1988, few elements within an Ohio community would protest if a new industry were to locate therein, even if it were granted tax abatements and other special considerations. It has become all too clear that a healthy economy is required to underwrite a healthy society.

This perception is clear to state and local legislators and officials. On the state level, Governor Celeste's administration continued to woo business, but the search shifted away from the conventional "smokestack" industries that once dominated Ohio's industrial scene. Rather, the emphasis was on serving industries already located in the state, and seeking new jobs in the "high tech" industries. To this end the administration used incentives such as favorable real estate deals and tax abatements to keep established industries and attract new ones. The state also emphasized providing quality education in Ohio schools and making the state a comfortable and attractive place for firms to locate their personnel.

Ohio and the Post-Industrial World

Changes in traditional industrial patterns have captured the attention of the public. One observer of the American scene, social historian Alvin

Toffler, has called the newly emerging economic conditions the "third wave." America's first wave, he said, had been its agriculturally based economy. In the nineteenth century the second wave, the industrially based economy, forged ahead. Now a "post-industrial" economy that emphasizes high technology and service industries is emerging to replace the second wave. While Toffler's scheme provides a convenient frame of reference in which to theorize about the new developments, he raised more questions than he answered about this post-industrial society.

Offsetting somewhat Ohio's loss of manufacturing jobs has been a commensurate growth of new jobs in the so-called service sector. Unfortunately, they seldom pay as well as the industrial jobs that were lost. In the mid-eighties, Ohio was among the leading states in creating new jobs, but they were disproportionately in the service sector.

While it is clear that American industry generally, and Ohio industry specifically, are in transition, it is impossible to determine what the long-term ramifications of this transition might be. One thing appears certain. It is possible to exaggerate the demise of American industry. In the Buckeye State a number of threatened industries remained relatively strong by streamlining their operations, cutting out the "fat" to make their companies lean and competitive in domestic and world markets. Another noteworthy trend has been the move away from huge companies, which try to produce a wide variety of products, toward smaller specialty firms. In the steel industry, for example, many such specialty firms prospered while the massive firms continued to flounder.

Ohio's Image in the Contemporary World

In his provocative book *The Image: A Guide to Pseudoevents in America*, Daniel Boorstin reveals how often the image becomes more "real" than reality. One can see that tendency at work in the way the national media portrayed Ohio during the difficult years after 1970. This portrayal was all too often a case of selective reporting, in which emphasis was on the state's problems ranging from the erosion of its industrial base to concerns over air and water pollution. Ohio was charged with everything from dull politics to dreary weather. While some of the unfavorable imagery was based on realities, the unrelenting focus on the negative unfairly distorted the state's image. In poll after poll, those who knew the state best, the people who lived in it, overwhelmingly supported Ohio as a desirable place to make one's life in.

There is a momentum in human affairs. States, like nations, have their day in the sun and then suffer from an accumulation of problems which slow further growth and development. In a sense that described Ohio. From its earliest settlement, it had been a productive land supporting a large and energetic population. Now it is clear that the state's economic base was shifting, and with that shift came adjustments in the social and political realms. It is not clear, however, what precise direction that shift might take. But the past is still a reasonable guide to what the future holds, and it suggests that the new Ohio which was emerging would continue to be the productive and promising place to live and work that it had been for so many generations.

18.

Toward Two Hundred Years

As Ohio approached its bicentennial, it retained much of its character, making it one of the nation's most representative states. That representative character rested upon the diversity of its people and their wide distribution across the state, upon an uncommon balance between rural and urban interests and between agriculture and industry, and upon its central location in the mainstream of national social and intellectual currents.

The fluid nature of contemporary American society makes it difficult to document Ohio's typicality. However, in the 1990s political pundits still flocked to this hard-to-predict state seeking clues to forthcoming voting patterns; test marketers used Ohio cities and towns as trial markets for new products; social analysts continued to search the state for hints about national trends. In poll after poll, ranging from religious affiliation to ranking of social attitudes, Ohio came as close as any state to matching the national profile.

As we examine Ohio's most recent decade, it will be apparent that a number of the state's historically distinguishing features have remained intact. One such feature is its political behavior, especially in presidential contests.

The Political Realm

Ohio's importance in presidential contests rests on two realities. First, as the seventh-most-populous state, its electoral college vote is eagerly sought. In postwar times population surges in Texas, Florida, and other western and southern states cost Ohio seats in the U.S. House of Representatives, hence electoral votes. The loss of two seats after the 1990 census reduced its representation to nineteen. But with twenty-one electoral votes (two senators and nineteen representatives), Ohio was still a significant prize. Second, regardless of what party registration figures revealed, in statewide contests Ohio was a two-party state, a state in which neither Democrats nor Republicans can take success for granted. For example, it is said that John F. Kennedy never understood how he lost the state in 1960 when it fit the Democratic profile so well and registered Democrats far outnumbered Republicans. In addition to these realities, cracker-barrel folklore about Ohio's political role remained intact, one bit of folklore being that no Republican has ever been elected president without Ohio's vote.

In 1988 the state lived up to its reputation by giving its support to Republican George Bush, who reached his peak of popularity when he sent American troops to the Near East during the short, technologically advanced Persian Gulf War of 1991. Among them were Ohio men and women; and save the sixteen who were killed, most of those who served returned to enthusiastic homecomings staged in nearly every sizable town. This outburst of patriotic sentiment is said to have been a way of assuaging national guilt over the shabby treatment shown Vietnam veterans.

President Bush's popularity took a nosedive in the wake of the war as the nation's economy faltered and presidential rhetoric did not address hard realities. When Bush sought reelection in 1992, Ohio again played its bellwether role. Democratic challenger Bill Clinton carried the state with 40.2 percent of the vote; Bush received 38.3 percent; and third-party candidate Ross Perot got a surprising 21 percent. Once again Ohio's presidential election figures closely paralleled the national distribution.

Another three-way battle shaped up in 1996 as President Clinton sought reelection. His challengers were Bob Dole, longtime Republican senator and party leader, and the persistent Ross Perot. Ohio's crucial role in this election was evident in the extraordinary amount of time spent by candidates and their supporters seeking to sway Buckeye voters. Each major party acted as though it could sell its candidate to the nation if only it could find a winning formula in Ohio. Clinton won with 47 percent of Ohio's vote; Dole received 42 percent and Perot 11 percent. Once again, the state's vote distribution closely matched the nation's.

State Politics: Time for a Change

The traditional political pendulum swings of Ohio politics were again evident in the early 1990s. Richard Celeste's eight years as governor marked a

high point of Democratic success in the recent era: all statewide elected executive officers were Democrats, and the party controlled the Ohio House.
Only the Senate, Republican-controlled during the governor's last six years,
spoiled the all-Democrat symmetry. When he left office, Celeste could point
to substantive accomplishments. Prominent among them were the securing of
much-needed new revenue, solving critical financial problems (Ohio's own
savings and loan scandal), securing enhanced support for the state's public
institutions, encouraging job growth and redirecting it into more promising
directions, and initiating innovative programs that established productive relationships between business and universities.

There was another side to the Celeste record, however. In his early years as
governor, party enthusiasms seemed to run out of control, with loyalty figuring
largely in the "pay-to-play" ambience of the Statehouse. The governor accepted bad advice in making his appointments, many of which came back to
embarrass him through their ineptness or even outright criminal conduct. The
governor's critics had a field day when, in a last-minute action, he pardoned a
number of "battered" women prisoners who had not been allowed to cite
their abuse in their own defense, and he also commuted death sentences for a
number of convicts. The governor acted out of conviction, but law enforcement officials, newspaper editorialists, and citizens sensitized to crime protested vigorously.

Celeste's admirers and supporters (nicknamed "Celestials") were confident
that he had a bright future in political office. Even some critics admitted that
his attractive personal qualities made him a prospect, but Celeste chose to
retire from the political scene, at least temporarily, to open a business office in
Columbus.

Ohio Democrats succeeded just twice in the 20th century in replacing
one of their own in the governor's chair, and both of those times were during
prolonged periods of crisis. This hard-luck pattern continued to plague the
Democrats in the 1990 elections. Their candidate for governor was Anthony J.
Celebrezze, Jr., the attorney general of Ohio, a proven vote-getter with a well-
recognized, political name.

The Republicans nominated George V. Voinovich, whose political career
included three terms in the Ohio House, a brief stint as lieutenant governor,
and long service as mayor of Cleveland. He emerged from the same Cleveland
ethnic ambience that had spawned Frank Lausche and a number of other
successful political leaders. Cleveland businessmen approached Voinovich while
he was serving as lieutenant governor and encouraged him to run for mayor of
their city in order to "rescue" it from default and the mistakes of the Kucinich
administration. Voinovich's success as mayor earned him the gratitude and
continued support of business interests in Cleveland.

Despite predictions of a close race, Voinovich won the election handily with 55 percent of the vote. He proved strong in Democrat-leaning northeastern Ohio and, of course, carried Republican-leaning central and southwestern Ohio. Only Lucas, Montgomery, Clark, and the economically depressed counties of eastern and south-central Ohio supported Celebrezze. Voinovich's victory was the precursor of Republican victories to come.

Future Republican triumphs rested in part on the restructuring of electoral districts. With the victory of Robert A. Taft II in the 1990 race for secretary of state, the Republicans were assured of a three to two majority on the all-important state Apportionment Board. The new electoral district lines were, as customary, arranged to benefit the party controlling the redistricting process, so Republicans made the most of their opportunity to maximize GOP prospects.

The redistricting process revealed interesting population shifts. The heavily industrialized, Democratic-leaning northeast faced decreases in population, especially in the core cities, while the Republican-leaning central and southwestern counties' populations grew. One immediate result of redistricting was a Republican resurgence in the Ohio House and in the state's representation in the U.S. House of Representatives.

Governor Voinovich moved swiftly to put his stamp on state government. One immediate goal—to cut state spending—required the cooperation of the legislature and, since such cuts had always been popular, little political risk was involved. However, when the governor later merged spending cuts with a tax increase he had a much tougher sell. The skills of Stanley J. Aronoff, president of the senate, and House Speaker Vernal G. Riffe, Jr., were necessary to salvage his program.

New spending constraints fell unevenly on public institutions. The state's "rainy day" fund was enhanced to act, as the governor said, as a hedge against new expenses that could arise if federal welfare programs were turned over to the states.

The governor and the legislature cooperated on other politically sensitive issues, including a modest restructuring of Ohio's costly Workers' Compensation Fund, which had a record of poor management and inefficient service. Even organized labor criticized it for seemingly erratic claims settlements, though was leery about any fundamental changes to the system. Business interests, strongly favoring change, bore the basic cost of the program, which was the nation's third most expensive such program and which added considerably to the cost of doing business in Ohio. One example, revealed through figures issued by LTV Steel in Cleveland, described how the company's integrated facilities in Ohio cost the company $1.81 per ton shipped in 1993. In Indiana, the equivalent workers' compensation cost was 39 cents. The General Assembly enacted a compromise "reform" bill in 1993.

As 1994 approached, there was little doubt that George Voinovich would seek reelection. He seemed comfortable in office. Polls revealed that voters liked his low-key style (the public knew little of his bursts of temper), his pragmatism, and his willingness to take a stand on controversial subjects (abortion rights and casino gambling, both of which he opposed, and the privatization of liquor stores, which he favored). While political true believers prefer controversy to blandness, Voinovich was well served by avoiding the ideological shrillness then associated with a new generation of Republicans on Capitol Hill.

The governor's popularity was intimidating to would-be challengers. No front-line Democrat would risk taking him on, so state senator Robert Burch of Tuscarawas County took up the fight in 1994. Voinovich took 72 percent of the vote, losing only Jefferson and Harrison counties. Republicans won other significant victories, some historic: Kenneth Blackwell won a full term as state treasurer, becoming the first African American to win statewide elective office; Nancy Putnam Hollister, former mayor of Marietta, became Ohio's first woman lieutenant governor; and Betty Montgomery became the state's first woman attorney general. Republicans also won control of the Ohio House and named its first female Speaker, Jo Ann Davidson of Franklin County. The strength of the Republican surge also helped carry Michael DeWine to victory over the retired Howard Metzenbaum's hand-picked candidate in a race for the U.S. Senate, Joel Hyatt.

The significance of the Republican sweep was felt in the changing leadership of the Ohio House. For twenty years, Vernal G. Riffe, Jr., held undisputed sway over this body, earning much admiration for his skills. His political acumen and legendary ability to secure action on politically sensitive items served the state well. Not so flattering was his attention to special interests, especially during his annual fund-raising gatherings. He did not need much money for his own campaigns, so he used deep pockets to finance other Democrats who would likely be grateful to the Speaker when elected. As do all representatives, when possible, he funneled resources into his home region, and the locals appreciated it. Shawnee State University was perhaps his major monument. On approaching the Scioto County line, highway signs informed travelers that they were entering "Riffe Country."

Riffe's retirement, which he had announced before the 1994 elections, was bittersweet. Though earning praise for his long service, he was at the same time charged with failing to report certain monies received to the Joint Legislative Ethics Committee as required by new state law and was assessed a minor penalty for this action. His legislative colleague, senate president Stanley Aronoff, also fell afoul of the new ethics laws and was fined by the court for failure to file a proper report. A third legislator, state senator Eugene Watts, pleaded no contest to taking money for appearances not made and was fined, as were two consulting firms involved in the incidents.

Public disenchantment with politics and politicians grew during the 1980s as the roles of lobbyists, political action committees, and other interest groups were widely reported. This was a national phenomenon intensified in Ohio by the perception that the "pay-to-play" mentality was growing more powerful. In 1992, therefore, Ohio voters strongly supported a constitutional amendment limiting terms for its elected representatives in both executive and legislative positions. The governorship had been limited to two consecutive terms since 1954, and now this eight-year limit was imposed on all statewide elected executive officers and members of the General Assembly. The limit on U.S. representatives from Ohio was also set at eight consecutive years; for U.S. senators the limit was twelve years (two consecutive terms). Persons then in office, except for the governor, were exempt from these limits.

Opponents of term limits presented valid arguments that focused on the reality that experience counts in public office. In Congress, they argued, Ohio's delegation would lack the seniority so important in determining leadership roles. Only a handful of other states had so limited themselves. Term limits, in conjunction with Ohio's diminished numbers in the U.S. House, could seriously cripple the state's influence in national affairs, and Ohio had long prided itself on providing national political leadership. In 1995 the U.S. Supreme Court put a halt on enacting term limits on the federal level.

Term limits were clearly outside the state's political tradition, but in other regards—close presidential elections, party dominance shifts in Columbus, fragmented party structure, the primary influence of money issues in political life—the tradition endured. Many Ohioans regarded the broadening of racial and gender representation in executive and legislative offices as a healthy departure from previous practice; so too did they regard enactment in the early 1990s of an ethics code placing restraints upon familiar abuses of money and power.

The "good old days" of recent Ohio politics were celebrated symbolically during "Ohio Politics Day," observed in Columbus in October 1994 in conjunction with publication of *Ohio Politics,* edited by Alexander Lamis of Case Western Reserve University. The day's highlight was a panel featuring James Rhodes, John Gilligan, and Richard Celeste. Before a knowledgeable audience, the former governors discussed their personal and political outlooks. Rhodes, with characteristic assurance, reiterated his favorite job-related themes. When he listed some of his many building projects, Celeste responded good naturedly, "yes, and you left me to pay for them." When asked what persons had served as their political inspirations, Rhodes named Franklin D. Roosevelt and Dwight D. Eisenhower—"they got things done." Gilligan surprised some in the audience by naming Bobby Kennedy, whom he respected for focusing attention on the nation's social needs. Celeste chose Chester Bowles, former governor of Connecticut, as a political mentor and Thomas Jefferson as his intellectual ideal.

Erasing the Rust

As the twentieth century entered its final decade, Ohio was still struggling to reverse a twenty-five-year period of declining economic fortunes. The 1980s' unhappy legacy included high unemployment (including the loss of at least 230,000 high-paying factory jobs) and a decrease in average family income. Although some 360,000 more women had entered the work force, there were a disproportionate number in low-paying service jobs, many of them without benefits. The ranks of Ohio's poor grew substantially.

Both the public and private sector sought ways to reverse these discouraging conditions, and by the early 1990s the efforts appeared to be bearing fruit. Newspaper headlines trumpeted the good news: "Toledo Shakes Rust Belt Tarnish"; "Fortune 500 Firms Are Back Full Steam." Like its sister states of the Old Northwest (Indiana, Illinois, Michigan, Wisconsin), Ohio had absorbed much of its traumatic loss and was on the road to recovery. The 1990s saw a healthy growth in employment, manufacturing, export values, retail sales, and personal income levels (which rose 6 percent in 1994 but still remained below the national average). But even though the economic pendulum was swinging toward prosperity, tens of thousands of people who had lost their jobs during the lean years missed out on the recovery.

Growth in the manufacturing sector was especially encouraging since it produced substantial jobs and fit so well with the state's tradition. The national business magazine *Site Selection* reported that Ohio led the nation in 1993–94 in new facilities and existing plant expansion. One of every five Ohio workers was employed in manufacturing and earned the nation's third-highest hourly wage. The state ranked fourth in the value of its manufactured products.

It is tenuous in the extreme to try to describe Ohio's rapidly changing economic profile in the 1990s. We can bring some order to this complex picture, however, by using the analytical structure developed in chapters twelve and seventeen.

Location

Ohio has always profited from its fortuitous location. In the waning years of the twentieth century, it was fashionable for information-age enthusiasts to downplay location's importance. The apostles of change overstated their claim, however, at least in the short run.

Clearly Ohio's locational advantage in a competitive marketplace continued to serve it well. As in the past, transportation networks—road, rail, river, lake, and air—moved goods efficiently. Major distributors continued to construct new facilities to take advantage of this fact. The "just in time" delivery of parts to assembly plants, especially in the automotive business, encouraged suppliers to locate new plants in the state. One example must suffice. In the early 1990s Ohio outranked every state except California in attracting Japanese manufacturing firms. Many of these firms came to Ohio because it was conveniently located for the major Japanese automotive plants in Ohio, Kentucky, and Michigan, which meant short hauls over an excellent highway network.

Some strong, traditional Ohio industries had a magnet effect on out-of-state businesses working in the same field. Thus northeastern Ohio, historically strong in polymer-related industries, experienced an influx of foreign and domestic firms anxious to gain access to the basic research, applied skills, and general know-how of the region. "Polymer Valley" was more than just an attractive slogan describing the Cleveland-Akron corridor.

Mineral and Natural Resources

Mineral resources, so important to Ohio's early industrial growth, continued to flow primarily from outside the state. Local supplies of limestone, silica sandstone, and shale were still adequate, as was salt produced by a number of processes to serve different purposes. Dutch-owned Akzo, for instance, was one of the world's principal producers of road salt, and its mines on Cleveland's Whiskey Island boomed during adverse winter weather. The clay products industry showed few signs of expanding locally; oil and natural gas production continued to be small-scale. Coal, which had long been Ohio's principal mineral resource, faded in the nineties as mining of local high-sulphur-content coal gave way increasingly to cleaner coal imported from western states.

Natural resources—soil, water, timber—were as important as ever to the state's well-being, and their proposed uses attracted basic, continuing controversy that one can oversimplify as developer versus environmentalist. Only a few high points of this inordinately complicated subject can be mentioned here.

What was happening to the state's soils? On the positive side was the fact that Ohio in the 1990s remained one of the nation's premier agricultural states. In 1993 it ranked thirteenth in the nation in gross farm income. Soy beans (fifth in the nation), corn (tenth), and dairy products (ninth) were the largest money makers, as they had been for decades. Production, however, increasingly gravitated to large-scale agribusiness. And so while average farm size continued to increase, the number of family farms continued to decline and all but disappeared from the urban counties. Much abandoned farm land continued to return to woodlot, but within any reasonable distance from a population center it was apt to be developed residentially or commercially. Urban sprawl was no longer confined to main traffic arteries reaching out from major population centers. It now encroached on once-open countryside far removed from cities. This movement was national in scope, fueled by population increase, desire to escape city problems, longing for a little elbow room, and affluent retirees seeking a garden spot for their later years.

Family farmers—quintessentially the good guys of American folklore—continued to struggle in a market dominated by agribusiness. Periodically local opinion rallied to their cause, but in this essentially urban state the general public remained largely unaware of their plight. The concentration and centralization of agricultural production had far-reaching implications in more than price, however. Gene Logsdon, a popular writer of farm-related articles and himself a farmer, described the effects of a large-scale egg producing enterprise involving millions of hens in a region dominated by family farms. While neighbors complained about the stench, a broader problem was how best to dispose of incredible amounts of chicken manure without compromising water supplies.

Capital

Ohio businesses had traditionally looked beyond the state for the large capital infusions they required. As previously noted, however, Ohio banks became far more aggressive in taking advantage of relaxed legal constraints to create large, regional banks. In part this was to gain the efficiencies of size in an automated age; in part it was a defensive move designed to ward off acquisition attempts. Ohio businesses benefited from the ability of these large banks to make loans of greater magnitude than before. Although they were not the friendly neighborhood banker of folklore, borrowers assumed that Ohio-based banks would be more knowledgeable about, and more sympathetic to, local business conditions than would out-of-state banks. An increase in local venture capital was a boon to start-up businesses. Coupled with the low-cost support furnished by urban industrial incubators, things began looking up for risk-taking Ohio entrepreneurs.

Energy

One damper on Ohio's manufacturing rebound in the 1990s was the relatively high cost of energy. Industry relied on imported oil and gas. Electric power prices, especially in northeastern Ohio, were affected by the high cost of pollution controls, by the loss of industrial customers, and by costs lingering from nuclear power development. Complicating the picture were prospects of opening the utilities market to competition. Some communities examined the possibility of generating their own power or buying it wholesale from electric utilities for resale at lower cost to their residents. One striking reality of the nineties was the apparent lack of interest in expanding nuclear power. Extraordinary costs, operational glitches, and public fears coalesced to keep the status quo in nuclear power development.

Ohio had to rely on imported oil and natural gas. Local wells remained an important supplementary source, but the number of new drillings diminished yearly—from 6,082 new wells drilled in 1981 to 695 drilled in 1993. However, new horizontal and diagonal drilling techniques promised to make some Ohio wells more productive. And with many small players locally, the industry was constantly being rearranged through buy-outs, mergers, and relocations.

Some innovative energy efforts of the seventies and eighties remained in limbo during the nineties. Both Columbus and Akron abandoned once-promising efforts to generate steam by burning trash; accidents, coupled with the high cost of adapting to new environmental regulations, doomed these plants. Experiments with the clean-burning of Ohio's high-sulphur coal and with the burning of shredded tires led to no large permanent installations.

Labor

Organized labor remained on the defensive in the early 1990s, although new initiatives were geared toward reviving its influence. Union membership, some 25 percent of the 1983 work force, fell to 19 percent in just a decade. The private manufacturing sector, historically the heart of union strength in Ohio, experienced a decline in membership to 29 percent during that same period. Unions had found no clear strategy for halting this erosion, yet when tempers flared some returned to old-time militancy. That worked in 1995 when General Motors workers in Dayton struck, shutting down GM plants across the nation. The strikers were protesting GM's plans for contracting work out to non-GM (possibly nonunion) plants.

Militancy proved futile in other circumstances, as in a prolonged strike against Bridgestone-Firestone by the United Rubber Workers. Its strike was ineffective, however, as this once-powerful union had sustained great membership loss. The URW was amenable, therefore, when the United Steel Workers offered to absorb them, even though this meant that the URW would lose both its identity and its Ohio base. The now-augmented USW anticipated joining the United Auto Workers and the International Association of Machinists by the year 2000 to create a union strong enough to combat what they perceived as an anti-union bias in American industry.

The decline in union membership had political repercussions. Union political clout in Ohio had always been spotty (for reasons outlined in chapter

17), and problems continued in 1994 when unionists were unable to keep some normally sympathetic representatives in Congress from voting in favor of the North American Free Trade Agreement (NAFTA), a pact designed to remove trade barriers across the continent. Labor feared a job exodus to cheap-labor Mexico. Business supporters of NAFTA countered by claiming that open borders would expand business opportunities, creating new jobs, most of which would remain at home. Again, because it is both a major industrial-union state and a major exporting state, Ohio would be an optimum place to watch how things would play out with NAFTA.

Science and Technology

Initiatives in the scientific and technological realms changed little in the 1990s. Industrial research, always an Ohio strength, continued to provide the constant innovation and upgrading necessary to remain competitive. The Dayton area's huge Wright-Patterson airfield complex and the NASA Lewis Research Center in Cleveland remained important components of the federal research program, although both were threatened with possible funding cuts. The national rush toward electronic networking was highly visible in the state as industries, schools, and individuals scrambled to keep abreast of the latest technology. The partnership between industry and universities initiated in the Celeste administration continued to be a valuable stimulus to industries throughout the state.

Entrepreneurship

A surge of new entrepreneurial ventures was visible in the early nineties, much of it traceable to industrial and commercial downsizing. Able employees, let go through no fault of their own, often preferred to take a chance on themselves in a new venture rather than work for someone else. The largest number of these new businesses were in the service sector, and a large percentage of them were headed by women, as minorities benefited from government loan funds. Those making a product could secure support from city-operated industrial incubators that provided basic services at minimal cost. Entrepreneurs also emerged from established companies to start similar businesses on their own, and Ohio was home to a number of such offshoots.

Political and Social Climate

Ohio's economy in the 1990s operated in a political and social climate not unlike those of preceding decades. Governor Voinovich, while not as verbal about it as were his two immediate predecessors, was well aware that political leaders must create and maintain a favorable business climate if the state was to prosper in competitive times. Ohio business offices were extended overseas and in Washington, D.C. The governor led state officials on visits to future trading partners in countries that might welcome Ohio exports. However, there was no 1990s version of "Rhodes's Raiders" seeking to woo business away from neighboring states.

Within the state, legislation was sought to broaden the package of amenities offered to business. Any such effort generated opposition, much of it on the local level, since taxes, land use, and environmental issues were involved. But the hard fact remained: Ohio had to match what other states offered if it was to remain competitive. Just over the border, especially in Kentucky and Indiana, officials had set a fast pace. In 1993 Donald E. Jakeway, director of the Ohio Department of Development, said that "We need a level playing field" and then described a half-dozen changes, most of them tax related, that he thought would substantially enhance Ohio's competitive position.

Favorable tax adjustments for business had always drawn criticism from unions, farmers' organizations, and others who would not benefit directly. Probusiness spokespersons did have a point when they claimed that Ohio's business tax structure was not as favorable to them as were those of many other states. One should differentiate, however, between relatively high business taxes and the general level of taxation within the state. The oft-repeated charge that Ohio is "a high-tax state" was simply not true. For decades the state had consistently ranked below the national average in the per capita amount paid in state and local taxes. Property taxes were also below average, and the state sales tax was as low as (or lower than) those in surrounding states, and Ohioans paid no sales tax on food consumed off the premises.

The 1990s brought a breakthrough on another touchy issue—annexation. The growing political strength of suburban and exurban areas, coupled with the longtime opposition of township trustees, made it increasingly difficult for urban areas to annex property. As noted earlier in this book, Cleveland and Cincinnati here hedged in by surrounding municipalities. Dayton and Akron were nearly encircled. Only Columbus and Toledo had succeeded in annexing large amounts of surrounding countryside in which to grow and enhance their tax base. An innovative plan introduced by Akron mayor Don Plusquellic established Joint Economic Development Districts (JEDD) whereby the city and selected neighboring townships cooperated. With approval by the state legislature, Akron could extend its services to the township in return for part of the taxes generated by new development. The success of this approach led the legislature to extend the program statewide in 1995.

The Environment

Many business constraints were related to environmental issues. Ohio had done a poor job historically in protecting its most precious resources—its soil, water, and air. Because it had long been a principal mining and manufacturing state, it had an unusually large number of pollution hot spots. In 1995 at least ten of these problem areas were severe enough to be listed on the federal "superfund" cleanup list. The Fernauld site near Cincinnati and the Mound site near Dayton involved nuclear contamination; others, well distributed around the state, were old industrial dumps and landfills. No region seemed immune. In some cases the courts ordered the industries responsible to help with the cleanup costs. Yet, for example, former gas station sites remained vacant because new owners would have to bear the cost of cleaning contaminated soil before building. In 1994 the legislature enacted a "brownfield" law aimed at speeding up polluted industrial sites, but implementation was delayed pending negotiations among the Ohio Environmental Agency, environmentalists, and business representatives.

A bright spot in pollution control efforts was the improved water quality in Lake Erie, the Ohio River, and their tributaries. Support for clean water became easier to achieve as the economic benefits associated with this phenomenon became apparent. Not so easy to appreciate, however, was the value of protecting wetlands. Developers and local officials eager for new tax dollars sought to drain and fill the land but were increasingly stymied by people attuned to the vital role of wetlands in the natural cycle. Ohio, it was claimed, had lost more than 90 percent of its historic wetlands, second only to California. Another land-use conflict involved communities, seeking to preserve their historic character, placing restrictions on new development. Hudson in Summit County was one example among a growing number.

Air pollution remained a major environmental problem in the early 1990s. Environmental Protection Agency rules, plus a public concerned with its effects, especially the impact of acid rain on fish and forest, undergirded new controls. Ohio adopted a federally mandated program called locally "E Check," which required persons living in the greater Cleveland region and in southwestern Ohio to have their vehicles checked for harmful emissions and to pay a substantial fee for it. The intent was beneficial—to reduce ozone and other harmful emissions—but startup glitches infuriated many citizens.

Education

There was near unanimity in Ohio that its children were the hope of the future and that this future was tied to the quality of education in the public schools. But there unanimity ceased. This was not just a concern in Ohio—it was a national concern. Few states, however, had as complex a problem as Ohio did, with each of its 611 school districts (in 1995) jealously guarding its autonomy and its continued existence. George Voinovich, the "education governor," encouraged a one-time financial shot in the arm shortly after taking office, but his attempt to make the state Board of Education appointive failed. Beyond these measures he shied away from politically explosive radical reform, as did the legislature.

Few states could match Ohio's historic record of leadership in providing high-quality public education for its children, so it was particularly galling for persons who remembered better days to see once-splendid school systems mired in difficulty. Cleveland's system was a case in point. Once a model for the nation, this system was so deeply in debt ($155 million in 1996) that the state Board of Education appointed an officer to oversee its management. Mayor Michael White took political risks to back four "reform" candidates for school board positions, but their election changed little. In 1996, federal judge Robert Krupansky rescinded court-ordered busing that had once seemed a panacea but was then perceived as a failure by parents, both black and white, anxious to reestablish neighborhood schools.

Those trying to fix blame for Cleveland's problems had plenty of targets to choose from—unresponsive unions, political infighting on the city Board of Education, voter apathy—but the core problems lay deeper. They involved white flight to the suburbs and industrial decay, both of which cost the city a loss of tax revenues, a breakdown in family responsibility, drugs, and the whole litany of urban social malaise. These social pathogens were present in other places, of course, but they reached more children in Cleveland than they did in other Ohio cities.

In recounting what was wrong in public schooling, one all too often overlooks what went right in scores of well-funded, well-managed systems across the state. We do not have the luxury here of detailing these success stories, but it was apparent on the basis of national assessments that many districts performed exceptionally well—to be expected in a state with 611 separate districts. Indeed, fragmentation was part of the problem. The amount of money available per student varied dramatically among these districts. At the top of the financial scale in 1996 were a cluster of districts in the greater Cleveland region. Some were residential communities that taxed themselves heavily in support of quality education; others benefited from industrial tax revenue. These districts spent more than three times as much per pupil, as did districts near the bottom of the scale. A disproportionate number of the latter were found in poor rural or semirural areas, and many of these districts secured two-thirds of their revenue from the state. The poorer districts were also likely to be well represented on a shameful list, compiled nationally, that claimed

Ohio schools were in worse physical shape than any in the nation.

Since before World War II, Ohio had not ranked well in the amount of public money per capita spent on elementary, secondary, or higher education. In cooperation with the legislature, Governor Rhodes had secured money for vast capital improvement programs and had encouraged vocational education; Governor Gilligan had secured additional state funding; Governor Celeste had negotiated new financial support from enhanced income tax revenue; and early in his administration Governor Voinovich had supported a one-time financial shot in the arm. These panaceas to some extent concealed a growing disenchantment in the legislature directed at school administrators and teachers. Money already available was not being spent wisely, they claimed, and until spending was tightened they had no intention of considering a fundamental restructuring. Administrators throughout the state, confronted by undeniable needs, resented this attitude. The superintendent of a small city system responded to legislative charges of inefficiency by saying, "That's a crock. We're doing a better job than we ever did."

Allowing that some systems were poorly managed, it was a fact that more than a hundred districts had to seek state loan agreements during the 1984–94 decade, even though voters in nearly all of them had supported higher property taxes in their districts. Clearly periodic infusions of new funds were not getting at the root problems. Nor were lottery earnings, which were placed in the school fund but were not the supplement they were intended to be; rather, the legislature used lottery money to replace funds previously designated for the schools that they had diverted to other projects.

It would take a thick volume to describe the furor and confusion surrounding public school funding, but amid the clutter two initiatives stand out. The first of these rested in the courts. In 1991 a coalition of more than five hundred school districts filed suit in Perry County *(DeRolph vs. State of Ohio)* claiming that the legislature violated the state constitutional mandate to provide a thorough and efficient system of public education. Judge Linton Lewis, Jr., ruled three years later that a 1979 Ohio supreme court ruling asserting that local control took precedence over equal distribution of resources was in error. The governor and legislative leaders ordered the attorney general to appeal. Although the appeals court agreed that the public education system was a mess, they overturned Judge Lewis on the grounds that he did not have the authority to overrule the supreme court's 1979 decision. The coalition was then granted a hearing by the supreme court, which heard arguments in 1996 and took the case under advisement.

The second major initiative was proposed by those wanting the state to provide vouchers to students who chose to attend private schools (including parochial schools). The student making the move would take along to the new school $2,250 in public money that otherwise would have remained with the public school. Backers claimed it would allow less affluent students the same option available to more affluent ones, and competition for state money would force public schools to improve their programs and be more accountable. Few educators endorsed this concept. Neither did citizens who felt it was wishful thinking and was merely an avoidance of the real problems. Only the more competent parents would take advantage of the vouchers, they said, leaving the most troubled children trapped in increasingly depressed systems incapable of dealing with their sociological and psychological problems. And then there was the problem of irresponsible private schools cashing in on opportunity.

Governor Voinovich was a strong supporter of vouchers and encouraged the legislature to run a pilot program in 1996 for a limited number of Cleveland students. Only Milwaukee, Wisconsin, had previous experience with vouchers and assessments of that program varied. The issue involving separation of church and state was unresolved in the courts in 1996, but Ohio went forward anyway to include parochial schools in their program. Critics pointed out that this would exacerbate existing conditions in that Ohio already funneled more public money to church-related schools than did any other state.

Public higher education also faced difficult times in the early 1990s. Ohio's public universities and community and technical colleges expanded greatly during the Rhodes administrations and enjoyed enhanced funding under Celeste. But budget constraints in the early nineties forced spending cutbacks. Coupled with this austerity was a decline in student enrollment attributed to the smaller numbers of students coming out of high schools. Cuts in state spending plus loss of tuition encouraged universities to speed staff retirements and to replace salaried full-time professors with part-time instructors. This in turn raised another issue: were students getting their money's worth when many of their classes were taught by less qualified individuals? Meanwhile, Ohio students continued to pay a larger portion of their university expenses than did students in all but a handful of other states.

Several higher education issues centered around the state Board of Regents. In the thirty years since its establishment, the board had moved from its intended role as an advisory, coordinating body toward a more active role. In the mid-1990s, in conjunction with a panel appointed by Voinovich, the Regents cut off, or truncated, state support for a number of established doctoral programs, although peer reviews had shown some of them to be functioning well. In addition, law schools in those public universities in the populous northern part of the state had their state funding truncated and were placed under new mandates. Critics charged that a new elitism would put doctoral and legal education out of the reach of the very clientele the programs had been designed (with Regents' approval) to serve. The amount of money saved by these moves was modest, but the cuts were consistent with a longtime Ohio pattern of underfunding its public universities.

Another concern for the Regents was the revelation that Central State University, Ohio's historically black-dominated university, was in deep financial trouble and that physical facilities, including dormitories, were in serious disrepair. Newspapers asked why attention had not been focused on these problems long before they reached the crisis stage. African American legislators, alumni, and concerned citizens pressed for answers and for assurances that the institution would be spared the drastic cuts in programs some had suggested. Why Ohio should continue to have a racially aligned public university in a desegregated age was too emotional an issue to address.

No justice can be done to Ohio's complex educational issues in brief scope. Not since the establishment of the School Foundation Formula in 1935 had the state made radical changes in its funding of public education. As the twentieth century wound down, however, the old pattern of muddling through and of legislative avoidance was being challenged. Unlike its Michigan and Kentucky neighbors, Ohio had not yet taken the heroic steps necessary to overhaul its funding for public education.

Criminal Justice

Dealing more effectively with crime ranked with education as a public concern in the 1990s. State funding for the criminal justice system rose dramatically. New prisons were built at a record pace. The long-abandoned Ohio Penitentiary in Columbus, long a massive cornerstone of the state corrections system, was to be dismantled, and a new maximum security prison was under construction in the Youngstown area to provide relief for crowded Lucasville. Officials made an effort to locate new prisons near the population centers that provided the largest numbers of inmates. This was for the convenience of visitors and for alleviating the unemployment found in economically distressed regions.

A tougher criminal code was enacted in the early nineties. Voters supported a successful effort to reduce the number of appeals available to death row inmates. Public opinion also supported placing police officers on foot patrol in urban beats, a move made possible in some cities through new federal funding. Victims' assistance programs gained increased visibility and popular support, and domestic abuse and violence were treated with increased seriousness. People concerned about excesses in the "get tough on crime" mentality pushed for programs designed to deter criminal behavior rather than focusing so much money on punishment.

Often linking criminal behavior to mental or emotional distress, the state has historically maintained an extensive system of institutions for the mentally and emotionally stressed. This extensive network was revamped as support built for the deinstitutionalizing of patients. Concern was expressed that this process "dumped" marginally competent people on the streets, increasing homelessness and criminal activity. Ohioans could take heart, however, in learning from national surveys that the state's care of its custodial patients ranked well with that found elsewhere, a marked improvement over the record of the not-too-distant past.

Ohio's Cities—Looking Good

Politics, economics, and social conditions naturally preempt our attention and sometimes distract us from looking around to see what else is happening. The early 1990s provided much of interest, a good deal of it focused on the revival of the state's principal urban centers. Possibly the most dramatic of these was the resurgence of Cleveland, the self-styled "comeback city."

So long stigmatized by the national media, Clevelanders reveled in their new amenities, none of which was more successful than Jacobs Field, the strikingly appropriate new home of the city's baseball team, the Indians, and, adjacent to it, the Gund Arena, home of Cleveland's basketball team, the Cavaliers. Both facilities brought an economic revival to a formerly decrepit part of the inner city. The I. M. Pei–designed Rock and Roll Hall of Fame and Museum on the Lake Erie waterfront was an instant hit, hosting more than a million visitors in its first year. Adjacent to it on the landscaped waterfront was the new Great Lakes Science Center. A new football stadium would replace the cavernous Municipal Stadium and was to be the home of a reincarnated Browns team, promised to the city in the wake of losing its longtime favorites to Baltimore in 1996.

The waterfront attractions were made accessible by a new Rapid Transit rail link that also connected the lakefront with the flourishing entertainment complex in the "Flats" along the Cuyahoga River. New office buildings and hotels graced the downtown, and many old warehouse and commercial buildings were revamped into apartments and lofts. Some locals decried all the money spent downtown, urging that more be directed to the neighborhoods. This cry was echoed nationally as other cities tried to revive their core regions.

Much of Cleveland's revival was made during the administration of Mayor Michael White, Cleveland's second African American leader. In a sense, White represented how far the city's black citizens had come in the three decades since Carl Stokes broke the color barrier. In 1990 about 47 percent of Clevelanders were African American, the highest percentage among Ohio cities.

Columbus, Ohio's largest city, continued to benefit from its central loca-tion. Its fortuitous economic profile, buttressed by an unusual concentration of white-collar workers, continued to shield it from the extremes experienced by the industrial cities. Indeed, Columbus's well-being engendered some re-sentment and jealousy in other parts of the state. Some argued that govern-mental offices should be decentralized and their white-collar jobs distributed around the state, but there appeared to be little chance of that happening.

Sports-minded Columbus, like every large Ohio city, talked of building new athletic facilities. Local boosters envisioned it as a major-league city, ca-pable of supporting major teams, even though for the moment it ranked be-hind Cleveland and Cincinnati in the size of its metropolitan population. Mean-while the building cranes, so long absent in other Ohio cities, continued to grace the skyline; new commercial districts emerged; the city limits continued to engulf large chunks of adjacent land; the entertainment and cultural sectors maintained vitality. In short, Columbus continued on its path toward urban sophistication and was a vital focus for a state regaining its sense of optimism after years of readjustment.

Cincinnati, the grande dame of Ohio cities, continued in her distinctive way to display both a sociocultural conservatism along with a progressive busi-ness spirit. What other city would build an elaborate new cultural center when it already boasted fine, historic facilities long the envy of other communities? Both the Natural History Museum and the Cincinnati Historical Society found new homes and striking new display areas in the cavernous reaches of the former Union Station, though controversy surrounded attempts to redesign historic Fountain Square in the heart of the business district. And like Cleve-land, Cincinnati passed tax issues to provide money for new athletic stadiums. Although the Reds of the early nineties could not match the performance of the "Big Red Machine" of an earlier time, their colorful and controversial owner, Marge Schott, helped keep the baseball team in the news. The Bengals also hoped to recapture glory days and looked forward to a new football sta-dium. Through it all the city retained its customary political and economic influence on the life of the state and nation.

Toledo, Akron, and Dayton, each distinct in its own way, shared many of the problems growing out of years of economic malaise, but as the employ-ment picture brightened, so did their prospects. Toledo attracted new con-struction to its downtown, and a reconstituted Portside promised well for the future. The city continued to capitalize on its waterfront by extending efforts to clear out unsightly remnants of an earlier day when Maumee's shores were preempted by commerce and transportation. More than other Ohio cities, perhaps, Toledo felt neglected in its far-northern location and complained that it had no connector highway with Columbus. But the city's real spirit was reflected in its continuing improvements, including a striking addition to its world-class art museum, a key feature in the city's vital cultural life.

Akron's long-dormant plans for downtown renewal moved forward in the 1990s. Inventure Place, the new home of the National Inventors Hall of Fame, provided a stimulating environment for people—specially schoolchildren—who wanted to examine the world through hands-on activities. A new convention center anchored other improvements to the downtown section, including a new minor-league baseball stadium that replaced a block of aging buildings on Main Street. One of the city's prides was its dramatically enhanced park system, which included an upgrading of the historic Ohio and Erie Canal corridor.

While in the nineties downtown Dayton still looked like its once-vigorous self, it too had experienced the retailers' flight to the suburbs. A thriving Sinclair Community College buttressed the near-west side. NCR, Dayton's flagship industry, was first taken over by AT&T and its name changed but then regained its identity in the mid-1990s, restoring a proud name to Dayton. Commercial expansion was marked to the city's north and east, the latter involving neighboring Greene County. In 1995, the facilities of Wright-Patterson Field hosted an important international conference on the subject of troubled Bosnia, with the resulting agreements being termed "the Dayton Accords."

Canton, once a city of over 100,000 people, worried about its manufacturing base but saw continued commercial expansion in the Belden Village region to its north and in the vicinity of the Akron-Canton Airport, and the frequently expanded Professional Football Hall of Fame kept Canton in the national consciousness. Youngstown still struggled to overcome as devastating a series of economic blows as befell any Ohio city in the 1970s and 1980s. Much of its commercial vitality was found in the southern suburbs, and Youngstown State University continued to upgrade the central city with fine buildings and tasteful landscaping.

Ohio's unusual number of cities in the 25,000–75,000 population range defy simple generalizations. Some industrial centers such as Lima, Marion, and Mansfield had been dealt severe economic blows during the long period of economic malaise. By the mid-1990s, however, these hard-hit cities were fighting back with some success, although it seemed unlikely that they could ever recover the loss of all the well-paid industrial jobs. Other cities in this population category were older, close-in suburbs of the major cities. These cities—Lakewood, Parma, Cuyahoga Falls, Barberton, Kettering, for example—suffered many of the same problems as their larger neighbors, and some found their commercial base undercut by newer suburban development.

The commercial and industrial vitality shown by many cities in this population range was most evident on the city fringes where malls and clean industries tended to locate. Their presence in turn drew new housing and ultimately churches, schools, and other supporting institutions. Indeed, the most dramatic growth could be seen in the exurban developments that had profited from location along main highway arteries. Delaware, Medina, Greene, Clermont, and Wood counties are illustrative of this phenomenon.

Cultural Vitality

As noted in chapter 16, Ohio was home to an uncommon number of well-distributed fine cultural resources. In the mid-1990s only one other state had as many symphonic orchestras with million-dollar budgets as did Ohio, and, among the six located in the state, the Cleveland Orchestra remained preeminent, still considered by experts to be among the top three in the world. Groups featuring chamber music, opera, classical dance, and other special enthusiasms brought variety to the arts. However, supporters of the arts worried about funding, since established sources federal money were sharply curtailed.

Several of Ohio's major art museums were either expanded or rehabilitated in the early 1990s. The state's major galleries succeeded in attracting world-famous art shows, often being among just a handful of places in the United States where these treasures could be seen. Public libraries continued to thrive in the computer age. Cincinnati's system, with forty-one branches, had the nation's second-largest circulation in 1995, while Columbus ranked fourth and Dayton, Cleveland, and Akron showed to advantage as well.

The state's strong tradition in literature continued apace with both new and familiar contributors. Toni Morrison received the 1993 Nobel Prize for literature, and Rita Dove was named the Poet Laureate of the United States in 1993–94—singular professional honors for Ohio's daughters. And each year the Ohioana Library Association reviewed scores of qualified entries to determine prize awards to Ohio authors in a number of literary specialties.

A Bit of State Pride

People perform best when they are in a positive environment. Obviously, what attracts one might leave another cold, but in Ohio's diversity there was something for everyone if they just looked. A pleasant work environment, a nice neighborhood, a thriving farm, a clean stream, a theater or music hall, a college campus—whatever appealed and was accessible. For those who honored the Buckeye State, even some transient event could stir a sense of state pride. The 1995 launching of NASA'S "all Ohio" space shuttle crew could do it. The only non-Ohioan in the three-man, two-woman crew was made an honorary citizen of the state before launching, helping the state to retain its primacy in supplying space pioneers.

Pride, of course, is the motivating force behind great civic celebrations, and as Ohio moved toward its bicentennial some of its cities and regions were already observing two hundred years of accomplishment. It was appropriate that Marietta and Cincinnati led off the celebrations in 1988. A banner year was 1996 when Chillicothe, Cleveland, Dayton, and Youngstown celebrated their bicentennials, as did the Western Reserve region and some smaller communities.

That year also marked the reopening of Ohio's Statehouse after years of rehabilitation. Generations of relative neglect had left this venerable, stately building in disarray with some three-hundred-plus cubbyhole rooms created in spaces never designed for them. These intrusions were eliminated, and the interior of the building, including the dramatic rotunda, was restored to early glory.

History reports. It does not predict. One virtue ascribed to history is its capacity for giving the careful reader a feel for the rhythms that characterize human affairs in specific societies. And the rhythms that move America move Ohio. It is with assurance, therefore, that one can contemplate an Ohio moving along its traditional paths of diversity, balance, and conservatism. There may be an occasional lapse, but the Ohio that is emerging will continue to be the productive, promising place to live and work in that it has been for so many generations.

Appendixes

Appendix 1

Governors of Ohio

Name	Party	County of Residence	Period in Office
Edward Tiffin (resigned)	Republican[1]	Ross	1803–1807
*Thomas Kirker	Republican	Adams	1807–1808
Samuel Huntington	Republican	Geauga { In the part of Ohio now called Lake County	1808–1810
Return J. Meigs, Jr. (resigned)	Republican	Washington	1810–1814
*Othniel Looker	Republican	Hamilton	1814
Thomas Worthington	Republican	Ross	1814–1818
Ethan Allen Brown	Republican	Hamilton	1818–1822
*Allen Trimble	Republican	Highland	1822
Jeremiah Morrow	Republican	Warren	1822–1826
Allen Trimble	Republican	Highland	1826–1830
Duncan McArthur	National Republican	Ross	1830–1832
Robert Lucas	Democrat	Pike	1832–1836
Joseph Vance	Whig	Champaign	1836–1838
Wilson Shannon	Democrat	Belmont	1838–1840
Thomas Corwin	Whig	Warren	1840–1842

[1] The early Republicans, who endorsed the political principles of Thomas Jefferson, should not be confused with members of the present Republican Party, an organization that arose during the decade prior to the Civil War.

* Governors so indicated filled a vacancy due to a death or a resignation.

Name	Party	County of Residence	Period in Office
Wilson Shannon (resigned)	Democrat	Belmont	1842–1844
*Thomas Bartley	Democrat	Richland	1844
Mordecai Bartley	Whig	Richland	1844–1846
William Bebb	Whig	Butler	1846–1849
Seabury Ford	Whig	Geauga	1849–1850
Reuben Wood (resigned)	Democrat	Cuyahoga	1850–1853
*William Medill	Democrat	Fairfield	1853–1856
Salmon P. Chase	Republican	Hamilton	1856–1860
William Dennison	Republican	Franklin	1860–1862
David Tod	Unionist	Mahoning	1862–1864
John Brough (died in office)	Unionist	Cuyahoga	1864–1865
*Charles Anderson	Unionist	Montgomery	1865–1866
Jacob D. Cox	Unionist	Trumbull	1866–1868
Rutherford B. Hayes	Republican	Hamilton	1868–1872
Edward F. Noyes	Republican	Hamilton	1872–1874
William Allen	Democrat	Ross	1874–1876
Rutherford B. Hayes (resigned)	Republican	Sandusky	1876–1877
*Thomas L. Young	Republican	Hamilton	1877–1878
Richard M. Bishop	Democrat	Hamilton	1878–1880
Charles Foster	Republican	Seneca	1880–1884
George Hoadly	Democrat	Hamilton	1884–1886
Joseph B. Foraker	Republican	Hamilton	1886–1890
James E. Campbell	Democrat	Butler	1890–1892
William McKinley	Republican	Stark	1892–1896
Asa Bushnell	Republican	Clark	1896–1900
George K. Nash	Republican	Franklin	1900–1904
Myron T. Herrick	Republican	Cuyahoga	1904–1906
John M. Pattison (died in office)	Democrat	Clermont	1906
*Andrew L. Harris	Republican	Preble	1906–1909
Judson Harmon	Democrat	Hamilton	1909–1913
James M. Cox	Democrat	Montgomery	1913–1915
Frank B. Willis	Republican	Delaware	1915–1917
James M. Cox	Democrat	Montgomery	1917–1921
Harry L. Davis	Republican	Cuyahoga	1921–1923
A. Victor Donahey	Democrat	Tuscarawas	1923–1929
Myers Y. Cooper	Republican	Hamilton	1929–1931
George White	Democrat	Washington	1931–1935
Martin L. Davey	Democrat	Portage	1935–1939
John W. Bricker	Republican	Franklin	1939–1945
Frank J. Lausche	Democrat	Cuyahoga	1945–1947
Thomas J. Herbert	Republican	Cuyahoga	1947–1949
Frank J. Lausche	Democrat	Cuyahoga	1949–1957
*John W. Brown	Republican	Medina	Jan. 3–14, 1957
C. William O'Neill	Republican	Washington	1957–1959
Michael V. DiSalle	Democrat	Lucas	1959–1963
James A. Rhodes	Republican	Franklin	1963–1971
John J. Gilligan	Democrat	Hamilton	1971–1975
James A. Rhodes	Republican	Franklin	1975–1983
Richard F. Celeste	Democrat	Cuyahoga	1983–1991
George V. Voinovich	Republican	Cuyahoga	1991–

Appendix 2

Population of Ohio's Major Cities

	1820	1840	1860	1880	1900	1920	1940	1960	1980	Est. 1990
Akron			3,477	16,512	42,728	208,435	244,791	290,351	237,177	223,019
Canton			4,041	12,258	30,667	87,091	108,401	113,631	94,730	84,161
Cincinnati	9,642	46,338	161,044	255,139	325,902	401,247	455,610	502,550	385,457	364,040
Cleveland	606	6,071	43,417	160,146	381,768	796,841	878,336	876,050	573,822	506,616
Columbus		6,048	18,554	51,647	125,560	237,031	306,087	471,316	564,871	632,910
Dayton	1,000	6,067	20,081	38,678	85,333	152,559	210,718	262,332	203,371	182,044
Toledo		1,222	13,768	50,137	131,822	243,164	282,349	318,003	354,635	332,943
Youngstown			2,759	15,435	44,885	132,358	167,720	166,689	115,436	95,732

Sources: Ohio Almanac (1980); Census Data Book; Statistical Abstracts of U.S. (1988).

Appendix 3

Metropolitan Statistical Areas of Ohio (1994)

Akron	677,000
Canton–Massillon	402,000
Cincinnati	1,581,000
Cleveland, Lorain, Elyria	2,222,000
Columbus	1,423,000
Dayton–Springfield	954,000
Hamilton–Middletown	313,000
Toledo	614,000
Youngstown–Warren	604,000

Source: Statistical Abstracts of the United States, 1995.

Bibliography

Selected Readings

The historical literature of Ohio and its people is rich and diverse. No single bibliography lists more than a fraction of it. Among the most useful bibliographies are those found in Eugene H. Roseboom and Francis P. Weisenburger, *A History of Ohio,* 2nd rev. ed. (Columbus: Ohio Historical Society, 1967) and Raymond Boryczka and Lorin Lee Cary, *No Strength Without Union: An Illustrated History of Ohio Workers 1803–1980* (Columbus: Ohio Historical Society, 1982).

This list of selected readings is not intended to be all-inclusive. Nearly every book listed has been published since 1960. Most have been reviewed in professional journals. I consulted many of them in preparing this book.

No effort is made here to cite specific journal articles. One must search far afield in the periodical literature to find Ohio topics. Specialized journals in every field contain relevant material. Overwhelmingly, however, articles focusing on Ohio topics are found in Ohio-based journals. Among the most important are *Ohio History* (published continuously since 1887, under a variety of names by the Ohio Historical Society); the *Cincinnati Historical Society Bulletin* (published by the Cincinnati Historical Society, previously published as the *Historical and Philosophical Society of Ohio Bulletin*); the *Northwest Ohio Quarterly: A Journal of History and Civilization* (Maumee Valley Historical Society); *The Old Northwest* (Miami University); *Inland Seas* (Great Lakes Historical Society); *Hayes Historical Journal* (The Rutherford B. Hayes Presidential Center); *Museum Echoes* and *Timeline* (both published by the Ohio Historical Society). Many local historical societies publish newsletters and bulletins containing solid historical information, as do genealogical societies. The Western Reserve Historical Society *Tracts* (1870–1929) and *Publications* (1943–) contain valuable information.

Most general histories of Ohio are seriously out of date. The most recent multivolume history of substance is Carl Wittke (ed.), *History of the State of Ohio*, 6 vols. (Columbus: Ohio Historical Society, 1941–44). Volume 1 in this series is Beverley W. Bond, Jr., *The Foundations of Ohio*; volume 2, William T. Utter, *The Frontier State, 1803–1825;* volume 3, Francis P. Weisenburger, *The Passing of the Frontier, 1825–1850;* volume 4, Eugene H. Roseboom, *The Civil War Era, 1850–1873;* volume 5, Philip D. Jordan, *Ohio Comes of Age, 1873–1900;* and Volume 6, Harlow Lindley (ed.), *Ohio in the Twentieth Century* (each chapter written by a different specialist, and none containing material beyond 1940). Although now half a century old, this series is still the starting place for most serious inquiry into Ohio's pre-1940 history. The best one-volume history is also dated. Roseboom and Weisenberger's *A History of Ohio* (previously cited) was originally written in the early 1930s. It was updated and reissued by the Ohio Historical Society in 1953 and again in 1967, with James H. Rodabaugh doing the editorial work.

Books of General Interest on Statewide Themes

In the past quarter century a number of books based on broad themes have added much to a popular understanding of Ohio. A heavily illustrated volume designed for the general reader is George W. Knepper, *An Ohio Portrait* (Columbus: Ohio Historical Society for the Ohio American Revolution Bicentennial Advisory Commission, 1976). Thomas H. Smith, a former director of the Ohio Historical Society, produced the attractive *The Mapping of Ohio* (Kent, Ohio: Kent State University Press, 1977), and also edited *An Ohio Reader*, 2 vols. (Grand Rapids: William B. Eerdmans 1975). Allen G. Noble and Albert J. Korsok, *Ohio: An American Heartland*, Bulletin 65, Division of Geological Survey (Columbus: Ohio Department of Natural Resources, 1975) concentrates on geographical influences. Walter Havighurst, *Ohio: A Bicentennial History* (New York: W. W. Norton, 1976) offers a brief overview and interpretation. Michael B. Lafferty (ed.), *Ohio's Natural Heritage* (Columbus: Ohio Academy of Science, 1979) is a model work of its kind. Boryczka and Cary's *No Strength Without Union*, previously cited, is a comprehensive account of Ohio industry and Ohio workers which could serve as a model for similar work in other fields of special interest. A brief overview of Ohio industry may be found in Eugene C. Murdock, *The Buckeye Empire: An Illustrated History of Ohio Enterprise* (Northridge, Cal.: Windsor, 1988). William Coyle (ed.), *Ohio Authors and Their Books* (Cleveland: World, 1962) is most useful for information about Ohio writers. *The Ohioana Library Quarterly*, published by the Ohioana Library Association, keeps up with current Ohio writers.

Professional historians differ as to the proper use of historical fiction. The very best fiction, solidly based in research and presented in a manner faithful to the known facts, serves a valuable function. The novelist, freed from the constraints of valueless reporting, can give his reader a visual image, a sense of time and place, an emotional increment. Among the most impressive of recent works of fiction are the novels of Conrad Richter, especially the Awakening Land trilogy—*The Trees, The Fields, and The Town* (various editions). William D. Ellis's Bounty Land series—*The Bounty*

Lands, Johnathan Blair: Bountylands Lawyer, and *The Brooks Legend* give life to subjects such as pioneer currency and banking problems, medicine, and relations with the Indians. Helen Hooven Santmyer's . . . *And Ladies of the Club* is a tour de force. It portrays evolving small-town Ohio in the critical period from the Civil War to the 1930s: her story unfolds against a backdrop that is faithful to the historic record. A special case is Allan Eckert's *The Frontiersmen,* a story of the Ohio country during the American Revolution. Eckert's claim for historical authenticity is weakened somewhat by his characterization, but whatever its technical limitations as history, this book provides a gripping and reasonably accurate picture of the early Ohio frontier.

Significant Books on Ohio

Some of the most useful books published in the last quarter century are listed here.

Frontier and Pioneer Ohio

Berquist, Goodwin, and Paul C. Bowers, Jr. *The New Eden: James Kilbourne and the Development of Ohio.* Lanham, Md.: University Press of America, 1983.

Bird, Harrison. *War for the West, 1790–1813.* New York: Oxford University Press, 1971.

Bloom, John Porter, ed. *The American Territorial System.* Athens: Ohio University Press, 1973.

Brown, Jeffrey P., and Andrew R. L. Cayton, eds. *The Pursuit of Public Power: Political Culture in Ohio, 1787–1861.* Kent, Ohio: Kent State University Press, 1994.

Cayton, Andrew R. L. *The Frontier Republic: Ideology and Politics in the Ohio Country, 1780–1825.* Kent, Ohio: Kent State University Press, 1986.

Connor, Elizabeth. *Methodist Trail Blazer: Philip Gatch, 1751–1834; His Life in Maryland, Virginia and Ohio.* Cincinnati: Creative Publishers, Inc., 1970.

Edmunds, R. David. *The Shawnee Prophet.* Lincoln: University of Nebraska Press, 1983.

———. *Tecumseh and the Quest for Indian Leadership.* Boston: Little, Brown and Company, 1984.

Foster, Emily, ed. *The Ohio Frontier: An Anthology of Early Writings.* Lexington: University Press of Kentucky, 1996.

Gieck, Jack. *A Photo Album of Ohio's Canal Era, 1825–1913.* Kent, Ohio: Kent State University Press, 1988.

Horton, John J. *The Jonathan Hale Farm: A Chronicle of the Ohio Valley.* Cleveland: Western Reserve Historical Society, 1961.

Hutslar, Donald A. *The Architecture of Migration: Log Construction in the Ohio Country, 1750–1850.* Athens: Ohio University Press, 1986.

Jackle, John. *Images of the Ohio Valley: A Historical Geography of Travel.* New York: Oxford University Press, 1977.

Lottich, Kenneth V. *New England Transplanted: A Study of the Development of Educational and Other Cultural Agencies in the Connecticut Western Reserve in their National and Philosophical Setting.* Dallas: Royal Publishing Company, 1964.

McConnell, Michael N. *A Country Between: The Upper Ohio Valley and Its People, 1724–1774.* Lincoln: University of Nebraska Press, 1992.

Mahon, John K. *The War of 1812.* Gainesville: University of Florida Press, 1972.

Olmstead, Earl P. *Blackcoats among the Delaware: David Zeisberger on the Ohio Frontier.* Kent, Ohio: Kent State University Press, 1991.

Onuf, Peter S. *Statehood and Union: A History of the Northwest Ordinance.* Bloomington: Indiana University Press, 1987.

Pieper, Thomas I., and James B. Gidney. *Fort Laurens, 1778–1779: The Revolutionary War in Ohio.* Kent, Ohio: Kent State University Press, 1976.

Rohrbaugh, Malcolm J. *The Land Office Business: The Settlement and Administration of American Public Lands, 1789–1837.* New York: Oxford University Press, 1968.

———. *The Trans-Appalachian Frontier: People, Societies, and Institutions, 1775–1850.* New York: Oxford University Press, 1978.

Shriver, Phillip R., ed. *A Tour to New Connecticut in 1811: The Narrative of Henry Leavitt Ellsworth.* Cleveland: Western Reserve Historical Society, 1985.

Skaggs, David C., ed. *The Old Northwest in the American Revolution: An Anthology.* Madison: State Historical Society of Wisconsin, 1977.

Sugden, John. *Tecumseh's Last Stand.* Norman: University of Oklahoma Press, 1985.

Sword, Wiley. *President Washington's Indian War: The Struggle for the Old Northwest, 1790–1795.* Norman: University of Oklahoma Press, 1985.

Tanner, Helen Hornbeck, ed. *Atlas of Great Lakes Indian History.* Norman: University of Oklahoma Press for the Newberry Library, 1987.

Walker, Byron, comp. *Frontier Ohio: A Resource Guide for Teachers.* Columbus: Ohio Historical Society, 1968?.

———. *Indian Cultures of Ohio: A Resource Guide for Teachers.* Columbus: Ohio Historical Society, 1973.

Welsh, William Jeffrey, and David Curtis Skaggs, eds. *War on the Great Lakes: Essays Commemorating the 175th Anniversary of the Battle of Lake Erie.* Kent, Ohio: Kent State UniversityPress, 1991.

Weslager, C. A. *The Delaware Indians: A History.* New Brunswick, N.J.: Rutgers University Press, 1972.

———. *The Delaware Indian Westward Migration.* Wallingford, Pa.: Middle Atlantic Press, 1978.

Wheeler-Voegelin, Erminie, and Helen Hornbeck Tanner. *Indians of Ohio and Indiana Prior to 1795.* 2 vols. New York: Garland, 1974.

The Maturing State, 1850–1940

Bagby, Wesley M. *The Road to Normalcy: The Presidential Campaign and Election of 1920.* Baltimore: Johns Hopkins University Press, 1962.

Barnard, John. *From Evangelicalism to Progressivism at Oberlin College, 1866–1917.* Columbus: Ohio State University Press, 1969.

Blackford, Mansel G. *A Portrait Cast in Steel: Buckeye International and Columbus, Ohio, 1881–1980.* Westport, Conn.: Greenwood Press, 1982.

Bonadio, Felice. *North of Reconstruction: Ohio Politics, 1865–1870.* New York: New York University Press, 1970.

Bringhurst, Bruce. *Antitrust and the Oil Monopoly: The Standard Oil Cases, 1890–1911.* Westport, Conn.: Greenwood Press, 1979.

Byrne, Frank L., and Jean Powers Soman, eds. *Your True Marcus: The Civil War Letters of a Jewish Colonel.* Kent, Ohio: Kent State University Press, 1985.

Campen, Richard N. *Architecture of the Western Reserve, 1800–1900.* Cleveland: Press of Case Western Reserve University, 1971.

Chapman, Edmund H. *Cleveland: Village to Metropolis, A Case Study of Problems of Urban Development in Nineteenth-Century America.* Cleveland: Western Reserve Historical Society and Press of Western Reserve University, 1964.

Cigliano, Jan. *Showplace of America: Cleveland's Euclid Avenue, 1850–1910.* Kent, Ohio: Kent State University Press, 1991.

Coletta, Paolo E. *The Presidency of William Howard Taft.* Lawrence: University Press of Kansas, 1973.

Condit, Carl W. *The Railroad and the City: A Technological and Urbanistic History of Cincinnati.* Columbus: Ohio State University Press, 1977.

Dannenbaum, Jed. *Drink and Disorder: Temperance Reform in Cincinnati from the Washingtonian Revival to the WCTU.* Urbana: University of Illinois Press, 1984.

Daugherty, Robert L. *Weathering the Peace: The Ohio National Guard in the Interwar Years, 1919–1940.* Dayton, Ohio: Wright State University Press, 1992.

Doenecke, Justus D. *The Presidencies of James A. Garfield and Chester A. Arthur.* Lawrence: Regents Press of Kansas, 1981.

Easton, Loyd D. *Hegel's First American Followers, the Ohio Hegelians: John B. Stallo, Peter Kaufmann, Moncure Conway, and August Willich.* Athens: Ohio University Press, 1966.

English, Peter C. *Shock, Physiological Surgery, and George Washington Crile: Medical Innovation in the Progressive Era.* Westport, Conn.: Greenwood Press, 1980.

Ferrell, Robert H., ed. *Banners in the Air: The Eighth Ohio Volunteers and the Spanish-American War, by Curtis V. Hard.* Kent, Ohio: Kent State University Press, 1988.

Filler, Louis, ed. *An Ohio Schoolmistress: The Memoirs of Irene Hardy.* Kent, Ohio: Kent State University Press, 1980.

Gara, Larry. *The Liberty Line.* Lexington: University of Kentucky Press, 1961.

Gerber, David. *Black Ohio and the Color Line: 1860–1915.* Urbana: University of Illinois Press, 1976.

Good, Howard E. *Black Swamp Farm.* Columbus: Ohio State University Press, 1967.

Gold, Lewis L. *The Presidency of William McKinley.* Lawrence: Regents Press of Kansas, 1980.

Grebner, Constantin. *"We Were the Ninth": A History of the Ninth Regiment, Ohio Volunteer Infantry April 17, 1861, to June 7, 1864.* Translated and edited by Frederic Trautmann. Kent, Ohio: Kent State University Press, 1987.

Hard, Curtis V. *Banners in the Air: The Eighth Ohio Volunteers and the Spanish-American War.* Edited by Robert H. Ferrell. Kent, Ohio: Kent State University Press, 1988.

Harper, Robert S. *Ohio Handbook of the Civil War.* Columbus: Ohio Historical Society, 1964.

Jenkins, William D. *Steel Valley Klan: The Ku Klux Klan in Ohio's Mahoning Valley.* Kent, Ohio: Kent State University Press, 1990.

Jones, Robert Leslie. *The History of Agriculture in Ohio to 1880.* Kent, Ohio: Kent State University Press, 1983.

Kerr, K. Austin. *Organized for Prohibition: A New History of the Anti-Saloon League.* New Haven, Conn.: Yale University Press, 1985.

Klement, Frank L. *The Limits of Dissent: Clement L. Vallandigham and the Civil War.* Lexington: University Press of Kentucky, 1970.

Kleppner, Paul. *The Cross of Culture: A Social Analysis of Midwestern Politics, 1850–1900.* New York: Free Press, 1970.

Kusner, Kenneth. *A Ghetto Takes Shape: Black Cleveland, 1870–1930.* Urbana: University of Illinois Press, 1976.

Lasser, Carol, and Marlene Merrill, eds. *Soul Mates: The Oberlin Correspondence of Lucy Stone and Antoinette Brown, 1846–1850.* Oberlin, Ohio: Oberlin College, 1983.

Leet, Don R. *Population Pressure and Human Fertility Response: Ohio 1810–1860.* New York: Arno Press, 1978.

McTighe, Michael J. *A Measure of Success: Protestants and Public Culture in Antebellum Cleveland.* Albany: State University of New York Press, 1994.

Maizlish, Stephen E. *The Triumph of Sectionalism: The Transformation of Ohio Politics, 1844–1856.* Kent, Ohio: Kent State University Press, 1983.

Mee, Charles. *The Ohio Gang: The World of Warren G. Harding.* New York: M. Evans, 1981.

Miller, Zane L. *Boss Cox's Cincinnati: Urban Politics in the Progressive Era.* New York: Oxford University Press, 1968.

Monkkonen, Eric H. *The Dangerous Class: Crime and Poverty in Columbus, Ohio, 1860–1885.* Cambridge: Harvard University Press, 1975.

Mould, David H. *Dividing Lines: Canals, Railroads and Urban Rivalry in Ohio's Hocking Valley.* Dayton, Ohio: Wright State University Press, 1994.

Murdock, Eugene C. *One Million Men: The Civil War Draft in the North.* Madison: State Historical Society of Wisconsin, 1971.

———. *Patriotism Limited 1862–1865: The Civil War Draft and the Bounty System.* Kent, Ohio: Kent State University Press, 1967.

Nelson, Daniel. *American Rubber Workers and Organized Labor, 1900–1914.* Princeton, N.J.: Princeton University Press, 1988.

Pixton, John. *The Marietta and Cincinnati Railroad, 1845–1883: A Case Study in American Railroad Economics.* The Pennsylvania State University Studies No. 17. University Park: Pennsylvania State University Press, 1966.

Quarles, Benjamin. *Allies for Freedom: Blacks and John Brown.* New York: Oxford University Press, 1974.

Ross, Steven J. *Workers on the Edge: Work, Leisure and Politics in Industrializing Cincinnati, 1788–1890.* New York: Columbia University Press, 1985.

Sacks, Howard L., and Judith Rose Sacks. *Way Up North in Dixie: A Black Family's Claim to the Confederate Anthem.* Washington, D.C.: Smithsonian Institution Press, 1993.

Sawrey, Robert D. *Dubious Victory: The Reconstruction Debate in Ohio.* Lexington: University Press of Kentucky, 1992.

Scheiber, Harry N. *Ohio Canal Era: A Case Study of Government and the Economy, 1820–1861.* Athens: Ohio University Press, 1969.

Schwantes, Carlos A. *Coxey's Army: An American Odyssey.* Lincoln: University of Nebraska Press, 1985.

Toman, James A., and Blaine S. Hays. *Horse Trails to Regional Rails: The Story of Public Transit in Greater Cleveland.* Kent, Ohio: Kent State University Press, 1996.

Trani, Eugene, and David L. Wilson. *The Presidency of Warren G. Harding.* Lawrence: Regents Press of Kansas, 1977.

Warner, Hoyt Landon. *Progressivism in Ohio, 1897–1917.* Columbus: Ohio State University Press for the Ohio Historical Society, 1964.

Wheeler, Kenneth W., ed. *For the Union: Ohio Leaders in the Civil War.* Columbus: Ohio State University Press, 1968.

Wilcox, Frank. *The Ohio Canals.* Kent, Ohio: Kent State University Press, 1969.

Wortman, Roy T. *From Syndicalism to Trade Unionism: The IWW in Ohio 1913–1950.* New York: Garland, 1985.

Toward Contemporary Ohio

Baskin, John. *New Burlington: The Life and Death of an American Village.* New York: W. W. Norton and Company, 1976.

Bills, Scott L., ed. *Kent State/May 4: Echoes Through a Decade.* 1982. Reprint. Kent, Ohio: Kent State University Press, 1988.

Cleary, Edward J. *The Orsanco Story: Water Quality Management in the Ohio Valley under an Interstate Compact.* Baltimore: Johns Hopkins University Press, 1967.

Ehle, Jay C. *Cleveland's Harbor: The Cleveland–Cuyahoga County Port Authority.* Kent, Ohio: Kent State University Press, 1996.

Fligstein, Neil. *Going North: Migration of Blacks and Whites from the South, 1900–1950.* New York: Harcourt Brace Jovanovich, 1981.

Gargan, John J., and James G. Coke, eds. *Political Behavior and Public Issues in Ohio.* Kent, Ohio: Kent State University Press, 1972.

Jenkins, Hal. *A Valley Renewed: The History of the Muskingum Watershed Conservancy District.* Kent, Ohio: Kent State University Press, 1976.

Keating, Dennis W., et al., eds. *Cleveland, A Metropolitan Reader.* Kent, Ohio: Kent State University Press, 1995.

Lieberman, Carl, ed. *Government and Politics in Ohio.* Lanham, Md.: University Press of America, 1984.

Miller, Zane L. *Suburb: Neighborhood and Community in Forest Park, Ohio, 1935–1976.* Knoxville: University of Tennessee Press, 1981.

Taylor, Henry Louis, Jr., ed. *Race and the City: Work, Community, and Protest in Cincinnati, 1820–1970.* Urbana: University of Illinois Press, 1993.

Zannes, Estelle. *Checkmate in Cleveland: The Rhetoric of Confrontation During the Stokes Years.* Cleveland: Press of Case Western Reserve University, 1972.

Biographies and "Life and Times"

Abzug, Robert H. *Passionate Liberator: Theodore Dwight Weld and the Dilemma of Reform.* New York: Oxford University Press, 1980.

Anderson, David D. *Brand Whitlock.* New York: Twayne, 1968.

———. *Sherwood Anderson: An Introduction and Interpretation.* New York: Holt, Rinehart and Winston, 1967.

Austin, James C. *Petroleum V. Nasby.* New York: Twayne, 1965.

Baker, William J. *Jesse Owens: An American Life.* New York: Free Press, 1986.

Bernstein, Burton. *Thurber: A Biography.* New York: Dodd, Mead and Company, 1975.

Blue, Frederick J. *Salmon P. Chase: A Life in Politics.* Kent, Ohio: Kent State University Press, 1987.

Brown, Harry J., and Frederick D. Williams, eds. *The Diary of James A. Garfield.* 2 vols. East Lansing: Michigan State University Press, 1967.

Campbell, Thomas F. *Daniel E. Morgan, 1877–1949: The Good Citizen in Politics.* Cleveland: Press of Western Reserve University, 1967.

Cebula, James E. *James M. Cox: Journalist and Politician.* New York: Garland, 1985.

Cole, Charles C., Jr. *Lion of the Forest: James B. Finley, Frontier Reformer.* Lexington: University Press of Kentucky, 1994.

Conlin, Mary Lou. *Simon Perkins of the Western Reserve.* Cleveland: Western Reserve Historical Society, 1968.

Cramer, Clarence H. *Newton D. Baker: A Biography.* Cleveland: World Publishing Company, 1961.

Cruden, Robert. *James Ford Rhodes: The Man, the Historian, and His Work.* Cleveland: Press of Western Reserve University, 1961.

Curl, Donald W. *Murat Halstead and the Cincinnati Commercial.* Boca Raton: University Presses of Florida, 1980.

Davies, Richard O. *Defender of the Old Guard: John Bricker and American Politics.* Columbus: Ohio State University Press, 1993.

Davison, Kenneth E. *The Presidency of Rutherford B. Hayes.* Westport, Conn.: Greenwood Press, 1972.

Dillon, Merton L. *Benjamin Lundy and the Struggle for Negro Freedom.* Urbana: University of Illinois Press, 1966.

Dorn, Jacob H. *Washington Gladden: Prophet of the Social Gospel.* Columbus: Ohio State University Press, 1968.

Downes, Randolph C. *The Rise of Warren Gamaliel Harding, 1865–1920.* Columbus: Ohio State University Press, 1970.

Fleischmann, Harry. *Norman Thomas.* New York: W. W. Norton and Company, 1964.

Franklin, John Hope. *George Washington Williams: A Biography.* Chicago: University of Chicago Press, 1985.

Geer, Emily Apt. *First Lady: The Life of Lucy Webb Hayes.* Kent, Ohio: Kent State University Press, 1984.

Giglio, James N. *H. M. Daugherty and the Politics of Expediency.* Kent, Ohio: Kent State University Press, 1978.

Harrison, John M. *The Man Who Made Nasby: David Ross Locke.* Chapel Hill: University of North Carolina Press, 1969.

Harrold, Stanley. *Gamaliel Bailey and Antislavery Union.* Kent, Ohio: Kent State University Press, 1986.

Hoogenboom, Ari. *Rutherford B. Hayes: Warrior and President.* Lawrence: University Press of Kansas, 1995.

Horine, Emmet Field. *Daniel Drake (1785–1852): Pioneer Physician of the Midwest.* Philadelphia: University of Pennsylvania Press, 1961.

Horsman, Reginald. *Matthew Elliott, British Indian Agent.* Detroit: Wayne State University Press, 1964.

Howard, Fred. *Wilbur and Orville: A Biography of the Wright Brothers.* New York: Knopf, 1987.

Izant, Grace Goulder. *John D. Rockefeller: The Cleveland Years.* Cleveland: Western Reserve Historical Society, 1972.

Joyce, Rosemary O. *A Woman's Place: The Life History of a Rural Ohio Grandmother.* Columbus: Ohio State University Press, 1983.

Knepper, George W., ed. *Travels Through the Southland 1822–1823: The Journal of Lucius Versus Bierce.* Columbus: Ohio State University Press, 1966.

Leech, Margaret, and Harry Brown. *Garfield Orbit.* New York: Harper & Row, 1978.

Madden, Edward H., and James E. Hamilton. *Freedom and Grace: The Life of Asa Mahan.* Metuchen, N.J.: Scarecrow Press, 1982.

Magrath, C. Peter. *Morrison R. Waite: The Triumph of Character.* New York: Macmillan, 1963.

Marszalek, John F. *Sherman: A Soldier's Passion for Order.* New York: Free Press, 1993.

Morgan, Charles H. *George Bellows: Painter of America.* New York: Reynal and Company, 1965.

Morgan, H. Wayne. *Kenyon Cox, 1856–1919: A Life in American Art* Kent, Ohio: Kent State University Press, 1994.

———. *William McKinley and His America.* Syracuse: Syracuse University Press, 1963.

Murray, Robert K. *The Harding Era: Warren G. Harding and His Administration.* Minneapolis: University of Minnesota Press, 1969.

Nelson, Paul David. *Anthony Wayne: Soldier of the Early Republic.* Bloomington: Indiana University Press, 1969.

Oates, Stephen. *To Purge This Land with Blood: A Biography of John Brown.* New York: Harper & Row, 1970.

Patterson, James T. *Mr. Republican: A Biography of Robert A. Taft.* Boston: Houghton Mifflin, 1972.

Peskin, Allan. *Garfield: A Biography.* Kent, Ohio: Kent State University Press, 1978.

———, ed. *North Into Freedom: The Autobiography of John Malvin, Free Negro, 1795–1880.* Cleveland: Press of Western Reserve University, 1966. Reprint. Kent, Ohio: Kent State University Press, 1988.

Rickenbacker, Edward V. *Rickenbacker.* Englewood Cliffs, N.J.: Prentice-Hall, 1967.

Ross, Ishbel. *An American Family: The Tafts 1678 to 1964.* Cleveland: World Publishing Company, 1964.

Russell, Francis. *The Shadow of Blooming Grove: Warren G. Harding in His Times.* New York: McGraw-Hill, 1968.

Sinclair, Andrew. *The Available Man.* New York: Macmillan, 1965.

Swanberg, W. A. *Norman Thomas: The Last Idealist.* New York: Charles Scribners' Sons, 1976.

Tager, Jack. *The Intellectual as Urban Reformer: Brand Whitlock and the Progressive Movement.* Cleveland: Press of Case Western Reserve University, 1968.

Trefousse, Hans L. *Benjamin Franklin Wade: Radical Republican from Ohio.* New York: Twayne, 1963.

Tuve, Jeanette E. *First Lady of the Law, Florence Ellinwood Allen.* Lanham, Md.: University Press of America, 1984.

Williams, T. Harry, ed. *Hayes: The Diary of a President, 1875–1881, Covering the Disputed Election, the End of Reconstruction, and the Beginning of Civil Service.* New York: David McKay Company, 1964.

———, ed. *Hayes of the Twenty-Third: The Civil War Volunteer Officer.* New York: Alfred A. Knopf, 1965.

General

Albeck, Willard D. *A Century of Lutherans in Ohio.* Yellow Springs, Ohio: Antioch Press, 1966.

Beauregard, Erving E. *Old Franklin: The Eternal Touch, A History of Franklin College, New Athens, Harrison County, Ohio.* Lanham Md.: University Press of America, 1983.

Becker, Carl M. *The Village: A History of Germantown, Ohio, 1804–1976.* Germantown, Ohio: Historical Society of Germantown, 1981.

Blodgett, Geoffrey. *Oberlin Architecture, College and Town: A Guide to Its Social History.* Oberlin, Ohio: Oberlin College and Kent State University Press, 1985.

Cayton, Andrew R. L., and Peter S. Onuf. *The Midwest and the Nation: Rethinking the History of an American Region.* Bloomington: Indiana University Press, 1990.

Clark, Ricky, George W. Knepper, and Ellice Ronsheim. *Quilts in the Community: Ohio's Traditions.* Nashville: Rutledge Hill Press, 1991.

Cramer, Clarence H. *Case Western Reserve University: A History of the University, 1826–1976.* Boston: Little, Brown, 1976.

———. *Open Shelves and Open Minds: A History of the Cleveland Public Library.* Cleveland: Press of Case Western Reserve University, 1972.

Crile, George, Jr., M.D. *The Way It Was: Sex, Surgery, Treasure, and Travel, 1907–1987.* Kent, Ohio: Kent State University Press, 1992.

Curtin, Michael F., in collaboration with Julia Barry Bell. *The Ohio Politics Almanac.* Kent, Ohio: Kent State University Press, 1996.

Davis, Russell H. *Black Americans in Ohio's City of Cleveland.* Washington D.C.: Associated Publishers, 1972.

———. *Memorable Negroes in Cleveland's Past.* Cleveland: Western Reserve Historical Society, 1969.

Downard, William L. *The Cincinnati Brewing Industry: A Social and Economic History.* Athens: Ohio University Press, 1973.

Fenton, John H. *Midwest Politics.* New York: Holt, Rinehart, and Winston, 1966.

Gates, William C., Jr. *The City of Hills and Kilns: Life and Work in East Liverpool, Ohio.* East Liverpool: East Liverpool Historical Society, 1984.

Gavin, Donald P. *John Carroll University: A Century of Service.* Kent, Ohio: Kent State University Press, 1985.

Goggins, Lathardus. *Central State University: The First One Hundred Years, 1887–1987.* Kent, Ohio: Kent State University Press, 1987.

Hostetler, John A. *Amish Society.* Baltimore: Johns Hopkins University Press, 1963.

Izant, Grace Goulder. *Hudson's Heritage: A Chronicle of the Founding and the Flowering of the Village of Hudson, Ohio.* Kent, Ohio: Kent State University Press, 1985.

Kern, Richard. *Findlay College: The First Hundred Years.* Nappanee, Ind.: Evangel Press, 1984.

Kinnison, William A. *Building Sullivant's Pyramid: An Administrative History of the Ohio State University, 1870–1907.* Columbus: Ohio State University Press, 1970.

Knepper, George W. *New Lamps for Old: One Hundred Years of Urban Higher Education at the University of Akron.* Akron, Ohio: University of Akron, 1970.

Lamis, Alexander P., ed., with the assistance of Mary Anne Sharkey. *Ohio Politics.* Kent, Ohio: Kent State University Press, 1994.

Lieberman, Carl, ed. *Government, Politics, and Public Policy in Ohio.* Akron, Ohio: Midwest Press Incorporated, 1995.

Lupold, Harry F., and Gladys Haddad, eds. *Ohio's Western Reserve: A Regional Reader.* Kent, Ohio: Kent State University Press, 1988.

McGinnis, Frederick A. *The Education of Negroes in Ohio.* Wilberforce, Ohio: the author, 1962.

McGovern, Frances. *Written on the Hills: The Making of the Akron Landscape.* Akron, Ohio: University of Akron Press, 1996.

McMillen, Wheeler. *Ohio Farm.* Columbus: Ohio State University Press, 1974.

Miller, Larry L. *Ohio Place Names.* Bloomington: Indiana University Press, 1996.

Morton, Marian J. *Women in Cleveland: An Illustrated History.* Bloomington: Indiana University Press, 1995.

Ohio American Revolution Bicentennial Conference Series. Columbus: Ohio Historical Society, 1976–78.

    Buchman, Randall, ed. *The Historic Indian in Ohio.*

    Pearson, Ralph L., ed. *Ohio in Century Three.*

    Smith, Thomas, ed. *Ohio in the American Revolution.*

    Westin, Rubin F., ed. *Blacks in Ohio History.*

    Whitlock, Marta, ed. *Women in Ohio History.*

    Wunder, John, ed. *Toward an Urban Ohio.*

Peacefull, Leonard, ed. *A Geography of Ohio.* Kent, Ohio: Kent State University Press, 1996.

Petersen, Gene B., Laure M. Sharp, and Thomas F. Drury. *Southern Newcomers to Northern Cities: Work and Social Adjustment in Cleveland.* New York: Praeger Publishers, 1977.

Porter, Philip W. *Cleveland: Confused City on a Seesaw.* Columbus: Ohio State University Press, 1976.

Publications of the Ohio Civil War Centennial Commission. Columbus: Ohio State University Press, 1964.

    Abbott, Richard H. *Ohio's Civil War Governors.*

    Bond, Otto F., ed. *Under the Flag of the Nation: Diaries and Letters of a Yankee Volunteer in the Civil War.*

    Chessman, G. Wallace. *Ohio Colleges in the Civil War.*

    Coles, Harry L. *Ohio Forms an Army.*

    Davison, Kenneth E. *Cleveland during the Civil War.*

    Downer, Edward T. *Ohio Troops in the Field.*

    Ford, Harvey S., comp. *Civil War Letters of Petroleum V. Nasby.*

    Harper, Robert S. *The Ohio Press in the Civil War.*

    Jones, Robert L. *Ohio Agriculture during the Civil War.*

    Murdock, Eugene C. *Ohio's Bounty System in the Civil War.*

    Shriver, Phillip R., and Donald J. Breen. *Ohio's Military Prisons in the Civil War.*

    Simms, Henry H. *Ohio Politics on the Eve of Conflict.*

    Tucker, Louis Leonard. *Cincinnati during the Civil War.*

    Weisenburger, Francis T. *Columbus during the Civil War.*

    Wesley, Charles H. *Ohio Negroes in the Civil War.*

Raphael, Marc Lee. *Jews and Judaism in a Midwestern Community: Columbus Ohio, 1840–1975.* Columbus: Ohio Historical Society, 1979.

Reid, Robert L., ed. *Always a River: The Ohio River and the American Experience.* Bloomington: Indiana University Press, 1991.

Schmidlin, Thomas W., and Jeanne Applehans Schmidlin. *Thunder in the Heartland: A Chronicle of Outstanding Weather Events in Ohio.* Kent, Ohio: Kent State University Press, 1996.

Scheiber, Harry N., ed. *The Old Northwest: Studies in Regional History, 1787–1910.* Lincoln: University of Nebraska Press, 1969.

Schreiber, William I. *Our Amish Neighbors.* Chicago: University of Chicago Press, 1962.

Silberstein, Iola Hessler. *Cincinnati Then and Now.* Cincinnati: League of Women Voters, 1982.

Skardon, Alvin W. *Steel Valley University: The Origins of Youngstown State.* Youngstown, Ohio: Youngstown State University, 1983.

Van Tassel, David D., and John J. Grabowski, eds. *The Encyclopedia of Cleveland History.* Bloomington: Indiana University Press, 1987.

Vincent, Sidney Z., and Judah Rubinstein. *Merging Traditions—Jewish Life in Cleveland, A Pictorial Record 1839–1975.* Cleveland: Western Reserve Historical Society and the Jewish Community Federation of Cleveland, 1978.

Vitz, Robert C. *The Queen and the Arts: Cultural Life in Nineteenth-Century Cincinnati.* Kent, Ohio: Kent State University Press, 1989.

Wittke, Carl. *The First Fifty Years: The Cleveland Museum of Art, 1916–1966.* Cleveland: John Huntington Art and Polytechnic Trust and the Cleveland Museum of Art, 1966.

Wright, Richard J. *Freshwater Whales: A History of the American Ship Building Company and Its Predecessors.* Kent, Ohio: Kent State University Press, 1970.

Wynear, Lubomyr, et al. *Ethnic Groups in Ohio with Special Emphasis on Cleveland.* Cleveland: Cleveland State University, Cleveland Ethnic Heritage Studies Development Program, 1975.

Index

DATE DUE

SEP 2 5 2000	
OCT 2 5 2000	AUG 2 1 2002
	JAN 2 7 2003
NOV 2 2 2000	
JAN 0 8 2001	SEP 2 3 2003
JUN 0 6 2001	APR 0 1 2004
SEP 2 0 2001	JUN 0 1 2004
DEC 1 0 2001	JUN 0 8 2004
	JAN 2 9 2005
JUN 1 0 2002	JUL 2 9 2005